SIGDIAL 2011 Conference

12th Annual Meeting of the Special Interest Group on Discourse and Dialogue

Co-located with ACL HLT 2011

Portland, Oregon, USA
17-18 June 2011

ISBN: 978-1-61839-242-8

Printed from e-media with permission by:

Curran Associates, Inc.
57 Morehouse Lane
Red Hook, NY 12571

CURRAN ASSOCIATES INC. proceedings.com

Some format issues inherent in the e-media version may also appear in this print version.

Printed by Curran Associates, Inc. (2011)

Association for Computational Linguistics
209 N. Eighth Street
Stroudsburg, Pennsylvania 18360

Phone: 1-570-476-8006
Fax: 1-570-476-0860

acl@aclweb.org

Additional copies of this publication are available from:

Curran Associates, Inc.
57 Morehouse Lane
Red Hook, NY 12571 USA
Phone: 845-758-0400
Fax: 845-758-2634
Email: curran@proceedings.com
Web: www.proceedings.com

Table of Contents

Strategic Conversation
Alex Lascarides 1

Spoken Dialog Challenge 2010: Comparison of Live and Control Test Results
Alan W Black, Susanne Burger, Alistair Conkie, Helen Hastie, Simon Keizer, Oliver Lemon, Nicolas Merigaud, Gabriel Parent, Gabriel Schubiner, Blaise Thomson, Jason D. Williams, Kai Yu, Steve Young and Maxine Eskenazi 2

What System Differences Matter? Using L1/L2 Regularization to Compare Dialogue Systems
José González-Brenes and Jack Mostow 8

A Two-Stage Domain Selection Framework for Extensible Multi-Domain Spoken Dialogue Systems
Mikio Nakano, Shun Sato, Kazunori Komatani, Kyoko Matsuyama, Kotaro Funakoshi and Hiroshi G. Okuno 18

A Comparison of Latent Variable Models For Conversation Analysis
Sourish Chaudhuri and Bhiksha Raj 30

Toward Learning and Evaluation of Dialogue Policies with Text Examples
David DeVault, Anton Leuski and Kenji Sagae 39

The Impact of Task-Oriented Feature Sets on HMMs for Dialogue Modeling
Kristy Boyer, Eun Young Ha, Robert Phillips and James Lester 49

Spoken Dialogue System based on Information Extraction using Similarity of Predicate Argument Structures
Koichiro Yoshino, Shinsuke Mori and Tatsuya Kawahara 59

Common Ground and Perspective-taking in Real-time Language Processing
Michael K. Tanenhaus 67

Giving instructions in virtual environments by corpus based selection
Luciana Benotti and Alexandre Denis 68

Optimising Natural Language Generation Decision Making For Situated Dialogue
Nina Dethlefs, Heriberto Cuayáhuitl and Jette Viethen 78

Regulating Dialogue with Gestures—Towards an Empirically Grounded Simulation with Conversational Agents
Kirsten Bergmann, Hannes Rieser and Stefan Kopp 88

Multiparty Turn Taking in Situated Dialog: Study, Lessons, and Directions
Dan Bohus and Eric Horvitz 98

Stability and Accuracy in Incremental Speech Recognition
Ethan Selfridge, Iker Arizmendi, Peter Heeman and Jason Williams 110

Predicting the Micro-Timing of User Input for an Incremental Spoken Dialogue System that Completes a User's Ongoing Turn
Timo Baumann and David Schlangen 120

An Empirical Evaluation of a Statistical Dialog System in Public Use
Jason Williams 130

"The day after the day after tomorrow?" A machine learning approach to adaptive temporal expression generation: training and evaluation with real users
Srinivasan Janarthanam, Helen Hastie, Oliver Lemon and Xingkun Liu 142

Detecting Levels of Interest from Spoken Dialog with Multistream Prediction Feedback and Similarity Based Hierarchical Fusion Learning
William Yang Wang and Julia Hirschberg 152

Exploring User Satisfaction in a Tutorial Dialogue System
Myroslava O. Dzikovska, Johanna D. Moore, Natalie Steinhauser and Gwendolyn Campbell . 162

Modeling and Predicting Quality in Spoken Human-Computer Interaction
Alexander Schmitt, Benjamin Schatz and Wolfgang Minker 173

Topics as Contextual Indicators for Word Choice in SMS Conversations
Ute Winter, Roni Ben-Aharon, Daniel Chernobrov and Ron Hecht 185

Multilingual Annotation and Disambiguation of Discourse Connectives for Machine Translation
Thomas Meyer, Andrei Popescu-Belis, Sandrine Zufferey and Bruno Cartoni 194

Commitments to Preferences in Dialogue
Anaïs Cadilhac, Nicholas Asher, Farah Benamara and Alex Lascarides 204

Using Performance Trajectories to Analyze the Immediate Impact of User State Misclassification in an Adaptive Spoken Dialogue System
Kate Forbes-Riley and Diane Litman 216

Comparing Triggering Policies for Social Behaviors
Rohit Kumar and Carolyn Rosé 227

Facilitating Mental Modeling in Collaborative Human-Robot Interaction through Adverbial Cues
Gordon Briggs and Matthias Scheutz 239

Embedded Wizardry
Rebecca J. Passonneau, Susan L. Epstein, Tiziana Ligorio and Joshua Gordon 248

Toward Construction of Spoken Dialogue System that Evokes Users' Spontaneous Backchannels
Teruhisa Misu, Etsuo Mizukami, Yoshinori Shiga, Shinichi Kawamoto, Hisashi Kawai and Satoshi Nakamura 259

Learning to Balance Grounding Rationales for Dialogue Systems
Joshua Gordon, Rebecca J. Passonneau and Susan L. Epstein 266

An Annotation Scheme for Cross-Cultural Argumentation and Persuasion Dialogues
Kallirroi Georgila, Ron Artstein, Angela Nazarian, Michael Rushforth, David Traum and Katia Sycara 272

An Approach to the Automated Evaluation of Pipeline Architectures in Natural Language Dialogue Systems
Eliza Margaretha and David DeVault 279

Perception of Personality and Naturalness through Dialogues by Native Speakers of American English and Arabic
Maxim Makatchev and Reid Simmons 286

Multi-Policy Dialogue Management
Pierre Lison 294

A Robotic World Model Framework Designed to Facilitate Human-robot Communication
Meghann Lomas, Ernest Cross, Jonathan Darvill, Robert Garrett, Michael Kopack and Kenneth Whitebread 301

Improving Pronominal and Deictic Co-Reference Resolution with Multi-Modal Features
Lin Chen, Anruo Wang and Barbara Di Eugenio 307

Examining the Impacts of Dialogue Content and System Automation on Affect Models in a Spoken Tutorial Dialogue System
Joanna Drummond and Diane Litman 312

Error Return Plots
Ron Artstein 319

PARADISE-style Evaluation of a Human-Human Library Corpus
Rebecca J. Passonneau, Irene Alvarado, Phil Crone and Simon Jerome 325

An Incremental Architecture for the Semantic Annotation of Dialogue Corpora with High-Level Structures. A case of study for the MEDIA corpus.
Lina Maria Rojas-Barahona and Matthieu Quignard 332

The CODA System for Monologue-to-Dialogue Generation
Svetlana Stoyanchev and Paul Piwek 335

Beetle II: an adaptable tutorial dialogue system
Myroslava Dzikovska, Amy Isard, Peter Bell, Johanna Moore, Natalie Steinhauser and Gwendolyn Campbell 338

Engagement-based Multi-party Dialog with a Humanoid Robot
David Klotz, Johannes Wienke, Julia Peltason, Britta Wrede, Sebastian Wrede, Vasil Khalidov and Jean-Marc Odobez 341

POMY: A Conversational Virtual Environment for Language Learning in POSTECH
Hyungjong Noh, Kyusong Lee, Sungjin Lee and Gary Geunbae Lee 344

Rapid Development of Advanced Question-Answering Characters by Non-experts
Sudeep Gandhe, Alysa Taylor, Jillian Gerten and David Traum 347

A Just-in-Time Document Retrieval System for Dialogues or Monologues
Andrei Popescu-Belis, Majid Yazdani, Alexandre Nanchen and Philip N. Garner 350

SIGDIAL 2011

Proceedings of the SIGDIAL 2011 Conference

The 12th Annual Meeting of the Special Interest Group on Discourse and Dialogue

June 17-18, 2011
Oregon Science & Health University
Portland, Oregon, USA

In cooperation with:

Association for Computational Linguistics (ACL)
International Speech Communication Association (ISCA)
Association for the Advancement of Artificial Intelligence (AAAI)

We thank our sponsors:

Honda Research Institutes	Microsoft Research	AVIOS
AT&T	Vlingo	IBM Research

Introduction

It is our great pleasure to present the Proceedings of the SIGDIAL 2011 Conference, the 12th Annual Meeting of the Special Interest Group on Discourse and Dialogue. The conference is held in Portland, Oregon, June 17-18, 2011, co-located with the ACL conference.

We received 68 paper submissions: 51 as long papers, 17 as short papers. The members of the Program Committee did a superb job in reviewing the submitted papers, providing helpful comments and contributing to discussions when required. We wish to thank all of them for their advice in selecting the accepted papers and for helping to maintain the high quality of the program. Special thanks go to Nicholas Asher, Dan Bohus, Deborah Dahl, Curry Guinn, Staffan Larsson, Andrei Popescu-Belis, and Antoine Raux for helping out with last minute review requests. Many submissions received strong recommendations from the Program Committee. In line with the SIGDIAL tradition, our aim has been to create a balanced program that could accommodate as many favorably rated papers as possible. Of the 68 submissions, 36 were accepted: 18 of 51 long paper submissions papers were accepted as full papers for plenary presentation, 7 were accepted as long papers for poster presentation, and 5 were accepted as as short papers for poster presentation. In addition, 6 of the 17 short paper submissions were accepted for poster presentation, for a total of 18 posters. Of special note this year, four papers were accepted as part of a Special Theme on situated dialogue. In addition, 7 of the 8 demo submissions were presented; the 8th was accepted but withdrawn.

This year, the review process continued the mentoring program that was initiated last year, and was coordinated by Ronnie Smith. The mentoring goal is to assist authors of papers that contain innovative ideas to improve their quality regarding English language usage or paper organization. Compared with the first year, reviewers accepted fewer papers that required mentoring, but we hope the initiative will continue and expand. Our thanks go to Ronnie Smith and the Program Committee members who volunteered to serve as mentors.

We are also grateful to the two keynote speakers whose topics expanded on the special theme of situated dialogue: Professor Alex Lascarides (The University of Edinburgh) and Professor Michael Tanenhaus (University of Rochester).

We would like to thank Peter Heeman, Local chair, and Pat Dickerson and Ethan Selfridge, the members of the local committee for taking care of the many details for the local arrangements. For on-site assistance, we thank the student volunteers, Lin Chen, Joanna Drummond, Joshua Gordon, Elnaz Nouri, Ethan Selfridge and William Wang. For help on the design of the conference bag, we thank Anabel-Franco-Heurta and Jennifer Wohlner.

We would like to thank Jason Williams, Sponsorships chair, for recruiting and liaising with our conference sponsors. The sponsorship program enables valuable aspects of the program, such as the invited speakers, conference reception and dinner, and best paper awards. We would also like to thank our sponsors. General conference sponsors include Microsoft Research, Vlingo, and AVIOS. The banquet is sponsored by Honda Research. AT&T Research sponsored the best paper award, and IBM Research sponsored the best student paper award.

We would like to thank last year's program co-chairs Raquel Fernández and Oliver Lemon for their advice, and responses to our questions. We thank last year's General co-chair Mikio Nakano for updates to the conference chair kit, and much helpful advice. Thanks also go to Kazunori Komatani and Guodong Zhou for answering our questions related to assembling the conference proceedings.

We would like to thank Priscilla Rasmussen at ACL for handling the financial transactions, including advance registration. We would also like to thank Drago Radev, ACL Secretary, for helpful advice. Thanks to SoftConf for use of the START conference management systems as well as helpful responses on its use. Thanks also to the SIGDIAL board, in particular Tim Paek, Amanda Stent, and Kristiina Jokinen, for their advice and support in all matters.

Finally, we thank all the authors of the papers in this volume, and all the conference participants for making this event such a great opportunity for new research in dialogue and discourse.

Johanna D. Moore and David R. Traum
General Co-Chairs

Joyce Y. Chai and Rebecca J. Passonneau
Technical Program Co-Chairs

Conference Organization

General Co-Chairs:

Johanna D. Moore, The University of Edinburgh, UK
David R. Traum, University of Southern California, USA

Technical Program Co-Chairs:

Joyce Y. Chai, Michigan State University, USA
Rebecca J. Passonneau, Columbia University, USA

Local Chair:

Peter A. Heeman, Oregon Health & Science University, USA

Sponsorship Chair:

Jason Williams, AT&T Labs - Research, USA

Mentoring Chair:

Ronnie Smith, East Carolina University, USA

SIGDIAL Officers:

President: Tim Paek, Microsoft Research, USA
Vice-President: Amanda Stent, AT&T Labs - Research, USA
Secretary/Treasurer: Kristiina Jokinen, University of Helsinki, Finland

Program Committee:

Hua Ai, Georgia Institute of Technology
Gregory Aist, Arizona State University
Jan Alexandersson, Deutsches Forschungszentrum für Künstliche Intelligenz (DFKI)
Jens Allwood, University of Göteborg
Nicholas Asher, Institut de Recherche en Informatique de Toulouse (IRIT)
Srinivas Bangalore, AT&T Labs Research
Nate Blaylock, Florida Institute for Human Machine Cognition
Dan Bohus, Microsoft Research
Johan Boye, KTH Royal Institute of Technology
Harry Bunt, University of Tilburg
Donna Byron, Northeastern University
Sandra Carberry, University of Delaware
Justine Cassell, Carnegie Mellon University
Yejin Choi, Stony Brook University

Jennifer Chu-Carroll, IBM T. J. Watson Research Center
Mark Core, University of Southern California Institute for Creative Technologies
Deborah Dahl, Conversational Technologies
David DeVault, University of Southern California Institute for Creative Technologies
Barbara Di Eugenio, University of Illinois at Chicago
Jens Edlund, KTH Royal Institute of Technology
Maxine Eskenazi, Carnegie Mellon University
Raquel Fernandez, University of Amsterdam
Katherine Forbes-Riley, University of Pittsburgh
Matthew Frampton, Stanford University
Sadaoki Furui, Tokyo Institute of Technology
Kallirroi Georgila, University of Southern California Institute for Creative Technologies
Genevieve Gorrell, University of Sheffield
Agustin Gravano, University of Buenos Aires
Nancy Green, University of North Carolina at Greensboro
Alexander Gruenstein, Massachusetts Institute of Technology
Curry Guinn, University of North Carolina at Wilmington
Joakim Gustafson, KTH Royal Institute of Technology
Helen Hastie, Heriot Watt University
Julia Hirschberg, Columbia University
Beth Ann Hockey, University of California at Santa Cruz
Michael Johnston, AT&T Labs Research
Kristiina Jokinen, University of Helsinki
Arne Jonsson, Linköping University
Pamela Jordan, University of Pittsburgh
Simon Keizer, University of Cambridge
John Kelleher, Dublin Institute of Technology
Alistair Knott, University of Otago
Geert-Jan Kruijff, Deutsches Forschungszentrum für Künstliche Intelligenz (DFKI)
Ivana Kruijff-Korbayova, University of Saarlandes
Ian Lane, Carnegie Mellon University
Staffan Larsson, Göteborg University
Gary Lee, Pohang University of Science and Technology (Postech)
Fabrice Lefevre, Cambridge University
Diane Litman, University of Pittsburgh
Ramon Lopez-Cozar, University of Granada
Susann Luperfoy, Massachusetts Institute of Technology
Wolfgang Minker, University of Ulm
Sebastian Moller, Deutsche Telekom Laboratories
Mikio Nakano, Honda Research Institute
Yukiko Nakano, Seikei University
Ani Nenkova, University of Pennsylvannia
Vincent Ng, University of Texas at Dallas
Tim Paek, Microsoft Research
Shimei Pan, IBM T. J. Watson Research Center
Patrick Paroubek, LIMSI-CNRS

Paul Piwek, Open University
Andrei Popescu-Belis, Idiap Research Institute
Matthew Purver, University of London
Antoine Raux, Honda Research Institute
Norbert Reithinger, Deutsches Forschungszentrum für Künstliche Intelligenz (DFKI)
Alex Rudnicky, Carnegie Mellon University
Yoshinori Sagisaka, Waseda University
David Schlangen, University of Potsdam
Stephanie Seneff, Massachusetts Institute of Technology
Elizabeth Shriberg, Microsoft
Candace Sidner, Worcester Polytechnic Institute
Gabriel Skantze, KTH Royal Institute of Technology
Manfred Stede, University of Potsdam
Amanda Stent, AT&T Labs Research
Matthew Stone, Rutgers University
Svetlana Stoyanchev, Open University
Michael Strube, Heidelberg Institute for Theoretical Studies
Marc Swerts, Tilburg University
Tokunaga Takenobu, Tokyo Institute of Technology
Thora Tenbrink, University of Bremen
Joel Tetrault, Educational Testing Service
Gokhan Tur, Microsoft
Marilyn Walker, University of California at Santa Cruz
Nigel Ward, University of Texas El Paso
Janyce Wiebe, University of Pittsburgh
Jason Williams, AT&T Labs Research
Teresa Wilson, University of Edinburgh
Steve Young, University of Cambridge
Michelle Zhou, IBM Almaden Research Center
Ingrid Zukerman, Monash University

Invited Speakers:

Professor Alex Lascarides, University of Edinburgh
Professor Michael Tanenhaus, University of Rochester

Strategic Conversation

Alex Lascarides

School of Informatics
University of Edinburgh
Edinburgh, EH8 9AB, Scotland, UK
alex@inf.ed.ac.uk

Models of conversation that rely on a robust notion of cooperation don't model dialogues where the agents' goals conflict; for instance, negotiation over restricted resources, courtroom cross examination and political debate. We aim to provide a framework in which both cooperative and non-cooperative conversation can be analyzed. We develop a logic that links the public commitments that agents make through their utterances to private attitudes---e.g., belief, desire and intention. This logic incorporates a qualitative model of human action and decision making that approximates principles from game theory: e.g., choose actions that maximize expected utility. However, unlike classical game theory, our model supports reasoning about action even when knowledge of one's own preferences and those of others is incomplete and/or changing as the dialogue proceeds---an essential feature of many conversations. The logic validates decidable inferences from utterances to mental states during interpretation, and from mental states to dialogue actions during language production. In a context where the agents' preferences align we derive axioms of co-operativity that are treated as primitive in BDI logics for analyzing dialogue. Thus models of cooperative conversation are a special case in our framework.

The research presented in this talk is joint work with Nicholas Asher.

Proceedings of the SIGDIAL 2011: the 12th Annual Meeting of the Special Interest Group on Discourse and Dialogue, page 1,
Portland, Oregon, June 17-18, 2011.

Spoken Dialog Challenge 2010: Comparison of Live and Control Test Results

Alan W Black[1], Susanne Burger[1], Alistair Conkie[4], Helen Hastie[2], Simon Keizer[3], Oliver Lemon[2], Nicolas Merigaud[2], Gabriel Parent[1], Gabriel Schubiner[1], Blaise Thomson[3], Jason D. Williams[4], Kai Yu[3], Steve Young[3] and Maxine Eskenazi[1]

[1]Language Technologies Institute, Carnegie Mellon University, Pittsburgh, USA
[2]Dept of Mathematical and Computer Science, Heriot-Watt University, Edinburgh, UK
[3]Engineering Department, Cambridge University, Cambridge, UK
[4]AT&T Labs – Research, Florham Park, NJ, USA
awb@cs.cmu.edu

Abstract

The Spoken Dialog Challenge 2010 was an exercise to investigate how different spoken dialog systems perform on the same task. The existing Let's Go Pittsburgh Bus Information System was used as a task and four teams provided systems that were first tested in controlled conditions with speech researchers as users. The three most stable systems were then deployed to real callers. This paper presents the results of the live tests, and compares them with the control test results. Results show considerable variation both between systems and between the control and live tests. Interestingly, relatively high task completion for controlled tests did not always predict relatively high task completion for live tests. Moreover, even though the systems were quite different in their designs, we saw very similar correlations between word error rate and task completion for all the systems. The dialog data collected is available to the research community.

1 Background

The goal of the Spoken Dialog Challenge (SDC) is to investigate how different dialog systems perform on a similar task. It is designed as a regularly recurring challenge. The first one took place in 2010. SDC participants were to provide one or more of three things: a system; a simulated user, and/or an evaluation metric. The task chosen for the first SDC was one that already had a large number of real callers. This had several advantages. First, there was a system that had been used by many callers. Second, there was a substantial dataset that participants could use to train their systems. Finally, there were real callers, rather than only lab testers. Past work has found systems which appear to perform well in lab tests do not always perform well when deployed to real callers, in part because real callers behave differently than lab testers, and usage conditions can be considerably different [Raux et al 2005, Ai et al 2008]. Deploying systems to real users is an important trait of the Spoken Dialog Challenge.

The CMU Let's Go Bus Information system [Raux et al 2006] provides bus schedule information for the general population of Pittsburgh. It is directly connected to the local Port Authority, whose evening calls for bus information are redirected to the automated system. The system has been running since March 2005 and has served over 130K calls.

The software and the previous years of dialog data were released to participants of the challenge to allow them to construct their own systems. A number of sites started the challenge, and four sites successfully built systems, including the original CMU system.

An important aspect of the challenge is that the quality of service to the end users (people in Pittsburgh) had to be maintained and thus an initial robustness and quality test was carried out on contributed systems. This control test provided scenarios over a web interface and required researchers from the participating sites to call each of the systems. The results of this control test were published in [Black et al. 2010] and by the individual participants [Williams et al. 2010, Thomson et al. 2010, Hastie et al, 2010] and they are repro-

Proceedings of the SIGDIAL 2011: the 12th Annual Meeting of the Special Interest Group on Discourse and Dialogue, pages 2–7,
Portland, Oregon, June 17-18, 2011.

duced below to give the reader a comparison with the later live tests.

Important distinctions between the control test callers and the live test callers were that the control test callers were primarily spoken dialog researchers from around the world. Although they were usually calling from more controlled acoustic conditions, most were not knowledgeable about Pittsburgh geography.

As mentioned above, four systems took part in the SDC. Following the practice of other challenges, we will not explicitly identify the sites where these systems were developed. We simply refer to them as SYS1-4 in the results. We will, however, state that one of the systems is the system that has been running for this task for several years. The architectures of the systems cover a number of different techniques for building spoken dialog systems, including agenda based systems, VoiceXML and statistical techniques.

2 Conditions of Control and Live tests

For this task, the caller needs to provide the departure stop, the arrival stop and the time of departure or arrival in order for the system to be able to perform a lookup in the schedule database. The route number can also be provided and used in the lookup, but it is not necessary. The present live system covers the East End of Pittsburgh. Although the Port Authority message states that other areas are not covered, callers may still ask for routes that are not in the East End; in this case, the live system must say it doesn't have information available. Some events that affect the length of the dialog include whether the system uses implicit or explicit confirmation or some combination of both, whether the system has an open-ended first turn or a directed one, and whether it deals with requests for the previous and/or following bus (this latter should have been present in all of the systems).

Just before the SDC started, the Port Authority had removed some of its bus routes. The systems were required to be capable of informing the caller that the route had been canceled, and then giving them a suitable alternative.

SDC systems answer live calls when the Port Authority call center is closed in the evening and early morning. There are quite different types and volumes of calls over the different days of the week. Weekend days typically have more calls, in part because the call center is open fewer hours on weekends. Figure 1 shows a histogram of average calls per hour for the evening and the early morning of each day of the week.

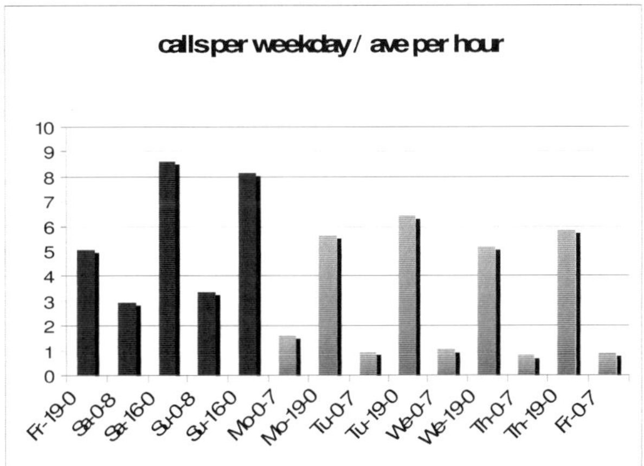

Figure 1: average number of calls per hour on weekends (dark bars) and weekdays. Listed are names of days and times before and after midnight when callers called the system.

The control tests were set up through a simple web interface that presented 8 different scenarios to callers. Callers were given a phone number to call; each caller spoke to each of the 4 different systems twice. A typical scenario was presented with few words, mainly relying on graphics in order to avoid influencing the caller's choice of vocabulary. An example is shown in Figure 2.

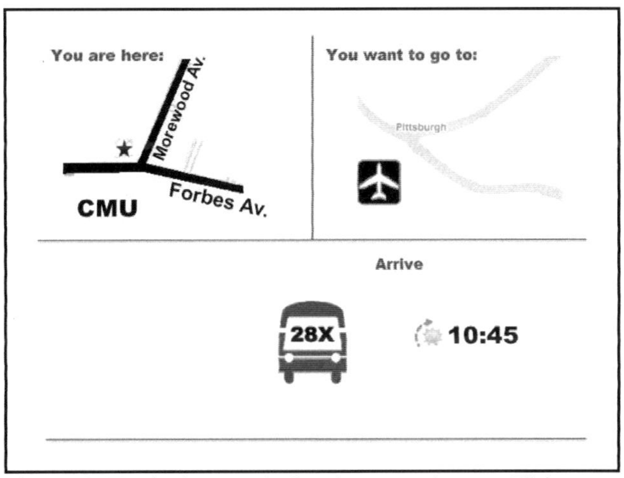

Figure 2: Typical scenario for the control tests. This example requests that the user find a bus from the corner of Forbes and Morewood (near CMU) to the airport, using bus route 28X, arriving by 10:45 AM.

3 Control Test Results

The logs from the four systems were labeled for task success by hand. A call is successful if any of the following outputs are correctly issued:

- Bus schedule for the requested departure and arrival stops for the stated bus number (if given).
- A statement that there is no bus available for that route.
- A statement that there is no scheduled bus at that time.

We additionally allowed the following boundary cases:

- A departure/arrival stop within 15 minutes walk.
- Departure/arrival times within one hour of requested time.
- An alternate bus number that serves the requested route.

In the control tests, SYS2 had system connection issues that caused a number of calls to fail to connect, as well as a poorer task completion. It was not included in the live tests. It should be pointed out that SYS2 was developed by a single graduate student as a class project while the other systems were developed by teams of researchers. The results of the Control Tests are shown in Table 1 and are discussed further below.

	SYS1	SYS2	SYS3	SYS4
Total Calls	91	61	75	83
no_ info	3.3%	37.7%	1.3%	9.6%
donthave	17.6%	24.6%	14.7%	9.6%
donthave_corr	*68.8%*	*33.3%*	*100.0%*	*100.0%*
donthave_incorr	*31.3%*	*66.7%*	*0.0%*	*0.0%*
pos_out	79.1%	37.7%	84.0%	80.7%
pos_out_corr	*66.7%*	*78.3%*	*88.9%*	*80.6%*
pos_out_incorr	*33.3%*	*21.7%*	*11.1%*	*19.4%*

Table 1. Results of hand analysis of the four systems in the **control test**

The three major classes of system response are as follows. **no_info**: this occurs when the system gives neither a specific time nor a valid excuse (bus not covered, or none at that time). **no_info** calls can be treated as errors (even though there maybe be valid reasons such as the caller hangs up because the bus they are waiting for arrives). **donthave**: identifies calls that state the requested bus is not covered by the system or that there is no bus at the requested time. **pos_out**: identifies calls where a specific time schedule is given. Both **donthave** and **pos_out** calls may be correct or erroneous (e.g the given information is not for the requested bus, the departure stop is wrong, etc).

4 Live Tests Results

In the live tests the actual Pittsburgh callers had access to three systems: SYS1, SYS3, and SYS4. Although engineering issues may not always be seen to be as relevant as scientific results, it is important to acknowledge several issues that had to be overcome in order to run the live tests.

Since the Pittsburgh Bus Information System is a real system, it is regularly updated with new schedules from the Port Authority. This happens about every three months and sometimes includes changes in bus routes as well as times and stops. The SDC participants were given these updates and were allowed the time to make the changes to their systems. Making things more difficult is the fact that the Port Authority often only releases the schedules a few days ahead of the change. Another concern was that the live tests be run within one schedule period so that the change in schedule would not affect the results.

The second engineering issue concerned telephony connectivity. There had to be a way to transfer calls from the Port Authority to the participating systems (that were run at the participating sites, not at CMU) without slowing down or perturbing service to the callers. This was achieved by an elaborate set of call-forwarding mechanisms that performed very reliably. However, since one system was in Europe, connections to it were sometimes not as reliable as to the US-based systems.

	SYS1	SYS3	SYS4
Total Calls	678	451	742
Non-empty calls	633	430	670
no_ info	18.5%	14.0%	11.0%
donthave	26.4%	30.0%	17.6%
donthave_corr	*47.3%*	*40.3%*	*37.3%*
donthave_incorr	*52.7%*	*59.7%*	*62.7%*
pos_out	55.1%	56.0%	71.3%
pos_out_corr	*86.8%*	*93.8%*	*91.6%*
pos_out_incorr	*13.2%*	*6.2%*	*8.4%*

Table 2. Results of hand analysis of the three systems in the **live tests**. Row labels are the same as in Table 1.

We ran each of the three systems for multiple two day periods over July and August 2010. This design gave each system an equal distribution of weekdays and weekends, and also ensured that repeat-callers within the same day experienced the same system.

One of the participating systems (SYS4) could support simultaneous calls, but the other two could not and the caller would receive a busy signal if the system was already in use. This, however, did not happen very often.

Results of hand analysis of real calls are shown in Table 4 alongside the results for the Control Test for easy comparison. In the live tests we had an additional category of call types – empty calls (0-turn calls) – which are calls where there are no user turns, for example because the caller hung up or was disconnected before saying anything. Each system had 14 days of calls and external daily factors may change the number of calls. We do suspect that telephony issues may have prevented some calls from getting through to SYS3 on some occasions.

Table 3 provides call duration information for each of the systems in both the control and live tests.

	Length (s)	Turns/call	Words/turn
SYS1 control	155	18.29	2.87 (2.84)
SYS1 live	111	16.24	2.15 (1.03)
SYS2 control	147	17.57	1.63 (1.62)
SYS3 control	96	10.28	2.73 (1.94)
SYS3 live	80	9.56	2.22 (1.14)
SYS4 control	154	14.70	2.25 (1.78)
SYS4 live	126	11.00	1.63 (0.77)

Table 3: For live tests, average length of each call, average number of turns per call, and average number of words per turn (numbers in brackets are standard deviations).

Each of the systems used a different speech recognizer. In order to understand the impact of word error rate on the results, all the data were hand transcribed to provide orthographic transcriptions of each user turn. Summary word error statistics are shown in Table 4. However, summary statistics do not show the correlation between word error rate and dialogue success. To achieve this, following Thomson et al (2010), we computed a logistic regression of success against word error rate (WER) for each of the systems. Figure 3 shows the regressions for the Control Tests and Figure 4 for the Live Tests.

	SYS1	SYS3	SYS4
Control	38.4	27.9	27.5
Live	43.8	42.5	35.7

Table 4: Average dialogue word error rate (WER).

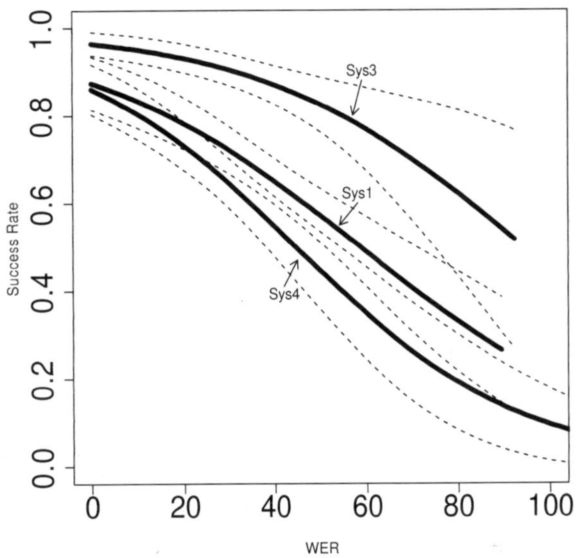

Figure 3: Logistic regression of control test success vs WER for the three fully tested systems

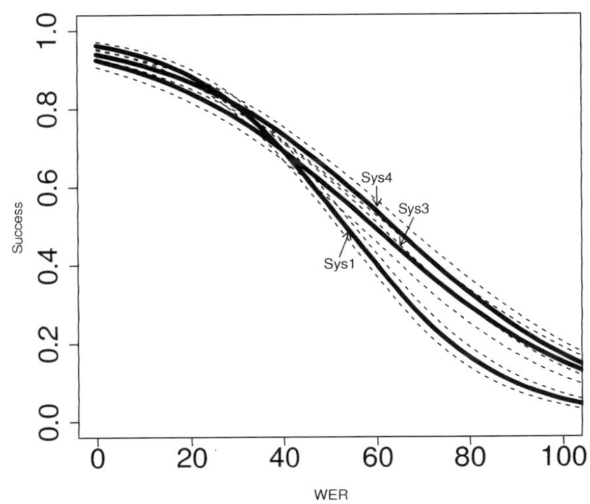

Figure 4: Logistic regression of live success vs WER for the three fully tested systems

In order to compare the control and live tests, we can calculate task completion as the percentage of calls that gave a correct result. We include only non-empty calls (excluding 0-turn calls), and treat all no_info calls as being incorrect, even though some may be due to extraneous reasons such as the bus turning up (Table 5).

	SYS1	SYS3	SYS4
Control	64.9% (5.0%)	89.4% (3.6%)	74.6% (4.8%)
Live	60.3% (1.9%)	64.6% (2.3%)	71.9% (1.7%)

Table 5: Live and control test task completion (std. err).

5 Discussion

All systems had lower WER and higher task completion in the controlled test vs. the live test. This agrees with past work [Raux et al 2005, Ai et al 2008], and underscores the challenges of deploying real-world systems.

For all systems, dialogs with controlled subjects were longer than with live callers – both in terms of length and number of turns. In addition, for all systems, live callers used shorter utterances than controlled subjects. Controlled subjects may be more patient than live callers, or perhaps live callers were more likely to abandon calls in the face of higher recognition error rates.

Some interesting differences between the systems are evident in the live tests. Looking at dialog durations, SYS3 used confirmations least often, and yielded the fastest dialogs (80s/call). SYS1 made extensive use of confirmations, yielding the most turns of any system and slightly longer dialogs (111s/call). SYS4 was the most system-directed, always collecting information one element at a time. As a result it was the slowest of the systems (126s/call), but because it often used implicit confirmation instead of explicit confirmation, it had fewer turns/call than SYS1.

For task completion, SYS3 performed best in the controlled trials, with SYS1 worst and SYS4 in between. However in the live test, SYS4 performed best, with SYS3 and SYS1 similar and worse. It was surprising that task completion for SYS3 was the highest for the controlled tests yet among the lowest for the live tests. Investigating this, we found that much of the variability in task completion for the live tests appears to be due to WER. In the control tests SYS3 and SYS4 had similar error rates but the success rate of SYS3 was higher. The regression in Figure 3 shows this clearly. In the live tests SYS3 had a significantly higher word error rate and average success rate was much lower than in SYS4.

It is interesting to speculate on why the recognition rates for SYS3 and SYS4 were different in the live tests, but were comparable in the control tests. In a spoken dialogue system the architecture has a considerable impact on the measured word error rate. Not only will the language model and use of dialogue context be different, but the dialogue design and form of system prompts will influence the form and content of user inputs. Thus, word error rates do not just depend on the quality of the acoustic models – they depend on the whole system design. As noted above, SYS4 was more system-directed than SYS3 and this probably contributed to the comparatively better ASR performance with live users. In the control tests, the behavior of users (research lab workers) may have been less dependent on the manner in which users were prompted for information by the system. Overall, of course, it is user satisfaction and task success which matter.

6 Corpus Availability and Evaluation

The SDC2010 database of all logs from all systems including audio plus hand transcribed utterances, and hand defined success values is released through CMU's Dialog Research Center (http://dialrc.org).

One of the core goals of the Spoken Dialog Challenge is to not only create an opportunity for researchers to test their systems on a common platform with real users, but also create common data sets for testing evaluation metrics. Although some work has been done on this for the control test data (e.g. [Zhu et al 2010]), we expect further evaluation techniques will be applied to these data.

One particular issue which arose during this evaluation concerned the difficulty of defining precisely what constitutes task success. A precise definition is important to developers, especially if reinforcement style learning is being used to optimize the success. In an information seeking task of the type described here, task success is straightforward when the user's requirements can be satisfied but more difficult if some form of constraint relaxation is required. For example, if the user asks if there is a bus from the current location to the airport – the answer "No." may be strictly correct but not necessarily helpful. Should this dialogue be scored as successful or not? The answer "No, but there is a stop two blocks away where you can take the number 28X bus direct to the airport." is clearly more useful to the user. Should success therefore be a numeric measure rather than a binary decision? And if a measure, how can it be precisely defined? A second and related issue is the need for evaluation algorithms which determine task success automatically. Without these, system optimization will remain an art rather than a science.

7 Conclusions

This paper has described the first attempt at an exercise to investigate how different spoken dialog systems perform on the same task. The existing Let's Go Pittsburgh Bus Information System was used as a task and four teams provided systems that were first tested in controlled conditions with speech researchers as users. The three most stable systems were then deployed "live" with real callers. Results show considerable variation both between systems and between the control and live tests. Interestingly, relatively high task completion for controlled tests did not always predict relatively high task completion for live tests. This confirms the importance of testing on live callers, not just usability subjects.

The general organization and framework of the evaluation worked well. The ability to route audio telephone calls to anywhere in the world using voice over IP protocols was critical to the success of the challenge since it provides a way for individual research labs to test their in-house systems without the need to port them to a central coordinating site.

Finally, the critical role of precise evaluation metrics was noted and the need for automatic tools to compute them. Developers need these at an early stage in the cycle to ensure that when systems are subsequently evaluated, the results and system behaviors can be properly compared.

Acknowledgments

Thanks to AT&T Research for providing telephony support for transporting telephone calls during the live tests. This work was in part supported by the US National Science foundation under the project "Dialogue Research Center".

References

Ai, H., Raux, A., Bohus, D., Eskenzai, M., and Litman, D. (2008) "Comparing spoken dialog corpora collected with recruited subjects versus real users", Proc SIGDial, Columbus, Ohio, USA.

Black, A., Burger, S., Langner, B., Parent, G., and Eskenazi, M. (2010) "Spoken Dialog Challenge 2010", SLT 2010, Berkeley, CA.

Hastie, H., Merigaud, N., Liu, X and Oliver Lemon. (2010) " 'Let's Go Dude', Using The Spoken Dialogue Challenge to Teach Spoken Dialogue Development", SLT 2010, Berkeley, CA.

Raux, A., Langner, B., Bohus, D., Black, A., Eskenazi, M. (2005) "Let's go public! Taking a spoken dialog system to the real world", Interspeech 2005, Lisbon, Portugal.

Raux, A., Bohus, D., Langner, B., Black, A., and Eskenazi, M. (2006) "Doing Research on a Deployed Spoken Dialogue System: One Year of Let's Go! Experience", Interspeech 2006 - ICSLP, Pittsburgh, PA.

Thomson B., Yu, K. Keizer, S., Gasic, M., Jurcicek, F., Mairesse, F. and Young, S. "Bayesian Dialogue System for the Let's Go Spoken Dialogue Challenge", SLT 2010, Berkeley, CA.

Williams, J., Arizmendi, I., and Conkie, A. "Demonstration of AT&T 'Let's Go': A Production-Grade Statistical Spoken Dialog System." SLT 2010, Berkeley, CA.

Zhu, Y., Yang, Z., Meng, H., Li, B., Levow, G., and King, I. (2010) "Using Finite State Machines for Evaluating Spoken Dialog Systems", SLT 2010, Berkeley, CA.

Which System Differences Matter? Using ℓ_1/ℓ_2 Regularization to Compare Dialogue Systems

José P. González-Brenes and **Jack Mostow**
Project LISTEN
Language Technologies Institute
School of Computer Science
Carnegie Mellon University
Pittsburgh, PA 15213, USA
{joseg,mostow}@cs.cmu.edu

Abstract

We investigate how to jointly explain the performance and behavioral differences of two spoken dialogue systems. The Join Evaluation and Differences Identification (JEDI), finds differences between systems relevant to performance by formulating the problem as a multi-task feature selection question. JEDI provides evidence on the usefulness of a recent method, ℓ_1/ℓ_p-regularized regression (Obozinski et al., 2007). We evaluate against manually annotated success criteria from real users interacting with five different spoken user interfaces that give bus schedule information.

1 Introduction

This paper addresses the problem of how to determine which differences between two versions of a system affect their behavior. Researchers in Spoken Dialogue Systems (SDSs) can be perplexed as to which of the differences between alternative systems affect performance metrics (Bacchiani et al., 2008). For example, when testing on real users at different periods of time, the variance of the performance metrics might be higher than the difference between systems, causing (i) significantly different scores in identical systems deployed at different times, and (ii) the same score on different systems (González-Brenes et al., 2009).

We approach the problem of finding which system differences matter by describing dialogues as feature vectors constructed from the logs of dialogs generated by the SDSs interacting with real users. Hence, we aim to identify features that jointly characterize the system differences and the performance of the SDS being evaluated. These features should be able to (i) predict a performance metric and (ii) distinguish between the two SDS being evaluated.

The main contribution of this paper is a novel algorithm for detecting differences between two systems that can explain performance. Additionally, we provide details on how to implement state-of-the-art multi-task learning for SDSs.

The rest of this manuscript is organized as follows. Section 2 reviews multi-task feature selection. Section 3 describes two algorithms to find which system differences matter. Section 4 describes the specific SDS used to illustrate our algorithms. Section 5 presents some experimental results. Section 6 reviews related prior work. Section 7 presents some concluding remarks and future work. Appendix A provides implementation details of the multi-task learning approach we used.

2 Feature Selection

In this section we describe how we use regression to perform feature selection. Feature selection methods construct and select subsets of features in order to build a good predictor. We focus our attention on feature selection methods that use complexity (regularization) penalties, because of their recent theoretical and experimental success (Yuan and Lin, 2006; Park and Hastie, 2007). We provide a more rigorous description of how to implement this formulation as an optimization problem in Appendix A.

We use labels to encode the output we want to predict. For example, if our performance metric is binary, we label successful dialogues with a $+1$, and unsuccesful dialogues with a -1. Given a training set consisting of labeled dialogues, we want to learn

Proceedings of the SIGDIAL 2011: the 12th Annual Meeting of the Special Interest Group on Discourse and Dialogue, pages 8–17,
Portland, Oregon, June 17-18, 2011.

a model that assigns a label to unseen dialogues. We follow an approach called empirical risk minimization (Obozinski et al., 2007), that aims to minimize the error of fitting the training data, while penalizing the complexity of the model:

$$\textbf{Minimize} \ \boxed{\text{Model loss}} + \lambda \boxed{\text{Complexity}} \quad (1)$$

Here the hyper-parameter λ controls the trade-off between a better fit to the training data (with a higher risk of over-fitting it), and a simpler model, with fewer features selected (and less predictive power). We now review the two components of risk minimization, model loss and complexity penalty.

2.1 Model Loss

We model probabilistically the loss of our model against the real-life phenomenon studied. Given a dialogue x, with correct label l, its loss using a model $\boldsymbol{\beta}$ is:

$$\text{loss}_{\beta}(\hat{y}, x) \equiv P(y = l|x; \text{reality}) - P(\hat{y} = l|x; \boldsymbol{\beta}) \quad (2)$$

Here $\hat{y}$ is the predicted value of the event y. Since l is the true label, $P(y = l|x; \text{reality}) = 1$. To get the overall loss of the model, we aggregate over the prediction loss of each of the dialogues in the training set by summing their individual loss calculated with Equation 2. Let $X = \{x^{(1)}, x^{(2)}, \ldots x^{(n)}\}$ be the n dialogues in the training set. Then the overall loss of model $\boldsymbol{\beta}$ is:

$$\text{loss}_{\beta}(y^{(1)}, x^{(1)}) + \cdots + \text{loss}_{\beta}(y^{(n)}, x^{(n)})$$

Since we use discrete labels, we use a logistic function to model their probability. Let $x_1, \ldots x_k$ be the k features extracted from dialogue x. Then the logistic regression model is:

$$P(\hat{y} = +1|x; \boldsymbol{\beta}) = \frac{1}{Z}\exp(\beta_1 x_1 + \cdots + \beta_k x_k)$$

Here $\beta_1 \ldots \beta_k$ are the parameters of the model, and Z simply normalizes P to ensure that P is a valid probability function (the range of P should be 0 to 1):

$$Z = 1 + \exp(\beta_1 x_1 + \cdots + \beta_k x_k)$$

Multi-task learning solves related regression problems at the same time using a shared representation. We now describe the risk-minimization formulation for multi-task learning. Let y^m be the value of the performance metric. Let y^s be the label of the system that generated the dialogue. The individual dialogue loss of using models $\boldsymbol{\beta}^m$ and $\boldsymbol{\beta}^s$ is:

$$\text{loss}_{\beta^m}(\hat{y}^m, x) + \text{loss}_{\beta^s}(\hat{y}^s, x)$$

2.2 Complexity Penalties

We consider a feature x_i to be selected into the model if its regression coefficient β_i is non-zero. Complexity penalties encourage selecting only a few features. We review several commonly used penalties (Zou and Hastie, 2005):

- **ℓ_2 Penalty.** Under some circumstances ℓ_2 penalties perform better than other types of penalties (Zou and Hastie, 2005). The ℓ_2 penalty for a model $\boldsymbol{\beta}$ is:

$$||\boldsymbol{\beta}||_{\ell_2} \equiv \sqrt{(\beta_1)^2 + \cdots + (\beta_k)^2}$$

- **ℓ_1 Penalty.** An ℓ_1 penalty induces sparsity by setting *many* parameters of the model $\boldsymbol{\beta}$ to exactly zero (Tibshirani, 1996).

$$||\boldsymbol{\beta}||_{\ell_1} \equiv |\beta_1| + \cdots + |\beta_k|$$

- **ℓ_1/ℓ_2 Penalty.** Yuan and Lin (2006) proposed a group penalty for penalizing groups of features simultaneously. Previous work has shown that grouping features between tasks encourages features to be used either by all tasks or by none (Turlach et al., 2005; Obozinski et al., 2007; Lounici et al., 2009; Puniyani et al., 2010). Our ℓ_1/ℓ_2 penalty is:

$$\left|\sqrt{(\beta_1^m)^2 + (\beta_1^s)^2}\right| + \ldots + \left|\sqrt{(\beta_k^m)^2 + (\beta_k^s)^2}\right|$$

3 Finding Features that Predict Performance and System Differences

We find system differences that are predictive of SDS performance, relying on:

- *Describing dialogues as feature vectors.* The behavior of the systems must be describable by features extracted from the logs of the systems. A discussion of feature engineering for dialogue systems is found in (González-Brenes and Mostow, 2011).

- *Finding system differences.* The features of a classifier that distinguishes between SDSs, can be used to identify their differences (González-Brenes et al., 2009). When comparing two SDSs, we label the baseline system with -1, and the alternate version with $+1$.

- *Modeling performance.* Although our approach does not depend on a specific performance metric, in this paper we use dialogue success, a binary indicator that triggers that the user's query was answered by the SDS. Task completion is cheaper to compute than dialogue success, as it does not require a manual human labeled reference, but we consider that dialogue success is a more accurate metric. Task completion is used in commercial applications (Bacchiani et al., 2008), and has been extensively studied in the literature (Walker et al., 2001; Walker et al., 2002; Hajdinjak and Mihelic, 2006; Levin and Pieraccini, 2006; Möller et al., 2007; Möller et al., 2008; Schmitt et al., 2010). We encode success of dialogues by manually annotating them with a binary variable that distinguishes if the user query is fulfilled by the SDS.

We now present two algorithms to find what differences matter between systems. We introduce Serial EvaluatioN Analysis (SERENA) as a scaffold for the Join Evaluation and Differences Identification (JEDI) algorithm.

3.1 SERENA algorithm

The input to SERENA is a collection of log files created by two different SDSs and two functions that represent the correct label for the regression tasks. In our case these functions should return binary labels $(+1, -1)$: one task distinguishes between successful and unsuccessful dialogues, and the other task distinguishes a baseline from an alternative SDS version. SERENA's objective is to select features from one task, and use them to predict the other task. For example, SERENA selects features that predict differences between versions, and uses them to predict performance.

Algorithm 1 provides the pseudo-code for SERENA. Line 1 builds the training set $\mathbf{X}$ from parsing the logs of the SDSs. Lines 2 and 3 create the output

Algorithm 1 SERENA algorithm

Require: $\mathbf{Logs_1}, \mathbf{Logs_2}$ are the collections of SDS logs of two systems. $\mathbf{task_1}, \mathbf{task_2}$ are functions that return the value of a performance metric, and which system is being evaluated (-1 if is the baseline, $+1$ otherwise).

1: $\mathbf{X} \leftarrow \text{extract\_features}(\mathbf{Log}_1, \mathbf{Log}_2)$

2: $\boldsymbol{y}^{t_1} \leftarrow \begin{bmatrix} \text{task}_1(\mathbf{Logs}_1) \\ \text{task}_1(\mathbf{Logs}_2) \end{bmatrix}$

3: $\boldsymbol{y}^{t_2} \leftarrow \begin{bmatrix} \text{task}_2(\mathbf{Logs}_1) \\ \text{task}_2(\mathbf{Logs}_2) \end{bmatrix}$

4: // Select features that explain both tasks:

5: **for** $\lambda = \{0.1, 0.2, \dots\}$ **do**

6: $\quad \boldsymbol{\beta}^{t_1} \leftarrow \text{regression}_{\ell_1}(\mathbf{X}, \boldsymbol{y}^{t_1}, \lambda)$

7: $\quad$ // Get feature weights:

8: $\quad \mathbf{X}' \leftarrow \mathbf{X}$; where $x_k | \forall x_k \in \mathbf{X}', \beta_k^{t_1} \neq 0$

9: $\quad \boldsymbol{\beta}^* \leftarrow \text{regression}_{\ell_2}(\mathbf{X}', \boldsymbol{y}^{t_2}, \lambda_c)$

10: **end for**

11: **return** $\boldsymbol{\beta}^*$

variables y for the regression tasks. Line 6 returns the most predictive features using ℓ_1 regularization as described in Section 2. Line 8 builds a new training set, removing the features that were not selected in line 6. Line 9 builds the final coefficients by fitting a ℓ_2-regularized model using a constant λ_c. We calculate the coefficients using an ℓ_2 penalty, because it has a better fit to the data (Zou and Hastie, 2005). Moreover, by using the same penalty, we control for the idiosyncrasies different penalties have in parameter learning. In the experiments described in Section 5, all of our experiments are reported fitting a ℓ_2-regularized models.

SERENA is not conmutative with regards to the order of the tasks: selecting the features that predict performance and using them to predict system differences is not the same as the reverse. More importantly, SERENA only searches in one of the tasks at a time. We are interested in finding the features that explain both tasks *simultaneously*. In the next subsection we describe JEDI which makes use of recent advances in multi-task feature selection in order to find the features for both tasks at the same time.

3.2 JEDI algorithm

Algorithm 2 provides the pseudo-code for JEDI. JEDI uses multi-task regression to find the features that affect performance and system differences

Algorithm 2 JEDI algorithm

Require: $\mathbf{Logs_1}, \mathbf{Logs_2}$ are the collections of SDS logs of two systems. $\mathbf{task_1}$, $\mathbf{task_2}$ are functions that return the value of a performance metric, and which system is being evaluated (-1 if is the baseline, $+1$ otherwise).

$\mathbf{X} \leftarrow \text{extract\_features}(\mathbf{Log}_1, \mathbf{Log}_2)$

$\boldsymbol{y}^{t_1} \leftarrow \begin{bmatrix} \text{task}_1(\mathbf{Logs}_1) \\ \text{task}_1(\mathbf{Logs}_2) \end{bmatrix}$

$\boldsymbol{y}^{t_2} \leftarrow \begin{bmatrix} \text{task}_2(\mathbf{Logs}_1) \\ \text{task}_2(\mathbf{Logs}_2) \end{bmatrix}$

// Select features that explain both tasks:

for $\lambda = \{0.1, 0.2, \ldots\}$ **do**

  $\boldsymbol{\beta}^{\mathbf{t_1}} \boldsymbol{\beta}^{\mathbf{t_2}} \leftarrow \text{regression}_{\ell_1/\ell_2}(\mathbf{X}, \vec{\mathbf{y}}^{t_1}, \vec{\mathbf{y}}^{t_2}, \lambda)$

  // Get feature weights:

  $\mathbf{X}' \leftarrow \mathbf{X}$; where $x_k | \forall x_k \in \mathbf{X}', \beta_k^{t_1} \neq 0$

  $\boldsymbol{\beta}^* \leftarrow \text{regression}_{\ell_2}(\mathbf{X}', \boldsymbol{y}^{t_2}, \lambda_c)$

end for

return $\boldsymbol{\beta}^*$

jointly. To ensure a sparse feature set across the tasks, it applies a ℓ_1/ℓ_2 penalty. In this way, a feature is either selected to predict performance and system differences, or it is not selected at all. In the next section we review a concrete example of a SDS in which we apply SERENA and JEDI.

4 Case Study

We use data collected from *Let's Go!*, an experimentary SDS available for research purposes[1] that provides bus planning information to the Pittsburgh East End community (Raux et al., 2006). Figure 1 shows a sample dialogue.

We assembled three disjoint datasets to have dialogues just before and after what we considered important architectural differences of Let's Go's implementation. By going through the change log, we realize that the magnitude of the differences varies widely. Table 1 describes the date the systems were deployed, the description of the change in the SDS, and the number of dialogues in each set. From the 86 dialogues of "Set A", half are a random sample of the logs before the acoustic model was retrained ($\mathbf{Log_1}$), and the other half is a sample after the acoustic model was retrained ($\mathbf{Log_2}$). In the case of the 84 dialogues of "Set B", half of the logs

[1] `http://www.dialrc.org/`

System:	Welcome to the CMU Let's Go! Bus Information System. How may I help you?
User:	I'd like to go to Forbes and Murray.
System:	To Forbes and Murray. Where are you leaving from?
User:	Carnegie Mellon.
System:	From Carnegie Mellon. There are five buses running between Carnegie Mellon and Forbes and Murray: the 501, the 59U, the 61A, the 61B, and the 61C. What else can I do for you?
User:	When is the next one?
System:	The next 61C going to Forbes and Murray will leave Carnegie Mellon at 5:13 PM.

Figure 1: Example of a *Let's Go* dialogue, from (Raux et al., 2006)

use an older version of the Olympus SDS infrastructure (Bohus et al., 2007), and the other half uses Olympus II. Since each system was deployed in a different period of time, we want to corroborate that we are modeling the differences among systems, and not seasonal. Hence, for control conditions, we also chose a data set that contained no major change to the system or to other conditions (Set C).

Sets were built by randomly sampling from the collection of logs. They have the same number of dialogues from each SDS version (baseline/alternate). Each dialogue was manually annotated to indicate whether the user's query was fulfilled, and we removed from our analysis the two dialogues that were only partially fulfilled. The number of successful dialogues is different from the number of unsuccessful dialogues.

We created a script to extract features from the log files of Let's Go!. The script has an explicit list of features to extract from the event logs, such as the words that were identified by the Automatic Speech Recognizer. Although this script is dependent on our specific log format, it should be a simple programming task to adapt it to a different dialogue system, provided its logs are comprehensive enough. The

Table 1: **Dataset Description**

Set	Size	Description	Date	
A	86	Baseline	8/05	10/05
		New acoustic model	12/05	2/05
B	86	Baseline	8/06	10/06
		New SDS architecture	6/07	7/07
C	84	Baseline	10/07	11/07
		No change	11/07	12/07

script performs the standard transformation of centering feature values as z-scores with mean zero and standard deviation one.

Table 2 summarizes the properties we are interested to model. Dialogue properties are the features that summarize the behavior of the whole dialogue, and turn properties work at a finer-grain. We encode turn properties into features in the following way:

- **Global average.** Turn properties are averaged over the entire dialogue.

- **Beginning window.** Turn properties are averaged across an initial window. Based on preliminary experiments, we defined the window as the first 5 turns.

- **State.** We relied on the fact that SDSs are often engineered as finite state automata (Bohus et al., 2007). Properties are averaged across the states that belong to a specific dialogue state (for example, asking departure place). Because we are interested in early identification of differences, we restricted state features to be inside the beginning window.

5 Evaluation

We assess the performance of our algorithms by evaluating the classification accuracy using the features selected. To facilitate assessment of SDS, we only consider models that select up to 15 features. Figure 2 reports mean classification accuracy using five-fold cross-validation. Its first column describes how well the features selected perform on detecting system differences, and the second column describes how well they predict task success as a performance metric. We compare JEDI and SERENA against the following approaches:

Table 2: **Features**

Dialogue Properties
# of re-prompted turns
# of turns
Mean Dialogue length
is evening?, is weekend?, 0-23 hour
Turn Properties
Occurrences of word w
# of parse errors
# of unrecognized words
# of words
# of repeated words
# of unique words
Turn length
Words per minute
Failed prompts (number and percentage)
Mean Utterance Length
Barge-in (in seconds)
Machine-user pause (in seconds)
User-machine pause (in seconds)
Amplitude (power) statistics

- **Majority classifier baseline.** A classifier that always selects the majority class (datasets B and C are not balanced in the number of successful dialogues).

- **Same Task Classifier** We report the classification accuracy of the model trained and tested on the *same* task. Features are selected using an ℓ_1 penalty, and the coefficients are estimated with ℓ_2-regularized logistic regression. For example, in the column of the left, SERENA uses the most predictive features of system differences to predict success, while the same task classifier uses them to predict system differences. The same task classifier does not answer "which system differences matter", it is just an interesting benchmark.

We used a one-sample t-test to check for statistically significant differences against the classification accuracy of the majority classifier baseline. We used a paired-sample t-test to check for significant differences in classification accuracy between classifiers. Paired samples have the same λ hyper-parameter, which was described in the risk-

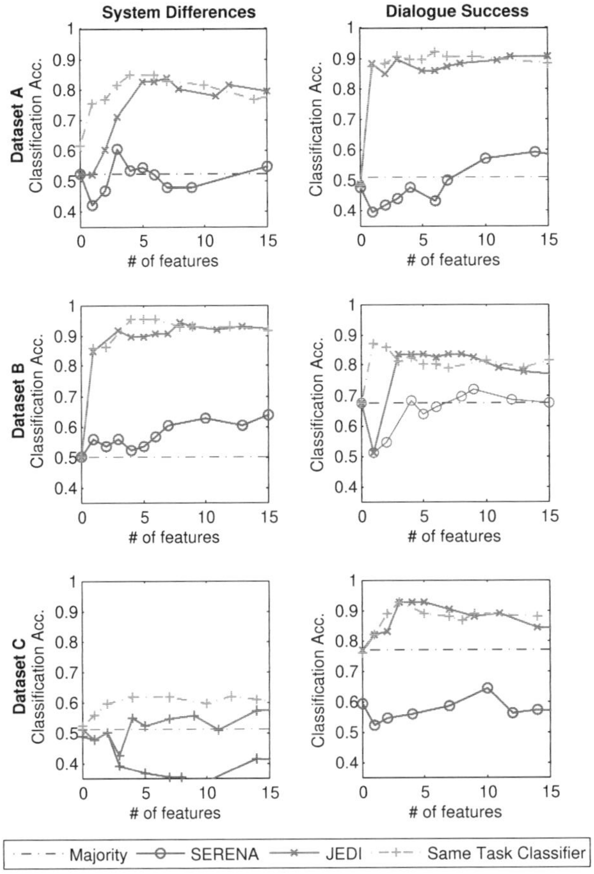

Figure 2: Classification accuracy of different feature selection techniques

minimization formulation explained in Section 2. This hyper-parameter is related to the number of features selected – as λ increases, the number of features selected decreases. We use 5% as the significance level at which to reject the null hypothesis. When checking for statistical differences, we tested on the range of λs computed[2].

First we investigate the performance of the simpler algorithm SERENA. For Dataset A, SERENA does not yield significant differences over the majority classifier baseline. For Dataset B, SERENA is significantly better than the majority classifier in predicting system differences, but is significantly worse for predicting success. This means that the order in which we choose the tasks in SERENA affects its performance. SERENA performs significantly worse in the Control Set C. We conclude that SERENA is not very reliable in predicting which system differences matter.

We now discuss how well JEDI is able to fill-in for the deficiencies of SERENA. As an "upper-bound", we will compare it to a classifier trained and tested in the same task. This classifier significantly dominates over the majority baseline, even for the the Control Set C, where there were no changes in the SDS. This suggests that the classifier might be picking up on seasonal differences. For Set A, JEDI performs significantly better than the majority classifier and than SERENA. For Set B, there are no significant differences between the upper-bound classifier and JEDI when predicting for changes in the SDS. Again, JEDI dominates over SERENA and the majority baseline. For the Control Set C, JEDI is not statistically different from the majority baseline. This is the expected behavior, since the difference in performance cannot be explained by the differences between the SDS. We hypothesize that the classification accuracy of JEDI could be used as a distance function between SDS: The closer the accuracy of distinguishing SDS is to 50%, the more similar the SDSs are. Conversely, when JEDI is able to classify system differences closer to 100%, it is because the SDSs are more different.

Tables 3 and 4 describe the features selected for Sets A and B respectively. The numbers indicate

[2] $\lambda = \{100, 30, 25, 20, 19, 18, \ldots, 1, 0.5, 0.25, 0.1\}$

Table 3: **Features selected in Dataset A**

Feature	Suc.	Diff.	JEDI
System-user pause	5		5
Weekend night?	3		
% of failed prompts	4		
"Forbes_St." word		5	3
User's max. power		5	

Table 4: **Features selected in Dataset B**

Feature	Suc.	Diff.	JEDI
% of failed prompts	5		4
User's power std.dev.	5		
Weekend night?	3		
Unrecognized word		5	
Words/min.		4	
User-system pause		5	
Turn length		5	5

in how many folds the feature was selected by JEDI and by classifiers trained to predict Success and SDS differences using five-fold cross validation. The λ used is selected to contain the closest to five features (ties are resolved randomly). We only report features that appeared in at least three folds. In Dataset A we see that time of day is selected to predict dialogue success. Anecdotally, we have noticed that many users during weekend nights appear to be intoxicated when calling the system. JEDI does not select "is weekend night" as a feature, because it has little predictive power to detect system differences. In Dataset A, JEDI selects a speech recognition feature (the token "Forbes_St" was recognized), and an end-pointing feature. Since in Dataset A, the difference between systems correspond to a different acoustic model, these features make sense intuitively. In Dataset B, JEDI detected that the features most predictive with system differences and success are percentage of failed prompts and the length of the turn. The models for both systems make sense after the fact. However, neither model was known beforehand, nor did we know which of many features considered would turn out to be informative. Anecdotally, the documentation of the history of changes of Let's Go! is maintained manually. Sometimes, because of human error, this history is incomplete. The ability of JEDI to identify system differences has been able to help completing the history of changes (González-Brenes et al., 2009).

6 Relation to Prior Work

The scientific literature offers several performance metrics to assess SDS performance (Polifroni et al., 1992; Danieli and Gerbino, 1995; Bacchiani et al., 2008; Suendermann et al., 2010). SDS are evaluated using different objective and subjective metrics. Examples of objective metrics are the mean number of turns in the dialogue, and dialogue success. Subjective evaluations study measure satisfaction through controlled user studies. Ai et al. (2007) studied the differences in using assessment metrics with real users and paid users.

PARADISE, a notable example of a SDS subjective evaluation, finds linear predictors of a satisfaction score using automatic and hand-labeled features (Hajdinjak and Mihelic, 2006; Walker et al., 2001), or only automatic features (Hastie et al., 2002). Satisfaction scores are calibrated using surveys in controlled experiments (Möller et al., 2007; Möller et al., 2008). Alternatively, Eckert et al. (1998) proposed simulated users to evaluate SDSs. Their performance metric has to be tuned with a subjective evaluation as well, in which they refer to the PARADISE methodology. Our approach does not require user surveys to be calibrated. Moreover, it would be feasible to adapt JEDI to regress to PARADISE, or other performance metrics. Our work extends previous studies that define performance metrics, in proposing an algorithm that finds how system differences are related to performance.

7 Conclusions and Future Work

We have presented JEDI, a novel algorithm that finds features describing system differences relevant to a success metric. This is a novel, automated "glass box" assessment in the sense of linking changes in overall performance to specific behavioral changes. JEDI is an application of feature selection using regularized regression.

We have presented empirical evidence suggesting that JEDI's use of multi-task feature selection performs better than single-task feature selection. Future work could extend JEDI to quantify the variability in performance explained by the differences found. Common techniques in econometrics, such as the Seemingly Unrelated Regressions (SUR) formulation (Zellner, 1962), may prove useful for this.

In our approach we used a single binary evaluation criterion. By using a different loss function, JEDI can be extended to allow continuous-valued metrics. Moreover, previous work has argued that evaluating SDSs should not be based on just a single criterion (Paek, 2001). JEDI's multi-task formulation can be extended to include more than one performance criterion at the same time, and may prove helpful to understand trade-offs among different evaluation criteria.

A Implementation Details of Feature Selection

In this appendix we review how to set-up multi-task feature selection as an optimization problem.

A.1 ℓ_1-Regularized Regression for Single-Task Feature Selection

We first review using regression with ℓ_1 regularization for single-task feature selection. Given a training set represented by $\mathbf{X}$, denoting a $n \times k$ matrix, where n is the number of dialogues, and k is the number of features extracted for each dialogue, we want to find the coefficients of the parameter vector $\vec{\beta}$, that can predict the output variables described in the vector $\vec{\mathbf{y}}$ of length n.

For this, we find the parameter vector that minimizes the loss function J, penalized by a regularization term (Tibshirani, 1996):

$$\underset{\vec{\beta}}{\operatorname{argmin}}\, J(\mathbf{X}, \vec{\beta}, \vec{\mathbf{y}}) + \lambda ||\vec{\beta}||_{\ell_1} \quad (3)$$

In the case of binary classification, outputs are binary (any given $y = \pm 1$). A commonly used loss function J is the Logistic Loss:

$$J_{\log}(x, \beta, y) \equiv \frac{1}{1 + e^{y(x \cdot \beta)}} \quad (4)$$

The ℓ_p-norm of a vector $\vec{\beta}$ is defined as:

$$||\vec{\beta}||_{\ell_p} \equiv \Big(\sum_{i=1}^{k} |\beta_i|^p\Big)^{1/p}$$

The ℓ_∞-norm is defined as $||\vec{\beta}||_{\ell_\infty} \equiv \max(\beta_1, \beta_2, \ldots, \beta_k)$.

The regularization term $||\vec{\beta}||_{\ell_1}$ in Equation 3 controls model complexity: The higher the value of the hyper-parameter λ, the smaller number of features selected. Conversely, the smaller the value of λ, the better the fit to the training data, with higher risk of over-fitting it. Thus, Equation 3 jointly performs feature selection and parameter estimation; it induces sparsity by setting *many* coefficients of $\vec{\beta}$ to zero (Tibshirani, 1996). Features with non-zero coefficients are considered the features selected.

A.2 ℓ_1-Regularized Regression for Multi-Task Feature Selection

ℓ_1 regularization can be used to learn a classifier for each of T prediction task *independently*. In our case we are interested in only two prediction tasks: version and success. We will index tasks with superscript t, and we define $\mathbf{X^t}$ as the $n \times k$ training data for task t, used to predict the output variable $\vec{\mathbf{y}}^t$. Learning each model separately yields the following optimization problem (Obozinski et al., 2007):

$$\underset{\vec{\beta}^t}{\operatorname{argmin}} \sum_{t=1}^{T} J(\mathbf{X^t}, \vec{\beta}^t, \vec{\mathbf{y}}^t) + \lambda ||\vec{\beta}^t||_{\ell_1} \quad (5)$$

Solving this problem leads to individual sparsity in each task (each $\vec{\beta}^t$ has many zeros), but the model does not enforce a common subset of features for all of the related output variables simultaneously (Turlach et al., 2005). In the next subsection we study how to achieve global sparsity across tasks.

A.3 ℓ_1/ℓ_p-Regularized Regression for Multi-task Feature Selection

Although ℓ_1-regularization is very successful at selecting individual features, it does not perform adequately when a group of features should enter or leave the model simultaneously (Yuan and Lin, 2006). Group LASSO (Yuan and Lin, 2006), which relies on ℓ_1/ℓ_p-regularization to overcome this limitation, by allowing groups of feature entering or leaving the model simultaneously. ℓ_1/ℓ_p regularization has been studied for multi-task learning by grouping each of the k features across the T learning tasks (Turlach et al., 2005; Obozinski et al., 2007; Lounici et al., 2009; Puniyani et al., 2010).

Let us define $\mathbf{B}$ as a $n \times T$ matrix, whose t^{th} column is the parameter vector for the task t. For example, since we have two tasks $\mathbf{B} = [\vec{\beta}^{t=1}, \vec{\beta}^{t=2}]$. Let $\vec{\beta}_g$ denote the gth row of $\mathbf{B}$. In the context of multi-task learning, the ℓ_1/ℓ_p-norm of a matrix $\mathbf{B}$ is defined as (Obozinski et al., 2007; Puniyani et al., 2010):

$$||\mathbf{B}||_{\ell_1/\ell_p} \equiv \sum_{g=1}^{k} ||\vec{\beta}_g||_{\ell_p} \quad (6)$$

Multi-task feature selection with ℓ_1/ℓ_p regularization is formulated as (Obozinski et al., 2007; Puniyani et al., 2010):

$$\underset{\mathbf{B}}{\operatorname{argmin}} \sum_{t=1}^{T} J(\mathbf{X}^t, \vec{\beta}^t, \vec{\mathbf{y}}^t) + \lambda ||\mathbf{B}||_{\ell_1/\ell_2} \quad (7)$$

When $T = 1$, the multi-task problem of Equation 7 reduces to the single-task problem of Equation 5.

A.4 Optimization procedure

Puniyani et al. (2010) describe that finding the parameter coefficients $\mathbf{B}$ of Equation 7 can be achieved more easily by transforming the problem into an equivalent single-task multivariate regression. We follow their procedure to create $\vec{y_g}$, $\vec{\beta_g}$ and $\mathbf{X_g}$:

1. Concatenate the vectors $\vec{\mathbf{y}}^t$'s into a single vector $\vec{\mathbf{y}}_g$ of length $n \times T$. In our case, since we have only two tasks ($T = 2$), we get the vector $\vec{\mathbf{y_g}} = \left[\begin{smallmatrix} \vec{\mathbf{y}}^{t=1} \\ \vec{\mathbf{y}}^{t=2} \end{smallmatrix}\right]$.

2. Similarly, we concatenate the $\vec{\beta}^t$'s into a $k \times T$ vector $\vec{\beta_g}$, in our case $\vec{\beta_g} = \left[\begin{smallmatrix} \vec{\beta}^{t=1} \\ \vec{\beta}^{t=2} \end{smallmatrix}\right]$.

3. Build a $(n \cdot T) \times (k \cdot T)$ block-diagonal matrix $\mathbf{X_g}$, where $\mathbf{X}^t$'s are placed along the diagonal, and the rest of the elements are set to zero. In our case since we only have two tasks this is $\mathbf{X_g} = \left[\begin{smallmatrix} \mathbf{X^{t=1}} & \emptyset \\ \emptyset & \mathbf{X^{t=2}} \end{smallmatrix}\right]$, where each $\emptyset$ denotes a $n \times k$ zero-matrix. The expanded notation of $\mathbf{X_g}$ is:

$$\mathbf{X_g} \equiv \begin{bmatrix} \mathrm{x}^{t=1}{}_1^{(1)} & \dots & \mathrm{x}^{t=1}{}_k^{(1)} & 0 & \dots & 0 \\ \vdots & & \vdots & \vdots & & \vdots \\ \mathrm{x}^{t=1}{}_1^{(n)} & \dots & \mathrm{x}^{t=1}{}_k^{(n)} & 0 & \dots & 0 \\ 0 & \dots & 0 & \mathrm{x}^{t=2}{}_1^{(1)} & \dots & \mathrm{x}^{t=2}{}_k^{(1)} \\ \vdots & & \vdots & \vdots & & \vdots \\ 0 & \dots & 0 & \mathrm{x}^{t=2}{}_1^{(n)} & \dots & \mathrm{x}^{t=2}{}_k^{(n)} \end{bmatrix}$$

Thus, the multi-task learning problem from Equation 7 is equivalent to (Yuan and Lin, 2006; Puniyani et al., 2010):

$$\underset{\mathbf{B}}{\operatorname{argmin}}\, J(\mathbf{X_g}, \vec{\beta_g}, \vec{\mathbf{y_g}}) + \lambda ||\mathbf{B}||_{\ell_1/\ell_2} \quad (8)$$

In this work we solve this optimization problem using an existing[3] implementation of Block Coordinate Descent (Schmidt et al., 2008) that solves regression problems with a ℓ_1/ℓ_p penalty.

Acknowledgments

This work was supported by the Institute of Education Sciences, U.S. Department of Education, through Grant R305A080628 to Carnegie Mellon University. The opinions expressed are those of the authors and do not necessarily represent the views of the Institute or U.S. Department of Education. We thank the educators, students, and LISTENers who helped generate, collect, and analyze our data, and the reviewers for their helpful comments. The first author was partially supported by the Costa Rican Ministry of Science and Technology (MICIT).

[3]Source code: `http://www.cs.ubc.ca/~murphyk/Software/L1CRF/`

References

H. Ai, A. Raux, D. Bohus, M. Eskenazi, and D. Litman. 2007. Comparing spoken dialog corpora collected with recruited subjects versus real users. In *Proc. of the 8th SIGdial workshop on Discourse and Dialogue*.

M. Bacchiani, F. Beaufays, J. Schalkwyk, M. Schuster, and B. Strope. 2008. Deploying GOOG-411: Early lessons in data, measurement, and testing. In *IEEE International Conference on Acoustics, Speech and Signal Processing, 2008. ICASSP 2008*, pages 5260–5263.

D. Bohus, A. Raux, T. Harris, M. Eskenazi, and A. Rudnicky. 2007. Olympus: an open-source framework for conversational spoken language interface research. In *HLT-NAACL 2007 Workshop on Bridging the Gap: Academic and Industrial Research in Dialog Technology*.

M. Danieli and E. Gerbino. 1995. Metrics for evaluating dialogue strategies in a spoken language system. In *Proceedings of the 1995 AAAI Spring Symposium on Empirical Methods in Discourse Interpretation and Generation*, pages 34–39.

W. Eckert, E. Levin, and R. Pieraccini. 1998. Automatic evaluation of spoken dialogue systems. *TWLT13: Formal semantics and pragmatics of dialogue*, pages 99–110.

J. P. González-Brenes and J. Mostow. 2011. Classifying dialogue in high-dimensional space. *Transactions of Speech and Language Processing; Special Issue on Machine Learning for Robust and Adaptive Spoken Dialogue Systems*. In press.

J. P. González-Brenes, A. W. Black, and M. Eskenazi. 2009. Describing Spoken Dialogue Systems Differences. In *International Workshop on Spoken Dialogue Systems*, Irsee, Germany. Springer–Verlat.

M. Hajdinjak and F. Mihelic. 2006. The PARADISE evaluation framework: Issues and findings. *Computational Linguistics*, 32(2):263–272.

H. W. Hastie, R. Prasad, and M. Walker. 2002. Automatic evaluation: Using a date dialogue act tagger for user satisfaction and task completion prediction. In *In LREC 2002*, pages 641–648.

E. Levin and R. Pieraccini. 2006. Value-based optimal decision for dialog systems. In *Spoken Language Technology Workshop, 2006. IEEE*, pages 198 –201.

K. Lounici, A.B. Tsybakov, M. Pontil, and van de Geer. 2009. Taking advantage of sparsity in multi-task learning. In *Conference on Learning Theory*, volume 1050, page 9, Montreal, Quebec.

S. Möller, P. Smeele, H. Boland, and J. Krebber. 2007. Evaluating spoken dialogue systems according to defacto standards: A case study. *Computer Speech and Language*, 21(1):26 – 53.

S. Möller, K.P. Engelbrecht, and R. Schleicher. 2008. Predicting the quality and usability of spoken dialogue services. *Speech Communication*, 50(8-9):730–744.

G. Obozinski, B. Taskar, and M.I. Jordan. 2007. Multi-task feature selection. In *The Workshop of Structural Knowledge Transfer for Machine Learning in the 23rd International Conference on Machine Learning (ICML)*, Pittsburgh, PA.

T. Paek. 2001. Empirical methods for evaluating dialog systems. In *ACL 2001 Workshop on Evaluation Methodologies for Language and Dialogue systems*, pages 3–10.

M.Y. Park and T. Hastie. 2007. L1-regularization path algorithm for generalized linear models. *Journal of the Royal Statistical Society: Series B (Statistical Methodology)*, 69(19):659–677.

J. Polifroni, L. Hirschman, S. Seneff, and V. Zue. 1992. Experiments in evaluating interactive spoken language systems. In *Proceedings of the workshop on Speech and Natural Language*, pages 28–33. Association for Computational Linguistics.

K. Puniyani, S. Kim, and E.P. Xing. 2010. Multi-population GWA mapping via multi-task regularized regression. *Bioinformatics*, 26(12):208.

A. Raux, D. Bohus, B. Langner, A.W. Black, and M. Eskenazi. 2006. Doing research on a deployed spoken dialogue system: one year of Let's Go! experience. In *Ninth International Conference on Spoken Language Processing*. ISCA.

M. Schmidt, K. Murphy, G. Fung, and R. Rosales. 2008. Structure learning in random fields for heart motion abnormality detection. In *Computer Vision and Pattern Recognition, 2008. CVPR 2008. IEEE Conference on*, pages 1 –8.

A. Schmitt, M. Scholz, W. Minker, J. Liscombe, and D. Suendermann. 2010. Is it possible to predict task completion in automated troubleshooters? In *INTERSPEECH*, pages 94–97.

D. Suendermann, J. Liscombe, R. Pieraccini, and K. Evanini. 2010. "How am I Doing?": A new framework to effectively measure the performance of automated customer care contact centers. In A. Neustein, editor, *Advances in Speech Recognition: Mobile Environments, Call Centers, and Clinics*, pages 155–180. Springer.

R. Tibshirani. 1996. Regression shrinkage and selection via the lasso. *Journal of the Royal Statistical Society. Series B (Methodological)*, 58(1):267–288.

B.A. Turlach, W.N. Venables, and S.J. Wright. 2005. Simultaneous variable selection. *Technometrics*, 47(3):349–363.

M. Walker, C. Kamm, and D. Litman. 2001. Towards developing general models of usability with PARADISE. *Natural Language Engineering*, 6(3):363–377.

M. A. Walker, I. Langkilde-Geary, H. W. Hastie, J. Wright, and A. Gorin. 2002. Automatically training a problematic dialogue predictor for a spoken dialogue system. *Journal of Artificial Intelligence Research*, 16:293–319.

M. Yuan and Y. Lin. 2006. Model selection and estimation in regression with grouped variables. *Journal of the Royal Statistical Society: Series B (Statistical Methodology)*, 68(1):49–67.

A. Zellner. 1962. An efficient method of estimating seemingly unrelated regressions and tests for aggregation bias. *Journal of the American Statistical Association*, 57(298):pp. 348–368.

H. Zou and T. Hastie. 2005. Regularization and variable selection via the Elastic Net. *Journal of the Royal Statistical Society*, 67:301–320.

A Two-Stage Domain Selection Framework for Extensible Multi-Domain Spoken Dialogue Systems

Mikio Nakano
Honda Research Institute Japan
Wako, Saitama, Japan
nakano@jp.honda-ri.com

Shun Sato
Tokyo Denki University
Hatoyama, Saitama, Japan
rela.relakuma@gmail.com

Kazunori Komatani
Nagoya University
Nagoya, Aichi, Japan
komatani@nuee.nagoya-u.ac.jp

Kyoko Matsuyama*
Kyoto University
Kyoto, Kyoto, Japan
matuyama@kuis.kyoto-u.ac.jp

Kotaro Funakoshi
Honda Research Institute Japan
Wako, Saitama, Japan
funakoshi@jp.honda-ri.com

Hiroshi G. Okuno
Kyoto University
Kyoto, Kyoto, Japan
okuno@i.kyoto-u.ac.jp

Abstract

This paper describes a general and effective domain selection framework for multi-domain spoken dialogue systems that employ distributed domain experts. The framework consists of two processes: deciding if the current domain continues and estimating the probabilities for selecting other domains. If the current domain does not continue, the domain with the highest activation probability is selected. Since those processes for each domain expert can be designed independently from other experts and can use a large variety of information, the framework achieves both extensibility and robustness against speech recognition errors. The results of an experiment using a corpus of dialogues between humans and a multi-domain dialogue system demonstrate the viability of the proposed framework.

1 Introduction

As spoken dialogue interfaces are becoming more widely utilized, they will be expected to be able to engage in dialogues in a wide variety of topics. Particularly, spoken dialogue interfaces for office robots (Asoh et al., 1999) and multimodal kiosk systems (Gustafson and Bell, 2000) are expected to deal with people's various requests, unlike automated call center systems that are dedicated to specific tasks.

One effective methodology to build such a system is to integrate systems in small domains by employing *distributed multi-domain system architecture*. This architecture has distributed modules that independently manage their own dialogue state and knowledge for speech understanding and utterance generation (e.g., Lin et al. (1999)). From an engineering viewpoint, such architecture has an advantage in that each domain expert can be designed independently and that it is easy to add new domains. It enables each domain expert to employ a dialogue strategy very different from those for other domains. For example, the strategy may be frame-based mixed-initiative, finite-state-based system-initiative, or plan-based dialogue management (McTear, 2004).

One of the crucial issues with distributed multi-domain spoken dialogue systems is how to select an appropriate domain for each user utterance so that the system can appropriately understand it and answer it. So far several methods have been proposed but none of them satisfy two basic requirements at the same time: the ability to be used with a variety of domain experts (**extensibility**) and being robust against ASR (Automatic Speech Recognition) errors (**robustness**). We suspect that this is one of the main reasons why not many multi-domain spoken dialogue systems have been developed even though their utility is widely recognized.

This paper presents a new general framework for domain selection that satisfies the above two requirements. In our framework, each expert needs to have two additional submodules: one for estimating the probability that it is newly activated, and one for deciding domain continuation when it is already activated. Since these submodules can be designed independently from those of other experts, there is no restriction on designing experts in our framework,

*Currently with Panasonic Corporation.

Proceedings of the SIGDIAL 2011: the 12th Annual Meeting of the Special Interest Group on Discourse and Dialogue, pages 18–29,
Portland, Oregon, June 17-18, 2011.

and thus extensibility is achieved. Robustness is also achieved because those submodules can be designed so that they can utilize domain-dependent information, including information on speech understanding and dialogue history, without detracting from extensibility. Especially the submodule for deciding domain continuation has the ability to utilize dialogue history to avoid erroneous domain shifts that often occur in previous approaches. Note that we do not focus on classifying each utterance without contextual information (e.g., Chu-Carroll and Carpenter (1999)). Rather, we try to estimate the user intention with regard to continuing and shifting domains in the course of dialogues.

In what follows, Section 2 explains the distributed multi-domain spoken dialogue system architecture and requirements for domain selection. Section 3 discusses previous work, and Section 4 presents our proposed framework. Section 5 describes an example implementation and its evaluation results, and Section 6 concludes the paper.

2 Domain Selection in Multi-Domain Spoken Dialogue Systems

2.1 Distributed Architecture

In distributed multi-domain spoken dialogue architecture (Figure 1), distributed modules independently manage their own dialogue state and knowledge for speech understanding and utterance generation (Lin et al., 1999; Salonen et al., 2004; Pakucs, 2003; Nakano et al., 2008). Although those modules are referred to with various names in that literature, we call them *domain experts* in this paper. In this architecture, when an input utterance is received, its ASR results are sent to domain experts. They try to understand the ASR results using their own knowledge for understanding. The domain selector gathers information from those experts and decides which expert should deal with the utterance and then decide on the system utterances. In this paper, the domain expert engaging in understanding user utterances and deciding system utterances is called *activated*.

2.2 Example Systems

So far many multi-domain spoken dialogue systems based on distributed architecture have been

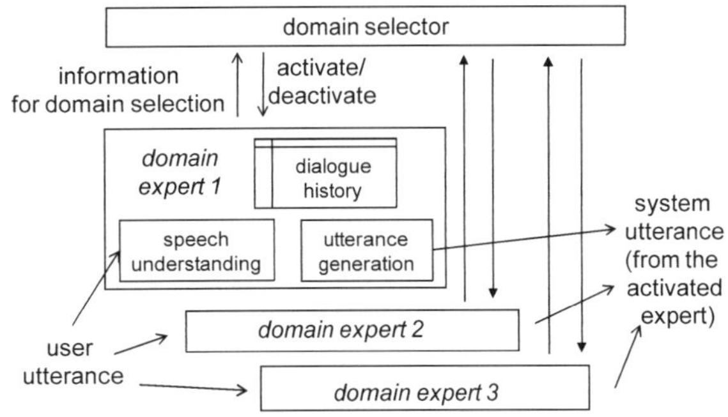

Figure 1: Distributed multi-domain spoken dialogue system architecture.

built and have demonstrated their ability to engage in dialogues in a variety of domains. For example, several systems integrated information providing and database searches in multiple domains (Lin et al., 1999; Komatani et al., 2006; O'Neill et al., 2004; Gustafson and Bell, 2000). Some other systems integrated domain experts that employ very different dialogue strategies. Lee et al. (2009) and Nakano et al. (2006) integrated task-oriented and non-task-oriented dialogue managements. Nakano et al. (2008) integrated domain experts for not only dialogues but also tasks requiring physical actions.

Below we explain an example system that we used to collect dialogue data for the domain selection experiment described in Section 5. It is a Japanese system that can provide information on UNESCO World Heritage Sites using speech, slides, and Microsoft Agent[1] gestures. It employs the following ten domain experts:

A *question answering (QA) expert*: It has a database consisting of question-answer pairs on World Heritage Sites (Narimatsu et al., 2010). Each question-answer pair consists of a set of example question sentences and answers to them. The answers consist of one or more utterances, plus slides. Keyphrase-based matching is used to select an example question that matches the input utterance.

Eight *interactive presentation (IP) experts*: Each of them explains in detail a famous World Heritage Site and adds a detailed explanation or skips some explanation according to the user's interruptions (Nishimura et al., 2007). Patterns of interruption utterances are described in the expert's knowledge base.

[1] http://www.microsoft.com/MSAgent/

	utterance	expert
S1:	Hello. I can answer questions about famous World Heritage Sites in Italy, Germany, Greece, and other areas. I can also explain some World Heritage Sites in detail. Please ask me anything.	QA
U1:	Show me the list of the World Heritage Sites in Italy.	QA
S2:	(show a slide of the list) I can tell you about the World Heritage Sites in these areas in Italy.	QA
U2:	Can you show me the list of World Heritage Sites you can explain in detail?	QA
S3:	(show a slide of the list) I can explain these in detail.	QA
U3:	Can you explain Maritime Greenwich?	RU
S4:	Maritime Greenwich, right?	RU
U4:	Yes.	RU
S5:	(show a slide on Greenwich) Okay. I'll explain Maritime Greenwich, a historic port town known for Greenwich Mean Time.	IP1
U5:	What is Greenwich Mean Time?	IP1
S6:	Greenwich Mean Time is the mean solar time at the Royal Greenwich Observatory.	IP1

S means system utterance and U means user utterance. IP1 is one of the IP experts.

Figure 2: An example dialogue with the system for data collection (translation from Japanese).

A *request understanding (RU) expert*: It understands the user's request to start one of the interactive presentations explained above, and engages in a dialogue to confirm the request. When the understanding finishes, the understood request is sent to a module called *task planner* (Nakano et al., 2008; Nakano et al., 2011). The task planner then activates another expert to perform the requested presentation (S5 in Figure 2).

Figure 2 shows an example dialogue between a human and this system. Note that user utterances are relatively short and include words related to specific World Heritage Sites or area names. If those words are misrecognized, domain selection is difficult unless dialogue context information is used.

This figure also indicates the domain experts that understood each user utterance and selected each system utterance. The domain expert that should deal with a user utterance is decided based on the set of user utterances that the expert is designed to deal with. The domains of utterances U1 and U3 are different because the QA expert has knowledge for understanding U1 and the RU expert has knowledge for understanding U3. Thus, in this study, the domain of each utterance is determined based on the design of the experts employed in the system. If none of the experts can deal with an utterance, it is considered as an out-of-domain utterance. Sometimes the correct domain needs to be determined using contextual information. For example, utterance U4 "Yes" can appear in all domains, but, since this is a reply to S4, its domain is RU.

This definition of domain is different from that of domain (or topic) recognition and adaptation studies in text, monologue, and human-human conversation processing, in which reference domains are annotated based on human perspectives rather than system perspectives. From a human perspective, all user utterances in Figure 2 may be in "World Heritage Site" domain. However, it is not always easy to build domain experts according to such domain definitions, because different dialogue tasks in one such domain may require different dialogue strategies (such as question answering and request understanding).

2.3 Requirements for Domain Selection

We pursue a method for domain selection that can be used in distributed architecture. Such a method must satisfy the following two requirements.

Extensibility It must not detract from the extensibility of distributed architecture, that is, any kind of expert must be able to be incorporated, and each expert must be able to be designed independently from other experts. This requires the interface between each domain expert and the domain selector to be as simple as possible.

Robustness It needs to be robust against ASR errors; that is, the system needs to be able to avoid erroneous domain transition caused by ASR errors.

3 Previous Work

So far various methods for domain selection have been proposed, but, as far as we know, no method satisfies both extensibility and robustness. Isobe et al. (2003) estimate a score for each domain from the

ASR result and select the domain with the highest score (hereafter referred to as RECSCORE). Since each domain expert has only to output a numeric score, it satisfies extensibility. However, because this method does not take into account dialogue context, it tends to erroneously shift domains when the score of some experts becomes high by chance. For example, if U4:"Yes" in Figure 2 is recognized as "Italy" with a high recognition score in the QA expert, the domain erroneously shifts to QA and the system explains about World Heritage Sites in Italy. Thus this method is not robust.

To avoid erroneous domain shifts, Lin et al. (1999) give preference to the *preceding domain* (the domain in which the previous system utterance was made) by adding a certain value to the score of the preceding domain (hereafter called RECSCORE+BIAS). However, to what extent the domain tends to continue varies depending on the dialogue context. For example, if a dialogue task in one domain finishes (e.g., when an IP expert finishes its presentation and says "This is the end of the presentation. Do you have any questions?"), the domain is likely to shift. So, adding a fixed score does not always work. O'Neill et al.'s (2004) system does not change the dialogue domain until it finishes a task in the domain, but it cannot recover from erroneous domain shifts.

To achieve robustness against ASR errors, several domain selection methods based on a classifier that uses features concerning dialogue history as well as ones concerning speech understanding results have been developed (Komatani et al., 2006; Ikeda et al., 2008; Lee et al., 2009). These studies, however, use some features available only in some specific type of domain experts, such as features concerning slot-filling, so they cannot be used with other kinds of domain experts. That is, these methods do not satisfy extensibility.

Methods that use classifiers based on word (and n-gram) frequencies have been developed for utterance classification (e.g., Chu-Carroll and Carpenter (1999)), topic estimation for ASR of speech corpora (e.g., Hsu and Glass (2006) and Heidel and Lee (2007)) and human-human dialogues (Lane and Kawahara, 2005). These methods can be applied to domain selection in multi-domain spoken dialogue systems. However, since they require training data in the same set of domains as the target system, it detracts from extensibility. In addition, they are not robust because they cannot utilize a variety of dialogue and understanding related features. Word frequencies are not always effective when two domains share words as in our system described in Section 2.2.

4 Proposed Framework

4.1 Basic Idea

To achieve extensibility, we need to restrict the information that each expert sends to the domain selector to a simple one such as numeric scores. Although RECSCORE and RECSCORE+BIAS satisfy this, they would not achieve high accuracy as explained above.

One possible extension to those methods to improve accuracy is to use not only recognition scores but also various expert-dependent features such as ones concerning dialogue history and speech understanding. Each expert first estimates the probability that the input utterance is in its domain using such features, and then the expert with the highest probability is selected (hereafter called MAXPROB). This method retains extensibility because the domain selector does not directly use those expert-dependent features. However, it suffers from the same problem as RECSCORE and RECSCORE+BIAS; if one of the experts other than the preceding domain's expert outputs a high probability by mistake, the domain shifts regardless of the dialogue state in the preceding domain's expert.

We focus attention on the fact that the domain does not often shift. Our idea is to decide if the domain continues or not by using information available in the preceding domain's expert. This prevents erroneous domain shifts when the utterance is considered not to change the domain. When it is decided that the currently active domain does not continue, each remaining expert estimates the probability of being newly activated using information available in the expert, and the expert whose probability is the highest is selected as the new domain expert.

We further refine this idea in two ways. One is by taking into account how likely the input utterance is to activate one of the other domain experts. We propose to use the maximum value of probabilities for other experts' activation (*maximum activation prob-*

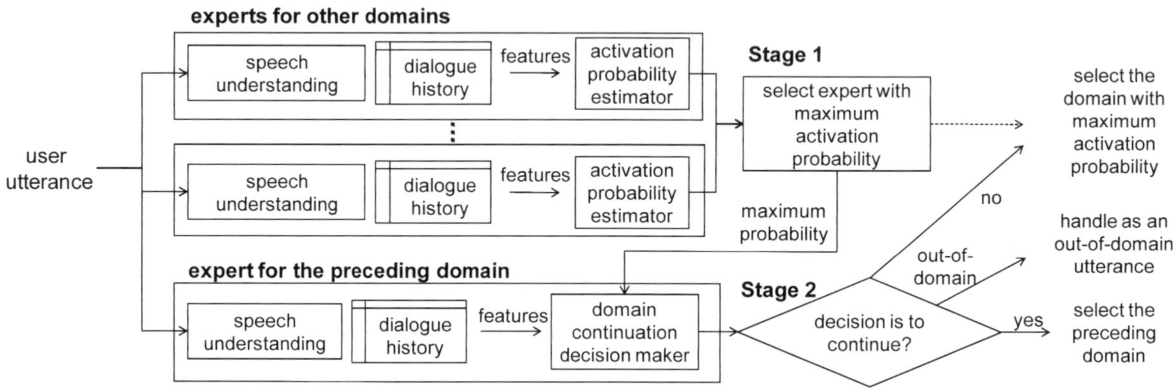

Figure 3: Two-stage domain selection framework.

ability) in the decision regarding domain continuation. Since the maximum activation probability is just a numeric score, this does not spoil extensibility. Unlike RECSCORE and RECSCORE+BIAS, in our method, even if the maximum activation probability is very high, the preceding domain's expert can decide to continue or not to continue based on its internal state. This makes it possible to retain robustness.

The other refinement is to explicitly deal with utterances that are not in any domains (*out-of-domain (OOD) utterances*). They include fillers and murmurs. They should be treated separately, because they appear context-independently. So we make the expert detect OOD utterances when deciding domain continuation. That is, it performs three-fold classification, *continue*, *not-continue*, and *OOD*.

4.2 Two-Stage Domain Selection Framework

This idea can be summarized as a domain selection framework which consists of two stages (Figure 3). It assumes that each domain expert has two submodules: *activation probability estimator* and a *domain continuation decision maker*, which use information available in the expert itself.

When a new input utterance is received, at Stage 1, the activation probability estimators of all non-activated experts estimate probabilities and send them to the domain selector. Then at Stage 2, the domain selector sends their maximum value to the expert of the preceding domain and asks it to decide whether it continues to deal with the new input utterances or does not continue, or it deals with the utterance as out-of-domain. If it decides not to continue, the domain selector selects the expert that outputs the highest probability at Stage 1.

The reason we use the term "framework" is that it does not specify the details of the algorithm and features used in each domain expert's submodules for domain selection. It rather specifies the interfaces of those submodules. Note that RECSCORE, RECSCORE+BIAS, and MAXPROB can be considered as one of the implementations of this framework. This framework, however, allows developers to use a wider variety of features and gives flexibility in designing those submodules.

5 Example Implementation and Evaluation

Since the proposed framework is an extension of the previous methods, if the activation probability estimator and domain continuation decision maker for each expert are designed well and trained using enough data, it should outperform previous methods that satisfy extensibility. We believe that this theoretical consideration and an experimental result using a human-system dialogue corpus show the viability of the framework. Below we explain our implementation and an experiment.

5.1 Data

For the implementation and evaluation, we used a corpus of dialogues between human users and the World Heritage Site information system described in Section 2.2. Domain selection of this system was performed using hand-crafted rules.

35 participants (17 males and 18 females) whose ages range from 19 to 57 were asked to engage in

domain	preceding domain	training data A	training data B	test data
RU	RU	134	169	145
	QA	51	102	59
	IP	21	16	23
	subtotal	206	287	227
QA	RU	46	55	51
	QA	783	870	888
	IP	59	87	66
	subtotal	888	1,012	1,005
IP	RU	2	1	3
	QA	7	11	18
	IP	311	305	277
	subtotal	320	317	298
OOD	RU	24	19	39
	QA	168	155	183
	IP	66	68	113
	subtotal	258	242	335
total		1,672	1,858	1,865

Table 1: Number of utterances in each domain in the training and test data.

conversation with the system four times. Each session lasted eight minutes. For each utterance, the correct domain or an OOD label was manually annotated. We also annotated its preceding domain, i.e., the domain in which the previous system utterance was made. It can be different from the previous user utterance's domain because of the system's erroneous domain selection. Utterances including requests in two domains at the same time should be given an OOD label but there are no such utterances. We used data from 23 participants (3,530 utterances) for training and those from the remaining 12 participants (1,865 utterances) for testing. We further split the training data into training data A (1,672 utterances) and B (1,858 utterances) to train each of the two submodules. Each training data set includes data from two sessions for each participant. Table 1 shows detailed numbers of utterances in the data sets.

5.2 Implementation

5.2.1 Expert Classes

Among the ten experts, eight IP (Interactive Presentation) experts have the same dialogue strategy and most of the predicted user utterance patterns. In addition, the number of training utterances for each IP expert's domain is small. We therefore used all training utterances in the IP domains to build a common ASR language model (LM), a common activation probability estimator, and a common domain continuation decision maker for all IP experts. Hereafter we call the set of IP experts *the IP expert class*. The RU (Request Understanding) expert and the QA (Question Answer) expert are themselves also expert classes.

expert class	QA	IP	RU
LM for ASR	trigram	trigram	finite-state grammar
language understanding	keyphrase -based	keyphrase -based	finite-state transducer
vocabulary size (word)	1,140	407	79
phone error rate (%)	10.95	19.47	23.60

Table 2: Speech understanding in each expert.

5.2.2 Speech Understanding

For all experts, we used the Julius speech recognizer and the acoustic model in the Japanese model repository (Kawahara et al., 2004).[2] Features of speech understanding in each expert class are shown in Table 2. Compared to the system used for data collection, LMs are enhanced based on the training data. We obtained the ASR performance on the utterances in each domain in the test data in terms of phone error rates. This is because Japanese has no standard word boundaries so it is not easy to correctly compute word error rates. The poor performance of ASR for IP is mainly due to the small amount of training utterances for LM and that for RU is mainly due to out-of-grammar utterances.

5.2.3 Stage 1

For Stage 1, we used logistic regression to estimate the probability that a non-activated expert would be activated by a user utterance. Features for logistic regression include those concerning speech recognition and understanding results as well as dialogue history (see Table 5 for the full list of features). These features are *expert-dependent*. This makes it possible to estimate how the input utterance is suit-

[2]Multiple LMs can be used at the same time with Julius.

able to the dialogue context more precisely than using just features available in any kind of expert.

To train the activation probability estimators, we fitted logistic regression coefficients using Weka data mining toolkit ver.3.6.2 (Witten and Frank, 2005)[3] and training data A. In the training for each expert class, we used utterances whose preceding domain was not that of the class because activation probabilities are estimated only for such utterances during domain selection. If the utterance is in a domain of the expert class, it is assigned an *activate* label and otherwise *not-activate*. Next, we performed feature selection to avoid overfitting. We used backward stepwise selection so that the weighted (by the sizes of *activate* and *not-activate* labels) average of the F_1 scores for training set B could be maximized. Table 6 lists the remaining features and their significances in terms of the F_1 score obtained when each feature is removed. Then, we duplicated the *activate*-labeled utterances in the training data A so that the ratio of *activate*-labeled utterances to *not-activate*-labeled utterances became 1 to 3. This is because the training data include a larger number of *not-activate*-labeled utterances and thus the results would be biased. The ratio was decided by trial and error so that the weighted average of the F_1 scores for training data B becomes high.

5.2.4 Stage 2

For Stage 2, we used multi-class support vector machines (SVMs)[4] to decide if the activated expert should continue to be activated, should not continue, or should regard the input utterance as OOD. We used the same set of features as Stage 1 as well as the maximum activation probability obtained at Stage 1. The training data for the SVM of each expert class is the set of utterances in training data B whose preceding domain is in that expert class, because domain continuation is decided only for such utterances during domain selection. They are labeled *continue*, *not-continue*, or *OOD*. Next, we performed backward stepwise feature selection so that the weighted average of F_1 scores for *continue*, *not-continue*, and *OOD* utterance detection on training data A could be maximized. Remaining features are listed in Table 7. The maximum activation probability was found to be significant in all expert classes. This suggests our two-stage framework that uses maximum activation probability is viable. Then, we duplicated utterances with *not-continue* label and *OOD* label in the training data so that the ratio of *continue*, *not-continue*, and *OOD* utterances became 3:1:1. This is because the number of utterances with the *continue* label is far greater than others. The ratio was experimentally decided by trial and error so that the weighted average of F_1 scores on training data A becomes high.

5.3 Evaluation

5.3.1 Compared Methods

We compared the *full implementation* described in Section 5.2 (FULLIMPL hereafter) with the following four methods which satisfy *extensibility*. Note that the first three methods were mentioned in Section 4.

RECSCORE: This chooses the expert class whose recognition score is the maximum (Isobe et al., 2003). We used the ASR acoustic score normalized by the duration of the utterance. If the IP expert class was chosen, the IP expert that had been most recently activated was chosen, because, in this system, domain shifts to other IP experts never occur due to the system constraints and the user did not try to do it. If none of the experts had a higher score than a fixed threshold, it recognized the utterance as OOD. The threshold was experimentally determined using the training data so that the weighted (by the sizes of OOD and non-OOD utterances) average of the F_1 scores of OOD/non-OOD classification is maximized.

RECSCORE+BIAS: This is the same as RECSCORE except that a fixed value (bias) is added to the score used in RECSCORE for the expert of the preceding domain. This is basically the same as Lin et al.'s (1999) method but we use a different recognition score since the recognition score they used cannot be used in our system due to the difference of speech understanding methods. The most appropriate bias for each expert class was decided using the training data so that the weighted average of the F_1 scores could be maximized. OOD detection was done in the same way as RECSCORE.

[3]Multinominal logistic regression model with a ridge estimator with Weka's default values.

[4]Weka's SMO with the linear kernel and its default values.

method	class	recall	precision	F_1	weighted ave. F_1
RECSCORE	cont.	0.763	0.867	0.812	
	shift	0.559	0.239	0.335	
	OOD	0.501	0.848	0.630	0.789
RECSCORE +BIAS	cont.	0.917	0.824	0.868	
	shift	0.400	0.421	0.410	
	OOD	0.501	0.848	0.630	0.838
MAXPROB	cont.	0.925	0.843	0.882	
	shift	0.282	0.264	0.273	
	OOD	0.275	0.477	0.348	0.832
NOACTIV PROB	cont.	0.875	0.890	0.882	
	shift	0.464	0.385	0.421	
	OOD	0.785	0.843	0.813	0.849
FULLIMPL	cont.	0.902	0.907	0.904	
	shift	0.591	0.565	0.578	
	OOD	0.824	0.829	0.826	**0.883**
CLASSIFIER (reference)	cont.	0.956	0.881	0.917	
	shift	0.545	0.759	0.635	
	OOD	0.755	0.885	0.815	0.899

Table 3: Evaluation results ("cont." means "continue.").

MAXPROB: The activation probabilities for all experts were obtained using logistic regression and the expert whose probability was the maximum was selected. IP experts that had never been activated were excluded because they cannot be activated due to system constraint. For logistic regression, in addition to the features used in FULLIMPL, the previous domain was used as a feature so that domain continuity was taken into account. Feature selection was also performed. The probability that the utterance is OOD was estimated in the same way using the features concerning speech understanding. If the maximum probability of OOD detection was greater than the maximum activation probability, then the utterance was considered to be OOD.

NOACTIVPROB: This is the same as FULLIMPL except that Stage 2 does not use the result of Stage 1, i.e., maximum activation probability.

5.3.2 Evaluation Results

To evaluate the domain selection, we focused on domain shifts rather than the selected domain. We classified the domain selection results into domain continuations, domain shifts, and OOD utterance detection. As the evaluation metric, we used the weighted average of F_1 scores for those classes. Here the weight is the ratio of those classes of correct labels. Note that shifting to an incorrect domain is counted as a false positive when calculating precision for domain shifts. Table 3 shows the results. In addition, the confusion matrices for the three best methods are shown in Table 4. We found FULLIMPL outperforms the other four methods. We also found that the differences between the results of the compared methods are all statistically significant ($p < .01$) by two-tailed binomial tests.

For reference, we also evaluated a classifier-based method that uses features from all the experts. Note that this method does not satisfy extensibility because it requires training data in the same set of domains as the target system. We evaluated this just for estimating how well our proposed method works while satisfying extensibility. It classifies each utterance into one of four categories: the QA expert's domain, the RU expert's domain, the most recently activated IP expert's domain, and OOD. If no IP expert has been activated before the utterance, threefold classification was performed. The training and test data were split depending on whether one of the IP experts has been activated before, and training and testing were separately conducted. The training data A was used for training SVM classifiers. Then feature selection was performed using the training data B. The performance of this method is shown as CLASSIFIER in Tables 3 and 4. Although this method outperforms FULLIMPL, FULLIMPL's performance is close to this method. This shows that our method does not degrade its performance very much even though it satisfies extensibility.

5.3.3 Discussion

One of the reasons why FULLIMPL outperforms other methods is that its precision for domain shifts is relatively higher than the other methods. This suggests it can avoid erroneous domain shifts, thus the proposed two-stage framework is more *robust*. RECSCORE+BIAS performed relatively well despite it used only limited features. We guess this is because adding preferences to the preceding domain was effective since domain shifts are rare in these data. Its low F_1 score for OOD utterances suggests using just recognition scores is insufficient to detect them. The comparison of FULLIMPL with NOACTIVPROB shows the effectiveness of using maximum activation probability in the second stage.

The F_1 score for domain shifts is low even with

RecScore+Bias:

correct	estimated result				total
	cont.	correct shift	wrong shift	OOD	
continue	1,201	-	82	27	1,310
shift	115	88	14	3	220
OOD	142	-	25	168	335
total	1,458	88	121	198	1,865

NoActivProb:

correct	estimated result				total
	cont.	correct shift	wrong shift	OOD	
continue	1,146	-	123	41	1,310
shift	92	102	18	8	220
OOD	50	-	22	263	335
total	1,288	102	163	312	1,865

FullImpl:

correct	estimated result				total
	cont.	correct shift	wrong shift	OOD	
continue	1,181	-	77	52	1,310
shift	70	130	15	5	220
OOD	51	-	8	276	335
total	1,302	130	100	333	1,865

Classifier (reference):

correct	estimated result				total
	cont.	correct shift	wrong shift	OOD	
continue	1,252	-	30	28	1310
shift	92	120	3	5	220
OOD	77	-	5	253	335
total	1,421	120	38	286	1,865

Table 4: Confusion matrices for the domain shifts.

FullImpl, although it is higher than those with other methods. One typical reason for this is that when one keyword in the ASR result of an utterance to shift the domain is also in the vocabulary of the preceding domain's expert, the selection tends to continue the previous domain by mistake. For example, an utterance "tell me about other World Heritage Sites" to shift from an IP domain to the QA domain is sometimes misclassified as an IP domain utterance, because "World Heritage Sites" is also in IP domains' vocabulary. We think this is because the training data do not include a sufficient amount of utterances that shift domains, and that a larger amount of training data would solve this problem.

6 Concluding Remarks

This paper presented a novel general framework for domain selection in extensible multi-domain spoken dialogue systems. This framework makes it possible to build a robust domain selector because of its flexibility in exploiting features and taking into account domain continuity. An experiment with data collected with an example multi-domain system supported the viability of the proposed framework. We believe that this framework will promote the development of multi-domain spoken dialogue systems and conversational robots/agents.

Among future work is to investigate how accurate the activation probability estimator and the domain continuation decision maker in each domain expert should be for achieving a reasonable accuracy in domain selection. We also plan to conduct experiments with systems that have a larger number of domain experts to verify the scalability of this framework. In addition, we will explore a way to estimate the confidence of the domain selection to reduce erroneous domain selections.

Acknowledgments

The authors would like to thank Hiroshi Tsujino, Yuji Hasegawa, and Hiromi Narimatsu for their support for this research.

References

Hideki Asoh, Toshihiro Matsui, John Fry, Futoshi Asano, and Satoru Hayamizu. 1999. A spoken dialog system for a mobile office robot. In *Proc. 6th Eurospeech*, pages 1139–1142.

Jennifer Chu-Carroll and Bob Carpenter. 1999. Vector-based natural language call routing. *Computational Linguistics*, 25(3):361–388.

Joakim Gustafson and Linda Bell. 2000. Speech technology on trial: Experiences from the August system. *Natural Language Engineering*, 6(3&4):273–286.

Aaron Heidel and Lin-shan Lee. 2007. Robust topic inference for latent semantic language model adaptation. In *Proc. ASRU-07*, pages 177–182.

Bo-June (Paul) Hsu and James Glass. 2006. Style and topic language model adaptation using HMM-LDA. In *Proc. EMNLP '06*, pages 373–381,.

Satoshi Ikeda, Kazunori Komatani, Tetsuya Ogata, and Hiroshi G. Okuno. 2008. Extensibility verification of robust domain selection against out-of-grammar utterances in multi-domain spoken dialogue system. In *Proc. Interspeech-2008 (ICSLP)*, pages 487–490.

T. Isobe, S. Hayakawa, H. Murao, T. Mizutani, K. Takeda, and F. Itakura. 2003. A study on domain recognition of spoken dialogue systems. In *Proc. Eurospeech-2003*, pages 1889–1892.

Tatsuya Kawahara, Akinobu Lee, Kazuya Takeda, Katsunobu Itou, and Kiyohiro Shikano. 2004. Recent progress of open-source LVCSR engine Julius and Japanese model repository. In *Proc. Interspeech-2004 (ICSLP)*, pages 3069–3072.

Kazunori Komatani, Naoyuki Kanda, Mikio Nakano, Kazuhiro Nakadai, Hiroshi Tsujino, Tetsuya Ogata, and Hiroshi G. Okuno. 2006. Multi-domain spoken dialogue system with extensibility and robustness against speech recognition errors. In *Proc. 7th SIGdial Workshop*, pages 9–17.

Ian R. Lane and Tatsuya Kawahara. 2005. Incorporating dialogue context and topic clustering in out-of-domain detection. In *Proc. ICASSP-2005*, pages 1045–1048.

Cheongjae Lee, Sangkeun Jung, Seokhwan Kim, and Gary Geunbae Lee. 2009. Example-based dialog modeling for practical multi-domain dialog system. *Speech Communication*, 51(5):466–484.

Bor-shen Lin, Hsin-ming Wang, and Lin-shan Lee. 1999. A distributed architecture for cooperative spoken dialogue agents with coherent dialogue state and history. In *Proc. ASRU-99*.

Michael F. McTear. 2004. *Spoken Dialogue Technology*. Springer.

Mikio Nakano, Atsushi Hoshino, Johane Takeuchi, Yuji Hasegawa, Toyotaka Torii, Kazuhiro Nakadai, Kazuhiko Kato, and Hiroshi Tsujino. 2006. A robot that can engage in both task-oriented and non-task-oriented dialogues. In *Proc. Humanoids-2006*, pages 404–411.

Mikio Nakano, Kotaro Funakoshi, Yuji Hasegawa, and Hiroshi Tsujino. 2008. A framework for building conversational agents based on a multi-expert model. In *Proc. 9th SIGdial Workshop*, pages 88–91.

Mikio Nakano, Yuji Hasegawa, Kotaro Funakoshi, Johane Takeuchi, Toyotaka Torii, Kazuhiro Nakadai, Naoyuki Kanda, Kazunori Komatani, Hiroshi G. Okuno, and Hiroshi Tsujino. 2011. A multi-expert model for dialogue and behavior control of conversational robots and agents. *Knowledge-Based Systems*, 24(2):248–256.

Hiromi Narimatsu, Mikio Nakano, and Kotaro Funakoshi. 2010. A classifier-based approach to supporting the augmentation of the question-answer database for spoken dialogue systems. In *Proc. 2nd IWSDS*, pages 182–187.

Yoshitaka Nishimura, Shinichiro Minotsu, Hiroshi Dohi, Mitsuru Ishizuka, Mikio Nakano, Kotaro Funakoshi, Johane Takeuchi, Yuji Hasegawa, and Hiroshi Tsujino. 2007. A markup language for describing interactive humanoid robot presentations. In *Proc. IUI'07*, pages 333–336.

Ian O'Neill, Philip Hanna, Xingkun Liu, and Michael McTear. 2004. Cross domain dialogue modelling: an object-based approach. In *Proc. Interspeech-2004 (ICSLP)*, pages 205–208.

Botond Pakucs. 2003. Towards dynamic multi-domain dialogue processing. In *Proc. Eurospeech-2003*, pages 741–744.

Esa-Pekka Salonen, Mikko Hartikainen, Markku Turunen, Jaakko Hakulinen, and J. Adam Funk. 2004. Flexible dialogue management using distributed and dynamic dialogue control. In *Proc. Interspeech-2004 (ICSLP)*, pages 197–200.

Ian H. Witten and Eibe Frank. 2005. *Data Mining: Practical machine learning tools and techniques, 2nd Edition*. Morgan Kaufmann, San Francisco.

expert class		Features
all classes $i = ru$, ip, qa	$F_{i,r1}$	If $\text{SRR}_{i,1}$ is obtained or not
	$F_{i,r2}$	If $\text{SRR}_{i,1}$ contains a filler or not
	$F_{i,r3}$	min (CMs of words in $\text{SRR}_{i,1}$)
	$F_{i,r4}$	avg (CMs of words in $\text{SRR}_{i,1}$)
	$F_{i,r5}$	(acoustic score of $\text{SRR}_{i,1}$) / duration
	$F_{i,r6}$	LM score of $\text{SRR}_{i,1}$
	$F_{i,r7}$	# of words in $\text{SRR}_{i,1}$
	$F_{i,r8}$	# of words in $\text{SRR}_{i,all}$
	$F_{i,r9}$	($F_{i,r5}$ - (acoustic score of $\text{SRR}_{lv,1}$)) / duration
RU	$F_{ru,r10}$	If $\text{SRR}_{ru,1}$ is an affirmative response
	$F_{ru,r11}$	If $\text{SRR}_{ru,1}$ is a denial response
	$F_{ru,r12}$	# of ASR results with LM_{ru}
	$F_{ru,r13}$	If $\text{SRR}_{ru,1}$ contains the name of a World Heritage Site
	$F_{ru,r14}$	max (CMs of words comprising the name of a World Heritage Site)
	$F_{ru,r15}$	ave (CMs of words comprising the name of a World Heritage Site)
	$F_{ru,h1}$	If $\text{SRR}_{ru,1}$ is an affirmative response (Stage 2 only)
	$F_{ru,h2}$	# of turns since this expert is activated
	$F_{ru,h3}$	# of denial responses recognized since this expert is activated
	$F_{ru,h4}$	$F_{ru,h4}/F_{ru,h3}$
	$F_{ru,h5}$	If the previous system utterance is a confirmation request to a user request for starting a presentation
	$F_{ru,h6}$	If the previous system utterance is an utterance to react to a non-understandable user utterance
	$F_{ru,h7}$	If the system has made a confirmation request to a user request for starting a presentation since this expert was activated
	$F_{ru,h8}$	If the system has made an utterance to react to a non-understandable user utterance since this expert was activated
	$F_{ru,h9}$	If the system has made a confirmation request to a user request for starting a presentation before
	$F_{ru,h10}$	If the system has made an utterance to react to a non-understandable user utterance before
IP	$F_{ip,r10}$	If the $\text{SRR}_{ip,1}$ is out of database
	$F_{ip,r11}$	$\sum_j$((# of keyphrases in $\text{SRR}_{ip,j}$) / (# of words in $\text{SRR}_{ip,j}$)) / (# of ASR results)
	$F_{ip,r12}$	$\min_i$(# of keyphrase$_i$ in $\text{SRR}_{ip,all}$ / (# of ASR results))
	$F_{ip,r13}$	$\max_i$(# of keyphrase$_i$ in $\text{SRR}_{ip,all}$ / (# of ASR results))
	$F_{ip,r14}$	avg(CM of keyphrase$_i$ in $\text{SRR}_{ip,1}$)
	$F_{ip,r15}$	$\min_i$ (CM of keyphrase$_i$ in $\text{SRR}_{ip,1}$)
	$F_{ip,r16}$	$\max_i$ (CM of keyphrase$_i$ in $\text{SRR}_{ip,1}$)
	$F_{ip,h1}$	If this expert has been activated before
	$F_{ip,h2}$	Same as $F_{ru,h2}$
	$F_{ip,h3}$	If the previous system utterance is the final utterance of the presentation
	$F_{ip,h4}$	If the previous system utterance is an utterance to react to a user interruption
	$F_{ip,h5}$	Same as $F_{ru,h6}$
	$F_{ip,h6}$	If the system has made the final utterance of the presentation since this expert was activated
	$F_{ip,h7}$	If the system has made an utterance to react to a user interruption since this expert was activated
	$F_{ip,h8}$	Same as $F_{ru,h8}$
	$F_{ip,h9}$	If the system has made the final utterance of the presentation before
	$F_{ip,h10}$	If the system has made an utterance to react to a user interruption before
	$F_{ip,h11}$	Same as $F_{ru,h10}$
QA	$F_{qa,r10}$	Same as $F_{ip,r12}$
	$F_{qa,r11}$	Same as $F_{ip,r13}$
	$F_{qa,r12}$	Same as $F_{ip,r14}$
	$F_{qa,r13}$	Same as $F_{ip,r15}$
	$F_{qa,r14}$	Same as $F_{ip,r16}$
	$F_{qa,r15}$	Same as $F_{ip,r17}$
	$F_{qa,r16}$	If $\text{SRR}_{qa,1}$ is an acknowledgment
	$F_{qa,h1}$	Same as $F_{ru,h1}$
	$F_{qa,h2}$	Same as $F_{ru,h2}$
	$F_{qa,h3}$	Same as $F_{ru,h3}$
	$F_{qa,h4}$	$F_{qa,h4}/F_{qa,h3}$
	$F_{qa,h5}$	If the previous system utterance is the final utterance of an answer
	$F_{qa,h6}$	Same as $F_{ru,h6}$
	$F_{qa,h7}$	If the system has made the final utterance of an answer since this expert was activated
	$F_{qa,h8}$	Same as $F_{ru,h8}$
	$F_{qa,h9}$	If the system has made the final utterance of an answer before
	$F_{qa,h10}$	Same as $F_{ru,h10}$

$\text{SRR}_{i,j}$ means j-th speech recognition result with the language model (LM) for expert class i. $\text{SRR}_{i,all}$ means all the recognition results in the n-best list. F_{i,r_x} are speech understanding related features and F_{i,h_x} are dialogue history related features. $\text{SRR}_{lv,j}$ is an ASR result with a large-vocabulary (60,250 words) statistical model (Kawahara et al., 2004), which we used for utterance verification. CM means confidence measure.

Table 5: Features used in the experiment.

expert class (F_1 score obtained after feature selection)	remaining features (F_1 score obtained when each feature is removed)
RU(0.948)	$F_{ru,r9}$ (0.922), $F_{ru,h8}$ (0.939), $F_{ru,r5}$ (0.940), $F_{ru,r14}$ (0.941), $F_{ru,r2}$ (0.944), $F_{ru,h9}$ (0.944), $F_{ru,h5}$ (0.944), $F_{ru,r13}$ (0.945), $F_{ru,h10}$ (0.945), $F_{ru,r10}$ (0.946), $F_{ru,r8}$ (0.946), $F_{ru,r7}$ (0.946)
IP(0.837)	$F_{ip,r7}$ (0.771), $F_{ip,r6}$ (0.772), $F_{ip,h9}$ (0.781), $F_{ip,h7}$ (0.781), $F_{ip,h11}$ (0.786), $F_{ip,r4}$ (0.79), $F_{ip,r2}$ (0.799), $F_{ip,r16}$ (0.809), $F_{ip,r5}$ (0.809), $F_{ip,r3}$ (0.809), $F_{ip,h4}$ (0.809), $F_{ip,r9}$ (0.814), $F_{ip,r15}$ (0.833), $F_{ip,r12}$ (0.834), $F_{ip,r13}$ (0.835), $F_{ip,h10}$ (0.836)
QA(0.836)	$F_{qa,r14}$ (0.813), $F_{qa,r7}$ (0.817), $F_{qa,r16}$ (0.817), $F_{qa,r10}$ (0.818), $F_{qa,h6}$ (0.820), $F_{qa,r6}$ (0.822), $F_{qa,r3}$ (0.831), $F_{qa,r5}$ (0.832)

Table 6: Features that remained after feature selection at Stage 1 and their significances in terms of the F_1 score obtained when each feature is removed.

expert class (F_1 score obtained after feature selection)	remaining features (F_1 score obtained when each feature is removed)
RU(0.773)	$F_{ru,r3}$ (0.728), $F_{ru,a}$ (0.737), $F_{ru,h5}$ (0.743), $F_{ru,h1}$ (0.751), $F_{ru,r9}$ (0.754), $F_{ru,h10}$ (0.757), $F_{ru,h8}$ (0.757), $F_{ru,r5}$ (0.758), $F_{ru,r2}$ (0.759), $F_{ru,r13}$ (0.762), $F_{ru,r14}$ (0.763), $F_{ru,h9}$ (0.767), $F_{ru,r15}$ (0.768), $F_{ru,r10}$ (0.768), $F_{ru,h3}$ (0.772)
IP(0.827)	$F_{ip,h5}$ (0.808), $F_{ip,r5}$ (0.809), $F_{ip,r4}$ (0.810), $F_{ip,r6}$ (0.811), $F_{ip,a}$ (0.812), $F_{ip,h4}$ (0.812), $F_{ip,r13}$ (0.813), $F_{ip,h3}$ (0.817), $F_{ip,r15}$ (0.818), $F_{ip,r3}$ (0.818), $F_{ip,h10}$ (0.819), $F_{ip,r12}$ (0.820), $F_{ip,h7}$ (0.821), $F_{ip,r11}$ (0.822), $F_{ip,r10}$ (0.822), $F_{ip,h8}$ (0.822), $F_{ip,h6}$ (0.822), $F_{ip,r2}$ (0.824), $F_{ip,r8}$ (0.824), $F_{ip,h9}$ (0.824), $F_{ip,h2}$ (0.825)
QA(0.873)	$F_{qa,a}$ (0.838), $F_{qa,r5}$ (0.857), $F_{qa,h1}$ (0.859), $F_{qa,r3}$ (0.862), $F_{qa,r6}$ (0.865), $F_{qa,h8}$ (0.867), $F_{qa,r7}$ (0.868), $F_{qa,r15}$ (0.870), $F_{qa,r8}$ (0.870), $F_{qa,h7}$ (0.870), $F_{qa,r12}$ (0.871), $F_{qa,r2}$ (0.871), $F_{qa,r16}$ (0.871), $F_{qa,h4}$ (0.871), $F_{qa,h3}$ (0.871), $F_{qa,r11}$ (0.872), $F_{qa,h6}$ (0.872), $F_{qa,h5}$ (0.872)

Table 7: Features that remained after feature selection at Stage 2 and their significances in terms of the F_1 score obtained when each feature is removed. $F_{ru,a}$, $F_{ip,a}$, and $F_{qa,a}$ are the maximum activation probabilities obtained at Stage 1.

A Comparison of Latent Variable Models For Conversation Analysis

Sourish Chaudhuri and Bhiksha Raj
Language Technologies Institute,
School of Computer Science,
Carnegie Mellon University,
Pittsburgh, PA - 15213.
{sourishc, bhiksha} @ cs.cmu.edu

Abstract

With the evolution of online communication methods, conversations are increasingly handled via email, internet forums and other such methods. In this paper, we attempt to model lexical information in a context sensitive manner, encoding our belief that the use of language depends on the participants in the conversation. We model the discourse as a combination of the speaker, the addressee and other participants in the conversation as well as a context specific language model. In order to do this, we introduce a novel method based on an HMM with an exponential state space to capture speaker-addressee context. We also study the performance of topic modeling frameworks in conversational settings. We evaluate the models on the tasks of identifying the set of people present in any conversation, as well as identifying the speaker for every utterance in the conversation, and they show significant improvement over the baseline models.

1 Introduction

In this paper, we experiment with different methods of automatically analyzing discourse. We present and validate hypotheses on how conversations can be better analyzed using information about the speakers, as well as other participants in the conversation. We present a novel method of modeling discourse using an exponential state Hidden Markov Model where states are based on speakers and addressees. We also cast the problem into the popular topic modeling frameworks, and compare the various approaches.

Consider a small group of people that a person knows well. Given a transcript of a discussion on a topic of mutual interest, that person would likely be able to identify who is likely to have said what, based on his knowledge of the speakers and their inclinations on various topics. We would like to be able to encode similar intelligence into a system that could automatically learn about speakers based on transcripts of prior conversations, and use that information to analyze new conversations.

The scenario we consider in this work is as follows: we have a known set of characters, any subset of whom could be present in a conversation. Given the transcript of a conversation only, without speaker annotations, we would like to : 1. Predict the *set* of participants in the conversation from the characteristics of the entire conversation, and 2. Identify the *individual* speakers at each conversation turn.

In order to do this, we model each utterance in a conversation as dependent on the speaker, the addressee and the other people present. As we shall describe, our models encode the belief that people speak/behave differently depending on other participants in the conversation. This has a two-fold benefit: first, it can help us discover social (or even, professional) relationship structures; second, it can help us understand how to respond to different people, and incorporate that information into automated conversational agents which can then behave in a more context sensitive manner. The ability to automatically model discourse as context specific in this manner is also useful for other tasks such as directed advertising and duplicity detection.

In Section 2, we describe relevant related work.

Proceedings of the SIGDIAL 2011: the 12th Annual Meeting of the Special Interest Group on Discourse and Dialogue, pages 30–38,
Portland, Oregon, June 17-18, 2011.

Section 3 describes the dataset for our experiments, Section 4 describes the problem, our use of topic models, and the novel HMM based method, while Section 5 summarizes the results and we conclude in Section 6.

2 Related Work

The task of automatically segmenting speech and then identifying speakers from audio (Reynolds and Torres-Carrasquillo, 2005) is referred to as diarization and has been well-studied (Tranter and Reynolds, 2006). More recently, approaches have been developed to fuse information from both the audio and video modalities (Noulas et al., 2011) to improve diarization systems when video information is available. In this paper, we attempt to understand just how much information is available in the text alone. Systems that can work with text only can be used to improve audio-based systems which can provide speech recognition output to a text-based system. They can also be used to work with closed caption streams, or on human-generated transcriptions of meeting recordings.

Research on identifying speakers from text or lexical information is limited in comparison to work with audio data. However, efforts have been made to use discourse level information to automatically identify speakers to calibrate idiolectal differences between speakers (Doddington, 2001). (Canseco et al., 2005,) investigated the use of lexical features to automatically diarize (but not actually identify) transcripts to determine if a current speaker continued or a previous speaker spoke or the next speaker spoke. Lei and Mirghafori (2 007) attempted to incorporate idiolect based speaker information by using word conditioning of phone N-grams to recognize speakers in dialogs with 2 speakers.

In our work, the models we use to identify speakers are powerful enough to predict the addressee as well. In this context, we note that several attempts have been made recently to automatically identify addressees in dialog settings. These approaches have used information about the context and content of the utterance, using dialog acts and information about the speaker's gaze to aid classifier performance (Jovanovic et al., 2006). Den Akker and Traum (2009) proposed rule-based methods for addressee classification. Unlike in these works, we attempt to jointly model both the speaker and the addressee as one of our proposed approaches. This is similar to the approach employed by (Otsuka et al., 2005,), who proposed a Dynamic Bayesian Network model to understand multiparty conversation structure using non-verbal cues only– eye gaze, facial expression, gesticulations and posture.

3 Data

The data for our experiments consists of fan-sourced transcripts of the episodes of the sitcom F.R.I.E.N.D.S. The structure of the data is as follows: we have a set of conversations as training data. Each conversation contains a sequence of turns, with each turn annotated with its speaker. We do not have any information about the addressee from the dataset. We do, however, have implicit information of the set of speakers within a conversation segment (we make the assumption here that if a character doesn't speak in a segment, he is not present). Annotator notes appear periodically to indicate that the scene changed or that new characters entered the scene or that some characters left the scene. We treat these annotator notes as conversation boundaries and the segment of turns between two such boundaries constitutes one conversation instance.

The set of characters used for our experiments is finite. The 6 primary characters in the sitcom (Chandler, Joey, Monica, Phoebe, Rachel and Ross) are retained. In addition to these 6 primary characters, there are a number of supporting characters who appear occasionally. We use *Other* to denote all other characters, as the amount of data for a number of the supporting characters is quite small and would not result in learning useful patterns regarding their behavior. As a result, we treat all of these characters as one character that can be thought of as a universal supporting character. Hence, we have a total of 7 possible characters. Any subset of these 7 characters could be part of a conversation. Below is an example of a pair of conversations from our dataset:

[EVENT]
Paul: thank you! thank you so much!
Monica: stop!
Paul: no, i'm telling you last night was like umm, all my birthdays, both graduations, plus the barn

raising scene in witness.

Monica: we'll talk later.

Paul: yeah. thank you.

[EVENT]

Joey: that wasn't a real date?! what the hell do you do on a real date?

Monica: shut up, and put my table back.

All: okayyy!

[EVENT]

The *event* markers are tags inserted at preprocessing time, to denote transcriber annotations such as characters entering or leaving scenes. The sequence of turns between two *event* markers are treated as one conversation. Also, note the character Paul in the first conversation in the example above – when training the system, the content of Paul's utterances are used to train the model for *Other*, since Paul is not one of the primary characters that we track. At test time, the input looks similar to the above, except that the turns are not annotated by speaker.

The transcripts used in our experiments are segmented by speaker turns, so that consecutive turns are uttered by different speakers. The entire set of 230 episodes was split randomly into training, development and test splits. Sequential information for the individual conversations were not used. Each episode was further divided into conversations based on the scene boundaries denoted by the transcribers. For training, overall, we used 195 episodes from F.R.I.E.N.D.S, with a total of 9,171 conversations and a total 52,516 turns. The average length in number of turns for each conversation was 5.73. The test set consisted of a total of 20 episodes with 855 conversations and 4,981 turns. The average length of a conversation in the test set was 5.83. The remaining 15 episodes were used as development data to tune hyperparameters – this set consisted of 529 conversations and 2,984 turns in total. The distribution of the number of utterances by speakers across the training, test and development set are shown in Figure 1. As one can observe, the distribution is not particularly skewed for any of the speakers across the splits of the dataset.

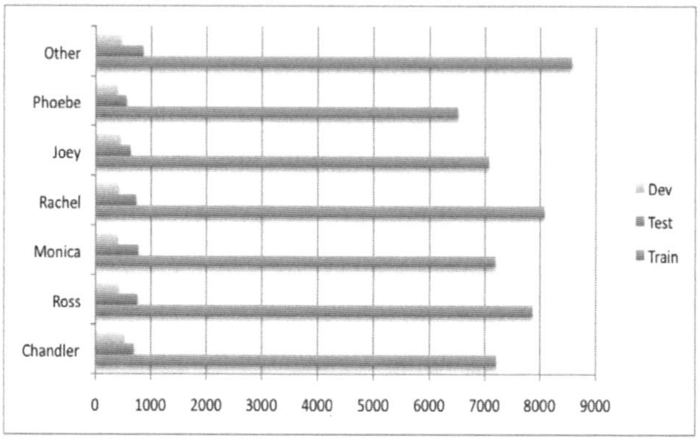

Figure 1: Distribution of #utterances for each speaker in the dataset.

4 Conversation Models

Previous work in analyzing participants in a conversation have used meeting data, with a fixed number of participants. In our task, the total number of possible participants is finite, but we do not have information on how many of them are present at any particular instant. Thus, our model first attempts to detect the participants in a segment of conversation, and then attempts to attribute speaker turns to individuals.

Our model for discourse structure is based on two premises. First, we believe that what a person says will depend on who he or she is speaking to. Intuitively, consider a person trying to make the same point to his boss and (at a different time and place) to his friend. It is likely that he will be more formal with his boss than his friend. Second, if the speaker addresses someone specifically in a group of people, knowing who he addressed would likely help us predict better who would speak next. We assume that the first hypothesis above also holds for groups of people in conversations, where the topics and their distribution in discussions (and words that affect the tone of the discussion) depend on the participants.

As described earlier, we evaluate our models on two tasks. First, we would like to identify the set of characters present in any conversation. Given segments of conversation, we attempt to understand the distribution of topics for specific subsets of characters present in that segment. To do this, we cast this problem into a topic modeling framework – we experiment with the Author-Topic model (Rosen-

Zvi et al., 2004), described in Section 4.1, for this task. We use the Author Topic Model to link the co-occurrence information of characters with the words in the conversation.

Second, we attempt to attribute speakers to utterances, described in Section 4.2. We introduce a novel approach using an HMM with an exponential state space to model speakers and addressees, described in Section 4.2.1. We also use the Author Topic Model and the Author-Recipient Topic Model (McCallum et al., 2007), described in Section 4.2.2 for this task. The key difference between the HMM-based model and the topic model based approaches is that the former explicitly takes sequence information into account.

4.1 Identifying Character Subset Presence

The premise behind attempting to model subsets of characters is that the nature of the conversation depends on the group of people participating. For instance, it seems intuitively likely that the content of a conversation between two friends would be different if they were the only ones present than it would be if their families were also present. To extend this hypothesis to a general scenario, the content of each speaker's turn depends not only on the speaker, but also on the person being spoken to as well as the other people present. To model this, we require a model that captures the distribution of the text for entire conversation, for each possible subset of characters. In this section, we describe the training of a generic model for conversations, and use it to produce features for a discriminative classifier.

Let there be N characters who could participate in a conversation. We assume a general scenario, where any subset of these characters may be present. Thus, there are $2^N - 1$ character subsets that are possible. We can model this as a multi-class classification problem (we will refer to this as *subset modeling*, henceforth).

The generative model for this task is as follows: Each conversation segment is associated with a set of utterances, and a set of characters. For each such set of characters, we associate a distribution over topics. For each word that is present in the segment, we select a topic from the subset-specific topic distribution, and then we select the word from that topic. Figure 2 shows the graphical model for this in plate notation.

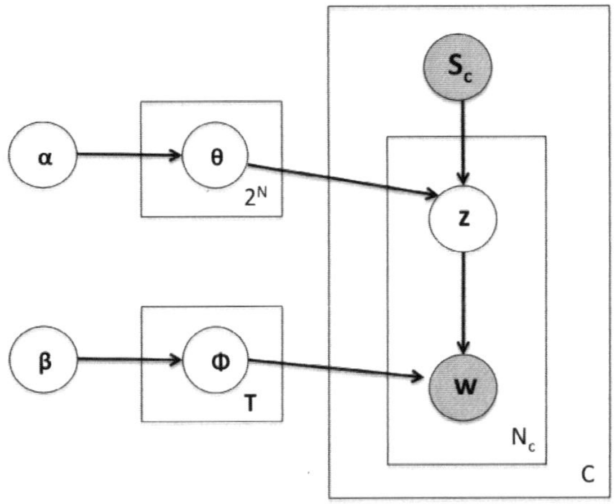

Figure 2: Graphical representation of the subset model in plate notation

In the plate notation, the observed variables are shaded and the latent variables are unshaded. Plates encapsulate a set of variables which are repeatedly sampled a fixed number of times, and the number at the bottom right indicates this fixed number.

S_c represents a subset of the characters who were present in the conversation segment. We have C such conversations, and each conversation contains N_c words. z represents the latent topic variable, and θ represents the multinomial topic distribution for each subset of characters (there are 2^N such subsets). The multinomial distribution of topics has a prior distribution characterized by α. Similarly, every topic (there are a set of T topics) has a multinomial distribution ϕ over the words in the vocabulary, and ϕ has a prior distribution characterized by β.

For every conversation in the training corpus, the set of characters present is known. The content of the conversation is treated as a bag of words. From the topic distribution for the subset of characters present, we sample a topic. Based on the word distributions for this topic, we sample a word. This process is repeated N_c times corresponding to the number of words in the conversation. The entire process of generating a conversation is repeated C times, corresponding to the number of conversations in the training corpus.

Depending on the value of N, the number of possible classes may be very high. Training a large number of models may lead to a data scarcity, especially given the high dimensionality of language data. We therefore slightly modify the model, so that instead of topic distributions for each possible subset, we have a topic distribution for each character, and the distribution of topics in the conversation is a mixture of the topic distributions for each character. This leads us to a graphical model that has been well-studied in the past – the Author-Topic model (ATM, henceforth) and is shown in Figure 3.

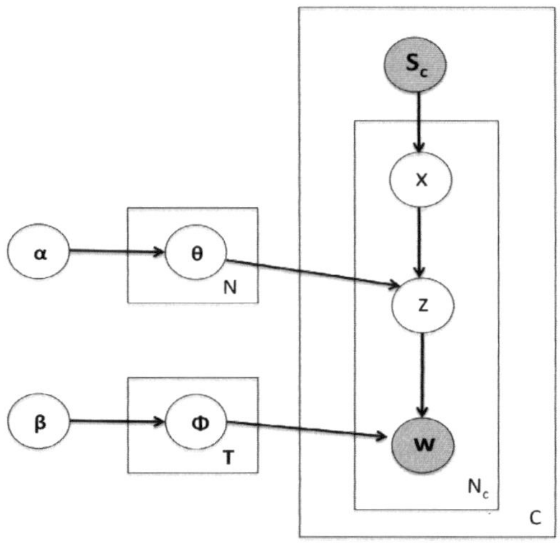

Figure 3: Graphical representation of the simplified subset model in plate notation

Thus, given the set of characters present, we sample one of them (x) from a uniform distribution. Then we generate a topic by sampling from the distribution of topics for that speaker. The rest of the process remains the same.We use this model to help us predict which subset of characters was present in a given conversation.

We learn speaker-specific topic distributions using the ATM. In order to predict characters present in a test conversation, we train binary SVM (Shawe-Taylor and Cristianini, 2000) classifiers for each speaker in the following manner: we compute the distribution of the speaker-specific topics in each conversation, and use these as the features of the data point. If the speaker was present in the conversation, the data point corresponding to the conversation has a class label of +1, else -1. A linear SVM classifier is trained over the data. At test time, we compute the distribution of the speaker's topics in the conversation, and use the SVM to predict if the speaker was present or not.

4.2 Identifying Speakers From Utterances

In this section, we describe our approach to identifying speakers from the text of the utterance. The ATM (as described above) treats all the participants in the conversation as being potential contributors to each turn. However, we can also use the ATM to predict speakers directly. In this case, we will use each turn as analogous to a document. Each such *document* has only one *author* and the author topic model can be used to learn models for each author. The plate notation for this would look very similar to the one in Figure 2, except that instead of a subset of characters being observed, only one would be observed, and the number of possible topic distributions would be equal to the number of characters.

The ATM for this task does not take any context information into account. In the following subsection, we introduce a novel HMM based approach that seeks to leverage information from the sequence of turns.

4.2.1 Exponential State Hidden Markov Model

In this model, we assign a state to each speaker-addressee combination possible. If our data consists of N characters, only one of the N characters will be speaking at any given point. He/She may be speaking to any combination of the remaining $N-1$ characters. Thus, the number of states in this model is $N \times 2^{(N-1)}$. Note that the addressee is not observed directly from the data.

The sequence of turns in a conversation is modeled by a Hidden Markov Model (Rabiner, 1989). At each time instant, the speaker corresponding to the state speaks a turn, which is the observed emission, before transitioning to another state at the next time instant. The state at the next time instant is constrained to have a different speaker.

The model is trained using the standard Baum-Welch training. The emission probabilities are captured by a trigram language model, trained using the SRILM toolkit (Stolcke, 2002). The parameters of the model are initialized as follows: for emission probabilities, we take all the utterances by a speaker and distributing them uniformly among the states that have that speaker, since we do not have direct information about the addressees. For transition probabilities, we initialize with a bias instead of uniformly. Given a conversation, for a state with speaker A and set of addressees (R, say – Note that R may have multiple characters), we give equal probabilities of transitioning to all states that have one of the characters in R as the speaker. Now, we pick the set of speakers (call it M) that uttered the next three turns (essentially, we look ahead in the data stream to see who the next 3 speakers are while training). We add a bias to every state with A as the speaker, and every possible combination of the speakers in M, to encode the hypothesis that the addressee would be likely to speak pretty soon, if not directly after.

The large state space in this model makes computation extremely expensive. However, an examination of the posterior probabilities show that a number of states are rarely, or never, entered. We prune away such states after every 5 iterations in the following manner – we use the current parameters of the model after each iteration to identify the speakers of each turn on the development set. Decoding of a sequence of turns at test time is done using the Viterbi algorithm. However, instead of using the best path only, we keep track of the top 10 best paths. Thus, after an iteration of training, we test on the development data, and obtain 10 possible sequences of speakers for each conversation. Over 5 iterations, we have the 50 best paths for each conversation. We then compute the average number of states entered in all the decoded paths obtained. If the average number of times a state was entered is μ, then any state that was entered less than $k \times \mu$ times ($k = 0.02$, for our experiments), according to the posterior probabilities was pruned out. In order to set the value of k, the development set was split into 2 halves, with one half being used to compute the average number of times a state is entered across the 10 best decodes for data in that half. For different values of k, accuracy of speaker identification on the 1-best decode was computed on the other half of the development set, for values of k from 0.005 to 0.1.

The optimal state sequence at test time also contains information about the addressee. For the tasks we evaluate, this information is not directly used. However, in other applications, such as those involving automated agents, this information could be valuable in triggering the agent.

4.2.2 Author-Recipient Topic Model

The Author Recipient Topic Model (McCallum et al., 2007) (ARTM, henceforth) was used for discovering topics and roles in social networks. It is built over the Author-Topic Model discussed previously, with the exception that messages are conditioned on the sender as well as the receivers. The graphical model in plate notation is shown in Figure 4.

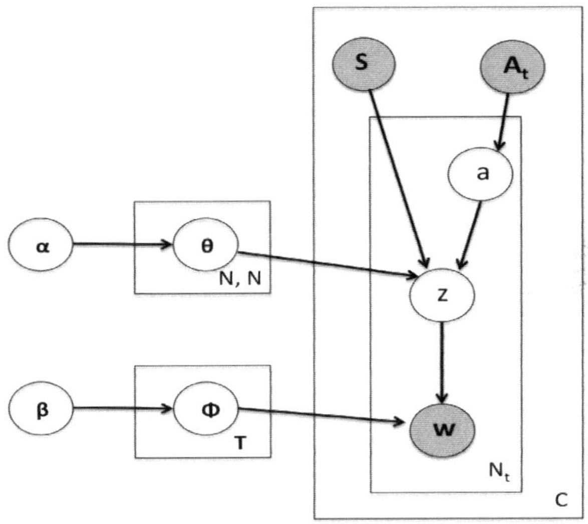

Figure 4: Graphical representation of the Author-Recipient Topic model in plate notation

Here, we model each turn as having a set of N_t words. Each turn has one speaker S, and a set of addressees A_t. The generative model works as follows: For each word in a turn, sample an addressee a from the set of addressees. Topic distributions are now conditioned over speaker-addressee pairs, instead of only the speaker as we saw in the ATM. A topic is now sampled from the speaker-addressee specific topic distribution. A word is now sampled from this topic using the topic specific word distributions. The parameters α, β, and z have the same meaning as in the ATM described earlier.

Note that the set of addressees in our setting is not explicitly observed. We know the participants in the conversation at training time, and we know the speaker, but we do not know who was addressed. Since we do not have information to make a better choice of addressee, we model the entire set of participants without the speaker as the set of addressees, in this model.

For the task of identifying the speaker who uttered the turn, we employ an approach, similar to the one used for ATM. We train speaker-addressee-specific models. The feature set for this task includes features not only from the turn itself, but also from the context. Thus, we have the distribution of the topics in the turn for *every* speaker-addressee pair with the right speaker, the speakers of the previous two turns, and the distribution of topics of the speaker of the current turn over the previous two turns. (Thus, while the model does not explicitly model sequence, as an HMM does, it utilizes context information in its feature space.) Using these features, we train a linear SVM to predict whether or not the speaker uttered the turn. In this case, we could potentially have multiple speakers (or none of them) predicted to have uttered the same turn. In that case, we choose the speaker with the maximum distance from the margin.

4.3 Baseline Models

In this section, we set up simple baseline models to evaluate our performance against. We describe how we set up a random baseline, a Naive Bayes baseline and an HMM baseline model.

4.3.1 Random Baseline

For the task of identifying the set of characters present in a conversation, the random baseline would work as follows: it knows that the number of characters present in any conversation lies between 1 and *N* (N = 7, in this case). (Note that monologues, with only 1 person being present, are possible. Typically, in our data, they happen at the beginning or end of scenes.) Thus, it randomly decides if each of these characters are present or not in any given conversation.

Suppose that the total number of characters are *n* and *r* of them are actually present in the conversation. Let us say the random guess system predicts *t* of the characters to be present. If we use the uniform distribution for picking t, then $P(t) = \frac{1}{7}, \forall t \in [1, 2, ..., 7]$, in this case. For any given t, the probability that we get k correct is given by:

$$P(k|t) = \frac{\binom{r}{k} \times \binom{n-r}{t-k}}{\binom{n}{t}} \quad (1)$$

To compute the probability of getting k right, we marginalize out the number of characters guessed to be present, t:

$$P(k) = \sum_t P(k,t) = \sum_t P(k|t).P(t) \quad (2)$$

Now we can compute the probability of getting k correct by randomly guessing, for all k from 0 to r. Using these, we can compute the expected number of correct guesses, which turns out to be $0.571.r$ for an average recall would be 57.1%.

For the task of identifying the characters, every turn could have been uttered by one of the n characters ($n = 7$, for our case). Thus, the average accuracy at identifying turns would be $\frac{1}{7}$ or 14.29%.

4.3.2 Naive Bayes Classifier

For the task of predicting the subset of speakers, we set up a Naive Bayes using words as features. We build up a term-document matrix, with each conversation treated as a document. For each character, we train a binary classifier using the training data- conversations where the character was present were marked as a positive instance for that character, and ones where he was not present were marked as negative instances. We experimented both with using priors based on the empirical distribution in the training data and with using uniform prior (i.e. $P(character) = 0.5$). Given a test conversation, we use individual classifiers for each of the characters to determine whether he/she was present or not.

For the task of identifying speakers, given an utterance, the Naive Bayes classifier is set up as follows: Again, we create term-document matrices for each of the speakers, where a document is a turn uttered by the speaker. Turns uttered by that speaker are positive instances and those uttered by someone else are negative instances. For each speaker, we compute the Naive Bayes probability ratio (odds) of him uttering the turn and not uttering the turn, in order to decide. If multiple speakers are classified as having uttered the turn, or no speaker is classified as having uttered the turn, the speaker with the best odds of having uttered the turn is selected.

System	Precision	Recall
Author Topic Model	63.22%	74.71%
NB	52.33%	44.19%
NB-prior	68.31%	36.25%
Random Baseline	28.05%	57.1%

Table 1: Results for predicting subset of characters present

System	Accuracy
ESHMM	27.13%
Speaker-LM HMM	25.04%
ARTM	23.64%
Author Topic Model	26.2%
NB	23.41%
NB-prior	21.39%
Random Baseline	14.29%

Table 2: Results for predicting speakers of utterances

4.3.3 Single Speaker HMM

This model is only used to attribute speakers to turns. Section 4.2.1 described an HMM model that captures speaker-addressee information. In the single- speaker HMM, we have a state for each speaker. Emission probabilities are given by a trigram language model that is trained on the speaker's utterances in the training data. The transition probabilities are initialized as per the empirical transitions between speakers in the data. This model does not capture any kind of addressee information.

5 Results

In this section, we present results of our experiments with the models we described earlier, on the two tasks, identifying the set of speakers in any given conversation and identifying individual speakers who uttered each turn in a conversation.

For the task of identifying the set of speakers in any given conversation, we evaluate performance using precision and recall, which are defined as follows: If the conversation actually contained r characters, the system predicted that it contained t characters, and got k right, then:

$$Precision = \frac{k}{t}; Recall = \frac{k}{r} \quad (3)$$

The results are summarized in Table 1. In the table, NB-prior indicates that the prior for the binary classifier was determined based on the number of conversations each character appeared in, while NB indicates that the prior was uniform (i.e., for each character, $P(present) = P(absent) = 0.5$). We find that the results obtained using the author-topic model are significantly better than each of the other three models.

On average, the number of speakers in each conversation in the test data was 2.44 (the corresponding number in the training data appears to be somewhat higher at 2.65). Our attempts to restrict the set of characters in a real setting plays a significant role here as we shall discuss later.

The Naive Bayes classifier with empirical priors on average predicted that there were 1.3 characters present per conversation, while the version with uniform priors predicted 2.2 characters to be present per conversation on average. The author-topic model, on average, over-estimated the number of characters at 2.86 characters per conversation.

For the task of predicting the speaker, given an utterance, we have two kinds of Hidden Markov Models, the Exponential State HMM (ESHMM) and and HMM with emission probabilities based on individual speaker language models (Speaker LM HMM). We also have the topic model based systems- the ARTM and the ATM. Finally, we have the baseline models- the Naive Bayes with empirical priors and with uniform priors, and the random baseline. Table 2 summarizes their performance. In this case, we only report accuracy. Since each turn has only one speaker, we can constrain each of the models to produce one speaker, in order to calculate the accuracy.

The HMM and topic based models all incorporate sequence information in some form. In the case of the HMM based models, state transitions are conditioned on the previous speaker. In the case of the topic model based systems, the feature vectors contain context, although the task is modeled as a discriminative classification task. The ESHMM model worked the best on this dataset. With the exception of the ATM and the speaker LM HMM ($p < 0.10$), the improvements obtained by using the ESHMM over all other models were statistically significant ($p < 0.05$). Surprisingly, the single speaker LM

HMM and the ATM both outperform the ARTM on this task. One of the reasons for this could be that the ARTM does not suitably capture what we hoped it would, perhaps because of the fact that the recipients (addressees) are not observed.

6 Conclusion

In this paper, we presented a set of latent variable model based approaches to analyzing conversation structure using the text transcript of the conversations only. The initial set of experiments show promising improvements over simple baseline methods, though the overall results leave considerable room for improvement. Conversations are a dynamic process, with the content varying significantly with time, and the use of formulations such as dynamic topic modeling (Blei and Lafferty, 2006) may help.

We believe that the concept of modeling speakers and addressees would be a powerful one in modeling conversation structure and useful in applications such as those involving automated agents, or in understanding discourse on discussion forums, as well as understanding development of authority in such forums. The state sequences predicted by the ESHMM implicitly predict addressees for each turn. This is not directly used in our tasks, but could be useful for automated agents, in understanding appropriate moments to take its turn.

The dataset used in this case introduced some noise. We decided to subsume everyone aside from the 6 main characters under the moniker *other*, in order to keep the state space manageable. In reality, it was a collection of a few dozen characters, some of whom appeared intermittently through the episodes. As a result, the emission model for this state was not a stable one. The system rarely predicted this class, and had very low accuracy when it did.

Further, development of datasets with annotations specifying the addressees explicitly would probably accelerate development of methods that work well in such settings.

References

Andrew McCallum, Xuerui Wang and Andres Corrada-Emmanuel. 2007. Topic and Role Discovery in Social Networks with Experiments on Enron and Academic Email. In *Journal of Artificial Intelligence Research.*.

Andreas Stolcke. 2002. SRILM an Extensible Language Modeling Toolkit. In *ICSLP*.

D. A. Reynolds and P. Torres-Carrasquillo. 2005. Approaches and applications of audio diarization. In *Proc. of ICASSP*.

David M. Blei and John D. Lafferty. 2006. Dynamic Topic Models. In *Proceedings of ICML*.

George Doddington. 2001. Speaker Recognition based on Idiolectal Differences between Speakers. In *Eurospeech.*.

S.E. Tranter and D.A. Reynolds. 2006. An overview of automatic speaker diarization systems. In *IEEE Transactions on Audio, Speech and Language Processing.*.

Athanasios Noulas, Gwenn Englebienne, Ben J.A. Krse 2011. Multimodal Speaker Diarization. In *IEEE Transactions on Pattern Analysis and Machine Intelligence.*.

Howard Lei and Nikki Mirghafori. 2007. *Word-Conditioned Phone n-grams For Speaker Recognition.* In *Proceedings of ICASSP*

John Shawe Taylor and Nello Cristianini. 2000. *Support Vector Machines and other Kernel Based Learning Methods.* Cambridge University Press..

Kazuhiro Otsuka, Yoshinao Takemae and Junji Yamato. 2005. A probabilistic inference of multiparty-conversation structure based on Markov-switching models of gaze patterns, head directions, and utterances. In *Proceedings of the 7th international conference on Multimodal interfaces.*

L.R. Rabiner. 1989. A tutorial on Hidden Markov Models and selected applications in speech recognition. In *Proceedings of IEEE.*

Leonardo Canseco, Lori Lamel and Jean-Luc Gauvain 2005. A Comparative Study using Manual and Automatic Transcriptions for Diarization. In *Proceedings of ASRU.*

Michal Rosen-Zvi, Thomas Griffiths, Mark Steyvers and Padhraic Smyth. 2004. The Author-Topic Model for Authors and Documents. In *20th Conference on Uncertainty in Artificial Intelligence.*

Natasa Jovanovic, Rieks op den Akker and Anton Nijholt. 2006. Addressee Identification in Face-to-Face Meetings In *Proc. of EACL.*

Rieks op den Akker and David Traum. 2009. A Comparison of Addressee Detection Methods for Multiparty Conversations. In *Proc. of Diaholmia 2009.*

Thomas Hofmann. 1999. Probabilistic latent semantic analysis. In *Proc of UAI.*.

Xavier Anguera, Chuck Wooters and Javier Hernando 2005. Speaker Diarization for Multi-Party Meetings using Acoustic Fusion In *IEEE Workshop on Automatic Speech Recognition and Understanding.*.

Toward Learning and Evaluation of Dialogue Policies with Text Examples

David DeVault and **Anton Leuski** and **Kenji Sagae**
Institute for Creative Technologies
University of Southern California
Playa Vista, CA 90094
{devault,leuski,sagae}@ict.usc.edu

Abstract

We present a dialogue collection and enrichment framework that is designed to explore the learning and evaluation of dialogue policies for simple conversational characters using textual training data. To facilitate learning and evaluation, our framework enriches a collection of role-play dialogues with additional training data, including paraphrases of user utterances, and multiple independent judgments by external referees about the best policy response for the character at each point. As a case study, we use this framework to train a policy for a limited domain tactical questioning character, reaching promising performance. We also introduce an automatic policy evaluation metric that recognizes the validity of multiple conversational responses at each point in a dialogue. We use this metric to explore the variability in human opinion about optimal policy decisions, and to automatically evaluate several learned policies in our example domain.

1 Introduction

There is a large class of potential users of dialogue systems technology who lack the background for many of the formal modeling tasks that typically are required in the construction of a dialogue system. The problematic steps include annotating the meaning of user utterances in some semantic formalism, developing a formal representation of information state, writing detailed rules that govern dialogue management, and annotating the meaning of system utterances in support of language generation, among other tasks.

In this paper, we explore data collection and machine learning techniques that enable the implementation of domain-specific conversational dialogue policies through a relatively small data collection effort, and without any formal modeling. We present a case study, which serves to illustrate some of the possibilities in our framework. In contrast to recent work on data-driven dialogue policy learning that learns dialogue behavior from existing data sources (Gandhe and Traum, 2007; Jafarpour et al., 2009; Ritter et al., 2010), we address the task of authoring a dialogue policy from scratch with a specific purpose, task and scenario in mind. We examine the data collection, learning and evaluation steps.

The contributions of this work include a data collection and enrichment framework without formal modeling, and the creation of dialogue policies from the collected data. We also propose a framework for evaluating learned policies. We show, for the scenario in our case study, that these techniques deliver promising levels of performance, and point to possible future developments in data-driven dialogue policy creation and evaluation.

2 Case study

For our case study we selected an existing dialogue system scenario designed for Tactical Questioning training (Traum et al., 2008). The character targeted in our study, Amani, is modeled closely after the Amani Tactical Questioning character described by Gandhe et al. (2009) and Artstein et al. (2009). Tactical Questioning dialogues are those in which small unit military personnel, usually on patrol, hold conversations with individuals to produce information of military value. A tactical questioning dialogue

Proceedings of the SIGDIAL 2011: the 12th Annual Meeting of the Special Interest Group on Discourse and Dialogue, pages 39–48,
Portland, Oregon, June 17-18, 2011.

system is a simulation training environment where virtual characters play the role of a person being questioned. Tactical questioning characters are designed to be non-cooperative at times. They may answer some of the interviewers questions in a cooperative manner, but may refuse to answer other questions, or intentionally provide incorrect answers. Therefore the interviewer is encouraged to conduct the interview in a manner that induces cooperation from the character: building rapport with the character, addressing their concerns, making promises and offers, as well as threatening or intimidating the character; the purpose of the dialogue system is to allow trainees to practice these strategies in a realistic setting (Gandhe et al., 2009).

This type of scenario is a good testbed for our proposed learning and evaluation framework, since it involves both flexible conversational choices and well-defined constraints regarding the disclosure of specific information. In the Amani scenario, the user plays the role of a commander of a small military unit in Iraq whose unit had been attacked by sniper fire. The user interviews a character named Amani who was a witness to the incident and is thought to have some information about the identity of the attackers. Amani is willing to tell the interviewer everything she knows provided that the user promises her safety, secrecy, and small monetary compensation for the information (Artstein et al., 2009).

An exhaustive formal definition of Amani's ideal dialogue policy might include a large number of rules covering a wide range of user utterance types. The key constraints for the training simulation, however, can be stated simply with a few rules governing the release of five pieces of information that Amani knows. Amani will only reveal one of these pieces of information if a precondition is met. Table 1 shows how certain information relates to each of the preconditions in Amani's dialogue policy. Amani can only reveal a fact from the first column if the user promised her an item from the second column. For example, Amani can only tell the user the shooter's name if the user promised her safety. If the user has not promised safety, Amani will ask him for safety. If the user refuses to promise safety, Amani will either decline to answer the question or lie to the interviewer. Amani does keep track of the user's promises and once she is promised safety, she would not ask for it again.

information	precondition
about shooter's name	safety
about shooter's description	safety
about shooter's location	secrecy
about the occupant of the shop	secrecy
about shooter's daily routine	money

Table 1: Amani's dialogue policy.

While the key constraints for Amani's policy, as summarized in Table 1, may be easily expressed in terms of rules involving dialogue-acts, the rest of Amani's behavior is more open-ended and underspecified. Ideally, the system designers would like for the character to obey conversational conventions (such as responding appropriately to greetings, thankings, etc.). Her responses to other user utterances should match human intuition about what a good response would be, but specific responses are not generally dictated by the goals for the training simulation. There is therefore room for some flexibility, and also for the character to reply that she does not understand. Of course, her conversational repertoire is inevitably limited by the available authoring and development effort as well as language processing challenges.

3 Data collection

The exponential number of possible utterances and dialogue paths in even a simple conversational dialogue scenario such as the Amani scenario suggests that learning acceptable dialogue behavior from surface text examples without annotation or formal modeling would require a seemingly insurmountable quantity of dialogues to serve as training data. We address this problem in a data collection framework with four main characteristics: (1) we sidestep the problem of learning natural language generation by using a fixed predefined set of utterances for the Amani character. This so-called "utterance selection" approach has been used in a number of dialogue systems (Zukerman and Marom, 2006; Sellberg and Jnsson, 2008; Kenny et al., 2007, for example) and often serves as a reasonable approximation to generation (Gandhe and Traum, 2010); (2) we collect dialogues from human participants who play the parts of Amani and the commander in a *structured role play* framework (Section 3.1); (3) we enrich the dialogues collected in the structured role play step with additional paraphrases for the utterances of the commander, in an attempt to deal with large variability of natural language input, even for a limited domain conversational dialogue scenario (Section 3.2); (4) we further augment the existing dialogue data by adding acceptable alternatives to the dialogue acts of the Amani role through the use of *external referees* (Section 3.3).

Our data collection procedure is designed to capture the necessary information for learning dialogue policies and evaluating their quality by approximating the exponentially large dialogue variability while keeping the data collection effort tractable.

3.1 Structured role play

To examine the hypothesis that dialogue policies such as Amani's can be learned from examples without explicit rules or any kind of formal modeling, we collected dialogue data through a constrained form of role play, which we call *structured role play*, where the person playing the role of Amani is encouraged, whenever possible, to only use utterances from a fixed set. Each utterance in the available set of Amani replies corresponds roughly to one of the dialogue acts (consisting of an illocutionary force and some semantic content) described by Artstein et al. (2009) for their version of the Amani character.

The players in the roles of Amani and the commander take turns producing one utterance at a time, each in a separate terminal. The commander player, who receives a natural language description of the scenario and the goal of the commander, enters utterances through a teletype (chat) interface. The Amani player, who receives a natural language description of the scenario and of Amani's dialogue policy, chooses an utterance from a list for each dialogue turn. The Amani player is encouraged to use an utterance from this list whenever possible; however, for user utterances that the Amani player judges cannot possibly be handled by any existing response, a new response can be authored (as English text) and immediately used in the role play. Each player sees the other's utterance as text in their own terminal. This closely resembles a Wizard-of-Oz setup, with they key difference being that both dialogue participants believe they are interacting with another person, which is in fact the case, and the idea of a wizard controlling a system is not part of the exercise. However, because the Amani player is encouraged to limit Amani's responses to a fixed utterance set, and the dialogue is constrained to a strict turn-taking setup that interleaves utterances from each participant, the situation also differs from conventional role play.

We collected a total of 19 dialogues and 296 utterances for Amani, for an average of 15.6 Amani utterances per dialogue.

3.2 Paraphrase generation

The dialogues collected through structured role play are intended for serving as training data from which Amani's dialogue policy can be learned. However, to cover the natural language variability with which dialogue acts from the commander can be expressed would require a much larger number of dialogues than it would be practical to collect, since a learned system that deals only with the surface text in the dialogues would need to deal both with the dialogue policy and natural language understanding for the scenario. Instead, we require only that the dialogues collected cover the desired dialogue acts for the player role in the scenario. To address the language understanding problem (indirectly), we attempt to cover the variability of expression of these dialogue acts through the collection of paraphrases for the commander utterances in the set of dialogues.

For each commander utterance in the 19 dialogues we collected, we had annotators create a set of paraphrases. In creating paraphrases, annotators were asked to take not just the original utterance into account, but also its context in the dialogue. We did not specify a fixed number of paraphrases per utterance, but instead asked for as many paraphrases as the annotator could quickly think of.

Figure 1 exemplifies the paraphrases created during this process, for a target user utterance of *can you tell me what you know of the incident?*. For this utterance, a total of 6 paraphrases were generated.

We used a total of 9 annotators, who created paraphrases for the 296 utterances in the 19 dialogues. Most annotators were responsible for no more than two dialogues, and took on average less than 30 minutes per dialogue. The average number of para-

Previous Dialogue History	
Lieutenant:	*hi amani*
Amani:	*hello.*
Lieutenant:	*how are you doing?*
Amani:	*fine thank you.*
Lieutenant:	*thank you for meeting with me*
Amani:	*you're welcome.*
Target User Utterance	
Lieutenant:	*can you tell me what you know of the incident?*
	Paraphrases:
	please tell me what information you have about the incident
	could you please tell me what you saw?
	what can you tell me about the incident?
	can you tell me about the incident?
	please, tell me what you know about the incident
	tell me what you saw, please
System Response	
Amani:	*i saw all the shooting from my window. what do you want to know about it?*
	External Referees:
	(3 referees) *i saw all the shooting from my window. what do you want to know about it?*
	(2 referees) *i remember that the gun fire was coming from the window on the second floor of assad's shop. the shop is only one story but there are apartments on top of the shop.*
	(1 referee) *what is it you want to know about the incident?*

Figure 1: An enriched dialogue turn from an Amani structured role play.

phrases collected per user utterance was 5.5.

Our 9 annotators had differing backgrounds, ranging from transcribers and summer interns to experienced NLP researchers. It should be noted that all had at least some experience working with natural language processing technologies. In future work, we would like to explore using less experienced annotators for paraphrasing.

3.3 External referee annotation

Although the paraphrase generation step helps with coverage of the language used by the commander in our scenario, the combination of the original dialogues collected through structured role play and the paraphrases do not address one crucial issue in learning of data-driven dialogue policies, and their automated evaluation: at each turn, a dialogue participant has multiple valid dialogue acts that can be performed, not a single correct one. In other words, given the same dialogue history up to a given point, multiple human dialogue participants following the same underspecified policy may choose different dialogue acts to continue the dialogue, and each of these different choices may be perfectly acceptable and coherent. This is one of main challenges in creation and evaluation of data-driven policies, since the exponentially many acceptable dialogue paths are both difficult to model explicitly, and difficult to recognize automatically when performed during testing. Of course, the degree to which this is a practical problem in a specific dialogue scenario depends on several factors, including how underspecified the targeted dialogue policy is. In our case study, the policy has a high level of underspecification, since only behaviors related to the information in Table 1 are mentioned directly, and even those are only described in natural language, without formal rigor. The rest of the policy dictates only that human players in the part of Amani act according to their commonsense in playing the role of the Amani character. However, we limit the otherwise potentially infinite possibilities for dialogue behavior by strongly encouraging the Amani player to perform only one of a set of predefined utterances corresponding to certain dialogue acts in the scenario. In our experiments, the number of utterances available for Amani was 96.

We first investigate this issue by attempting to characterize the amount of human variation in the choice of one of the 96 available dialogue acts at any given point in a dialogue. To this end, we introduce the idea of the *external referee*, who essentially provides a "second opinion" for dialogue acts performed by the original role player. The external referee annotation task works as follows: (1) Starting with an existing dialogue containing n utterances

$\langle u_1, u_2, ..., u_n \rangle$ for the participant whose utterances will be externally refereed (one of the dialogues collected through structured role play, in our case study, where we externally referee the Amani utterances), produce n dialogue histories $h_1, h_2, ..., h_n$, with each h_i consisting of every utterance from each dialogue participant from the beginning of the dialogue down to, but not including, the ith utterance in the dialogue. (2) For each dialogue history h_i, the external referee (who must not be the person who played a part in the original dialogue) chooses an utterance u'_i from the choices available for the scenario, without knowledge of the original utterance u_i in the dialogue from which the history was produced.

Figure 1 provides an example of the choices made by 6 external referees for a single target user utterance. Given the previous dialogue history and the target user utterance (*can you tell me what you know of the incident?*), each external referee independently chose a single best utterance for the character to respond with. In the example in the figure, it can be seen that 3 of the 6 external referees chose the same response as the original Amani player, asserting that Amani did indeed witness the incident and asking what the commander would like to know. The other three chose alternative responses; two of these selected a response asserting information about where the gun fire was coming from, while a third referee chose a response simply asking what the commander would like to know. It is important to note that all three of these alternative responses would be acceptable from a design and training perspective.

In this annotation task, the task is not to provide alternative dialogues, but simply one character response to each individual utterance, assuming the fixed history of the original dialogue. In other words, the annotator has no control or impact over the dialogue history at any point, and provides only additional reference utterances for possible immediate continuations for each dialogue history. It is for this reason we call the annotator an external referee.

Annotations from multiple external referees for the dialogues collected through structured role play do not result in a representation of the lattice of the many possible dialogue paths in the scenario, but rather an approximation that represents the possible options in the immediate future of a given dialogue history. The main difference is that the available histories are limited to those in the original dialogues from structured role play. While this may be a limiting factor if one attempts to model dialogue behavior based on entire dialogue histories, since the available histories represent only a very sparse sample of the space of valid histories, it is possible that good approximate models can be achieved with factorization of dialogues by sequences of a fixed number of consecutive turns, e.g. a model that makes a second-order Markov assumption, considering only the previous two turns in the dialogue as an approximation of the entire history (Gandhe and Traum, 2007). This is in a way the same approximation used in n-gram language models, but at the level of granularity of sentences, rather than words.

We collected annotations from 6 different external referees, with each individual referee annotating the entire set of 19 dialogues, and taking on average about two hours to complete the annotation of the entire set. All of our external referees were very familiar with the design of the Amani character, and most had natural language processing expertise.

4 Evaluation of dialogue policies with multiple external referees

4.1 External referee agreement

The dialogues and external referee annotations collected using the procedure described in Section 3 provide a way to characterize the targeted policy with respect to human variability in choosing utterances from a fixed set, since the annotations include the choices made by multiple external referees.

From the annotations of utterances chosen for Amani in our 19 dialogues, we see that human annotators agree only 49.2% of the time when choosing an utterance in the external referee framework. That is, given the same dialogue history, we expect that two human role players would agree on average slightly less than 50% of the time on what the next utterance should be[1].

Based on this level of pairwise agreement, one might conclude that using these data for either policy learning or policy evaluation is a lost cause. How-

[1]This represents the averaged agreement over all pairs of external referees.

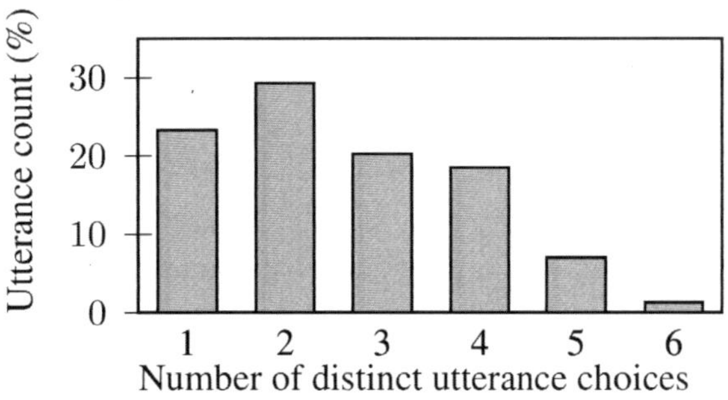

Figure 2: Distribution in number of distinct choices by external referees

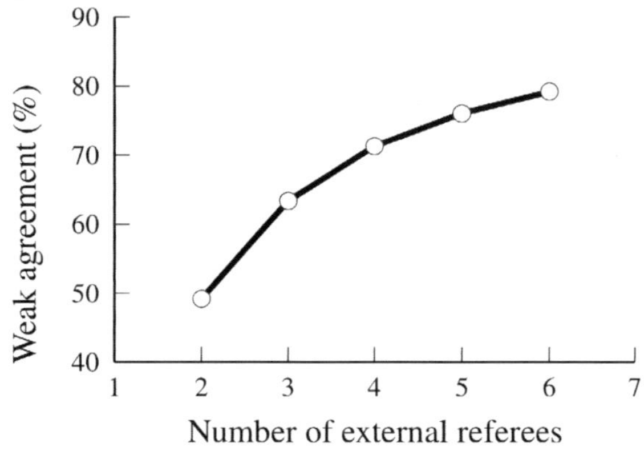

Figure 3: Weak agreement between external referees

ever, this result does not necessarily indicate that human raters disagree on what the correct choice is; it is more likely to reflect that there are in fact multiple "correct" (acceptable) choices, which we can capture through multiple annotators.

The annotations from multiple external referees in our case study support this view: Figure 2 shows the number of distinct utterance choices made by each of the six external referees for each specific utterance in the 19 dialogues collected through structured role play. Each external referee chooses only one utterance (out of 96 options) per Amani turn in the 19 dialogues. Over the 296 Amani utterances in the entire set of dialogues, all six referees agreed unanimously on their utterance choice only 23.3% of the time. The most frequent case, totaling almost 30% of all utterances, was that the set composed by the single choice from each of the six wizards for an utterance had exactly two distinct elements. For only 1.3% of the 296 utterances did that set contain the maximum number of distinct elements (six), indicating complete disagreement among the external referees. We note that, in this case, very low agreement to complete disagreement reflects a situation in dialogue where it is likely that there are many dialogue act choices considered acceptable by the collective body of external referees. In our scenario, there were at most two choices from the six referees for more than 50% of the Amani turns, indicating that in the majority of the cases there is only a small set of acceptable dialogue acts (from the 296 available), while five or more options were chosen for less than 10% of all Amani turns.

For a more direct characterization of dialogue scenarios, and also for the purposes of evaluation, we now define a metric that reflects overall agreement in a group of external referees. Instead of comparing one choice from a single referee to another single choice, we instead check for membership of a single choice c_{ij} from a single referee R_i for utterance u_j in the set of choices $\{c_{kj} | k \neq i\}$ from all of the other referees $\{R_k | k \neq i\}$. In the positive case, we say that R_i *weakly agrees* with the rest of the raters $\{R_k | k \neq i\}$ on the annotation of utterance u_j. We define the *weak agreement* agr_n for a set of N external referees over a set of m utterances to be rate at which each rater R_i weakly agrees with the $n-1$ raters $\{R_k | k \neq i\}$, for all integer values of i ranging from 1 to N, inclusive. Intuitively, weak agreement reflects two important questions: (1) how often is the choice of a referee supported by the choice of at least one more referee? and (2) given a set of $n-1$ referees, how much new information (in the form of unseen choices) should I expect to see from a new n^{th} referee? Figure 3 addresses these questions for the scenario in our case study by showing the weak agreement figures obtained for sets of increasing numbers of external referees, from 2 to 6. Each point in the graph corresponds to the average of the weak agreement values obtained for all possible ways of holding out one external referee R_i, and computing the weak agreement between R_i and the other referees, assuming an overall pool containing the given number of external referees.

We note that with the dialogue act choices of a single person, coverage of the possible acceptable options is quite poor, corresponding only to an average of 50% of the choices made by another person.

The coverage increases rapidly as two more external referees are added, and more slowly, although still steadily from there. The rightmost point in Figure 3 indicates that with a set of five external referee we should expect to cover almost 80% of the choices of a sixth referee.

4.2 Dialogue policy evaluation with multiple external referees

The weak agreement metric defined in the previous section can be used to measure the quality of automatically learned policies, and to provide insight into how a learned policy compares to human-level performance. Because it recognizes the validity of multiple responses, the weak agreement metric can help distinguish true policy errors from policy choices that are consistent with the intuitions of at least some human referees about what the character should say.

In particular, given the choices made by five external referees for our 19 Amani dialogues, we can expect their choices to cover about 80% of the choices a sixth person would make for what Amani should say at each turn in these dialogues. (I.e., we know that the weak agreement among a group of six human referees is about 80% for this Amani scenario.)

We proceed to rate the quality of an automatic policy by computing a one-vs-others version of weak agreement—intuitively treating our policy as if it were such a "sixth person", and comparing it to the other five. Instead of computing the average weak agreement for referees randomly selected from an entire group, as in the previous section, to evaluate a policy, we compute its weak agreement compared to the combined set of human external referees, as follows. For every system utterance u_j in our set of role play dialogues, a given automatic policy P is used to select a response c'_j (corresponding to a dialogue act in the domain). We then check for membership of c'_j in the set that contains only and all dialogue act choices c_{kj} for k ranging from 1 to N, inclusive, where N is the number of external referees and c_{kj} corresponds to the kth referee's choice for the jth utterance. Another way to interpret this evaluation metric is to consider it a form of accuracy that computes the number of correct choices made by the policy divided by the total number of choices made by the policy, where a choice is considered "correct" if it matches any of the external referees' choices for a specific utterance. For this reason, we refer to this evaluation-focused one-vs-all version of weak agreement as *weak accuracy*.

Based on the definition above, an automatic policy with quality indistinguishable from that of a person choosing utterances for the Amani character would have a weak accuracy of about 80% or higher when measured using a set of five external referees. We see then that this metric is far from perfect, since it cannot rank two policies with weak accuracy levels of, say, 80% and 90%. It is also possible for a policy that results in dialogue behavior noticeably inferior to that of a human referee to be rated at the same weak accuracy value for a human referee (80%). In practice, however, weak accuracy with five or six external referees has far greater power for discriminating between policies of varying quality, and ranking them correctly, than a naive version of accuracy, which corresponds to weak accuracy using a single referee. Furthermore, the addition of only a few more external referees would very likely increase the efficacy of the weak agreement metric.

Despite the shortcomings of weak accuracy as a metric for evaluation of quality of dialogue policies, it opens up a wide range of opportunities for development of learned policies. Without an automated metric, development of such techniques can be only vaguely incremental, relying on either costly or, more likely, infrequent human evaluations with results that are difficult to optimize toward with current machine learning techniques. The use of imperfect automated metrics in situations where ideal metrics are unavailable or are impractical to deploy is fairly common in natural language processing. PARSEVAL (Abney et al., 1991), commonly used for parser evaluation, and BLEU (Papineni et al., 2002), commonly used in machine translation, are two examples of well-known imperfect metrics that have been the subject of much criticism, but that are widely agreed to have been necessary for much of the progress enjoyed by their respective fields. Unlike BLEU, however, which has been shown to correlate with certain types of human judgment on the quality of machine translation systems, our notion of weak accuracy has not yet been demonstrated to correlate with human judgments on the quality of dialogue policies, and as such it is only hypothesized to have this property. We leave this important step of validation as future work.

5 Learning dialogue policies from examples without formal modeling

Equipped with a dataset with 19 dialogues in the Amani scenario (including paraphrases for the unconstrained commander utterances, and external referee annotations for the constrained Amani utterances), and an automatic evaluation framework for distinguishing quality differences in learned policies, we now describe our experiments on learning dialogue policies from data collected in structured role play sessions, and enriched with paraphrases and external referee annotations.

In each of our experiments we attempt to learn a dialogue policy as a maximum entropy classifier (Berger et al., 1996) that chooses one utterance out of the 96 possible utterances for Amani after each commander utterance, given features extracted from the dialogue history. This policy could be integrated in a dialogue system very easily, since it chooses system utterances directly given previous user and system utterances. We evaluate the dialogue policies learned in each experiment through 19-fold cross-validation of our set of 19 dialogues: in each fold, we hold out one dialogue (and all of its related information, such as external referee annotations and user utterance paraphrases) and use the remaining 18 dialogues as training data.

5.1 Learning from examples

Using only the dialogues collected in structured role play sessions, and no additional information from external referees or paraphrases, we train the maximum entropy classifier to choose a system utterance s_i based on features extracted from the two previous user utterances u_i and u_{i-1} and the previous system utterance s_{i-1}. The features extracted from these utterances are the words present in each user utterance, and the complete text of each system utterance. Low frequency words occurring fewer than 5 times in the corpus are excluded.

The weak accuracy for this simple policy is 43%, a low value that indicates that for more than half its turns the policy chooses an utterance that was not chosen by any of the referees, giving us a reasonable level of confidence that this policy is of poor quality.

5.2 Enhanced training with external referees

The next experiment expands the training set available to the maximum entropy classifier by adding training instances based on the utterances chosen by the external referees. For each of the training instances (target utterance coupled with features from u_i, s_{i-1} and u_{i-1}) we add six new training instances, each using the same features as the original training instance, but replacing the target class with the choice made by an external referee. Note that this creates identical training instances for cases when the same utterance is chosen by multiple annotators, which has the effect of weighting training examples. With the additional information, weak accuracy for this policy improves to 56%, which is a large gain that still results in a mediocre dialogue policy.

5.3 Expanding training examples with paraphrases

To help determine how much of difficulty in our policy learning task is due to the related problem of natural language understanding (NLU), and how much is due to modeling dialogue behavior regardless of NLU, we performed manual annotation of dialogue acts for the user utterances, and trained a policy as in the previous section, but using manually assigned dialogue acts instead of the words for user utterances in the dialogue history. With this gold-standard NLU, weak accuracy improves from 56% to 67%, approaching the level of human performance, and already at a level where two out of every three choices made by the learned policy matches the choice of a human referee.

To bridge the gap between learning purely from surface text (with no formal modeling) and learning from manually assigned dialogue acts specifically designed to capture important information in the scenario, we turn to the paraphrases collected for user utterances in our 19 dialogues. These paraphrases are used to create additional synthetic training material for the classifier, as follows: for each training instance produced from a chosen system utterance s_i and previous utterances u_i, s_{i-1} and u_{i-1} (see previous section), we create additional training instances keeping the target system utterance s_i and previous system utterance s_{i-1} the same, but using a paraphrase u'_i in the place of u_i, and a paraphrase u'_{i-1} in the place of u_{i-1}. Training instances are added for all possible combinations of the available paraphrases for u_i and u_{i-1}, providing some (artificial) coverage for parts of the space of possible dialogue paths that would be otherwise completely ignored during training.

Training the classifier with material from the external referees (see previous section) and additional synthetic training examples from paraphrases as described above produces a dialogue policy with weak accuracy of 66%, at the same level as the policy learned with manually assigned speech acts. It is noteworthy that this was achieved through a very simple and intuitive paraphrase annotation task that requires no technical knowledge about dialogue systems, dialogue acts or domain modeling. As mentioned in section 3.2, paraphrases for each of the 19 dialogues were generated in less than 30 minutes on average.

6 Conclusion and future work

We introduced a framework for collection and enrichment of scenario-specific dialogues based only on tasks that require no technical knowledge. Data collected in this framework support novel approaches not just for learning dialogue policies, but perhaps more importantly for evaluating learned policies, which allows us to examine different techniques using an objective automatic metric.

Although research on both learning and evaluating dialogue policies is still in early stages, this case study and proof-of-concept experiments serve to illustrate the basic ideas of external referee and paraphrase annotation, and the use of multiple reference dialogue act choices in evaluation of dialogue policies, in a way similar to how multiple reference translations are used in evaluation of machine translation systems. We do not consider this line of research a replacement for or an alternative to formal modeling of domains and dialogue behavior, but rather as an additional tool in the community's collective arsenal. There are many unexplored avenues for including data-driven techniques within rule-based frameworks and vice-versa.

In future work we intend to further validate the ideas presented in this paper by performing additional collection of dialogues in the Amani domain to serve as a virgin test set, and applying these techniques to other dialogue domains and scenarios. We also plan to refine the weak accuracy and weak agreement metrics to take into account the level of agreement within utterances to reflect that some parts of dialogues may be more open-ended than others. Finally, we will conduct human evaluations of different policies to begin validating weak accuracy as an automatic metric for evaluation of dialogue policies.

Acknowledgments

The project or effort described here has been sponsored by the U.S. Army Research, Development, and Engineering Command (RDECOM). Statements and opinions expressed do not necessarily reflect the position or the policy of the United States Government, and no official endorsement should be inferred. We would also like to thank Ron Artstein, Sudeep Gandhe, Fabrizio Morbini, Angela Nazarian, Susan Robinson, Michael Rushforth, and David Traum.

References

S. Abney, S. Flickenger, C. Gdaniec, C. Grishman, P. Harrison, D. Hindle, R. Ingria, F. Jelinek, J. Klavans, M. Liberman, M. Marcus, S. Roukos, B. Santorini, and T. Strzalkowski. 1991. Procedure for quantitatively comparing the syntactic coverage of english grammars. In E. Black, editor, *Proceedings of the workshop on Speech and Natural Language*, HLT '91, pages 306–311, Stroudsburg, PA, USA. Association for Computational Linguistics.

Ron Artstein, Sudeep Gandhe, Michael Rushforth, and David R. Traum. 2009. Viability of a simple dialogue act scheme for a tactical questioning dialogue system. In *DiaHolmia 2009: Proceedings of the 13th Workshop on the Semantics and Pragmatics of Dialogue*, page 43–50, Stockholm, Sweden, June.

Adam L. Berger, Stephen D. Della Pietra, and Vincent J. D. Della Pietra. 1996. A maximum entropy approach to natural language processing. *Computational Linguistics*, 22(1):39–71.

Sudeep Gandhe and David R. Traum. 2007. Creating spoken dialogue characters from corpora without annotations. In *Proceedings of Interspeech-07*, 08/2007.

Sudeep Gandhe and David R. Traum. 2010. I've said it before, and i'll say it again: An empirical investigation of the upper bound of the selection approach to dialogue. In *11th annual SIGdial Meeting on Discourse and Dialogue*.

Sudeep Gandhe, Nicolle Whitman, David R. Traum, and Ron Artstein. 2009. An integrated authoring tool for tactical questioning dialogue systems. In *6th Workshop on Knowledge and Reasoning in Practical Dialogue Systems*, Pasadena, California, July.

Sina Jafarpour, Chris Burges, and Alan Ritter. 2009. Filter, rank, and transfer the knowledge: Learning to chat. In *Proceedings of the NIPS Workshop on Advances in Ranking*.

Patrick Kenny, Thomas D. Parsons, Jonathan Gratch, Anton Leuski, and Albert A. Rizzo. 2007. Virtual patients for clinical therapist skills training. In *Proceedings of the 7th international conference on Intelligent Virtual Agents*, IVA '07, pages 197–210, Berlin, Heidelberg. Springer-Verlag.

Kishore Papineni, Salim Roukos, Todd Ward, and Wei-Jing Zhu. 2002. Bleu: a method for automatic evaluation of machine translation. In *Proceedings of the 40th Annual Meeting on Association for Computational Linguistics*, ACL '02, pages 311–318, Stroudsburg, PA, USA. Association for Computational Linguistics.

Alan Ritter, Colin Cherry, and Bill Dolan. 2010. Unsupervised modeling of twitter conversations. In *Proceedings of HLT-NAACL.*

Linus Sellberg and Arne Jnsson. 2008. Using random indexing to improve singular value decomposition for latent semantic analysis. In *Proceedings of the Sixth International Language Resources and Evaluation (LREC'08)*, Marrakech, Morocco, may.

David R. Traum, Anton Leuski, Antonio Roque, Sudeep Gandhe, David DeVault, Jillian Gerten, Susan Robinson, and Bilyana Martinovski. 2008. Natural language dialogue architectures for tactical questioning characters. In *Army Science Conference*, Florida, 12/2008.

Ingrid Zukerman and Yuval Marom. 2006. A corpus-based approach to help-desk response generation. *Computational Intelligence for Modelling, Control and Automation, International Conference on*, 1:23.

The Impact of Task-Oriented Feature Sets on HMMs for Dialogue Modeling

Kristy Elizabeth Boyer **Eun Young Ha** **Robert Phillips*** **James Lester**

Department of Computer Science
North Carolina State University
*Dual affiliation with Applied Research Associates, Inc.
Raleigh, North Carolina, USA
{keboyer, eha, rphilli, lester}@ncsu.edu

Abstract

Human dialogue serves as a valuable model for learning the behavior of dialogue systems. Hidden Markov models' sequential structure is well suited to modeling human dialogue, and their theoretical underpinnings are consistent with the conception of dialogue as a stochastic process with a layer of implicit, highly influential structure. HMMs have been shown to be effective for a variety of descriptive and predictive dialogue tasks. For task-oriented dialogue, understanding the learning behavior of HMMs is an important step toward building unsupervised models of human dialogue. This paper examines the behavior of HMMs under six experimental conditions including different task-oriented feature sets and preprocessing approaches. The findings highlight the importance of providing HMM learning algorithms with rich task-based information. Additionally, the results suggest how specific metrics should be used depending on whether the models will be employed primarily in a descriptive or predictive manner.

1 Introduction

Human dialogue serves as a valuable model for learning the behavior of dialogue systems. For this reason, corpus-based approaches to dialogue management tasks have been an increasingly active area of research (Bangalore, Di Fabbrizio, & Stent, 2006; Di Eugenio, Xie, & Serafin, 2010; Georgila, Lemon, Henderson, & Moore, 2009; Rotaru & Litman, 2009). Modeling the dialogue policies that humans employ permits us to directly extract conversational and task-based expertise. These techniques hold great promise for scaling gracefully to large corpora, and for transferring well across domains.

The richness and flexibility of human dialogue introduce nondeterministic and complex patterns that present challenges for machine learning approaches. One approach that has been successfully employed in dialogue modeling is the hidden Markov model (HMM) (Rabiner, 1989). These models are well suited to the sequential nature of dialogue (Stolcke et al., 2000). Moreover, their theoretical underpinnings are consistent with the conception of dialogue as a stochastic process whose observations are influenced by a layer of implicit, yet highly relevant, structure (Boyer et al., 2009; Woszczyna & Waibel, 1994).

HMMs have been shown to perform well on important dialogue management tasks such as automatic dialogue act classification (Stolcke et al., 2000). Our work has employed HMMs for a different goal: learning dialogue policies, or strategies, from corpora (Boyer, Phillips, et al., 2010; Boyer, Phillips, Ingram, et al., in press). This work can be viewed from two perspectives. First, a *descriptive* goal of the work is to learn models that describe the nature of human dialogues in succinct probabilistic terms, in a way that facilitates important qualitative investigations. The second and complementary goal is *predictive*: learning models that accurately predict the dialogue moves of humans, in order to capture a dialogue policy that can be used within a system.

Proceedings of the SIGDIAL 2011: the 12th Annual Meeting of the Special Interest Group on Discourse and Dialogue, pages 49–58,
Portland, Oregon, June 17-18, 2011.

Both of these goals are of paramount importance in *tutorial dialogue*, in which tutors and students engage in dialogue in support of a learning task (Boyer, Ha, et al., 2010; VanLehn et al., 2007). Descriptive modeling represents a critical step toward more fully understanding the phenomena that contribute to the high effectiveness of human tutoring, which has to date been unmatched by tutorial dialogue systems. Predictive models, on the other hand, may be used directly as dialogue policies within systems.

The HMMs considered here were learned from an annotated corpus of textual human-human tutorial dialogue. In this domain, HMMs have been shown to correspond qualitatively to widely held conceptions of tutorial dialogue strategies, and adjacency pair analysis before model learning has been shown to enhance this qualitative correspondence (Boyer et al., 2009). Moreover, HMMs can identify in an unsupervised fashion structural components that correlate with student knowledge gain (Boyer, Phillips, Ingram, et al., in press).

However, to date, several important questions have not been explored. The answers to these questions have implications for learning HMMs for task-oriented dialogues. The questions include the following: 1) How reliably does the HMM learning framework converge to the hyperparameter N, the best-fit number of hidden states? 2) What are the effects of preprocessing approaches, specifically, adjacency pair analysis, on the resulting HMMs? 3) How do different feature sets for task-oriented dialogue impact the descriptive fit and predictive power of learned HMMs? This paper addresses these questions. The findings suggest that model stability and predictive power benefit from the richest possible input sequences, which include not only dialogue acts but also information about the task state and the absence of particular tutor dialogue moves. Additionally, we find that traditional measures of HMM goodness-of-fit may not identify the most highly predictive models under some conditions.

2 Background

HMMs have been used for dialogue modeling tasks for many years. Early work utilized HMMs to model underlying linguistic structure for the purposes of identifying speech acts and reducing perplexity for speech recognition (Stolcke et al., 2000; Woszczyna & Waibel, 1994). These projects treated underlying dialogue structure as the hidden layer, and dialogue utterances as observations. This treatment is analogous to the work presented in this paper, except that our observations are dialogue act tags only, rather than being constituent words in each utterance. Our goals are also different: to create a qualitatively interpretable model of dialogue structure that corresponds to widely accepted notions of task-oriented dialogue, and to learn a highly predictive dialogue policy from a human-human dialogue corpus.

HMMs rely on treating dialogue as a sequential Markov process in which each observation depends only on a finite set of preceding observations. Some other approaches that rely on this assumption treat dialogue as a Markov decision process or partially observable Markov decision process, in which state changes are associated with actions and rewards (e.g., Young et al., 2010). Such work focuses on learning an optimal policy, typically utilizing a combination of human and simulated dialogue corpora. Reinforcement learning techniques can then be applied to learn the optimal policy based on the observed rewards. In contrast, we start with a rich corpus of human-human dialogue, which may have poor coverage in some areas (though the dialogue act tags were empirically derived and therefore mitigate this problem to some extent), and subsequently learn a model that explains the variance in that human corpus as well as possible.

Capturing the dialogue policy implicit within a corpus of human-human dialogue has been explored in other work in a catalogue-ordering domain (Bangalore, Di Fabbrizio, & Stent, 2006). That work utilized maximum entropy modeling to predict human agents' dialogue moves within a vector-based framework. Although a vector-based approach differs in many regards from the sequential HMM approach described here, both approaches assume a dependence only on a finite history. HMMs accomplish this through graphical dependencies, while vector-based approaches accomplish it by including features for a restricted window of left-hand context. The results of this catalogue-ordering project highlight how challenging it is to predict human agents' dialogue moves in a task-oriented domain.

3 Corpus

The corpus was collected during a human-human tutoring study. Students solved an introductory computer programming problem in the Java programming language. Tutors were located in a separate room and communicated with students through textual dialogue while viewing a synchronized view of the student's problem-solving workspace. Forty-eight students interacted for approximately one hour each with a tutor. Students exhibited statistically significant learning gains from pretest to posttest, indicating that the tutoring was effective (Boyer, Phillips, Ingram, et al., in press). The corpus contains 1,468 student moves and 3,338 tutor moves. Overlapping utterances, which are common in dialogue platforms such as instant messaging, were prevented by permitting only one user to construct a dialogue message at a time. Because the corpus is textual, utterances were segmented at textual message boundaries except when the lead dialogue annotator noted the presence of two separate dialogue acts within non-overlapping chunks of text. In these events the utterance was segmented by the primary annotator prior to being tagged by the second dialogue act annotator.

In addition to dialogue act annotation, the corpus was manually annotated for task structure and correctness (Section 3.2), and for delayed tutor feedback (Seciton 3.3). The appendix displays an excerpt from the annotated corpus.

3.1 Dialogue Act Annotation

As part of prior work, the corpus was annotated with dialogue acts for both tutor (Boyer, Phillips, Ingram, et al., in press) and student (Boyer, Ha, et al., 2010) utterances (Table 1). One annotator tagged the entire corpus, while a second annotator independently tagged a randomly selected 10% of tutoring sessions. The inter-annotator agreement Kappa score was 0.80.

3.2 Task Annotation

The corpus includes 97,509 keystroke-level task events (computer programming actions), all taken by the student. Tutors viewed synchronously, but could not edit, the computer program. The task actions were manually clustered and labeled for subtask structure (Boyer, Phillips, et al., 2010). The task structure annotation was hierarchical, with leaves corresponding to specific subtasks such as creating a temporary variable in order to swap two variables' values (subtask *3-c-iii-2*). Each problem-solving cluster, or subtask, was then labeled for correctness (Table 2). These correctness labels are utilized in the models presented in this paper. The Kappa agreement statistic for the correctness annotation on 20% of the corpus was 0.80.

Table 1. Dialogue act tags

Dialogue Act	Tutor Example
ASSESSING Q.	*Which type should that be?*
EXTRA-DOMAIN	*A coordinator will be there soon.*
GROUNDING	*Ok.*
LUKEWARM FDBK	*That's close.*
LUKEWARM CONTENT FDBK	*Almost there, but the second parameter isn't quite right.*
NEGATIVE FDBK	*That's not right.*
NEGATIVE CONTENT FDBK	*No, the counter has to be an int.*
POSITIVE FDBK	*Perfect.*
POSITIVE CONTENT FDBK	*Right, the array is a local variable.*
QUESTION	*Which approach do you prefer?*
RESPONSE	*It will be an int.*
STATEMENT	*They start at 0.*

Table 2. Task correctness tags

Correctness Tag	Description
CORRECT	*Fully conforming to the requirements of the task.*
BUGGY	*Violating the requirements of the task. These task events typically require tutorial remediation.*
INCOMPLETE	*Not violating, but not yet fulfilling, the requirements of the task.*
DISPREFERRED	*Technically fulfilling requirements but not utilizing the target concepts being tutored. These events typically require tutorial remediation.*

3.3 Annotation for Delayed Tutor Feedback

The dialogue act and task annotations reflect positive evidence regarding what *did* occur in the dialogues. An additional annotation was introduced for what *did not* occur—specifically, instances in which tutors did not to make a dialogue move in response to students' relevant task actions. The task in our corpus is computer programming, so bugs in the task correspond to errors either in syntax or semantics of the computer program compared to the desired outcome. The human tutors were working with only one student at a time and were carefully monitoring student task actions during the dialogue, so we take the absence of a dialogue move at a relevant point to be an intentional choice by the tutor to delay feedback as part of the tutorial strategy. The automatic annotation for delayed feedback introduced two new event tags: NO-MENTION of correctly completed subtasks, and NO-REMEDIATION of existing bugs within the task.

The intuition behind these tags is that within a learned dialogue policy, specifically modeling when *not* to intervene is crucial. Typically human tutors mention correctly completed subtasks, but at times other tutorial goals eclipse the importance of doing so. The NO-MENTION tag captures these instances. On the other hand, typically when working with novices, human tutors remediate an existing bug quickly. However, tutors may choose to delay this remediation for a variety of reasons such as remediating a different bug instead or asking a conceptual question to encourage the student to reflect on the issue. The NO-REMEDIATION tag captures these instances of the absence of remediation given that a bug was present. These two annotations for delayed feedback were performed automatically (Boyer, Phillips, Ha, et al., in press).

3.4 Adjacency Pair Modeling

Prior work has demonstrated that adjacency pairs can be identified in an unsupervised fashion from a corpus (Midgley, Harrison, & MacNish, 2006). This technique relies on statistical analysis to determine the significant dependencies that exist between pairs of dialogue acts, or in our task-oriented corpus, pairs of dialogue acts or task actions. After the pairs of dependent events are identified, they are joined within the corpus algorithmically (Boyer et al., 2009). Joining a pair of dependent moves in this way is equivalent to introducing a deterministic (probability=1) succession between observation symbols. This type of dependency cannot be learned in the traditional first-order HMM framework, but is desirable when two observations are strongly linked.[1]

[1] Enhanced HMM structures, such as autoregressive HMMs, which allow for direct graphical links between observation symbols, can learn such a dependency but only in stochastic terms.

The experiment that is described in Section 4 utilizes different feature sets to learn and compare HMMs. Table 3 shows these feature sets and their most highly statistically significant adjacency pairs.

Table 3. Experimental conditions and top three adjacency pairs (subscripts denote speaker, <u>S</u>tudent or <u>T</u>utor)

Condition	Description	Significant Adjacency Pairs
DAONLY	*Dialogue acts only*	Q_S~Rsp_T $Ground_S$~$Ground_T$ $AssessQ_T$~$PosFdbk_S$
DATASK	*Dialogue acts & task correctness events*	*Q_S~Rsp_T* $CorrectTask_S$~$CorrectTask_S$ $Ground_S$~$Ground_T$
DATASK-DELAY	*Dialogue acts, task correctness, & delayed feedback*	*Q_S~Rsp_T* $NoRemediate_T$~$BuggyTask_S$ $CorrectTask_S$~$CorrectTask_S$

4 Models

HMMs were selected as the modeling framework for this work because their sequential nature is well suited to the structure of human dialogue, and their "hidden" variable corresponds to widely held conceptions of dialogue as having an unobservable, but influential, layer of stochastic structure. For example, in tutoring, an "explanation" mode is common, in which the tutor presents new information and the student provides acknowledgments or takes task actions accordingly. Although the presence of the "explanation" goal is not directly observable in most dialogues, it may be inferred from the observations. These sequences correspond to the input observations for learning an HMM.

4.1 Hidden Markov Models

HMMs explicitly model hidden states within a doubly stochastic structure (Rabiner, 1989). A first-order HMM, in which each hidden state depends only on the immediately preceding hidden state, is defined by the following components:

- $\Sigma = \{\sigma_1, \sigma_2, ..., \sigma_M\}$, the observation symbol alphabet
- $S = \{s_1, s_2, ..., s_N\}$, the set of hidden states

- $\Pi=[\pi_i]$, $i=1,...,N$, the initial probability distribution, where π_i is the probability of the model beginning in hidden state s_i in S
- $A=[a_{ij}]$, a transition probability distribution, where a_{ij} is the probability of the model transitioning from hidden state i to hidden state j for $i,j=1,...,N$
- $B=[b_{ik}]$, an emission probability distribution where b_{ik} is the probability of state i $(i=1,...,N)$ emitting (or generating) observation symbol k $(k=1,...,M)$.

4.2 Dialogue Modeling with HMMs

In this work, the observation symbol alphabet $\sum$ is given. For each experimental condition, $\sum$ is either 1) all dialogue act tags, 2) all dialogue acts plus task correctness tags, or 3) dialogue act, task correctness, and delayed feedback tags. The transition probability distribution A, emission probability distribution B, and initial probability distribution Π are learned by the standard Baum-Welch algorithm for optimizing HMM parameters (Rabiner, 1989). This algorithm is susceptible to becoming trapped in local optima, so our approach uses ten-time random restart with new initial parameters for each model to reduce the probability of selecting a model that represents only a local optimum.

The hyperparameter N, which is the best number of hidden states, is also learned rather than fixed. This process involves running the full HMM training algorithm, including random restarts in ten-fold cross-validation, across the data and selecting the N that corresponds to the best mean goodness-of-fit measure. For HMMs, a typical goodness-of-fit measure is log-likelihood, which captures how likely the observations would be under the current model. The log is taken for practical reasons, to avoid numerical underflow. Higher log-likelihood corresponds to improved model fit. However, typically it is desirable to penalize a higher number of hidden states, since increasing the model complexity results in tradeoffs that may not be fully warranted by the improvement in model fit. In this work, we utilize the Akaike Information Criterion (AIC), a standard penalized log-likelihood metric (Akaike, 1976).

$$AIC = 2*N - 2*ln(likelihood)$$

Lower values of AIC indicate better model fit.

4.3 Experimental Conditions

HMMs were learned using three separate feature sets, each providing a progressively more complete picture of the task-oriented dialogues: dialogue acts only (DAONLY), dialogue acts and task events (DATASK), and dialogue acts with both task correctness events and tags for delayed tutor feedback (DATASKDELAY).

In addition to the three different feature sets, each condition included one of two types of preprocessing. Each type of model was trained on unaltered sequences of the annotated tags, which we refer to as the UNIGRAM condition. Additionally, each type of model was trained on sequences with statistically dependent adjacency pairs joined in a preprocessing step as described in Section 3.4. The UNIGRAM and ADJPAIR conditions were explored for each of the three feature sets, resulting in six experimental conditions. These conditions were chosen in order to explore the convergence behavior of HMMs under the different feature sets and preprocessing, and to compare measures of descriptive fit with measures of predictive power.

4.4 Learned HMMs

Figures 1 and 2 show a subset of the DAONLY UNIGRAM model and the DATASKDELAY ADJPAIR model. These figures depict the structure of our HMMs: each hidden state is associated with an emission probability distribution over the possible observation symbols.

5 Goodness-of-Fit Curves

The learning algorithm described in Section 4.2 was applied to input sequences under the six experimental conditions to learn the best-fit HMM parameters. Figure 3 displays these AIC results, which are discussed in detail in the remainder of this section.

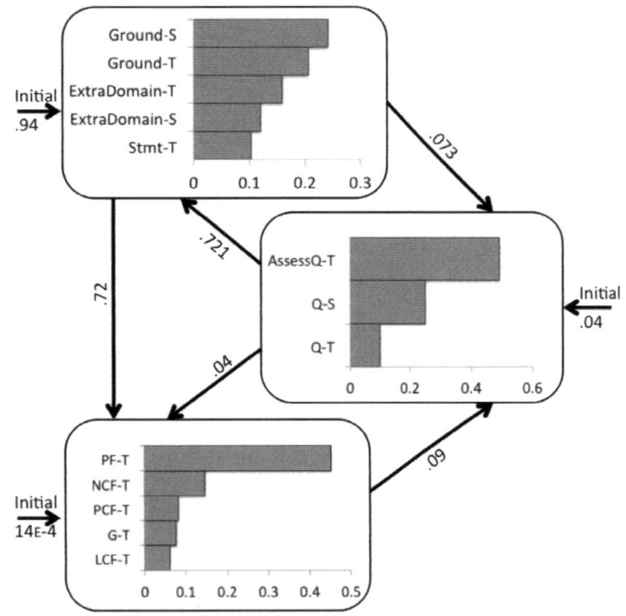

Figure 1. Subset of learned HMM (N=13) for DAONLY UNIGRAM condition

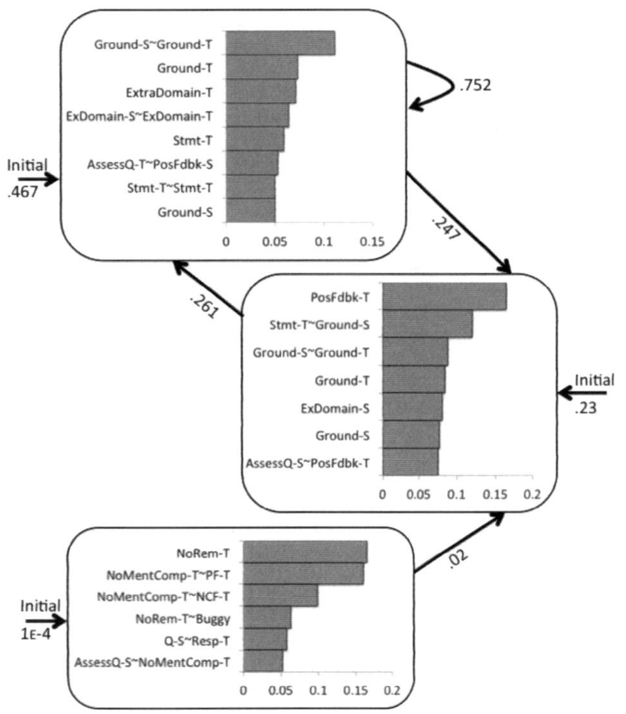

Figure 2. Subset of learned HMM (N=9) for DATASKDELAY ADJPAIR condition

5.1 Impact of Experimental Conditions

For the DAONLY condition, both the UNIGRAM and ADJPAIR models generally improve until N=12 or 13, after which the fit generally worsens. A different pattern emerges for the DATASK condition, in which the UNIGRAM sequences are optimally fit to a model with 16 states, while the ADJPAIR sequences are fit to a model with 8 states. Finally, for the DATASKDELAY condition, the UNIGRAM sequences are best fit by a model with 10 hidden states, while the ADJPAIR sequences are fit best by 9. Typically, we see that ADJPAIR sequences are fit to slightly simpler models in terms of the hyperparameter N, number of hidden states.

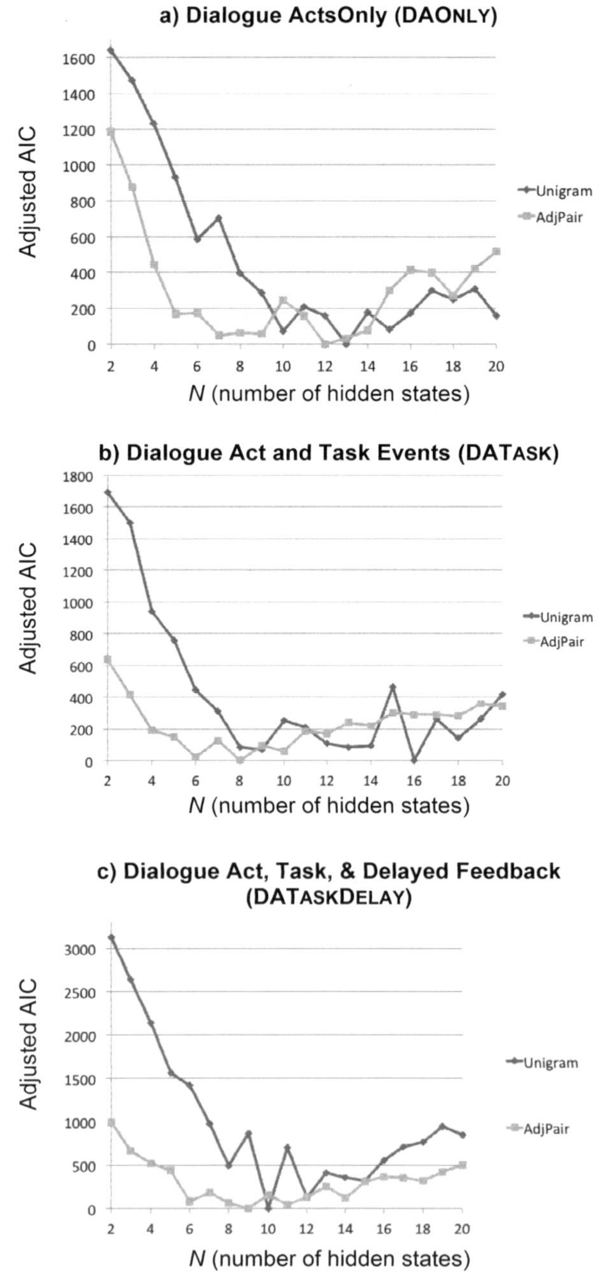

Figure 3. Number of hidden states and corresponding adjusted AIC, shifted to a minimum score of zero indicating the best-fit N

Stability in the hyperparameter N is an important consideration because an underlying assumption of our work is that the hidden states correspond to unobserved stochastic structures of the *real world process*—that is, we hypothesize that a "true" value for N exists. We would like models to exhibit decreasing variation in goodness of fit measures around this true N. To examine this stability we consider the three best AIC values for each condition and their corresponding Ns: the set $\{N_{k\text{-}best} \mid k=1,2,3\}$. The range of this set indicates how "far apart" the best three Ns are: for example, in the DAONLY UNIGRAM condition, the top three models have Ns of $\{13,10,15\}$, yielding a range of 5. Intuitively, a small value for this metric indicates that the model has converged tightly on N.

Figure 4 shows the stability results for the six different experimental conditions. As shown in the figure, for the DATASK and DATASKDELAY conditions, the ADJPAIR models achieve the smallest range among the top three values of N; these models converge most tightly to the "best" value.

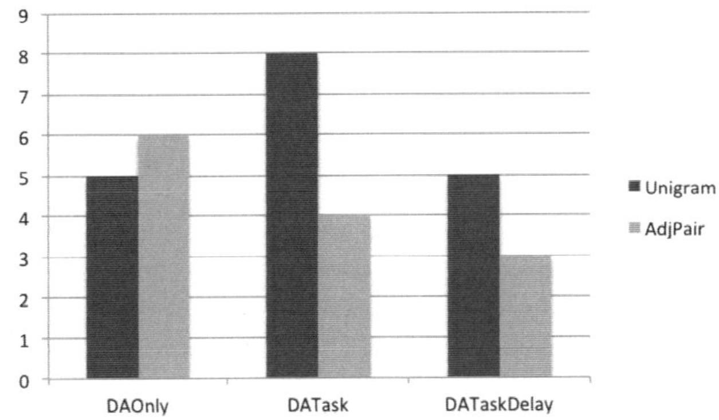

Figure 4. Stability of N (range of $\{N_{1best}, N_{2best}, N_{3best}\}$) – smaller implies tighter convergence to "best" N

6 Predictive Analysis

Section 5 presented an analysis of the goodness-of-fit curves of HMMs learned from the corpus. The measures of stability and discrimination for N capture important aspects of the behavior of HMMs toward this parameter, which is conceived of as representing "true" real-world stochastic behavior. In this way, Section 5 has presented a descriptive view of HMM dialogue models.

This section presents a predictive view of the models. Specifically, we consider *prediction accuracy*, defined as the percent of tutor dialogue moves that the model is able to correctly predict given the dialogue history sequence up to that point.

6.1 Impact of Dependent Adjacency Pairs

We first explore whether the preprocessing step of joining dependent adjacency pairs impacted prediction accuracy. The prediction accuracy of the best-fit model in each condition is displayed in Figure 5. This figure includes prediction accuracy on training data, which were used to learn model parameters, as well as prediction accuracy on testing data, which were withheld from model training.

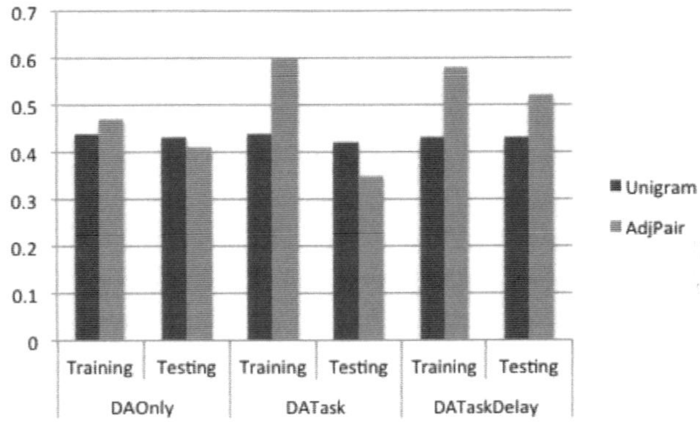

Figure 5. Prediction accuracy for tutor moves

As shown in Figure 5, joining the adjacency pairs improved model performance on the training sets of all three conditions, indicating that the variation within the training data was better explained by ADJPAIR models. (This measure of predictive power is different from a goodness-of-fit criterion as described in the previous section, a relationship that will be discussed further in Section 7.) In contrast to the training set performance, the ADJPAIR models performed better than UNIGRAM models for the testing set only in the DATASKDELAY condition.

6.2 Impact of Task-Oriented Feature Sets

As illustrated in Figure 5, the three feature sets perform similarly under the UNIGRAM condition. This performance is slightly above baseline (DAONLY and DATASK baselines = 0.38; DATASKDELAY baseline = 0.30), and diminishes little between the training and testing sets. In contrast, under the ADJPAIR condition, performance between conditions and across training and testing sets varies. The DATask model performs far better on predicting observations in the training than the testing set, suggesting possible overfitting to the training set. This relationship is discussed further in Section 7. The DATASKDELAY model performs well during both training and testing, though with a slight decrease in accuracy on the testing set.

6.3 Relationship Between Predictive and Descriptive Metrics

Measures of fit such as log-likelihood and AIC capture the likelihood of observing the data given a model. Predictive accuracy, on the other hand, measures the probability that the model can predict the next observation given a partial sequence. In general, we would expect these measures to correlate well; however, there is not perfect correlation between these metrics because the mechanism by which log-likelihood (and thereby AIC) is derived involves maximizing likelihood over complete sequences, while prediction is performed over partial sequences.

To examine how well AIC and prediction accuracy correlate, Figure 6 displays these values for a subset of the models in the DAONLY UNIGRAM condition and the DATASKDELAY ADJPAIR condition. These two conditions represent the extremes of the experimental conditions, with DAONLY containing the least information about the task-oriented dialogue while DATASKDELAY contains the most information.

As shown in Figure 6, the correlation for DAONLY UNIGRAM roughly conforms to what would be expected: lower AIC, indicating better model fit, is associated with the highest prediction accuracies. The relationship is less clear for the DATASKDELAY ADJPAIR condition. While its worst AIC is associated with the lowest prediction accuracy as expected, the best AIC is not associated with the highest prediction accuracy. This phenomenon may be due to the lack of spread among AIC values overall for this condition; as seen in Figure 3, the DATASKDELAY ADJPAIR condition has the flattest AIC curve of all conditions, indicating that for this condition the difference between best-fit and worst-fit models is smaller than for any other condition. The inconsistent relationship between AIC and prediction accuracy, therefore, may be the product of noise surrounding a large set of "good" models, whereas for the DAONLY UNIGRAM condition, the set of good models is smaller.

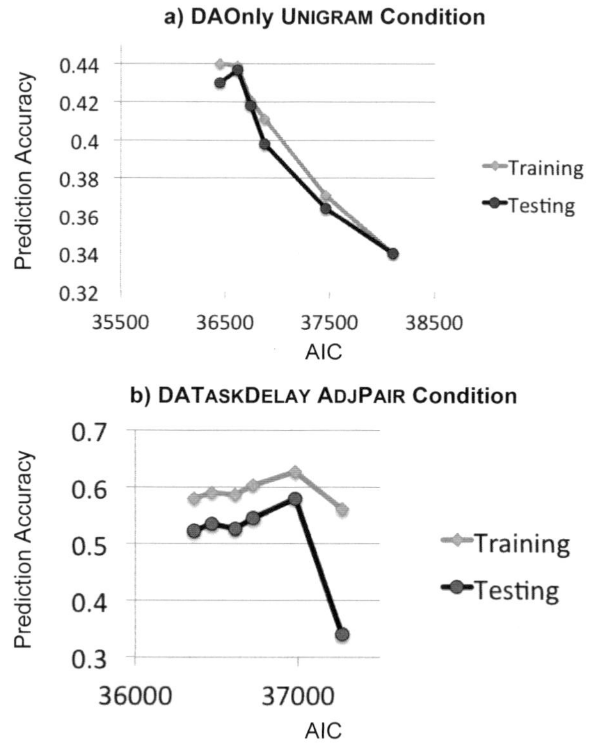

Figure 6. Prediction accuracy vs. AIC

7 Discussion

The results suggest several important findings regarding feature sets and preprocessing for learning HMMs of task-oriented dialogue. First, the models' convergence patterns to a best-fit N, number of hidden states, indicate that more information embedded within the sequences may correspond with a flatter goodness-of-fit curve. Adding more information to the input sequences may introduce some regularities that partly mitigate the limitations of even a poorly fit HMM. This additional information may come in the form of adjacency pairs discovered in an unsupervised fashion, which improved the stability of convergence on the best-fit N under the DATASK and DATASKDELAY conditions. This increased stability is likely due to the fact that under these conditions, leveraging adjacency pair information augments the HMM's structure with contextual dependencies that could otherwise not be learned under the traditional HMM framework.

For predictive accuracy, the benefits of richer input sequences are also highlighted. The most highly predictive models included all three sources of information: dialogue acts, task events, and delayed feedback tags. However, with the addition of this rich information to the input sequences and the accompanying flatter goodness-of-fit curve as discussed above, we noted an irregular pattern of correlation between goodness-of-fit and predictive accuracy that is worthy of future exploration. Specifically, it appears that the most highly predictive DATASKDELAY ADJPAIR model, which is the most highly predictive of all models in all conditions, does *not* correspond to the best (lowest) AIC for that condition (Figure 3). This finding suggests that when a predictive task is the primary goal, a predictive metric should be used to select the best-fit model. Additional support for such an approach is provided by the close correspondence between training and testing set prediction accuracy.

8 Conclusion

Understanding how HMMs behave under different feature sets is an important step toward learning effective models of task-oriented dialogue. This paper has examined how HMMs converge to a best number of hidden states under different experimental conditions. We have also considered how well HMMs under these conditions predict tutor dialogue acts within a corpus of task-oriented tutoring, a crucial step toward learning dialogue policies from human corpora. The findings highlight the importance of adding rich task-based features to the input sequences in order to learn HMMs that converge tightly on the best-fit number of hidden states. The results also indicate that caution should be used when utilizing traditional goodness-of-fit metrics, which are appropriate for descriptive applications, if the goal is to learn a highly predictive model.

This line of research is part of a larger research program of learning unsupervised models of human task-oriented dialogue that can be used to define the behavior of dialogue systems. Developing a framework for learning a dialogue policy from human corpora, as discussed here, is a critical step toward that goal. Future work should focus on unsupervised dialogue act classification, and address the challenges of user plan recognition.

Acknowledgments. This work is supported in part by National Science Foundation through Grants REC-0632450, IIS-0812291, DRL-1007962 and the STARS Alliance Grant CNS-0739216. Any opinions, findings, conclusions, or recommendations expressed in this report are those of the participants, and do not necessarily represent the official views, opinions, or policy of the National Science Foundation.

References

Akaike, H. (1976). An information criterion (AIC). *Math. Sci., 14*(153), 5-9.

Bangalore, S., Di Fabbrizio, G., & Stents, A. (2006). Learning the structure of task-driven human-human dialogs. *Proceedings of ACL '06*, 201-208.

Boyer, K. E., Ha, E. Y., Phillips, R., Wallis, M. D., Vouk, M. A., & Lester, J. C. (2010). Dialogue Act Modeling in a Complex Task-Oriented Domain. *Proceedings of SIGDIAL* (pp. 297-305).

Boyer, K. E., Phillips, R., Ha, E. Y., Wallis, M. D., Vouk, M. A., & Lester, J. C. (in press). Learning a Tutorial Dialogue Policy for Delayed Feedback. *Proceedings of the 24th International FLAIRS Conference.*

Boyer, K. E., Phillips, R., Ha, E. Y., Wallis, M. D., Vouk, M. A., & Lester, J. C. (2009). Modeling dialogue structure with adjacency pair analysis and hidden Markov models. *Proceedings of NAACL HLT, Companion Volume*, 49-52.

Boyer, K. E., Phillips, R., Ha, E. Y., Wallis, M. D., Vouk, M. A., & Lester, J. C. (2010). Leveraging Hidden Dialogue State to Select Tutorial Moves. *Proceedings of the NAACL HLT 2010 Fifth Workshop on Innovative Use of NLP for Building Educational Applications* (pp. 66-73).

Boyer, K. E., Phillips, R., Ingram, A., Young, E., Wallis, M., Vouk, M., et al. (in press). Investigating the Relationship Between Dialogue Structure and Tutoring Effectiveness: A Hidden Markov Modeling Approach. *International Journal of Artificial Intelligence in Education.*

Di Eugenio, B., Xie, Z., & Serafin, R. (2010). Dialogue Act Classification, Higher Order Dialogue Structure, and Instance-Based Learning. *Dialogue & Discourse, 1*(2), 1-24.

Georgila, K., Lemon, O., Henderson, J., & Moore, J. D. (2009). Automatic annotation of context and speech acts for dialogue corpora. *Natural Language Engineering, 15*(3), 315-353.

Midgley, T. D., Harrison, S., & MacNish, C. (2006). Empirical verification of adjacency pairs using dialogue segmentation. *Proceedings of SIGDIAL*, 104-108.

Rabiner, L. R. (1989). A tutorial on hidden Markov models and selected applications in speech recognition. *Proceedings of the IEEE, 77*(2), 257-286.

Rotaru, M., & Litman, D. J. (2009). Discourse Structure and Performance Analysis : Beyond the Correlation. *Proceedings of SIGDIAL* (pp. 178-187).

Stolcke, A., Ries, K., Coccaro, N., Shriberg, E., Bates, R., Jurafsky, D., et al. (2000). Dialogue Act Modeling for Automatic Tagging and Recognition of Conversational Speech. *Computational Linguistics*, *26*(3), 339-373.

VanLehn, K., Graesser, A. C., Jackson, G. T., Jordan, P., Olney, A., & Rose, C. P. (2007). When Are Tutorial Dialogues More Effective Than Reading? *Cognitive Science: A Multidisciplinary Journal*, *30*(1), 3-62.

Woszczyna, M., & Waibel, A. (1994). Inferring linguistic structure in spoken language. *Proceedings of the International Conference on Spoken Language Processing* (pp. 847-850).

Young, S., Gašić, M., Keizer, S., Mairesse, F., Schatzmann, J., Thomson, B., et al. (2010). The Hidden Information State model: A practical framework for POMDP-based spoken dialogue management. *Computer Speech & Language*, *24*(2), 150-174.

Appendix. Excerpt from task-oriented textual human-human tutoring corpus.

Speaker	Utterance or Event	Tag
Student:	*[Task action on subtask 3-c-i-4]*	BUGGY
Student:	*[Task action on subtask 3-c-ii-5]*	CORRECT
Tutor:	*[Does not provide remediation for existing bug]*	NOREMEDIATION
Student:	*[Task action on subtask 3-c-iii-1]*	BUGGY
Student:	i don't remember off the top of my head how the swap function worked. most of the time i just copied and pasted it from some of my older code	NEGATIVECONTENTFDBK
Tutor:	The easiest way to swap x and y is to make a temporary variable	
Student:	Ok	ACK
Student:	do i need to pass the entire array and the indecies of the items to swap?	ASSESSQ
Tutor:	if you want to use a seperate method to swap, then yes, you'll have to pass those things	POSCONTENTFDBK
Tutor:	*[Does not mention a correctly completed subtask]*	NOMENTIONCOMP
Student:	oh. i guess i could just swap it in the same method. it is problably easier that way, and less code. we were showed in class how to do it separately, but i had never thought of doing it the other way.	STMT
Student:	*[Task action on subtask 3-c-iii-2]*	DISPREFERRED
Tutor:	Both ways work, but it's definitely less code to just do it inside this method.	STMT
Student:	Ok	ACK

Spoken Dialogue System based on Information Extraction using Similarity of Predicate Argument Structures

Koichiro Yoshino, Shinsuke Mori and Tatsuya Kawahara
School of Informatics, Kyoto University
Sakyo-ku, Kyoto, 606-8501, Japan

Abstract

We present a novel scheme of spoken dialogue systems which uses the up-to-date information on the web. The scheme is based on information extraction which is defined by the predicate-argument (P-A) structure and realized by semantic parsing. Based on the information structure, the dialogue system can perform question answering and also proactive information presentation. Feasibility of this scheme is demonstrated with experiments using a domain of baseball news. In order to automatically select useful domain-dependent P-A templates, statistical measures are introduced, resulting to a completely unsupervised learning of the information structure given a corpus. Similarity measures of P-A structures are also introduced to select relevant information. An experimental evaluation shows that the proposed system can make more relevant responses compared with the conventional "bag-of-words" scheme.

1 Introduction

Recently, a huge amount of information is accumulated and distributed on the web day by day. As a result, many people get information via web rather than the conventional mass media. On the other hand, the amount of information on the web is so huge that we often encounter the difficulty in finding information we want. Keyword search is the most widely-used means for the web information access. However, this style is not necessarily the best for information demands of all users who do not have definite goals or just want to know what would be interesting. To cope with user's vague information demands is an important mission for interactive spoken dialogue systems. Moreover, supporting user's information collection in a small-talk style is one of the new directions of spoken dialogue systems.

Existing spoken dialogue systems can be classified into two types (T.Kawahara, 2009): those using relational databases (RDB) such as the Airline Travel Information System (ATIS) (D.A.Dahl, 1994), and those using information retrieval techniques based on statistical document matching (T.Misu and T.Kawahara, 2010). The first scheme can achieve a well-defined task by using a structural database, but this scheme cannot be applied to the web information in which the structure and task are not well defined. The second scheme has been studied to handle large-scale texts such as web, but most of the conventional systems adopt a "bag-of-words" model, and naive statistical matching often generates irrelevant responses which have nothing to do with the user's requests. Our proposed scheme solves this problem by using information extraction based on semantic parsing from web texts, without constructing an RDB. We adopt the predicate-argument (P-A) structure generated by a parser as a baseline, but every P-A structure is not useful for information extraction and retrieval(Y.Kiyota et al., 2002; M.O.Dzikovska et al., 2003; S.Harabagiu et al., 2005). In fact, the useful information structure is dependent on domains. Conventionally, the templates for information extraction were hand-crafted (R.Grishman, 2003), but this heuristic process is so costly that it cannot be applied to a variety of domains on the web. In this paper, therefore, we pro-

Proceedings of the SIGDIAL 2011: the 12th Annual Meeting of the Special Interest Group on Discourse and Dialogue, pages 59–66,
Portland, Oregon, June 17-18, 2011.

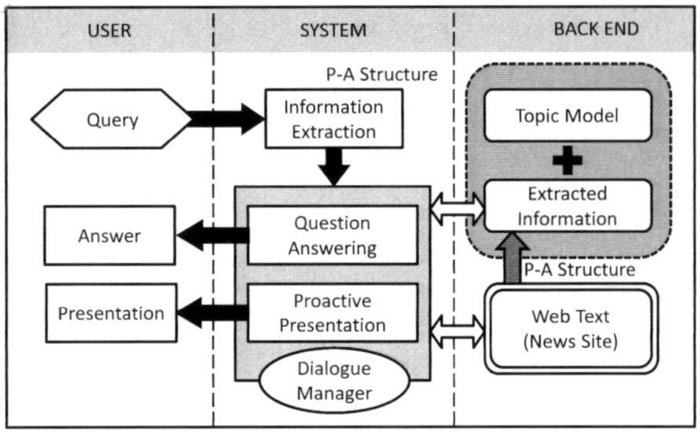

Figure 1: *System overview.*

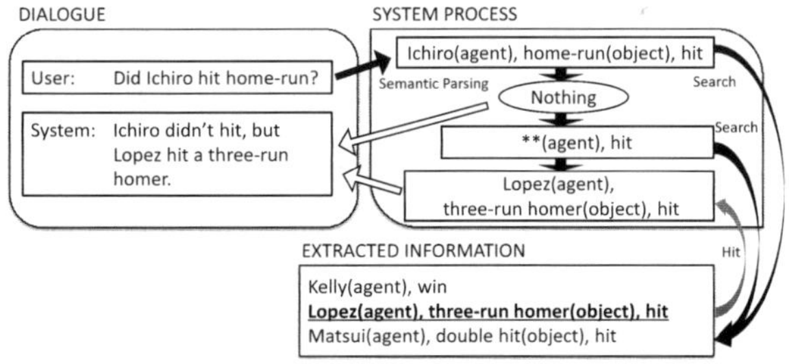

Figure 2: *Example of information extraction and dialogue.*

pose a filtering method of predicate-argument (P-A) patterns generated by the parser, in order to automatically define the domain-dependent useful information structure.

We also address flexible matching based on the P-A structure, because the exact matching often fails and does not generate any outputs. In order to retrieve most relevant information, we define similarity measures of predicates and arguments, which are also learned from a domain corpus.

In this paper, the proposed scheme is applied to a domain of baseball news, and implemented as a spoken dialogue system which can reply to the user's question as well as make proactive information presentation using a news website. An overview of this system is described in Section 2, and the template filtering method is presented in Section 3. Then, system response generation based on flexible matching is explained in Section 4. Finally, an evaluation of the system is presented in Section 5.

2 System Overview

2.1 Architecture

The architecture of the proposed spoken dialogue system is depicted in Fig. 1. First, information extraction is conducted by parsing web texts in advance. A user's query is also parsed to extract the same information structure, and the system matches the extracted information against the web information. According to the matching result, the system either answers the user's question or makes proactive presentation of information which should be most relevant to the user's request.

If the system finds some information which completely matches the user's query, the system makes a response using the corresponding web text. When the system cannot find exact information, it searches for some information which matches partially. For example, in Fig. 2, when a user asked "Did Ichiro hit a home-run?", the system cannot find exact information "[Ichiro (agent), home-run (object), hit]", but finds "[Lopez (agent), three-run homer (object), hit]" which is partially matched and most relevant. This information is used to generate a relevant response that the user would expect.

In the conventional RDB-based dialogue scheme, the system hardly makes relevant responses if it finds no matched entries, thus usually replies "There is no matched entries". In the conventional question-answering scheme, the same situation often happens. Occasionally, a set of close-matched answers may be found by statistical matching, but the found answers may not be relevant to the user's query. In the proposed scheme, we guarantee that the answer is at least partially matched to the user's query in terms of the information structure.

2.2 Information Extraction based on P-A Structure

We use the predicate argument (P-A) structure to define the information structure from web texts. The P-A structure represents a sentence with a predicate, arguments and their semantic cases, as shown in the previous examples. There are some required semantic cases depending on the type of the predicate (verb), and also arbitrary semantic cases like time, place, and other modifications. This structure is a classic concept in natural language processing, but recently, automatic semantic parsing has reached a practical level thanks to corpus-based learning techniques (D.Kawahara and S.Kurohashi, 2006) and has been used for several large-scale tasks (D.Shen and M.Lapata, 2007; R.Wang and Y.Zhang, 2009; D.Wu and P.Fung, 2009). We use KNP[1] as a syntactic and semantic parser.

3 Extraction of Domain-Dependent P-A Templates

The P-A structure automatically generated by the semantic parser provides useful information structure as a baseline. However, every P-A pair is not meaningful in information navigation; actually, only a fraction of the patterns are useful, and they are domain-dependent. For example, in the baseball domain, key patterns include "[A (agent) beat B (object)]" and "[A (agent) hit B (object)]", and in the business domain, "[A (agent) sell B (object)]" and "[A (agent) acquire B (object)]". We propose a method to automatically extract these useful patterns given a domain corpus. We assume each article in the newspaper corpus/websites is annotated with a domain such as sports-baseball and economy-stock.

The method is to filter P-A structure patterns (=templates) based on some statistical measure which accounts for the domain. The filtering process is also expected to eliminate inappropriate patterns caused by parsing errors. Moreover, in spoken dialogue systems, errors in automatic speech recognition (ASR) may result in erroneous matching. By eliminating irrelevant patterns, we expect robust information extraction for spoken input.

Specifically, the following two significance measures are investigated in this work.

3.1 TF-IDF Measure

First, we use the TF-IDF measure to evaluate importance of word w_i in a particular domain or topic t.

$$tfidf(w_i, t) = P(w_i|t) \log \frac{C(d)}{C(d : w_i \in d)} \quad (1)$$

The TF term is the occurrence probability of word w_i, defined as:

$$P(w_i|t) \approx \frac{C(w_i, t) + \alpha}{\sum_j (C(w_j, t) + \alpha)} \quad (2)$$

[1]http://nlp.kuee.kyoto-u.ac.jp/nl-resource/knp.html

where $C(w_i, t)$ is the occurrence count of word w_i in the domain t in the corpus, and α is a smoothing factor given by the Dirichlet process prior. The IDF term is the inverse log probability of documents containing word w_i:

$$\frac{C(d)}{C(d : w_i \in d)} \approx \frac{C(d) + \beta}{C(d : w_i \in d) + \beta} \quad (3)$$

where $C(d)$ is the number of documents (=newspaper articles) in the corpus and $C(d : w_i \in d)$ is the number of documents which contain w_i. β is a smoothing factor given by the Dirichlet process prior. We estimate α and β by a likelihood function using the training corpus. We compute the TF-IDF value for a predicate and each argument, and then compute their geometric mean to define the evaluation measure for a P-A template.

3.2 Naive Bayes (NB) Model

The second measure is based on the Naive Bayes model.

$$P(t|w_i) = \frac{C(w_i, t) + D_t \gamma}{C(w_i) + \gamma} \quad (4)$$

Here, γ is a smoothing factor and D_t is a normalization coefficient of the corpus size of the domain t.

$$D_t = \frac{\sum_j C(w_j, t)}{\sum_k C(w_k)}. \quad (5)$$

The evaluation measure for a P-A pattern is obtained by taking a geometric mean of the component words.

3.3 Clustering of Named Entities

The statistical learning often falls in the data sparseness problem, especially for proper nouns, for example, name of persons. Moreover, there may be mismatch in the set of named entities between the training corpus and the test phase. For robust estimation, we introduce classes for named entities (name of persons, organizations, places). Note that unifying all named entities in the corpus before computing the evaluation measure would weaken the significance of these entities. Thus, we compute statistics for every proper noun before clustering, and sum up values for the class afterwards. For example, the score for "[[person](agent), hit]" is computed as a sum over all persons of this pattern.

Table 1: Evaluation of template filtering.

model	feature	Precision	Recall	F
Baseline	-	0.444	1	0.615
TF-IDF	Predicate	0.587	0.840	0.691
	Argument	0.658	0.730	0.692
	P + A	0.513	0.843	0.638
NB	Predicate	0.601	0.879	0.714
	Argument	0.661	0.794	0.722
	P + A	**0.878**	0.726	**0.795**

3.4 Evaluation of Template Filtering

We performed an experimental evaluation to compare the effectiveness of the two significance measures (TF-IDF and Naive Bayes (NB)) in the Japanese professional baseball domain. The models are trained with the Mainichi Newspaper corpus 2008. The clustering of named entities is applied to both methods. The P-A templates having larger significance scores are selected. We determined a threshold for selecting templates using a development set which was held out from the test set by 10%. The test set was made from Mainichi newspaper's website which talks about games played between April 21-23, 2010. Manual annotation was made on typical predicates and semantic cases which can be used for question answering and proactive presentation. The filtering was performed on the test set by matching the patterns defined by each measure, and evaluated against the annotated answers in terms of recall, precision and F-measure (F). Table 1 lists the result for the two measures using predicate-only, argument-only, and both of them.

In this result, using both predicates and arguments in the Naive Bayes (NB) model performs the best. Compared with the baseline without any filtering, the proposed methods significantly improved precision with some degradation of recall. This property is important in realizing informative response generation robust against ASR and parsing errors. Among the selected templates, we can find typical and important patterns like "have a win", "come into pitch", and "make it consecutive wins". Most of recall errors are infrequent patterns, and majority of precision errors are those patterns that are frequently observed but not useful for presentation.

4 Presentation of Relevant Information

When the system fails to find exact information that matches the user's query, or the user does not speak for a while, the system tries to make proactive information presentation. It is based on the partially matched entries of the current or latest query. The fall-back is similar to collaborative response generation in the conventional spoken dialogue systems (D.Sadek, 1999), but it is intended for proactive information presentation using general documents.

4.1 Response generation based on partial matching

For preference among multiple components in the P-A pattern of the user query, we make use of the significance measure defined in Section 3. Specifically, we relax (=ignore) the component of the least significance score, then search for relevant information. If any entry is not still matched, we relax the next less significant component. If multiple entries are found with this matching, we need to select the most relevant entry. Thus, we introduce two scores of relevance. The relevance measure is defined in different manners for predicates (=verbs) and arguments (=nouns). The measure for arguments is defined based on the co-occurrence statistics in the corpus. The measure for predicate is defined based on distributional analysis of arguments.

4.2 Relevance measure of arguments

The relevance of argument words (=nouns) w_i and w_j is defined as

$$sim_{arg}(w_i, w_j) = \frac{\{C(w_i, w_j)\}^2}{C(w_i) \times C(w_j)}. \quad (6)$$

Here, w_i is in the original query, and relaxed (ignored) in the partial matching, and w_j of the best relevance score is retrieved for response generation. In the example of Fig. 2, w_i is "Ichiro" and w_j is "Lopez".

4.3 Relevance measure of predicates

Distributional analysis (Z.Harris, 1951; Lin, 1998) has been used to define similarity of words, assuming that similar words have similar contexts. In this paper, we use the distribution of arguments which have a modification relation to predicates (Fig. 3)

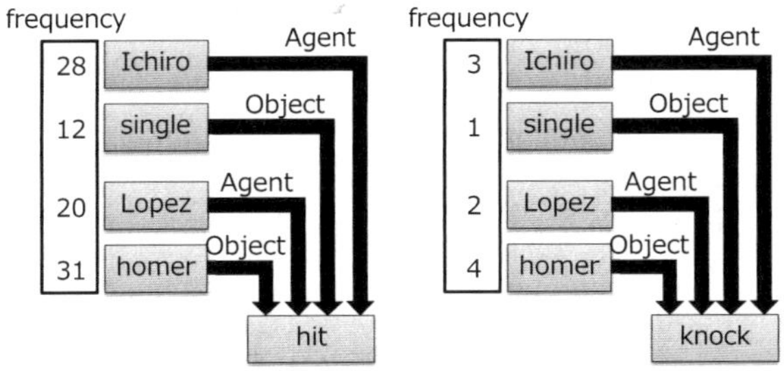

Figure 3: *Distribution analysis of P-A structure.*

(T.Shibata et al., 2008; P.Pantel et al., 2009). The relevance of predicate words w_{pre_i} and w_{pre_j} is defined as a cosine distance of occurrence vectors of the modifying arguments(J.Mitchell and M.Lapata, 2008; S.Thater et al., 2010). Here, argument entries are distinguished by their semantic cases such as Agent and Object, as shown in Fig 3. As the distribution of arguments is sparse and its reliable estimation is difficult, we introduce smoothing by using another distributional analysis of arguments, which is similar to the one in the previous section.

4.4 Bag-of-Words (BOW) Model

If no entry is matched with all possible partial matching, we resort to the naive "bag-of-words" (BOW) model, in which a sentence is represented with a vector of word occurrence and matching is done based on this vector. This method is widely used for document retrieval. We count only content words. In this method, we make use of the significance score for preference of the words when multiple candidates are matched for a short query.

The overall matching strategy of the proposed scheme is summarized in Fig. 4.

4.5 Selection of Relevant Information from Sentence

Answer or information presentation is generated based on the matched sentence in a newspaper article. As a sentence is often complex or made of multiple predicates, simple presentation of the sentence would be redundant or even irrelevant. Therefore, we select the portion of the matched P-A structure, to generate a concise response relevant to the user's query. For example, when a sentence "Ichiro hit a three-run homer in the seventh inning and Mariners won the game" is matched by the pattern "[Ichiro(agent), hit]", we select the former portion of the sentence which exactly answers the user's query, and generate a response "Ichiro hit a three-run homer in the seventh inning."

1. **Exact Matching** of P-A templates.
2. **Partial Matching** using significance measure for query relaxation and relevance score for candidate selection.
3. Back-off to **"Bag-of-Words" (BOW) model** with significance measure for disambiguation.

Figure 4: *Strategy for flexible matching in steps.*

5 System Evaluation

We have implemented a spoken dialogue system based on the significance measure (Naive Bayes model) and the relevance measures, which were learned using the Mainichi Newspaper corpus of ten years (2000-2009). For evaluation of the system, we prepared 201 questions from news articles (September 19-26, 2010) seen at the website of Mainichi Newspaper[2]. Correct answers to the test queries were annotated manually. Evaluation was done with the text input as well as speech input. A word N-gram language model for ASR dedicated to the domain was trained using the relevant newspaper article corpus. The word error rate was approximately 24%.

The system responses for the test queries are categorized into one of the following four: correct answer only ("Correct"), case which includes the correct answer but also other redundant answers ("Ambiguous"), incorrect answer ("Incorrect"), and ("No Answer"). The ambiguous cases occur when multiple sentences or predicates are matched. We also calculate recall, precision and F-measure by counting individual answers separately even when multiple answers are output. The results based on these evaluation measures are summarized in Table 2 and Table 3 for text input and speech input.

In the tables, the proposed method is broken down into three phases as shown in Fig. 4: exact matching of P-A structure (Section 3), incorporation of the partial matching (Section 4.1), and back-off to the "bag-of-words" (BOW) model (Section 4.4). For comparison, we also tested the BOW model and

[2] http://www.mainichi.jp

Table 2: Evaluation of system response.

Input	Model	Correct	Ambiguous	Incorrect	No Answer
Text	Exact	29.9%	0.5%	1.5%	68.1%
	Exact+Partial	66.2%	5.0%	20.3%	8.5%
	Exact+Partial+BOW	69.7%	5.0%	25.3%	0.0%
	(cf) Bag-of-words (BOW)	46.8%	13.9%	39.3%	0.0%
	(cf) Sequence-of-words (SOW)	54.2%	11.4%	34.3%	0.0%
Speech (ASR)	Exact	19.4%	1.0%	0.5%	79.1%
	Exact+Partial	57.2%	6.0%	18.9%	17.9%
	Exact+Partial+BOW	64.1%	6.5%	28.9%	0.0%
	(cf) Bag-of-words (BOW)	39.8%	9.4%	48.8%	0.0%
	(cf) Sequence-of-words (SOW)	46.3%	10.4%	43.3%	0.0%

Table 3: Accuracy of system response.

Input	Model	Precision	Recall	F
Text	Exact	93.8%	30.3%	45.8%
	Exact+Partial	72.5%	71.1%	71.8%
	Exact+Partial+BOW	70.1%	74.6%	72.3%
	(cf) Bag-of-words (BOW)	49.8%	60.7%	54.7%
	(cf) Sequence-of-words (SOW)	55.2%	65.6%	60.0%
Speech (ASR)	Exact	89.1%	20.4%	33.2%
	Exact+Partial	65.8%	63.2%	64.5%
	Exact+Partial+BOW	61.7%	70.6%	65.9%
	(cf) Bag-of-words (BOW)	42.9%	49.3%	45.9%
	(cf) Sequence-of-words (SOW)	48.3%	56.7%	52.2%

"sequence-of-words" (SOW) model, which consider the sequence order in the BOW model. The exact matching assumes strong constraint of P-A patterns, so the generated answers are almost correct, but no answers are generated very often. By incorporating the partial matching and BOW model, the system can output more relevant answers. Compared with the BOW model, the proposed method achieves much higher ratio or precision of correct answers. F-measure is also higher by 17% absolute.

A similar tendency is observed for speech input, although the overall accuracy is degraded because of the ASR errors. However, degradation is relatively small considering the word accuracy of 76%. The partial matching works effectively even if the exact matching fails due to ASR errors. Moreover, the back-off to the BOW model is effective in ASR input.

The proposed method generates concise responses by selecting the relevant portion as described in Section 4.5, while the BOW method often generates long responses which includes many redundant portions. This property is particularly important in the speech interface.

We show a dialogue example in Fig. 5 which is in Japanese and translated to English for reference (=Italic).

6 Domain Portability

In the proposed scheme, we construct a domain-dependent system in a pre-determined domain. It is straightforward to port the system to other domains just by preparing a domain corpus. This system uses a newspaper corpus for training domain-dependent statistical models. Newspaper articles are classified according to domain categories such as sports/baseball and business/finance. Therefore, it is straightforward to select relevant articles for a particular domain. In the proposed scheme, we do not need any further annotations and all statistical models are trained in an unsupervised manner.

User:	Hanshin ha katta? *(Did Hanshin win the game?)*
System:	Hanshin ha nanakai ni Kanemoto, Hiyama no daida kousei de katta yo. *(Hanshin won the game by Kanemoto and Hyama's pinch-hiting in the seventh inning.)*
User:	Noumi ha touban shita? *(Did Noumi come in to pitch?)*
System	Noumi ga nanakai mushitten de kachitousyu ni natta yo. *(Noumi was the winning pitcher, by shutting out for seven innings.)*
User:	Sanshin wo tori mashita ka? *(Did he get strikeout? ("he" is omitted.))*
System:	Noumi ha nishi ichi-nirui deha Abe wo naikaku suraida- de sanshin ni totta yo. *(Noumi struck out Abe on a slider with two out two-on jam.)*

Figure 5: *Dialogue example (original in Japanese, translated to English).*

7 Conclusions

We have presented a new scheme of spoken dialogue systems which can talk about web texts in an interactive manner. The information extraction technique is adopted to conduct question answering as well as proactive information presentation. Filtering based on a statistical significant measure is introduced to automatically select useful templates in a given domain. Relevance measures are also defined for predicate and argument in order to retrieve relevant entries when the exact matching does not succeed. In experimental evaluations, we have demonstrated that the filtering works effectively and the system generates more relevant responses than the conventional method.

Ongoing works include application to other domains to demonstrate generality of the scheme.

References

D.A.Dahl. 1994. Expanding the scope of the ATIS task: The ATIS-3 corpus. In *Proc. ARPA Human Language Technology Workshop*, pages 43–48.

D.Kawahara and S.Kurohashi. 2006. A fully-lexicalized probabilistic model for japanese syntactic and case structure analysis. In *Proc. HLT-NAACL*, pages 176–183.

D.Sadek. 1999. Design consideration on dialogue systems: From theory to technology - the case of Artimis -. In *Proc. ESCA workshop on Interactive Dialogue in Multi-Modal Systems*, pages 173–187.

D.Shen and M.Lapata. 2007. Using semantic roles to improve question answering. In *Proc. EMNLP-CoNLL*, pages 12–21.

D.Wu and P.Fung. 2009. Can semantic role labeling improve SMT? In *Proc. EAMT*, pages 218–225.

J.Mitchell and M.Lapata. 2008. Vector-based models of semantic composition. In *Proc. ACL-HLT*, pages 236–244.

Dekang Lin. 1998. Automatic retrieval and clustering of similar words. In *Proc. ACL and COLING*, pages 768–774.

M.O.Dzikovska, M.D.Swift, and J.F.Allen. 2003. Integrating linguistic and domain knowledge for spoken dialogue systems in multiple domains. In *Proc. of IJCAI-03 Workshop on Knowledge and Reasoning in Practical Dialogue Systems.*

P.Pantel, E.Crestan, A.Borkovsky, A.-M.Popescu, and V.Vayas. 2009. Web-scale distributional similarity and entity set expansion. In *Proc. EMNLP*, pages 938–947.

R.Grishman. 2003. Discovery methods for information extraction. In *Proc. ISCA & IEEE Workshop on Spontaneous Speech Processing and Recognition*, pages 243–247.

R.Pieraccini, E.Tzoukermann, Z.Gorelov, J-L.Gauvain, E.Levin, C.-H Lee, and J.G.Wilpon. 1992. A speech understanding system based on statistical representation of semantics. In *Proc. IEEE-ICASSP*, volume 1, pages 193–196.

R.Wang and Y.Zhang. 2009. Recognizing textual relatedness with predicate-argument structure. In *Proc. EMNLP*, pages 784–792.

S.Harabagiu, A.Hickl, J.Lehmann, and D.Moldovan. 2005. Experiments with interactive question-answering. In *Proc. ACL*, pages 205–214.

S.Thater, H.Fürstenau, and M.Pinkal. 2010. Contextualizing semantic representations using syntactically enriched vector models. In *Proc. ACL*, pages 948–957.

T.Kawahara. 2009. New perspectives on spoken language understanding: Does machine need to fully understand speech? In *Proc. IEEE-ASRU*, pages 46–50.

T.Misu and T.Kawahara. 2010. Bayes risk-based dialogue management for document retrieval system with speech interface. *Speech Communication*, 52(1):61–71.

T.Shibata, M.Odani, J.Harashima, T.Oonishi, and S.Kurohashi. 2008. Syngraph: A flexible matching method based on synonymous expression extraction from an ordinary dictionary and a web corpus. In *Proc. IJCNLP*, pages 787–792.

Y.Kiyota, S.Kurohashi, and F.Kido. 2002. "dialog navigator" : A question answering system based on large text knowledge base. In *Proc. COLING*, pages 460–466.

Z.Harris. 1951. *Structural Linguistics*. University of Chicago Press.

Common Ground and Perspective-taking in Real-time Language Processing

Michael K. Tanenhaus

Department of Brain and Cognitive Sciences
University of Rochester
Rochester, NY 14627
mtan@bcs.rochester.edu

Successful communication would seem to require that speakers and listeners distinguish between their own knowledge, commitments and intentions, and those of their interlocutors. A particularly important distinction is between shared knowledge (common ground) and private knowledge (privileged ground). Keeping track of what is shared and what is privileged might seem too computationally expensive and too memory intensive to inform real-time language processing--a position supported by striking experimental evidence that speakers and listeners act egocentrically, showing strong and seemingly inappropriate intrusions from their own privileged ground. I'll review recent results from my laboratory using unscripted conversation demonstrating that (1) speaker's utterances provide evidence about whether they believe information is shared or privileged; and (2) addressees are extremely sensitive to this evidence. I'll suggest an integrative framework that explains discrepancies in the literature and might be informative for researchers in the computational dialogue community.

Proceedings of the SIGDIAL 2011: the 12th Annual Meeting of the Special Interest Group on Discourse and Dialogue, page 67,
Portland, Oregon, June 17-18, 2011.

Giving instructions in virtual environments by corpus based selection

Luciana Benotti
PLN Group, FAMAF
National University of Córdoba
Córdoba, Argentina
luciana.benotti@gmail.com

Alexandre Denis
TALARIS team, LORIA/CNRS
Lorraine. Campus scientifique, BP 239
Vandoeuvre-lès-Nancy, France
alexandre.denis@loria.fr

Abstract

Instruction giving can be used in several applications, ranging from trainers in simulated worlds to non player characters for virtual games. In this paper we present a novel algorithm for rapidly prototyping virtual instruction-giving agents from human-human corpora without manual annotation. Automatically prototyping full-fledged dialogue systems from corpora is far from being a reality nowadays. Our approach is restricted in that only the virtual instructor can perform speech acts while the user responses are limited to physical actions in the virtual worlds.

We have defined an algorithm that, given a task-based corpus situated in a virtual world, which contains human instructor's speech acts and the user's responses as physical actions, generates a virtual instructor that robustly helps a user achieve a given task in the virtual world. We explain how this algorithm can be used for generating a virtual instructor for a game-like, task-oriented virtual world. We evaluate the virtual instructor with human users using task-oriented as well as user satisfaction metrics. We compare our results with both human and rule-based virtual instructors hand-coded for the same task.

1 Introduction

Virtual human characters constitute a promising contribution to many fields, including simulation, training and interactive games (Kenny et al., 2007; Jan et al., 2009). The ability to communicate using natural language is important for believable and effective virtual humans. Such ability has to be good enough to engage the trainee or the gamer in the activity. Nowadays, most conversational systems operate on a dialogue-act level and require extensive annotation efforts in order to be fit for their task (Rieser and Lemon, 2010). Semantic annotation and rule authoring have long been known as bottlenecks for developing conversational systems for new domains.

In this paper, we present a novel algorithm for generating virtual instructors from automatically annotated human-human corpora. Our algorithm, when given a task-based corpus situated in a virtual world, generates an instructor that robustly helps a user achieve a given task in the virtual world of the corpus. There are two main approaches toward automatically producing dialogue utterances. One is the selection approach, in which the task is to pick the appropriate output from a corpus of possible outputs. The other is the generation approach, in which the output is dynamically assembled using some composition procedure, e.g. grammar rules. The selection approach to generation has only been used in conversational systems that are not task-oriented such as negotiating agents (Gandhe and Traum, 2007a), question answering characters (Kenny et al., 2007), and virtual patients (Leuski et al., 2006). To the best of our knowledge, our algorithm is the first one proposed for doing corpus based generation and interaction management for task-oriented systems.

The advantages of corpus based generation are many. To start with, it affords the use of complex and human-like sentences without detailed analysis. Moreover, the system may easily use recorded audio clips rather than speech synthesis and recorded video for animating virtual humans. Finally, no

Proceedings of the SIGDIAL 2011: the 12th Annual Meeting of the Special Interest Group on Discourse and Dialogue, pages 68–77,
Portland, Oregon, June 17-18, 2011.

rule writing by a dialogue expert or manual annotations is needed. The disadvantage of corpus based generation is that the resulting dialogue may not be fully coherent. For non-task oriented systems, dialogue management through corpus based methods has shown coherence related problems. Shawar and Atwell (2003; 2005) present a method for learning pattern matching rules from corpora in order to obtain the dialogue manager for a chatbot. Gandhe and Traum (2007b) investigate several dialogue models for negotiating virtual agents that are trained on an unannotated human-human corpus. Both approaches report that the dialogues obtained by these methods are still to be improved because the lack of dialogue history management results in incoherences. Since in task-based systems, the dialogue history is restricted by the structure of the task, the absence of dialogue history management is alleviated by tracking the current state of the task.

In the next section we introduce the corpora used in this paper. Section 3 presents the two phases of our algorithm, namely automatic annotation and dialogue management through selection. In Section 4 we present a fragment of an interaction with a virtual instructor generated using the corpus and the algorithm introduced in the previous sections. We evaluate the virtual instructor in interactions with human subjects using objective as well as subjective metrics. We present the results of the evaluation in Section 5. We compare our results with both human and rule-based virtual instructors hand-coded for the same task. Finally, Section 7 discusses the weaknesses of the approach for developing instruction giving agents, as well as its advantages and drawbacks with respect to hand-coded systems. In this last section we also discuss improvements on our algorithms designed as a result of our error analysis.

2 The GIVE corpus

The Challenge on Generating Instructions in Virtual Environments (GIVE; Koller et al. (2010)) is a shared task in which Natural Language Generation systems must generate real-time instructions that guide a user in a virtual world. In this paper, we use the GIVE-2 Corpus (Gargett et al., 2010), a freely available corpus of human instruction giving in virtual environments. We use the English part of the corpus which consists of 63 American English written discourses in which one subject guided another in a treasure hunting task in 3 different 3D worlds.

The task setup involved pairs of human partners, each of whom played one of two different roles. The "direction follower" (DF) moved about in the virtual world with the goal of completing a treasure hunting task, but had no knowledge of the map of the world or the specific behavior of objects within that world (such as, which buttons to press to open doors). The other partner acted as the "direction giver" (DG), who was given complete knowledge of the world and had to give instructions to the DF to guide him/her to accomplish the task.

The GIVE-2 corpus is a multi-modal corpus which consists of all the instructions uttered by the DG, and all the object manipulations done by the DF with the corresponding timestamp. Furthermore, the DF's position and orientation is logged every 200 milliseconds, making it possible to extract information about his/her movements.

3 The unsupervised conversational model

Our algorithm consists of two phases: an annotation phase and a selection phase. The *annotation phase* is performed only once and consists of automatically associating the DG instruction to the DF reaction. The *selection phase* is performed every time the virtual instructor generates an instruction and consists of picking out from the annotated corpus the most appropriate instruction at a given point.

3.1 The automatic annotation

The basic idea of the annotation is straightforward: associate each *utterance* with its corresponding *reaction*. We assume that a reaction captures the semantics of its associated instruction. Defining reaction involves two subtle issues, namely *boundary* determination and *discretization*. We discuss these issues in turn and then give a formal definition of reaction.

We define the *boundaries* of a reaction as follows. A reaction R_k to an instruction U_k begins right after the instruction U_k is uttered and ends right before the next instruction U_{k+1} is uttered. In the following example, instruction 1 corresponds to the reaction $\langle 2, 3, 4\rangle$, instruction 5 corresponds to $\langle 6\rangle$, and instruction 7 to $\langle 8\rangle$.

DG(1): hit the red you see in the far room
DF(2): [enters the far room]
DF(3): [pushes the red button]
DF(4): [turns right]
DG(5): hit far side green
DF(6): [moves next to the wrong green]
DG(7): no
DF(8): [moves to the right green and pushes it]

As the example shows, our definition of boundaries is not always semantically correct. For instance, it can be argued that it includes too much because 4 is not strictly part of the semantics of 1. Furthermore, misinterpreted instructions (as 5) and corrections (e.g., 7) result in clearly inappropriate instruction-reaction associations. Since we want to avoid any manual annotation, we decided to use this naive definition of boundaries anyway. We discuss in Section 5 the impact that inappropriate associations have on the performance of a virtual instructor.

The second issue that we address here is *discretization* of the reaction. It is well known that there is not a unique way to discretize an action into sub-actions. For example, we could decompose action 2 into 'enter the room' or into 'get close to the door and pass the door'. Our algorithm is not dependent on a particular discretization. However, the same discretization mechanism used for annotation has to be used during selection, for the dialogue manager to work properly. For selection (i.e., in order to decide what to say next) any virtual instructor needs to have a *planner* and a *planning problem*: i.e., a specification of how the virtual world works (i.e., the actions), a way to represent the states of the virtual world (i.e., the state representation) and a way to represent the objective of the task (i.e., the goal). Therefore, we decided to use them in order to discretize the reaction.

For the virtual instructor we present in Section 4 we used the planner LazyFF and the planning problem provided with the GIVE Framework. The planner LazyFF is a reimplementation (in Java) of the classical artificial intelligence planner FF (Hoffmann and Nebel, 2001). The GIVE framework (Gargett et al., 2010) provides a standard PDDL (Hsu et al., 2006) planning problem which formalizes how the GIVE virtual worlds work. Both the LazzyFF planner and the GIVE planning problem are freely available on the web[1].

Now we are ready to define *reaction* formally. Let S_k be the state of the virtual world when uttering instruction U_k, S_{k+1} be the state of the world when uttering the next utterance U_{k+1} and $Acts$ be the representation of the virtual world actions. The *reaction* to U_k is defined as the sequence of actions returned by the planner with S_k as the initial state, S_{k+1} as the goal state and $Acts$ as the actions.

Given this reaction definition, the annotation of the corpus then consists of automatically associating each utterance to its (discretized) reaction. The simple algorithm that implements this annotation is shown in Figure 1. Moreover, we provide a fragment of the resulting annotated corpus in Appendix A.

$Acts \leftarrow$ *world possible actions*
for all utterance U_k in the corpus **do**
    $S_k \leftarrow$ *world state at* U_k
    $S_{k+1} \leftarrow$ *world state at* U_{k+1}
    $U_k.Reaction \leftarrow$ plan(S_k, S_{k+1}, $Acts$)
end for

Figure 1: Annotation algorithm

3.2 Selecting what to say next

In this section we describe how the selection phase is performed every time the virtual instructor generates an instruction.

The instruction selection algorithm, displayed in Figure 2, consists in finding in the corpus the set of candidate utterances C for the current task plan P (P is the sequence of actions that needs to be executed in the current state of the virtual world in order to complete the task). We define $C = \{U \in \text{Corpus} \mid P \text{ starts with } U.Reaction\}$. In other words, an utterance U belongs to C if the first actions of the current plan P exactly match the reaction associated to the utterance U. All the utterances that pass this test are considered paraphrases and hence suitable in the current context.

Whenever the plan P changes, as a result of the actions of the DF, we call the selection algorithm in order to regenerate the set of candidate utterances C.

[1] `http://www.give-challenge.org/`

$C \leftarrow \emptyset$
$Plan \leftarrow$ *current task plan*
for all utterance U in the corpus **do**
  if $Plan$ starts with $U.Reaction$ **then**
    $C \leftarrow C \cup \{U\}$
  end if
end for
return C

Figure 2: Selection algorithm

While the plan P doesn't change, because the DF is staying still, the virtual instructor offers alternative paraphrases of the intended instruction. Each paraphrase is selected by picking an utterance from C and verbalizing it, at fixed time intervals (every 3 seconds). The order in which utterances are selected depends on the length of the utterance reaction (in terms of number of actions), starting from the longest ones. Hence, in general, instructions such as "go back again to the room with the lamp" are uttered before instructions such as "go straight", because the reaction of the former utterance is longer than the reaction of the later.

It is important to notice that the discretization used for annotation and selection directly impacts the behavior of the virtual instructor. It is crucial then to find an appropriate granularity of the discretization. If the granularity is too coarse, many instructions in the corpus will have an empty reaction. For instance, in the absence of the representation of the user orientation in the planning domain (as is the case for the virtual instructor we evaluate in Section 5), instructions like "turn left" and "turn right" will have empty reactions making them indistinguishable during selection. However, if the granularity is too fine the user may get into situations that do not occur in the corpus, causing the selection algorithm to return an empty set of candidate utterances. It is the responsibility of the virtual instructor developer to find a granularity sufficient to capture the diversity of the instructions he wants to distinguish during selection.

4 A virtual instructor for a virtual world

We implemented an English virtual instructor for one of the worlds used in the corpus collection we presented in Section 2. The English fragment of the corpus that we used has 21 interactions and a total of 1136 instructions. Games consisted on average of 54.2 instructions from the human DG, and took about 543 seconds on average for the human DF to complete the task.

On Figures 4 to 7 we show an excerpt of an interaction between the system and a user. The figures show a 2D map from top view and the 3D in-game view. In Figure 4, the user, represented by a blue character, has just entered the upper left room. He has to push the button close to the chair. The first candidate utterance selected is "red closest to the chair in front of you". Notice that the referring expression uniquely identifies the target object using the spatial proximity of the target to the chair. This referring expression is generated without any reasoning on the target distractors, just by considering the current state of the task plan and the user position.

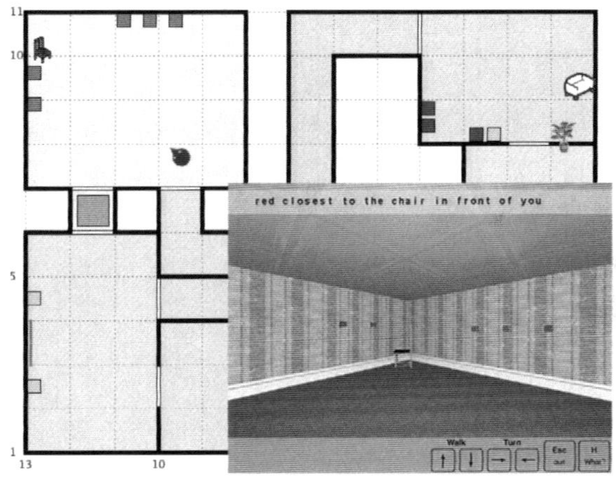

Figure 4: "red closest to the chair in front of you"

After receiving the instruction the user gets closer to the button as shown in Figure 5. As a result of the new user position, a new task plan exists, the set of candidate utterances is recalculated and the system selects a new utterance, namely "the closet one".

The generation of the ellipsis of the button or the chair is a direct consequence of the utterances normally said in the corpus at this stage of the task plan (that is, when the user is about to manipulate this object). From the point of view of referring expression algorithms, the referring expression may not be optimal because it is over-specified (a pronoun would

L	go
yes	left
straight	now go back
go back out	now go back out
closest the door	down the passage
go back to the hallway	nowin to the shade room
go back out of the room	out the way you came in
exit the way you entered	ok now go out the same door
back to the room with the lamp	go back to the door you came in
Go through the opening on the left	okay now go back to the original room
okay now go back to where you came from	ok go back again to the room with the lamp
now i ned u to go back to the original room	Go through the opening on the left with the yellow wall paper

Figure 3: All candidate selected utterances when exiting the room in Figure 7

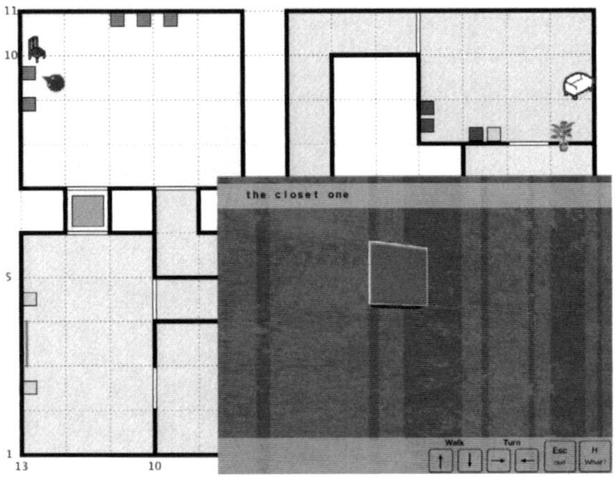

Figure 5: "the closet one"

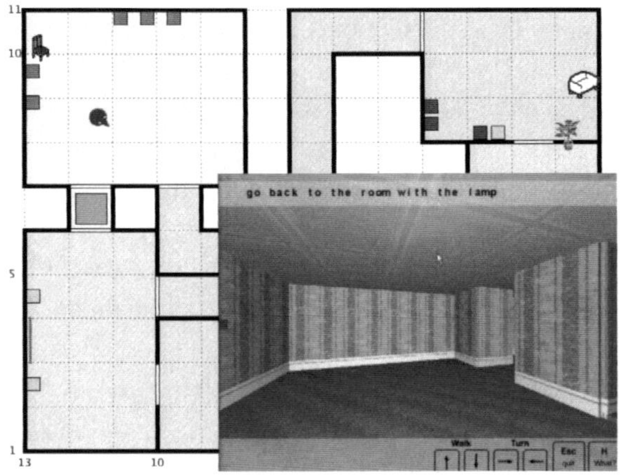

Figure 7: "go back to the room with the lamp"

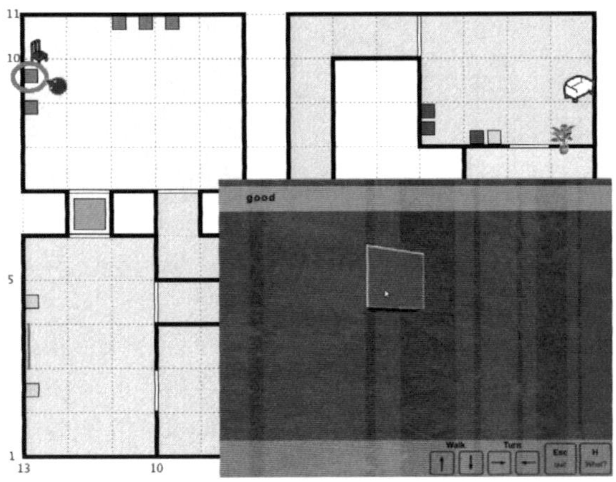

Figure 6: "good"

be preferred as in "click it"), Furthermore, the instruction contains a spelling error ('closet' instead of 'closest'). In spite of this non optimality, the instruction led our user to execute the intended reaction, namely pushing the button.

Right after the user clicks on the button (Figure 6), the system selects an utterance corresponding to the new task plan. The player position stayed the same so the only change in the plan is that the button no longer needs to be pushed. In this task state, DGs usually give acknowledgements and this is then what our selection algorithm selects: "good".

After receiving the acknowledgement, the user turns around and walks forward, and the next action in the plan is to leave the room (Figure 7). The system selects the utterance "go back to the room with the lamp" which refers to the previous interaction. Again, the system keeps no representation of the past actions of the user, but such utterances are the ones that are found at this stage of the task plan.

We show in Figure 3 all candidate utterances selected when exiting the room in Figure 7. That is, for our system purposes, all the utterances in the figure are paraphrases of the one that is actually uttered in Figure 7. As we explained in Section 3.2, the utterance with the longest reaction is selected first ("go back to the room with the lamp"), the second utterance with the longest reaction is selected second ("ok go back again to the room with the lamp"), and so on. As you can observe in Figure 3 the utterances in the candidate set can range from telegraphic style like "L" to complex sentences like "Go through the opening on the left with the yellow wall paper". Several kinds of instructions are displayed, acknowledgements such as "yes", pure moving instructions like "left" or "straight", instructions that refer to the local previous history such as "go back out the room" or "ok now go out the same door" and instructions that refer back to the global history such as "okay now go back to the original room".

Due to the lack of orientation consideration in our system, some orientation dependent utterances are inappropriate in this particular context. For instance, "*left*" is incorrect given that the player does not have to turn left but go straight in order to go through the correct door. However, most of the instructions, even if quite different among themselves, could have been successfully used in the context of Figure 7.

5 Evaluation and error analysis

In this section we present the results of the evaluation we carried out on the virtual instructor presented in Section 4 which was generated using the dialogue model algorithm introduced in Section 3.

We collected data from 13 subjects. The participants were mostly graduate students; 7 female and 6 male. They were not English native speakers but rated their English skills as near-native or very good.

The evaluation contains both objective measures which we discuss in Section 5.1 and subjective measures which we discuss in Section 5.2.

5.1 Objective metrics

The objective metrics we extracted from the logs of interaction are summarized in Table 1. The table compares our results with both human instructors and the three rule-based virtual instructors that were top rated in the GIVE-2 Challenge. Their results correspond to those published in (Koller et al., 2010) which were collected not in a laboratory but connecting the systems to users over the Internet. These hand-coded systems are called NA, NM and Saar. We refer to our system as OUR.

	Human	NA	Saar	NM	OUR
Task success	100%	47%	40%	30%	70%
Canceled	0%	24%	n/a	35%	7%
Lost	0%	29%	n/a	35%	23%
Time (sec)	543	344	467	435	692
Mouse actions	12	17	17	18	14
Utterances	53	224	244	244	194

Table 1: Results for the *objective* metrics

In the table we show the percentage of games that users completed successfully with the different instructors. Unsuccessful games can be either canceled or lost. We also measured the average time until task completion, and the average number of utterances users received from each system. To ensure comparability, we only counted successfully completed games.

In terms of task success, our system performs better than all hand-coded systems. We duly notice that, for the GIVE Challenge in particular (and probably for human evaluations in general) the success rates in the laboratory tend to be higher than the success rate online (this is also the case for completion times) (Koller et al., 2009). Koller et al. justify this difference by stating that the laboratory subject is being discouraged from canceling a frustrating task while the online user is not. However, it is also possible that people canceled less because they found the interaction more natural and engaging as suggested by the results of the subjective metrics (see next section).

In any case, our results are preliminary given the amount of subjects that we tested, but they are indeed encouraging. In particular, our system helped users to identify better the objects that they needed to manipulate in the virtual world, as shown by the low number of mouse actions required to complete the task (a high number indicates that the user must have manipulated wrong objects). This correlates with the subjective evaluation of referring expression quality (see next section).

We performed a detailed analysis of the instructions uttered by our system that were unsuccessful, that is, all the instructions that did not cause the intended reaction as annotated in the corpus. From the 2081 instructions uttered in total (adding all the utterances of the 13 interactions), 1304 (63%) of them were successful and 777 (37%) were unsuccessful.

Given the limitations of the annotation discussed in Section 3.1 (wrong annotation of correction utterances and no representation of user orientation) we classified the unsuccessful utterances using lexical cues into 1) correction like "no" or "wrong", 2) orientation instruction such as "left" or "straight", and 3) other. We found that 25% of the unsuccessful utterances are of type 1, 40% are type 2, 34% are type 3 (1% corresponds to the default utterance "go" that our system utters when the set of candidate utterances is empty). In Section 7 we propose an improved virtual instructor designed as a result of this error analysis.

5.2 Subjective metrics

The subjective measures were obtained from responses to the GIVE-2 questionnaire that was presented to users after each game. It asked users to rate different statements about the system using a continuous slider. The slider position was translated to a number between -100 and 100. As done in GIVE-2, for negative statements, we report the reversed scores, so that in Tables 2 and 3 greater numbers indicates that the system is better (for example, Q14 shows that OUR system is less robotic than the rest). In this section we compare our results with the systems NA, Saar and NM as we did in Section 5.1, we cannot compare against human instructors because these subjective metrics were not collected in (Gargett et al., 2010).

The GIVE-2 Challenge questionnaire includes twenty-two subjective metrics. Metrics Q1 to Q13 and Q22 assess the effectiveness and reliability of instructions. For almost all of these metrics we got similar or slightly lower results than those obtained by the three hand-coded systems, except for three metrics which we show in Table 2. We suspect that the low results obtained for Q5 and Q22 relate to the unsuccessful utterances identified and discussed in Section 5.1 (for instance, corrections were sometimes contradictory causing confusion and resulting in subjects ignoring them as they advanced in the interaction). The high unexpected result in Q6, that is indirectly assessing the quality of referring expressions, demonstrates the efficiency of the referring process despite the fact that nothing in the algorithms is dedicated to reference. This good result is probably correlated with the low number of mouse actions mentioned in Section 5.1.

NA	Saar	NM	OUR
Q5: I was confused about which direction to go in			
29	5	9	-12
Q6: I had no difficulty with identifying the objects the system described for me			
18	20	13	40
Q22: I felt I could trust the system's instructions			
37	21	23	0

Table 2: Results for the significantly different *subjective* measures assessing the effectiveness of the instructions (the greater the number, the better the system)

Metrics Q14 to Q20 are intended to assess the naturalness of the instructions, as well as the immersion and engagement of the interaction. As Table 3 shows, in spite of the unsuccessful utterances, our system is rated as more natural and more engaging (in general) than the best systems that competed in the GIVE-2 Challenge.

NA	Saar	NM	OUR
Q14: The system's instructions sounded robotic			
-4	5	-1	28
Q15: The system's instructions were repetitive			
-31	-26	-28	-8
Q16: I really wanted to find that trophy			
-11	-7	-8	7
Q17: I lost track of time while solving the task			
-16	-11	-18	16
Q18: I enjoyed solving the task			
-8	-5	-4	4
Q19: Interacting with the system was really annoying			
8	-2	-2	4
Q20: I would recommend this game to a friend			
-30	-25	-24	-28

Table 3: Results for the *subjective* measures assessing the naturalness and engagement of the instructions (the greater the number, the better the system)

6 Portability to other virtual environments

The hand-coded systems, which we compared to, do not need a corpus in a particular GIVE virtual world in order to generate instructions for any GIVE virtual world, while our system cannot do without such corpus. These hand-coded systems are designed to work on different GIVE virtual worlds without the need of training data, hence their algorithms are more complex (e.g. they include domain independent algorithms for generation of referring expressions) and take a longer time to develop.

Our algorithm is independent of any particular virtual world. In fact, it can be ported to any other instruction giving task (where the DF has to perform a physical task) with the same effort than required to port it to a new GIVE world. This is not true for the hand-coded GIVE systems. The inputs of our algorithm are an off-the-shelf planner, a formal planning problem representation of the task and a human-human corpus collected on the very same task the system aims to instruct. It is important to notice that any virtual instructor, in order to give instructions that are both causally appropriate at the point of the task and relevant for the goal cannot do without such planning problem representation. Furthermore, it is quite a normal practice nowadays to collect a human-human corpus on the target task domain. It is reasonable, then, to assume that all the inputs of our algorithm are already available when developing the virtual instructor, which was indeed the case for the GIVE framework.

Another advantage of our approach is that virtual instructor can be generated by developers without any knowledge of generation of natural language techniques. Furthermore, the actual implementation of our algorithms is extremely simple as shown in Figures 1 and 2. This makes our approach promising for application areas such as games and simulation training.

7 Future work and conclusions

In this paper we presented a novel algorithm for automatically prototyping virtual instructors from human-human corpora without manual annotation. Using our algorithms and the GIVE corpus we have generated a virtual instructor for a game-like virtual environment. A video of our virtual instructor is available in `http://cs.famaf.unc.edu.ar/~luciana/give-OUR`. We obtained encouraging results in the evaluation with human users that we did on the virtual instructor. In our evaluation, our system outperforms rule-based virtual instructors hand-coded for the same task both in terms of objective and subjective metrics. We plan to participate in the GIVE Challenge 2011[2] in order to get more evaluation data from online users and to evaluate our algorithms on multiple worlds.

The algorithms we presented solely rely on the plan to define what constitutes the context of uttering. It may be interesting though to make use of other kinds of features. For instance, in order to integrate spatial orientation and differentiate "turn left" and "turn right", the orientation can be either added to the planning domain or treated as a context feature. While it may be possible to add orientation in the planning domain of GIVE, it is not straightforward to include the diversity of possible features in the same formalization, like modeling the global discourse history or corrections. Thus we plan to investigate the possibility of considering the context of an utterance as a set of features, including plan, orientation, discourse history and so forth, in order to extend the algorithms presented in terms of context building and feature matching operations.

In the near future we plan to build a new version of the system that improves based on the error analysis that we did. For instance, we plan to take orientation into account during selection. As a result of these extensions however we may need to enlarge the corpus we used so as not to increase the number of situations in which the system does not find anything to say. Finally, if we could identify corrections automatically, as suggested in (Raux and Nakano, 2010), we could get an increase in performance, because we would be able to treat them as corrections and not as instructions as we do now.

In sum, this paper presents the first existing algorithm for fully-automatically prototyping task-oriented virtual agents from corpora. The generated agents are able to effectively and naturally help a user complete a task in a virtual world by giving her/him instructions.

[2] `http://www.give-challenge.org/research`

References

Sudeep Gandhe and David Traum. 2007a. Creating spoken dialogue characters from corpora without annotations. In *Proceedings of 8th Conference in the Annual Series of Interspeech Events*, pages 2201–2204, Belgium.

Sudeep Gandhe and David Traum. 2007b. First steps toward dialogue modelling from an un-annotated human-human corpus. In *IJCAI Workshop on Knowledge and Reasoning in Practical Dialogue Systems*, Hyderabad, India.

Andrew Gargett, Konstantina Garoufi, Alexander Koller, and Kristina Striegnitz. 2010. The GIVE-2 corpus of giving instructions in virtual environments. In *Proceedings of the 7th International Conference on Language Resources and Evaluation (LREC)*, Malta.

Jörg Hoffmann and Bernhard Nebel. 2001. The FF planning system: Fast plan generation through heuristic search. *JAIR*, 14:253–302.

Chih-Wei Hsu, Benjamin W. Wah, Ruoyun Huang, and Yixin Chen. 2006. New features in SGPlan for handling soft constraints and goal preferences in PDDL3.0. In *Proceedings of ICAPS*.

Dusan Jan, Antonio Roque, Anton Leuski, Jacki Morie, and David Traum. 2009. A virtual tour guide for virtual worlds. In *Proceedings of the 9th International Conference on Intelligent Virtual Agents*, IVA '09, pages 372–378, Berlin, Heidelberg. Springer-Verlag.

Patrick Kenny, Thomas D. Parsons, Jonathan Gratch, Anton Leuski, and Albert A. Rizzo. 2007. Virtual patients for clinical therapist skills training. In *Proceedings of the 7th international conference on Intelligent Virtual Agents*, IVA '07, pages 197–210, Berlin, Heidelberg. Springer-Verlag.

Alexander Koller, Kristina Striegnitz, Donna Byron, Justine Cassell, Robert Dale, Sara Dalzel-Job, Johanna Moore, and Jon Oberlander. 2009. Validating the web-based evaluation of nlg systems. In *Proceedings of ACL-IJCNLP 2009 (Short Papers)*, Singapore.

Alexander Koller, Kristina Striegnitz, Andrew Gargett, Donna Byron, Justine Cassell, Robert Dale, Johanna Moore, and Jon Oberlander. 2010. Report on the second NLG challenge on generating instructions in virtual environments (GIVE-2). In *Proceedings of the International Natural Language Generation Conference (INLG)*, Dublin.

Anton Leuski, Ronakkumar Patel, David Traum, and Brandon Kennedy. 2006. Building effective question answering characters. In *Proceedings of the 7th SIGdial Workshop on Discourse and Dialogue*, SigDIAL '06, pages 18–27, Stroudsburg, PA, USA. Association for Computational Linguistics.

Antoine Raux and Mikio Nakano. 2010. The dynamics of action corrections in situated interaction. In *Proceedings of the SIGDIAL 2010 Conference*, pages 165–174, Tokyo, Japan, September. Association for Computational Linguistics.

Verena Rieser and Oliver Lemon. 2010. Learning human multimodal dialogue strategies. *Natural Language Engineering*, 16:3–23.

Bayan Abu Shawar and Eric Atwell. 2003. Using dialogue corpora to retrain a chatbot system. In *Proceedings of the Corpus Linguistics Conference*, pages 681–690, United Kingdom.

Bayan Abu Shawar and Eric Atwell. 2005. Using corpora in machine-learning chatbot systems. volume 10, pages 489–516.

A Automatically annotated fragment of the GIVE corpus

Utterance: make a left and exit the room
Reaction: ⟨move(b2-room-1-9,room-1-9), move(room-1-9,room-1-8), move(room-1-8,room-1-7), move(room-1-7,room-1-6), move(room-1-6,room-1-3), move(room-1-3,room-1-4), move(room-1-4,room-1-5), move(room-1-5,d3-room-1-5)⟩

Utterance: go forward and turn 90 degrees
Reaction: ⟨move(d3-room-1-5,d3-room-2), move(d3-room-2,room-2)⟩

Utterance: go into the room on the right
Reaction: ⟨move(room-2,d6-room-2), move(d6-room-2,a2-d6-room-3), move(a2-d6-room-3,room-3)⟩

Utterance: push the green button to the left of the red button
Reaction: ⟨move(room-3,b6-room-3), manipulate-stateless(b6), move(b6-room-3,room-3)⟩

Utterance: go into the room on your right
Reaction: ⟨move(room-3,d11-room-3), move(d11-room-3,d11-room-7), move(d11-room-7,room-7)⟩

Utterance: turn 90 degrees right and push the red button
Reaction: ⟨move(room-7,b11-room-7), manipulate(b11), move(b11-room-7,room-7)⟩

Utterance: on your right, push the yellow button
Reaction: ⟨move(room-7,b10-room-7), manipulate-stateless(b10), move(b10-room-7,room-7)⟩

Utterance: turn 180 degrees and push the red button next to the plant
Reaction: ⟨move(room-7,b12-room-7), manipulate-stateless(b12), move(b12-room-7,room-7)⟩

Utterance: turn 180 degrees and push the blue button in the middle of the yellow and blue button
Reaction: ⟨move(room-7,b8-b9-room-7), manipulate-stateless(b9), move(b8-b9-room-7,room-7)⟩

Utterance: turn 90 degrees left
Reaction: ⟨⟩

Utterance: go into the room on the right
Reaction: ⟨move(room-7,d10-room-7), move(d10-room-7,d10-room-6), move(d10-room-6,room-6)⟩

Utterance: turn right and proceed down the room
Reaction: ⟨⟩

Utterance: push the red button next to the blue button on your right
Reaction: ⟨move(room-6,b13-b14-room-6), manipulate(b14), move(b13-b14-room-6,room-6)⟩

Utterance: turn left 120 degrees left
Reaction: ⟨⟩

Utterance: and walk through the hall
Reaction: ⟨move(room-6,d9-room-6), move(d9-room-6,d9-room-5), move(d9-room-5,room-5)⟩

Optimising Natural Language Generation Decision Making For Situated Dialogue

Nina Dethlefs
Department of Linguistics,
University of Bremen
dethlefs@uni-bremen.de

Heriberto Cuayáhuitl
German Research Centre
for Artificial Intelligence (DFKI)
heriberto.cuayahuitl@dfki.de

Jette Viethen
Centre for Language Technology
acquarie University
jviethen@ics.mq.edu.au

Abstract

Natural language generators are faced with a multitude of different decisions during their generation process. We address the joint optimisation of navigation strategies and referring expressions in a situated setting with respect to task success and human-likeness. To this end, we present a novel, comprehensive framework that combines supervised learning, Hierarchical Reinforcement Learning and a hierarchical Information State. A human evaluation shows that our learnt instructions are rated similar to human instructions, and significantly better than the supervised learning baseline.

1 Introduction

Natural Language Generation (NLG) systems are typically faced with a multitude of decisions during their generation process due to nondeterminacy between a semantic input to a generator and its realised output. This is especially true in situated settings, where sudden changes of context can occur at anytime. Sources of uncertainty include (a) the situational context, such as visible objects, or task complexity, (b) the user, including their behaviour and reactions, and (c) the dialogue history, including shared knowledge or patterns of linguistic consistency (Halliday and Hasan, 1976) and alignment (Pickering and Garrod, 2004).

Previous work on context-sensitive generation in situated domains includes Stoia et al. (2006) and Garoufi and Koller (2010). Stoia et al. present a supervised learning approach for situated referring expression generation (REG). Garoufi and Koller use techniques from AI planning for the combined generation of navigation instructions and referring expressions (RE). More generally, the NLG problem of non-deterministic decision making has been addressed from many different angles, including PENMAN-style choosers (Mann and Matthiessen, 1983), corpus-based statistical knowledge (Langkilde and Knight, 1998), tree-based stochastic models (Bangalore and Rambow, 2000), maximum entropy-based ranking (Ratnaparkhi, 2000), combinatorial pattern discovery (Duboue and McKeown, 2001), instance-based ranking (Varges, 2003), chart generation (White, 2004), planning (Koller and Stone, 2007), or probabilistic generation spaces (Belz, 2008) to name just a few.

More recently, there have been several approaches towards using Reinforcement Learning (RL) (Rieser et al., 2010; Janarthanam and Lemon, 2010) or Hierarchical Reinforcement Learning (HRL) (Dethlefs and Cuayáhuitl, 2010) for NLG decision making. All of these approaches have demonstrated that HRL/RL offers a powerful mechanism for learning generation policies in the absence of complete knowledge about the environment or the user. It overcomes the need for large amounts of handcrafted knowledge or data in rule-based or supervised learning accounts. On the other hand, RL can have difficulties to find an optimal policy in a large search space, and is therefore often limited to small-scale applications. Pruning the search space of a learning agent by including prior knowledge is therefore attractive, since it finds solutions faster, reduces computational demands, incorporates expert knowledge, and scales to complex problems. Sug-

Proceedings of the SIGDIAL 2011: the 12th Annual Meeting of the Special Interest Group on Discourse and Dialogue, pages 78–87,
Portland, Oregon, June 17-18, 2011. ©2011 Association for Computational Linguistics

gestions to use such prior knowledge include Litman et al. (2000) and Singh et al. (2002), who hand-craft rules of prior knowledge obvious to the system designer. Cuayáhuitl (2009) suggests using Hierarchical Abstract Machines to partially pre-specify dialogue strategies, and Heeman (2007) uses a combination of RL and Information State (IS) to also pre-specify dialogue strategies. Williams (2008) presents an approach of combining Partially-Observable Markov Decision Processes with conventional dialogue systems. The Information State approach is well-established in dialogue management (e.g., Bohlin et al. (1999) and Larsson and Traum (2000)). It allows the system designer to specify dialogue strategies in a principled and systematic way. A disadvantage is that random design decisions need to be made in cases where the best action, or sequence of actions, is not obvious.

The contribution of this paper consists in a comprehensive account of constrained Hierarchical Reinforcement Learning through a combination with a hierarchical Information State (HIS), which is informed by prior knowledge induced from decision trees. We apply our framework to the generation of navigation strategies and referring expressions in a situated setting, jointly optimised for task success and linguistic consistency. An evaluation shows that humans prefer our learnt instructions to the supervised learning-based instructions, and rate them equal to human instructions. Simulation-based results show that our semi-learnt approach learns more quickly than the fully-learnt baseline, which makes it suitable for large and complex problems. Our approach differs from Heeman's in that we transfer it to NLG and to a hierarchical setting. Although Heeman was able to show that his combined approach learns more quickly than pure RL, it is limited to small-scale systems. Our 'divide-and-conquer' approach, on the other hand, scales up to large search spaces and allows us to address complex problems.

2 The Generation Tasks

2.1 The GIVE-2 Domain

Our domain is the generation of navigation instructions and referring expressions in a virtual 3D world in the GIVE scenario (Koller et al., 2010). In this task, two people engage in a 'treasure hunt', where an instruction giver (IG) navigates an instruction follower (IF) through the world, pressing a sequence of buttons and completing the task by obtaining a trophy. Pairs take part in three dialogues (in three different worlds); after the first dialogue, they switch roles. The GIVE-2 corpus (Gargett et al., 2010) provides transcripts of such dialogues in English and German. For this paper, we complemented the English dialogues of the corpus with a set of semantic annotations.[1] The feature set is organised in five groups (Table 1). The first two groups cover manipulation instructions (i.e., instructions to press a button), including distractors[2] and landmarks (Gargett et al., 2010). The third group describes high- and low-level navigation, the fourth group describes the user. The fifth group finally contains grammatical information.

2.2 Navigation and Manipulation Instructions

Navigation instructions can take many forms, even for the same route. For example, a way to another room can be described as 'go to the room with the lamp', 'go left and through the door', or 'turn 90 degrees, left, straight'. Choosing among these variants is a highly context- and speaker-dependent task. Figure 1 shows the six user strategies we identified from the corpus based on an analysis of the combination of navigation level (*'high'* vs. *'low'*) and content (*'destination'*, *'direction'*, *'orientation'*, *'path'*, *'straight'*). User models are based on the navigation level and content decisions made in a sequence of instructions, so that different sequences, with a certain distribution, lead to different user model classifications. The proportions are shown in Figure 1. We found that 75% of all speakers use the same strategy in consecutive rounds/games. 62.5% of pairs are consistent over all three dialogues, indicating inter-speaker alignment. These high measures of human consistency suggest that this phenomenon is worth modelling in a learning agent, and therefore provides the motivation of including linguistic consistency in our agent's behaviour. Manipulation instructions were treated as an REG task, which needs to be sensitive to the properties of the referent and distractors (e.g, size, colour, or spatial relation

[1]The annotations are available on request.

[2]Distractors are objects of the same type as the referent.

ID	Feature	Type	Description
f_1	absolute_property(referent)	*boolean*	Is the colour of the referent mentioned?
f_2	absolute_property(distractor)	*boolean*	Is the colour of the distractor mentioned?
f_3	discriminative_colour(referent)	*boolean*	Is the colour of the referent discriminating?
f_4	discriminative_colour(distractor)	*boolean*	Is the colour of the distractor discriminating?
f_5	mention(distractor)	*boolean*	Is a distractor mentioned?
f_6	first_mention(referent)	*boolean*	Is this the first reference to the referent?
f_7	mention(macro_landmark)	*boolean*	Is a macro (non-movable) landmark mentioned?
f_8	mention(micro_landmark)	*boolean*	Is a micro (movable) landmark mentioned?
f_9	num(distractors)	*integer*	How many distractors are present?
f_{10}	num(micro_landmarks)	*integer*	How many micro landmarks are present?
f_{11}	spatial_rel(referent,obj)	*string*	Which spatial relation(s) are used in the RE?
f_{12}	taxonomic_property(referent)	*boolean*	Is the type of the distractor mentioned?
f_{13}	within_field_of_vision(referent)	*boolean*	Is the referent within the user's field of vision?
f_{14}	mention(colour, lm)	*boolean*	Is the colour of a macro- / micro lm mentioned?
f_{15}	mention(size, lm)	*boolean*	Is the size of a macro- / micro lm mentioned?
f_{16}	abstractness(nav_instruction)	*string*	Is the instruction *explicit* or *implicit*?
f_{17}	content(nav_instruction)	*string*	Vals: *destination, direction, orientation, path, straight*
f_{18}	level(nav_instruction)	*string*	Is the instruction *high-* or *low-level*?
f_{19}	position(user)	*string*	Is the user *on_track* or *off_track*?
f_{20}	reaction(user)	*string*	Vals: *take_action, take_wrong_action, wait, req_help*
f_{21}	type(user)	*string*	Vals: *likes_waiting, likes_exploring, in_between*
f_{22}	waits(user)	*boolean*	Is the user waiting for the next instruction?
f_{23}	model(user)	*string*	User model/navig. strategy used (cf. Fig.1)?
f_{24}	actor(instruction)	*boolean*	Is the actor of the instruction inserted?
f_{25}	mood(instruction)	*boolean*	Is the mood of the instruction inserted?
f_{26}	process(instruction)	*boolean*	Is the process of the instruction inserted?
f_{27}	locational_phrase(instruction)	*boolean*	Is the loc. phrase (path, straight, etc.) inserted?

Table 1: *Corpus annotation features that were used as knowledge of the learning agent and the Information State. Features are presented in groups, describing the properties of referents in the environment ($f_1...f_{13}$) and their distractors ($f_{14}...f_{15}$), features of high- and low-level navigation ($f_{16}...f_{18}$), the user ($f_{19}...f_{23}$), and grammatical information about constituents ($f_{24}...f_{27}$).*

with respect to the referent) to be natural and distinguishing. We also considered the visual salience of objects, and the type of spatial relation involved, since recent studies indicate the potential relevance of these features (Viethen and Dale, 2008). Given these observations, we aim to optimise the **task success** and **linguistic consistency** of instructions. Task success is measured from user reactions after each instruction (Section 5.1). Linguistic consistency is achieved by rewarding the agent for generating instructions that belong to the same user model as the previous one. The agent has the same probability for choosing any pattern, but is then rewarded for consistency. Table 3 (in Section 5.2) presents an example dialogue generated by our system.

3 Constrained Hierarchical Reinforcement Learning for NLG

3.1 Hierarchical Reinforcement Learning

Our idea of *language generation as an optimisation problem* is as follows: given a set of generation states, a set of actions, and an objective reward function, an optimal generation strategy maximises the objective function by choosing the actions leading to the highest reward for every reached state. Such states describe the system's knowledge about

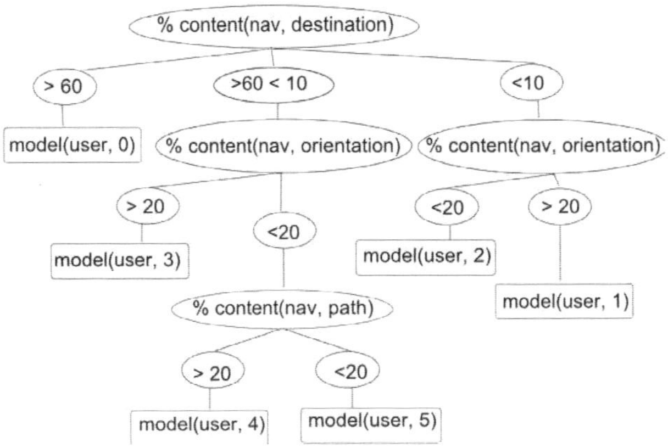

Figure 1: *Decision tree for the classification of user models (UM) defined by the use of navigation level and content. UM 0=high-level, UM 1=low-level (LL), UM 2=orientation-based LL, UM 3=orientation-based mixture (M), UM 4=path-based M, UM 5=pure M.*

the generation task (e.g. navigation strategy, or referring expressions). The action set describes the system's capabilities (e.g. *'use high level navigation strategy'*, *'mention colour of referent'*, etc.). The reward function assigns a numeric value for each action taken. In this way, language generation can be seen as a finite sequence of states, actions and rewards $\{s_0, a_0, r_1, s_1, a_1, ..., r_{t-1}, s_t\}$, where the goal is to find an optimal strategy automatically. To do this we use RL with a divide-and-conquer approach in order to optimise a hierarchy of generation policies rather than a single policy. The hierarchy of RL agents consists of L levels and N models per level, denoted as M^i_j, where $j \in \{0, ..., N-1\}$ and $i \in \{0, ..., L-1\}$. Each agent of the hierarchy is defined as a Semi-Markov Decision Process (SMDP) consisting of a 4-tuple $< S^i_j, A^i_j, T^i_j, R^i_j >$. S^i_j is a set of states, A^i_j is a set of actions, T^i_j is a transition function that determines the next state s' from the current state s and the performed action a, and R^i_j is a reward function that specifies the reward that an agent receives for taking an action a in state s lasting τ time steps. The random variable τ represents the number of time steps the agent takes to complete a subtask. Actions can be either primitive or composite. The former yield single rewards, the latter correspond to SMDPs and yield cumulative discounted rewards. The goal of each SMDP is to find an optimal policy that maximises the reward for each visited state, according to $\pi^{*i}_j(s) = \arg\max_{a \in A^i_j} Q^{*i}_j(s, a)$, where $Q^{*i}_j(s, a)$ specifies the expected cumulative reward for executing action a in state s and then following policy π^{*i}_j. We use HSMQ-Learning (Dietterich, 1999) for learning a hierarchy of generation policies. This hierarchical approach has been applied successfully to dialogue strategy learning by Cuayáhuitl et al. (2010).

3.2 Information State

The notion of an Information State has traditionally been applied to dialogue, where it encodes all information relevant to the current state of the dialogue. This includes, for example, the context of the interaction, participants and their beliefs, and the status of grounding. An IS consists of a set of *informational components*, encoding the information of the dialogue, *formal representations* of these components, a set of *dialogue moves* leading to the update of the IS, a set of *update rules* which govern the update, and finally an *update strategy*, which specifies which update rule to apply in case more than one applies (Larsson and Traum (2000), p. 2-3). In this paper, we apply the theory of IS to language generation. For this purpose we define the informational components of an IS to represent the (situational and linguistic) knowledge of the generator (Section 4.2). Update rules are triggered by generator actions, such as the decision to insert a new constituent into the current logical form, or the decision to prefer one word order sequence over another. We use the DIPPER toolkit (Bos et al., 2003)[3] for our implementation of the IS.

3.3 Combining Hierarchical Reinforcement Learning and Information State

Previous work has suggested the HSMQ-Learning algorithm for optimizing text generation strategies (Dethlefs and Cuayáhuitl, 2010). Because such an algorithm uses all available actions in each state, an important extension is to constrain the actions available with some prior expert knowledge, aiming to combine behaviour specified by human designers and behaviour automatically inferred by reinforcement learning agents. To that end, we sug-

[3]http://www.ltg.ed.ac.uk/dipper

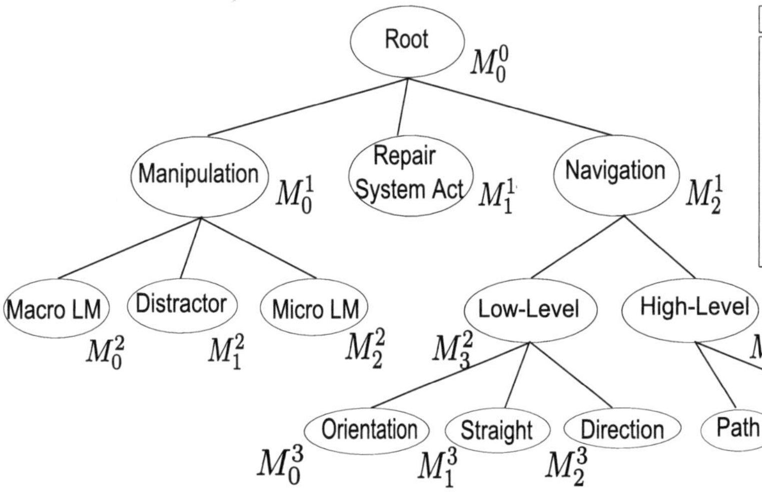

Model	State variables (features)
M_0^0	$f_{19}...f_{22}$
M_0^1	$f_1...f_{10}$, $f_{12}...f_{13}$, $f_{19}...f_{20}$, f_{22}
M_1^1	$f_{16}...f_{22}$
M_2^1	$f_{17}...f_{23}$
M_0^2	f_7, $f_1 1$, $f_{13}...f_{15}$
M_1^2	$f_1...f_5$, f_{11}, f_{13}
M_2^2	f_8, f_{11}, f_{13}, f_{20} ,f_{22}
M_3^2, M_4^2	f_{16}, f_{21}, f_{20} ,$f_{22}...f_{23}$
$M_0^3...M_4^3$	$f_{24}...f_{27}$

Figure 2: (Left:) Hierarchy of learning agents executed from top to bottom for generating instructions. (Right:) State representations for the agents shown in the hierarchy on the left. The features $f_1...f_{27}$ refer back to the features used in the annotation given in the first column of Table 1. Note that agents can share information across levels.

gest combining the Information State approach with hierarchical reinforcement learning. We therefore re-define the characterisation of each Semi-Markov Decision Process (SMDP) in the hierarchy as a 5-tuple model $M_j^i =< S_j^i, A_j^i, T_j^i, R_j^i, I_j^i >$, where S_j^i, A_j^i, T_j^i and R_j^i are as before, and the additional element I_j^i is an Information State used as knowledge base and rule-based decision maker. In this extended model, action selection is based on a constrained set of actions provided by the IS update rules. We assume that the names of update rules in I_j^i represent the agent actions A_j^i. The goal of each SMDP is then to find an optimal policy that maximises the reward for each visited state, according to $\pi^{*i}_j(s) = \arg\max_{a \in A_j^i \cap I_j^i} Q^{*i}_j(s,a)$, where $Q_j^{*i}(s,a)$ specifies the expected cumulative reward for executing constrained action a in state s and then following π^{*i}_j thereafter. For learning such policies we use a modified version of HSMQ-Learning. This algorithm receives subtask M_j^i and Information State I_j^i used to initialise state s, performs similarly to Q-Learning for primitive actions, but for composite actions it invokes recursively with a child subtask. In contrast to HSMQ-Learning, this algorithm chooses actions from a subset derived by applying the IS update rules to the current state of the world. When the subtask is completed, it returns a cumulative reward $r_{t+\tau}$, and continues its execution until finding a goal state for the root subtask. This process iterates until convergence occurs to optimal context-independent policies, as in HSMQ-Learning.

4 Experimental Setting

4.1 Hierarchy of Agents

Figure 2 shows a (hand-crafted) hierarchy of learning agents for navigating and acting in a situated environment. Each of these agents represents an individual generation task. Model M_0^0 is the root agent and is responsible for ensuring that a set of navigation instructions guide the user to the next referent, where an RE is generated. Model M_0^1 is responsible for the generation of the RE that best describes an intended referent. Subtasks M_0^2 ... M_2^2 realise surface forms of possible distractors, or macro- / micro landmarks. Model M_2^1 is responsible for the generation of navigation instructions which smoothly fit into the linguistic consistency pattern chosen. Part of this task is choosing between a low-level (model M_3^2) and a high-level (model M_4^2) instruction. Subtasks $M_0^3...M_4^3$ realise the actual instructions, destination, direction, orientation, path, and 'straight', respectively.[4] Finally, model M_1^1 can repair previous system utterances.

[4]Note that navigation instructions and REs correspond to sequences of actions, not to a single one.

Model(s)	Actions
M_0^0	navigation, manipulation, confirmation, stop, repair_system_act, repair_no_system_act
M_0^1	insert_distractor, insert_no_distractor, insert_no_absolute_property, insert_micro_relatum, insert_macro_relatum
	insert_no_taxonomic_property, insert_absolute_property, insert_no_macro_relatum, insert_taxonomic_property
M_2^1	choose_high_level, choose_low_level, get_route, choose_easy_route, choose_short_route
M_0^2... M_2^2	exp_head, exp_no_head, insert_colour, insert_no_colour, insert_size, insert_no_size, exp_spatial_relation
M_3^2	choose_explicit_abstractness, choose_implicit_abstractness, destination_instruction, path_instruction
M_4^2	choose_explicit_abstractness, choose_implicit_abstractness, direction_instr, orientation_instr, straight_instr
M_0^3... M_4^3	exp_actor, exp_no_actor, exp_mood, exp_loc_phrase, exp_no_loc_phrase, exp_process, exp_no_process

Table 2: *Action set of the learning agents and Information States.*

4.2 State and Action Sets

The HRL agent's knowledge base consists of all situational and linguistic knowledge the agent needs for decision making. Figure 2 shows the hierarchy of learning agents together with the knowledge base of the learning agent with respect to the semantic features shown in Table 1 that were used for the annotation of the GIVE-2 corpus dialogues. The first column of the table in Figure 2 indicates the respective model, also referred to as agent, or subtask, and the second column refers to the knowledge variable it uses (in the form of the feature index given in the first column of Table 1). In the agent, boolean values and strings were represented as integers. The HIS shares all information of the learning agent, but has an additional set of relational feature-value pairs for each slot. For example, if the agent knows that the slot $content(nav\_instruction)$ has value 1 (meaning 'filled'), the HIS knows also which value it was filled with, such as $path$. Such additional knowledge is required for the supervised learning baseline (Section 5). The action set of the hierarchical learning agent and the hierarchical information state is given in Table 2. The state-action space size of a flat learning agent would be $|S \times A| = 10^{11}$, the hierarchical setting has a state-action space size of 2.4×10^7. The average state-action space size of all subtasks is $|S \times A|/14 = 1.7 \times 10^7$. Generation actions can be primitive or composite. While the former correspond to single generation decisions, the latter represent separate generation subtasks (Fig. 2).

4.3 Prior Knowledge

Prior knowledge can include decisions obvious to the system designer, expert knowledge, or general intuitions. In our case, we use a supervised learning approach to induce prior knowledge into our HRL agent. We trained decision trees on our annotated corpus data using Weka's (Witten and Frank, 2005) J48 decision tree classifer. A separate tree was trained for each semantic attribute (cf. Table 1). The obtained decision trees represent our supervised learning baseline. They achieved an accuracy of 91% in a ten-fold cross-validation. For our semi-learnt combination of HRL and HIS, we performed a manual analysis of the resulting rules to assess their impact on a learning agent.[5] In the end, the following rules were used to constrain the agent's behaviour: (1) In REs, always use a referent's colour, except in cases of repair when colour is not discriminating; (2) mention a distractor or micro landmark, if the colour of the referent is not discriminating; (3) in navigation, always make orientation instructions explicit. All remaining behaviour was subject to learning.

4.4 Reward Function

We use the following reward function to train the hierarchy of policies of our HRL agent. It aims to reduce discourse length at maximal task success[6] using a consistent navigation strategy.

$$R = \begin{cases} 0 & \text{for} \quad \text{reaching the goal state} \\ \text{-2} & \text{for} \quad \text{an already invoked subtask} \\ +1 & \text{for} \quad \text{generating instruction } u \text{ consistent with instruction } u_{-1} \\ \text{-1} & \quad\quad\quad \text{otherwise.} \end{cases}$$

[5]We excluded rules that always choose the same value, since they would work against our aim of generating consistent, but variable instructions.

[6]Task success is addressed by that the user has to 'accept' each instruction for a state transition.

The third reward that encourages consistency of instructions rewards a sequence of actions that allow the last generated instruction to be classified as belonging to the same navigation strategy/user model as the previously generated instruction (cf. 2.2).

5 Experiments and Results

5.1 The Simulated Environment

The simulated environment contains two kinds of uncertainties: (1) uncertainty regarding the state of the environment, and (2) uncertainty concerning the user's reaction to a system utterance. The first aspect is represented by a set of contextual variables describing the environment, [7] and user behaviour.[8] Altogether, this leads to 115 thousand different contextual configurations, which are estimated from data (cf. Section 2.1). The uncertainty regarding the user's reaction to an utterance is represented by a Naive Bayes classifier, which is passed a set of contextual features describing the situation, mapped with a set of semantic features describing the utterance.[9] From these data, the classifier specifies the most likely user reaction (after each system act) of *perform_desired_action, perform_undesired_action, wait* and *request_help*.[10] The classifier was trained on the annotated data and reached an accuracy of 82% in a ten-fold cross validation.

5.2 Learnt Policies

With respect to REs, the **fully-learnt policy** (only HRL) uses colour when it is discriminating, and a distractor or micro landmark otherwise. The **semi-learnt policy** (HRL with HIS) behaves as defined in Section 4.3. The **supervised learning policy** (only HIS) uses the rules learnt by the decision trees. Both learnt policies learn to maximise task success, and to generate consistent navigation strategies.[11] The supervised learning policy generates successful instructions from the start. Note that we are not actually learning dialogue strategies, but rather generation strategies using dialogue features. Therefore the described policies, fully-learnt, semi-learnt and supervised-learning, exclusively guide the system's behaviour in the interaction with the simulated user. An example dialogue is shown in Table 3. We can observe that the agent starts using a low level navigation strategy, and then switches to high level. When the user gets confused, the system temporarily switches back to low level. For referring expressions, it first attempts to locate the referent by reference to a distractor, and then repairs by using a micro landmark. The surface forms of instructions were realised from templates, since the NLG system so far only generates a sequence of content selection decisions. We address surface realisation in Dethlefs and Cuayáhuitl (2011).

[7] previous system act, route length, route status (known/unknown), objects within vision, objects within dialogue history, number of instructions, alignment(proportion)

[8] previous user reaction, user position, user waiting(true/false), user type(explorative/hesitant/medium)

[9] navigation level(high / low), abstractness(implicit / explicit), repair(yes / no), instruction type(destination / direction / orientation / path / straight)

[10] User reactions measure the system's task success.

[11] They thereby also learn to adapt their semantic choices to those most frequently made by humans.

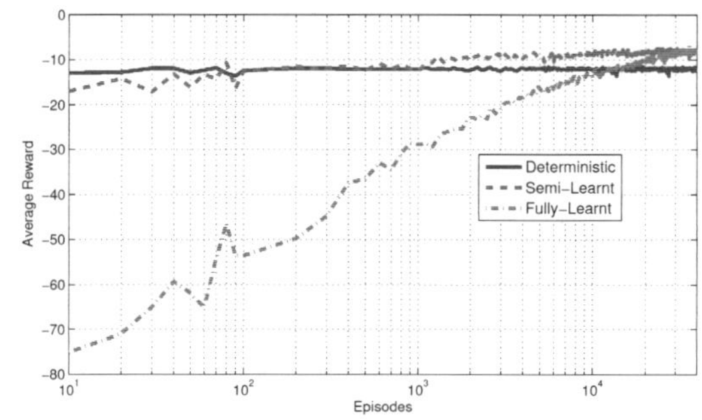

Figure 3: Comparison of fully-learnt, semi-learnt, and supervised learning (deterministic) behaviours.

We compared our semi-learnt policy against a fully-learnt, and a supervised learning baseline. All policies were trained for 40 thousand episodes. For training, the step-size parameter α, which indicates the learning rate, was initiated with 1 and then reduced over time by $\alpha = \frac{1}{1+t}$, where t is the time step. The discount rate γ, which indicates the relevance of future rewards in relation to immediate rewards, was set to 0.99, and the probability of a random action ϵ was 0.01. See (Sutton and Barto, 1998) for details on these parameters.

5.3 Comparison of Policies

Figure 3 compares the rewards averaged over 10 runs. In terms of **learning speed**, we can see that

Agent	Policy	Action (composite in italics)	Utterance
Usr		*request_route*	How do I get to the trophy?
Sys	π_0^0, π_2^1	*root, navigation*, dontRepair, orientation	
	π_3^2, π_0^3	*low level navigation*, add direction+degrees	First, turn 90 degrees left.
	π_3^2, π_1^3	*low level navigation*, 'straight'	Then go straight ahead.
Usr			*perform_desired_action*
Sys	π_0^0	confirmation	OK.
	$\pi_4^2, \pi_4^3, \pi_2^3$	*high level navigation*, destination, direction,	
	$\pi_4^2, \pi_4^3, \pi_2^3$	addLocation	Turn left at the end of the hallway.
Usr			*wait*
Sys	π_1^1	*repair system act*, change navigation strategy	
	π_3^2, π_2^3	*low level navigation*, direction	Turn right
	π_4^2, π_3^3	*high level navigation*, path	and go down the hallway.
Usr			*perform_desired_action*
Sys	π_3^2, π_2^3	*low level navigation*, direction	Now turn left.
Usr			*perform_desired_action*
Sys	π_0^0	confirmation	OK.
	π_4^2, π_4^3	*high level navigation*, destination,	
	π_4^2, π_4^3	addLocation	Enter to the room in front of you.
Usr			*perform_desired_action*
Sys	π_0^1, π_1^2	*manipulation*, use colour, use distractor	Press the red button beside the blue.
Usr			*request_help*
Sys	π_1^1	*repair system act*, change granularity	
	π_4^2, π_0^1	*high level navigation, manipulation*	
	π_4^3, π_2^2	destination, use colour, use micro landmark	Go to the red button beside the chair.
Usr			*perform_desired_action*
Sys	π_0^1	*manipulation*	Press it.
Usr			*perform_desired_action*
Sys	π_0^0	confirmation	Well done.

Table 3: Sample dialogue in the GIVE-2 scenario showing the dynamics of generation policies. See Figure 2 for the corresponding hierarchy models, and Table 2 for the action set. See Section 5.2 for an explantation of the dialogue.

while the semi-learnt behaviour is able to follow a near-optimal policy from the beginning, the fully-learnt policy takes about 40 thousand episodes to reach the same performance. In terms of simulated **task success**, we see that while the supervised learning behaviour follows a good policy from the start, it is eventually beaten by the learnt policies.

5.4 Human Evaluation Study

We asked 11 participants[12] to rate altogether 132 sets of instructions, where each set contained a spatial graphical scene containing a person, mapped with one human, one learnt, and one supervised learning instruction. Instructions consisted of a navigation instruction followed by a referring expression. Subjects were asked to rate instructions on a 1-5 Likert scale (where 5 is the best) for their helpfulness on guiding the displayed person from its origin to pressing the intended button. We selected six different scenarios for the evaluation: (a) only one button is present, (b) two buttons are present, the referent and a distractor of the same colour as the referent, (c) two buttons are present, the referent and a distractor of a different colour than the referent, (d) one micro landmark is present and one distractor of the same colour as the referent, (e) one micro landmark is present and one distractor of a different colour than the referent. All scenarios oc-

[12] 6 female, 5 male with an age average of 26.4.

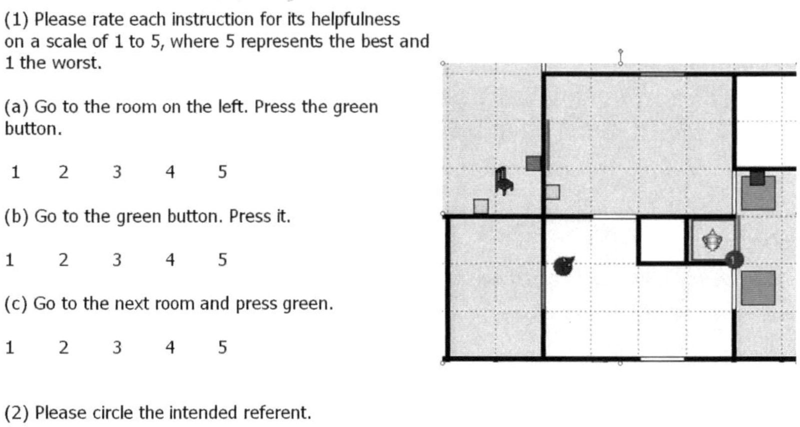

Figure 4: Example scenario of the human evaluation study.

curred twice in each evaluation sheet, their specific instances were drawn from the GIVE-2 corpus at random. Scenes and instructions were presented in a randomised order. Figure 4 presents an example evaluation scene. Finally, we asked subjects to circle the object they thought was the intended referent. Subjects rated the human instructions with an average of 3.82, the learnt instructions with an average of 3.55, and the supervised learning instructions with an average of 2.39. The difference between human and learnt is not significant. The difference between learnt and supervised learning is significant at $p < 0.003$, and the difference between human and supervised learning is significant at $p < 0.0002$. In 96% of all cases, users were able to identify the intended referent.

6 Conclusion and Discussion

We have presented a combination of HRL with a hierarchical IS, which was informed by prior knowledge from decision trees. Such a combined framework has the advantage that it allows us to systematically pre-specify (obvious) generation strategies, and thereby find solutions faster, reduce computational demands, scale to complex domains, and incorporate expert knowledge. By applying HRL to the remaining (non-obvious) action set, we are able to learn a flexible, generalisable NLG policy, which will take the best action even under uncertainty. As an application of our approach and its generalisability across domains, we have presented the joint optimisation of two separate NLG tasks, navigation instructions and referring expressions, in situated dialogue under the aspects of task success and linguistic consistency. Based on an evaluation in a simulated environment estimated from data, we showed that our semi-learnt behaviour outperformed a fully-learnt baseline in terms of learning speed, and a supervised learning baseline in terms of average rewards. Human judges rated our instructions significantly better than the supervised learning instructions, and close to human quality. The study revealed a task success rate of 96%. Future work can transfer our approach to different applications to confirm its benefits, and induce the agent's reward function from data to test in a more realistic setting.

Acknowledgments

Thanks to the German Research Foundation DFG and the Transregional Collaborative Research Centre SFB/TR8 'Spatial Cognition' and the EU-FP7 project ALIZ-E (ICT-248116) for partial support of this work. Also, thanks to John Bateman for comments on an earlier draft of this paper.

References

Srinivas Bangalore and Owen Rambow. 2000. Exploiting a probabilistic hierarchical model for generation. In *Proceedings of the 18th conference on Computational linguistics - Volume 1*, pages 42–48.

Anja Belz. 2008. Automatic generation of weather forecast texts using comprehensive probabilistic generation-space models. *Natural Language Engineering*, 1:1–26.

Peter Bohlin, Robin Cooper, Elisabet Engdahl, and Staffan Larsson. 1999. Information states and dialogue move engines. In *IJCAI-99 Workshop on Knowledge and Reasoning in Practical Dialogue Systems*.

Johan Bos, Ewan Klein, Oliver Lemon, and Tetsushi Oka. 2003. DIPPER: Description and Formalisation of an Information-State Update Dialogue System Architecture. In *4th SIGDial Workshop on Discourse and Dialogue*, pages 115–124.

Heriberto Cuayáhuitl, Steve Renals, Oliver Lemon, and Hiroshi Shimodaira. 2010. Evaluation of a hierarchical reinforcement learning spoken dialogue system. *Computer Speech and Language*, 24(2):395–429.

Heriberto Cuayáhuitl. 2009. *Hierarchical Reinforcement Learning for Spoken Dialogue Systems*. Ph.D. thesis, School of Informatics, University of Edinburgh.

Nina Dethlefs and Heriberto Cuayáhuitl. 2010. Hierarchical Reinforcement Learning for Adaptive Text Generation. *Proceedings of INLG '10*.

Nina Dethlefs and Heriberto Cuayáhuitl. 2011. Hierarchical Reinforcement Learning and Hidden Markov Models for Task-Oriented Natural Language Generation. In *Proceedings of ACL-HLT 2011, Portland, OR*.

Thomas G. Dietterich. 1999. Hierarchical reinforcement learning with the maxq value function decomposition. *Journal of Artificial Intelligence Research*, 13:227–303.

Pablo A. Duboue and Kathleen R. McKeown. 2001. Empirically estimating order constraints for content planning in generation. In *ACL '01*, pages 172–179.

Andrew Gargett, Konstantina Garoufi, Alexander Koller, and Kristina Striegnitz. 2010. The give-2 corpus of giving instructions in virtual environments. In *LREC*.

Konstantina Garoufi and Alexander Koller. 2010. Automated planning for situated natural language generation. In *Proceedings of the 48th Annual Meeting of the Association for Computational Linguistics*, pages 1573–1582, July.

Michael A. K. Halliday and Ruqaiya Hasan. 1976. *Cohesion in English*. Longman, London.

Peter Heeman. 2007. Combining reinforcement learning with information-state update rules. In *Human Technology Conference (HLT)*, pages 268–275.

Srinivasan Janarthanam and Oliver Lemon. 2010. Learning to adapt to unknown users: referring expression generation in spoken dialogue systems. In *ACL '10*, pages 69–78.

Alexander Koller and Matthew Stone. 2007. Sentence generation as planning. In *Proceedings of ACL-07*.

Alexander Koller, Kristina Striegnitz, Donna Byron, Justine Cassell, Robert Dale, Johanna Moore, and Jon Oberlander. 2010. The first challenge on generating instructions in virtual environments. In M. Theune and E. Krahmer, editors, *Empirical Methods on Natural Language Generation*, pages 337–361, Berlin/Heidelberg, Germany. Springer.

Irene Langkilde and Kevin Knight. 1998. Generation that exploits corpus-based statistical knowledge. In *ACL-36*, pages 704–710.

Staffan Larsson and David R. Traum. 2000. Information state and dialogue management in the TRINDI dialogue move engine toolkit. *Nat. Lang. Eng.*, 6(3-4):323–340.

Diane J. Litman, Michael S. Kearns, Satinder Singh, and Marilyn A. Walker. 2000. Automatic optimization of dialogue management. In *Proceedings of the 18th conference on Computational linguistics*, pages 502–508.

William Mann and Christian M I M Matthiessen. 1983. NIGEL: A systemic grammar for text generation. Technical report, ISI/RR-85-105.

Martin J. Pickering and Simon Garrod. 2004. Toward a mechanistc psychology of dialog. *Behavioral and Brain Sciences*, 27.

Adwait Ratnaparkhi. 2000. Trainable methods for surface natural language generation. In *Proceedings of NAACL*, pages 194–201.

Verena Rieser, Oliver Lemon, and Xingkun Liu. 2010. Optimising information presentation for spoken dialogue systems. In *ACL '10*, pages 1009–1018.

Satinder Singh, Diane Litman, Michael Kearns, and Marilyn Walker. 2002. Optimizing Dialogue Management with Reinforcement Learning: Experiments with the NJFun System. *Journal of Artificial Intelligence Research*, 16:105–133.

Laura Stoia, Darla Magdalene Shockley, Donna K. Byron, and Eric Fosler-Lussier. 2006. Noun phrase generation for situated dialogs. In *Proceedings of INLG '06*, pages 81–88.

Richard S Sutton and Andrew G Barto. 1998. *Reinforcement Learning: An Introduction*. MIT Press, Cambridge, MA, USA.

Sebastian Varges. 2003. *Instance-based Natural Language Generation*. Ph.D. thesis, School of Informatics, University of Edinburgh.

Jette Viethen and Robert Dale. 2008. The use of spatial relations in referring expression generation. In *Proceedings of INLG '08*, INLG '08, pages 59–67.

Michael White. 2004. Reining in CCG chart realization. In *In Proc. INLG-04*, pages 182–191.

Jason Williams. 2008. The best of both worlds: Unifying conventional dialog systems and POMDPs. In *Interspeech*, Brisbane.

Ian H. Witten and Eibe Frank. 2005. *Data Mining: Practical Machine Learning Tools and Techniques*. 2. edition.

Regulating Dialogue with Gestures—Towards an Empirically Grounded Simulation with Conversational Agents

Kirsten Bergmann[1,2] **Hannes Rieser**[1] **Stefan Kopp**[1,2]

[1] Collaborative Research Center 673 „Alignment in Communication", Bielefeld University
[2] Center of Excellence „Cognitive Interaction Technology"(CITEC), Bielefeld University

{kbergman,skopp}@TechFak.Uni-Bielefeld.DE
hannes.rieser@Uni-Bielefeld.DE

Abstract

Although not very well investigated, a crucial aspect of gesture use in dialogues is to regulate the organisation of the interaction. People use gestures decisively, for example to indicate that they want someone to take the turn, to 'brush away' what someone else said, or to acknowledge others' contributions. We present first insights from a corpus-based investigation of how gestures are used to regulate dialogue, and we provide first results from an account to capture these phenomena in agent-based communication simulations. By advancing a model for autonomous gesture generation to also cover gesture interpretation, this account enables a full gesture turn exchange cycle of generation, understanding and acceptance/generation in virtual conversational agents.

1 Motivation

Research on gestures must combine empirical, theoretical and simulation methods to investigate form, content and function of gestures in relation to speech. Our work is based on a corpus of multimodal data, the Bielefeld Speech and Gesture Alignment corpus of route-description dialogues (SAGA corpus, Lücking et al. 2010). The point of departure of our research has been work on iconic and deictic gestures over many years. In this paper we focus on a not very well investigated function of gestures which we have repeatedly observed in this corpus, namely, the regulation of dialogue.

Most of current gesture research is oriented towards the semiotics of a Peircean tradition as can for instance be seen from McNeill's "Kendon's continuum" (McNeill 1992, p. 37). As a consequence of this Peircian orientation, gestures have been viewed as single signs interfacing with speech. Going beyond the integration of input/output modalities in *single* speech-gesture compositions (Johnston and Bangalore, 2005), little effort has been spent on the investigation of *sequences* of gestures and speech-gesture composition both within and across speakers (Hahn and Rieser 2010, Rieser 2010). Furthermore, research of gesture meaning was restricted to the contribution of gesture content to propositional content. An exception to this research line has been the work of Bavelas et al. (1992, 1995). It is characterised by two features, a functional perspective on gesture in opposition to purely classificatory and typological ones and an interest to systematically investigate the role of gesture in interaction. In particular, Bavelas et al. (1992) proposed a distinction between 'topic gestures' and 'interactive gestures': Topic gestures depict semantic information directly related to the topic of discourse, while interactive gestures refer to some aspect of the process of conversing with another person. Interactive gestures include *delivery* gestures (e.g. marking information status as new, shared, digression), *citing* gestures (acknowledging others' prior contributions), *seeking* gestures (seeking agreement, or help in finding a word), and *turn coordination* ges-

Proceedings of the SIGDIAL 2011: the 12th Annual Meeting of the Special Interest Group on Discourse and Dialogue, pages 88–97,
Portland, Oregon, June 17-18, 2011.

tures (e.g. taking or giving the turn). Gill et al. (1999) noted similar functions of gesture use, adding body movements to the repertoire of pragmatic acts used in dialogue act theory (e.g. turn-taking, grounding, acknowledgements).

We aim to find out how gestures are related to and help regulate the structure of dialogue. We will call these gestures `discourse gestures´. Relevant research questions in this respect are the following: How can gesture support next speaker selection if this follows regular turn distribution mechanisms such as current speaker selects next? From the dialogues in SAGA we know that averting next speaker's self-selection is of similar importance as handing over the floor to the next speaker. So, how can averting self-selection of other be accomplished gesturally? A still different problem is how gesture is utilised to establish an epistemically transparent, reliable common ground, say a tight world of mutual belief. A precondition for that is how gesture can help to indicate a gesturer's stance to the information he provides. Natural language has words to indicate degrees of confidence in information such as *probably*, *seemingly*, *approximately*, *perhaps, believe, know, guess* etc. Can gestures acquire this function as well?

All these issues can be synopsised as follows: How can gestures↓apart from their manifest contribution to propositional content↓be used to push the dialogue machinery forward? In our research, gesture simulation and theory of speech-gesture integration are developed in tandem. Up to now, both have been tied to occurrences of single gestures and their embedding in dialogue acts. In this paper, we present first steps along both methodological strands to explore the use and function of gesture in dialogue. We start with an empirical perspective on discourse gestures in section 2. In section 3 we briefly describe our gesture simulation model which so far simulates gesture use employing the virtual agent MAX independent of discourse structures. Section 4 analyses a corpus example of a minimal discourse which is regulated mainly by gestures of the two interactants. This provides the basis for our proposed extension of the gesture generation approach to capture the discourse function of gestures as described in section 5. This extension will encompass a novel approach to employ the very generation model used for gesture production, and hence all the heuristic gesture knowledge it captures, also for gesture interpretation in dialogue. Section 6 discusses the difference between pure interactive gestures and discourse gestures and proposes further steps that need to be taken to elucidate how gestures are used as a vehicle for regulating dialogue.

2 Empirical Work on Discourse Gestures

In looking for discourse gestures we started from the rated annotation of 6000 gestures in the SAGA corpus. We managed to annotate and rate about 5000 of them according to traditional criteria using practices and fine-grained gesture morphology like hand-shape and wrist-movement. About 1000 gestures could not be easily subsumed under the traditional gesture types (iconics, deictics, metaphorics, beats). Furthermore, they were observed to correlate with discourse properties such as current speaker's producing his contribution or non-regular interruption by other speaker.

For purposes of the classification of the remaining 1000 gestures we established the following functional working definition: `Discourse gestures´ are gestures tied up with properties or functions of agents' contributions in dialogue such as successfully producing current turn, establishing coherence across different speakers' turns by gestural reference or indicating who will be next speaker.

What did we use for dialogue structure? Being familiar with dialogue models such as SDRT (Asher and Lascarides, 2003), PTT (Poesio and Traum, 1997), and KoS (Ginzburg, 2011) we soon found that these were too restricted to serve descriptive purposes. So we oriented our "classification of dialogue gesture enterprise" on the well known turn taking organisation model of Sacks et al. (1974) and Levinson's (1983) discussion of it. However, it soon turned out that even these approaches were too normative for the SAGA data: This is due to the fact that dialogue participants develop enormous creativity in establishing new rules of content production and of addressing violations of *prima facie* rules.

Rules of turn-taking, for example, are not hard and fast rules, they can be skirted if the need arises, albeit there is a convention that this has to be acknowledged and negotiated. A very clear example of an allowed interruption of an on-going production is a quickly inserted clarification request serving the communicative goals of current speaker and the aims of the dialogue in general. Another

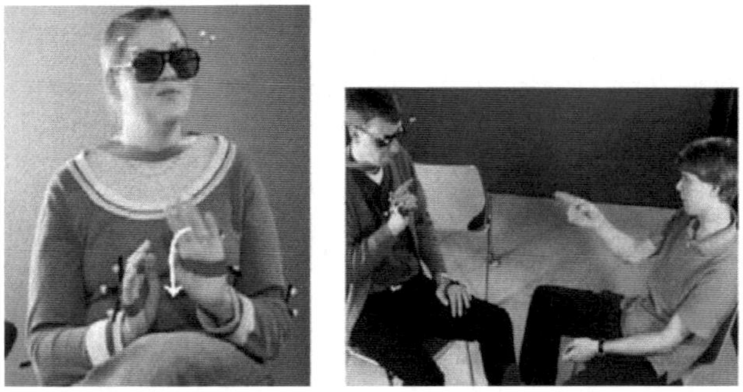

Figure 1: Examples of discourse gestures: the brush-away gesture (left) and situated pointing to the upper part of the interlocutor's torso (right) used for next speaker selection in a "Gricean" sense (see text for explanation).

problem with the Sacks et al. model consists in the following fact: Since its origination many dialogue regularities have been discovered which cannot be easily founded on a phenomenological or observational stratum which is essentially semantics-free. This can for example be seen from the development of the notion of grounding and common ground as originally discussed by Stalnaker (1978), Clark (1996) and others. Nevertheless, grounding (roughly, coming to agree on the meaning of what has been said (see e.g. Traum, 1999; Roque and Traum, 2008; Ginzburg 2011, ch. 4.2 for the options available) generates verbal structure and verbal structure interfaces with gesture. Other examples in this class are acknowledgements or accepts discussed in more detail below.

How did we decide on which distinctions of gesture annotation have to be used for characterising discourse gestures? In other words, how did we conceive of the map between gestures of a certain sort and discourse structures? First of all we observed that two types of discourse gestures emerge from the SAGA data. Some of them come with their own global shape and are close to emblems, (i.e. conveyors of stable meaning like the victory sign). This is true for example of the "brush aside or brush away" gesture shown in Figure 1 (left), indicating a gesturer's assessment of the downrated relevance of information, actions or situations. Discourse gestures of the second class exploit the means of, for instance, referring gestures or iconic gestures. An example of an iconic gesture in this role will be discussed to some extent in section 4. Its simulation will be described in sections 3 and 5.

Here we explain the phenomenon with respect to referring pointing gestures which are easier to figure out (see Figure 1 (right)). Their usage as under focus here is not tied to the information under discussion but to objects in the immediate discourse situation, preferably to the participants of the dialogue. These uses have a Gricean flavour in the following way: Only considerations of relevance and co-occurrence with a turn transition relevance place together indicate that *prima facie* not general reference is at stake but indication of next speaker role. It wouldn't make sense to point to the other person singling her or him out by indexing, because her or his identity is clear and well established through the on-going interaction. Thus we see that a gestural device associated with established morphological features, pointing, acquires a new function, namely indicating the role of next-speaker.

Now both classes of gestures, "brush away" used to indicate informational or other non-relevance and pointing, indicating the role of being next speaker exploit the motor equipment of the hands. For this reason, annotation of discourse gestures can safely be based on the classification schemas we have developed for practices like indexing, shaping or modelling and for the fine-grained motor behaviour of the hands as exhibited by palm orientation, back-of-hand trajectory etc. In work by Hahn & Rieser (2009-2011) the following broad classes of discourse gestures were established. We briefly comment upon these classes of gestures found in the SAGA corpus relevant for dialogue structure and interaction:

- **Managing of own turn**: A speaker may indicate how successful he is in editing out his current production.
- Mechanisms of **next-speaker selection** as proposed in classical CA research, for instance, pointing to the other's torso is often used as a means to indicate next speaker.
- In **grounding acts and feed-back** especially iconic gestures are used to convey propositional content.
- **Clarification requests** to work on contributions: An addressee may indicate the need for a quick interruption using a pointing to demand a clarification. In contrast, a current speaker can ward off the addressee's incipient interruption using a palm-up gesture di-

rected against the intruder thus setting up a "fence".

- **Evidentials for establishing a confidence leve:** There are fairly characteristic gestures indicating the confidence a speaker has in the information he is able to convey.
- **Handling of non-canonical moves by discourse participants**: Interaction sequences consisting of attempts by other speaker to interrupt and to thwart this intention by current speaker or to give way to it show how discourse participants handle non-canonical moves.
- **Assessment of relevance by discourse participants**: Speakers provide an assessment of which information is central and which one they want to consider as subsidiary.
- An **indication of topical information with respect to time, place or objects** is frequently given by pointing or by "placing objects" into the gesture space.

We know that this list is open and could, moreover, depend on the corpus. In this paper the focus will be on grounding acts and feedback (see sections 3-5). The reason is that this way we can provide an extension of existing work on the simulation of gesture production in a fairly direct manner.

3 Simulating Gesture Use: The Generation Perspective

Our starting point to simulate gestural behavior in dialogue is a gesture generation system which is able to simulate speaker-specific use of iconic gestures given (1) a communicative intention, (2) discourse contextual information, and (3) an imagistic representation of the object to be described. Our approach is based on empirical evidence that iconic gesture production in humans is influenced by several factors. Apparently, iconic gestures communicate through iconicity, that is their physical form depicts object features such as shape or spatial properties. Recent findings indicate that a gesture's form is also influenced by a number of contextual constraints such as information structure (see for instance Cassell and Prevost, 1996), or the use of more general gestural representation techniques such as shaping or drawing is decisive.

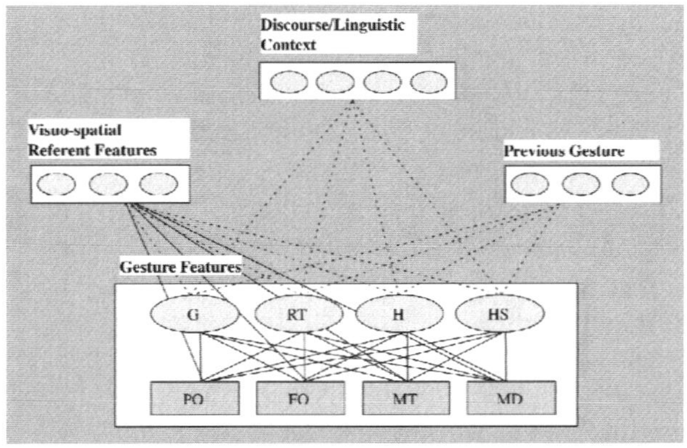

Figure 2: Schema of a gesture generation network in which gesture production choices are considered either probabilistically (chance nodes drawn as ovals) or rule-based (decision nodes drawn as rectangles). Each choice is depending on a number of contextual variables. The links are either learned from speaker-specific corpus data (dotted lines) or defined in a set of if-then rules (solid lines).

In addition, inter-subjective differences in gesturing are pertinent. There is, for example, wide variability in how much individuals gesture when they speak. Similarly, inter-subjective differences are found in preferences for particular representation techniques or low-level morphological features such as handshape or handedness (Bergmann & Kopp, 2009).

To meet the challenge of considering general and individual patterns in gesture use, we have proposed GNetIc, a gesture net specialised for iconic gestures (Bergmann & Kopp, 2009a), in which we model the process of gesture formulation with Bayesian decision networks (BDNs) that supplement standard Bayesian networks by decision nodes. This formalism provides a representation of a finite sequential decision problem, combining probabilistic and rule-based decision-making. Each decision to be made in the formation of an iconic gesture (e.g., whether or not to gesture at all or which representation technique to use) is represented in the network either as a decision node (rule-based) or as a chance node with a specific probability distribution. Factors which contribute to these choices (e.g., visuo-spatial referent features) are taken as input to the model (see Figure 2) The structure of the network as well as local conditional probability tables are learned from the SAGA corpus by means of automated machine learning techniques and supplemented with rule-based decision making. Individual as well as general networks are learned from the SAGA corpus by means of automated machine learning techniques and supplemented with rule-based decision making. So far, three different factors have been incorporated into this model: discourse context, the previously performed gesture, and features of the referent. The latter are extracted from a hierarchical representation called Imagistic Description Trees (IDT), which is designed to cover all decisive visuo-spatial features of objects one finds in iconic gestures (Sowa & Wachsmuth, 2009). Each node in an IDT contains an imagistic description which holds a schema representing the shape of an object or object part. Features extracted from this representation in order to capture the main characteristics of a gesture's referent are whether an object can be decomposed into detailed subparts (whole-part relations), whether it has any symmetrical axes, its main axis, its position in the VR stimulus, and its shape properties extracted on the basis of so called multimodal concepts (see Bergmann & Kopp, 2008).

Analyzing the GNetIc modelling results enabled us to gain novel insights into the production process of iconic gestures: the resulting networks for individual speakers differ in their structure and in their conditional probability distributions, revealing that individual differences are not only present in the overt gestures, but also in the production process they originate from.

The GNetIc model has been extensively evaluated. First, in a prediction-based evaluation, the automatically generated gestures were compared against their empirically observed counterparts, which yielded very promising results (Bergmann & Kopp, 2010). Second, we evaluated the GNetIc models in a perception-based evaluation study with human addressees. Results showed that GNetIc-generated gestures actually helped to increase the perceived quality of object descriptions given by MAX. Moreover, gesturing behaviour generated with individual speaker networks was rated more positively in terms of likeability, competence and human-likeness (Bergmann, Kopp & Eyssel, 2010).

GNetIc gesture formulation has been embedded in a larger production architecture for speech and gesture production. This architecture comprises modules that carry out content planning, formulation, and realisation for speech and gesture separately, but in close and systematic coordination (Bergmann & Kopp, 2009). To illustrate gesture generation on the basis of GNetIc models, consider the following example starting upon the arrival of a message which specifies the communicative intent to describe the landmark townhall with respect to its characteristic properties:

```
lmDescrProperty (townhall-1).
```

Based on this communicative intention, the imagistic description of the involved object gets activated and the agent adopts a spatial perspective towards it from which the object is to be described (see Figure 3). The representation is analyzed for referent features required by the GNetIc model: position, main axis, symmetry, number of subparts, and shape properties. Regarding the latter, a unification of the imagistic townhall-1 representation and a set of underspecified shape property representations (e.g. for „longish", „round" etc.) reveals „U-shaped" as the most salient property to be depicted. All evidence available (referent features, discourse context, previous gesture and linguistic context) is propagated through the network (learned from the data of one particular speaker) resulting in a posterior distribution of probabilities for the values in each chance node.

Figure 3: The townhall in the virtual world (left) and schematic of the corresponding IDT content (right); activated parts are marked.

This way, it is first decided to generate a gesture in the current discourse situation at all, the representation technique is decided to be „drawing", to be realized with both hands and the pointing handshape ASL-G. Next, the model's decision nodes are employed to decide on the palm and back of hand (BoH) orientation as well as movement type and direction: as typical in drawing gestures, the palm is oriented downwards and the BoH away from the speaker's body. These gesture features are combined with a linear movement consisting of two segments per hand (to the right and backwards with the right hand; accordingly mirror-symmetrical with the left hand) to depict the shape of the townhall.

Accompanying speech is generated from selected propositional facts using an NLG engine. Synchrony between speech and gesture follows co-expressivity and is set to hold between the gesture stroke (depicting the U-shape property) and corresponding linguistic element. These values are used to fill the slots of a gesture feature matrix which is transformed into an XML representation to be realized with the virtual agent MAX (see Figure 4).

Figure 4: Specification (left) and realization (right) of an autonomously generated drawing gesture which depicts the U-shaped townhall.

4 Example of a Minimal Discourse

To start with the analysis of how gestures are not only employed to carry referential content but also to regulate dialogue and discourse, we first present a datum from the SAGA corpus showing how the Follower's gesture aligns with the Router's gesture to indicate acknowledgement or accept. The situation is as follows: the Router describes to the Follower that he would approach the town-hall and how it looks to him. A transcription of the initial dialogue passage by the Router and the subsequent crucial speech-gesture annotation, including the Follower, in ELAN looks as displayed in Figure 5 (*placing*, *drawing*, and *shaping* are names of annotated gestural representation techniques).

A short comment on the data might be in order: When introducing the townhall as a U-shaped building, the Router draws the boundary of it, namely a "U". He then goes on to describe how the on-looker apprehends the building. This is accompanied by a forward-oriented direction gesture with both hands, mimicking *into it*. In principle, all the information necessary to identify the townhall from a front perspective is given by then. There is a short pause and we also have a turn transition relevance place here. However, there is no feedback by the Follower at this point. Therefore the Router selects a typical pattern for self-repairs or continuations in German, a *that is* construction in the guise of a propositional apposition. Overlapping the production of *kind*, he produces a three-dimensional partial U-shaped object maintaining the same perspective as in his first drawing of the U-shaped border.

Observe that the Follower already gives feedback after *front*. The most decisive contribution is the Follower's acknowledgement, however. She imitates the Router's gesture but from her perspective as a potential observer. Also, at the level of single form features, she performs the gesture differently. (different movement direction, different symmetry) The imitating gesture overlaps with her nod and her contribution *OK*. It is important to see that her gesture provides more than a repetition of the word *townhall* could possibly give. It refers at the same time to the town-hall (standing for a discourse referent) and provides the information of a U-shape indicating property, in other words, it expresses the propositional information "This building being U-shaped" with *this building* acting as a definite anaphora to the occurrence of *a building* in the first part of the Router's contribution. Hence, assessed from a dialogue perspective the following happens: The grounding process triggered by the Follower's acknowledgement amounts to mutual belief among Router and Follower that the town hall is U-shaped and the approaching on-looker on the route perceives it from the open side of the U.

Router: Das ist dann das Rathaus [placing].
This is then the townhall [placing].
Das ist ein u-förmiges Gebäude [drawing].
That is a U-shaped building [drawing].
Du blickst praktisch da rein [shaping]. *Yo*
look practically there into it [shaping].
Das heisst, es hat vorne so zwei Buchtungei
That is, it has to the front kind of two bulges.
und geht hinten zusammen dann. *and closes i*
the rear then.

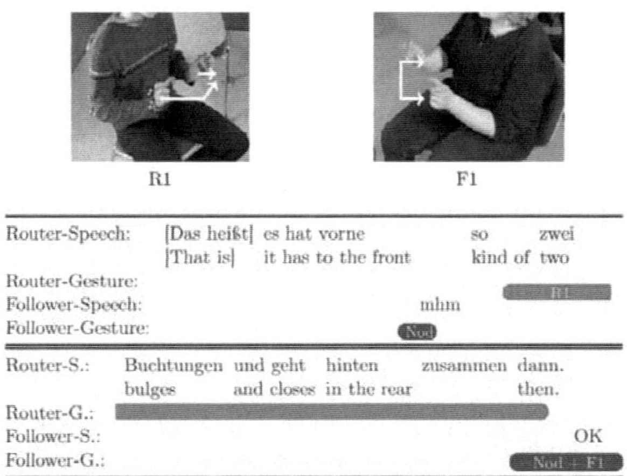

Figure 5: Example showing the Router's and the Follower's gestures and their crucial exchange in terms of the Router's assertion and the Follower's acknowledgement.

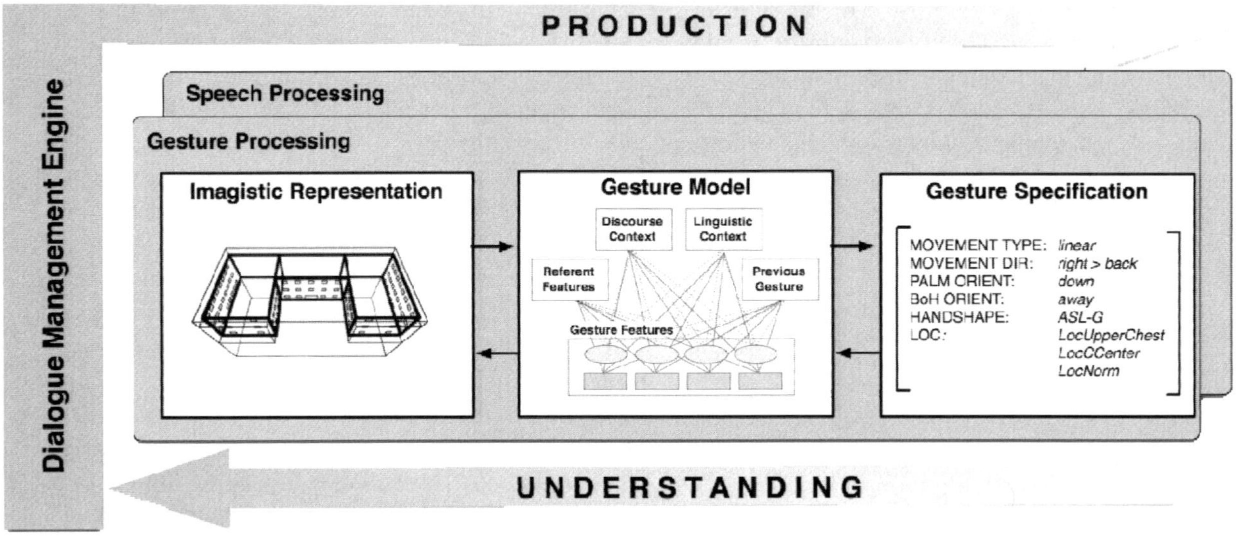

Figure 6: Overview of the production and understanding cycle in the simulation model.

5 Extending the Simulation: The Understanding-Acceptance/Generation Cycle

How can we go beyond the simulation of isolated speaker-specific gestures towards the generation of gestures in dialogues? We build on our findings in the corpus study, briefly taken up here again (see list in section 2 and the respective comments): Gesture helps in structuring the dialogue supporting next speaker selection or indicating non-regular contributions of other speaker. It enables assessment of the current speaker's (Router's or Follower's) communicative intentions by the addressee, for example of whether the Router wants to keep the turn but indicates current memory and recapitulation problems thus appealing to the addressee's cooperation. In addition, appraisal of the reliability of the information given by the Router can be read off from some of the Router's gestures. Finally, as shown in section 4, gestures complementing or even replacing verbal information is used in acknowledgements.

Building on these observations, our goal is to simulate such dialogic interaction with two virtual agents (Router and Follower), each of whom provided with a speaker-specific GNetIc model. In the minimal discourse example Router and Follower use similar gestures which, notably, differ with respect to some details (e.g. speaker's perspective). In the simulation we essentially capture the Router's contribution in Figure 5 (R1) and the subsequent acknowledgement by the Follower (F1). In order to vary the Router's gesturing behavior we use the representation technique of drawing instead of shaping in the simulation.

What we need to extend the model with is an analysis of the Follower's understanding of the Router's gesture. Psychologically plausible but beyond commonly specialised technical approaches, we want to employ the same model of an agent's „gesture knowledge" for both generating and understanding gestures. For an overview of the production and understanding cycle see Figure 6.

Here we can make use of the fact that the BDN formalism allows for two different types of inference, causal inferences that follow the causal inter actions from cause to effect, and diagnostic inferences that allow for introducing evidence for effects and infer the most likely causes of these effects. This bi-directional use of BDNs could be complementary to approaches of plan/intention recognition such as in Geib and Goldman (2003).

To model a use of gestures for regulation as observed with the Follower F1, the Router agent's gestural activity is set as evidence for the output nodes of the Follower's BDN. A diagnostic inference then yields the most likely causes, that is, the most likely referent properties and values of discourse contextual variables. In other words, we employ the same speaker-specific GNetIc model for generation and for understanding. That is, information about the physical appearance of the

Router's gesture (as specified in Figure 4) is provided as evidence for the Follower's GNetIc model revealing↓correctly↓that the gesture's representation technique is "drawing" and the shape property is "U-shaped".
Notably, just as the gesture generation process has to make choices between similarly probable alternatives, not all diagnostic inferences which are drawn by employing the Follower agent's GNetIc model are necessarily in line with the evidence from which the Router agent's gesture was originally generated. For instance, the communicative goal as inferred by the Follower agent is "lmDescrPosition" (with a likelihood of .65) instead of "lmDescrProperty". Nevertheless, the inferred knowledge reveals an underspecified representation of the referent (see Figure 7) as well as the most likely specification of the discourse context. That way, the Follower agent develops his own hypothesis of the Router agent's communicative goal and the content being depicted gesturally.
This hypothesis is forwarded to the follower agent's dialogue manager, which responds to such declaratives by the Router with an acknowledgement grounding act. Now the very same generation process as described in section 3 sets in. The Follower agent's feedback is generated by employing his GNetIc model for causal inference. The resulting gesture is, notably, different from the Router agent's gesture: it is a two-handed shaping gesture with handshape ASL-C. Movement type and movement features are the same as in the Router agent's drawing gesture. Palm and BoH orientation are different due to representation technique specific patterns which are implemented in the decision nodes (see Figure 7). This case of using iconic gesture for regulating dialogue has been successfully implemented using GNetIc and the overall production architecture.

6 Discussion and further research agenda

In this paper we addressed the dialogue-regulating function of gestures. Based on empirical observations of interactional patterns from the SAGA corpus, the starting points for the simulation of these gestures were non-interactional propositional ones such as iconics used to describe routes or landmarks. We achieved to simulate such iconic gestures used in their function as acknowledgements shown in section 3 which clearly transcends their mere representational task.

Figure 7: Imagistic representation of what the Follower understood from the Router's gestural depiction of the townhall (left) and the simulation of the Follower's autonomously generated shaping gesture used as an acknowledgement.

We first note that we draw a distinction between gestures relevant for dialogue structure such as next speaker selection or acknowledgement and those which focus on influencing the social climate among the dialogue participants. We did not have many of the latter in SAGA but observed some which we classified as "calming down" and "don't bother". In certain communication cultures also touching the other's body is accepted.
As for a research agenda to elucidate further the functions of gestures in dialogue, we do not go too deeply into matters of dialogue theory here. We already have shown that gestures accompanying base-line information, being part of the Router's report or the Follower's uptake can be modelled in PTT (Poesio and Rieser 2009, Rieser and Poesio 2009), if one assumes a unified representation for verbal and gestural meaning. Here we concentrate on how the simulation work can be pushed forward based on theoretical analyses of empirical data.
Note that on the list of discourse gestures given in section 2 the following items are tied to Router's behaviour and can be generated in an autonomous fashion:

- managing of own turn
- evidentials for establishing a confidence level
- assessment of relevance by discourse participants
- indication of topicality with respect to time, place or objects.

Observe, however, that these will also have an impact on the mental state of the Follower as is e.g., obvious for evidentials or the "brush away gesture" (Figure 1). Relevant for the sequencing of multimodal contributions are clearly the following:

- mechanisms of next-speaker selection as proposed in classical CA research
- grounding acts and feedback
- handling of non-canonical moves by discourse participants

- clarification requests to work on contributions.

These are intrinsically involved in the production of adjacency pairs, having a current and a next contribution and it is on these that simulation will focus on in future work. In combination with an information state-based multimodal discourse record (Traum & Larsson, 2003), the implementated cycle of generation, understanding and acceptance/generation provides the basis for modeling this kind of gesture-based discourse regulation.

Acknowledgments

This research is partially supported by the DFG in the CRC 673 "Alignment in Communication" and the Center of Excellence "Cognitive Interaction Technology".

References

Asher, N. and Lascarides, A. (2003). *The Logic of Conversation.* Cambridge University Press

Bavelas, J., Chovil, N., Lawrie, D., and Wade, A. (1992). Interactive gestures. *Discourse Processes*, 15(4):469–491.

Bavelas, J., Chovil N., Coated, L., Roe, L. (1995). Gestures Specialised for Dialogue. *Personality and Social Psychology Bulletin*, 21(4):394–405

Bergmann, K., & Kopp, S. (2010). Modelling the Production of Co-Verbal Iconic Gestures by Learning Bayesian Decision Networks. *Applied Artificial Intelligence,* 24(6):530–551.

Bergmann, K. & Kopp, S. (2009). Increasing expressiveness for virtual agents–Autonomous generation of speech and gesture in spatial description tasks. In *Proceedings of AAMAS 2009*, pages 361–368.

Bergmann, K. & Kopp, S. (2009a). GNetIc–Using Bayesian Decision Networks for iconic gesture generation. In *Proceedings of the 9th International Conference on Intelligent Virtual Agents*, pages 76–89.

Bergmann, K., Kopp, S., and Eyssel, F. (2010). Individualized gesturing outperforms average gesturing–Evaluating gesture production in virtual humans. In *Proceedings of IVA 2010*, pages 104–117, Berlin/Heidelberg. Springer.

Cassell, J. and S. Prevost (1996). Distribution of Semantic Features Across Speech and Gesture by Humans and Computers. Proceedings of the Workshop on the Integration of Gesture in Language and Speech.

Clark, H.H. (1996). *Using Language.* CUP

Geib, C., Goldman, R.,(2003). Recognizing Plan/Goal Abandonment. In *Proceedings of the International Joint Conference on Artificial Intelligence (IJCAI)*, pp. 1515–1517.

Gill, S. P., Kawamori, M., Katagiri, Y., and Shimojima, A. (1999). Pragmatics of body moves. In *Proceedings of the 3rd International Cognitive Technology Conference*, pages 345–358.

Ginzburg, J. (2011). The Interactive Stance. Meaning for Conversation. Oxford University Press (in press).

Hahn, F. and Rieser, H. (2009-2011): Dialogue Structure Gestures and Interactive Gestures. Manual, 1st version. CRC 673 Working Paper. Bielefeld University

Hahn, F. and Rieser, H. (2010): Explaining Speech-Gesture Alignment in MM Dialogue Using Gesture Typology. In P. Lupowski and M. Purver (Eds.), *Aspects of Semantics and Pragmatics of Dialogue.* SemDial 2010, pp. 99–111.

Levinson, St. C. (1983). *Pragmatics.* Cambridge University Press.

Lücking, A., Bergmann, K., Hahn, F., Kopp, S., & Rieser, H. (2010): The Bielefeld Speech and Gesture Alignment Corpus (SaGA). In M. Kipp et al. (Eds.), *LREC 2010 Workshop: Multimodal Corpora.*

McNeill, D. (1992). *Hand and Mind.* Chicago University Press.

Poesio, M. & Rieser, H. (2009). Anaphora and Direct Reference: Empirical Evidence from Pointing. In J. Edlund et al. (Eds.), *Proceedings of the 13th Workshop on the Semantics and Pragmatics of Dialogue (DiaHolmia)* (pp. 35–43). Stockholm, Sweden.

Rieser, H. (2010). On Factoring out a Gesture Typology from the Bielefeld Speech-And-Gesture-Alignment Corpus (SAGA). In Kopp and Wachsmuth (Eds.), *Proceedings of GW 2009.* Springer, pp. 47–61.

Rieser, H. & Poesio, M. (2009). Interactive Gesture in Dialogue: a PTT Model. In P. Healey et al. (Eds.), Proceedings of the SIGDIAL 2009 Conference (pp. 87–96). London, UK: ACL.

Poesio, M. and Rieser, H. (2010). Completions, coordination and alignment in dialogue. *Dialogue and Discourse* 1(1), 1–89

Poesio, M. and Traum, D. (1997). Conversational actions and discourse situations. *Computational Intelligence*, 13(3): 309–347

Roque, A. and Traum, D. (2008). Degrees of Grounding Based on Evidence of Understanding. In *Proceedings of the 9th SIGdial Workshop on Discourse and Dialogue*, pp. 54–63

Sacks, H., Schegloff, E., Jefferson, G. (1974). A simplest systematics for the organization of turn-taking for conversation. *Language*, 50: 696–735

Stalnaker, R. (1978): Assertion. In Cole, P. (Ed.) *Syntax and Semantics 9: Pragmatics,* pp. 315–322.

Sowa, T. and Wachsmuth, I. (2009). A computational model for the representation an processing of shape in coverbal iconic gestures. In K. Coventry et al. (Eds.), *Spatial Language and Dialogue*, pages 132–146. Oxford University Press.

Traum, D. (1999). Computational models of grounding in collaborative systems. In *Working Notes of AAAI Fall Symposium on Psychological Models of Communication*, pp. 124–131.

Traum, D., & Larsson, S. (2003). The information state approach to dialogue management. In R.W. Smith and J.C.J. van Kuppevelt (Eds.), *Current and New Directions in Discourse & Dialogue* (pp. 325–353). Kluwer Academic Publishers.

Multiparty Turn Taking in Situated Dialog: Study, Lessons, and Directions

Dan Bohus
Microsoft Research
One Microsoft Way
Redmond, WA, 98052
dbohus@microsoft.com

Eric Horvitz
Microsoft Research
One Microsoft Way
Redmond, WA, 98052
horvitz@microsoft.com

Abstract

We report on an empirical study of a multiparty turn-taking model for physically situated spoken dialog systems. We present subjective and objective performance measures that show how the model, supported with a basic set of sensory competencies and turn-taking policies, can enable interactions with multiple participants in a collaborative task setting. The analysis brings to the fore several phenomena and frames challenges for managing multiparty turn taking in physically situated interaction.

1. Introduction

Effective dialog relies on the coordination of contributions by participants in a conversation via turn taking. The complexity of understanding and managing turns grows significantly in moving from dyadic to multiparty settings, including situations where groups of people converse as they collaborate on shared goals. We are exploring computational methods that can endow dialog systems with the ability to participate in a natural, fluid manner in conversations involving several people.

In Bohus and Horvitz (2010a), we presented a computational model for managing multiparty turn taking. The model harnesses multisensory perception and reasoning and includes a set of components and representations. These include methods for tracking multiparty conversational dynamics, for making turn-taking decisions, and for rendering decisions about turns into an appropriate set of low-level, coordinated gaze, gesture and speech behaviors. We implemented the model and have been testing it in several domains. The investigations have been aimed at characterizing the system's performance in complex multiparty settings.

In Bohus and Horvitz (2010b), we examine data collected during a user study to evaluate the ability of the system to shape the flow of multiparty conversational dynamics. In this paper, we focus our attention on the performance of the inference and decision-making models. We analyze the accuracy of current turn-taking inferences, the influence of inference errors on decisions, and the overall effectiveness of the system's decision making. We report on subjective and objective measures of the system's turn-taking performance. We find that the turn-taking methodology enables our system to successfully participate in multiparty interactions, even when relying on relatively coarse models for inference and decision making. The analysis highlights several general phenomena including standing bottlenecks and difficulties, and opportunities for enhancing multiparty turn taking in dialog systems. Based on the results, we discuss challenges and directions for research on turn taking in physically situated dialog.

2. Related Work

We begin by placing this work within the larger context of research on multiparty interaction and turn taking. In a seminal paper on turn taking in natural conversations, Sacks, Schegloff and Jefferson (1974) proposed a basic model for the organi-

Proceedings of the SIGDIAL 2011: the 12th Annual Meeting of the Special Interest Group on Discourse and Dialogue, pages 98–109,
Portland, Oregon, June 17-18, 2011. ©2011 Association for Computational Linguistics

zation of turns in conversation. The model is centered on the notion of *turn-constructional-units*, separated by *transition relevance places* that provide opportunities for speaker changes. In later work, Schegloff (2000) elaborates on several aspects of this model, including interruptions and overlap resolution devices. Other researchers in conversational analysis and psycho-linguistics have highlighted the important role played by gaze, gesture, and other non-verbal communication channels in regulating turn taking. For instance, Duncan (1972) discusses the role of non-verbal signals, and proposes that turn taking is mediated via a set of verbal and non-verbal cues. Wiemann and Knapp (1975) survey prior investigations on turn-taking cues in several conversational settings, in an effort to elucidate differences. Goodwin (1980) discusses various aspects of the relationship between turn taking and attention. More recently, Hjalmarsson (2011) investigates the additive effect turn-taking cues have on listeners in both human and synthetic voices.

Within the dialog systems community, efforts have been made on designing and implementing computational models for managing turn taking (e.g., Traum, 1994; Thorrissön, 2002; Raux and Eskenazi, 2009; Selfridge and Heeman, 2010). Moving beyond the dyadic setting, Traum and Rickel (2002) describe a turn management component for supporting dialog between a trainee and multiple virtual humans. Kronlid (2006) describes a Harel state-chart implementation of the original SSJ model. Researchers studying human-robot interaction have developed prototype robots that can interact with multiple human participants (e.g. Matsusaka et al., 2001; Bennewitz et al., 2005). In our previous work Bohus and Horvitz (2009; 2010a; 2010b), we describe a platform that leverages multimodal perception and reasoning to support multiparty dialog in open-world settings.

3. Multiparty Turn-Taking Model

We engaged in a set of experiments to probe the inference and decision making competencies of a computational model for multiparty turn taking (Bohus and Horvitz 2010a; 2010b). To set the stage for the analysis to follow, we briefly review the proposed approach.

We model turn taking as an interactive, collaborative process by which participants in a conversation monitor one another and take coordinated actions to ensure that (generally) only one person speaks at a given time. The participant ratified to speak via this process is said to have the *floor*. Each participant engaged in the interaction continuously produces (*i.e.* at every time tick) one of four *floor management actions*: a *hold* action indicates that a participant is maintaining the floor; a *release* action indicates that the participant is yielding the floor to a set of other participants (which could be void, allowing for self-selection next turn allocation); a *take* action indicates that the participant is trying to acquire the floor; finally, a *null* action indicates that a participant is not making any floor claims. The floor shifts from one participant to another as the result of the joint, cooperative floor management actions taken by the participants. Specifically, a *release* action must be met with a *take* action for a floor shift to occur; in all other cases the floor stays with the participant that currently holds it.

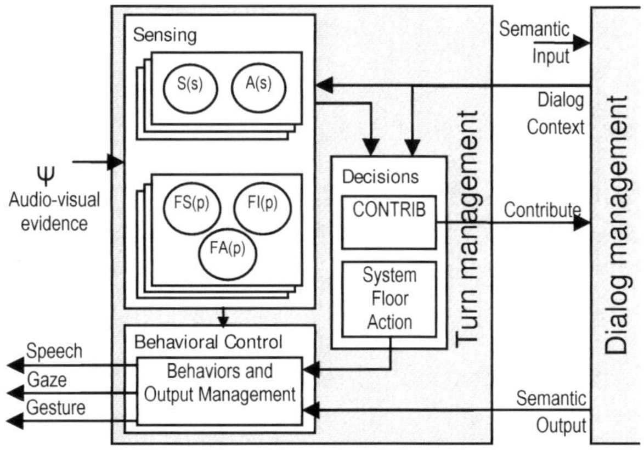

Figure 1. Components of turn-taking model.

Figure 1 illustrates the main components and key abstractions in the model. The sensing subcomponent tracks the conversational dynamics, and includes models for detecting spoken signals *s*, inferring the source *S(s)* and the set of addressees *A(s)* for each signal, as well as the floor state *FS(p)*, actions *FA(p)* and intentions *FI(p)* of each participant *p* engaged in a conversation. This information is used in conjunction with higher-level dialog context to decide when the system should generate new contributions and which floor action should be produced at each point in time. Finally, floor actions are rendered by a behavioral component into a set of coordinated gaze, gesture and speech behaviors. By harnessing these different components, the proposed model can enable an embodied conversational agent to handle a broad spectrum of turn-taking phenomena.

4. User Study

We implemented an initial set of turn-taking inference and decision making models in the context of a multiparty dialog system, and we conducted a large-scale multiparty interaction user study with this system. The study, described in more detail below, was designed to fulfill two goals: (1) to ascertain an initial performance baseline and identify current bottlenecks and challenges to be addressed moving forward, and (2) to collect a large set of multiparty human-computer dialog data that can be used to study and improve multiparty turn taking in dialog systems.

4.1. System

The platform used in these experiments, described in detail in Bohus and Horvitz (2009), takes the form of a multimodal interactive kiosk that displays an avatar head which plays a questions game with multiple participants. The system leverages audiovisual information and employs components for visually tracking multiple people in the scene, sound source localization, speech recognition, conversational scene analysis, behavioral control and dialog management. Figure 2 shows a screen generated by the system, with the rendered avatar and a sample challenge question. Users can collaborate on selecting an answer, and, after a confirmation, the system provides an explanation if the answer is incorrect, before moving on to the next question. Sample interactions are found in Appendix C and videos are available online (Situated Interaction, 2011).

4.2. Turn-Taking Inference and Decisions

In the current system, a voice activity detector is used to identify and segment spoken utterances. The source of each utterance is assumed to be the participant who is closest in the horizontal plane to the sound direction identified by the microphone array. The set of addressees is identified by fusing information probabilistically about the focus of attention of the source, as obtained through face detection and head pose tracking, while the utterance is being detected. In addition, the system assumes that non-understandings are addressed to other engaged participants, since initial tests indicated that in this domain about 80% of utterances that led to non-understandings were in fact addressed to others. Similarly, the system assumes that utterances longer than three seconds are addressed to others (responses addressed to the system tend to be short in this domain)

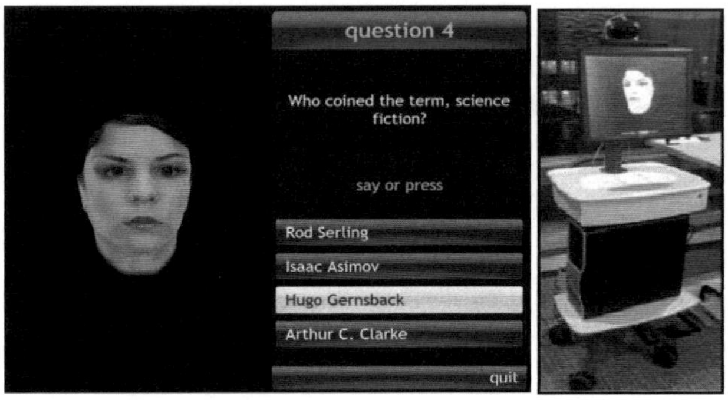

Figure 2. Questions game: screen and kiosk.

Floor management actions are inferred as follows. If a participant has the floor, we assume they are performing a hold action if speaking and a release action otherwise. The release is assumed to be towards the addressees of the last spoken utterance. Although the latter assumption on releases may not hold in the most general case, it is a reasonable one for the questions game domain. If a participant does not have the floor, the system assumes they perform a take action if speaking or a null action otherwise. The system also assumes that the floor intentions are fully reflected by the floor actions, i.e., a participant intends to have the floor if and only if she performs a hold or take action. Floor states are updated based on the joint, coordinated floor actions of all participants, as described earlier.

Turn-taking decisions are based on a simple heuristic policy. The system takes the floor if (1) the floor is being released to it or (2) a participant releases the floor to someone else, but no one claims the floor for a preset duration. In most cases, this duration is set to 3.5 seconds. However, if the floor is released to someone else after the system is interrupted during a *question* dialog act, the system will try to quickly reacquire the floor should no one else be speaking, so as to finish or restate its question. The waiting duration is set in the latter case to 500 milliseconds. If after 500ms, when the system tries to take the floor another conflict occurs (followed by a floor release to someone else), the waiting duration is increased again to 3.5 seconds. Finally, if a third consecutive conflict occurs when the system tries to acquire the floor, the waiting duration is set to a longer, 20 seconds.

The system releases the floor at the end of its own outputs. In addition, it has to decide whether it should release the floor when a user performs a take action (i.e. barges in) while the system is speaking. The heuristic policy currently implemented by the system releases the floor only for barge-ins occurring during question dialog acts.

Finally, the behavioral models employ policies informed by the existing literature on the role of gaze in regulating turn taking. In particular, the system's gaze is directed towards the speaking participant, or, if the system is speaking, towards the addressees of the system's utterance. During silences, the system's gaze is directed towards the participants that the floor is being released to.

The models and policies described above represent a starting point for inference and action, constructed to enable data collection and an initial evaluation in this domain. We are working to update the turn-taking architecture with more sophisticated evidential reasoning and utility-theoretic decision making. Nevertheless, when harnessed as an ensemble within the turn-taking approach that we have described, the current procedures provide for an array of complex, multiparty turn-taking behaviors. For instance, the system can address each participant individually or all participants as a group via controlling the orientation of its head pose. When participants talk amongst themselves, the system can monitor their exchanges and wait until the floor is being released back to it. If an answer is heard during such a side conversation (e.g., one participant suggests an answer to another), the system highlights it on the screen (see Figure 2). If a significant pause is detected during this side conversation, the avatar takes the floor and the initiative, e.g., *"So, what do you think is the correct answer?"* Once a participant provides an answer, the system seeks confirmation from another participant before moving on. In some cases, the avatar passes back the floor and seeks confirmation non-verbally, by simply turning towards another participant and raising its eyebrows. The system can try to require the floor immediately after being interrupted, but can also back off, giving the participants a chance to finish a side conversation, if successive floor conflicts occur. Sample interactions can be viewed in Appendix C and online (Situated Interaction, 2011).

4.3. Study Design

The user study was conducted in a usability lab and involved a total of 60 participants recruited as pairs of people from the general population who previously knew one another (30 male and 30 female, with ages between 18 and 61). The study was structured in 15 one-hour sessions, with each session involving four participants, i.e., two pairs of two previously acquainted participants. In each session, we formed all possible subgroups of size two (6 subgroups) and of size three (4 subgroups) with the four participants. Each subgroup played one game with the system. This setup allowed us to collect a large set of multiparty interactions under diverse conditions (e.g., all-male, all-female, mixed-gender groups; groups where people were previously acquainted *vs.* not, etc.). At the end of each session, participants filled in a subjective assessment survey.

4.4. Corpus, Annotations, and Cost Assessment

In total, 150 multiparty interactions were collected: 90 with two participants and the system, and 60 with three participants and the system. A professional annotator transcribed the utterances detected by the system at runtime, and labeled them with *source* and *addressee* information.

The system was noted to commit several types of turn-taking errors. To expand the error analysis beyond occurrence statistics and to characterize the impact of various types of errors, we conducted a follow-up study. In this second study, a set of additional participants were recruited to review videos of interactions from the first study and asked to (1) identify the turn-taking errors committed by the system and (2) to assess the costliness of the error on a five-point scale.

A total of 9 interactions (5 with two participants and system; 4 with three participants and system) were randomly sampled from the collected corpus, while ensuring that each turn-taking outcome of interest (discussed in Section 5 and summarized in Table 1) was sufficiently represented. Nine participants were recruited via an email request to employees at our organization. Each participant reviewed three interactions, and each interaction was reviewed by three different participants. Prior to the experiment, each of the annotators received a brief review of the turn-taking process in human-human interaction. Next, they used a multimodal annotation tool that we created to review the interaction videos. As each video played, the annotator pushed a button at each point they believed that the system had committed a turn-taking error. In a second pass, each annotator was asked to review the errors that they had previously identified and to assess the relative cost of the error, on a scale from 0 ("no error") to 5 ("worst error"). In a final step, the authors manually aligned each identified turn-taking error with a turn-taking decision made by the system and its corresponding outcome.

5. Evaluation

We now focus on the various types of turn-taking errors, the outcomes that these errors lead to, and the costs assessed for the outcomes. We begin by focusing on diarization challenges described in Section 5.1. In Sections 5.2 and 5.3, we review the accuracy of the system's turn-taking inferences and decisions, and their corresponding outcomes. Finally, in Section 5.4, we turn our attention to the subjective assessment results obtained via the post-experiment user survey.

Before diving into the details, we note that we eliminated 7 out of the total 150 interactions from the analysis due to significant problems with acoustic echo cancellation. In the remaining 143 interactions, we also identified and eliminated 24 utterances in the transitional engagement stages, e.g., when the users were not ready or properly setup in front of the system. The analysis below is based on the remaining 4379 utterances.

5.1. Diarization

The system uses a voice activity detector which leverages energy, acoustics and grammar to detect spoken utterances. Our experiments indicate that this type of black-box solution can make diarization errors, especially in multiparty settings where people may speak simultaneously, at a fast pace, and address each other with language outside the system's grammar. Results show that only 72% of the detected segments contain speech from a single participant. Another 2% contain background noises incorrectly identified as speech. Most often these are instances where the system heard itself due to acoustic echo-cancellation problems; the ratio grows to about 6% among all utterances detected while the system is speaking. The remaining 26% contain overlapping or successive utterances from multiple speakers. Inspection of the data reveals that some utterances spoken softly by participants were not detected and that segmentation boundary errors are also sometimes present. While such errors may be mitigated by inferences at higher levels in the turn-taking model, they can significantly influence the system's ability to track the conversational dynamics and make appropriate turn-taking decisions. We plan to pursue more robust audiovisual diarization methods that integrate sound localization as detected by a microphone array, along with higher-level interaction context.

5.2. *Take* versus *Null*

We now turn our attention to the system's floor control decisions. The analysis below is based on the utterances and segmentation *detected by the system at runtime*. We note that a more precise analysis could be conducted with a ground truth segmentation of utterances. Utterances detected by the system can be classified into three categories, based on their relationship to system outputs, as shown in Figure 3: *overlaps*, which start and end during a system's output, *continuers*, which begin during but finish after a system output has ended, and *responses*, which do not overlap anywhere.

With the current policy, the system chooses whether it should take the floor following each detected *continuer* and *response*. The dataset contains a total of 3265 such instances. The system's decision at each of these points hinges on the results of its inferences about the participants' floor actions, and thus of inferences about the addressees of each utterance. Table 1 displays a tabulation of the release actions performed by the participants versus the actions identified by the system. The release actions are determined from labels assigned manually by the professional annotator. Recall that we make an assumption that the release is towards the set of addressees of an utterance. For segments that were labeled as containing multiple utterances, the release is made to the addressee of the last utterance. The last row in Table 1 corresponds to background noises and system speech incorrectly

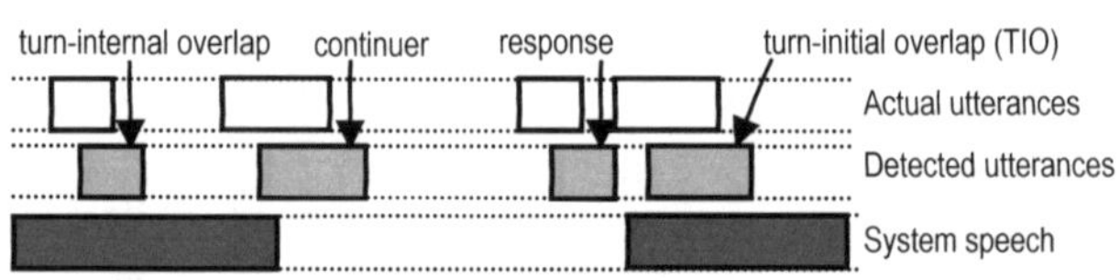

Figure 3. Schematic of different classes of overlap.

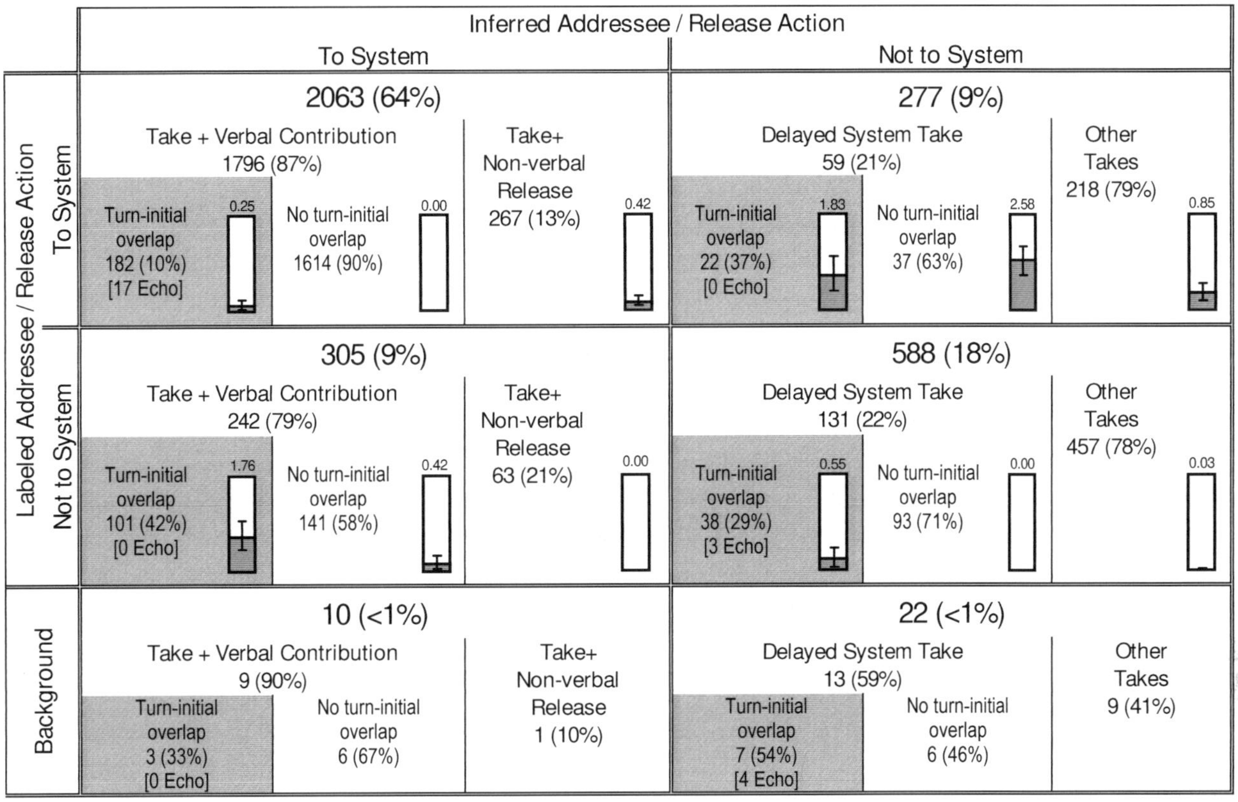

Table 1. Decisions to *take* floor (vs. *null*), outcomes, and estimated costs (bar graph with confidence intervals). *Echo* denotes cases where the turn initial overlap is created by utterances where the system hears itself because of errors with echo cancellation.

identified as utterances.

On the task of detecting addressees, and thus floor release actions, the results show an error rate of 18%, including 305 false-positives (erroneous detections) and 277 false-negatives (missed detections) of floor releases to the system. These errors influence the quality of turn taking in a variety of ways and underscore the need for more robust inferences about speech source and target, and floor release actions. We believe that more sophisticated models learned from audiovisual information (e.g., prosody, head and body pose, etc.) and attributes of the interaction context (e.g., who spoke last, where is the system looking, etc.) can reduce errors significantly.

Table 1 indicates that in 305 (9%) of the cases the system incorrectly inferred that the floor was being released to it. In 79% of these cases, the system took the floor and produced a verbal contribution. Since the floor was not released to the system, such errors can lead to significant turn-taking problems, which often manifest as floor conflicts marked by *turn-initial overlaps*, where a participant and the system start speaking around the same time (see Figure 3). Operationally, we define *turn-initial overlaps* as all detected overlaps with an actual onset of less than 300 milliseconds from the beginning of the system's utterance (see discussion in Appendix A); the other overlaps are dubbed *turn-internal.* We note that the time at which an overlap is *detected* by the system lags behind the actual onset of the utterance by an average of about 700 milliseconds, due to core latencies in our audio and speech processing pipeline. Accounting for these computational lags, and others arising at different places in processing pipelines, raise challenges for turn taking in spoken dialog systems.

42% of the verbal takes performed incorrectly by the system led to turn-initial overlaps. This is not surprising, as the system starts speaking when the floor was not released to it. In some of these cases the same participant continues (e.g., diarization errors incorrectly segmented the utterance), or someone else starts speaking. The cost assessment experiment confirmed the impact of these errors – the average estimated cost was 1.76. If no turn-initial overlap occurred after the system incorrectly took the floor, the average cost was 0.42. Clearly floor conflicts come with a cost. The specific cost assessments we obtained are perhaps influenced to a degree by the role of *game mediator* played by the system. With this role, taking the floor in cases when the system was not addressed is perhaps not as costly as it might be in other domains.

Note that 182 turn-initial overlaps also occur when the system takes the floor after correctly identifying that the floor was released to it (upper-left quadrant in Table 1). 17 of them are created by the system hearing itself as it starts speaking, due to errors in acoustic echo cancellation; these instances are marked *Echo* in Table 1. While the relative percentage of turn-initial overlaps is smaller after a floor release to the system (~10%), the majority of all turn-initial overlaps (shaded cells in Table 1) occur in this context, because of the larger incidence of the situation. Often, these utterances contain an immediate answer or a short confirmation from another participant. The cost of these turn-initial overlaps is also much lower: 0.25 versus 1.76 (again, the cost structure is probably sensitive to details of the domain).

We believe the turn-initial overlaps that occur when the floor is released to the system can be explained in part by the interpretation of the system's short delay in responding (per processing) as a signal that the system is not taking the floor, leading other participants to take initiative. As another factor, turn taking is a mixed-initiative process, and other participants might vie for the floor and issue their own contributions immediately after an answer directed to the system. These observations bring to the fore two questions: (1) how can we minimize the number of turn-initial overlaps, and (2) how can the system gracefully handle such overlaps once they occur?

One approach to minimizing turn-initial overlaps is to reduce the system's response delays via faster processing or via the use of predictive models to anticipate the end of turns (e.g. Ferrer et al., 2003; Schlangen, 2006; Raux and Eskenazi, 2008; Skantze and Schlangen, 2009). Multiparty settings require methods for forecasting not only when a current speaker will finish, but also whether any participant will try to take (or release) the floor within a small window of time in the future, i.e., accurately modeling all floor intentions. Our turn-taking framework includes components for representing and modeling floor intentions, but these are not used in the current system. We believe there is promise in learning models to predict floor intentions and the timing of ends of utterances from interaction data. The availability of such predictions can fuel additional turn-taking strategies and also pave the way to more graceful handling of turn-initial overlaps after they occur. For instance, if the system can anticipate that someone else might start speaking, it might still decide to take the floor but it might start with a filler, e.g., *"So* [pause] *What do you think?"* constructing a natural opportunity for resolving a potential conflict after *"So"* We plan to investigate the use of decision-theoretic methods to anticipate and resolve such conflicts by introducing and modulating an array of strategies, including the use of fillers, restarts, and acknowledgment gestures.

In 21% of the 305 incorrectly detected floor releases to the system, our system immediately performed a non-verbal floor release to another participant by turning the avatar's face towards them and raising its eyebrows (Take + Non-verbal Release in Table 1). These situations are not costly, as the system's action does not interrupt the flow of the conversation. Indeed they were never penalized in the cost assessment experiment that we conducted. However, the same action, performed when the floor is actually released to the system (13% of 2063 cases), has the potential to create problems if not properly recognized by the targeted participant as a floor release by the system; the average cost assessed in this case was 0.42.

The right-hand column in Table 1 shows cases where the system detected that the floor was not released to it. In these cases, the system waits (performs null) for a specified duration. The cost assessment indicates that waiting in this situation is overall costly, and the cost depends on the ultimate outcome. If no one else takes the floor, the system will eventually do so (Delayed System Take cases in Table 1). In some of these cases, turn-initial overlaps also occur. The 277 cases in which the system fails to detect that the floor was in fact released to it lead to no immediate response from the system. In these cases the system can be perceived as unresponsive and the participants eventually repeat themselves. We believe that performance can be improved with the use of an ongoing decision-theoretic analysis that continuously reassesses the situation while the system waits. Such an analysis would consider the delay, floor holder's previous actions, inferences about participants' floor intentions, and cost-benefit tradeoffs of different floor actions.

5.3. *Release* versus *Hold*

We now turn our attention to the system's decisions to release the floor. Recall that, according to the current policy, the system performs a floor hold while it is speaking and a floor release at the end of its outputs. In addition, if an overlap (i.e., barge-in) was detected during question dialog acts, the system performed a floor release immediately, interrupting its own output and allowing for the user barge-in.

Since such barge-ins were allowed only during the question dialog acts, as Table 2 shows, the current policy leads to an abundance of cases in which the system performs hold when an overlap is detected. Some of these cases are continuers: the overlap only happens at the very end of the system's output. These cases do not create significant turn-taking problems, as the floor still transitions to the participant relatively quickly (the system releases at the end of its output). However, in a significant number of cases the system appears to ignore the participants (shaded cells in Table 2). About three quarters of these overlaps occur while the system is providing an explanation after an incorrect answer. Observations of the data indicate that in these cases participants may discuss or give their opinion on the answer or some aspect of the system's explanation, while ignoring the system as it blindly continues the explanation.

We have separated in Table 2 turn-initial from turn-internal overlaps. The two types of overlaps reflect different phenomena. As we have discussed, turn-initial overlaps mark floor conflicts, and various strategies could be used to negotiate such conflicts (e.g., Yang and Heeman, 2010). In contrast, turn-internal overlaps may reflect efforts by other participants to take the floor, or might simply be

		Action performed by system when overlap detected		
		HOLD		RELEASE
Overlap Type	Turn Initial	315 (23%)		43 (3%) [7 Echo]
		Overlap 285 (90%) [14 Echo]	Continuer 30 (10%) [3 Echo]	
	Turn Internal	968 (69%)		73 (5%) [13 Echo]
		Overlap 828 (86%) [44 Echo]	Continuer 140 (14%) [7 Echo]	

Table 2. Decisions to *release* floor (vs. *hold*).

backchannels, laughter, exclamations or other lexical or non-lexical events that do not mark a claim for the floor. Making appropriate floor control decisions in this case will require models for reliably distinguishing between the two, i.e., between the take or null floor actions of the participants. This is an especially challenging inference problem as decisions need to be made as early as possible after the onset of an utterance.

We note the relatively large incidence of failures in echo cancellation in our microphone array. On the utterances marked *Echo* in Table 2, the system heard itself and thought a user was speaking. We believe these failures could be significantly reduced with better acoustic echo cancellation.

5.4. Subjective Assessment

Finally, we present results from a subjective assessment of the system by participants, based on a post-experiment survey. The survey included several 7-point Likert scale questions related to turn taking, which are displayed in Figure 4, together with the mean user responses and the corresponding 95% confidence intervals. Generally, participants rated the system's turn-taking abilities favorably, with scores around 4.5-5. No statistically significant differences were detected in assessments across the participant's gender or previous familiarity with speech recognition systems. We also note that a parallel human—human interaction study would help us characterize better the system's performance relative to human dialog.

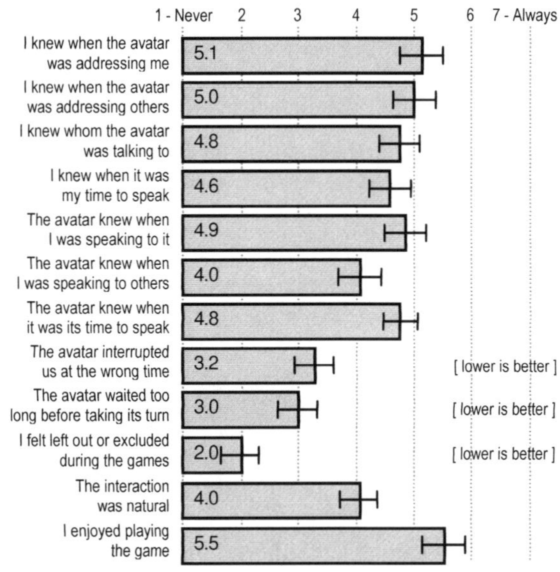

Figure 4. Results of subjective assessments.

In addition to the survey questions, participants were invited to describe in their own words what they liked best and the first thing they would change about the system. 21 of the 60 participants mentioned aspects of multiparty interaction in the "what I liked best" category, such as the system's ability to track the speaking participant and address people individually. Other frequent answers to this question called out the overall experience with the integrative intelligence of the system (15 answers), the fun/educational nature of the game (14), and aspects of speech recognition (11). On the "first thing you would change," the majority of answers (32) included references to shortcomings in rendering the avatar, while 13 answers included references to problematic aspects of the multiparty turn taking. Other answers included task domain suggestions (6) and comments about improving the speech recognition (5). A sampling of answers is presented in Appendix B.

6. Summary and Future Work

We reported on a user study of a multiparty turn-taking model. Objective measures of system performance and subjective assessments by participants indicate that the approach can enable successful multiparty turn taking in the questions game domain. When the correct turn-taking decisions are made, the multiparty interaction is seamless and resembles human-human collaboration. The conversations exhibit fluid exchanges among people and the system, including mixed-initiative, multiparty floor control, fluid back offs and restarts, natural use of non-verbal cues, such as participants' utterances being triggered by a turn of the avatar's head or a lift of the eyebrows. In contrast, turn-taking failures lead to a striking loss of fluidity and a qualitative jump out of an engaged process, where the system rapidly shifts from a collaborating *participant* into a distant and uncoordinated *appliance*.

The results we have discussed are based on an initial set of coarse perceptual and decision-making models and thus reflect an initial baseline; there is significant room for improvements. A careful dissection of the outcomes demonstrates the subtleties of multiparty turn taking and highlights several directions we plan to address in future work. First, our experiments have highlighted the importance of accurate diarization in multiparty dialog settings. Minimizing errors requires rich perceptual and inferential competencies, leveraging audiovisual evidence, general patterns of human discourse, and attributes of the task-specific goals and context. We plan to explore the use of machine learning procedures for constructing predictive models that harness richer streams of evidence to identify and segment utterances, and to make inferences about their sources and targets, and the floor state, actions and intentions of all participants. Better turn-taking decisions can also be supported by inferences about social norms, roles and dynamics, pace of interaction, and engagement.

Although handcrafted turn-taking policies went a long way in this domain, enabling more general multiparty turn taking will require continuous inference and decision making under uncertainty that considers subtleties of intention and timing, and that takes into consideration tradeoffs associated with different courses of actions. We foresee the value of extending the current decision models with richer temporal reasoning for performing such ongoing analyses. Challenges include a more in-depth understanding of the cost of different types of turn-taking errors; the development of a wider array of graded strategies and behaviors for taking, releasing, or holding the floor, and for gracefully negotiating floor conflicts; and finally, the ability to reason about uncertainty in the world as well as in the system's own processing delays in order to resolve tradeoffs between taking timely action and delaying for additional evidence that promises to enhance the accuracies of decisions.

Much also remains to be done with the corresponding generation of subtle verbal and non-verbal cues for enhanced signaling and naturalness of conversation, including the use of fillers, restarts, backchannels, and envelope feedback. We are excited about tackling these and other challenges on the path to fielding systems that can engage in fluid multiparty dialog.

Acknowledgments

We thank Anne Loomis Thompson, Ece Kamar, Qin Cai, Cha Zhang, and Zicheng Liu for their contributions. We also thank our colleagues who participated in pilot experiments for the user study.

References

Bennewitz, M., Faber, F., Joho, D., Schreiber, M., and Behnke, S., 2005. Integrating vision and speech for Conversations with Multiple Persons, in *Proc. of IROS'05*

Bohus, D., and Horvitz, E., 2009. Dialog in the Open-World: Platform and Applications, in *Proc ICMI'09.*

Bohus, D., and Horvitz, E., 2010a. Computational Models for Multiparty Turn Taking, Microsoft Research Technical Report MSR-TR 2010-115.

Bohus, D., and Horvitz, E., 2010b. Facilitating Multiparty Dialog with Gaze, Gesture and Speech, in *Proc ICMI'10.*

Duncan, S. 1972. Some Signals and Rules for Taking Speaking Turns in Conversation, *Journal of Personality and Social Psychology* 23, 283-292.

Ferrer, L., Shriberg, E., and Stolcke, A. 2003. A Prosody-Based Approach to End-Of-Utterance Detection That Does Not Require Speech Recognition, in *Proc. ICASSP'03.*

Goodwin, C. 1980. Restarts, pauses and the achievement of mutual gaze at turn-beginning, *Sociological Inquiry*, 50(3-4).

Hjalmarsson, A., 2011. The additive effect of turn-taking cues in human and synthetic voice, *in Speech Communication,* vol. 53, issue 1.

Kronlid, F., 2006. Turn Taking for Artificial Conversational Agents, *in Cooperative Information Agents X*, LNAI 4149, Springer-Verlag

Matsusaka, Y., Fujie, S., and Kobayashi, T., 2001. Modeling of conversational strategy for the robot participating in the group conversation, in *Proc of EuroSpeech'01.*

Raux, A., and Eskenazi, M. 2008. Optimizing endpointing thresholds using dialogue features in a spoken dialogue system, *in Proc of SIGdial-2008.*

Raux, A. and Eskenazi, M., 2009. A Finite-State Turn-Taking Model for Spoken Dialog Systems, in *Proc. HLT'09.*

Sacks, H., Schegloff. E., and Jefferson, G. 1974. A simplest systematics for the organization of turn-taking in conversation, *Language*, 50, 696-735.

Schegloff, E. 2000. Overlapping talk and the organization of turn-taking in conversation, *Language in Society*, 29, 1-63.

Schlangen, D., 2006. From reaction to prediction: Experiments with computational models of turn-taking, in *Proc. Interspeech'06, Panel on Prosody of Dialogue Acts and Turn-Taking*

Selfridge, E., and Heeman, P., 2010. Importance-Driven Turn-Bidding for Spoken Dialogue Systems, *in Proc. of ACL-2010*, Uppsala, Sweden

Skantze, G., and Schlangen, D., 2009. Incremental dialogue processing in a micro-domain, *in Proc. of EACL-2009.*

Situated Interaction, 2011. Project web page: http://research.microsoft.com/~dbohus/si.html

Thorisson, K.R. 2002. Natural Turn-Taking Needs No Manual: Computational Theory and Model, from Perceptions to Action, *Multimodality in Language and Speech Systems*, Kluwer Academic Publishers.

Traum, D., 1994. *A Computational Theory of Grounding in Natural Language Conversation*, TR-545, U. of Rochester.

Traum, D., and Rickel, J., 2002. Embodied Agents for Multi-party Dialogue in Immersive Virtual World, in *Proc. AAMAS'02.*

Wiemann, J., and Knapp, M., 1975. Turn-taking in conversation, *Journal of Communication*, 25, 75-92.

Yang, F., and Heeman, P., 2010. Initiative Conflicts in Task-Oriented Dialogue, *in Computer, Speech and Language,* vol. 24, issue 2.

Appendix A. Details on derivation of operational definition of turn-initial overlaps.

As described in Section 5.2, we operationally define *turn-initial* overlaps as detected user utterances that have an actual onset of less than 0.3 seconds from the beginning of a system utterance. Figure 5 shows the histogram of the onset time for user speech with respect to system utterances (start of system utterance is at 0 seconds), for overlapping utterances, where this onset is between -2 and +5 seconds. If multiple user utterances overlap with a single system utterance, only the first user utterance, i.e. the first overlap, is considered in computing this histogram. As Figure 5 shows, the onset distribution has a bimodal character. We believe that the two modes may reflect two different phenomena in terms of the floor transition. The early-onset mode corresponds to situations in which a user starts to speak right around (before or immediately after) the time the system also started speaking; this indicates a situation where there is contention for the floor and the system cannot assume it has successfully acquired the floor. In contrast, user utterances starting at later times represent cases where the floor did first transition to the system and the user is aware of this transition. In producing an utterance the user is attempting to barge-in and take the floor back from the system (unless the user utterance is a backchannel). The threshold of 0.3 seconds on the onset for turn-initial overlaps was selected based on the shape of this distribution.

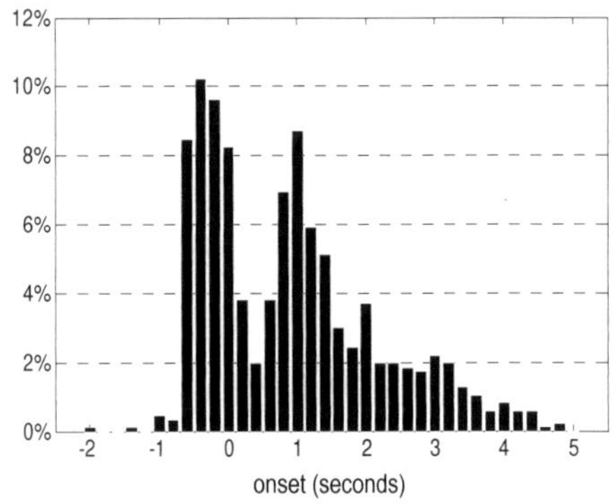

Figure 5. Histogram of onsets for first overlaps.

Appendix B. Sample responses from survey

Category	#	Example comment
Please describe what you liked best about interacting with the system		
Multiparty interaction prowess	21	- I enjoyed how it recognized who was speaking and actually looked at you - I liked how the avatar tracked the players; how it understood speech - It was great to play a game where you don't have to use your hands, just your mind. The way the avatar would recognize position of who spoke was nice. The blinking action at the avatar made her more realistic but she needed more than her face. - That it would look right at you and ask a question - I liked how the avatar made eye contact with each person playing the game
Overall experience with system	15	- It was very new and thus it was fun. I don't play computer games often and I did enjoy this one. Which is rare for me. - It was different than any other trivia game I've played in the past - I think this is a great way for a human to interact with a computer - It's cool interacting with the avatar
Rewarding task	14	- I liked the challenge of the questions - It's a great fun way to improve knowledge - New experience that I found enjoyable. I enjoyed thinking about choices and having an interaction with the avatar
Speech and language	11	- Voice recognition was fairly accurate, no need to repeat - The ability of it to understand what I was saying. Plus it's pretty cool. - I liked it because it wasn't really hard for the system to understand what we were saying. Even though we have an accent.
If there was one thing you could change about this system, what would it be?		
Avatar rendering	32	- The avatar should be more friendly – she came off a bit austere – she didn't smile even when we got 5 out of 6 questions right, it was only "pretty good". - The way it moves its lips needs to be better - The avatar seemed a little to "stiff". It needs to be more natural in movement and speech - The face was a "warmer face". Smiling perhaps.
Multiparty failures	13	- Extend the time limit when questions haven't been fully answered. It would sometimes say we were correct or false before we had confirmed our answer - Sometimes it skips and pauses and making it difficult to understand - Consistency in waiting and asking player to confirm answer instead of overhearing conversations and choosing an answer itself
Task domain	6	- It would be cool if it could remember our names. Also, 6 questions was a little short. I think 8 or 10 questions would be better. - I think the questions should be more pop culture related
Speech and language	5	- I enjoyed her. I would like her to understand a little easier. We had to repeat answers on occasion which wasn't too bad. Overall I really liked it. Perhaps it could ask our names and call us by name when speaking to us

Appendix C. Excerpts from interactions with the system. We present and discuss two segments from an interaction with the questions game system. The segments illustrate challenges for diarization, tracking conversational dynamics (e.g. inferring speech source, target, floor actions, etc.) and decisions making for multiparty turn taking. The video for this entire interaction, as well as an additional interaction are available online at (Situated Interaction, 2011)

1	$S \rightarrow P_1$	Hi. Would you like to play a questions game?	Immediately after the system's greeting, the two participants also say *"Hi"* and *"Hello"*. Their greetings are detected as a single utterance by the system which partially overlaps with the beginning of the system's follow-up question (overlaps are underlined in the examples to the left). According to the current policy, the system does not release the floor on this interruption and continues with its question. The *"Yes"* responses from (4) and (5) are overlapping with each other and are detected by the system as a single utterance which is correctly decoded.
2	$P_{17} \rightarrow S$	*Hi*	
3	$P_{16} \rightarrow S$	*Hello*	
4	$P_{17} \rightarrow S$	*Yes*	
5	$P_{18} \rightarrow S$	*Yes*	
6	$S \rightarrow P_{16}$	Here is the first question. The study of the size and shape of the skull as an indicator of a person's character is known as: telepathy, graphology, or phrenology?	The system correctly infers the floor was addressed to it, and therefore takes the floor and produces the first question
7	$P_{16} \rightarrow S$	*I'll go... Graphology*	Given the pause between *"I'll go"* and *"Graphology"* the response in (7) is in fact detected as two separate utterances by the system. The first part is non-understood, hence assumed addressed to other and the system does not take the floor. The system correctly understands and takes the floor after *"Graphology"*, and moves to ask for confirmation (8). Next, while the system asks the other participant for confirmation, due to imperfections in echo cancellation, the system hears a noise at the beginning of its utterance, but ignores the detected "barge-in".
8	$S \rightarrow P_{17}$	What do you think?	
9	$P_{17} \rightarrow P_{17}$	*graph-*	P_{17} softly says to herself *"graph-"*. This utterance is not actually detected by the system.
10	$P_{16} \rightarrow P_{17}$	*That doesn't sound right but*	Next, the system misunderstands the utterance in (10) as "that sounds right" and incorrectly infers that the utterance was addressed to it. It therefore takes the floor and continues. This leads to a turn-initial overlap with the *"Phrenology"* utterance immediately produced by P_{17} (11)
11	$P_{17} \rightarrow S$	*Phrenology*	
12	$S \rightarrow P_{16},P_{17}$	I'm sorry but that's incorrect. Popular during the 19th century but not discredited, phrenology is a theory that a person's character and intelligence can be determined by the size and shape of their skull.	
13	$P_{16} \rightarrow P_{17}$	*phrenology*	The follow-up utterances and discussion between participants (13-16) overlap with portions of the system's explanation. They indicate the high cost of the misunderstanding and of the system's incorrect inference and decision to take the floor (admonished by the user in (16) ❶, as well as the shortcomings of the current policy to not release the floor for barge-ins detected during explanations. This example highlights the need for more robust inferences, but also better policies for releasing back the floor and for machinery that would allow the system to gracefully backing from detected floor conflicts.
14	$P_{16} \rightarrow P_{17}$	*She did not wait for your answer*	
15	$P_{17} \rightarrow P_{16}$	*I guess not*	
16	$P_{16} \rightarrow S$	*You didn't wait for my answer*	
17	$S \rightarrow P_{16},P_{17}$	Next question [...]	The system then moves on to the next question

1	$S \rightarrow P_{16}$	In the USA hospitals have a red cross, what sign do they use in the Arab World?	This segment starts with the system asking a question
2	$P_{16} \rightarrow P_{16}$	Hospitals have a red cross what sign do they user in the Arab World...	P_{16} echoes back the question to himself in a low voice. The system detects this utterance, correctly inferred that the floor is not being released to it (the utterance leads to a non-understanding), and the system turns towards the other participant, which produces *"Solid blue circle"* (3). The utterance and corresponding floor release to the system are correctly understood, and the system turns back to P_{16} for confirmation. Next, the system detects an utterance from P_{17}, who has changed her mind (5). The system takes the floor and asks both participants (by directing gaze towards them) what the correct answer is (6), and releases the floor to both participants ❷. P_{17} speaks first towards P_{16} (7) – this utterance is low energy and not detected by the system, and then towards the system (8). The system recognizes the floor is released to it after (8), takes the floor and directs it back towards P_{16} non-verbally, by turning towards him and raising eyebrows. P_{16} responds immediately, and the system takes the floor and continues to the next question.
3	$P_{17} \rightarrow S$	Solid blue circle	
4	$S \rightarrow P_{16}$	Is that correct?	
5	$P_{17} \rightarrow S$	No	
6	$S \rightarrow P_{16},P_{17}$	So what's the correct answer?	
7	$P_{17} \rightarrow P_{16}$	Red crescent moon	
8	$P_{17} \rightarrow S$	Red crescent moon	
9	$S \rightarrow P_{16}$	[turns to P_{16}, lifts eyebrows]	
10	$P_{16} \rightarrow S$	Yes	
11	$S \rightarrow P_{16},P_{17}$	That's right. Okay, so far you're two out of three [...]	

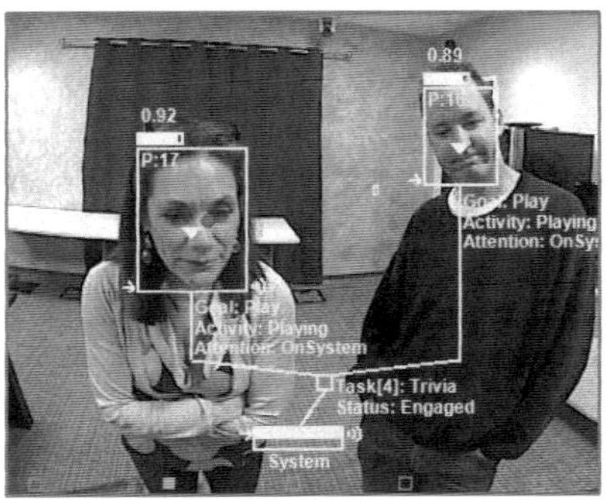

❶ In the first segment, while the system is speaking to both participants (12), P_{17} leans in as she produces utterance (16)

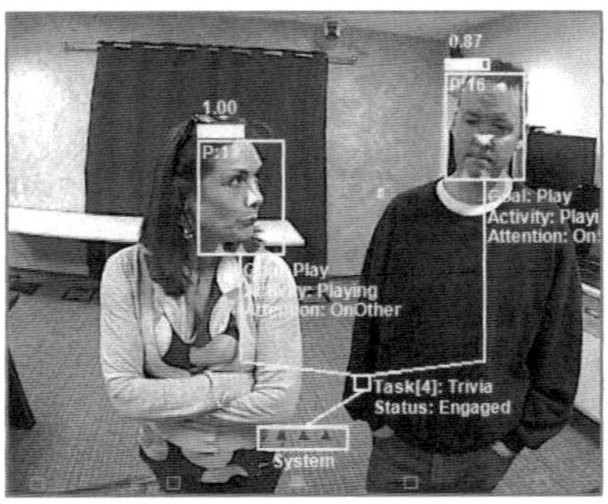

❷ In the second segment, the system releases the floor to both participants after producing (6)

Illustrations of conversational scene analysis performed by the system in real-time, at runtime.

Stability and Accuracy in Incremental Speech Recognition

Ethan O. Selfridge[†], **Iker Arizmendi**[‡], **Peter A. Heeman**[†], **and Jason D. Williams**[‡]

[†] Center for Spoken Language Understanding, Oregon Health & Science University, Portland, OR
[‡]AT&T Labs – Research, Shannon Laboratory, Florham Park, NJ
{selfridg,heemanp}@ohsu.edu {iker,jdw}@research.att.com

Abstract

Conventional speech recognition approaches usually wait until the user has finished talking before returning a recognition hypothesis. This results in spoken dialogue systems that are unable to react while the user is still speaking. Incremental Speech Recognition (ISR), where partial phrase results are returned during user speech, has been used to create more reactive systems. However, ISR output is unstable and so prone to revision as more speech is decoded. This paper tackles the problem of stability in ISR. We first present a method that increases the *stability* and *accuracy* of ISR output, without adding delay. Given that some revisions are unavoidable, we next present a pair of methods for predicting the stability and accuracy of ISR results. Taken together, we believe these approaches give ISR more utility for real spoken dialogue systems.

1 Introduction

Incremental Speech Recognition (ISR) enables a spoken dialogue system (SDS) to react quicker than when using conventional speech recognition approaches. Where conventional methods only return a result after some indication of user completion (for example, a short period of silence), ISR returns partial phrase results while the user is still speaking. Having access to a real-time stream of user speech enables more natural behavior by a SDS, and is a foundation for creating systems which take a more active role in conversations.

Research by Fink et al.(1998) and Skantze & Schlangen (2009), among others, has demonstrated the efficacy of ISR but has also drawn attention to a significant obstacle to widespread use: partial phrase results are generally unstable and so, as more speech is decoded, are prone to revision. For example, the ISR component in a bus information SDS may return the partial "leaving from Hills", where "Hills" is a neighborhood name. It may then return the revision "leaving from Pittsburgh", which the system must handle gracefully. Given this propensity to revise, a Stability Measure (SM) — likelihood of a partial result remaining unchanged compared to the final result — is necessary for optimal incremental system behavior. Furthermore, since a stable partial may still be inaccurate, a Confidence Measure (CM) — likelihood of partial correctness — is also necessary.

Effective ISR enables systems to participate in more dynamic turn-taking. For instance, these two measures would enable an SDS to identify inaccurate recognition results while the user is still speaking. The SDS could then interrupt and prompt the user to start again. On the other hand, ISR allows systems to handle pauses gracefully. If the SDS recognizes that an utterance is incomplete (though stable and accurate), it could give the user more time to speak before reacting.

We present two contributions specific to the use of ISR. First, we characterize three approaches to ISR which make different trade-offs between stability and the number of partials generated. We then present a novel hybrid approach that combines their strengths to increase

Proceedings of the SIGDIAL 2011: the 12th Annual Meeting of the Special Interest Group on Discourse and Dialogue, pages 110–119,
Portland, Oregon, June 17-18, 2011. ©2011 Association for Computational Linguistics

stability without adding latency. However, even with this method, some partial results are still later revised. The second contribution of the paper is to present a pair of methods which predict the stability and accuracy of each partial result. These two measures are designed for use in concert by dialogue systems, which must decide whether to act on each partial result in real time.

2 Background and Related Work

We now describe modern speech recognition methodology, the production of partial phrase results, and the advantages and deficiencies of ISR. In this we seek only to provide a topical foundation, and not a comprehensive review.

Most modern speech recognition engines use Hidden-Markov Models and the Viterbi algorithm to decode words from audio. Decoding employs three models: an acoustic model, which assigns probabilities to speech audio given a phone; a lexicon, which specifies phone sequences for a word; and a language model, which specifies the probability of a word sequence. The aim of the decoding process is to find the N most probable word sequences given the audio spoken and these three models.

Two useful but different forms of language models are commonly used in spoken dialogue systems. A *Rule-based Language Model* (RLM) specifies a list of valid sentences which may be recognized, usually via expansion rules. By contrast, a *Statistical Language Model* (SLM) specifies a vocabulary of words, allowing arbitrary sentences to be formed. Both models specify probabilities over their respective sets — RLMs via whole-sentence probabilities, and SLMs via probabilities of short word sequences called N-grams. In an SLM, special word symbols are used to represent the beginning and end of the phrase, so the probability of beginning or ending phrases with words can be modeled.

As speech frames are received, the recognizer builds up a *lattice* which compactly describes the probable sequences of words decoded from the audio. In conventional turn-based speech recognition, decoding continues until the user finishes speaking. Once the user has finished, the engine searches the lattice for the most probable word sequence and returns this to the dialogue manager. By contrast, in ISR the engine inspects the lattice *as it is being built*, and returns *partial* results to the dialogue manager as they become available. A key issue for ISR is that partial results may later be revised, because as more speech is received and the lattice is extended, a different path may become the most probable. In other words, partial results are *unstable* in the sense that they may later be revised. Note that stability is not the same as accuracy: a partial result may be accurate (correct so far) but unstable, because it is later revised. Similarly, a stable result may not be accurate.

In the literature, ISR has been proposed for dialogue systems to enable them to engage in more natural, human-like interactions. Studies have shown that incremental systems react faster than non-incremental ones, and are well-liked by users because of their naturalness (Aist et al., 2007; Skantze and Schlangen, 2009). Aist et al. (2007) found that incremental speech recognition yielded 20% faster task completion. Moreover, adding ISR improved users' satisfaction with the interaction; the authors attributed this improvement to "naturalness": "incremental systems are more like human-human conversation than their non-incremental counterparts." Skantze & Schlangen (2009) observed a similar trend, finding that an incremental system was "clearly preferred" since it "was experienced as more pleasant and human-like", though it did not actually outperform the non-incremental system in a number dictation task.

Some recent work has focused on incremental natural language understanding (NLU). DeVault et al. (2009) showed that when using a relatively small number of semantic possibilities the correct interpretation could be predicted by early incremental results. Schlangen et al. (2009) demonstrated that an incremental reference resolver could identify the correct reference out of 12 more than 50% of the time. This type of NLU can use context and other information to be somewhat resilient to errors, and word recognition inaccuracies may not yield a change in understanding. In this paper we focus on improving accuracy and stability at the word level; we belief that improvements at the word level are likely to improve performance at the understanding level, although we do not evaluate this here.

A number of researchers have described methods for evaluating and improving the stability of ISR results (Baumann et al., 2009; Fink et al., 1998). Baumann, Atterer, & Schlangen spoke directly to stability by comparing partial phrase results against the "final hypothesis produced by the ASR". They show that increasing the amount of "right context" — the amount of speech after the end of the putative partial result — increases the stability of the partials. Fink et al. (1998) also used a right context delay to decrease the word error rate of ISR results.

A key limitation of these past efforts to improve stability is that adding right context necessarily incurs *delay*, which degrades responsiveness and erodes the overall benefits of ISR. Furthermore, past work has not addressed the problem of identifying which partials are likely to be revised. In this paper, we tackle both of these problems. We first present a method for improving stability by considering features of the lattice itself, without incurring the delay associated with adding right context. Additionally, since some partials will still be revised, we then propose a method of scoring the stability of partial speech recognition results.

3 Three approaches to ISR

We now describe three approaches to ISR: Basic, Terminal, and Immortal. Basic ISR simply returns the most likely word sequence observed after some number of speech frames has been decoded (in our case every 3 frames or 30ms). This is the least restrictive approach, and we believe is the method used by recent ISR research.

Terminal ISR, a more restrictive approach, finds a partial result if the most likely path through the (partially-decoded) lattice ends at a *terminal* node in the language model. The intuition is that if a partial result finishes a complete phrase expected by the language model, it is more likely to be stable. The meaning of *terminal* is slightly different for rule-based language models (RLMs) and statistical language models (SLMs). For a rule-based grammar, the terminal node is simply one that ends a valid phrase ('Pittsburgh' in 'leaving from Pittsburgh'). For an SLM, a terminal node indicates that the most likely successor state is the special end-of-sentence symbol. In other words, in an SLM Terminal partial result, the language model assigns the highest probability to ending the phrase.

A third method, Immortal ISR, is the most restrictive method (Spohrer et al., 1980). If all paths of the lattice come together into a node — called an *immortal* node — then the lattice structure before that node will be unchanged by any subsequent decoding. This structure guarantees that the best word sequence prior to an immortal node is stable. Immortal ISR operates identically for both RLMs and SLMs.[1]

To compare these approaches we evaluate their performance. Utterances were extracted from real calls to the Carnegie Mellon "Lets Go!" bus information system for Pittsburgh, USA (Raux et al., 2005; Parent and Eskenazi, 2009). We chose this domain because this corpus is publicly available, and this domain has recently been used as a test bed for dialogue systems (Black et al. , 2010). The AT&T WATSON speech recognition engine was used, modified to output partials as described above (Goffin et al., 2005). We tested these three approaches to ISR on three different recognition tasks. The first two tasks used rule-based language models (RLM), and the third used a statistical language model (SLM).

The two rule-based language models were developed for AT&T "Let's Go" dialogue system, prior to its deployment (Williams et al. , 2010). The first RLM (RLM1) consisted

[1]The choice of search beam size affects both accuracy and the number of immortal nodes produced: a smaller beams yields a sparser lattice with more immortal nodes and lower accuracy; a larger beam yields a richer lattice with fewer immortal nodes and higher accuracy. In this work we used our recognizer's default beam size, which allows recognition to run in less than real time and yields near-asymptotic accuracy for all experiments.

of street and neighborhood names, built from the bus timetable database. The second RLM (RLM2) consisted of just neighborhood names. Utterances to test RLM1 and RLM2 were selected from the corpus provided by Carnegie Mellon to match the expected distribution of speech at the dialogue states where RLM1 and RLM2 would be used. RLM1 was evaluated on a set of 7722 utterances, and RLM2 on 5411 utterances. To simulate realistic use, both RLM test sets were built so that 80% of utterances are in-grammar, and 20% are out-of-grammar. The SLM was a 3-gram trained on a set of 140K utterances, and is tested on a set of 42620 utterances.

In past work, Raux et al. (2005) report word error rates (WERs) of 60-68% on data from the same dialogue system, though on a different set of utterances. By comparison, our SLM yields a WER of 35%, which gives us some confidence that our overall recognition accuracy is competitive, and that our results are relevant.

Table 1 provides a few statistics of the LMs and test sets, including *whole-utterance accuracy*, computed using an exact string match. Results are analyzed in two groups: *All*, where all of the utterances are analyzed, and *Multi-Word (MW)*, where only utterances whose transcribed speech (what was actually said) has more than one word. Intuitively, these utterances are where ISR would be most effective. That said, ISR is beneficial for both short and long utterances — for example, ISR systems can react faster to users regardless of utterance length.

ISR was run using each of the three approaches (Basic, Terminal, Immortal) in each of the three configurations (RLM1, RLM2, SLM). The mean number of partials per utterance is shown in Table 2. For all ISR methods, the more flexible SLM produces more partials than the RLMs. Also as expected, multi-word utterances produce substantially more partials per utterance than when looking at the entire utterance set. The Basic approach produces nearly double the number of partials than Terminal ISR does, and Immortal ISR production highlights its primary weakness: in many utterances, no immortal nodes are found. Given this however, immortal node occurrence is directly related to the number of words, as indicted by the greater number of immortal partials in multi-word utterances.

Table 1: Statistics for Recognition Tasks. In all tables, *All* refers to all utterances in a test set, and *MW* refers to the subset of multi-word utterances in a test set.

	RLM1	RLM2	SLM
Num. Utts All	7722	5411	42620
Num. Utts MW	3213	1748	20396
Words/Utt All	1.7	1.5	2.3
Words/Utt MW	2.8	2.6	3.8
Utt. Acc. All.	50 %	60 %	62 %
Utt. Acc. MW	53 %	56 %	44 %

Stability is assessed by comparing the partial to the final recognition result. For simplicity, we restrict our analysis to 1-Best hypotheses. If the *partial* 1-Best hypothesis is a prefix (or full exact match) of the *final* 1-Best hypothesis then it is considered stable. For instance, if the partial 1-Best hypothesis is "leaving from Forbes" then it would be stable if the final 1-Best is "leaving from Forbes" or "leaving from Forbes and Murray" but not if it is "from Forbes and Murray" or "leaving". Accuracy is assessed similarly except that the transcribed reference is used instead of the final recognition result.

We report stability and accuracy in Table 3. Immortal partials are excluded from stability since they are guaranteed to be stable. The first four rows report stability, and the second six report accuracy. The results show that Terminal Partials are relatively unstable, with 23%-

Table 2: Average Number of Partials per utterance

ISR	Group	RLM1	RLM2	SLM
Basic	All	12.0	9.9	11.6
	MW	14.6	12.3	29.7
Terminal	All	5.4	3.3	6.2
	MW	6.4	4.1	8.8
Immortal	All	0.22	0.32	0.55
	MW	0.42	0.67	0.63

Table 3: Stability and Accuracy Percentages

ISR	Group	RLM1	RLM2	SLM
Stability				
Basic	All	10 %	11 %	7 %
	MW	14 %	15 %	9 %
Terminal	All	23 %	31 %	37 %
	MW	20 %	28 %	36 %
Accuracy				
Basic	All	9 %	1 %	5 %
	MW	11 %	13 %	6 %
Terminal	All	13 %	21 %	24 %
	MW	12 %	17 %	21 %
Immortal	All	91 %	93 %	55 %
	MW	90 %	90 %	56 %

37% of partials being stable, and that their stability drops off when looking at multi-word utterances. SLM stability seems to be somewhat higher than that of the RLM. Basic partials are even more unstable (about 10% of partials are stable), with extremely low stability for the SLM. Unlike Terminal ISR, their stability grows when only multi-word utterances are analyzed, though the maximum is still quite low.

The results also show that partials are always less accurate than they are stable, indicating that not all stable partials are accurate. Immortal partials are rare, but when they are found, they are much more accurate than Terminal or Basic partials. The RLM accuracy is very high, and we suspect that immortal nodes are correlated with utterances which are easier to recognize. Terminal ISR is far more accurate than Basic ISR for all of the utterances, but its improvement declines for multi-word RLMs.

We have shown three types of ISR: Basic, Terminal and Immortal ISR. While Basic and Terminal ISR are both highly productive, Terminal ISR is far more stable and accurate than Basic. Furthermore, there are far more Basic partials than Terminal partials, implying that the dialogue manager would have to handle more unstable and inaccurate partials more often. Given this, Terminal ISR is a far better "productive ISR" than the Basic method. Taking production and stability together, there is a double dissociation between Terminal and Immortal ISR. Terminal partials are over produced and relatively unstable. Furthermore, they are even less stable when the transcribed reference is greater than one word. On the other hand, Immortal partials are stable and quite accurate, but too rare for use alone. By integrating the Immortal Partials with the Terminal ones, we may be able to increase the stability and accuracy overall.

Table 4: Lattice-Aware ISR (LAISR) Example

1-best	Partial Type
yew	Terminal
sarah	Terminal
baum	Terminal
dallas	Terminal
downtown	Terminal
downtown	Immortal
downtown pittsburgh	Terminal
downtown pittsburgh	Immortal

4 Lattice-Aware ISR (LAISR)

We introduce *Lattice-Aware ISR* (LAISR — pronounced "laser"), that integrates Terminal and Immortal ISR by allowing both types of partials to be found. The selection procedure works by first checking for an Immortal partial. If one is not found then it looks for a Terminal. Redundant partials are returned when the partial type changes. An example recognition is shown in Table 4. Notice how the first four partials are completely unstable. This is very common, and suppressing this noise is one of the primary benefits of using more right context. Basic ISR has even more of this type of noise.

LAISR was evaluated on the three recognition tasks described above (see Table 5). The first two rows show the average number of partials per utterance for each task and utterance group. Unsurprisingly, these numbers are quite similar to Terminal ISR. The stability percentage of LAISR is shown in the second two rows. For all the utterances, there appears to be a very slight improvement when compared to Terminal ISR in Table 3. The improvement increases for MW utterances, with LAISR improving over

Table 5: Lattice-Aware ISR Stats

	RLM1	RLM2	SLM
Partials per Utterance			
All	5.6	3.5	6.7
MW	6.7	4.5	9.6
Stability Percentage			
All	24 %	33 %	40 %
MW	24 %	35 %	41 %
Accuracy Percentage			
All	15 %	23 %	26 %
MW	16 %	22 %	24 %

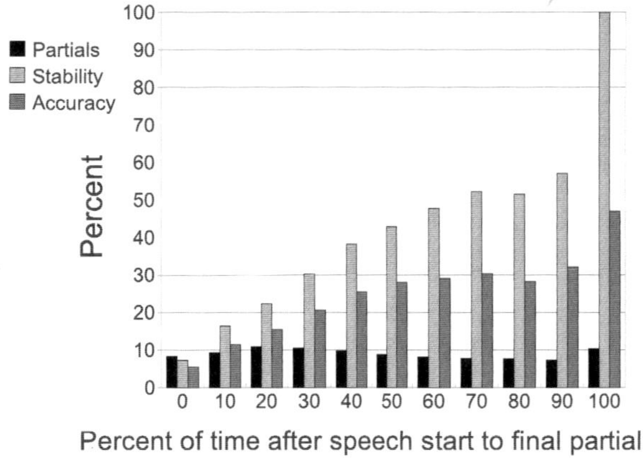

Figure 1: Percent of LAISR partials returned from the start of detected speech to the final partial using the SLM. The percentage of partials returned that are stable/accurate are also shown.

Terminal ISR by 4–7 percentage points. This is primarily because there is a higher occurrence of Immortal partials as the utterance gets longer. Accuracy is reported in the final two rows. Like the previous ISR methods described, the accuracy percentage is lower than the stability percentage. When compared to Terminal ISR, LAISR accuracy is slightly higher, which confirms the benefit of incorporating immortal partials with their relatively high accuracy. To be useful in practice, it is important to examine *when* in the utterance ISR results are being produced. For example, if most of the partials are returned towards the end of utterances, than ISR is of little value over standard turn-based recognition. Figure 1 shows the percent of partials returned from the start of speech to the final partial for MW utterances using the SLM. This figure shows that partials are returned rather evenly over the duration of utterances. For example, in the first 10% of duration of each utterance, about 10% of all partial results are returned. Figure 1 also reports the stability and accuracy of the partials returned. These numbers grow as decoding progresses, but shows that mid-utterance results do yield reasonable accuracy: partials returned in the middle of utterances (50%-60% duration) have an accuracy of near 30%, compared to final partials 47% percent.

For use in a real-time dialogue system, it is also important to assess *latency*. Here we define latency as the difference in (real-world) time between (1) when the recognizer receives the last frame of audio for a segment of speech, and (2) when the partial that covers that segment of speech is returned from the recognizer. Measuring latencies of LAISR on each task, we find that RLM1 has a median of 0.26 seconds and a mean of 0.41s; RLM2 has a median of 0.60s and a mean of 1.48s; and SLM has a median of 1.04s and a mean of 2.10s. Since reducing latency was not the focus on this work, no speed optimizations have been made, and we believe that straightforward optimization can reduce these latencies. For example, on the SLM, simply turning off N-Best processing reduces the median latency to 0.55s and the mean to 0.79s. Human reaction time to speech is roughly 0.20 seconds (Fry, 1975), so even without optimization the RLM latencies are not far off human performance.

In sum, LAISR produces a steady stream of partials with relatively low latency over the course of recognition. LAISR has higher stability and accuracy than Terminal ISR, but its partials are still quite unstable and inaccurate. This means that in practice, dialogue systems will need to make important decisions about which partials to use, and which to discard. This need motivated us to devise techniques for predicting when a partial is stable, and when it is accurate, which we address next.

Table 6: Equal Error Rates: Significant improvements in bold. Basic at $p < 0.016$, Terminal at $p < 0.002$, and LAISR at $p < 0.00001$

		All			Multi-Word		
Stability Measure (SM) Equal Error Rate							
		RLM 1	RLM 2	SLM	RLM 1	RLM 2	SLM
Basic	WATSON Score	13.3	13.3	12.8	15.6	16.4	15.2
	Regression	**10.7**	**11.3**	**12.3**	**13.2**	**15.2**	15.1
Terminal	WATSON Score	24.3	29.1	34.4	26.6	26.0	34.1
	Regression	**19.7**	**26.5**	**26.5**	**23.0**	24.3	**24.7**
LAISR	WATSON Score	24.7	29.3	35.0	24.0	27.0	35.3
	Regression	**19.2**	**25.6**	**25.0**	**18.4**	**23.3**	**22.7**
Confidence Measure (CM) Equal Error Rate							
Basic	WATSON Score	11.3	11.7	9.9	14.1	14.0	11.6
	Regression	**9.8**	**9.8**	9.7	**12.3**	**12.9**	**11.0**
Terminal	WATSON Score	15.1	21.1	30.6	15.7	17.4	29.3
	Regression	**11.7**	**16.8**	**20.8**	**12.1**	**14.5**	**18.4**
LAISR	WATSON Score	15.8	21.8	32.3	18.4	19.5	31.8
	Regression	**11.6**	**16.6**	**21.0**	**11.6**	**14.2**	**18.7**

5 Stability and Confidence Measures

As seen in the previous section, partial speech recognition results are often revised and inaccurate. In order for a dialogue system to make use of partial results, measures of both stability and confidence are crucial. A Stability Measure (SM) predicts whether the current partial is a prefix or complete match of the final recognition result (regardless of whether the final result is accurate). A Confidence Measure (CM) predicts whether the current partial is a prefix or complete match of what the user actually said. Both are useful in real systems: for example, if a partial is likely stable but unlikely correct, the system might interrupt the user and ask them to start again.

We use logistic regression to learn separate classifiers for SM and CM. Logistic regression is appealing because it is well-calibrated, and has shown good performance for whole-utterance confidence measures (Williams and Balakrishnan, 2009). For this, we use the BXR package with default settings (Genkin et al., 2011). For Terminal and Basic ISR we use 11 features: the raw WATSON confidence score, the individual features which affect the confidence score, the normalized cost, the normalized speech likelihood, the likelihoods of competing models, the best path score of word confusion network (WCN), the length of WCN, the worst probability in the WCN, and the length of N-best list. For LAISR, four additional features are used: three binary indicators of whether the partial is Terminal, Immortal or a Terminal following an Immortal, and one which gives the percentage of words in the hypothesis that are immortal.

We built stability and confidence measures for Basic ISR, Terminal ISR, and LAISR. Each of the three corpora (RLM1, RLM2, SLM) was divided in half to form a train set and test set. Regression models were trained on *all* utterances in the train set. The resulting models were then evaluated on both All and MW utterances. As a baseline for both measures, we compare to AT&T WATSON's existing confidence score. This score is used in numerous deployed commercial applications, so we believe it is a fair baseline. Although the existing confidence score is designed to predict accuracy (*not stability*), there is no other existing mechanism for predicting stability.

We first report "equal error rate" for the measures (Table 6). Equal error rate (EER) is the sum of false accepts and false rejects at the rejec-

Figure 2: True accept percentages for stability measure (a) and confidence measure (b), using a fixed false accept rate of 5%. LAISR yields highest true accept rates, with $p < 0.0001$ in all cases.

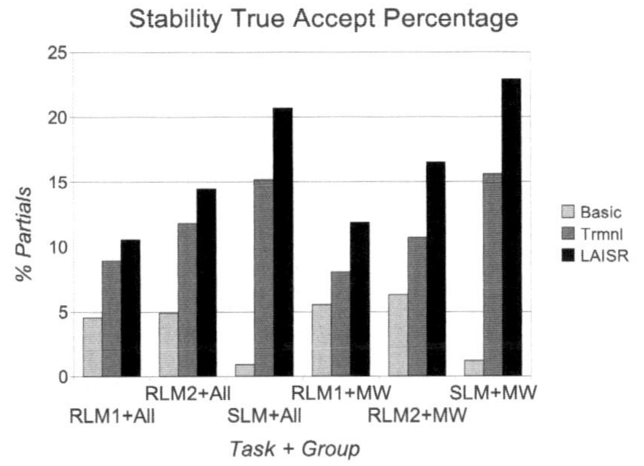

(a) Stability measure

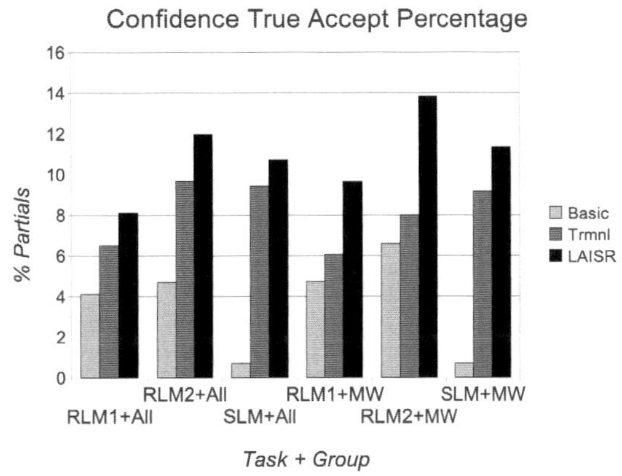

(b) Confidence measure

tion threshold for which false accepts and false rejects are equal. Equal error rate is a widely used metric to evaluate the quality of scoring models used for accept/reject decisions. A perfect scoring model would yield an EER of 0. For statistical significance we use χ^2 contingency tables with 1 degree of freedom. It is inappropriate to compare EER across ISR methods, since the total percentage of stable or accurate partials significantly effects the EER. For example, Basic ISR has relatively low EER, but this is because it also has a relatively low number of stable or accurate partials.

The top six rows of Table 6 show EER for the Stability Measure (SM). The left three columns show results on the entire test set (all utterances, of any length). On the whole, the SM outperforms the WATSON confidence scores, and the greatest improvement is a 10.0 point reduction in EER for LAISR on the SLM task. The right three columns show results on only multi-word (MW) utterances. Performance is similar to the entire test set, with a maximum EER reduction of 12.6 percent. The SLM MW performance is interesting, suggesting that it is easier to predict stability after at least one word has been decoded, possibly due to higher probability of immortal nodes occurring. This suggests there would be benefit in combining our method with past work that adds right-context, perhaps using more context early in the utterance. This idea is left for future work.

The bottom six rows show results for the Confidence Measure (CM). We see that that even when comparing our CM against the WATSON confidence scores, there is significant improvement, with a maximum of 13.1 for LAISR in the MW SLM task.

The consistent improvement shows that logistic regression is an effective technique for learning confidence and stability measures. It is most powerful when combined with LAISR, and only slightly less so with Terminal. Furthermore, though the gains are slight, it is also useful with Basic ISR, which speaks to the generality of the approach.

While equal error rate is useful for evaluating discriminative ability, when building an actual system a designer would be interested to know how often the correct partial is accepted. To evaluate this, we assumed a fixed false-accept rate of 5%, and report the resulting percentage of partials which are correctly accepted (true-accepts). Results are shown in Figure 1. LAISR accepts substantially more correct partials than other methods, indicating that LAISR would be more useful in practice. This result also shows a synergy between LAISR and our regression-based stability and confidence measures: not only does LAISR improve the fraction of stable and correct partials, but the regression is able to identify them better than for Terminal ISR. We believe this shows the usefulness of the additional lattice features used by the regression model built on LAISR results.

6 Discussion and Conclusion

The adoption of ISR is hindered by the number of revisions that most partials undergo. A number of researchers have proposed the use of right context to increase the stability of partials. While this does increase stability, it mitigates the primary gain of ISR: getting a relatively real-time stream of the user's utterance. We offer two methods to improve ISR functionality: the integration of low-occurring Immortal partials with higher occurring Terminal partials (LAISR), and the use of logistic regression to learn stability and confidence measures.

We find that the integrative approach, LAISR, outperforms Terminal ISR on three recognition tasks for a bus timetable spoken dialogue system. When looking at utterances with more than one word this difference becomes even greater, and this performance increase is due to the addition of immortal partials, which have a higher occurrence in longer utterances. This suggests that as dialogue systems are used to process multi-phrasal utterances and have more dynamic turn-taking interactions, immortal partials will play an even larger roll in ISR and partial stability will further improve.

The Stability and Confidence measures both have lower Equal Error Rates than raw recognition scores when classifying partials. The improvement is greatest for LAISR, which benefits from additional features describing lattice structure. It also suggests that other incremental features such as the length of right context could be useful for predicting stability. The higher number of True Accept partials by LAISR indicates that this method is more useful to a dialogue manager than Basic or Terminal ISR. Even so, for all ISR methods there are still more useful stable partials than there are accurate ones. This suggests that both of these measures are important to the downstream dialogue manager. For example, if the partial is predicted to be stable but not correct, than the agent could possibly interrupt the user and ask them to begin again.

There are a number of avenues for future work. First, this paper has examined the *word* level; however dialogue systems generally operate at the *intention* level. Not all changes at the word level yield a change in the resulting intention, so it would be interesting to apply the confidence measure and stability measures developed here to the (partial) intention level. These measures could also be applied to later stages of the pipeline – for example, tracking stability and confidence in the dialogue state resulting from the current partial intention. Features from the intention level and dialogue state could be useful for these measures – for instance, indicating whether the current partial intention is incompatible with the current dialogue state.

Another avenue for future work would be to apply these techniques to non-dialogue real-time ASR tasks, such as transcription of broadcast news. Confidence and stability measures could be used to determine whether/when/how to display recognized text to a viewer, or to inform down-stream processes such as named entity extraction or machine translation.

Of course, an important objective is to evaluate our Stability and Confidence Measures with LAISR in an actual spoken dialogue system. ISR completely restructures the conventional turn-based dialogue manager, giving the agent the opportunity to speak at any moment. The use of reinforcement learning to make these turn-taking decisions has been shown in a small simulated domain by Selfridge and Heeman (2010), and we believe this paper builds a foundation for pursuing these ideas in a real system.

Acknowledgments

Thanks to Vincent Goffin for help with this work, and the anonymous reviewers for their thoughtful suggestions and critique. We acknowledge funding from the NSF under grant IIS-0713698.

References

G. Aist, J. Allen, E. Campana, C. Gallo, S. Stoness, Mary Swift, and Michael K. Tanenhaus. 2007. Incremental understanding in human-computer dialogue and experimental evidence for advantages over nonincremental methods. In *Proc. DECALOG*, pages 149–154.

T. Baumann, M. Atterer, and D. Schlangen. 2009. Assessing and improving the performance of speech recognition for incremental systems. In *Proc. NAACL: HLT*, pages 380–388.

A. Black, S. Burger, B. Langner, G. Parent, and M. Eskenazi, 2010. Spoken dialog challenge 2010, In *Proc. Workshop on Spoken Language Technologies (SLT), Spoken Dialog Challenge 2010 Special Session.*

David DeVault, Kenji Sagae, and David Traum. 2009. Can i finish? learning when to respond to incremental interpretation results in interactive dialogue. In *Proc. SIGdial 2009 Conference*, pages 11–20,

G.A. Fink, C. Schillo, F. Kummert, and G. Sagerer. 1998. Incremental speech recognition for multimodal interfaces. In *Industrial Electronics Society, 1998. IECON'98* volume 4, pages 2012–2017.

D.B. Fry. 1975. Simple reaction-times to speech and non-speech stimuli.. *Cortex* volume 11, number 4, page 355.

A. Genkin, L. Shenzhi, D. Madigan, and DD. Lewis. 2011. Bayesian logistic regression. *http://www.bayesianregression.org.*

V. Goffin, C. Allauzen, E. Bocchieri, D. Hakkani-Tur, A. Ljolje, S. Parthasarathy, M. Rahim, G. Riccardi, and M. Saraclar. 2005. The AT&T WATSON speech recognizer. In *Proc. of ICASSP*, pages 1033–1036.

G. Parent and M. Eskenazi. 2009. Toward Better Crowdsourced Transcription: Transcription of a year of the Let's Go Bus Information System Data. *Proc. of Interspeech 2005, Lisbon, Portugal.*

A. Raux, B. Langner, D. Bohus, A.W. Black, and M. Eskenazi. 2005. Lets go public! taking a spoken dialog system to the real world. In *Proc. of Interspeech 2005.*

D. Schlangen, T. Baumann, and M. Atterer. 2009. Incremental reference resolution: The task, metrics for evaluation, and a Bayesian filtering model that is sensitive to disfluencies. In *Proc. SIGdial*, pages 30–37.

E.O. Selfridge and P.A. Heeman. 2010. Importance-Driven Turn-Bidding for spoken dialogue systems. In *Proc. of ACL 2010*, pages 177–185.

G. Skantze and D. Schlangen. 2009. Incremental dialogue processing in a micro-domain. In *Proc. EACL 2009*, pages 745–753

J.C. Spohrer, PF Brown, PH Hochschild, and JK Baker. 1980. Partial traceback in continuous speech recognition. In *Proc. of the IEEE International Conference on Cybernetics and Society.*

J.D. Williams, I. Arizmendi and A. Conkie. 2010. Demonstration of AT&T "Let's Go": A production-grade statistical spoken dialog system. In *Proc Demonstration Session at IEEE Workshop on Spoken Language Technology*

J.D. Williams and S. Balakrishnan. 2009. Estimating probability of correctness for ASR N-Best lists. In *Proc. of SIGdial 2009*, pages 132–135.

Predicting the Micro-Timing of User Input for an Incremental Spoken Dialogue System that Completes a User's Ongoing Turn

Timo Baumann
Department of Linguistics
Potsdam University
Germany
timo@ling.uni-potsdam.de

David Schlangen
Faculty of Linguistics and Literature
Bielefeld University
Germany
david.schlangen@uni-bielefeld.de

Abstract

We present the novel task of predicting temporal features of continuations of user input, while that input is still ongoing. We show that the remaining duration of an ongoing word, as well as the duration of the next can be predicted reasonably well, and we put this information to use in a system that synchronously completes a user's speech. While we focus on collaborative completions, the techniques presented here may also be useful for the alignment of back-channels and immediate turn-taking in an incremental SDS, or to synchronously monitor the user's speech fluency for other reasons.

1 Introduction

Turn completion, that is, finishing a user's ongoing utterance, can be considered an ideal test-case of *incremental* spoken language processing, as it requires that all levels of language understanding and production are carried out in real time, without any noticeable lags and with proper timing and even with the ability to predict what will come. Spoken dialogue systems, especially incremental ones, have come a long way towards reducing lags at turn changes (e. g. (Raux and Eskenazi, 2009; Skantze and Schlangen, 2009)), or even predicting upcoming turn changes (Schlangen, 2006; Baumann, 2008; Ward et al., 2010). Compared to regular turn changes, where short pauses or overlaps occur frequently (Weilhammer and Rabold, 2003), turn completions in natural dialogues are typically precisely aligned and prosodically highly integrated with the turn that is being completed (Local, 2007). With ever more incremental (and hence quicker) spoken dialogue systems, the phenomenon of completion comes into reach for SDSs, and hence questions of micro-timing become important.

While completing someone else's turn – especially for a computer – may be considered impolite or even annoying, *being able* to do so can be a useful capability. Some tasks where it might be helpful are

- negotiation training to induce stress in a human trainee as presented by DeVault et al. (2009), or
- pronunciation aids for language learners, in which hard to pronounce words could be spoken simultaneously by the system.

A system should certainly not try to complete all or even many user turns, but having the capability to do so means that the system has a very efficient interactional device at its disposal.

Furthermore, monitoring the user's timing, as is required for the temporal prediction of turn continuations, can also be used for other conversational tasks such as producing back-channels that are precisely aligned to the user's back-channel inviting cues, to enable micro-alignment of turn-onsets, or to quickly react to deviations in the user's fluency.

In this paper, we concentrate on the temporal aspects of turn completion, that is, the prediction of the precise temporal alignment of a turn continuation and the technical realization of this timing. We assume the task of predicting the completion itself to be handled by some other system component. Such components are indeed under development (see Section 2). However, previous work has left out the question of how the precise timing of turn completions can be accomplished, which is what we try to answer here.

The remainder of this paper is structured as follows: In Section 2 we review literature on turn completion and related work in spoken dialogue systems,

Proceedings of the SIGDIAL 2011: the 12th Annual Meeting of the Special Interest Group on Discourse and Dialogue, pages 120–129,
Portland, Oregon, June 17-18, 2011. ©2011 Association for Computational Linguistics

before we explain what exactly our task is in Section 3. In Section 4 we present our system's overall architecture and the duration modelling technique that we use, before describing the corpus that we use in Section 5. In Section 6 we first analyse whether enough time to output a completion is available sufficiently often, before turning to the question for the actual sub-tasks of *when* and *how* to complete. We wrap up with concluding remarks and ideas for future work.

2 Related Work

The general phenomenon of turn completion can be broken down into cases where the completion is spoken simultaneously with the original speaker (*turn sharing*, (Lerner, 2002)) and where the floor changes in mid-utterance (*collaborative turn sequences* (Lerner, 2004) or *split utterances* (Purver et al., 2009)). In this paper, a differentiation between the two cases is not important, as we only deal with the question of when to start speaking (for the previously non-speaking system) and not the question of whether the current turn owner will stop speaking. Moreover, whether the other speaker will stop is beyond the system's control. Lerner (2004) distinguishes turn *co-optation*, in which a listener joins in to come first and win the floor, and turn *co-completion*, in which the completion is produced in chorus. Both of these phenomena relate to the current speaker's speech: either to match it, or to beat it. While we focus on matching in this work, the methods described similarly apply to co-optation.

As Lerner (2002) notes, attributing this view to Sacks et al. (1974), simultaneous speech in conversation is often treated exclusively as a turn taking problem in need of repair. This is exactly the point of view taken by current spoken dialogue systems, which avoid overlap and interpret all simultaneous speech as *barge-in*, regardless of content. However, Lerner (2002) also notes that simultaneous speech systematically occurs without being perceived as a problem, e. g. in greetings, or when saying good bye, which are relevant sub-tasks in deployed SDSs.

Two corpus studies are available which investigate split utterances and their frequency: Skuplik (1999) looked at *sentence cooperations* in a corpus of task-oriented German (Poesio and Rieser, 2010) and found 3.4 % of such utterances. Purver et al. (2009) find 2.8 % of utterance boundaries in the BNC (as annotated by Fernández and Ginzburg (2002)) to meet their definition of utterances split between speakers. Thus, while the absolute frequency may seem low, the phenomenon does seem to occur consistently across different languages and corpora.

Local (2007) describes phonetic characteristics at utterance splits (he calls the phenomenon *turn co-construction*) which distinguish them from regular turn handovers, namely temporal alignment and close prosodic integration with the previous speaker's utterance. In this paper, we focus on the temporal aspects (both alignment and speech rate) when realizing turn completions, leaving pitch integration to future work.

Cummins (2009) analyses speech read aloud by two subjects at the same time (which he calls *synchronous speech*): Synchrony is slightly better in a live setting than with a subject synchronizing to a recording of speech which was itself spoken in synchrony and this is easier than to a recording of unconstrained speech. Cummins (2009) also experiments with reduced stimuli: eliminating f_0-contour had no significant impact on synchrony, while a carrier without segmental information (but including f_0-contour) fared significantly better than speaking to an uninformative hiss. (The first sentence of each recording was always left unmodified, allowing subjects to estimate speech rate even in the HISS condition.) Thus, pitch information does not seem necessary for the task but may help in the absence of segmental information.

On a more technical level and as mentioned above, much work has been put into speeding up end-of-turn detection and reducing processing lags at turn changes (Raux and Eskenazi, 2009) and more recently into end-of-turn prediction: Ward et al. (2010) present a model of turn-taking which estimates the remaining duration of a currently ongoing turn. We extend the task to predicting the remaining duration of any currently ongoing *word* in the turn. Of course, for this to be possible, words must be recognized while they are still being uttered. We have previously shown (Baumann et al., 2009) that this can be achieved with incremental ASR for the vast majority of words and with an average of 102 ms between when a word is first recognized and the word's end.

As mentioned above, our work relies on other incremental components to form a meaningful, turn completing application and such components are being developed: Incremental understanding is well underway (Sagae et al., 2009; Heintze et al., 2010), as is decision making on whether full understanding of an utterance has been reached (DeVault et al., 2009), and Purver et al. (2011) present an incremental semantics component aimed explicitly at split utterances. In fact, DeVault et al. (2009) provide exactly the counterpart to our work, describing a method that, given the words of an ongoing utterance, decides when the point of maximum understanding has been reached and with what words this utterance is likely to end. However, in their system demonstration, Sagae et al. (2010) use short silence time-outs to trigger system responses. Our work eliminates the need for such time-outs.

Hirasawa et al. (1999) present a study where immediate, overlapping back-channel feedback from the system was found to be inferior to acknowledging information only after the user's turn. However, they disregarded the back-channels' micro-temporal alignment as explored in this study (presumably producing back-channels as early as possible), so their negative results cannot be taken as demonstrating a general shortcoming of the interactional strategy.

3 The Task

The general task that our timing component tackles is illustrated in Figure 1. The component is triggered into action when an understanding module signals that (and with what words) a turn should be completed. At this *decision point*, our component must estimate (a) *when* the current word ends and (b) *how* the user will speak the predicted continuation. Ideally, the system will start speaking the continuation precisely when the next word starts and match the user's speech as best as possible. Thus, our component must estimate the time between decision point and ideal onset (which we call *holding time*) and the user's *speech rate* during the following words.

In order for the system to be able to produce a continuation ("*five six seven*" in Figure 1) in time, of course the decision point must come sufficiently early (i. e. during "*four*") to allow for a completion to be output in due time. This important precondition must be met by-and-large by the employed ASR. However, it is not a strict requirement: If ASR results are lagging behind, the timing component's estimated holding time should turn negative. Depending on the estimated lag, a completion can be suppressed or, if it is small, fairly good completions can still be realized by shortening the first (few) phonemes of the completion to be synthesized.

We will now present our overall system before describing two strategies we developed for solving the task just described, and further on present the experiments we conducted with the system and their results in Sections 5 and 6.

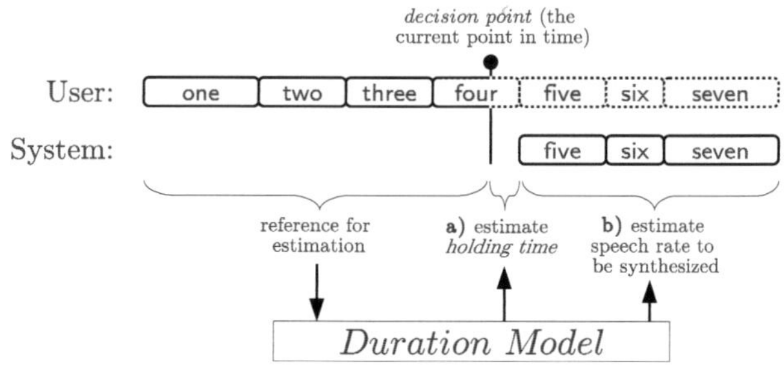

Figure 1: The task: When notified that the ongoing utterance should be completed with "*five six seven*" after the word "*four*", the first three words are used to (a) estimate the remaining duration of "*four*" and to (b) estimate the speech rate for the completion.

4 System Description

Our system is based on the InproTK toolkit for incremental spoken dialogue systems (Schlangen et al., 2010) which uses Sphinx-4 (Walker et al., 2004) and MaryTTS (Schröder and Trouvain, 2003) as underlying ASR and TTS engines, respectively. The core of our system is a component that incrementally receives rich speech recognition input (words, their durations and a pitch track) from an incremental ASR and computes the timing of completions.

When receiving a new word from ASR, our component queries an understanding component whether a completion can be predicted, and if so, whether such a completion should be performed. In order to not duplicate the work of DeVault et al. (2009), we use a mock implementation of an understanding module, which actually knows what words are going to be spoken (from a transcript file) and aims to complete after *every* word spoken.

We have implemented two strategies for the timing module, which we will describe in turn, after first discussing a simple baseline approach.

Baseline: Speak Immediately A first, very simple approach for our timing component is to never wait between the decision point and outputting a completion right away. We believe that this was the strategy taken by Hirasawa et al. (1999) and we will show in our evaluation in Section 6.2 that it is not very good.

Strategy 1: Estimating ASR Lookahead In our ASR-based strategy (illustrated in Figure 2, top) the system estimates what we call its *lookahead* rate, i. e. the average time between when a word is first recognized by ASR and the word's end in the signal. This lookahead is known for the words that have been recognized so far and the average lookahead can then be used as an estimate of the remaining duration of the word that is currently being detected (i. e. its *holding time*). Once the currently spoken word is expected to end, the system should start to speak.

The strategy just described, as well as the baseline strategy, only solve half of the task, namely, when the continuation should be started, but not the question of *how* to speak, which we will turn to now. Both sub-tasks can be solved simultaneously by estimating the speech rate of the current speaker, based on what she already said so far, and considering this speech rate when synthesizing a completion. Speech rate estimation using some kind of duration model thus forms the second strategy's main component. For the purpose of this work, we focus on duration models in the context of TTS, where they are used to assign durations to the phones to be uttered. Rule-based approaches (Klatt, 1979) as well as methods using machine learning have been used (primarily CART (Breiman et al., 1984)); for HMM-based speech synthesis, durations can be generated from Gaussian probability density functions (PDFs) (Yoshimura et al., 1998). We are not aware of any work that uses duration models to predict the remaining time of an ongoing word or utterance.

In our task, we need the duration model to make estimations based on limited input (instead of providing plausibility ratings as in most ASR-related applications). As it turns out, a TTS system in itself is an excellent duration model because it potentially ponders all kinds of syntactic, lexical, post-lexical, phonological and prosodical context when assigning durations to words and their phones. Also, our task already involves a TTS system to synthesize the turn

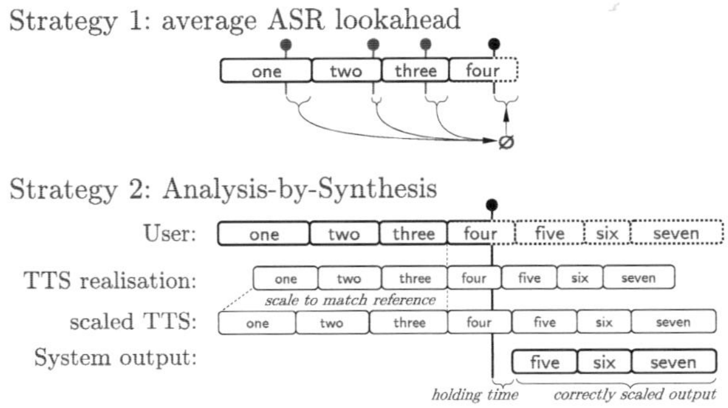

Figure 2: Our strategies to estimate holding time (*when* to speak), and speech rate (*how* to speak; only Strategy 2).

completion – in our case MaryTTS (Schröder and Trouvain, 2003). The durations can be accessed in symbolic form in MaryTTS, and the system allows to manipulate this information prior to acoustic synthesis. Depending on which voice is used, MaryTTS uses machine-learned duration models (CART or PDFs) or an optimized version of Klatt's (1979) rules which have been shown to perform only marginally worse than the CART-based approach (Brinckmann and Trouvain, 2003).

Strategy 2: Analysis-by-Synthesis As just described, we hence employ the TTS' duration model in an analysis-by-synthesis approach in this second strategy, as illustrated in Figure 2 (bottom): When triggered to complete an ongoing utterance, we query the TTS for the durations it would assign to a production of the predicted full utterance, i. e. the prefix that was heard plus the predicted continuation of the turn. In that way, the TTS can take the full utterance into account when assigning prosodic patterns which may influence durations. We then compute the factor that is needed to scale the TTS's duration of the words already finished by the user (in the example: "*one two three*") to the duration of the actual utterance and apply this scaling factor to the remaining words in the synthesized completion. We can then read off the expected duration of the currently spoken word from the scaled TTS output and, by subtracting the time that this word is already going on, find out the *holding time*. Similarly, the completion of the turn which is now scaled to match the user's speech rate can be fed back to the synthesis system in order to generate the acoustic waveform which is to be output to the speakers once the system should start to speak.

5 Corpus and Experiment Setup

In order to evaluate the accuracy of the individual components involved in the specific subtasks, we conducted a controlled offline experiment. We have not yet evaluated how actual users of our system would judge its performance at outputting collaborative completions.

As evaluation corpus we use recordings of the German version of the story *The North Wind and the Sun* (IPA, 1999) from the Kiel Corpus of Read Speech (IPDS, 1994). The story (including title) consists of 111 words and is read by 16 speakers, giving a total of 1776 words in 255 inter-pausal-units (IPUs), altogether resulting in about 12 minutes of speech. (In the following, we will equate "turns" with IPUs, as our corpus of read speech does not contain true turns.) Words and phones in our corpus have a mean/median/std dev duration of 319/290/171 ms and 78/69/40 ms, respectively.

We assume that every word can be a possible completion point in a real system, hence we evaluate the performance of our timing component for all words in the corpus. (This generalization may have an influence on our results: real collaborative completions are sometimes invited by the speaker, probably by giving cues that might simplify co-completion; if that is true, the version tackled here is actually harder than the real task.)

Good turn completions (and good timings) can probably only be expected in the light of high ASR performance. We trained a domain-specific language model (based on the test corpus) and used an acoustic model trained for conversational speech which was not specifically tuned for the task. The resulting WER is 4.2 %. While our results could hence be considered too optimistic, Baumann et al. (2009) showed that incremental metrics remained stable in the light of varying ASR performance. We expect that lower ASR performance would not radically change prediction quality itself; rather, it would have an impact on how often continuations could be predicted, since that is based on correct understanding of the prefix of the utterance, limiting the amount of data points for our statistics.

Even though we simulated the understanding and prediction module, we built in some constraints that are meant to be representative of real implementations of such a module: it can only find the right completion if the previous two words are recognized correctly and the overall WER is lower than 10 %. (Coming back to Figure 1, if the system had falsely recognized "*on two three*", no completion would take place: Even though the last two words "*two three*" were recognized correctly, the WER between "*on two three*" and "*one two three*" is too high.) Under this constraint, the timing component generated data for 1100 IPU-internal and 223 IPU-final words in our corpus.

The main focus of this paper is turn completion and completions can only take place if there is something left to complete (i. e. after turn-internal words). It is still useful to be able to predict the duration of turn-final words, though, as this is a prerequisite for the related task of timing speaker changes. For this reason, we include both turn-internal and turn-final words in the analyses in Section 6.2.

In the evaluation, we use the ASR's word alignments from recognition as gold standard (instead of e. g. hand-labelled timings), which are essentially equal to output from forced alignment. However, when evaluating how well our timing component predicts the following word's duration, we need that word to also be correctly recognized by ASR. This holds for 1045 words in our corpus, for which we report results in Section 6.3.

6 Results

We evaluate the timing of our system with regards to whether completions are possible in general, when a completion should be produced, and what the speech rate of the completion should be in the subsections below.

6.1 Availability of Time to Make a Decision

While it is strictly speaking not part of the timing component, a precondition to being able to speak *just-in-time* is to ponder this decision sufficiently early as outlined above.

Figure 3 shows a statistic of when our ASR first hypothesizes a correct word relative to the word's end (which can be determined post-hoc from the final recognition result) on the corpus. Most words are hypothesized before their actual endings, with a mean of 134 ms (median: 110 ms) ahead. This leaves

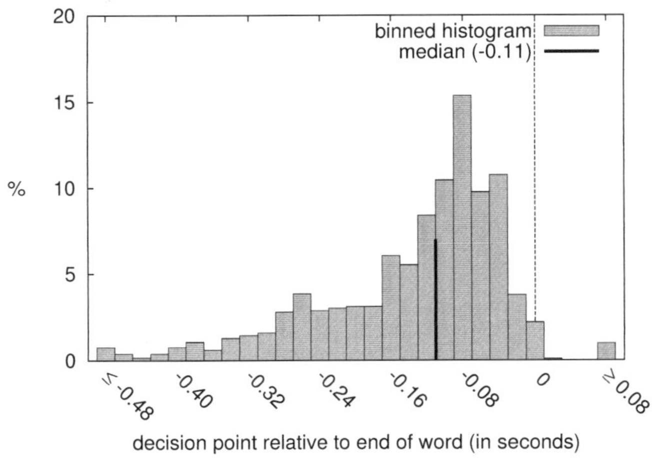

Figure 3: Statistics of when decisions can be first taken relative to the word's end (determined post-hoc).

enough lookahead to synthesize a completion and for some delays that must be taken into account for input and output buffering in the sound card, which together take around 50 ms in our system.

Interestingly, lookahead differs widely for the speakers in our corpus with means between 97 and 237 ms. As can be seen in Figure 3, some words are only hypothesized *after the fact*, or at least too late to account for the inevitable lags, which renders impossible successful turn-completions following these words. However, the timing component should know when it is too late – the holding time should be negative – and could either not output the completion at this point or e. g. back off to setting in one or more phones or syllables later (actually, back off until the holding time turns positive).

6.2 When to Start Speaking

We evaluate the strategies from Section 4 by comparing the predicted holding times with the ideal holding time, i. e. the time necessary to match the ASR's lookahead.

Figure 3 can also be taken as depicting the error distribution of our baseline strategy to find out when to start a completion: on average, the completion will be early by 134 ms if it is uttered immediately and the distribution is somewhat skewed. An unbiased baseline strategy is obtained by subtracting the global mean from the holding times. This however requires the mean to be known in advance and is hence inflexible: the global mean may very well be different for other data sets as it already differs between

model	error distribution metrics (in ms)			
	mean	median	std dev	MAE
baseline: all	-134	-110	107	110
baseline $-\mu$	0	23	107	63
ASR-based : all	-2	19	105	60
IPU-internal	26	33	82	51
IPU-final	-148	-143	87	142
TTS-based : all	-3	4	85	45
IPU-internal	12	11	77	41
IPU-final	-78	-76	83	79

Table 1: Descriptive statistics of the error distributions over estimated onset times for different duration models.

speakers in our corpus. The two other strategies' error distributions are less skewed, so we just report the distributions' mean, median, and standard deviation,[1] as well as the median absolute error (MAE) for the ASR-based, the TTS-based and the baseline strategies in Table 1.

As can be seen in Table 1, both strategies are similarly effective in predicting the average remaining time of a currently uttered word, reducing the mean error close to zero, a significant improvement over starting a completion or next turn immediately. (ANOVA with post-hoc Tukey's honest significance differences test.) While our two approaches perform similarly when comparing the performance for all words, there actually are differences when looking separately at IPU-internal and IPU-final words. In both cases the TTS-based approach has a significantly lower bias (paired Student's t-tests, $p < 0.01$).

The bias of both strategies differs depending on whether the current word is IPU-internal or -final. We believe this to be due to final lengthening: phones are about 40 % longer in IPU-final words. This is not captured by the ASR-based strategy and the lengthening may be stronger than what is predicted by the pronunciation model of the TTS we use.

A low standard deviation of the error distribution is probably even more important than a low mean error, as it is variability, or *jitter*, that makes a system unpredictable to the user. While there is no significant improvement of the ASR-based approach over the baseline, the TTS-based approach significantly outperforms the other approaches with a 20 % re-

[1] We prefer to report mean and std dev for bias and jitter separately; notice that RMSE= $\sqrt{\mu^2 + \sigma^2}$.

task	error distribution metric (in ms)			
	mean	median	std dev	MAE
TTS-based : duration	-5	4	75	45
+ **ASR-based** : onset	26	33	82	51
= end of word	25	30	100	81
+ **TTS-based** : onset	12	11	77	41
= end of word	7	10	94	74

Table 2: Descriptive statistics of the error distributions for the first spoken word of a completion.

duction of jitter down to about the average phone's length (Browne-Forsythe's modified Levene's test, $p < 0.001$).

Regarding human performance in synchronous speech, Cummins (2002) reports an MAE of 30 ms for the synchronous condition. However, MAE increased to 56 ms when synchronizing to an (unsynchronously read) recording, a value which is in the range of our results (and with our system relying on similar input).

6.3 How to Speak

As explained in the task description, knowing when to speak is only one side of the medal, as a turn completion itself must be integrated with the previous speech in terms of duration, prosodic shape and loudness.

Only our TTS-based strategy is capable of outputting predictions for a future word; our ASR-based approach does not provide this information. However, both duration and onset estimation (the next onset is identical to the end of the current word as estimated in Section 6.2) together determine the error at the word's end. Hence, we report the error at the next word's end for the TTS strategy's duration estimate combined with both strategies' onset estimates in Table 2.

Duration prediction for the next word with the TTS-based strategy works similarly well as for ongoing words (as in Section 6.2), with an MAE of 45 ms (which is again in the range of human performance). However, for the next word's end to occur when the speaker's word ends, correct onset estimation is just as important. When we combine onset estimation with duration prediction, errors add up and hence the error for the next word's end is somewhat higher than for either of the tasks alone, with a standard deviation of 94 ms and an MAE of 74 ms for the TTS-based model, which again outperforms the ASR-based model.

So far, we have not evaluated the matching of prosodic characteristics such as loudness and intonation (nor implemented their prediction). We believe that simple matching (as we implemented for onset and speech rate) is not as good a starting point for these as they are more complex. Instead, we believe these phenomena to mostly depend on communicative function, e. g. a co-optation having a wide pitch-range and relatively high loudness regardless of the current speaker's speech. Additionally, pitch-range would have to be incrementally speaker-normalized which results in some implementation difficulties.[2]

7 Demo Application: Shadowing

To get a feeling for the complete system and to demonstrate that our timing component works on live input, we implemented a shadowing application which completes – or rather shadows – a user utterance word-by-word. Given the prediction for the next word's onset time and duration it prepares the output of that next word while the user is still speaking the preceding word. As the application expects to know what the user is going to speak, the user is currently limited to telling the story of *North Wind and the Sun*.

Two examples of shadowings are shown in Appendix A.[3] As can be seen in the screenshots, the decision points for all words are sufficiently early before the next word, allowing for the next word's output generation to take place. Overall, shadowing quality is good, with the exception of the second "*die*" in the second example. However, there is an ASR error directly following ("*aus*" instead of "*luft*") and the ASR's alignment quality for "*sonne die*" is already sub-optimal. Also, notice that the two words following the ASR error are not shadowed as per our error recovery strategy outlined in Section 5.

[2]Edlund and Heldner (2007) report that for a reliable pitch-range estimation 10 to 20 seconds of *voiced* speech and hence – in our view – twice the amount of audio is necessary. This would have reduced our corpus size by too much.

[3]Audio files of the examples are available at `http://www.ling.uni-potsdam.de/~timo/pub/shadowing/`.

8 Discussion and Future Work

We described the task of micro-timing, or micro-aligning a system response (in our case a turn completion and shadowing a speaker) to the user's speech based on incremental ASR output and with both ASR and symbolic TTS output as duration models to predict when and how a completion should be uttered.

We have shown first of all, that a completion is possible after most words, as an incremental ASR in a small-enough domain can have a sufficient lookahead. Additionally, we have shown that the TTS-based duration model is better than both the baseline and the ASR-based model. Both the next word's onset and duration can be predicted relatively well ($\sigma = 77$ ms and $\sigma = 75$ ms, respectively), and within the margin of human performance in synchronously reading speech. It is interesting to note here that synchronous speech is simplified in prosodic characteristics (Cummins, 2002), which presumably facilitates the task. Errors in speech rate estimation add up, so that the deviation at the next word's end is somewhat higher ($\sigma = 94$ ms). Deviation will likely increase for longer completions, underlining the need for an incremental speech synthesis system which should allow to instantly adapt output to changes in speech rate, content, and possibly sentiment of the other speaker.

Clearly, our duration modelling is rather simplistic and could likely be improved by combining ASR and TTS knowledge, more advanced (than a purely linear) mapping when calculating relative speech rate, integration of phonetic and prosodic features from the ASR, and possibly more. As currently implemented, improvements to the underlying TTS system (e. g. more "conversational" synthesis) should automatically improve our model. The TTS-based approach integrates additional, non-ASR knowledge, and hence it should be possible to single out those decision points after which a completion would be especially error-prone, trading coverage against quality of results. Initial experiments support this idea and we would like to extend it to a full error estimation capability.

We have focused the analysis of incrementally comparing expected to actual speech rate to the task of micro-aligning a turn-completion and shadowing a speaker. However, we believe that this capability can be used in a broad range of tasks, e. g. in combination with word-based end-of-turn detection (Atterer et al., 2008) to allow for swift turn taking.[4] In fact, precise micro-alignment of turn handovers could be used for controlled testing of linguistic/prosodic theory such as the oscillator model of the timing of turn-taking (Wilson and Wilson, 2005).

Finally, duration modelling can be used to quickly detect deviations in speech rate (which may indicate hesitations or planning problems of the user) *as they happen* (rather than post-hoc), allowing to take the speaker's fluency into account in understanding and turn-taking coordination as outlined by Clark (2002).

Acknowledgments

This work was funded by a DFG grant in the Emmy Noether programme. We wish to thank the anonymous reviewers for their very helpful comments.

References

Michaela Atterer, Timo Baumann, and David Schlangen. 2008. Towards incremental end-of-utterance detection in dialogue systems. In *Proceedings of Coling*, Manchester, UK.

Timo Baumann, Michaela Atterer, and David Schlangen. 2009. Assessing and improving the performance of speech recognition for incremental systems. In *Proceedings of NAACL*, Boulder, USA.

Timo Baumann. 2008. Simulating spoken dialogue with a focus on realistic turn-taking. In *Proceedings of the 13th ESSLLI Student Session*, Hamburg, Germany.

Leo Breiman, Jerome H. Friedman, Richard A. Olshen, and Charles J. Stone. 1984. *Classification and regression trees*. Wadsworth, Monterey.

Caren Brinckmann and Jürgen Trouvain. 2003. The role of duration models and symbolic representation for timing in synthetic speech. *International Journal of Speech Technology*, 6(1):21–31.

Herbert H. Clark. 2002. Speaking in time. *Speech Communication*, 36(1):5–13.

Fred Cummins. 2002. On synchronous speech. *Acoustic Research Letters Online*, 3(1):7–11.

Fred Cummins. 2009. Rhythm as entrainment: The case of synchronous speech. *Journal of Phonetics*, 37(1):16–28.

[4] Additionally, both our models consistently under-estimate the duration of IPU-final words. It should be possible to turn this into a feature by monitoring whether a word actually has ended when it was predicted to end. If it is still ongoing, this may be an additional indicator that the word is turn-final.

David DeVault, Kenji Sagae, and David Traum. 2009. Can I finish? Learning when to respond to incremental interpretation results in interactive dialogue. In *Proceedings of SIGDIAL*, London, UK.

Jens Edlund and Mattias Heldner. 2007. Underpinning /nailon/: Automatic Estimation of Pitch Range and Speaker Relative Pitch. In *Speaker Classification II*, volume 4441 of *LNCS*, pages 229–242. Springer.

Raquel Fernández and Jonathan Ginzburg. 2002. Non-sentential utterances: A corpus-based study. *Traitement automatique des languages*, 43(2):13–42.

Silvan Heintze, Timo Baumann, and David Schlangen. 2010. Comparing local and sequential models for statistical incremental natural language understanding. In *Proceedings of SIGDIAL*, Tokyo, Japan.

Jun-ichi Hirasawa, Mikio Nakano, Takeshi Kawabata, and Kiyoaki Aikawa. 1999. Effects of system barge-in responses on user impressions. In *Proceedings of Eurospeech*, Budapest, Hungary.

International Phonetic Association, IPA. 1999. *Handbook of the International Phonetic Association*. Cambridge University Press.

Institut für Phonetik und digitale Sprachverarbeitung, IPDS. 1994. The Kiel corpus of read speech. CD-ROM.

Dennis H. Klatt. 1979. Synthesis by rule of segmental durations in English sentences. *Frontiers of Speech Communication Research*, pages 287–299.

Gene H. Lerner. 2002. Turn sharing: The choral co-production of talk in interaction. In C. Ford, B. Fox, and S. Thompson, editors, *The Language of Turn and Sequence*, chapter 9. Oxford University Press.

Gene H. Lerner. 2004. Collaborative turn sequences. In Gene H. Lerner, editor, *Conversation Analysis: Studies from the First Generation*, Pragmatics & Beyond, pages 225–256. John Benjamins, Amsterdam.

John Local. 2007. Phonetic detail and the organisation of talk-in-interaction. In *Proceedings of the 16th ICPhS*, Saarbrücken, Germany.

Massimo Poesio and Hannes Rieser. 2010. Completions, coordination, and alignment in dialogue. *Dialogue and Discourse*, 1(1):1–89.

Matthew Purver, Christine Howes, Patrick G. T. Healey, and Eleni Gregoromichelaki. 2009. Split utterances in dialogue: a corpus study. In *Proceedings of SIGDIAL*, London, UK.

Matthew Purver, Arash Eshghi, and Julian Hough. 2011. Incremental semantic construction in a dialogue system. In *Proceedings of the 9th IWCS*, Oxford, UK.

Antoine Raux and Maxine Eskenazi. 2009. A finite-state turn-taking model for spoken dialog systems. In *Proceedings of NAACL*, Boulder, USA.

Harvey Sacks, Emanuel A. Schegloff, and Gail A. Jefferson. 1974. A simplest systematic for the organization of turn-taking in conversation. *Language*, 50:735–996.

Kenji Sagae, Gwen Christian, David DeVault, and David Traum. 2009. Towards natural language understanding of partial speech recognition results in dialogue systems. In *Proceedings of NAACL*, Boulder, USA.

Kenji Sagae, David DeVault, and David Traum. 2010. Interpretation of partial utterances in virtual human dialogue systems. In *Proceedings of NAACL*.

David Schlangen, Timo Baumann, Hendrik Buschmeier, Okko Buß, Stefan Kopp, Gabriel Skantze, and Ramin Yaghoubzadeh. 2010. Middleware for incremental processing in conversational agents. In *Proceedings of SIGDIAL*, Tokyo, Japan.

David Schlangen. 2006. From reaction to prediction: Experiments with computational models of turn-taking. In *Proceedings of Interspeech*, Pittsburgh, USA.

Marc Schröder and Jürgen Trouvain. 2003. The German text-to-speech synthesis system MARY: A tool for research, development and teaching. *International Journal of Speech Technology*, 6(3):365–377.

Gabriel Skantze and David Schlangen. 2009. Incremental dialogue processing in a micro-domain. In *Proceedings of EACL*, Athens, Greece.

Kristina Skuplik. 1999. Satzkooperationen. Definition und empirische Untersuchung. Technical Report 1999/03, SFB 360, Universität Bielefeld.

Willie Walker, Paul Lamere, Philip Kwok, Bhiksha Raj, Rita Singh, Evandro Gouvea, Peter Wolf, and Joe Woelfel. 2004. Sphinx-4: A flexible open source framework for speech recognition. Technical Report SMLI TR2004-0811, Sun Microsystems Inc.

Nigel Ward, Olac Fuentes, and Alejandro Vega. 2010. Dialog prediction for a general model of turn-taking. In *Proceedings of Interspeech*, Tokyo, Japan.

Karl Weilhammer and Susen Rabold. 2003. Durational aspects in turn taking. In *Proceedings of the 15th ICPhS*, Barcelona, Spain.

Margaret Wilson and Thomas P. Wilson. 2005. An oscillator model of the timing of turn-taking. *Psychonomic Bulletin & Review*, 12(6):957–968.

Takayoshi Yoshimura, Keiichi Tokuda, Takashi Masuko, Takao Kobayashi, and Tadashi Kitamura. 1998. Duration modeling for HMM-based speech synthesis. In *Proceedings of the 5th ICSLP*, Sydney, Australia.

Appendix A Examples of Shadowing

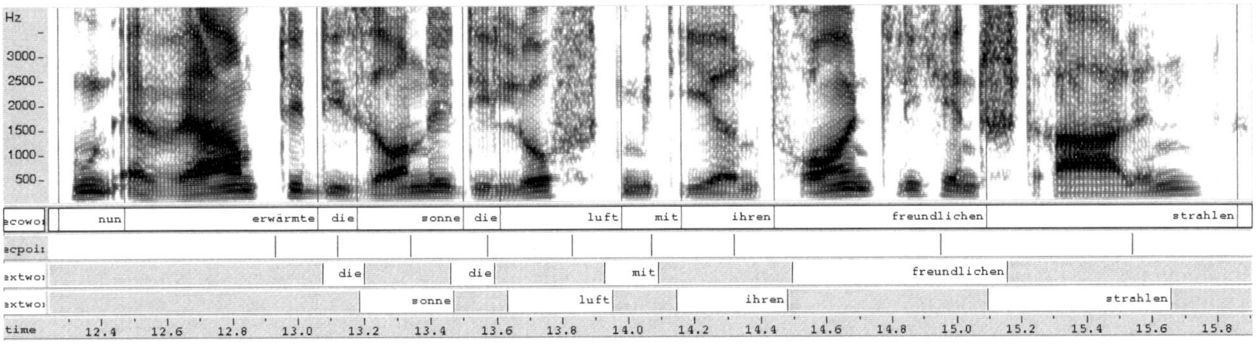

Figure 4: Example of shadowing for a file in our corpus (k73nord2). The first line of labels shows the final ASR output, the second line shows the decision points for each word and the third and fourth lines show the system's output (planned output may overlap, hence two lines; in the system, an overlapped portion of a word is replaced by the following word's audio).

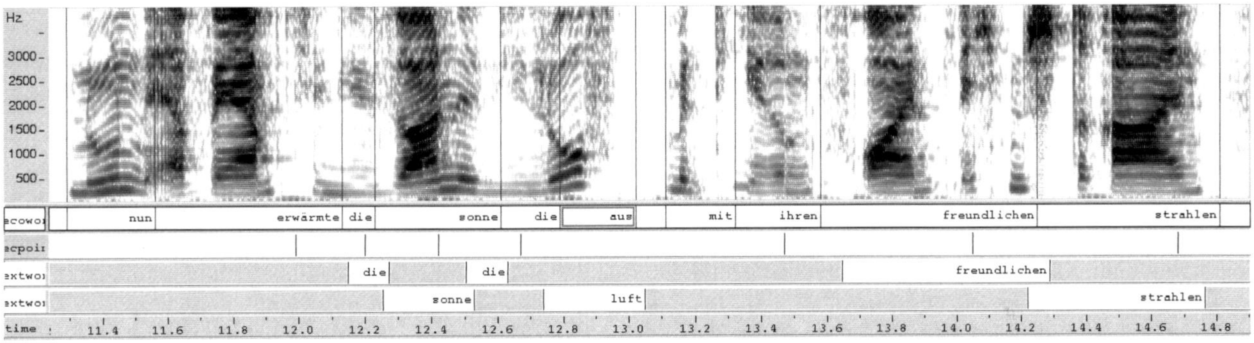

Figure 5: Example of shadowing with live input (verena2nord2). Notice that "*Luft*" is predicted and synthesized although it is (later) misunderstood by ASR as "*aus*", resulting in a missing shadowing of "*mit*" and "*ihren*". In order to not disturb the speaker, the system's audio output was muted.

An Empirical Evaluation of a Statistical Dialog System in Public Use

Jason D. Williams
AT&T Labs - Research, Shannon Laboratory, 180 Park Ave., Florham Park, NJ 07932, USA
jdw@research.att.com

Abstract

This paper provides a first assessment of a statistical dialog system in public use. In our dialog system there are four main recognition tasks, or slots – bus route names, bus-stop locations, dates, and times. Whereas a conventional system tracks a single value for each slot – i.e., the speech recognizer's top hypothesis – our statistical system tracks a distribution of many possible values over each slot. Past work in lab studies has showed that this distribution improves robustness to speech recognition errors; but to our surprise, we found the distribution yielded an increase in accuracy for only two of the four slots, and actually decreased accuracy in the other two. In this paper, we identify root causes for these differences in performance, including intrinsic properties of N-best lists, parameter settings, and the quality of statistical models. We synthesize our findings into a set of guidelines which aim to assist researchers and practitioners employing statistical techniques in future dialog systems.

1 Introduction

Over the past decade, researchers have worked to apply statistical techniques to spoken dialog systems, and in controlled laboratory studies, statistical dialog systems have been shown to improve robustness to errors compared to conventional approaches (Henderson and Lemon, 2008; Young et al., 2010; Thomson and Young, 2010). However, statistical techniques have not yet been evaluated in a publicly deployed system, and real users behave very differently to usability subjects (Raux et al., 2005; Ai et al., 2008). So there is an important open question whether statistical dialog systems improve performance *with real users*.

This paper provides a first evaluation of a publically deployed statistical dialog system, AT&T Let's Go (Williams et al., 2010). AT&T Let's Go provides bus times for Pittsburgh, and received approximately 750 calls from real bus riders during the 2010 Spoken Dialog Challenge (Black et al., 2010). AT&T Let's Go is based on a publicly available toolkit (Williams, 2010a) and achieved the highest rates of successful task completion on real callers in the challenge, so it provides a relevant exercise from which to draw inferences.

AT&T Let's Go collected four types of information, or *slots*: bus route names, bus-stop names, dates, and times. For each slot, we measured turn-level accuracy of the deployed statistical system and compared it to accuracy without application of the statistical techniques (i.e., the top speech recognition result).

To our surprise, we found that statistical techniques appeared to improve accuracy for only two of the four slots, and decreased accuracy for the other two. To investigate this, we considered four *mechanisms* by which statistical methods can differ from the top speech recognition result. Analyzing the effects of each mechanism on each slot enables underlying causes to be identified: for example, one mechanism performed exceptionally well when its statistical models was well matched to usage data, but rather poorly when its model diverged from real usage. We believe this analysis – the focus of this paper – is relevant to researchers as well as practi-

Proceedings of the SIGDIAL 2011: the 12th Annual Meeting of the Special Interest Group on Discourse and Dialogue, pages 130–141,
Portland, Oregon, June 17-18, 2011.

tioners applying statistical techniques to production systems.

In this paper, Section 2 reviews the operation of statistical spoken dialog systems. Section 3 then describes the AT&T Let's Go dialog system. Section 4 reports on overall accuracy, then analyzes the underlying reasons for accuracy gains and losses. Section 5 tackles how well error in the belief state can be *identified* compared to speech recognition errors. Section 6 concludes by summarizing lessons learned.

2 Statistical dialog systems

Statistical dialog systems maintain a distribution over a set of hidden dialog states. A dialog state includes information not directly observable to the dialog system, such as the user's overall goal in the dialog or the user's true action (e.g., the user's true dialog act). For each dialog state s, a posterior probability of correctness called a *belief* is maintained $b(s)$. The set of hidden dialog states and their beliefs is collectively called the *belief state*, and updating the belief state is called *belief tracking*. Here we will present belief tracking at a level sufficient for our purposes; for a more general treatment, see (Williams and Young, 2007).

At the start of the dialog, the belief state is initialized to a *prior* distribution $b_0(s)$. The system then takes an action a, and the user takes an action in response. The automatic speech recognizer (ASR) then produces a ranked list of N hypotheses for the user's action, $\mathbf{u} = (u_1, \ldots, u_N)$, called an *N-best list*. For each N-best list the ASR also produces a distribution $P_{\text{asr}}(u)$ which assigns a local, context-independent probability of correctness to each item, often called a *confidence score*. The belief state is then updated:

$$b'(s) = k \cdot \sum_{u} P_{\text{asr}}(u) P_{\text{act}}(u|s, a) b(s) \qquad (1)$$

where $P_{\text{act}}(u|s, a)$ is the probability of the user taking action u given the dialog is in hidden state s and the system takes action a. k is a normalizing constant.

In practice specialized techniques must be used to compute Eq 1 in real-time. The system in this paper uses *incremental partition recombination* (Williams, 2010b); alternatives include the Hidden Information State (Young et al., 2010), Bayesian Update of Dialog States (Thomson and Young, 2010), and particle filters (Williams, 2007). The details are not important for this paper – the key idea is that Eq 1 synthesizes a prior distribution over dialog states together with all of the ASR N-best lists and local confidence scores to form a cumulative, whole-dialog posterior probability distribution over all possible dialog states, $b(s)$.

In the system studied in this paper, slots are queried separately, and an independent belief state is maintained for each. Consequently, within each slot user actions u and hidden states s are drawn from the same set of slot values. Thus the top ASR result u_1 represents the ASR's best hypothesis for the slot value in the current utterance, whereas the top dialog state $\arg\max_s b(s) = s^*$ represents the belief state's best hypothesis for the slot value given all of the ASR results so far, a prior over the slot values, and models of user action likelihoods. The promise of statistical dialog systems is that s^* will (we hope!) be correct more often than u_1. In the next section, we measure this in real dialogs.

3 AT&T Let's Go

AT&T Let's Go is a statistical dialog system that provides bus timetable information for Pittsburgh, USA. This system was created to demonstrate a production-grade system built following practices common in industry, but which incorporates two statistical techniques: belief tracking with the AT&T Statistical Dialog Toolkit (Williams, 2010a), and regression-based ASR confidence scores (Williams and Balakrishnan, 2009).

As with most commercial dialog systems, AT&T Let's Go follows a highly directed flow, collecting one *slot* at a time. There are four types of slots: ROUTE, LOCATION, DATE, and TIME. The system can only recognize values for the slot being queried, plus a handful of global commands ("repeat", "go back", "start over", "goodbye", etc.) – mixed initiative and over-completion were not supported. As mentioned above, an independent belief state is maintained for each slot: this was an intentional design decision made in order to use statistical techniques within current commercial practices.

The system opens by asking the user to say a bus ROUTE, or to say "I'm not sure." The system next asks for the origin and destination LOCATIONs. The system then asks if the caller wants times for the "next few buses"; if not, the system asks for the DATE then TIME in two separate questions. Finally bus times are read out.

After requesting the value of a slot, the system receives an N-best list, assigns each item a confidence score $P_{\text{asr}}(u)$, and updates the belief in (only) that slot using Eq 1. The top dialog hypothesis s^* and its belief $b(s^*)$ are used to determine which action to take next, following a hand-crafted policy. This is in contrast to a conventional dialog system, in which the top ASR result and its confidence govern dialog flow. Figure 6 shows the design of AT&T Let's Go.

In the period July 16 – August 16 2010, AT&T Let's Go received 742 calls, of which 670 had one or more user utterances. These calls contained a total of 8269 user utterances, of which 4085 were in response to requests for one of the four slots. (The remainder were responses to yes/no questions, timetable navigation commands like "next bus", etc.)

Our goal in this paper is to determine whether tracking a distribution over multiple dialog states improved turn-level accuracy compared to the top ASR result. To measure this, we compare the accuracy of the top belief state and the top ASR result. A transcriber listened to each utterance and marked the top ASR hypothesis as *correct* if it was an exact lexical or semantic match, or *incorrect* otherwise. The same was then done for the top dialog hypothesis in each turn.

Accuracy of the top ASR hypothesis and the top belief state are shown in Table 1, which indicates that belief monitoring improved accuracy for ROUTE and DATE, but degraded accuracy for LOCATION and TIME. We had hoped that belief tracking would improve accuracy for all slots; seeing that it hadn't prompted us to investigate the underlying causes.

Slot	ROUTE	LOCATION	DATE	TIME
Utts	1520	2235	173	157
ASR	769	1326	124	80
correct	50.6%	59.3%	71.7%	51.0 %
Belief	799	1246	139	63
correct	52.6%	55.7%	80.3%	40.1%
Belief	+30	-80	+15	-17
– ASR	+2.0%	-3.6%	+8.7%	-10.8%

Table 1: Accuracy of the top ASR result and top belief state. LOCATION includes both origin and destination utterances. Most callers requested the next bus so few were asked for DATE and TIME.

4 Belief tracking analysis

When an ASR result is provided to Eq 1 and a new belief state is computed, the top dialog state hypothesis s^* may differ from top ASR result u_1. Formally, these differences are simply the result of evaluating this equation. However, *intuitively* there are four *mechanisms* which cause differences, and each difference can be explained by the action of one or more mechanisms. These mechanisms are summarized here; the appendix provides graphical illustrations.[1]

- **ASR re-ranking**: When computing a confidence score $P_{\text{asr}}(u)$, it is possible that the entry with the highest confidence $u^* = \arg\max_u P_{\text{asr}}(u)$ will not be the first ASR result, $u_1 \neq u^*$. In other words, if the confidence score *re-ranks* the N-best list, this may cause s^* to differ from u_1 (Figure 7).
- **Prior re-ranking**: Statistical techniques use a prior probability for each possible dialog state – in our system, each slot value – $b_0(s)$. If an item recognized lower-down on the N-best list has a high prior, it can obtain the most belief, causing s^* to differ from u_1 (Figure 8).
- **Confidence aggregation**: If the top belief state s^* has high belief, then subsequent low-confidence recognitions which do not contain s^* will not dislodge s^* from the top position, causing s^* to differ from u_1 (Figure 9).
- **N-best synthesis**: If an item appears in two N-best lists, but is not in the top ASR N-best position in the latter recognition, it may still obtain the highest belief, causing s^* to differ from u_1 (Figure 10).

[1] This taxonomy was developed for belief tracking over a single slot. For systems which track joint beliefs over multiple slots, additional mechanisms could be identified.

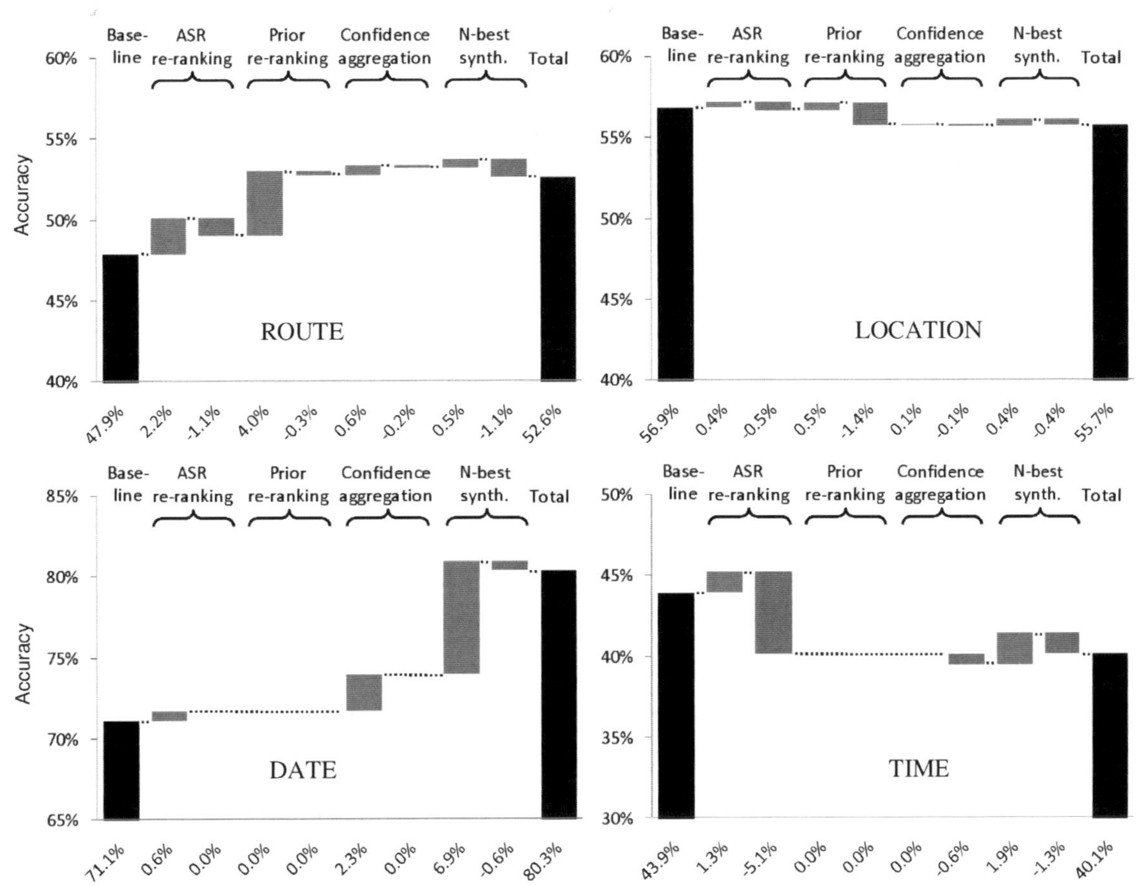

Figure 1: Differences in accuracy between ASR and belief monitoring. "Baseline" indicates accuracy among utterances where belief monitoring had no effect – where ASR and belief monitoring are both correct, or both incorrect. Blue bars show cases where the top belief state s^* is correct and the top ASR result u_1 is not; red bars show cases where u_1 is correct and s^* is not. The plot is arranged to show a running total where blue bars increase the total and red bars decrease the total. Percentages under blue and red bars show the change in accuracy due to each mechanism. The black bar on the right shows the resulting accuracy in deployment.

We selected utterances where the correctness of the top ASR result and top dialog hypothesis differed – where one was correct and the other was not – and labeled these by hand to indicate which of the four mechanisms was responsible for the difference. In a few cases multiple mechanisms were responsible; these were labeled with the first contributing mechanism in the order listed above.

Figures 1 shows results. Of the four mechanisms, prior re-ranking occurred most often, and confidence aggregation occurred least often. Interestingly, some mechanisms provided a performance gain for certain slots and a degradation for others. This led us to look at each mechanism in detail.

4.1 Evaluation of ASR Re-ranking

The recognizer used by AT&T Let's Go produced an N-best list ordered by decoder cost. After decoding, a confidence score was assigned to each item on the N-best list using a regression model that operated on features of the recognition (Williams and Balakrishnan, 2009). The purpose of this regression was to assign a probability of correctness to each item on the N-best list; while it was not designed to re-rank the N-best list, the design of this model did allow it to assign a higher score to the $n = 2$ hypothesis than the $n = 1$ hypothesis. When this happens, we say the N-best list was *re-ranked*. Table 2 shows how often ASR re-ranking occurred, and how often the

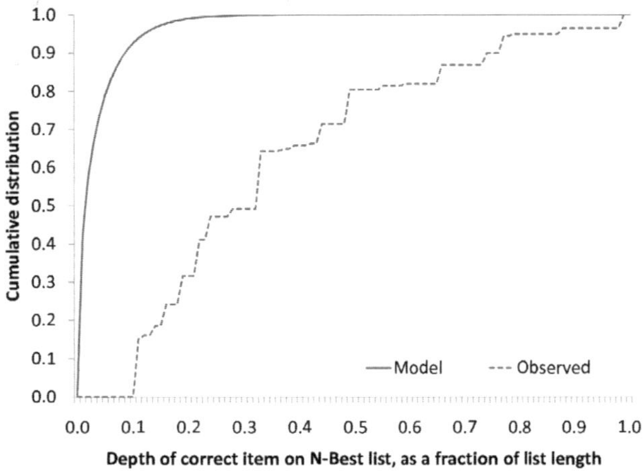

Figure 2: Cumulative distribution of the position of the correct item on N-Best lists for the ROUTE when the correct item is in position $2 \ldots N$. Depth is shown as a fraction of the N-Best list length.

ASR re-ranking helped and hurt ASR accuracy. We found that re-ranking degraded ASR accuracy for all slots, except DATE where it had a trivial positive impact. This suggested a problem with our confidence score; examining ROUTE, LOCATION, and TIME we found that the distributions used by the confidence score that apportions mass to items $2 \ldots N$ were far more concentrated on the N=2 entry than observed in deployment (Figure 2). Investigation revealed a bug in the model estimation code for these slots.

Where ASR re-ranking decreased ASR accuracy, we'd expect to see it also decrease belief state accuracy. Indeed, for the TIME slot, ASR re-ranking causes a substantial decrease in belief state accuracy, highlighting the importance of an accurate confidence score to statistical techniques. However, for the ROUTE slot, we see an *increase* in belief state accuracy attributed to ASR re-ranking. This can be explained by interaction between ASR re-ranking and prior re-ranking, discussed next.

4.2 Evaluation of prior re-ranking

Whereas N-best re-ranking affects $b'(s)$ via P_{asr}, *prior re-ranking* affects $b'(s)$ via the *prior probability* in a slot $b_0(s)$ – i.e., the initial belief, at the start of the dialog, for each value the slot may take. If the slot's prior is uniform (non-informative), we expect to see no effect on accuracy due to the prior – indeed, Figure 1 shows that priors had no effect on belief accuracy for DATE and TIME, which used uniform priors.

ROUTE and LOCATION employed a non-uniform prior, and here we'd expect to see a gain in performance if the prior matches actual use. Both priors were computed using a simple heuristic in which the prior was proportional to the number of distinct bus-stops on the route or covered by the location expression, smoothed with a smoothing factor. For example, the phrase "downtown" covered 17 stops and its prior was 0.018; the phrase "airport" covered 1 stop and its prior was 0.00079. Even though historical usage data was available to Spoken Dialog Challenge 2010 participants (Parent and Eskenazi, 2010), we instead chose to base priors on bus-stop counts as a test of whether effective priors could be constructed without access to usage data.

Overall the prior for ROUTE fit actual usage data well (Figure 3), and we see a corresponding net gain in belief accuracy of $3.7\% = 4.0\% - 0.3\%$ in Figure 1. However the prior for LOCATION was a poor match with actual usage (Figure 4), and this caused a net degradation in belief accuracy of $-0.9\% = 0.5\% - 1.4\%$. The key problem is that the heuristic wrongly assumed all stops are equally popular: for example, although the airport contained a single stop (and thus received a very low prior), it was very popular. This suggests that it would be better to estimate priors based on usage data rather than the bus-stop count heuristic. More broadly, it also underscores the importance of accurate priors to statistical dialog techniques.

In the previous section, for ROUTE, it was observed that ASR re-ranking degraded ASR accuracy, yet caused an improvement in belief accuracy. The effects of the prior explain this: the prior was often stronger, such that an error introduced by ASR re-ranking was cancelled by prior re-ranking. Examining cases where ASR re-ranking occurred but the belief state was still correct confirmed this. Where ASR re-ranking and prior re-ranking agreed, the ASR re-ranking received credit. Looking at LOCATION, the prior was essentially noise, so ASR re-ranking errors could not be systematically canceled by prior re-ranking in the same way – indeed, LOCATION belief accuracy was degraded by both ASR re-ranking and prior re-ranking. More broadly, this provides a nice illustration of how statistical tech-

Slot	ROUTE	LOCATION	DATE	TIME
All utterances	1520	2235	173	157
Utterances with	505	305	3	40
ASR re-ranking	33.2%	13.6%	1.7%	25.5%
ASR re-ranked; N=2 correct	36	11	1	3
(ASR re-ranking helped)	+2.4%	+0.5 %	+0.6 %	+1.9 %
ASR re-ranked; N=1 correct	63	33	0	9
(ASR re-ranking hurt)	-4.1%	-1.5 %	0 %	-5.7 %
Net gain from	-27	-22	+1	-6
ASR re-ranking	-1.8 %	-1.0%	+0.6%	-3.8%

Table 2: ASR re-ranking.

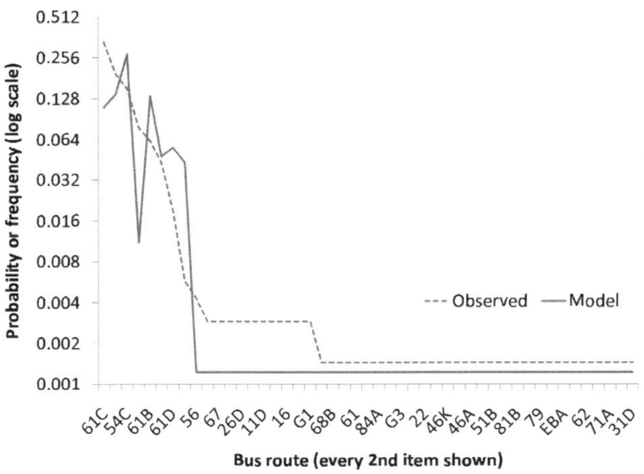

Figure 3: Modeled prior for ROUTE vs. observed usage. The modeled prior was a relatively good predictor of actual usage.

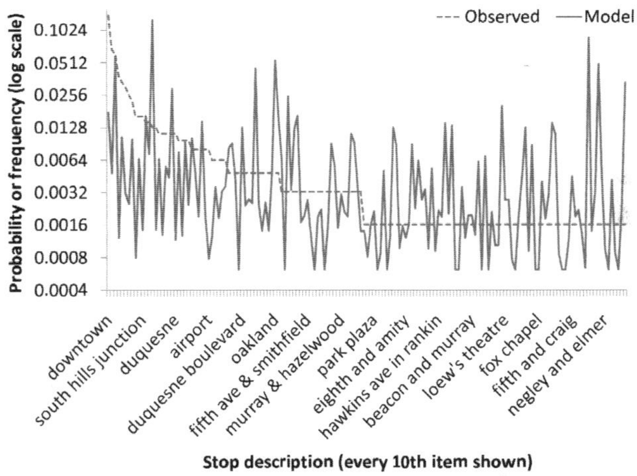

Figure 4: Modeled prior for LOCATION vs. observed usage. The modeled prior was essentially noise compared to actual usage.

niques can combine conflicting evidence – in this case, from the prior and ASR.

4.3 Evaluation of confidence score aggregation

The conditions for confidence score aggregation occur somewhat rarely: for no slot did it have the greatest effect on belief accuracy. It had the largest effect on DATE; investigation revealed that belief scores for DATE were relatively lower than for other slots (Table 3). Since all slots used the same thresholds to make accept/reject decisions, DATE had proportionally more retries in which the top belief hypothesis was correct, yielding more opportunities for confidence aggregation to have an effect.

But why were belief values for DATE lower than for other slots? Investigation revealed that a bug was causing priors for DATE to be nearly an order of magnitude too small, so that each recognized date was artificially improbable. As a result, DATE effectively had a more stringent threshold for accept/reject decisions. Although caused by a bug, this case study provides a more general illustration: obtaining sufficient belief to meet higher thresholds requires more ASR evidence in the form of more re-

Slot	ROUTE	LOCATION	DATE	TIME
Correct	0.90	0.89	0.60	0.73
Incorrect	0.52	0.59	0.34	0.53

Table 3: Average belief in the top dialog state hypothesis when that hypothesis was correct or incorrect.

Slot	ROUTE	LOCATION	DATE	TIME
Average N-best list length	5.0	2.8	2.1	4.3
N-best accuracy	27.9%	10.6%	46.0%	34.7%
Average position of correct item ($n > 1$)	3.3	3.2	2.6	2.9

Table 4: Descriptive statistics for N-best lists. *Average N-best list length* indicates the average length of all N-best lists, regardless of accuracy. *N-best accuracy* indicates how often the correct item appeared in any position $n > 1$ among cases where the top ASR result $n = 1$ was not correct. *Average position of correct item* refers to the average n among cases where the correct item appeared with $n > 1$.

tries.

4.4 Evaluation of N-best synthesis

For DATE, N-best synthesis had a large positive effect, TIME and LOCATION a small positive effect (or no effect), and ROUTE a small negative effect. N-best synthesis occurs when commonality exists across N-best lists, so we next examined the N-best lists for each slot.

Table 4 shows three key properties of the N-best lists. ROUTE and DATE had the most extreme values: ROUTE had the longest N-best lists, comparatively poor N-best accuracy, and the correct item appeared furthest down the N-best list. By contrast, DATE had the shortest N-best lists, the best N-best accuracy, and the correct item appeared closest to the top. LOCATION and TIME were between the two. This relative ordering aligns with the observed effect that N-best synthesis had on belief accuracy, where DATE enjoyed a large improvement and ROUTE suffered a small degradation.

This correlation suggests that basic properties of the N-best list govern the effectiveness of N-best synthesis: when N-best lists are shorter, more often contain the correct answer, and when the correct answer is closer to the top position, N-best synthesis can lead to large gains. When N-best lists are longer, less often contain the correct answer, and when the correct answer is farther from the top position, N-best synthesis can lead to small gains or even degradations.

5 Identifying belief state errors

The analysis in the preceding section assessed the *accuracy* of the belief state. In practice, a system must decide whether to accept or reject a hypothesis, so it is also important to evaluate the ability of the belief state to discriminate between correct and incorrect hypotheses. We studied this by plotting receiver operating characteristic (ROC) curves for each slot, in Figure 5.

Where the belief state has higher accuracy (ROUTE, DATE), the belief state shows somewhat better ROC results, especially at higher false-accept rates. However, gains in ROC performance appear to be due entirely to gains in accuracy: In LOCATION, belief tracking made nearly no difference to accuracy, and the belief state shows virtually no difference to ASR in ROC performance. TIME suffered degradations in both accuracy and ROC performance. The trend appears to be that if belief tracking does not improve over ASR 1-best, then it seems that belief tracking does not enable better accept/reject decision to made. Perhaps addressing the model deficiencies mentioned above will improve discrimination – this is left to future work.

6 Conclusions

This paper has provided a first assessment of statistical techniques in a spoken dialog system under real use. We have found that belief tracking is not guaranteed to improve accuracy – its effects vary depending on the operating conditions:

- Overall the effects of prior re-ranking and N-best synthesis are largest; confidence aggregation has the smallest effect.
- When N-best lists are *useful*, N-best synthesis can have a large positive effect (DATE); when N-best lists are more noisy, N-best synthesis has a small or even negative effect (ROUTE).
- In the presence of more rejection, confidence aggregation can have a positive effect (DATE),

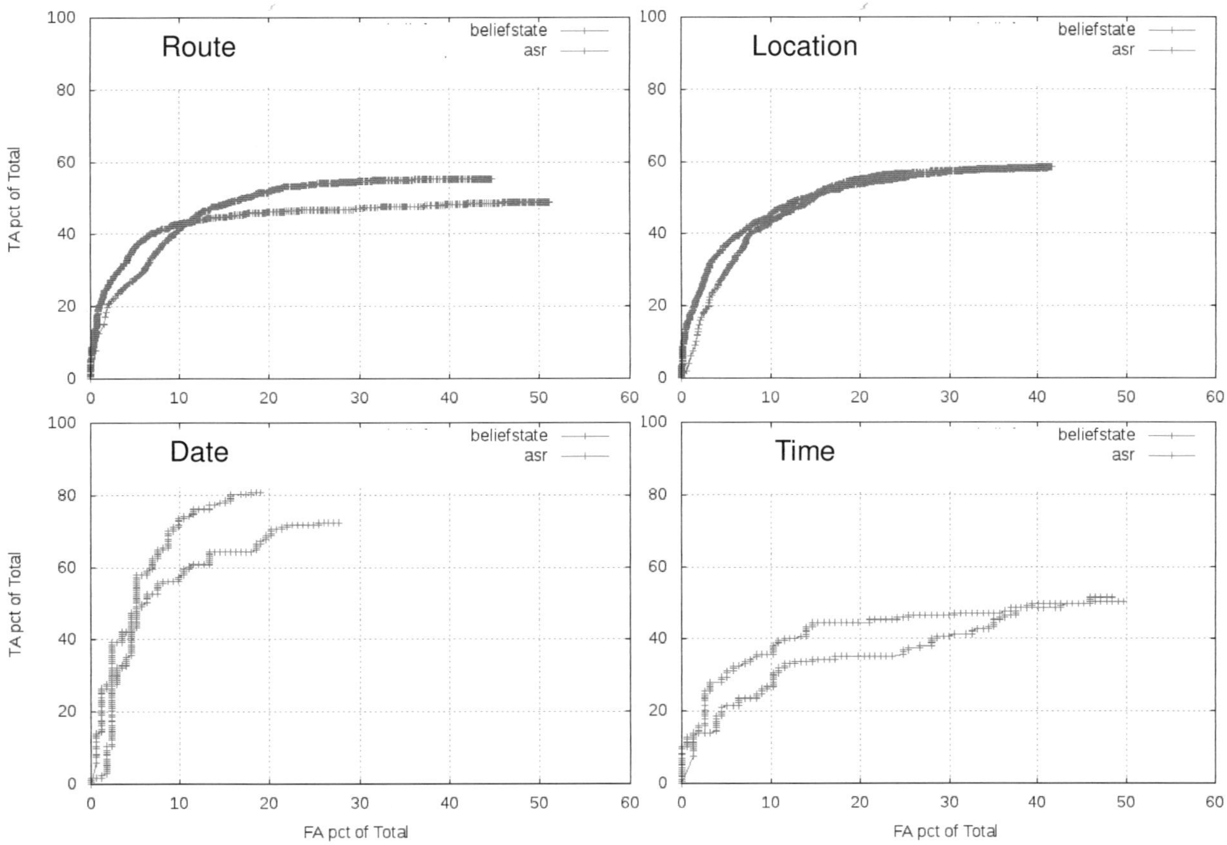

Figure 5: ROC curves. Red curves show the top-scored ASR hypothesis u^* with accept/reject decisions made using the confidence score $P_{\text{asr}}(u)$; blue curves show the top belief state s^* with accept/reject decisions made using its belief $b(s^*)$.

but otherwise plays a small role.

- When there exists an informative prior and it is estimated correctly, prior re-ranking produces an accuracy gain (ROUTE); when estimated poorly, it degrades accuracy (LOCATION).

- The belief state, at least when using our current models, improves accept/reject decisions only when belief tracking produces a gain in accuracy over ASR. Absent an accuracy increase, the belief state is no more informative than a good confidence score for making accept/reject decisions.

We believe these findings validate that statistical techniques – properly employed – have the capability to improve ASR robustness under real use. This paper has focused on descriptive results; in future work, we plan to test whether correcting the model deficiencies and re-running belief tracking does indeed improve performance. For now, we hope that this work serves as a guide to practitioners building statistical dialog systems, providing some instruction on the importance of accurate model building, and examples of the effects of different design decisions.

Acknowledgments

Thanks to Barbara Hollister and the AT&T labeling lab for their excellent work on this project.

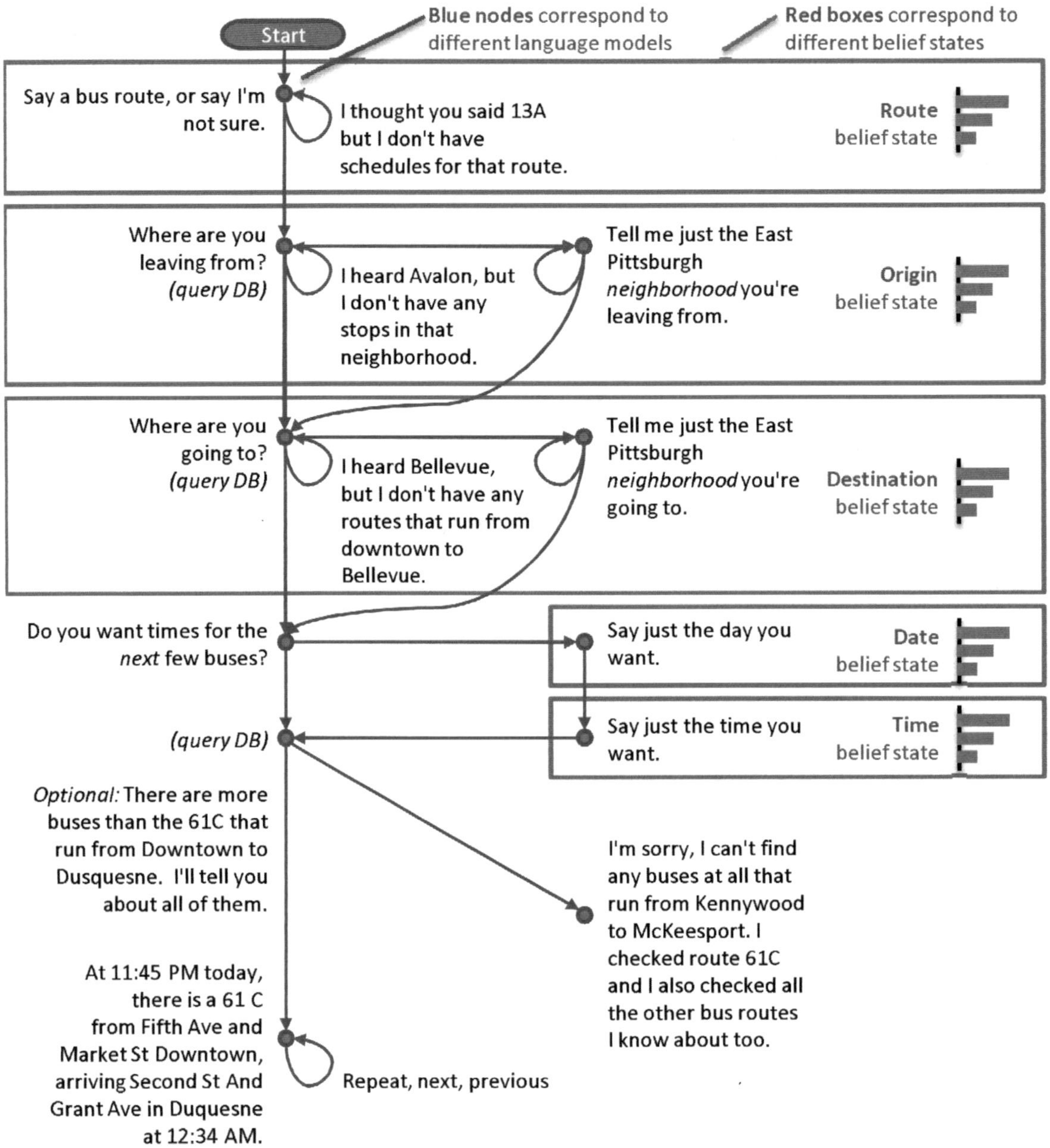

Figure 6: Flowchart of AT&T Let's Go. The system asks for the bus route, then the origin bus stop, then the destination bus stop. If the user does not want the next few buses, the system also asks for the date and time. Prompts shown are paraphrases; actual system prompts include example responses and are tailored to dialog context. Different language models are used for each slot, and separate belief states are maintained over each of these 5 slots. In the analysis in this paper, results for the origin and destination slots have been combined to form the LOCATION slot.

References

H Ai, A Raux, D Bohus, M Eskenzai, and D Litman. 2008. Comparing spoken dialog corpora collected with recruited subjects versus real users. In *Proc SIGdial, Columbus, Ohio, USA*.

AW Black, S Burger, B Langner, G Parent, and M Eskenazi. 2010. Spoken dialog challenge 2010. In *Proc SLT, Berkeley, CA*.

J Henderson and O Lemon. 2008. Mixture model POMDPs for efficient handling of uncertainty in dialogue management. In *Proc ACL-HLT, Columbus, Ohio*.

G Parent and M Eskenazi. 2010. Toward better crowdsourced transcription: Transcription of a year of the let's go bus information system data. In *Proc SLT, Berkeley, CA*.

A Raux, B Langner, D Bohus, A Black, and M Eskenazi. 2005. Let's go public! Taking a spoken dialog system to the real world. In *Proc INTERSPEECH, Lisbon*.

B Thomson and SJ Young. 2010. Bayesian update of dialogue state: A POMDP framework for spoken dialogue systems. *Computer Speech and Language*, 24:562–588.

JD Williams and S Balakrishnan. 2009. Estimating probability of correctness for ASR N-best lists. In *Proc SIGdial, London, UK*.

JD Williams and SJ Young. 2007. Partially observable Markov decision processes for spoken dialog systems. *Computer Speech and Language*, 21(2):393–422.

JD Williams, I Arizmendi, and A Conkie. 2010. Demonstration of AT&T "Let's Go": A production-grade statistical spoken dialog system. In *Proc SLT, Berkeley, CA*.

JD Williams. 2007. Using particle filters to track dialogue state. In *Proc IEEE Workshop on Automatic Speech Recognition and Understanding (ASRU), Kyoto, Japan*.

JD Williams, 2010a. *AT&T Statistical Dialog Toolkit*. `http://www.research.att.com/people/Williams_Jason_D`.

JD Williams. 2010b. Incremental partition recombination for efficient tracking of multiple dialog states. In *Proc Intl Conf on Acoustics, Speech, and Signal Processing (ICASSP), Dallas, USA*.

SJ Young, M Gašić, S Keizer, F Mairesse, J Schatzmann, B Thomson, and K Yu. 2010. The hidden information state model: a practical framework for POMDP-based spoken dialogue management. *Computer Speech and Language*, 24(2):150–174, April.

Appendix: Mechanism illustrations

This appendix provides graphical illustrations of each of the four *mechanisms* that can cause the top ASR hypothesis to be different from the top belief state hypothesis. These examples were taken from logs of calls with real users, although some surface forms have been simplified for space.

At the top of each panel is the system action taken. The user's true response is shown in italics in the left-most column. The second column shows the top 7 entries from the ASR N-best list, displayed in the order produced by the speech recognition engine. The third column shows the confidence score – the local probability of correctness assigned to each ASR N-best entry. The last column shows the resulting belief state, sorted by the magnitude of the belief. Correct entries are shown in bold red.

ASR re-ranking and prior re-ranking occur within one turn, and confidence aggregation and N-best synthesis occur across two turns. These examples all show cases where the belief state is correct and the ASR is incorrect; however, the opposite also occurs of course.

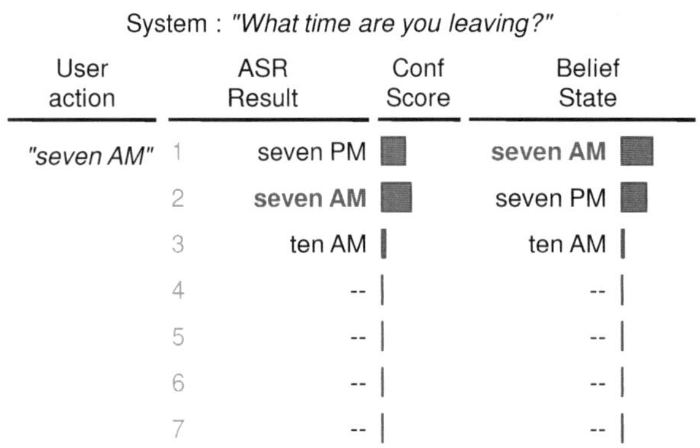

Figure 7: **Illustration of ASR re-ranking**: The correct ASR hypothesis ("seven AM") is in the $n = 2$ position, but it is assigned a higher confidence score than the misrecognized $n = 1$ entry "seven PM". TIME uses a flat prior, so the higher confidence score results in "seven AM" attaining the highest belief.

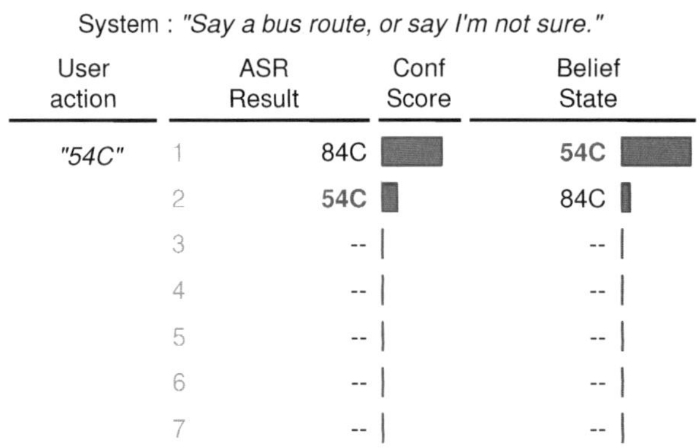

Figure 8: **Illustration of Prior re-ranking**: The correct ASR hypothesis ("54C") is in the $n = 2$ position, and it is assigned less confidence than the mis-recognized $n = 1$ entry, "84C". However, the prior on 54C is much higher than on 84C, so 54C obtains the highest belief.

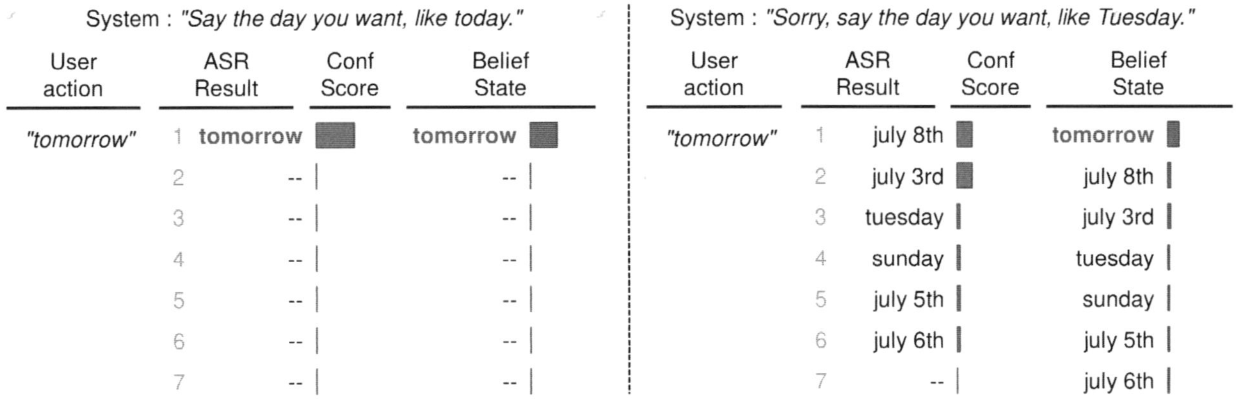

Figure 9: **Illustration of Confidence aggregation**: In the first turn, "tomorrow" is recognized with medium confidence. In the second turn, "tomorrow" does not appear on the N-best list; however the recognition result has very low confidence, so this misrecognition is unable to dislodge "tomorrow" from the top belief position. At the end of the second update, the belief state's top hypothesis of "tomorrow" is correct even though it didn't appear on the second N-best list.

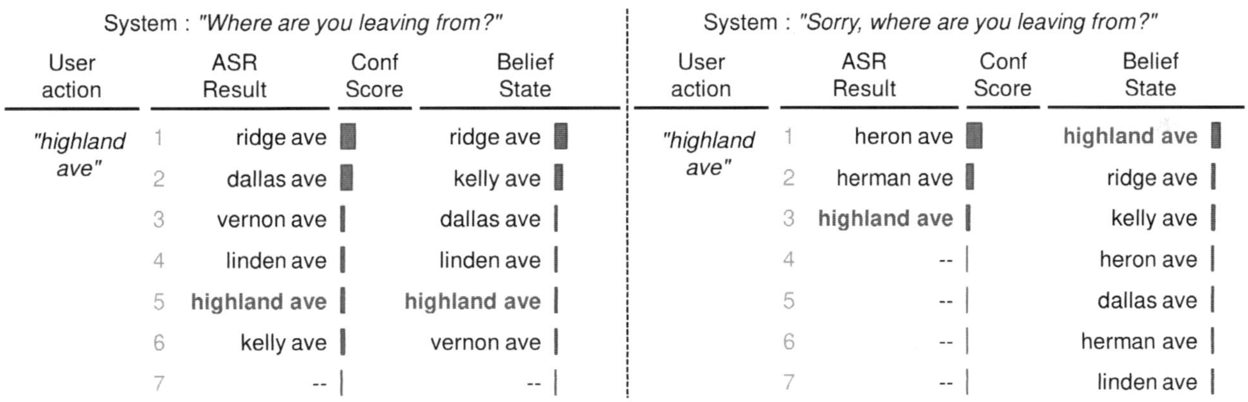

Figure 10: **Illustration of N-best synthesis**: In the first turn, the correct item "highland ave" is on the ASR N-best list but not in the top position. It appears in the belief state but not in the top position. In the second turn, the correct item "highland ave" is again on the ASR N-best list but again not in the top position. However, because it appeared in the previous belief state, it obtains the highest belief after the second update. Even though "highland ave" was mis-recognized twice in a row, the commonality across the two N-best lists causes it to have the highest belief after the second update.

"The day after the day after tomorrow?" A machine learning approach to adaptive temporal expression generation: training and evaluation with real users

Srinivasan Janarthanam, Helen Hastie, Oliver Lemon, Xingkun Liu
Interaction Lab
School of Mathematical and Computer Sciences (MACS)
Heriot-Watt University
{sc445, h.hastie, o.lemon, x.liu}@hw.ac.uk

Abstract

Generating Temporal Expressions (TE) that are easy to understand, unambiguous, and reasonably short is a challenge for humans and Spoken Dialogue Systems. Rather than developing hand-written decision rules, we adopt a data-driven approach by collecting user feedback on a variety of possible TEs in terms of task success, ambiguity, and user preference. The data collected in this work is freely available to the research community. These data were then used to train a simulated user and a reinforcement learning policy that learns an adaptive Temporal Expression generation strategy for a variety of contexts. We evaluate our learned policy both in simulation and with real users and show that this data-driven adaptive policy is a significant improvement over a rule-based adaptive policy, leading to a 24% increase in perceived task completion, while showing a small increase in actual task completion, and a 16% decrease in call duration. This means that dialogues are more efficient and that users are also more confident about the appointment that they have agreed with the system.

1 Introduction

Temporal Expressions are linguistic expressions that are used to refer to a date and are often a source of confusion in human-human, human-computer and text interactions such as emails and instant messaging. For example, "Let's meet next Sunday"– "do you mean Sunday this week or a week on Sunday?". (Mccoy and Strube, 1999) state that changes in temporal structure in text are often indicated by either cue words and phrases (e.g. "next Thursday", "this week", "tomorrow"), a change in grammatical time of the verb (e.g. present tense versus future tense), or changes in aspect (e.g. atomic versus extended events versus states as defined by (Moens and Steedman, 1988)). In this study, we will concentrate on the first of these phenomena, generating TEs with the optimal content and lexical choice.

Much work in the field of Natural Language Processing concerns understanding and resolving these temporal expressions in text (Gerber et al., 2002; Pustejovsky et al., 2003; Ahn et al., 2007; Mazur and Dale, 2007; Han et al., 2006), however, little work has looked at how best to plan and realise temporal expressions in order to minimize ambiguity and confusion in a Spoken Dialogue System (SDS). (Reiter et al., 2005) presented a data driven approach to generating TEs to refer to time in weather forecast information where appropriate expressions were identified using contextual features using supervised learning. We adopt an adaptive, data-driven reinforcement learning approach instead. Similar data-driven approaches have been applied to information presentation (Rieser et al., 2010; Walker et al., 2007) where each Natural Language Generation (NLG) action is a sequential decision point, based on the current dialogue context and expected long-term reward of that action. A data-driven approach has also been applied to the problem of referring expression generation in dialogue for expert and novice-users of a SDS (Janarthanam and Lemon, 2010). However, to date, there has been no previous work on adaptive data-driven approaches for *temporal* referring expression generation, where uncertainty in

Proceedings of the SIGDIAL 2011: the 12th Annual Meeting of the Special Interest Group on Discourse and Dialogue, pages 142–151,
Portland, Oregon, June 17-18, 2011.

the stochastic environment is explicitly modelled.

The data-driven approach to temporal expression generation presented here is in the context of appointment scheduling dialogues. The fact that there are multiple ways that a time slot can be referred to leads to an interesting NLG problem of how best to realise a TE for a particular individual in a particular context for certain domains. For example, the following expressions all vary in terms of length, ambiguity, redundant information and users' preference: "next Friday afternoon" or "Friday next week at the same time", or "in the afternoon, a week on Friday".

Temporal Expressions contain two types of references: absolute references such as "Tuesday" and "12th January", and relative references such as "tomorrow" and "this Tuesday". Generating TEs therefore, involves both in selecting appropriate pieces of information (date, day, time, month, and week) to present and deciding how to present them (absolute or relative reference).

Our objective here is to convey a target appointment slot to users using an expression that is optimal in terms of the trade-off between understandability, length and user preference.

2 Methodology

We address the issue of generating TEs by adopting a data-driven approach that has four stages. Firstly, we define Temporal Expression Units (TEU) as described in Section 2.1. Secondly, we design and implement a web-based data collection, gathering metrics on the TEUs in various contexts for a variety of date types (Section 3). Thirdly, we train a user simulation and use it to learn a policy using reinforcement learning techniques that generates the optimal combination of TEUs for each context (Section 4). Finally, we deploy and evaluate this policy in a Spoken Dialogue System for appointment scheduling and show that our learned policy performs better than a hand-written, adaptive one (results presented in Section 5).

2.1 Temporal Expression Units

For this study, TEs are broken down into 5 categories or units (TEUs) presented in a fixed order: DAY, DATE, MONTH, WEEK and TIME. Each of these units can be expressed relative to the current day and to the current context (i.e. previously mentioned dates). Specifically, there are 3 unit attributes: absolute (e.g. DAY=abs "Tuesday"); relative to current day (e.g. DAY=rel "tomorrow"); and relative to context (e.g. DAY=rc "the following day").

TEU	Choices
DAY	abs, rel, rc, nn
DATE	abs, nn
MONTH	abs, nn
WEEK	abs, rel, nn
TIME	abs, rc

Table 1: TEU choices where abs is absolute, rel is relative, rc is relative to context and nn is none

Certain restrictions on possible TEU combinations were imposed, for example, DATE=rc and DAY=rel were combined to be just DAY=rel, and some combinations were omitted on the basis that it is highly unlikely that they would be uttered in natural speech, for example WEEK=rel and MONTH=abs would result in "this week in September". Finally, every TE has to contain a time (am or pm for this application). The possible combinations are summarised in Table 1.

3 Data Collection

The data collection experiment was in two parts (Task 1 and Task 2) and was designed using the Webexp experimental software[1]. Webexp is a client-server set up where a server application hosts the experiment and stores the experimental files, logs and results. The client side runs an applet on the user's web-browser.

In Task 1, participants listened to an audio file containing a TE generated from absolute and relative TEUs (see Figure 1). No relative-context (rc) TEUs were used in Task 1 since the dialogue excerpt presented was in isolation and therefore had no context. Each participant was asked to listen to 10 different audio files in a sequence corresponding to a variety of dates randomly chosen from 8 possible dates. The participant then had to identify the correct appointment slot that the system is referring to. There is scope for the participant to add multiple answers in order to capture potential ambiguity

[1] http://www.webexp.info

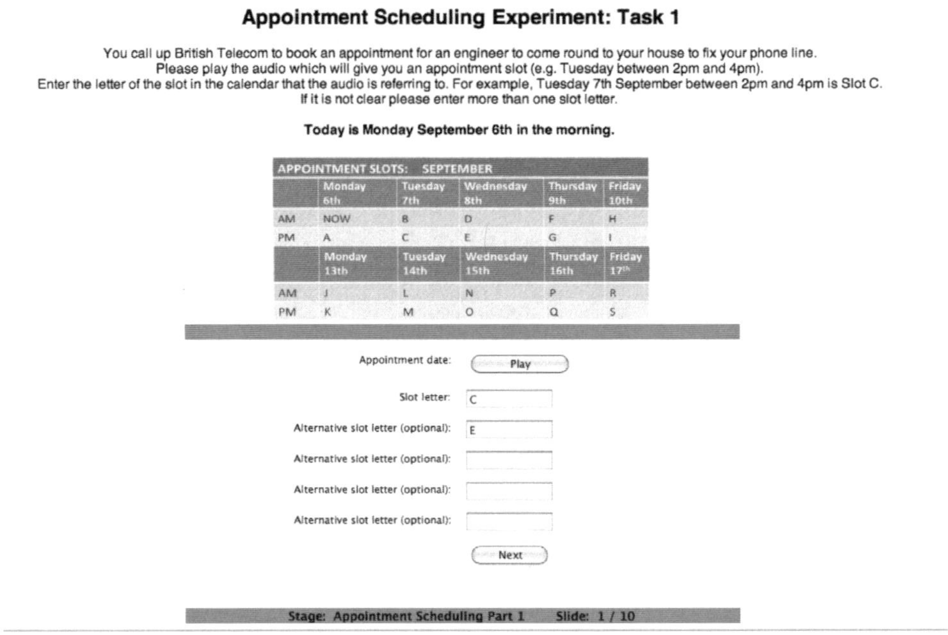

Figure 1: Screen shot of Task 1 in the on-line data collection experiment

of a TE, and we report on this below. The 8 dates that were used to generate the TEs fell into a two week period in a single month which is in-line with the evaluation set-up of the appointment scheduling SDS discussed in Section 5.3.

For each date, the TE was randomly picked from a set of 30 possible combinations of TEUs. Each TEU was generated by a rule-based realiser and synthesized using the Baratinoo synthesizer (France Telecom, 2011). This realiser generates text from a candidate list for each TEU based on the given date. For example, if the slot currently being discussed is Tuesday 7th, the realiser would generate "tomorrow" for DAY=rel; if the date in discussion was Wednesday 8th then DAY=rel would be realised as "the day after tomorrow". There was potential for overlap of stimuli, as any given TE for any given date may be assessed by more than one participant.

Task 2 of the experiment was in two stages. In the first stage (Task 2A), the participants are given today's date and the following dialogue excerpt; Operator: "We need to send out an engineer to your home. The first available appointment is ..." (see Figure 2). They are then asked to listen to 5 audio files of the system saying different TEs for the same date and asked to rate preference on a scale of 1-6 (where 1 is bad and 6 is great.) For the second stage (Task 2B), the dialogue is as follows; Operator: "so you can't do Wednesday 8th September in the morning." and then the participants are asked to listen to 5 more audio files that are generated TEs including relative context such as "how about Thursday at the same time?". This two-stage process is then repeated 4 times for each participant.

Table 2 summarizes the metrics collected in the different parts of the experiment. The metric *Distance* is calculated in terms of the number of slots from the current date to the target date (TD). Instances were grouped into four distance groups: G1: TD is 1-2 slots away; G2: TD is 3-6 slots away; G3: TD is 7-11 slots away and G4: TD more than 11 slots away. P_replay is calcuated by the total number of replays divided by the total number of plays for that temporal expression, i.e. the probability that the temporal expression played is requested to be replayed. P_ambiguous is calculated by the number of times a given temporal expression is given more than 1 interpretation divided by the total number of times that the same given referring expression is answered.

In total there were 73 participants for Task 1 and

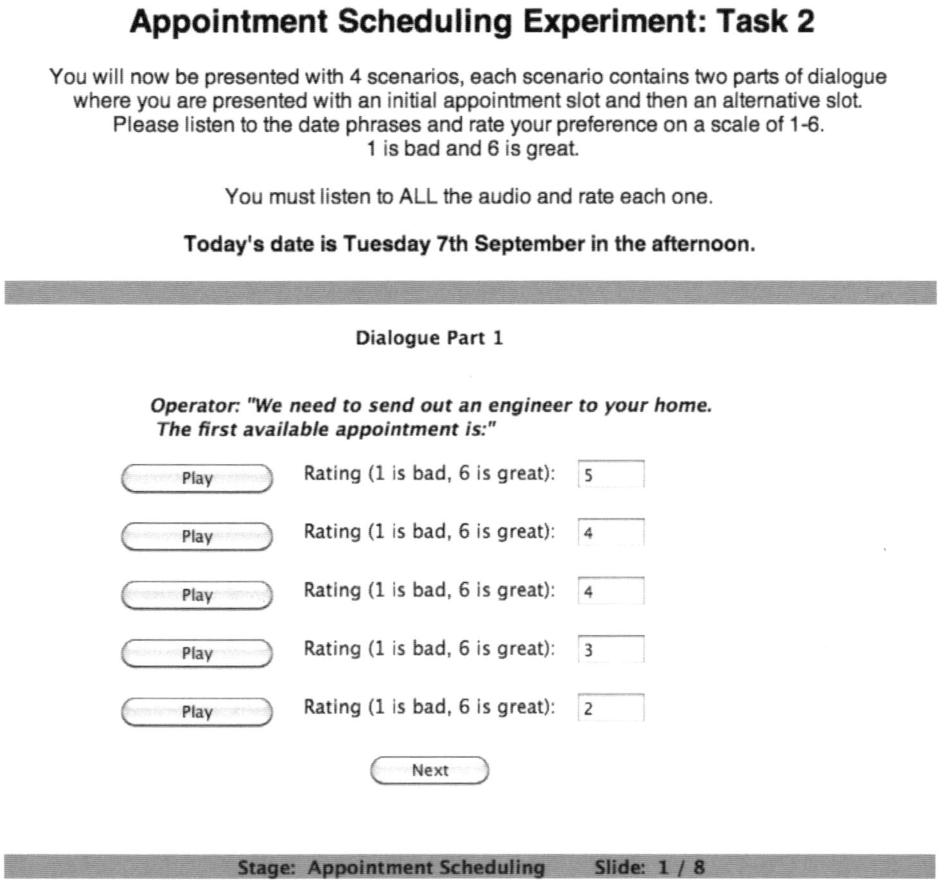

Figure 2: Screen shot of Task 2 in the on-line data collection experiment

730 TE samples collected. Although Task 2 directly followed on from Task 1, there was a significant drop out rate as only 48 participants completed the second task resulting in 1,920 TE samples. Participants who completed both tasks were rewarded by a chance to win an Amazon voucher.

3.1 Data Analysis

Figure 3 shows various metrics with respect to TE absoluteness and relativeness is the number of absolute and relative TEUs respectively. These two graphs represent the state space that the generation policy described in Section 4 is exploring, trading off between various features such as *Length, taskSuccess* and *userPref*.

As we can see, there is a tendency for average *taskSuccess* to increase as absoluteness increases whereas, for relativeness the distribution is more even. The TE with the greatest *taskSuccess* has an absoluteness of 4 and zero relativeness: DATE=abs, MONTH=abs, WEEK=abs, TIME=abs (e.g. "11th September, the week starting the 10th, between 8am and 10am") and the TE with the least *taskSuccess* has an absoluteness of only 2, again with no relativeness: DATE=abs, TIME=abs, (e.g. "8th between 8am and 10am").

Average *userPref* stays level and then decreases if absoluteness is 5. We infer from this that although long utterances that are completely explicit are more clear in terms of *taskSuccess*, they are not necessarily preferred by users. This is likely due to TE length increasing. On average, the inclusion of one relative expression is preferred over none at all or two. The most preferred TE has an absoluteness of 3 with a relativeness of 2: DAY=rel, DATE=abs, MONTH=abs, WEEK=rel, TIME=abs (e.g. "Tomorrow the 7th of September, this week, between 8am and 10am").

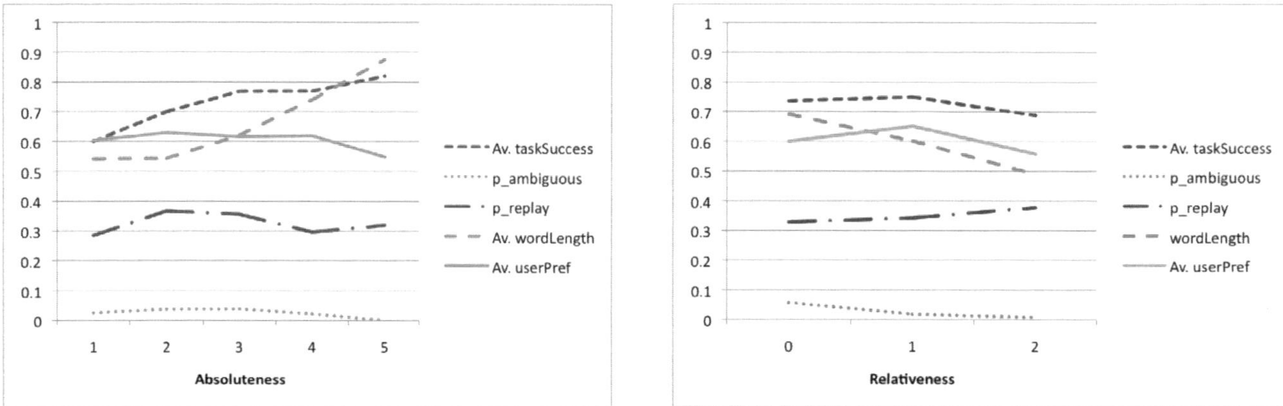

Figure 3: Graph showing the trade-offs between various metrics with respect to absoluteness and relativeness (number of absolute/relative TEUs) in terms of probabilities or normalised values.

Metric	Description	Task
P_ambiguous	Probability that the expression is ambiguous to the user	1
taskSuccess	Correct slot identified	1
P_replay	Probability of replay (measure of understandability)	1 & 2
Length	Expression length in terms of number of TEUs that are non null divided by the total number of possible TEUs (5)	1 & 2
wordLength	Expression length in words normalised over max num of words (15)	1 & 2
userPref	Preference rating of audio from 1-6	2
Distance	Distance from target date (TD) to current date in terms of number of slots	1 & 2

Table 2: Metrics collected in various parts of the experiment

The probability of ambiguity and replay does not seem to be affected by absoluteness. The most ambiguous TE has an absoluteness of 3 and zero relativeness: DAY=abs MONTH=abs TIME=abs, (e.g. "Tuesday September between 8am and 10am") indicating that a date is needed for precision. The TEs that the participants were most likely to replay tended to be short e.g. "Tomorrow at the same time". This may be due to the clarity of the speech synthesiser.

4 Learning a TE generation policy

Reinforcement learning is a machine learning approach based on trial and error learning, in which a learning agent learns to map sequences of "optimal" actions to environment or task states (Sutton and Barto, 1998). In this framework the problem of generating temporal expressions is presented as a Markov Decision Process. The goal of the learning agent is to learn to choose those actions that obtain maximum expected reward in the long run. In this section, we present the reinforcement learning setup for learning temporal expression generation policies.

4.1 Actions and States

In this learning setup, we focus only on generating the formal specification and treat the set of TEU choices as the sequential actions of the learning agent. Table 1 presents the choices that are available for each TEU.

The actions are taken based on two factors: the

distance (in terms of time slots: morning or afternoon appointments) between (1) the current date and the target slot and (2) the current date and the slot in context. Based on the distance, the target slot was classified to belong to one of the four distance groups (G1-G4). The slot in context represents whether there was any other slot already mentioned in the conversation so far, so that the system has an option to use "relative_context" expressions to present day and time information. Information concerning the target slot's group and the slot in context make up the state space of the Markov Decision Process (MDP).

4.2 User Simulation

We built a user simulation to simulate the dialogue behaviour of a user in appointment scheduling conversations based on the data from real users described in Section 3. It responds to the TE used by the system to refer to an appointment slot. It responds by either accepting, rejecting, or clarifying the offered slot based on the user's own calendar of available slots. For instance, the simulated user rejects an offered slot if the user is not available at that time. If they accept or reject an offered slot, the user is assumed to understand the TE unambiguously. However, if the user is unable to resolve the appointment slot from the TE, it responds with a clarification request. The simulation responded with a dialogue action ($A_{u,t}$) to TEs based on the system's dialogue act ($A_{s,t}$), system's TE ($TE_{s,t}$). The following probabilistic model was used to generate user dialogue actions:

$$P(A_{u,t}|A_{s,t}, TE_{s,t}, G, C, Cal)$$

In addition to $TE_{s,t}$ and $A_{s,t}$, other factors such as distance between the target slot and the current slot (G), the previous slot in context (C), and the user's calendar (Cal) were also taken into account. G is either G1, G2, G3 or G4 as explained in Section 3. The User's dialogue action ($A_{u,t}$) is one of the three: Accept_slot, Reject_slot or Request_Clarification. The probability of clarification request was calculated as the average of the ambiguity and replay probabilities seen in real user data.

4.3 Reward function

The learning agent was rewarded for each TE that it generated. The reward given to the agent was based on trade-offs between three variables: User preference (UP), Length of the temporal expression (L), and Clarification request probability (CR). UP for each TE is obtained from Task 2 of the data collection. In the following reward function, UP is normalised to be between 0 and 1. L is based on number of TEUs used. The maximum number of TEUs that can be used is 5 (i.e. DAY, DATE, WEEK, MONTH, TIME). L is calculated as follows:

$$\text{Length of TE (L)} = \frac{No.\ of\ used\ TEUs}{Max.\ no.\ of\ TEUs}$$

The clarification request (CR) is set to be 1 if the user responds to the TE with a Request_Clarification and 0 otherwise. Reward is therefore calculated on a turn-by-turn basis using the following formula:

$$Reward = UP * 10.0 - L * 10.0 - CR * 10.0$$

In short, we chose a reward function that penalises TEs that are long and ambiguous, and which rewards TEs that users prefer. It also indirectly rewards task success by penalising ambiguous TEs resulting in clarification requests. This trade-off structure is evident from the data collection where TEs that are too long are dispreferred by the users (see Figure 3). The maximum possible reward is 6 (i.e. UP=1, CR=0, L=2/5) and the minimum is -20 (i.e. UP=0, CR=1, L=1). Note that other reward functions could be explored in future work, for example maximising only for user preference or length.

4.4 Training

We trained a TE generation policy using the above user simulation model for 10,000 runs using the SARSA reinforcement learning algorithm (Sutton and Barto, 1998). During the training phase, the learning agent generated and presented TEs to the user simulation. When a dialogue begins, there is no appointment slot in context (i.e. C = 0). However, if the user rejects the first slot, the dialogue system sets C to 1 and presents the next slot. This is again reset at the beginning of the next dialogue. The agent was rewarded at the end of every turn based on the user's response, length of the TE, and user preference scores as shown above. It gradually explored all possible combinations of TEUs and identified those TEUs in different contexts that maximize

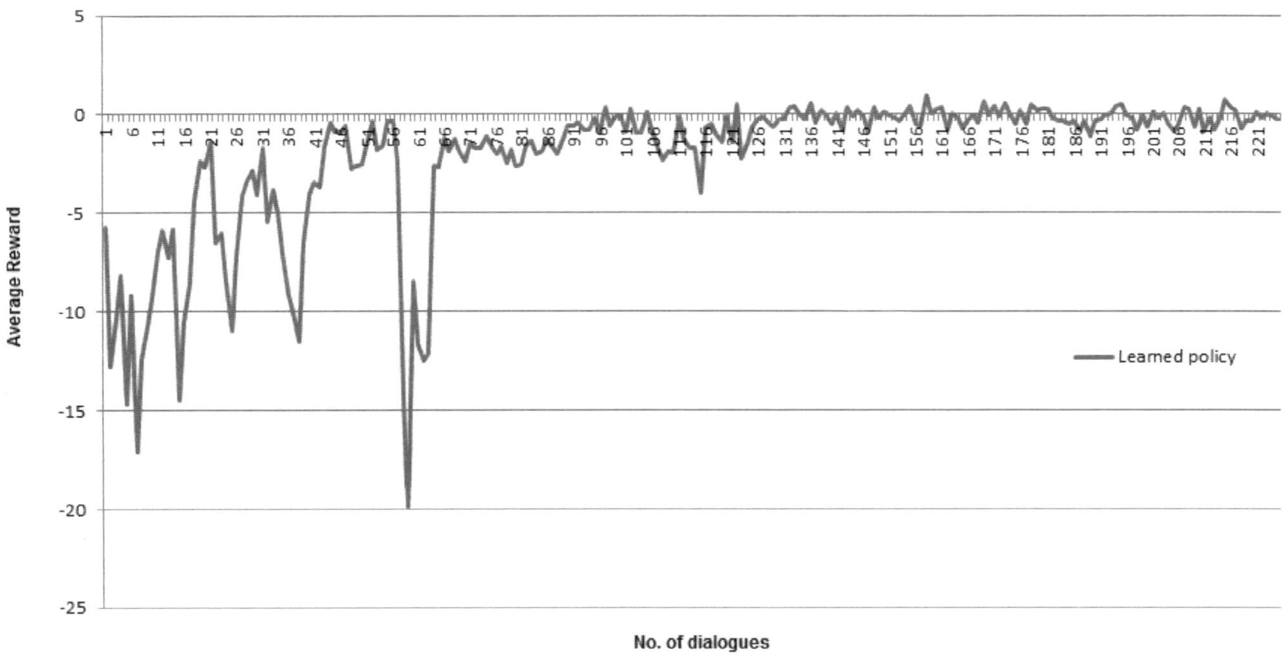

Figure 4: Learning curve

the long-term reward. Figure 4 shows the learning curve of the agent.

Table 3 presents the TE generation policy learned by the agent. As one can observe, it used a minimum number of TEUs to avoid length penalties in the reward. In all cases, MONTH and WEEK information have not been presented at all. For target slots that were closest (in group G1) and the farthest (in group G4), it used relative forms of day (e.g. "tomorrow", "next Tuesday", etc.). This is probably because users dispreferred day information for in-between slots (e.g. "the day after the day after tomorrow"). Also, MONTH information may have been considered to be irrelevant due to the fact that the two week window over which the data has been collected do not span over two different months.

Slots	Specification learned
1-2 > 11	DAY=rel;DATE=abs;MONTH=nn; WEEK=nn;TIME=abs
3-11	DAY=nn;DATE=abs;MONTH=nn; WEEK=nn;TIME=abs

Table 3: Learned policy

5 Evaluation

In this section, we present the baseline policies that were evaluated along with the learned policy. We then present the results of evaluation.

5.1 Baseline policies

The following are the baseline TEG policies:

1. **Absolute policy**: always use absolute formats for all TEUs (i.e. DAY=abs; DATE=abs; MONTH=abs; WEEK=abs; TIME=abs)

2. **Minimal policy**: always use a minimal format with only date, month and time information in their absolute forms (i.e. DAY=nn; DATE=abs; MONTH=abs; WEEK=nn; TIME=abs)

3. **Random policy**: select possible formats randomly for each TEU.

TEG Policy	Average reward
Learned	-0.071* (±3.75)
Absolute	-4.084 (±4.36)
Minimal	-1.340 (±4.2)
Random	-8.21 (±7.72)

Table 4: Evaluation with simulated users (* $p < 0.05$, two-tailed independent samples t-test)

5.2 Results

We evaluated the learned policy and the three other hand-coded baseline TE generation policies with our user simulation model. Each policy generated 1,000 TEs in different states. Table 4 present the results of evaluation with simulated users. On average, the learned policy scores higher than all the baseline policies and the differences between the average reward of the learned policy and the other baselines are statistically significant. This shows that target slots can be presented using different TEs depending on how far they are from the current date and such adaptation can produce less ambiguous, shorter and user preferred expressions.

5.3 Evaluation with real users

The policy was also integrated into an NLG component of a deployed Appointment Scheduling spoken dialogue system. Please note that this is different from the web environment in which the training data was collected. Our data-driven policy was activated when the system informs the user of an available time slot. This system was compared to the exact same system but with a *rule-based* adaptive baseline system. In the rule-based policy MONTH, DATE and TIME were always absolute, DAY was relative if the target date was less than three days away (i.e. "today, tomorrow, day after tomorrow"), and WEEK was always relative (i.e. "this week, next week"). All 5 information units were included in the realisation (e.g. "Thursday the 15th July in the afternoon, next week") although the order was slightly different (DAY-DATE-MONTH-TIME-WEEK).

In this domain, the user tries to make an appointment for an engineer to visit their home. Each user is given a set of 2-week calendars which shows their availability and the goal is to arrange an appointment when both they and the engineer are available.

There were 12 possible scenarios that were evenly rotated across participants and systems. Each scenario is categorised in terms of scheduling difficulty (Hard/Medium/Easy). Scheduling difficulty is calculated for User Difficulty (UD) and System Difficulty (SD) separately to assess the system's mixed initiative ability. Scheduling difficulty is calculated as the ordinal of the first session that is free for both the User and the System. Hard scenarios are with an ordinal of 3 or 4; Medium with an ordinal of 2, and Easy with an ordinal of 1. There are 4 scenarios in each of these difficulty categories for both the user and system. To give an example, in Scenario 10, the user can schedule an appointment on Wednesday afternoon but he/she also has one free session on the previous Tuesday afternoon when the engineer is busy therefore UD = 2. For the system, in this scenario, the first free session it has is on the Wednesday afternoon therefore SD=1. In this case, the scenario is easier for the system than the user because the system could just offer the first session that it has free.

605 dialogues were collected and analysed. The system was evaluated by employees at France Telecom and students of partner universities who have never used the appointment scheduling system before. After each scenario, participants were then asked to fill out a questionnaire on perceived task success and 5 user satisfaction questions on a 6-point Likert Scale (Walker et al., 2000). Results from the real user study are summarised in Table 5. The data-driven policy showed significant improvement in Perceived Task Success (+23.7%) although no significant difference was observed between the two systems in terms of Actual Task Success (Chi-square test, df=1). Perceived Task Success is users' perception of whether they completed the task successfully or not. Overall user satisfaction (the average score of all the questions) was also significantly higher (+5%)[2]. Dialogues with the learned policy were significantly shorter with lower Call Duration in terms of time (-15.7%)[2] and fewer average words per system turn (-23.93%)[2]. Figure 5 shows the length results in time for systems of varying UD and SD. We can see that the data-driven adaptive policy consistently results in a shorter dialogue across all levels of difficulty. In summary, these results show that using a policy trained on the data collected here

Parameters	Learned TEG	Baseline TEG
Actual Task Success	80.05%	78.57%
Perceived Task Success	74.86%*	60.50%
User satisfaction	4.51*	4.30
No. system turns	22.8	23.2
Words per system turn	13.16*	17.3
Call duration	88.60 sec *	105.11 sec

Table 5: Results with real users (* statistically significant difference at $p<0.05$)

results in shorter dialogues and greater confidence in the user that they have had a successful dialogue. Although the learned policy was trained to generate optimal TEs within a two week window and therefore is not general policy for all TE generation problems, we believe that the data-driven approach that we have followed can generalise to other TE generation tasks.

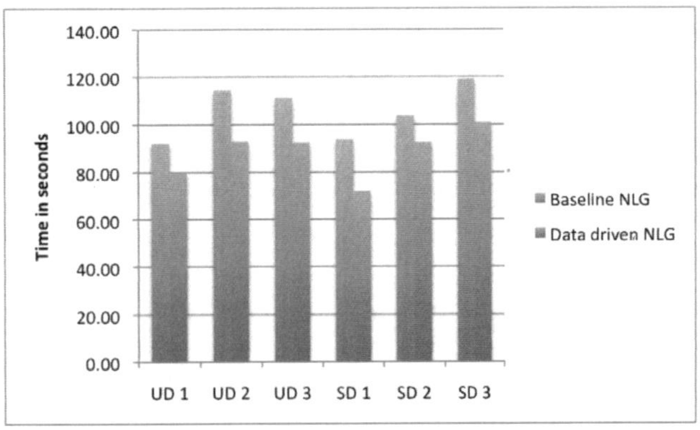

Figure 5: Graph comparing length of dialogues for user (UD) and system difficulty (SD)

6 Conclusion

We have presented a principled statistical learning method for generating Temporal Expressions (TEs) that refer to appointment slots in natural language utterances. We presented a method for gathering data on TEs with an on-line experiment and showed how we can use these data to generate TEs using a Markov Decision Process which can be optimised using reinforcement learning techniques. We showed that a TEG policy learned using our framework performs signifcantly better than hand-coded adaptive policies with real users as well as with simulated users.

[2]independent two-tailed t-test $p < 0.05$

The data collected in this work has been freely released to the research community in 2011[3].

Acknowledgements

The research leading to these results has received funding from the EC's 7th Framework Programme (FP7/2007-2013) under grant agreement no. 216594 (CLASSiC project `www.classic-project.org`), (FP7/2011-2014) under grant agreement no. 248765 (Help4Mood project), (FP7/2011-2014) under grant agreement no. 270435 (JAMES project), (FP7/2011-2014) under grant agreement no. 270019 (SpaceBook project), and from the EPSRC, project no. EP/G069840/1. We would also like to thank our CLASSiC project colleagues at Cambridge University and France Telecom / Orange Labs.

References

D. Ahn, J. van Rantwijk, and M. de Rijke. 2007. A Cascaded Machine Learning Approach to Interpreting Temporal Expressions. In *Proceedings of NAACL-HLT 2007*.

France Telecom. 2011. Baratinoo expressive speech synthesiser. *http://tts.elibel.tm.fr*.

L. Gerber, L. Ferro, I. Mani, B. Sundheim, G. Wilson, and R. Kozierok. 2002. Annotating Temporal Information: From Theory to Practice. In *Proceedings of HLT*.

B. Han, D. Gates, and L. Levin. 2006. Understanding temporal expressions in emails. In *HLT-NAACL 2006*.

Srinivasan Janarthanam and Oliver Lemon. 2010. Learning to adapt to unknown users: referring expression generation in spoken dialogue systems. In *ACL '10*.

P. Mazur and R. Dale. 2007. The DANTE Temporal Expression Tagger. In *Proceedings of the 3rd Language and Technology Conference, Poznan, Poland*.

Kathleen F. Mccoy and Michael Strube. 1999. Taking time to structure discourse: Pronoun generation beyond accessibility. In *Proc. of the 21th Annual Conference of the Cognitive Science Society*.

M. Moens and M. Steedman. 1988. Temporal ontology and temporal reference. In *Computational Linguistics*, volume 14(2), pages 15–28.

[3]Sec 2.6 at http://www.macs.hw.ac.uk/ilabarchive/classicproject/data/

J. Pustejovsky, J. Castano, R. Ingria, R. Sauri, R. Gaizauskas, A. Setzer, G. Katz, and D. Radev. 2003. TimeML: Robust specification of event and temporal expressions in text. In *AAAI Spring Symposium on New Directions in Question-Answering, Stanford, CA*.

E. Reiter, S. Sripada, J. Hunter, and J. Yu. 2005. Choosing words in computer-generated weather forecasts. *Artificial Intelligence*, 167:137169.

Verena Rieser, Oliver Lemon, and Xingkun Liu. 2010. Optimising information presentation for spoken dialogue systems. In *Proc. ACL 2010*.

R. Sutton and A. Barto. 1998. *Reinforcement Learning*. MIT Press.

Marilyn A. Walker, Candace A. Kamm, and Diane J. Litman. 2000. Towards Developing General Models of Usability with PARADISE. *Natural Language Engineering*, 6(3).

Marilyn Walker, Amanda Stent, François Mairesse, and Rashmi Prasad. 2007. Individual and domain adaptation in sentence planning for dialogue. *Journal of Artificial Intelligence Research (JAIR)*, 30:413–456.

Detecting Levels of Interest from Spoken Dialog with Multistream Prediction Feedback and Similarity Based Hierarchical Fusion Learning

William Yang Wang
Department of Computer Science
Columbia University
New York, NY 10027
yw2347@columbia.edu

Julia Hirschberg
Department of Computer Science
Columbia University
New York, NY 10027
julia@cs.columbia.edu

Abstract

Detecting **levels of interest** from speakers is a new problem in Spoken Dialog Understanding with significant impact on real world business applications. Previous work has focused on the analysis of traditional acoustic signals and shallow lexical features. In this paper, we present a novel hierarchical fusion learning model that takes feedback from previous multistream predictions of prominent seed samples into account and uses a mean cosine similarity measure to learn rules that improve reclassification. Our method is domain-independent and can be adapted to other speech and language processing areas where domain adaptation is expensive to perform. Incorporating Discriminative Term Frequency and Inverse Document Frequency (D-TFIDF), lexical affect scoring, and low and high level prosodic and acoustic features, our experiments outperform the published results of all systems participating in the 2010 Interspeech Paralinguistic Affect Subchallenge.

1 Introduction

In recent years, there has been growing interest in identifying speakers' emotional state from speech (Devillers and Vidrascu, 2006; Ai et al., 2006; Liscombe et al., 2005). For Spoken Dialog Systems (SDS), the motivation has been to provide users with improved over-the-phone services by recognizing emotions such as anger and frustration and directing users to a human attendant. Other forms of *paralinguistic* information which researchers have attempted to detect automatically include other classic emotions, charismatic speech (Biadsy et al., 2008), and deceptive speech (Hirschberg et al., 2005). More recently, the 2010 Interspeech Paralinguisic Affect Subchallenge sparked interest in detecting a speaker's **level of interest** (LOI), including both the speaker's interest in the topic and his/her willingness to participating in the dialog (Schuller et al., 2010). Sensing users' LOI in SDS should be useful in sales domains, political polling, or service subscription.

In this paper, we present a similarity-based hierarchical regression approach to predicting speakers' LOI. The system has been developed based on the hierarchical fusion learning of lexical and acoustic cues from speech. We investigate the contribution of a novel source of information, **Discriminative TFIDF**; lexical affect scoring; and prosodic event features. Inspired by the successful use of Pseudo Relevance Feedback (Tao and Zhai, 2006) techniques in Information Retrieval and the cosine similarity measure (Salton, 1989) in Data Mining, we design a novel learning model which takes the multistream prediction feedback that is initially returned from seed samples [1] and uses a mean cosine similarity measure to calculate the distance between the new instance and prominent seed data points in the Euclidean Space. We then add this similarity measure as a new feature to perform a reclassification. Our main contributions in this paper are: (1) *the novel Discriminative TFIDF approach for lexical modeling and keywords spotting;* (2) *using lexical affect scoring and language modeling techniques to augment lexical modeling;* (3) *combin-*

[1] Seed samples are from a random small subset in the test set.

Proceedings of the SIGDIAL 2011: the 12th Annual Meeting of the Special Interest Group on Discourse and Dialogue, pages 152–161,
Portland, Oregon, June 17-18, 2011. ©2011 Association for Computational Linguistics

ing (1) and (2) with additional low-level prosodic features together with voice quality and high-level prosodic event features; and (4) *introducing a multistream prediction feedback and mean cosine similarity based fusion learning approach.*

We outline related work in Section 2. The corpus, system features, and machine learning approaches are described in Section 3. We describe our experimental results in Section 4 and conclude in Section 5.

2 Related Work

Schuller et al. (2006) were among the first to study LOI from conversational speech. They framed this task as either a three-way or binary classification, extracting standard acoustic features and building a bag-of-words vector space model for lexical analysis. By linearly combining lexical features with acoustic features, they achieved high F-measures when using Support Vector Machine (SVM). Since a bag-of-words model is a naive model, there may be more valuable lexical information that it cannot capture. Moreover, as lexical and acoustic features are extracted from different domains, a single layer linear combination may not yield the optimal results.

In 2010, Interspeech launched a Paralinguistic Challenge (Schuller et al., 2010) that included the task of detecting LOI from speech as a subchallenge. Competitors were given conversational speech corpora with annotated LOI, baseline acoustic features, and two baseline results. The evaluation metric used for the challenge was primarily the cross correlation [2] (CC) measure (Grimm et al., 2008), with mean linear error [3] (MLE) also taken into consideration. The baseline was built only on acoustic features, and the CC and MLE for Training vs. Development sets were 0.604 and 0.118. For the test data, CC and MLE scores of 0.421 and 0.146 were observed.

Gajsek et al. (2010) participated in this challenge and proposed the use of Gaussian Mixture Models as Universal Background Model (GMM-UBM) with relevance MAP estimation for the acoustic data. This is based on the success of GMM-UBM modeling in the speaker identification tasks (Reynolds et al., 2000). They achieved CC and MLE of 0.630 and 0.123 in the training vs. development condition, but CC and MLE of only 0.390 and 0.143 in the testing condition. This performance may have been due to the fact that different subsets of the corpus include different speakers: acoustic features alone may not be robust enough to capture the speaker variation.

Jeon et al. (2010) approach won the 2010 Subchallenge for this task. In addition to the baseline acoustic features provided, they used term frequency and a subjectivity dictionary to mine the lexical information. In addition to a linear combination of all lexical and acoustic features, they designed a hierarchical regression framework with multiple level of combinations. Its first two combiners tackle the prediction problems from different acoustic classifiers and then uses a final stage SVM classifier to combine the overall acoustic predictions with lexical predictions to form the final output. They report a result of 0.622 for CC and 0.115 for MLE. On the test set, they report CC and MLE of 0.428 and 0.146 respectively.

3 Our System

Unlike previous approaches, we emphasize lexical modeling, to counter problems of speaker variation in acoustic features (Jeon et al., 2010). We propose an improved version of standard TFIDF (Spärck Jones, 1972) — Discriminative TFIDF — which computes the IDF score of the target word by discriminating its different mean LOI score tags during training to produce more informative keyword spotting in testing.

In addition to Discriminative TFIDF, we utilize the Dictionary of Affect in Language (DAL) (Whissell, 1989) to detect lexical affect and compute an utterance-level affect score. To maximize the coverage of lexical cues, we also train trigram language models on the training data to capture contextual information and use the test output log likelihoods and perplexities as features. Besides these lexical features and the 1582 baseline acoustic features from the Interspeech Paralinguistic Challenge, we extract 32 additional prosodic and voice quality features using Praat (Boersma, 2001). In order to model sentence-level prosodic events, we use Au-

[2]Pearson product-moment correlation coefficient is a measure of the linear dependence that is widely used in regression settings.

[3]MLE is a regression performance measure for the mean absolute error between an estimator and the true value.

ToBI (Rosenberg, 2010) to extract pitch accent and phrase-based features. These features are described in detail in Section 3.2.

The simplest approach to classification is to include all features in a single classifier. However, different features streams include different number of features, extracted and represented in different domains. The Sum Rule approach (Kittler et al., 1998) is an early solution to this classifier combination problem. Instead, we train 1st-tier classifiers for each of the feature streams and then train a 2nd-tier classifier to weight the posterior predictions of the 1st-tier classifiers. We further improve this method by integrating a novel model which considers the 1st-tier multistream prediction feedback from the seed samples and uses a mean cosine similarity method to measure the distance between a new instance and prominent seed samples. We use this similarity measure to improve classification.

3.1 Corpus

The corpus we use in our experiments is the 2010 Paralinguistic Challenge Affect Subchallenge corpus Technische Universtät Munchën Audiovisual Interest Corpus (TUM AVIC), provided by Schuller (2010). The corpus consists of 10 hours of audio-visual recordings of interviews in which an interviewer provides commercial presentations of various products to a subject. The subject and interviewer discuss the product, and the subject comments on his/her interest in it. Subjects were instructed to relax and not to worry about politeness in the conversation. 21 subjects participated (11 male, 10 female), including three Asians and the rest of European background. All interviews were conducted in English; while none of the subjects were native speakers, all were fluent. 11 subjects were younger than 30; 7 were between 30-40; and 3 were over 40. The subject portions of the recordings were segmented into speaker turns (continuous speech by one speaker with backchannels by the interviewer ignored). These were further segmented into sub-speaker turns at grammatical phrase boundaries such that each segment is shorter than 2sec.

These smaller segments were annotated by four male undergraduate psychology students for subject LOI, using a 5-point scale as follows: (-2) *Disinterest* (subject is totally tired of discussing this topic and totally passive); (-1) *Indifference* (subject is passive and does not want to give feedback); (0) *Neutrality* (subject follows and participates in the dialog, but it is not recognized if she/he is interested in the topic); (1) *Interest* (subject wants to talk about the topic, follows the interviewer and asks questions); (2) *Curiosity* (subject is strongly interest in the topic and wants to learn more.) A normalized mean LOI is then derived from mean LOI/2, to map the scores into [-1, +1]. (Note that no negative scores occur for this corpus.) In our experiments, we consider the normalized mean LOI score as the label for each sub-speaker turn segment; we refer to this as "mean LOI" below. The corpus was divided for the Sub-challenge into training, development, and test corpora; we use these divisions in our experimens.

3.2 Feature Sets

Table 1 provides an overview of the feature sets in our system.

Discriminative TFIDF

In the standard vector space model, each word is associated with its Term Frequency (TF) in the utterance. The Inverse Document Frequency (IDF) provides information on how rare the word is over all utterances. The standard TFIDF vector of a term t in an utterance u is represented as $V(t,u)$:

$$V(t,u) = TF * IDF = \frac{C(t,u)}{C(v,u)} * \log \frac{|U|}{\sum u(t)}$$

TF is calculated by dividing the number of occurrences of term t in the utterance u by the total number of tokens v in the utterance u. IDF is the log of the total number of utterances U in the training set, divided by the number of utterances in the training set in which the term t appears. $u(t)$ can be viewed as a simple function: if t appears in utterance u, then it returns 1, otherwise 0.

In Discriminative TFIDF we add additional information to the TFIDF metrics. When calculating IDF, we weight each word by the distribution of its labels in the training set. This helps us to weight words by the LOI of the utterances they are uttered in. An intuitive example is this: Although the words "chaos" and "Audi" both appear once in the corpus, the occurrence of "Audi" is in an utterance with a Mean LOI score of 0.9, while "chaos" appears in an utterance with a label of 0.1. A standard TFIDF approach

Feature Sets	Features
Discriminative TFIDF	Sum of word-level Discriminative TFIDF scores
Lexical Affect Scoring	Sum of word-level lexical affect scores
Language Modeling	Trigram language model log-likelihood and perplexity
Acoustic Features	1582 acoustic features. Detail see Schuller et. al, (2010)
Pulses	# Pulses, # Periods, Mean Periods, SDev Period
Voicing	Fraction, # Voice Breaks, Degree, Voiced2total Frames
Jitter	Local, Local (absolute), RAP, PPQ5
Shimmer	Local, Local (dB), APQ3, APQ5, APQ11
Harmonicity	Mean Autocorrelation, Mean NHR, Mean NHR (dB)
Duration	Seconds
Fundamental Frequency	Min, Max, Mean, Median, SDev, MAS
Energy	Min, Max, Mean, SDev
Prosodic Events	Pitch accents, intermediate phrase, and intonational boundaries.

Table 1: **Feature Sets**. *RAP: Relative Average Perturbation. PPQ5: five-point Period Perturbation Quotient. APQn: n-point Amplitude Perturbation Quotient. NHR: Noise-to-Harmonics Ratio. MAS: Mean Absolute Slope.*

will give these two terms the same score. To differentiate the importance of these two words, we define our Discriminative TFIDF measure as follow:

$$V(t,u) = \frac{C(t,u)}{C(v,u)} * \log \frac{|U|}{\sum u(t) * (1 - |MeanLOI|)}$$

Here, the Mean LOI score ranging from (0,1) is the label of each utterance. Instead of summing the *u(t)* scores directly, we now assign a weight to each utterance. The weight is $(1 - |MeanLOI|)$ in our task. The overall IDF score of words important to identifying the LOI of an utterance will thus be boosted, as the denominator of the IDF metric decreases compared to the standard TFIDF. Discriminative TFIDF can be viewed as a generalized version of Delta TFIDF (Martineau and Finin, 2009) that can be used in various regression settings.

Wang and McKeown (2010) show that adding Part-of-Speech (POS) information to text can be helpful in similar classification tasks. So we have also used the Stanford POS tagger (Toutanova and Manning, 2000) to tag these transcripts before calculating the Discriminative TFIDF score.

Lexical Affect Scoring

Whissell's Dictionary of Affect in Language (DAL) (Whissell, 1989) attempts to quantify emotional language by asking raters to judge 8742 words collected from various sources including college essays, interviews, and teenagers descriptions of their own emotional state. Its pleasantness (EE) score indicates the negative or positive valence of a word, rated on a scale from 1 to 3. For example, "abandon" scores 1.0, implying a fairly low level of pleasantness. A previous study (Agarwal et al., 2009) notes that one of the advantages of this dictionary is that it has different scores for various forms of a root word. For example, the words "affect" and "affection" have very different meanings; if they were given the same score, the lexical affect quantification might not be discriminative. To calculate an utterance's lexical affect score, we first remove the stopwords and then sum up [4] the EE score of each word in the utterance.

Statistical Language Modeling

In order to capture the contextual information and maximize the use of lexical information, we also train a statistical language model to augment the Discriminative TFIDF and lexical affect scores. We train trigram language models on the training set using the SRI Language Modeling Tookit (Stolcke, 2002). In the testing stage, the log likelihood and perplexity scores are used as language modeling features. Due to the data sparsity issue, we are not able to train language models on subsets of training data that correspond to different LOI scores.

[4] We have experimented with Min, Max and Mean scores, but the results were poor.

Acoustic, Prosodic and Voice Quality Features

As noted above, the TUM AVIC corpus includes acoustic features (Schuller et al., 2010) for all of the data sets. These include: PCM loudness, MFCC[0-14], log Mel Frequency Band[0-7], Line Spectral Pairs Frequency [0-7], F0 by Sub-Harmonic Sum., F0 Envelope, Voicing Probability, Jitter Local, Jitter Difference of Difference of Periods, and Shimmer local. We have extracted an additional 32 standard prosodic and voice quality features to augment these, including Glottal Pulses, Voicing, Jitter, Shimmer, Harmonicity, Duration, Fundamental Frequency, and Energy (See Table 1).

Prosodic Event Features

To examine the contribution of higher-level prosodic events, we have also experimented with AuToBI (Rosenberg, 2010) to automatically detect pitch accents, word boundaries, intermediate phrase boundaries, and intonational boundaries in utterances. AuToBI requires annotated word boundary information; since we do not have hand-annotated boundaries, we use the Penn Phonetics Lab Forced Aligner (Yuan and Liberman, 2008) to align each utterance with its transcription. We use AuToBI's models, which were trained on the spontaneous speech Boston Directions Corpus (BDC) (Hirschberg and Nakatani, 1996), to identify prosodic events in our corpus.

3.3 Fusion Learning Approaches

Assuming that our various lexical, acoustic and prosodic feature streams are informative to some extent when tested separately, we want to combine information from the streams in different domains to improve prediction. We experimented with several approaches, including Bag-of-Features, Sum Rule combination, Hierarchical Fusion, and a new approach. We present here results of each on our LOI prediction task. In the Bag-of-Features approach, a simple classification method includes all features in a single classifier. A potential problem with this method is that, when combining 1582 acoustic features with 10 lexical features, the classifier will treat them equally, so potentially more useful lexical features will not be evaluated properly. A second problem is that our features are extracted from different domains using different methods, and normalization across domains is not possible in a bag-of-features classification/regression approach. Another possible approach is the Sum Rule Combiner, which uses product or sum rules to combine the predictions from 1st-tier classifiers. Kittler et al. (1998) show that the Sum Rule approach outperforms the product rule, max rule and mean rule approaches when combining classifiers. Their sensitivity analysis shows that this approach is most resilient to estimation errors.

A third method of combining features is the Hierarchical Fusion approach of fusing multistream information, which involves multiple classifiers and performs classification/regression in multiple stages. This can be implemented by first training 1st-tier classifiers for each single stream of features, collecting the predictions from these classifiers, and training a 2nd-tier supervector classifier to weight the importance of predictions from the different streams and make a final prediction. The rationale behind this approach is to solve the cross-domain issue by letting the 2nd-tier classifier weight the streams, as the predictions from 1st-tier classifiers will be in a unified/normalized form (e.g. 0 to 1 in this task).

The Multistream Prediction Feedback and Mean Cosine Similarity based Hierarchical Fusion

Our Multistream Prediction Feedback and Mean Cosine Similarity based Hierarchical Fusion approach combines a similarity based two-stage approach with a multistream feedback approach. Figure 1 shows the architecture of this system. It is based on the intuition that, if we can identify the prominent samples (e.g. the samples that all 1st-tier classifiers assign high average prediction scores), then we can measure the average distance between a new sample and all these prominent samples in the Euclidean Space. Furthermore, we can use this average distance (average similarity) as a new feature to improve the 2nd-tier classifier's final prediction.

To implement this process, we first train five 1st-tier Additive Logistic Regression (Friedman et al., 2000) classifiers and a Random Subspace meta learning (Ho, 1998) 1st-tier classifier (for the acoustic stream), using six different feature streams in our training data. In the testing stage, we use a random subset of the test set as seed samples. Next, we run the seed samples for each of these 1st-tier classifiers

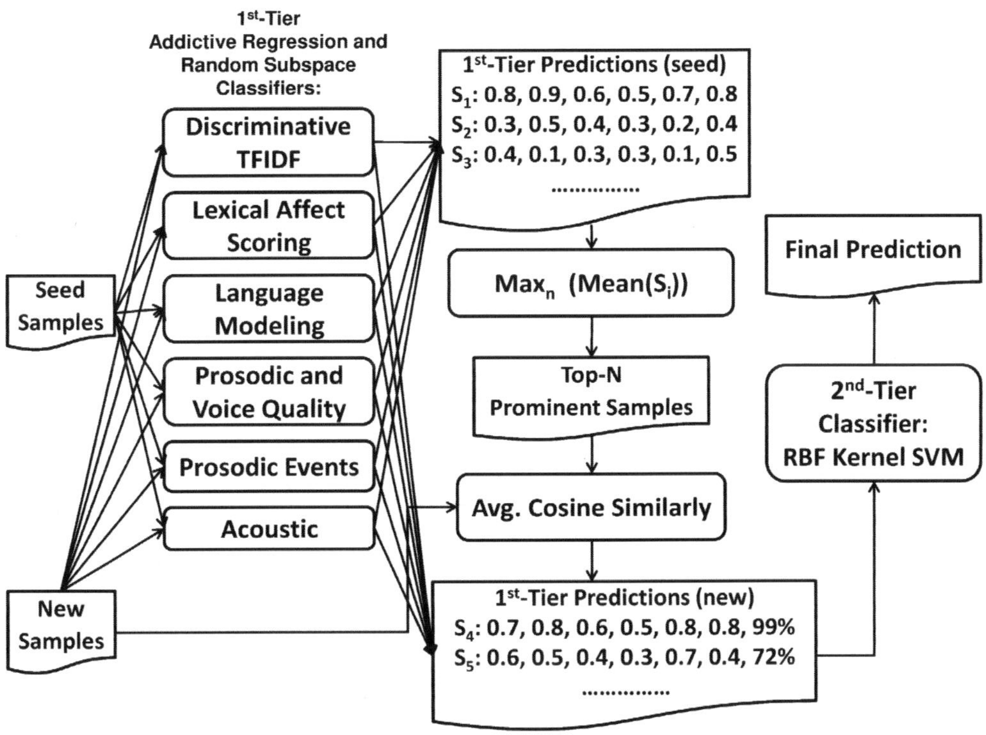

Figure 1: **The Overview of Multistream Prediction Feedback and Mean Cosine Similarity based Hierarchical Fusion Learning**

to obtain prediction scores ranging from 0 to 1. Now, we take the mean of these predicted scores for each sample, and use the following method to select the top n samples from the seed samples S as "prominent samples":

$$Prominent(S, n) = Max_n(Mean(S))$$

Recall that the cosine similarity (Salton, 1989) of two utterances U_i, U_j in the vector-space model is:

$$cos(U_i, U_j) = \frac{U_i \cdot U_j}{||U_i||_2 * ||U_j||_2}$$

where "·" indicates 'dot product'. Now, given our hypothesized prominent samples, for each of these samples and new samples, we choose the original Discriminative TFIDF, Lexical Affect Scoring, Language Modeling, Prosodic and Voice Quality, and Prosodic Event features as k vectors to represent all the samples in Euclidean Space. The reason we drop the acoustic features from the vector space model is because of the dimensionality issue — 1582 acoustic features. We substitute our 32 standard prosodic features instead. Now we use the mean cosine similarity score to represent how far a new sample U_n is from the prominent samples U_S in the space:

$$Sim(U_n, U_S) = Mean\left(\frac{\sum_{i=1}^{k} V_n * V_s}{\sqrt{\sum_{i=1}^{k} V_n^2} * \sqrt{\sum_{i=1}^{k} V_s^2}}\right)$$

In the next step, we add this mean cosine similarity measure as a new feature and include it in the 2nd-tier classifier for reclassification. Now, in the reclassification stage, all 1st-tier feature stream predictions will be re-weighted by the new 2nd-tier classifier that incorporated with Multistream Feedback information.

The reason why the Multistream Prediction Feedback is useful in this task is that, like many spoken language understanding tasks, in LOI detection, if we have a different set of speakers with different genders, ages, and speaker styles, the overall feature distribution for lexical, prosodic, and acoustic cues in the test set can be very different from the training set. Traditional speaker adaptation techniques typically focus only on the acoustic stream and may be very expensive to perform. So, by extracting more knowledge about the lexical, prosodic, and acoustic features distributions in test set using our novel approach, we will have a better understanding about the skewed distributions in the test set. In addition, our approach is inexpensive and does not require extra unlabeled data.

4 Experiments and Results

We conduct our experiments in three parts. First, we examine how well the Discriminative TFIDF feature performs, compared with standard TFIDF feature. Secondly, we look at how different feature sets influence our results. For the first two parts, we evaluate our features using the Subchallenge training vs. development sets only. Finally, we compare our similarity based multistream fusion feedback approach to other feature-combining approaches. We examine our final system first comparing training vs. development performance, and then combined training and development sets vs. the test set. WEKA (Witten and Frank, 2005) and LIBSVM (Chang and Lin, 2001) are used for regression.

4.1 TFIDF v.s. Discriminative TFIDF

Method	CC	MLE
TFIDF	0.296	0.142
D-TFIDF	0.368	0.140
S-D-TFIDF	**0.381**	**0.136**

Table 2: **Single TFIDF Feature Stream Single Regression Results** *(Train vs. Develop, Additive Logistic Regression). D-TFIDF: Discriminative TFIDF. S-D-TFIDF: the POS tagged version of D-TFIDF. CC: Cross Correlation. MLE: Mean Linear Error.*

When working with the training and development sets, we are able to access the label and transcriptions of each set to calculate the Discriminative TFIDF scores. For the testing scenario discussed in in Section 4.3, we do not have these annotations. So, we redefine the task as a keyword spotting task, where we can use the identified keywords in the training and development sets as keyword features in testing. We also sum up the word-level TFIDF scores and use the sentence-level TFIDF as a single feature for the classification experiment. The regression algorithm we use is Additive Logistic Regression with 50 iterations. Table 2 shows how different approaches perform in the experiment. We see that the Syntactic Discriminative TFIDF approach is much more informative than the standard TFIDF approach. Note that, after calculating the global IDF score, the standard TFIDF approach selects **732** terms as top-1 level keywords. In contrast, our Discriminative TFIDF has stronger discriminative power and picks a total number of **59** truly rare terms as top-1 level keywords.

4.2 Regression with Different Feature Streams

Table 3 shows performance using different feature streams in our system. We see that the acoustic and prosodic features are the dominating features in this task. The Prosodic Events feature stream also emerges as a new informative high-level prosodic feature in this task.

Feature Streams	CC	MLE
S-D-TFIDF	0.394	0.132
Language Modeling	0.404	0.141
Prosodic Events	0.458	0.133
Lexical Affect Scoring	0.459	0.132
Standard Prosody + VQ	0.591	0.122
Acoustic	**0.607**	**0.118**
Multistream Feedback (n=3)	0.234	0.150
Multistream Feedback (n=10)	0.262	0.149
Multistream Feedback (n=20)	**0.290**	**0.146**

Table 3: **Comparing Contributions of Different Feature Streams in the 2nd-tier Classifier** *(Training vs. Developmen, Random Subspace for the 1st-tier classifier of Acoustic Stream, and Additive Logistic Regression for other 1st-tier classifiers. Radial Basis Function (RBF) Kernel SVM as 2nd-tier Classifier.) S-D-TFIDF: the POS tagged version of D-TFIDF. VQ: Voice Quality. n: Top-n Feedback. CC: Cross Correlation. MLE: Mean Linear Error.*

When testing the multistream feedback information as a single feature stream, we see in the bottom half of Table 3 that CC and MLE are improved when we increase the number of prominent samples. Discriminative TFIDF and Language Modeling are also important, as seen from these results, but the Lexical Affect Scoring feature performs best among the lexical features in this task. We suspect that the reason may be a data sparsity issue, as we do not have a large amount of data for training robust global Discriminative IDF scores, language models, and the feedback stream. In contrast, the DAL is trained on much larger amounts of data.

4.3 Comparing with State-of-the-Art Systems

Table 4 compares our approach to alternative learning approaches. The first half of this table reports results on training vs. development sets, and the second half compares combined training and developemen vs. test set result.

Method	CC	MLE
Shuller et al.,(2010)	0.604	0.118
Jeon et al., (2010)	0.622	0.115
Gajsek et al. (2010)	0.630	0.123
Bag-of-features Fusion	0.602	0.118
Sum Rule Combination	0.617	0.117
SVM Hierarchical Fusion	0.628	0.115
Feedback + Hierarchical Fusion	**0.640**	**0.113**
Gajsek et al. (2010)	0.390	0.143
Shuller et al.,(2010)	0.421	0.146
Jeon et al., (2010)	0.428	0.146
Bag-of-features Fusion	0.420	0.145
Sum Rule Combination	0.422	0.138
SVM Hierarchical Fusion	0.450	0.131
Feedback + Hierarchical Fusion	**0.480**	**0.131**

Table 4: **Comparing Different Systems.** *Above: Training vs. Development. Bottom: Combined Training+ Development vs. Test. CC: Cross Correlation. MLE: Mean Linear Error.*

Note that, in order to transcribe the test data, we have trained a 20 Gaussian per state 39 MFCC Hidden Markov Model speech recognizer with HTK, using the training and development sets together with TIMIT (Fisher et al., 1986), the Boston Directions Corpus (BDC) (Hirschberg and Nakatani, 1996), and the Columbia Game Corpus (Hirschberg et al., 2005). The word error rate (WER) is 29% on the development set.

Note that a Bag-of-Features approach combining all features results in poorer performance than the use of acoustic features alone. The Sum Rule approach improves over this method by achieving CC score of 0.422. Although the improvement of CC seems small, it is extremely statistically significant (Paired t-test with two-tailed P-value less than 0.0001), comparing to the Bag-of-features model. However, when using the SVM as the 2nd-tier supervector classifier to weight different prediction streams, we achieve 0.628 CC and 0.115 MLE in training vs. development data, and 0.450 CC and 0.131 MLE on the test set; this result is significantly different from the Bag-of-features baseline (paired t-test, $p < 0.0001$), but it is not significantly different from the Sum Rule Combination approach.

Augmenting the SVM hierarchical fusion learning approach with multistream feedback, we observe a significant improvement over all other systems and methods. We obtain a final CC of 0.480 and MLE of 0.131 in the test mode, which is sigificantly different from the Bag-of-features approach (paired t-test $p < 0.0001$), but does not differ significantly from the SVM hierarchical fusion approach.

5 Conclusion

Detecting **levels of interest** from speakers is an important problem for Spoken Dialog Understanding. While earlier work, done in the 2010 Interspeech Paralinguistic Affect Subchallenge, employing traditional acoustic features and shallow lexical features, achieved good results, our new features — Discriminative TFIDF, lexical affect scoring, language modeling, prosodic event — when used with standard prosodic features and our new Multistream Prediction Feedback and Mean Cosine Similarity heuristic-based Hierarchical Learning method improves over all published results on the LOI corpus. Our method is domain-independent and can be adapted to other speech and language processing areas where domain adaptation is expensive to perform. In the future, we would like to experiment with different distributional similarity measures and bootstrapping strategies.

Acknowledgments

The first author was funded by Kathleen McKeown while conducting the research. We would also like to thank Andrew Rosenberg and three anonymous reviewers for their useful comments.

References

Agarwal, Apoorv and Biadsy, Fadi and Mckeown, Kathleen R. 2009. Contextual Phrase-Level Polarity Analysis Using Lexical Affect Scoring And Syntactic N-Grams. in *EACL 2009*.

Ai, Hua and Litman, Diane J. and Forbes-Riley, Kate and Rotaru, Mihai and Tetreault, Joel and Purandare, Amruta 2006. Using System and User Performance Features to Improve Emotion Detection in Spoken Tutoring Dialogs. in *INTERSPEECH 2006*.

Biadsy, Fadi and Rosenberg, Andrew and Carlson, Rolf and Hirschberg, Julia and Strangert, Eva. 2008. A Cross-Cultural Comparison of American, Palestinian, and Swedish Perception of Charismatic Speech. in *Proceedings of the Speech Prosody 2008*.

Boersma, Paul. 2001. Praat, a system for doing phonetics by computer. in *Glot International*.

Chang,Chih-Chung and Lin, Chih-Jen. 2001. LIBSVM: a library for support vector machines. Software available at *www.csie.ntu.edu.tw/~cjlin/libsvm*.

Devillers, Laurence and Vidrascu, Laurence 2006. Real-life Emotions Detection with Lexical and Paralinguistic Cues on Human-Human Call Center Dialogs. in *INTERSPEECH 2006*.

Fisher, William M. and Doddington, George R. and Goudie-Marshall, Kathleen M. 1986. The DARPA Speech Recognition Research Database: Specifications and Status. in *DARPA Workshop on Speech Recognition*.

Friedman, Jerome and Hastie, Trevor and Tibshirani, Robert. 2000. Additive logistic regression: a statistical view of boosting. in *Ann. Statist.*.

Gajšek, Rok and Žibert, Janez and Justin, Tadej and Štruc, Vitomir and Vesnicer, Boštjan and Mihelič, France. 2010. Gender and Affect Recognition Based on GMM and GMMUBM modeling with relevance MAP estimation. in *INTERSPEECH 2010*.

Grimm, Michael and Kroschel, Kristian and Narayana, Shrikanth. 2008. The Vera am Mittag German Audio-Visual Emotional Speech Database. in *IEEE ICME*.

Hirschberg, Julia and Nakatani, Christine H. 1996. A prosodic analysis of discourse segments in direction-giving monologues. in *ACL 1996*.

Hirschberg, Julia and Benus, Stefan and Brenier, Jason M. and Enos, Frank and Friedman, Sarah and Gilman, Sarah and Gir, Cynthia and Graciarena, Martin and Kathol, Andreas and Michaelis, Laura. 2005. Distinguishing Deceptive from Non-Deceptive Speech. in *INTERSPEECH 2005*.

Ho, Tin Kam. 1998. The Random Subspace Method for Constructing Decision Forests. *IEEE Transactions on PAMI*.

Jeon, Je Hun and Xia, Rui and Liu, Yang. 2010. Level of Interest Sensing in Spoken Dialog Using Multi-level Fusion of acoustic and Lexical Evidence. in *INTERSPEECH 2010*.

Kittler, Josef and Hatef, Mohamad and Duin, Robert P. W. and Matas, Jiri. 1998. On combining classifiers. *IEEE Transactions on PAMI*.

Laskowski, Kornel and Burger, Susanne. 2007. Analysis of the Occurrence of Laughter in Meetings. in *INTERSPEECH 2007*.

Liscombe, Jackson and Hirschberg, Julia and Venditti, Jennifer J.. 2005. Detecting Certainness in Spoken Tutorial Dialogues. in *Eurospeech*.

Martineau, Justin and Finin, Tim. 2009. Delta TFIDF: An Improved Feature Space for Sentiment Analysis. in *ICWSM*.

Reynolds, Douglas A. and Quatieri, Thomas F. and Dunn, Robert B. 2000. Speaker verication using adapted gaussian mixture models. in *Digital Signal Processing*.

Rosenberg, Andrew. 2010. AuToBI - A Tool for Automatic ToBI Annotation. in *INTERSPEECH 2010*.

Salto, Gerard 1989. *Automatic Text Processing: The Transformation, Analysis, and Retrieval of Information by Computer*.

Schuller, Bjöern, and Köhler, Niels and Müeller, Ronald and Rigoll, Gerhard. 2006. Recognition of Interest in Human Conversational Speech. in *INTERSPEECH 2006*.

Schuller, Bjöern, and Steidl, Stefan and Batliner, Anton and Burkhardt, Felix and Devillers, Laurence and Müeller, Christian and Narayanan, Shrikanth. 2010. The INTERSPEECH 2010 Paralinguistic Challenge. in *INTERSPEECH 2010*.

Spärck Jones, Karen. 1972. A statistical interpretation of term specificity and its application in retrieval. in *Journal of Documentation*.

Stolcke, Andreas. 2002. SRILM-an extensible language modeling toolkit. in *ICSLP 2002*.

Toutanova, Kristina and Manning, Christopher D.. 2000. Enriching the Knowledge Sources Used in a Maximum Entropy Part-of-Speech Tagger. in *EMNLP/VLC-2000*.

Tao, Tao and Zhai, ChengXiang 2006. Regularized estimation of mixture models for robust pseudo-relevance feedback. in *SIGIR 2006*.

Wang, William Yang and McKeown, Kathleen. 2010. "Got You!": Automatic Vandalism Detection in Wikipedia with Web-based Shallow Syntactic-Semantic Modeling. in *COLING 2010.*

Wang, Chingning and Zhang, Ping and Choi, Risook and DEredita, Michael. 2002. Understanding consumers attitude toward advertising. in *Eighth Americas conf. on Information System.*

Witten, Ian H. and Frank, Eibe 2005. *Data mining: Practical machine learning tools and techniques, 2nd Edition.* San Francisco: Morgan Kaufmann.

Whissell, Cynthia. 1989. The Dictionary of Affect in Language. in *R. Plutchik and H. Kellerman, Editors, Emotion: Theory Research and Experience.*

Yuan, Jiahong and Liberman, Mark. 2008. Speaker identification on the SCOTUS corpus. in *Proceedings of acoustics '08.*

Exploring User Satisfaction in a Tutorial Dialogue System

Myroslava O. Dzikovska, Johanna D. Moore
School of Informatics, University of Edinburgh
Edinburgh, United Kingdom
m.dzikovska,j.moore@ed.ac.uk

Natalie Steinhauser, Gwendolyn Campbell
Naval Air Warfare Center Training Systems Division
Orlando, Florida, USA
gwendolyn.campbell,natalie.steinhauser@navy.mil

Abstract

User satisfaction is a common evaluation metric in task-oriented dialogue systems, whereas tutorial dialogue systems are often evaluated in terms of student learning gain. However, user satisfaction is also important for such systems, since it may predict technology acceptance. We present a detailed satisfaction questionnaire used in evaluating the BEETLE II system (REVU-NL), and explore the underlying components of user satisfaction using factor analysis. We demonstrate interesting patterns of interaction between interpretation quality, satisfaction and the dialogue policy, highlighting the importance of more fine-grained evaluation of user satisfaction.

1 Introduction

User satisfaction is one of the primary evaluation measures for task-oriented spoken dialogue systems (SDS): the goal of an SDS is to accomplish the task, and to keep the user satisfied, so that they will want to continue using the system. Typically, the PARADISE methodology (Walker et al., 2000) is used to establish a performance function which relates user satisfaction measured through questionnaires to interaction parameters that can be derived from system logs. This function can then be used to better understand which properties of the interaction have the most impact on the users, and to compare different system versions.

In contrast, tutorial dialogue systems are typically evaluated in terms of student learning gain, by comparing student scores on standardized tests before and after interacting with the system. This is clearly an important evaluation metric, since it directly assesses the benefit students obtain from using the system. However, it is also important to evaluate user satisfaction, since it can influence students' willingness to use computer tutors in a long run. Thus, recent studies have looked at factors that could influence user satisfaction in tutorial dialogue, such as different tutoring policies (Forbes-Riley and Litman, 2011), quality of speech output (Forbes-Riley et al., 2006), and students' prior attitudes towards technology (Jackson et al., 2009).

Assessing user satisfaction, however, is not a straightforward task. As we discuss in more detail in Section 2, user satisfaction is known to be a complex multi-dimensional construct, composed of largely independent factors such as perceived ease of use and perceived usefulness. Therefore, questionnaires used for assessing satisfaction need to be validated through user studies, and different satisfaction dimensions should be assessed independently. Therefore, SDS researchers are now starting to use techniques from psychometrics for this purpose (Hone and Graham, 2000; Möller et al., 2007). However, user satisfaction studies tutorial dialogue currently rely on simple questionnaires adapted from either task-oriented SDS or non-dialogue intelligent tutoring systems (Michael et al., 2003; Forbes-Riley et al., 2006; Forbes-Riley and Litman, 2011; Jackson et al., 2009), and these questionnaires have not been validated for tutorial dialogue systems.

In this paper, we make the first step towards developing a better user satisfaction questionnaire for tutorial dialogue systems. We present a user satis-

Proceedings of the SIGDIAL 2011: the 12th Annual Meeting of the Special Interest Group on Discourse and Dialogue, pages 162–172,
Portland, Oregon, June 17-18, 2011. ©2011 Association for Computational Linguistics

faction evaluation of the BEETLE II tutorial dialogue system. Starting with a detailed user satisfaction questionnaire, we employ exploratory factor analysis to discover a set of dimensions for the students' satisfaction with a dialogue-based tutor. We then use the factors we derived to compare user satisfaction between two versions of our computer tutor that use different policies for generating the tutor's feedback. We investigate the relationships between the subjective satisfaction dimensions and the objective learning gain metric for the two systems. Finally, we carry out a more detailed investigation of our prior results on the relationship between user satisfaction and interpretation quality in tutorial dialogue. Our analysis also provides insights for further improving the questionnaire we developed and gives an example of how user satisfaction metrics developed for task-oriented dialogue can be adapted to different dialogue applications. It also opens new questions about how different properties of the interaction affect user satisfaction in tutorial dialogue, which can be investigated in future work.

The rest of the paper is organized as follows. We discuss the approaches for assessing user satisfaction with SDS in Section 2. In Section 3 we describe the BEETLE II tutorial dialogue system used in this evaluation. We describe our questionnaire design in Section 4, and describe its use in BEETLE II evaluation in Section 5. We conclude by discussing the implication of our analysis for tutorial dialogue system evaluation in Section 6.

2 Background

A typical approach to assessing user satisfaction in dialogue systems is collecting user survey data by asking users to rate their agreement with statements such as "the system was easy to use". In the simplest case of early PARADISE studies, the questionnaires contained 5 items assessing different dimensions of satisfaction, which were then summed to produce a total satisfaction score.

However, using simple questionnaires has drawbacks now recognized by the SDS community. First, if individual questions are expected to assess different dimensions of user satisfaction, they need to be validated first, or else they may be ambiguous and mean different things to different users. Second, summing or averaging over questions measuring different satisfaction components may not be the best approach, since it may conflate unrelated judgments (Hone and Graham, 2000).

To address this problem, SDS researchers have started using more complex questionnaires, where each underlying dimension of user satisfaction is assessed through multiple questions. Factor analysis is then used to determine which questions are related to one another (and therefore are likely to be assessing the same underlying satisfaction dimension), and to discard possibly ambiguous questions. Then, the PARADISE methodology can be used to relate different interaction parameters to individual components of user satisfaction.

Several such studies have been conducted recently (Hone and Graham, 2000; Larsen, 2003; Möller et al., 2007; Wolters et al., 2009), covering command-and-control and information-seeking dialogue. The questionnaires in those studies contained 25 to 50 items, and factor analyses typically resulted in 6- or 7-factor solutions, with dimensions such as acceptability, affect, system response accuracy and cognitive demand. The underlying factors found by those analyses tend to match up well, but not to overlap perfectly. In comparison, all user satisfaction questionnaires for tutorial dialogue systems that we are aware of contain 10-15 items which are either summed up for PARADISE studies, or compared individually to track system improvement (Michael et al., 2003; Forbes-Riley et al., 2006; Forbes-Riley and Litman, 2011; Jackson et al., 2009).

In this paper, we apply the more sophisticated SDS evaluation methodology to the BEETLE II tutorial dialogue system. We devise a more sophisticated user satisfaction questionnaire using SDS questionnaires for guidance and then apply factor analysis to investigate the underlying dimensions. We compare our results to analyses from two previous studies: SASSI (Hone and Graham, 2000), which is a validated questionnaire intended for use with a variety of task-oriented dialogue systems, and a more recent "modified SASSI" questionnaire which is a version of SASSI adapted for use with the INSPIRE home control system (Möller et al., 2007). Henceforth we will refer to this as INSPIRE.

3 BEETLE II Tutorial Dialogue System

The goal of BEETLE II (Dzikovska et al., 2010c) is to teach students conceptual knowledge in the domain of basic electricity and electronics. The system is built on the premise that encouraging students to explain their answers and to talk about the domain will lead to improved learning, a finding consistent with analyses of human-human tutoring in several domains (Purandare and Litman, 2008; Litman et al., 2009). BEETLE II has been engineered to test this hypothesis by eliciting contentful talk through explanation questions.

The BEETLE II learning material consists of two self-contained lessons suitable for college-level students with no prior knowledge of basic electricity and electronics. The lessons take 4 to 5 hours to complete, and consist of reading materials and interactive exercises. During the exercises, the students interact with a circuit simulator, building electrical circuits containing bulbs, batteries and switches, and using a multimeter to measure voltage. Then the tutor asks students to explain circuit behavior, for example, "Why was bulb A on when switch Y was open and switch Z was closed?" In addition, at different points in the lesson the tutor asks "summary" questions, asking students to define concepts such as voltage, and verbalize general patterns such as "What are the conditions that are required for a bulb to light?". At present, students use a typed chat interface to communicate with the system.[1]

We built and evaluated two versions of the system (Dzikovska et al., 2010a). The baseline non-adaptive tutor (BASE) requires students to produce answers, but does not provide any remediation and immediately states the correct answer. The fully adaptive version (FULL) engages in dialogue with the student, and tailors its feedback to the student's answer by confirming its correct parts and giving hints in order to help students fix missing or incorrect parts. The FULL system generates feedback automatically based on a detailed analysis of the student's input, and is capable of giving hints at different levels of specificity depending on the student's previous performance.

[1]A speech interface is being developed, but typed communication is common in online and distance learning, and therefore is an acceptable choice for tutorial dialogue as well.

These two system versions were designed to evaluate the impact of adaptive feedback (within the limitations of current language interpretation technology) on student learning and satisfaction. Our initial data analysis focused on the differences in student language depending on the condition (Dzikovska et al., 2010a), and on the impact of different types of interpretation errors on learning gain and user satisfaction (Dzikovska et al., 2010b). However, these initial results were based on an aggregate satisfaction score obtained by averaging over scores for all questions in our user satisfaction questionnaire. In this analysis, we take a more detailed look at the different factors that contribute to students satisfaction with the system, and their relationship with learning gain and interpretation quality.

4 Data Collection

4.1 Questionnaire Design

To support user satisfaction evaluation we developed a satisfaction questionnaire, REVU-IT (Report on the Enjoyment, Value, and Usability of an Intelligent Tutor). It consists of 63 items which cover all aspects of interaction with the tutoring system: the clarity and usefulness of the reading material; the graphical user interface to the circuit simulator; interaction with the dialogue tutor; and the overall impression of the BEETLE II system as a whole. The reading material, graphical user interface and interaction with the tutor sections are complementary, because they cover separate parts of the BEETLE II interface. We expect that all of these three components contribute to the overall impression score. For purposes of this paper, we will focus on the part of the questionnaire that relates to the natural language interaction with the tutor (REVU-NL), and its relationship to the overall impression score (REVU-OVERALL).

The REVU-IT questionnaire was developed by experienced cognitive psychologists (two of the authors of this paper). The REVU-NL section consists of 35 items shown in Appendix A. Its design was guided by questionnaires used in previous research, including INSPIRE and a questionnaire used to evaluate the ITSPOKE tutorial dialogue system (Forbes-Riley et al., 2006). REVU-NL contains a number of items from these, but omits items that are not relevant to the BEETLE II domain (e.g, "Domestic devices can be operated efficiently with the system" or "The tutor responded effectively after I was uncertain"), and adds extra questions related to tutoring (e.g., "Our dialogues quickly led to me having a deeper understanding of the material"), based on the authors' previous experience in human factors research. We also slightly rephrased all questions to refer to "the tutor" rather than "the system".

The REVU-OVERALL section of REVU-IT consists of 5 items assessing the student's satisfaction with their learning as a whole. The questions are: "Overall, I am satisfied with my experience learning about electricity from this system."; "Working in this learning environment was just like working one-on-one with a human tutor"; "I would have preferred to learn about electricity in a different way."; "I would use this system again in the future to continue to learn about electricity."; "I would like to be able to use a system like this to learn about other topics in the future.". We use the averaged score over these 5 items to represent the student's overall satisfaction with the learning environment, referring to it as "overall satisfaction".

Adding new questions to the REVU-NL questionnaire on top of already existing questions is the initial step in addressing the issues discussed in Section 2: validating the individual questions and discovering the underlying dimensions of user satisfaction. Having a large number of questions asking about the same aspects of the interaction will allow us to group related questions together into dimensions ("factors"), and also to discover ambiguous questions that will need to be improved in future studies. The detailed discussion of the technique and issues involved is presented in Hone and Graham (2000).

4.2 Participants

We used REVU-IT as part of a controlled experiment comparing the BASE and FULL versions of the system. We recruited 87 participants from a university in the Southern US, paid for participation. Participants had little knowledge of the domain. Each participant signed consent forms and completed a pre-test, then worked through both lessons (with breaks), and then completed a post-test and a REVU-IT questionnaire. Each session lasted 3.5 hours on average.

Out of 87 participants that completed the study, 13 had an inordinate amount of trouble with interface: they typed utterances that could not be interpreted by the tutor (defined as having more than 3 standard deviations in interpretation errors compared to the rest), did not follow tutor's instructions or experienced system crashes. In addition, two participants were learning gain outliers (again, more than 3 standard deviations from average). These participants were removed from the analysis. The questionnaires from the remaining 72 participants are used in our data analysis.

5 Analysis

5.1 Underlying satisfaction dimensions

Each item in the REVU-NL questionnaire used a 5-point Likert scale, from "completely disagree" (1) to "fully agree" (5). Most of the items were phrased so that the agreement with the statement meant a positive evaluation of the system. For a few items, however, the polarity was reversed (e.g., "The tutor was not helpful"). Those items were reverse-coded, with 1 meaning "fully agree" and 5 "completely disagree", to ensure that a lower score on all questions corresponds to a negative assessment.

Following Hone and Graham (2000), we used exploratory factor analysis to group questionnaire items into clusters representing different dimensions. One of the standard approaches in determining how many factors ("question clusters") to use is the *scree test* which checks the number of eigenvalues in the question covariance matrix which are greater than 1. These typically correspond to principal components which reflect the underlying questionnaire structure. The scree test showed 7 eigenvalues greater than 1, resulting in the 7-factor solution presented in Table 1.

The loadings in the table are the correlation coefficients between the individual question scores and the variables representing the factors. Most of the correlations are quite high, indicating that the questions are strongly correlated both among themselves and the underlying factor. However, the last two factors contain only non-loading questions according to the criteria in (Hone and Graham, 2000), i.e., questions for which the correlations are too weak to be

#	Question	Loading
1	t29: Knew what to say at each point	0.82
1	t22: Easy to interact with the tutor.	0.79
1	t9: Not sure what was expected.	0.73
1	t18: Knew what to say to the tutor.	0.70
1	t14: The tutor was too inflexible.	0.69
1	t19: Able to recover easily from errors	0.69
1	t24: Easy to learn to speak to tutor.	0.69
1	t16: Tutor didn't do what I wanted.	0.65
1	t3: Tutor understood me well.	0.65
1	t15: Working as easy as with a human.	0.64
1	t13: Had to concentrate when talking.	0.62
2	t31 Tutor was an efficient way to learn.	0.79
2	t32: Easy to learn from the tutor.	0.78
2	t34: Tutor was worthwhile	0.72
3	t28: Tutor was irritating.	0.76
3	t10: Tutor was fun.	0.74
3	t7: Enjoyed talking with tutor.	0.72
3	t30: Dialogues were boring.	0.66
4	t2: Tutor took too long to respond	0.84
4	t33: Tutor responded quickly	0.84
5	t26: Didn't always understand tutor	0.89
6	(t3: The tutor understood me well)	0.4
7	(t25: Comfortable talking with tutor)	0.59

Table 1: Factors derived from the REVU-NL questionnaire, with question loadings for the factor to which each question was assigned. Question text shortened due to space limitations, full text presented in the appendix. Non-loading questions in parentheses.

reliable. In addition, factors 4 and 5 had fewer than 3 questions. Since the number of subjects in our data set is small, such factors may not be reliable. Therefore, we focus our remaining analysis on the top 3 factors from the questionnaire, each of which contains 3 or more questions.

Twelve questions in REVU-NL were "cross-loading" according to criteria in Hone and Graham (2000), that is, their two top loadings differed by less than 0.2. This indicates questions that are likely to be ambiguous, since they are strongly correlated with two (theoretically independent) variables. Such questions should be refined and re-designed in future surveys. These were questions *t1*, *t4*, *t6*, *t11*, *t12*, *t17*, *t20*, *t21*, *t23*, *t25*, *t27*, *t35* from the appendix. We removed them from our solution, and discuss the implications for survey design in Section 6.

The first component in our analysis lines up well with the *Transparency* and *Cognitive load* factors from INSPIRE, and *Response accuracy*, *Cognitive demand* and *Habitability* from SASSI, though it was not split into individual factors as in those analyses. We will refer to this factor as *Transparency*. The second component contains questions specific to tutoring. However, it is similar to the *Acceptability* dimension from INSPIRE (the original SASSI questionnaire did not include similar questions), which asked users to rate statements such as "domestic devices can be operated efficiently with the system". Thus, we will refer to it as *Acceptability*. Finally, our third dimension lines up best with the *Affect* and *Annoyance* items from SASSI.[2] We will refer to it as *Affect*.

Although the correspondences between our factors and those derived from SASSI and INSPIRE are not perfect, the fact that similar underlying factors are derived from different user groups and systems indicates that they are likely to be measuring the same underlying constructs.

5.2 Comparing satisfaction in different systems

Recall that in this study we combined the data from two systems: FULL, where the system provided students with adaptive feedback and hints, and BASE, where the system simply acknowledged the student's answers and then provided a correct answer without engaging in dialogue. Table 2 separates out the average factor scores for these two conditions, where a factor score is computed by averaging over scores of all questions assigned to that factor.

When comparing learning gain and overall satisfaction between the two systems (which is the overall impression of the system behavior as a whole, including circuit simulation and lesson design), the difference is *not* statistically significant (learning gain $t(69) = -0.95, p = 0.35$, overall satisfaction $t(69) = -1.52, p = 0.13$). In contrast, on individual dimensions related to tutoring the scores for BASE is significantly higher than the score for FULL (*Transparency*, $t(69) = -7.19, p < 0.0001$; *Acceptability*: $t(69) = -3.24, p < 0.01$; *Affect*:

[2]The *acceptability* dimension from INSPIRE is split between our factors 2 and 3, but most of the questions correspond to our factor 2 questions.

	FULL	BASE
Transparency	2.15 (0.56)	3.36 (0.81)
Acceptability	3.11 (1.02)	3.80 (0.77)
Affect	2.43 (0.80)	2.86 (0.996)
Overall	3.39 (0.88)	3.70 (0.83)
Learning gain	0.61 (0.15)	0.65 (0.22)

Table 2: Average scores for different satisfaction dimensions in FULL and BASE (standard deviation in parentheses)

$t(69) = -1.97, p = 0.05$). Comparing the means, the biggest difference in student ratings shows on the *Transparency* scale, while the affective reaction for the two systems is more similar (though still rated higher for BASE).

It is somewhat unexpected to see that the students were equally satisfied overall with both systems but rated the tutor in BASE more highly than in FULL, since the tutor behavior was the only thing different between conditions. We are at present investigating the reasons for this result. One possibility is that when students did not get much feedback from the tutor (as in BASE), other factors became more important to overall satisfaction, such as course design and quality of user simulation.

5.3 Relationships between subjective and objective outcome measures

We investigated the correlations between learning gain and different user satisfaction factors for the two system versions. Results are presented in Table 3. As can be seen from the table, learning gain and user satisfaction are only significantly correlated in FULL, and only for the acceptability and overall satisfaction factors. None of the factors in the BASE system correlate with learning gain. This indicates that the student's affective reaction to the system is not necessarily linked directly to its objective benefits. We discuss these results further in Section 6

5.4 Impact of interpretation quality on user satisfaction

It is generally known in SDS research that measures of interpretation quality such as word error rate and concept accuracy are strongly correlated with user

	FULL	BASE
Transparency	0.32 (0.07)	0.06 (0.69)
Acceptability	**0.38** (0.03)	0.23 (0.16)
Affect	0.29 (0.08)	-0.10 (0.53)
Overall	**0.38** (0.02)	0.18 (0.28)

Table 3: Correlations between satisfaction factors and learning gain for two dialogue policies. Significance level in parentheses. Bold indicates significance at $p < 0.05$ level.

satisfaction (e.g., (Walker et al., 2000; Möller et al., 2007)). Our system uses typed input and produces complex logical representations (rather than simple slot-value pairs), thus, these measures cannot be computed directly. However, in an earlier study we showed that another measure of interpretation quality, namely, percentage of utterances that could not be interpreted by the system ("uninterpretable utterances") is negatively correlated with learning gain and user satisfaction (Dzikovska et al., 2010b).[3]

That study revealed an unexpected pattern. Although the system recorded the number of utterances it could not interpret in both FULL and BASE, students in BASE were never informed of any interpretation problems. Nevertheless, the proportion of such uninterpretable utterances was still significantly negatively correlated with user satisfaction in BASE. After analyzing correlations between different types of errors and user satisfaction, we hypothesized that this can be explained by the lack of alignment between the system and the student, in particular when students used terminology different from that used by the system (Dzikovska et al., 2010b).

We can now analyze this relationship in more detail, looking at correlations between interpretation problems and different components of user satisfaction. The results are presented in Table 4.

As can be seen from the table, the proportion of uninterpretable answers is significantly correlated with *Acceptability* in FULL, but not in BASE. This is not surprising, indicating that students who were told that they were not understood perceived the system as less useful for them. More surprisingly, *Transparency*, which is related to perceived ease of

[3]In that study, we computed user satisfaction with the tutor by averaging over the entire 35 questions in our questionnaire as an initial approximation.

	FULL	BASE
Transparency	-0.28 (0.1)	-0.25 (0.10)
Acceptability	**-0.58** (< 0.001)	-0.29 (0.07)
Affect	**-0.35** (0.04)	**-0.34** (0.04)
Overall	**-0.38** (0.03)	-0.27 (0.11)
Learning gain	**-0.38** (0.03)	-0.09(0.60)

Table 4: Correlations between satisfaction factors and uninterpretable utterances for two different policies. Significance level in parentheses.

use for the system, was not correlated with uninterpretable utterances. Finally, the proportion of uninterpretable utterances is significantly correlated with *Affect* for both systems. Moreover, the unexpected negative correlation we observed in the earlier study between satisfaction with the tutor and interpretation problems in BASE can be primarily attributed to the negative correlation with the *Affect* score.

6 Discussion

In this study, we attempted to apply insights from studies of user satisfaction in spoken dialogue systems to a different type of dialogue application: tutorial dialogue. We were looking to develop a better user satisfaction questionnaire for evaluating tutorial dialogue systems, and to implement an evaluation methodology which takes into account different underlying dimensions of user satisfaction.

The three dimensions we obtained based on exploratory factor analysis of REVU-NL align well with the dimensions reported in the SDS literature, which provides some evidence of their validity. However, the results are preliminary because of the small number of participants involved, and need to be replicated with additional participants and different tutoring systems. Regardless, our analysis highlighted important issues in designing satisfaction surveys for different dialogue genres.

When choosing which questions to include in a satisfaction questionnaire for a new system type, SASSI is a very attractive starting point, because it was validated across multiple SDS in two genres (command and control and information seeking). This also means that SASSI items are phrased very generally and therefore easier to adapt. In contrast, INSPIRE contains a number of questions specific to the command and control domain, asking whether the user thinks the system is useful in achieving their goals (i.e., operating the domestic devices). SASSI includes only one similar item, "The system was useful". It was classed as *Affect*, most likely because there were no other similar items. However, we think that such questions represent an important separate dimension, namely the "perceived usefulness" factor known to predict technology acceptance (Adams et al., 1989). Therefore we included several items in REVU-NL with similar intent, asking whether users thought the system was beneficial to their goal (i.e., learning the material). These items were clustered into a separate dimension by factor analysis, indicating that they should be included in other satisfaction surveys.

Moreover, some of the questions that appeared genre-independent to us proved to be cross-loading in our analysis, which is an indicator of ambiguity. Apparently, some of the items from task-oriented dialogue questionnaires did not transfer well. For example, statements like "The system didn't always do what I expected" are unambiguous for task-oriented dialogue, where the user is supposed to be in control of the interaction, and therefore has clear expectations of what the system should do. In contrast, in tutorial dialogue the tutor has control over the learning material. Thus, it may be more ambiguous as to what, if anything, students are expecting from the interaction.

Overall, our experience shows that it may not be possible, or indeed useful, to create completely generic surveys. However, we believe that questionnaires can be phrased generally enough to apply to a range of systems with similar goals, and REVU-NL in particular is useful starting point for comparing dialogue-based tutoring systems. We believe that the 18 questions that we retained as unambiguous in our analysis provide adequate assessment of user satisfaction, and are grouped into factors consistent with results of previous research. However, the questionnaire could be further improved by revisiting the cross-loading items we rejected as ambiguous, and seeing if their wording could be improved. We are also intending to use REVU-IT in evaluating a spoken version of BEETLE II, thus providing additional validation data on a different version of the interface.

With respect to evaluation methodology, our results highlight the need to look at different satisfaction dimensions separately. We used our factors to further investigate a pattern that we discovered in previous research, namely, that students who speak in a way that is difficult for the system to interpret tend to be less satisfied with the tutor, *even when they are not told of the interpretation problems.* Looking at correlations with individual dimensions shows that this relationship is primarily explained by the *Affect* dimension. Our working hypothesis is that the lack of alignment between incorrect student answers and the answers supplied by the system caused students to perceive the system as a less likeable or cooperative conversational partner.

We also observed that *Acceptability*, but no other dimensions, were correlated with learning gain in FULL. One possible explanation is that students who are learning more believe that the system is helping them reach their goals (our definition of *Acceptability*). The FULL condition provides students with more explicit feedback as to their learning; whereas in BASE students may have a less accurate estimate of how well they are doing, and hence no satisfaction dimensions are correlated with learning gain.

It is worth noting that an earlier study investigating the relationship between user satisfaction and learning in two different tutorial dialogue systems (Forbes-Riley and Litman, 2009) found little correlation between the answers to individual questions on their satisfaction questionnaire and learning gain. Only one correlation, with the question "The tutor helped me to concentrate", reached significance in only one of the 4 conditions they investigated. This adds further evidence that the relationship between learning gain and satisfaction is not straightforward. However, our results are difficult to compare since the questionnaires used are different, and Forbes-Riley and Litman (2009) are studying correlations with individual questions rather than grouping related questions together. Developing better validated questionnaires will make such results easier to compare and interpret, and we believe that REVU-NL makes a significant step in that direction.

7 Conclusion and Future Work

In this paper, we proposed an improved questionnaire (REVU-NL) for evaluating user satisfaction in tutorial dialogue systems, which is an important evaluation metric alongside learning gain. We used the methodology from SDS evaluations to investigate different dimensions of user satisfaction, and their relationship to learning gain and different interaction properties. Next, we are planning to use the PARADISE methodology to establish predictive models that relate satisfaction dimensions to measurable interaction properties, so that we can determine development priorities, and make it easier to compare different system versions. We are also planning to collect additional questionnaire data with a speech-enabled version of the system, and verify our analyses on this extended data set.

Acknowledgments

This work has been supported in part by US Office of Naval Research grants N000141010085 and N0001410WX20278. We would like to thank our sponsors from the Office of Naval Research, Dr. Susan Chipman and Dr. Ray Perez, and the Research Associates who worked on this project, Katherine Harrison, Leanne Taylor, Charles Scott, Simon Caine, Elaine Farrow and Charles Callaway for their contribution to this effort.

References

Dennis A. Adams, R. Ryan Nelson, and Peter A. Todd. 1989. Perceived usefulness, ease of use, and usage of information technology. *MIS Quarterly.*, 13:319–339.

Myroslava Dzikovska, Natalie B. Steinhauser, Johanna D. Moore, Gwendolyn E. Campbell, Katherine M. Harrison, and Leanne S. Taylor. 2010a. Content, social, and metacognitive statements: An empirical study comparing human-human and human-computer tutorial dialogue. In *Sustaining TEL: From Innovation to Learning and Practice - 5th European Conference on Technology Enhanced Learning (EC-TEL 2010)*, pages 93–108, Barcelona, Spain, October.

Myroslava O. Dzikovska, Johanna D. Moore, Natalie Steinhauser, and Gwendolyn Campbell. 2010b. The impact of interpretation problems on tutorial dialogue. In *Proceedings of the 48th Annual Meeting of the Association for Computational Linguistics(ACL-2010)*, Uppsala, Sweden, July.

Myroslava O. Dzikovska, Johanna D. Moore, Natalie Steinhauser, Gwendolyn Campbell, Elaine Farrow, and Charles B. Callaway. 2010c. Beetle II: a system for tutoring and computational linguistics experimentation. In *Proceedings of the 48th Annual Meeting of the Association for Computational Linguistics (ACL-2010) demo session*, Uppsala, Sweden, July.

Katherine Forbes-Riley and Diane J. Litman. 2009. Adapting to student uncertainty improves tutoring dialogues. In *Artificial Intelligence in Education: Building Learning Systems that Care: From Knowledge Representation to Affective Modelling, Proceedings of the 14th International Conference on Artificial Intelligence in Education (AIED 2009)*, pages 33–40, Brighton, UK, July.

Katherine Forbes-Riley and Diane J. Litman. 2011. Designing and evaluating a wizarded uncertainty-adaptive spoken dialogue tutoring system. *Computer Speech & Language*, 25(1):105–126.

Katherine Forbes-Riley, Diane J. Litman, Scott Silliman, and Joel R. Tetreault. 2006. Comparing synthesized versus pre-recorded tutor speech in an intelligent tutoring spoken dialogue system. In *Proceedings of the Nineteenth International Florida Artificial Intelligence Research Society Conference*, pages 509–514, Melbourne Beach, Florida, USA, May.

Kate S. Hone and Robert Graham. 2000. Towards a tool for the subjective assessment of speech system interfaces (SASSI). *Natural Language Engineering*, 6(3&4):287–303.

G. Tanner Jackson, Arthur C. Graesser, and Danielle S. McNamara. 2009. What students expect may have more impact than what they know or feel. In *Proceedings 14th International Conference on Artificial Intelligence in Education (AIED)*, Brighton, UK.

Lars Bo Larsen. 2003. Issues in the evaluation of spoken dialogue systems using objective and subjective measures. In *Proceedings of 2003 IEEE Workshop on Automatic Speech Recognition and Understanding (ASRU'03)*, pages 209 – 214, December.

Diane Litman, Johanna Moore, Myroslava Dzikovska, and Elaine Farrow. 2009. Using natural language processing to analyze tutorial dialogue corpora across domains and modalities. In *Proceedings of 14th International Conference on Artificial Intelligence in Education (AIED)*, Brighton, UK, July.

Joel Michael, Allen Rovick, Michael Glass, Yujian Zhou, and Martha Evens. 2003. Learning from a computer tutor with natural language capabilities. *Interactive Learning Environments*, 11:233–262(30).

Sebastian Möller, Paula Smeele, Heleen Boland, and Jan Krebber. 2007. Evaluating spoken dialogue systems according to de-facto standards: A case study. *Computer Speech & Language*, 21(1):26 – 53.

Amruta Purandare and Diane Litman. 2008. Content-learning correlations in spoken tutoring dialogs at word, turn and discourse levels. In *Proceedings of the 21st International FLAIRS Conference*, Coconut Grove, Florida, May.

Marilyn A. Walker, Candace A. Kamm, and Diane J. Litman. 2000. Towards Developing General Models of Usability with PARADISE. *Natural Language Engineering*, 6(3).

Maria Wolters, Kallirroi Georgila, Robert Logie, Sarah MacPherson, Johanna Moore, and Matt Watson. 2009. Reducing working memory load in spoken dialogue systems. *Interacting with Computers*, 21(4):276–287.

A REVU-NL **Questions**

t1 I felt in control of my conversations with the tutor.
t2 It took the tutor too long to respond to my statements.
t3 I felt that the tutor understood me well.
t4 The tutor didn't always do what I expected.
t5 The information that the tutor provided to me was incomplete.
t6 It was easy for me to become confused during our dialogue.
t7 I enjoyed talking with the tutor.
t8 The tutor interfered with my understanding of the topics in electricity and circuits.
t9 I was not always sure what the tutor expected of me.
t10 Conversing with the tutor was fun.
t11 It was easy to understand the things that the tutor said.
t12 The dialogue between me and the tutor was very repetitive.
t13 I had to really concentrate when I was talking with the tutor.
t14 The tutor was too inflexible.
t15 Working through the lessons with the computer tutor was as easy as working through the lessons with a human tutor.
t16 The tutor didn't always do what I wanted.
t17 I felt confident when talking with the tutor.
t18 I always knew what to say to the tutor.
t19 I was able to recover easily from errors during our dialogues.
t20 Talking with the tutor was frustrating.
t21 The information provided by the tutor was clear.
t22 It was easy to interact with the tutor.
t23 The tutor's dialogue was clumsy and unnatural.
t24 It was easy to learn how to speak to the tutor in a way that the tutor understood.
t25 I felt comfortable talking with the tutor.
t26 I didn't always understand what the tutor meant.
t27 The tutor was not helpful.
t28 I found conversing with the tutor to be irritating.
t29 I knew what I could say or do at each point in the conversation with the tutor.
t30 I found our dialogues to be boring.
t31 Having the tutor help me with the material was an efficient way to learn.
t32 It was easy to learn from the tutor.
t33 The tutor responded quickly.
t34 Having the tutor was worthwhile
t35 Our dialogues quickly led to me having a deeper understanding of the material.

B REVU-OVERALL **questions**

o1 Overall, I am satisfied with my experience learning about electricity from this system.
o2 Working in this learning environment was just like working one-on-one with a human tutor.
o3 I would have preferred to learn about electricity in a different way.
o4 I would use this system again in the future to continue to learn about electricity.
o5 I would like to be able to use a system like this to learn about other topics in the future.

C REVU-IT **questions related to GUI and reading material (mentioned but not analyzed in the paper)**

sl1 It was easy to navigate through the slides.
sl2 It took a long time for each new slide to be displayed.
sl3 The material on the slides was easy to understand.
sl4 The material on the slides was poorly written.
sl5 I would have benefited from more instrucion on how to move through the slides.
sl6 The material on the slides was interesting.
sl7 The slide navigation buttons didn't always work the way I expected them to.
sl8 The slides were annoying.
sl9 The material on the slides was written at a level far beneath my abilities.
sl10 I would prefer reading a text book over reading these slides.
e1 I found it difficult to learn how to build circuits and take measurements in the workspace.
e2 Completing exercises in the workspace was fun.
e3 Before beginning the lesson, I received the right amount of instruction on how to build circuits in the workspace and take measurements.
e4 The exercises were well designed to illustrate the important lesson concepts.
e5 Sometimes I didn't understand what I was supposed to do for an exercise.
e6 The method for connecting components with wires was counter-intuitive.
e7 Having to build all those circuits was annoying.
e8 I always knew exactly what to build and/or measure in the workspace, and how to do it.
e9 Circuits loaded quickly.
e10 Even if I didn't predict the outcome correctly ahead of time, once I completed an exercise, I always understood the point.
e11 It was easy to use the meter.
e12 There were more exercises than necessary to cover the lesson topics.
e13 I would have learned more if I had been able to build circuits with actual light bulbs and batteries.

Modeling and Predicting Quality in Spoken Human-Computer Interaction

Alexander Schmitt, Benjamin Schatz and Wolfgang Minker
Dialogue Systems Research Group
Institute for Information Technology
Ulm University, Germany

{alexander.schmitt, benjamin.schatz, wolfgang.minker}@uni-ulm.de

Abstract

In this work we describe the modeling and prediction of Interaction Quality (IQ) in Spoken Dialogue Systems (SDS) using Support Vector Machines. The model can be employed to estimate the quality of the ongoing interaction at arbitrary points in a spoken human-computer interaction. We show that the use of 52 completely automatic features characterizing the system-user exchange significantly outperforms state-of-the-art approaches. The model is evaluated on publically available data from the CMU Let's Go Bus Information system. It reaches a performance of 61.6% unweighted average recall when discriminating between 5 classes (good to very poor). It can be further shown that incorporating knowledge about the user's emotional state does hardly improve the performance.

1 Introduction

For years, the research community has been trying to model quality of Spoken Dialogue Systems (SDS) with statistical approaches. Most vividly discussed has been the PARADISE approach which tries to map objective performance metrics of an SDS to subjective user ratings (Walker et al., 2000). The paradigm assumes that task success and dialogue costs contribute to user satisfaction which is the target variable in the model. By that, an automatic evaluation of an SDS should be enabled. While the intention of PARADISE is to evaluate and compare SDS or different system versions among each other, it is not suited to evaluate a spoken dialogue at arbitrary points during an interaction. Such a model can be helpful for a number of reasons: Firstly, it allows for a prediction of critical dialogue situations. These predictions could be employed to adapt the dialogue strategy or - in telephone applications with human assistance - escalate to human operators. Secondly, it could help to uncover potentially weak dialogue design and point out problematic turns that need a re-design. Thirdly, user satisfaction models help understand the satisfaction of the users. In this study we present such a statistical model that is trained with a large set of domain-independent features taken from system logs and use additional manually created features, such as emotional state and dialogue acts, to create an upper baseline.

This paper is organized as follows: In Section 2 we present related work and discuss afterwards in Section 3 further issues that need to be addressed in this field. There, we also disambiguate the term user satisfaction from Interaction Quality. After that, we describe the annotation scheme as well as the rating process for modeling IQ and present, how we derive a generic label from the different raters' opinions in Section 4. The input feature groups along with their features are presented in Section 5. We anticipate that the problem is best modeled with Support Vector Machines (SVM), which is addressed in Section 6. Ensuing, the performance of the model is evaluated. In the first place, we analyze the impact of different feature groups on the SVM classifier in Section 7 and secondly, we optimize the model and determine the most relevant features for predicting the IQ score in Section 8. A linear modeling approach of IQ by use of multivariate linear regression will be

Proceedings of the SIGDIAL 2011: the 12th Annual Meeting of the Special Interest Group on Discourse and Dialogue, pages 173–184,
Portland, Oregon, June 17-18, 2011.

presented and discussed in Section 9 to obtain comparability with PARADISE. This study closes with a conclusion and a discussion in Section 10.

2 Related Work

Models predicting user satisfaction at any point in an SDS have only been deficiently explored to date. (Engelbrecht et al., 2009) modeled user satisfaction as process evolving over time with Hidden Markov Models (HMM). In the experiment, users were asked to interact with a Wizard-of-Oz restaurant information system. Each participant followed dialogues which have previously been defined following predefined scripts, i.e. specific scenarios. This resulted in equally long dialogue transcripts for each scenario. The users were constrained to rate their satisfaction on a 5-point scale with "bad", "poor", "fair", "good" and "excellent" after each dialogue step. The interaction was halted while the user voted.

In a similar spirit, (Higashinaka et al., 2010a) developed a model for predicting turn-wise ratings, which was evaluated on human-machine and human-human dialogues. The data employed was not spoken dialogue but text dialogues from a chat system and a transcribed conversation between humans. The labels in the model originated from two expert raters that listened to the recorded interactions and provided turn-wise scores from 1-7 on smoothness ("Smoothness of the conversation"), closeness ("Closeness perceived by the user towards the system") and willingness ("Willingness to continue the conversation"). Rater-independent performance scores of the model reached about 0.2-0.24 unweighted average recall, which is about 0.1 points above the baseline of app. 0.14.

(Hara et al., 2010) created n-gram models from dialogue acts (DA) to predict user satisfaction based on dialogues from real users interacting with a music retrieval system. The model is based on *overall* ratings from the users measuring their satisfaction on a five point scale *after* the interaction. The best result could be achieved with a 3-gram model that reached 34% accuracy in distinguishing between six classes at any point in the dialogue. It seems that the prediction of turn-level user satisfaction scores given only one overall dialogue-level score seems hardly possible and is close to random: The prediction of the five user satisfaction classes reach an average F-score as low as 0.252, which is only 0.052 score points above the baseline of 0.20. A similar result as (Hara et al., 2010) was obtained by (Higashinaka et al., 2010b). Using HMMs they derived turn-level ratings from dialogue-wide ratings. The model's performance when trained on dialogue-level ratings was closer to random than when trained on turn-level ratings. The open issues that arise from the cited work are addressed in the following.

3 Issues

Our aim is to create a general model that may be used to predict the quality of the interaction - or ideally the actual satisfaction of the user - at arbitrary system-user exchanges in an SDS. It has become obvious from the cited work that current models are not suited for deployment due to low prediction accuracy. Crucial for a successful recognition of user satisfaction is the choice and appropriateness of the input variables. (Higashinaka et al., 2010a), (Higashinaka et al., 2010b) and (Hara et al., 2010) employ a - mostly hand annotated - "dialogue act" feature to predict the target variable. Dialogue acts are frequently highly system-dependent and do not model the full bandwidth of the interaction. (Engelbrecht et al., 2009) additionally employed contextual appropriateness, confirmation strategy and task success, of which many require hand annotation. Yet it is mandatory for an automatic prediction of user satisfaction to design and derive completely automatic features that do not require manual intervention. It is further easy to comprehend that the modeling of user satisfaction in ongoing dialogues starts with a dilemma: tracking user satisfaction from real users in real environments performing real tasks is virtually impracticable. Consequently data for deriving models can either be obtained under laboratory conditions with real users performing fake tasks in an artificial environment, cf. (Engelbrecht et al., 2009), or by manual annotation of real-life data from experts that pretend to be the users.

It is thus vital for modeling "user satisfaction" to understand the term itself. In the literature there exists no rigorous definition, however, it seems obvious that it is the user himself who determines the satisfaction - and not expert annotators. According to (Doll and Torkzadeh, 1991) "user satisfaction" is the opinion of users about a specific computer application, which they use. Other terms for "user satisfaction" are common, such as "user information satisfaction", which is defined as "the extent to which users believe the information system available to them meets their information requirements" (Ives et al., 1983). User satisfaction and usability are closely interwoven. (ISO, 1998) subsumes under the definition "usability" a compound of efficiency, effectiveness and satisfaction. Yet satisfaction is often seen as a by-product of great usability in HCI literature (Lindgaard and Dudek, 2003). They could also show that user satisfaction ratings are subject to large fluctuations among different users and it can be further assumed that those fluctuations do also occur within a single dialogue of a user. As a result, general prediction models that mirror a universal, unbiased understanding of satisfaction can presumably hardly be derived from user's impressions. Large influence of subjectivity - and also randomness in assigning the scores - would prevent such a general model. Consequently, it seems unavoidable to employ expert annotations. In the proper meaning of the word, the scores then do not exactly mirror the subjective impression of users but the more objective impression of expert raters.

Thus we decide against the use of the term user satisfaction in the course of this work in contrast to (Higashinaka et al., 2010a) and instead opt for the expression *Interaction Quality*. It can be assumed that basic attitudes towards dialogue systems in general, opinions about the TTS voice, environmental factors etc. that would typically influence user satisfaction scores, and which are not of interest for our prediction, are not dominant in expert satisfaction scores in a series of annotated dialogues. Experts are expected to fade out such system-dependent and environment-dependent influences and instead focus on the dialogue behavior (i.e. the Interaction Quality) only.

As a result, two key issues are addressed in this work: First of all, the input feature set has to be designed as a generic, domain-independent set that can be derived from any spoken dialogue system log and that takes into account a maximum of available information about the interaction. Secondly, the target variable, i.e. the IQ score, needs to be determined in a guided rating process in order to be reproducible in future work and has to be empirically derived from several expert annotators that provide scores for each single system-user turn of an interaction.

4 Corpus Annotation

For our study we employ data from the Let's Go Bus information system (Raux et al., 2006). Three raters, advanced students of computer science and engineering, annotated respectively 200 dialogues comprising 4885 system-user exchanges from the 2006 corpus. The raters were asked to annotate the quality of the interaction at each system-user exchange with the scores 5 (very good), 4 (good), 3 (fair), 2 (poor) and 1 (very poor). Every dialogue is initially rated with a score of 5 since every interaction at the beginning can be considered as good until the opposite eventuates. Our model assumes that users are initially interacting with an SDS without bias, i.e. the basic attitude towards a dialogue system is positive. Other assumptions would not be statistically predictable. An example dialogue is depicted in Table 5 along with the ratings (cf. Figure 2 in the Appendix). (Higashinaka et al., 2010b) and (Higashinaka et al., 2010a) report low correlation among the ratings (Spearman's ρ 0.04-0.32), which motivated us to develop a set of basic guidelines that should be used by the raters (cf. Table 6 in the Appendix). The guidelines have been designed in such a way that the raters still have sufficient level of freedom when choosing the labels but preventing them from too strong variations among the neighboring system-user exchanges.

The distribution of the labels provided by the single raters is depicted in Figure 3. As expected, the distribution is skew towards label "5" since every dialogue initially is assumed to have a good IQ.

The inter-rater agreement shows that Interaction Quality is still a subjective metric, although guidelines seem to synchronize the labels to a certain extent. The overall mean agreement can be reported with Cohen's $\kappa = 0.31$ and the correlation among the raters can be reported with Spearman's $\rho = 0.72$ which depicts a by 0.4 points higher correlation as reported by (Higashinaka et al., 2010a). Since we aim to model a general opinion on Interaction Quality, i.e. the model should mirror the IQ score other raters - and in the last instance users - agree with, we determine the final label empirically. A majority voting for the distinction of the final label cannot be used since in 21% of the exchanges all three raters opted for different scores. Thus we consider the mean of all rater opinions as possible candidates for the final class label:

$$rating_{mean} = \lfloor \left(\frac{1}{R} \sum_{r=1}^{R} IQ_r \right) + 0.5 \rfloor$$

where IQ is the Interaction Quality score provided by rater r. $\lfloor y \rfloor$ denotes the biggest integer value smaller than y. Every value IQ_r contributes equally to the result that is finally rounded half up to an integer value. Furthermore we consider the median, which we define as

$$rating_{median} = select(sort(IQ_R), \frac{R+1}{2})$$

for an odd number of raters R, where $sort$ is a function that orders the ratings of all raters ascending and $select(X = [x_1, ..., x_n], i)$ chooses the item with index i from X.

The compliance of the single user ratings with the final label (calculated on mean and median) is depicted in Table 1. As can be seen, the agreement of the three raters with the median label is significantly higher than with the mean label. Consequently the median label represents the most objective measurement of Interaction Quality and commends itself for creating the model.

	Mean Label	Median Label
Cohen's κ		
Rater1	0.557	0.688
Rater2	0.554	0.679
Rater3	0.402	0.478
Mean	0.504	**0.608***
Spearman's ρ		
Rater1	0.901	0.900
Rater2	0.911	0.907
Rater3	0.841	0.814
Mean	**0.884**	0.874
Accuracy		
Rater1	0.651	0.755
Rater2	0.647	0.749
Rater3	0.539	0.598
Mean	0.612	**0.701***

Table 1: Agreement of single rater opinions to the merged label when determined by mean and median, measured in κ, ρ and accuracy. (*)=significantly higher ($\alpha < 0.05$)

5 Input Features

The system-user interaction is modeled on exchange level. Each system-user exchange consists of a set of fully automatic features that can be derived from system logs. We used parameters similar to the ones described in (Schmitt et al., 2008; Schmitt et al., 2010b). In the first place, we modeled each system-user exchange with a number of Speech Recognition (ASR), Spoken Language Understanding (SLU) and Dialog Manager (DM)-related features:

ASR ASRRECOGNITIONSTATUS: one of 'success', 'reject', 'timeout'; ASRCONFIDENCE: confidence of the ASR; BARGED-IN?: did the user barge-in?, MODALITY: one of 'speech', 'DTMF'; EXMO: the modality expected from the system ('speech', 'DTMF', 'both'); UNEXMO?: did the user employ another modality than expected?; GRAMMARNAMES: names of the active grammars; TRIGGEREDGRAMMAR: name of grammar that matched; UTTERANCE: raw ASR transcription; WPUT: number of words per user turn; UTD: utterance turn duration;

SLU SEMANTICPARSE: semantic interpretation of caller utterance; HELPREQUEST?: is the current turn a help request?; OPERATORREQUEST?: is the current turn an operator request?;

Dialog Manager ACTIVITY: identifier of the current system action; ACTIVITYTYPE: one of 'question', 'announcement', 'wait_for_user_feedback'; PROMPT: system prompt; WPST: number of words per system turn; REPROMPT?: is the current system turn a reprompt?; CONFIRMATION?: whether the current system prompt is a confirmation to elicit common ground between user and system due to low ASR confidence; TURNNUMBER: current turn; DD: dialog duration up to this point in seconds.

To account for the overall history of important system events we added running tallies, percentages and mean values for certain features symbolized with the suffixes '#', '%' and 'MEAN'. They are: MEANASRCONFIDENCE, the average of ASR confidence scores from all user utterances so far in the dialog, and #ASRSUCCESS, the number of succesfully parsed user utterances so far. Further we calculate #ASRREJECTIONS, #TIME-OUTPROMPTS, #BARGEINS, #UNEXMO and the respective normalized equivalents with the prefix '%' instead of '#'. We consider the immediate context within the previous 3 turns of the current turn as particularly relevant for the Interaction Quality. Hence, derived from the basic parameters we created further parameters that emphasize specific user behavior prior to the classification point. They are symbolized with the prefix {#} for a number and {Mean} for the mean value. A number of successive barge-ins or recognition problems might indicate a low IQ. Thus we add {MEAN}ASRCONFIDENCE, the mean confidence of the ASR within the window, {#}ASRSUCCESS, {#}ASRREJECTIONS and {#}TIME-OUTPROMPTS, i.e. the number of successfully and unsuccessfully parsed utterances within the window and the number of time-outs. The other counters are calculated likewise: {#}BARGEINS; {#}UNEXMO, {#}HELPREQUESTS, {#}OPERATORREQUESTS, {#}REPROMPT, {#}CONFIRMATIONS, {#}SYSTEMQUESTIONS.

To provide comparability to previous work (Higashinaka et al., 2010a), we further introduce a dialogue act feature group that we create semi-automatically:

DAct SYSTEMDIALOGUEACT: one of 28 distinct dialogue acts, such as *greeting, offer_help, ask_bus, confirm_departure, deliver_result, etc.* USERDIALOGUEACT: one of 22 distinct DAs, such as *confirm_departure, place_information, polite, reject_time, request_help*, etc.

To create an upper baseline of our model we further introduce the negative emotional state of the user that is manually annotated by a human rater who chooses one of the labels *garbage, non-angry, slightly angry, very angry* for each single user turn:

Emo EMOTIONALSTATE: emotional state of the caller in the current exchange. One of *garbage, non-angry, slightly angry, very angry.*

The same annotation scheme as in our previous work on anger detection has been applied, see e.g. (Schmitt et al., 2009). From all 4,832 user turns, 68.5% were non-angry, 14.3% slightly angry, 5.0% very angry and 12.2% contained garbage, i.e. non-speech events. In total, the number of interaction parameters servings as input variables for the model amounts to 52.

6 Non-Linear Modeling with Support Vector Machines

The IQ scores are classified with Support Vector Machines (Bennett and Campbell, 2000). In short, an SVM uses a set of training examples

$$(x_1, y_1) \ldots (x_n, y_n) | x_i \in \mathcal{X}, y_i \in \{-1, 1\}$$

to create a hyperplane that separates two classes $\{-1, 1\}$ in such a manner that the smallest margin between all training samples is maximized. The hyperplane is described by a normal vector w and a so-called bias b. To classify an unknown sample the following decision rule is applied:

$$Y = sgn[w^T x + b > 0] = \begin{cases} +1, & w^T x + b > 0 \\ -1, & w^T x + b \leq 0 \end{cases}$$

Depending on the position of the training sample in relation to the hyperplane, the class 1 or -1 is assigned to the unknown sample. Multi-class problems are solved by reducing the problem to several binary classification problems where usually a *one-versus-all* decision is applied.

The model is constructed with an SVM with linear kernel that uses the fast Sequential Minimal Optimization (SMO) algorithm (Platt, 1999). Input variables are features from the described groups, i.e. $x \in \{DAct, ASR, SLU, DM, Emo\}$. The target variable is the IQ score.

7 Feature Group Evaluation

The skew distribution of the five classes requires the employment of an evaluation metric that weights the prediction of all classes equally. Hence, a performance metric, such as *accuracy*, would not be a reliable measurement. We select the *unweighted average recall* (UAR) to assess the model performance. Although it does not consider the severity of the error, i.e. predicting "1" for an IQ of "5" is considered as fatal as predicting "4", it has been proven to be superior to other evaluation metrics, see (Higashinaka et al., 2010a), where the UAR is called *Match Rate per Rating* (MR/R). It is defined as follows:

$$MR/R(\mathbf{R},\mathbf{H}) = \frac{1}{K}\sum_{r=1}^{K}\frac{\sum_{i\in\{i|R_i=r\}} match(R_i,H_i)}{\sum_{i\in\{i|R_i=r\}} 1},$$

where K is the number of classes, here "5", and 'match' is either '1' or '0' depending on whether the classifier's hypothesis H_i for the class r matches the reference label R_i. In the course of this work we will stick to the expression MR/R by reason of clearness. We further list Cohen's κ and Spearman's ρ to make our work comparable to other studies but will use MR/R as central evaluation criterion and for feature selection.

We have split all available data into two disjoint subsets consisting of 60% of the dialogues for training and testing via 10-fold cross-validation and the remaining 40% of the dialogues for optimization. The dialogues have been selected randomly.

In order to assess the performance contribution of the single feature groups, we trained the SVM respectively with all features from the *DAct, ASR, SLU* and *DM* groups. Further, we subsumed the groups ASR, SLU and DM as *AUTO* features since they can automatically be derived from logs without manual intervention. In addition, the *AUTOEMO* group contains all *AUTO* features plus the emotion label. Finally, the *ALL* group contains the *AUTOEMO* features plus the *DAct* features. For all groups, the support vector classifier has been trained and evaluated in 10-fold cross validation with the 3110 exchanges from the 118 training/testing dialogues. The first turn of each dialogue has been excluded from the evaluation since each dialogue starts with a score of "5". Results are depicted in the *first half* of Table 2.

Input	*Feature Selection*	MR/R	κ	ρ
	Majority Baseline	0.200	0.0	NA
DAct	no	0.269	0.136	0.363
ASR	no	**0.605**	0.551	0.753
SLU	no	0.250	0.083	0.293
DM	no	0.429	0.334	0.653
AUTO	no	**0.584**	0.526	0.776
AUTOEMO	no	**0.606**	0.549	0.785
ALL	no	0.619	0.559	0.800
DAct	–	-	-	-
ASR	13/25	0.598	0.545	0.730
SLU	4/5	0.250	0.083	0.293
DM	10/17	0.436	0.338	0.649
AUTO	20/47	**0.616**	0.563	0.786
AUTOEMO	31/48	**0.604**	0.545	0.785
ALL	23/52	**0.625**	0.575	0.795

Table 2: Model performance after 10-fold cross validation on training/test set. The first half comprises results when all features of a group are employed. The second half contains results after feature selection on the optimization set ((x/y)=where x is the number of features used from all y available features.)

As can be seen, the model reaches a similar performance as (Higashinaka et al., 2010a) with MR/R=0.26, when trained with dialogue act features alone. The slightly higher performance of our model can potentially be explained by the lower number of classes (5 vs. 7), a different definition of the dialogue act set, the employment of Support Vector Machines instead of Hidden Markov Models or the difference in the target variable (IQ vs. closeness/smoothness/willingness). It can be noted that the utilization of other features considerably outperforms dialogue act features. Particularly the group of the *ASR* features alone reaches a performance of 60.5%. The employment of all *AUTO* features delivers 58.4% which is 2.1% below the *ASR* features. Consequently, other variables seem to be less meaningful for predicting the Interaction Quality and seem to harm the performance of the SVM. The knowledge of the emotional state of the user contributes with merely another 0.1% in comparison to the *ASR* features. It can be assumed that the emotion feature increases the recognition rate of the lower IQ scores "1" and "2". However, this could not be confirmed: even when considering class-wise performance values a significant contribution of the emotion feature cannot be observed. We also have to bear in mind that we employed hand-annotated emotions. Emotion recognition itself is error-prone and a distinction of the emotional state of the caller with the employed annotation scheme can be expected with approximately 70%-80% UAR, see e.g. (Schmitt et al., 2010a). The influence of emotion recognition on the IQ distinction can be considered as limited and is insofar not surprising as the occurrence of strong anger in the data is not dominant (5.0%). The contribution of the single features to the classification result (across the groups they are assigned to) is analyzed in the following.

8 Optimizing the Model by Feature Selection

Since too many (potentially irrelevant) features might harm the classifier's performance we perform feature selection with the optimization set. First, the features are ordered according to an Information Gain Ratio (IGR) ranking. The 10 most relevant features according to IGR for predicting IQ are depicted in Table 3.

	Feature	IGR
1	#ASRREJECTIONS	1
2	#TIMEOUT_ASRREJ	0.967288
3	#ASRSUCCESS	0.834238
4	#REPROMPTS	0.804752
5	%REPROMPTS	0.800462
6	#TIMEOUTPROMPTS	0.757596
7	#SYSTEMQUESTIONS	0.757596
8	ROLEINDEX	0.699246
9	DD	0.566836
10	#BARGE-INS	0.566836

Table 3: Top 10 features on optimization set according to IGR.

As can be seen the Interaction Quality is obviously heavily influenced by the performance of the ASR. In other words, it can be assumed that the raters themselves are influenced by the ASR's performance when assigning the IQ scores. All features belong to the group AUTO, i.e. they can be determined automatically during runtime. Furthermore, nearly all features are related to the overall interaction, i.e. features related to the current exchange, such as UTTERANCE, ASRSUCCESS? etc. do not even occur. It can also be noted that the emotional state and the dialogue acts are not listed as most relevant features. To determine the global maximum of the classifier, i.e. the best performing feature set, we incrementally select the k topmost features from the list and perform 10-fold cross validation on the optimization set. A plot of the iterative feature selection is depicted in Figure 1.

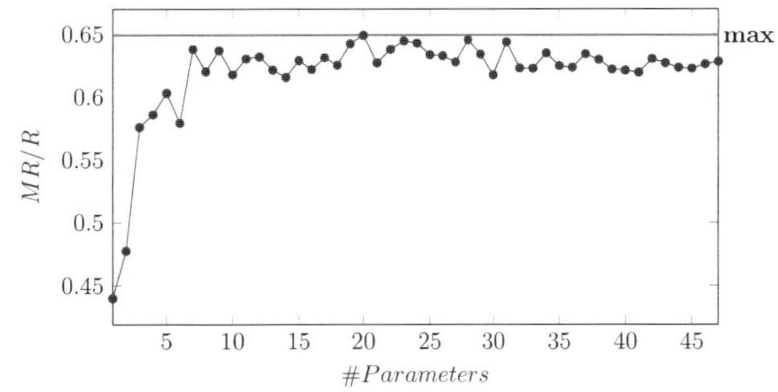

Figure 1: Performance of the SVM when iteratively increasing the size of the feature vector with the k topmost features according to IGR.

Several observations can be made: the best performing feature set consists of 20 features with an absolute performance of 65 % MR/R on the optimization set. However, a similar performance can already be gained with the 7 top-most features. All other features obviously neither significantly decrease nor increase the performance and can be considered irrelevant for predicting the IQ score. The impact of feature selection on the model when evaluated on the single feature groups from the test/training set using only the most relevant features from the optimization set can be seen in the lower part of Table 2. Again, 10-fold cross validation has been applied. The *AUTO* group benefits from the selection and delivers the highest performance with 20 features with an MR/R of 61.6%, which is an increase of 3.2%. The upper baseline with hand annotated features (*ALL* group) amounts to 62.5%. The fact that the *AUTOEMO* set underperforms with 60.4% - in comparison to the *AUTO* set - can be explained due to the potentially too small size of the optimization set.

The confusion matrix for the *AUTO* feature set is depicted in Table 4, along with the class-wise precision and recall values. The model yields the best performance in predicting the scores at the edge, i.e. "5" and "1". In between, the confusion is slightly higher and the model performance lower.

Table 4: Confusion matrix including class-wise precision and recall values after 10-fold cross validation (training/test set) using the AUTO set. A (weighted average) accuracy of 67.5% can be derived.

	true 5	true 4	true 3	true 2	true 1	prec.
pred. 5	**721**	154	42	9	5	0.774
pred. 4	89	**464**	104	44	19	0.644
pred. 3	17	63	**231**	49	38	0.580
pred. 2	2	15	39	**89**	33	0.500
pred. 1	4	23	29	27	**169**	0.670
rec.	0.865	0.645	0.519	0.408	0.640	

9 Linear Regression Modeling

Models from the initially mentioned PARADISE approach presume a linear relationship between input variables - quantifying the dialogue - and the target variable US, the user satisfaction. Assuming linearity, such linear models allow inferences such as "The longer the dialogue duration, the lower the satisfaction". While linear modeling is descriptive and easy to read it delivers poor performance when applied on non-linear problems. Such non-linear problems reach a better predictability using Support Vector Machines (SVM). Although we anticipate that a relationship between IQ and the interaction parameters is not given, we list a multivariate linear regression model for comparison reasons with PARADISE.

The linear regression model of Interaction Quality is calculated as follows:

$$IQ = \sum_{i=1}^{n} w_i \cdot \mathcal{N}(p_i)$$

where w_i is the weight for the interaction parameters p_i, and $\mathcal{N}$ the z-score normalization function. $\mathcal{N}$ normalizes the input variables to a mean of zero and a standard deviation of one. This eliminates the variying scales of the input variables.

From the CMU Let's Go dataset we obtained the following IQ function using the *ALL* feature set:

$$\begin{aligned}
IQ = \quad & 0.7797 \cdot \mathcal{N}(\text{TURNNUMBER}) \\
& + 0.7797 \cdot \mathcal{N}(\text{\#SYSTEMTURNS}) \\
& - 0.7386 \cdot \mathcal{N}(\textbf{\#ASRSuccess}) \\
& - 0.7175 \cdot \mathcal{N}(\text{\#USERTURNS}) \\
& - 0.3019 \cdot \mathcal{N}(\textbf{\%RePrompts}) \\
& - 0.2371 \cdot \mathcal{N}(\text{EMOTIONALSTATE}) \\
& - 0.2224 \cdot \mathcal{N}(\textbf{\#ASRRejections}) \\
& - 0.1961 \cdot \mathcal{N}(\text{\#TIMEOUTS_ASRREJ}) \\
& + 0.1912 \cdot \mathcal{N}(\text{ASRRECOGNITIONSTATUS}) \\
& + 0.1648 \cdot \mathcal{N}(\text{ASRCONFIDENCE}) \\
& - 0.1592 \cdot \mathcal{N}(\text{\#ASRSUCCESS}) \\
& - 0.1466 \cdot \mathcal{N}(\text{ACTIVITY}) \\
& + 0.1388 \cdot \mathcal{N}(\text{ACTIVITYTYPE}) \\
& + 0.1231 \cdot \mathcal{N}(\text{MEANASRCONFIDENCE}) \\
& - 0.0981 \cdot \mathcal{N}(\text{\#SYSTEMQUESTIONS}) \\
& + 0.0948 \cdot \mathcal{N}(\text{\%ASRREJECTIONS}) \\
& - 0.0918 \cdot \mathcal{N}(\text{\#TIMEOUTS_ASRREJ}) \\
& + 0.0835 \cdot \mathcal{N}(\textbf{\#Reprompts}) \\
& + 0.0812 \cdot \mathcal{N}(\text{\%BARGE-INS}) \\
& - 0.0567 \cdot \mathcal{N}(\text{\%TIME-OUTPROMPTS}) \\
& - 0.0555 \cdot \mathcal{N}(\text{\#TIMEOUTS·ASRREJ}) \\
& - 0.0467 \cdot \mathcal{N}(\textbf{\#Time-OutPrompts}) \\
& + 0.0461 \cdot \mathcal{N}(\text{WPST}) \\
& + 0.0432 \cdot \mathcal{N}(\text{HANDTRANSCRIPTION}) \\
& - 0.0425 \cdot \mathcal{N}(\text{LOOPNAME}) \\
& + 0.0375 \cdot \mathcal{N}(\textbf{\#SystemQuestions}) \\
& + 0.0374 \cdot \mathcal{N}(\text{SEMANTICPARSE}) \\
& - 0.0345 \cdot \mathcal{N}(\text{BARGED-IN?}) \\
& + 0.0338 \cdot \mathcal{N}(\textbf{RoleIndex}) \\
& - 0.0335 \cdot \mathcal{N}(\text{\#REPROMPTS}) \\
& - 0.0316 \cdot \mathcal{N}(\text{\#ASRREJECTIONS}) \\
& + 0.0302 \cdot \mathcal{N}(\text{REPROMPT?}) \\
& + 0.0249 \cdot \mathcal{N}(\text{WPUT}) \\
& + 0.0225 \cdot \mathcal{N}(\text{ROLENAME})
\end{aligned}$$

Parameters occurring in the top 10 feature list according to IGR (see Table 3) are printed in boldface. It is interesting to note that parameters related to the progress of the dialogue (TURNNUMBER, #SYSTEMTURNS, #USERTURNS) seem to play the most important role, which can easily be explained: the later in the dialogue, the higher the probability that the score is low, due to the nature of IQ. Remember that all dialogues have been annotated with high IQ scores ("5") in the beginning (see also

Table 5). However, many inconsistencies remain unexplained, e.g. the negative sign in "$-0.7175 \cdot \mathcal{N}$(#USERTURNS)" contradicting the positive sign in "$+0.7797 \cdot \mathcal{N}$(#SYSTEMTURNS)". The negative sign in "$-0.7386 \cdot \mathcal{N}$(#ASRSUCCESS)" would further imply that the more successful the ASR, the lower the IQ score. This corroborates our suspicion that IQ is not a linear problem.

To assess the performance of linear regression for predicting IQ we employed 10-fold cross validation, again with all 200 annotated dialogues. We obtained a root mean squared error of 0.594 and $R^2 = 0.646$.

Mapping the continuous values to discrete score classes from 1-5, we obtain $MR/R = 45.5\%$ (62.5% using SVM), $\kappa = 0.352$ (0.575) and $\rho = 0.46$ (0.795). All values finally suggest that IQ is better modeled with non-linear classifiers such as SVMs or Multilayer Perceptrons (MLP).

10 Conclusion and Discussion

In this work we have developed a statistical model that predicts Interaction Quality, an objective measure of user satisfaction, at arbitrary points in an SDS. The model targets on predicting critical situations on exchange level in ongoing dialogues. The classifier, an SVM, reaches a performance of 61.6% MR/R ($\kappa = 0.563, \rho = 0.786$) by use of an optimized feature set that can be automatically derived during the interaction. It could be further shown that linear modeling with multivariate linear regression is not appropriate for predicting IQ and reaches merely 45.5.% MR/R. Among all five feature groups comprising altogether 52 features, the ASR and DM groups contribute the most, while the EMOTIONALSTATE underperforms. We could further show that features requiring manual annotation, such as dialogue acts, do not significantly improve the model's performance. The model has been evaluated with 200 dialogues from the CMU Let's Go corpus comprising 4885 system-user exchanges where three annotators labeled the Interaction Quality on a score from 1-5. We could show that the median of all three opinions depicts the most generic view on the IQ and is thus chosen as final score for the model.

Some issues have to be addressed in future work: In the current study we assume that Interaction Quality is an objective metric for determining the satisfaction of users during the interaction. How far this assumption is justified has to be empirically proven in a laboratory study with real users. A corresponding study is in preparation and the results will be published in a follow-up work. Although the model's performance can be considered as satisfying, the direct deployment in dialogue systems cannot be recommended at this stage. For enabling a dialogue system to react on poor interaction quality, a correct prediction of the low IQ scores 1,2 and 3 is urgent, i.e. the classifier has to be optimized to deliver a very high *precision* on such low scores rather than towards a high general *MR/R* value. We assume that the performance can be further driven up by extending the feature space to the last n exchanges, which would take into account a larger dialogue history for the decision (cf. (Schmitt et al., 2010b)). The presented model can principally be trained on data from any dialogue system; however, we did not yet deliver the proof that the present model trained on Let's Go data is general enough for cross-domain and cross-system application without significant performance loss. Due to the general character of the ten most relevant features (cf. Table 3), portability can at least be assumed - without the need for domain-dependent and system-dependent re-training.

11 Acknowledgements

We would like to thank Maxine Eskenazi, Alan Black, Lori Levin, Rita Singh, Antoine Raux and Brian Langner from the Let's Go Lab at Carnegie Mellon University, Pittsburgh, for providing the Let's Go Sample Corpus. Further we would like to thank the reviewers for their constructive advices.

The research leading to these results has received funding from the Transregional Collaborative Research Centre SFB/TRR 62 "Companion-Technology for Cognitive Technical Systems" funded by the German Research Foundation (DFG).

References

K. P. Bennett and C. Campbell. 2000. Support vector machines: Hype or hallelujah? *Journal of SIGKDD Explorations*, 2(2):1–13.

W. J. Doll and G. Torkzadeh. 1991. The measurement of end-user computing satisfaction: theoretical and methodological issues. *MIS Q.*, 15:5–10, March.

K.-P. Engelbrecht, F. Gödde, F. Hartard, H. Ketabdar, and S. Möller. 2009. Modeling user satisfaction with hidden markov model. In *Proc. of SIGDIAL 2009 Conference*, pages 170–177. ACL.

S. Hara, N. Kitaoka, and K. Takeda. 2010. Estimation method of user satisfaction using n-gram-based dialog history model for spoken dialog system. In *Proc. of the Seventh conference on International Language Resources and Evaluation (LREC'10)*, Valletta, Malta.

R. Higashinaka, Y. Minami, K. Dohsaka, and T. Meguro. 2010a. Issues in predicting user satisfaction transitions in dialogues: Individual differences, evaluation criteria, and prediction models. In *Spoken Dialogue Systems for Ambient Environments*, Lecture Notes in Computer Science, pages 48–60. Springer Berlin / Heidelberg.

R. Higashinaka, Y. Minami, K. Dohsaka, and T. Meguro. 2010b. Modeling user satisfaction transitions in dialogues from overall ratings. In *Proceedings of the SIGDIAL 2010 Conference*, pages 18–27, Tokyo, Japan, September. ACL.

ISO. 1998. *Ergonomic requirements for office work with visual display terminals (VDTs), Part 11: Guidance on usability*. International Standardization Organization (ISO).

B. Ives, M. H. Olson, and J. J. Baroudi. 1983. The measurement of user information satisfaction. *Commun. ACM*, 26:785–793.

D. Larcker and V. P. Lessig. 1980. Perceived usefulness of information: A psychometric examination. *Decision Sciences*, pages 121–134, November.

G. Lindgaard and C. Dudek. 2003. What is this evasive beast we call user satisfaction? *Interacting with Computers*, 15(3):429–452.

J. C. Platt, 1999. *Fast training of support vector machines using sequential minimal optimization*, pages 185–208. MIT Press, Cambridge, MA, USA.

A. Raux, D. Bohus, B. Langner, A. W. Black, and M. Eskenazi. 2006. Doing research on a deployed spoken dialogue system: One year of lets go! experience. In *Proc. of the International Conference on Speech and Language Processing (ICSLP)*.

A. Schmitt, C. Hank, and J. Liscombe. 2008. Detecting problematic calls with automated agents. In *4th IEEE Tutorial and Research Workshop Perception and Interactive Technologies for Speech-Based Systems*, Irsee (Germany), June.

Alexander Schmitt, Tobias Heinroth, and Jackson Liscombe. 2009. On nomatchs, noinputs and bargeins: Do non-acoustic features support anger detection? In *Proceedings of the 10th Annual SIGDIAL Meeting on Discourse and Dialogue, SigDial Conference 2009*, London (UK), September. Association for Computational Linguistics.

Alexander Schmitt, Tim Polzehl, and Wolfgang Minker. 2010a. Facing reality: Simulating deployment of anger recognition in ivr systems. In *Second International Workshop on Spoken Dialogue Systems (IWSDS)*, September.

Alexander Schmitt, Michael Scholz, Wolfgang Minker, Jackson Liscombe, and David Sündermann. 2010b. Is it possible to predict task completion in automated troubleshooters? In *Proc. of the International Conference on Speech and Language Processing (ICSLP)*.

Marilyn Walker, Candace Kamm, and Diane Litman. 2000. Towards developing general models of usability with paradise. *Nat. Lang. Eng.*, 6(3-4):363–377.

Appendix

1	Welcome to the CMU Let's Go bus information system.
2	To get help at any time, just say Help or press zero.
3	What can I do for you?
	<DTMF-Zero>
4	I am an automated spoken dialogue system that can give you schedule information for bus routes in Pittsburgh's East End. You can ask me about the following buses: 28X, 54C, 56U, 59U, 61A, 61B, 61C, 61D, 61F, 64A, 69A, and 501.
5	What bus schedule information are you looking for?
6	For example, you can say, when is the next 28X from DOWNTOWN to THE AIRPORT? or I'd like to go from MCKEESPORT to HOMESTEAD tomorrow at 10 a.m..
	28X
7	The 56C . Is this correct?
	No, 28X
8	What can I do for you?
	I want to know whether /uh/ tomorrow the bus is available or not.
9	Leaving at 11 p.m. . Did I get that right?
	No, I just want to know is there any bus service for 28X tomorrow.
10	Please use shorter answers because I have trouble understanding long sentences.
11	Leaving at 11 p.m. . Is this correct?
	On twenty third november.
12	Leaving at 11 p.m. . Is this correct?
	No, I want to know the schedule on twenty third november
13	Leaving at 2 a.m. . Did I get that right?
	<noise>
14	If you want to leave at 2 a.m. say yes or press one, otherwise say no or press three.
	no <noise>
15	Going to NORTH AND CEDAR. Did I get that right?
	28x going to airport at seven a.m.
16	Please use shorter answers because I have trouble understanding long sentences.
17	Going to NORTH AND CEDAR. Is this correct?
	No.
18	Leaving from DYNAMO. Is this correct?
	No.
19	Leaving from DYNAMO. Is this correct?
	Leaving to airport.
20	Leaving from AIRPORT . Did I get that right?
	yes
21	Right
22	Where are you going?
	To airport.
23	Going to AIRPORT. Did I get that right?
	yeah, yep
24	Okay
25	When would you like to travel?
	yes
26	When would you like to travel?
	Twenty third November.
27	When would you like to travel?
	Tomorrow.
28	At what time do you wanna travel?
	Seven a.m.
29	Leaving at 7 a.m. . Is this correct?
	yep
30	Alright
31	Just a minute. I'll look that up.
32	AIRPORT and AIRPORT are both the same stop. Please provide a different start or end point.
33	To ask about a different trip, you can say, start a new query. If you are finished, you can say goodbye.
	Yes.
34	You can say start a new query, or goodbye.
	No.
35	To ask about a different trip, you can say, start a new query. If you are finished, you can say goodbye.
	<noise>
36	You can say start a new query, or goodbye.
	<noise>
	You can say start a new query, or goodbye.
	<hangup>

Table 5: Example dialogue (ID: 2061122025) from the CMU Let's Go System (2006 corpus) with low Interaction Quality. The user utterances are printed in italic.

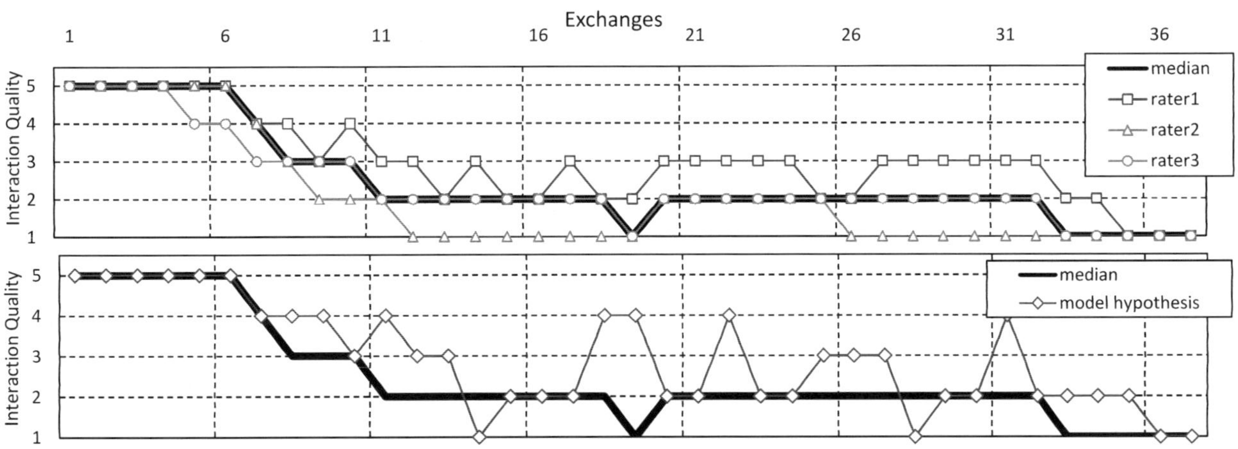

Figure 2: Upper chart: Turn-wise Interaction Quality (IQ) annotation from 3 raters. The final label is the median of all three opinions. Lower chart: median reference vs. hypothesis of the model trained with *AUTO* feature set.

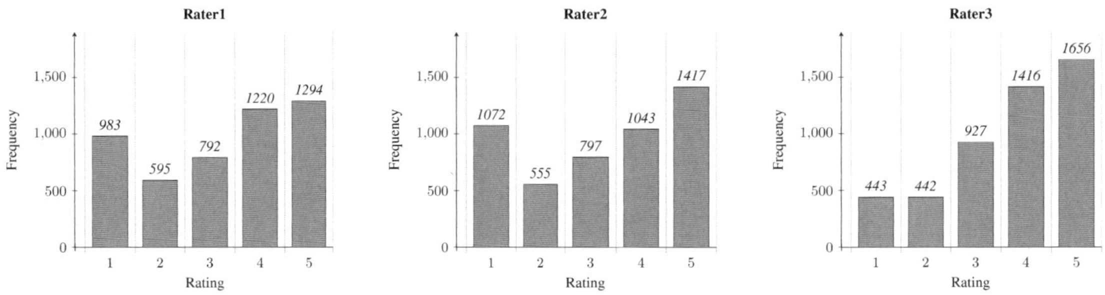

Figure 3: Rating distribution for Interaction Quality within the Let's Go Corpus for each rater.

Table 6: Rater guidelines for annotating Interaction Quality.

Rule	Description
1.	The rater should try to mirror the users point of view on the interaction as objectively as possible.
2.	An exchange consists of the system prompt and the user response. Due to system design, the latter is not always present.
3.	The IQ score is defined on a 5-point scale with "1=bad", "2=poor", "3=fair", "4=good" and "5=excellent".
4.	The Interaction Quality is to be rated for each exchange in the dialogue. The history of the dialogue should be kept in mind when assigning the score. For example, a dialogue that has proceeded fairly poor for a long time, should require some time to recover.
5.	A dialogue always starts with an Interaction Quality score of "5".
6.	The first user input should also be rated with 5, since until this moment, no rateable interaction has taken place.
7.	A request for help does not invariably cause a lower Interaction Quality, but can result in it.
8.	In general, the score from one exchange to the following exchange is increased or decreased by one point at the most.
9.	Exceptions, where the score can be decreased by two points are e.g. hot anger or sudden frustration. The rater's perception is decisive here.
10.	Also, if the dialogue obviously collapses due to system or user behavior, the score can be set to "1" immediately. An example herefore is a reasonable frustrated sudden hang-up.
11.	Anger does not need to influence the score, but can. The rater should try to figure out whether anger was caused by the dialogue behavior or not.
12.	In the case a user realizes that he should adapt his dialogue strategy to obtain the desired result or information and succeeded that way, the Interaction Quality score can be raised up to two points per turn. In other words, the user realizes that he caused the poor Interaction Quality by himself.
13.	If the system does not reply with a bus schedule to a specific user query and prompts that the request is out of scope, this can nevertheless be considered as "task completed". Therefore this does not need to affect the Interaction Quality.
14.	If a dialogue consists of several independent queries, each query's quality is to be rated independently. The former dialogue history should not be considered when a new query begins. However, the score provided for the first exchange should be equal to the last label of the previous query.
15.	If a dialogue proceeds fairly poor for a long time, the rater should consider to increase the score more slowly if the dialogue starts to recover. Also, in general, he should observe the remaining dialogue more critical.
16.	If a constantly low-quality dialogue finishes with a reasonable result, the Interaction Quality can be increased.

Topics as Contextual Indicators for Word Choice in SMS Conversations

Ute Winter[1], Roni Ben-Aharon, Daniel Chernobrov, Ron M Hecht[1]

[1]GM Advanced Technical Center, HaManofim Street 11, Herzeliya 46725, Israel

ute.winter@gm.com, r.ben.aharon@gmail.com,

daniel-cher@hotmail.com, ron.hecht@gm.com

Abstract

SMS dictation by voice is becoming a viable alternative providing a convenient method for texting in a variety of environments. Contextual knowledge should be used to improve performance. We propose to add topic knowledge as part of the contextual awareness of both texting partners during SMS conversations. Topics can be used for speech applications, if the relation between the conversed topics and the choice of words in SMS dialogs is measurable. In this study, we collected an SMS corpus, developed a topic annotation scheme, and built a topic hierarchy in a tree structure. We validated our topic assignments and tree structure by the Agglomerative Information Bottleneck method, which also proved the measurability of the interrelation between topics and wording. To quantify this relation we propose a naïve classification method based on the calculation of topic distinctive word lists and compare the classifiers' topic recognition capabilities for SMS dialogs with unigram language models. The results demonstrate that the relation between topic and wording is significant and can be integrated into SMS dictation.

1 Introduction

One of the largest growth areas in communication is the Short Message Service (SMS) or text messaging, as it is more popularly known. SMS grew out of what was initially a by-product of the mobile phone industry (Agar, 2003; Goggin, 2006). In fact, by 2009 text messaging has become the most frequently used communication means among teens in the US, supported by the mobile phone industry offering unlimited texting plans (Lenhart et. al., 2010).

For many reasons, voice enabled texting has become a desirable alternative in a variety of mobile scenarios. The number of speech applications for mobile phones including texting by voice is constantly growing. However, the challenges for SMS dictation by voice are multifold, from particular noise conditions, to the use of vocabulary and domain specific language, the dialogical nature of text messaging (Thurlow and Poff, 2009), and to error correction of imperfect recognition results.

Achieving a high and robust performance is crucial for the success of the application. For this purpose additional contextual factors can be integrated into the recognition process. One possible factor, the conversed topic, has influence on the speaker's choice of words. Hence, it is an important contextual factor for the prediction of the speaker's wording, since it originates in the speaker's mental concepts during a dialog situation, which is the nature of texting.

To date, research on text messaging has primarily examined socio-linguistic phenomena (e.g., Thurlow, 2003). With respect to language and communication, text messaging is still an underexamined research area. Thurlow and Poff (2009) provide a comprehensive overview of existing literature about SMS in linguistics. Moreover, there exists noteworthy work on SMS text normalization (Aw et. al., 2006; Fairon and Paumier, 2006; Cook and Stevenson, 2009; Kobus et. al., 2008; Pennell and Liu, 2010), for instance for the purpose of Machine Translation, Text-to-Speech engines or spell checking, work on SMS based question answering

Proceedings of the SIGDIAL 2011: the 12th Annual Meeting of the Special Interest Group on Discourse and Dialogue, pages 185–193, Portland, Oregon, June 17-18, 2011. ©2011 Association for Computational Linguistics services (Kothari, 2009), and work on predefined SMS replies in automobiles (Wu et. al., 2010). However, conversed topics in the context of SMS discourse have not been examined in the literature, neither in linguistics nor for any Natural Language Processing applications.

Hence, in this paper we have developed a new approach to make topics useful as context knowledge for SMS dictation by voice. We describe topic annotation of a novel SMS corpus and study the influence which SMS dialog topics may have on the choice of words. Based on the results, we are able to estimate and initially quantify its impact. This research can serve as the basis for developing algorithms that use topic knowledge for SMS dictation in speech applications.

2 Topic Annotation for SMS

2.1 SMS Corpus in US English

SMS data was collected from 250 participants who conversed with another 900. Participants were distributed almost evenly across gender, two age groups, and four US regions. Participants under 30 years comprised 48% of the dataset, and participants over 30 years comprised 52% of the dataset. Within each of these two age groups, there were equal number of men and women. The demographic spread contained datasets from participants from the various regions in the USA: east coast 19%, west coast 24%, central 29%, and south 28%.

The corpus dataset contains a total number of more than 51,000 messages, chosen randomly from a significantly larger set of data, for which participants provided authentic SMS conversations from their mobile phones to online SMS backup services. Besides demographic constraints, all text messages are part of SMS conversations, each composed at least by one message and a textual response, to preserve a contextual authentic situation. A conversation is considered to be ended if a time frame of 4 hours elapses without a response. The average length of SMS conversations in the corpus is between 8-9 messages, distributed over a notably higher number of shorter conversions than longer dialogs. Altogether the corpus contains more than 5800 conversations.

Personal information of the SMS conversations was removed. Nonetheless the corpus itself is currently not published, because identifying information can be indirectly present in SMS dialogs.

The SMS corpus is semi-automatically normalized following a general guideline to transform each texted message into one which could be dictated by the user. For all following research the normalized rather than the raw SMS textual utterances are used.

Table 1 shows representative examples for text normalization.

Raw	Normalized
Yea b workin for hospice	yeah be working for hospice
I am at vetran @at@8 am	I am at Veteran at eight ei-em
Lets go 2 eat	Let's go to eat
You wanna go to da b walk or sumthin?	You wanna go to the bee walk or something?

Table 1: Text messages in raw and normalized format.

2.2 Topic Annotation Method

A key point for usefulness of an annotated corpus is the abstraction which maps SMS conversations present in the corpus to an abstract model serving the research goals (Wallis and Nelson, 2001; Mc Enery et. al., 2006). In our research, the corpus shall be used to explore to what extent the knowledge of one or more discussed topics, for which both SMS dialog partners try to make progress, can contribute to the performance of a speech recognition engine, where we expect the engine to be based on Statistical Language Models (SLM). Consequently, the annotation needs to enable us to trace a path from discussed topics to the choice of words and phrases in SMS conversations. This abstraction leads to our definition of the term topic and to guidelines for the annotation which are identified to be essential, when incorporating topics into speech recognition.

Other than an agreement on "what is being talked about", the definition of topic in linguistics is a matter of viewpoint and dispute (Levinson, 1983; Li and Thompson, 1976; Chafe, 1976; Molnár, 1993; Stutterheim, 1997). Moreover, a literature review has not revealed existing topic annotations which can be used for our purpose (Mc Enery et. al., 2006; Meyer, 2002). Since the intention is to build a task driven, problem oriented annotation scheme we further specify a discourse topic as observable content or story line which discourse partners follow up in an SMS conversation. Hence, we understand a topic foremost as an attribute of an SMS dialog rather than of a single SMS, or of a phrase within the dialog. We assign at least one topic to each dialog. Since dialogs can in fact contain several distinct topics, we assign all explicitly mentioned topics to a conversation and mark separately all SMS which belong doubtlessly to each topic in the context of the conversation,

Topics describe the content only, not any other level of discourse. The example in figure 1 shows a conversation with the topic 'meeting arrangement'.

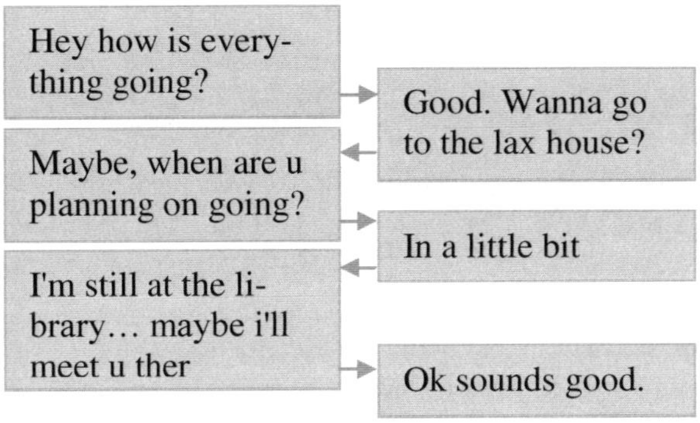

Figure 1: Example of SMS dialog about "meeting arrangement".

2.3 Topic Annotation Procedure

Discourse topics are highly domain dependent in their nature and may differ from the SMS domain to other domains, even to computer mediated communication services, like e-mail, Twitter, or Instant Messaging. Because of that, the list of SMS relevant topics evolves from the data itself. Additionally the list of possible topics always remains an open tag list, although one can expect recurring topics after a while with sparse extension of an existing topic list. Hence, the approach for annotating the SMS corpus must be manual. For this purpose a team of four annotators marked the conversations with the help of an annotation tool developed specifically for the topic annotation. To ensure annotator agreement a linguist verified and confirmed the growing topic list and all topic assignments in several iterations. Further annotation of a larger corpus may be semi-automated based on the achieved topic list.

Assigning topics to a dialog remains intuitive to a certain extent, because any mutual understanding of the dialog's content and pragmatic meaning is supported by social cues, situation awareness and world knowledge of dialog partners (Levinson, 1983; Lambert and Carberry, 1992). These knowledge dimensions need to be reconstituted during the annotation process, when assigning a new topic. One criterion is to ask if the topic is distinct from other topics with regard to describing pieces of our world knowledge dimensions, e.g. scripts and events that people repeatedly experience, or subjects, they are recurrently dealing with.

Furthermore, a task driven approach demands to determine the level of specialization and detail for topics. Even if broad topics, such as "food" or "appointment", may prove themselves to be distinct and meaningful enough for speech recognition, the annotation is done to one degree more detailed. Each topic is composed by a term and one restrictive attribute which divides a major topic into more distinctive topics. Thus "appointment" appears in the corpus divided into "cancel appointment", "attending an appointment", "meeting arrangements", and other. The advantage of the annotation procedure is twofold; it leads to a list of topics, which can be depicted in a tree structure with several levels of specialization, and, even though the annotation is targeted to a special problem, there is sufficient information to make the corpus useful for a broader range of research.

3 Corpus Analysis for Topic Usage

3.1 Properties of Topics

SMS conversations may follow up on one or more topics. Multiple topic conversations may make progress on topics even in parallel, either switching topics or addressing both within the same SMS. In general, we avoid topics which are suspected to describe the intention or strategy for the conversation rather than the content. There are a few exceptions, where the topic is implicitly or explicitly present in the dialog not only on content level but also as driving force for texting, e.g. "maintain friendship/relationship" or "small talk" (see example (2) in figure 2). The border cannot be clearly drawn in these cases.

Two topic assignments require explanation. "Small talk" is used for a group of short SMS dialogs, for which one cannot identify a topic. One is able to understand the dialog as a short form of friendship maintenance though, where both parties achieve mutual positive feedback about their current situation, e.g. via salutation. Therefore "small talk" is expected to be of interest regarding word usage contrary to "undefined topic". The latter is assigned to all conversations, where we do not share enough knowledge about the background and situation of the texters to understand and identify the topic of the dialog (example (3) in figure 2).

1 **Missed phone call, planned schedule**

Texter 1: Hi, sorry I missed your call. I'm actually at an appointment right now.
Texter 1: I will call you about 12:45pm. Please answer, so we can finally connect, if not I will call after 17:00.
Texter 2: O.K no problem, call me when you're free :)
Texter 1: The appointment is over, I tried calling you but you didn't answer, will talk when I'm on my way home
Texter 2: Thankyou.

2 **Small talk**

Texter 1: What's up?
Texter 2: I'm good, u?
Texter 1: I'm fine, talk to you later
Texter 2: Sure :)

3 **Topic undefined**

Texter 1: df
Texter 2: what?
Texter 1: don't forget
Texter 2: Lol :-) I won't

Figure 2: SMS dialogs with (1) multiple topics, (2) small talk, and (3) undefined topic.

All in all, the corpus contains 42.1% of dialogs with one annotated topic and 46.6% with multiple topics. The remaining 11.3% of dialogs are tagged as "undefined".

3.2 Building a Topic Tree

The identification of similar or related topics in our corpus allow for grouping them together in specific topic clusters, such as "human relations", "technology", and "transportation", and represent them in a tree structure hierarchy. The assignment to a topic cluster for each topic is determined by the relation between topics, which humans define based on their world knowledge and based on the semantic meaning of the topic.

The topic tree hierarchy consists of four levels. The nodes in the first two levels build the tree structure and represent the topic clusters. Therefore they have not been used during the annotation process. Only from level three and above the topic names are assigned to the corpus and may be leaves of the tree. A forth level is used, when third level topics are frequently used in SMS dialogs and can further be divided into meaningful sub topics.

Figure 3: Topic tree branch related to "shopping".

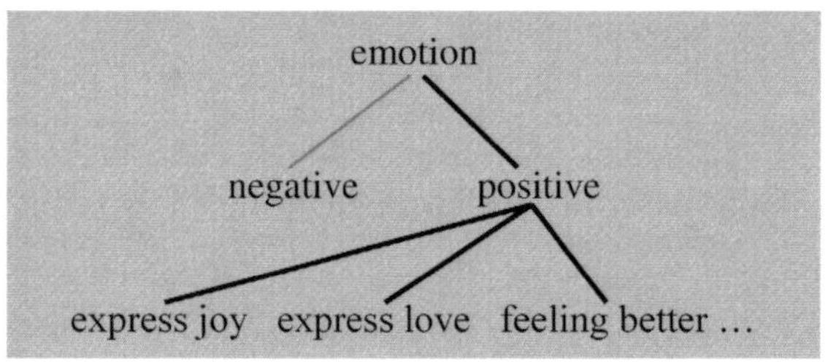

Figure 4: Topic tree branch for "positive emotion".

3.3 Topic Distribution in SMS Corpus

87.1% of all text messages are categorized in nine preferably conversed topic clusters (see figure 5), the remaining messages belong either to SMS dialogs, where the topic is labeled as undefined, or to miscellaneous, rarely conversed topics, e.g. "weather" or "religious belief".

More than 55% of all text messages are motivated by interpersonal and emotional matters. About 45% of all text messages deal with "human relations", mainly including sub topics regarding relation maintenance (36% of "human relations", e.g. "make promise", "make apology", "health condition", "small talk", a. o.), regarding relations with friends (14%), concerning relationship issues with a partner (11%). The latter 10% converse about negative or positive emotions, nearly 50% of these dialogs expressing love. SMS dialogs from "human relations" contain 9.3 messages per dialog in the average, which is significantly more than the average of 4-6 messages in all other topic clusters.

The second most discussed topic is "activities & events" (14% of all messages), such as "going out" (32% of "activities & events" labeled messages), or "going shopping" (15%). Interestingly, the topic of "appointment & scheduling" is only the third most popular, consisting of less than 13% of all text messages.

Figure 5 shows the topic distribution in the corpus with respect to the topic tree's first hierarchy.

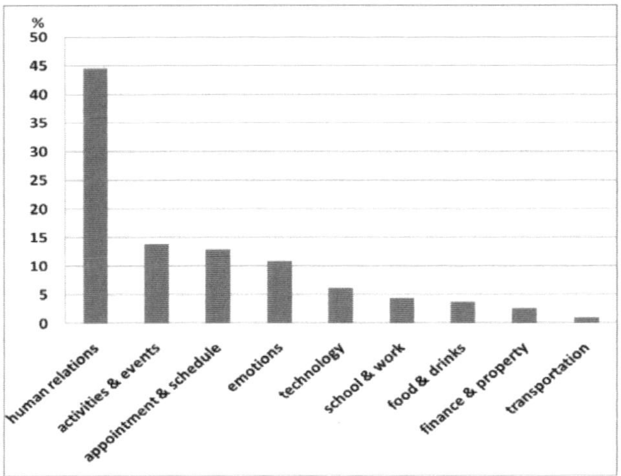

Figure 5: Topic distribution on first tree level.

Thurlow (2003) has presented a study about the communicative intent of US English text messages, describing their functional orientation rather than the content. Thurlow's findings concur in that the amount of SMS with relational and intimate orientation vs. transactional orientation is similar to the amount of SMS with interpersonal and emotional content vs. all other topic clusters.

Finally, we examine if distribution differences depend on the demographic data of the users regarding gender, age groups (18-23, 24-28, 29-35, 36-42) and regions. Users older than 42 years are not taken into account because of the limited number of text messages in the corpus.

Generally, males and females talk about the same topics in SMS conversations through all age groups and regions. However, there are still some differences between those groups worth mentioning and shown in figure 6.

While interpersonal and emotional text messages together are present in fairly equal quantity for both gender groups, females tend to express their "emotion" via text messages much more frequently than males (12.5% compared to 8.5%); likely on the expense of non-emotional "human relations" messages (46.8% for males compared to 41.9%). Furthermore, males and females have contradicting trends in "emotion" talk over ages. Females tend to express emotions more with age progression, while males have the opposite tendency. In both genders, the corpus suggests a tradeoff between the topics "human relations" and "emotion", i.e. age may change the portion of one topic on the expense of the other one.

4 Relation between Topic and Wording

4.1 Automated Validation of Topic Tree

A human annotation process is highly effective due to people's ability to exploit their mental knowledge base and mind concepts, and thus a broad range of information sources. However, even

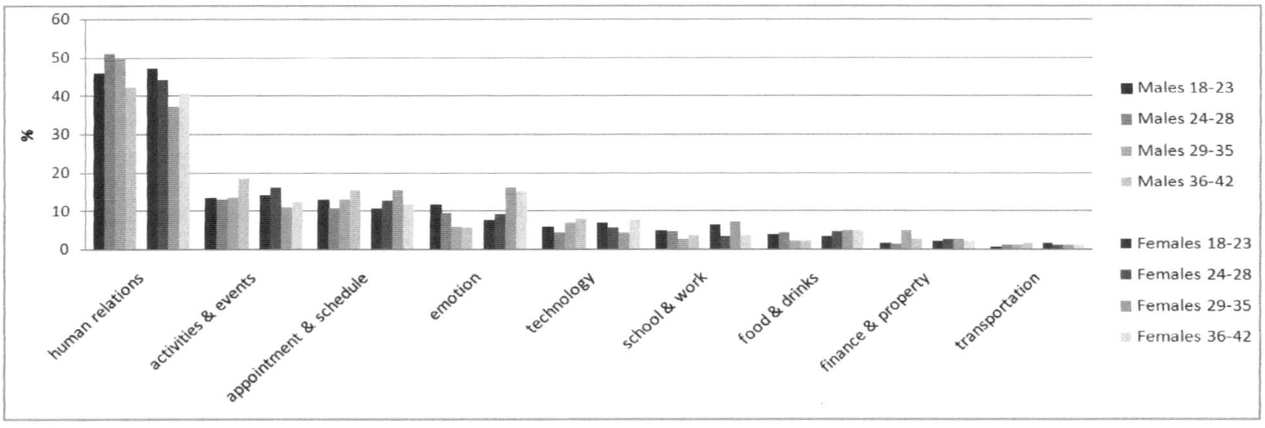

Figure 6: Topic distribution by gender (males left, females right) and age groups

in a most rigorous procedure errors may occur, especially regarding annotation and tree consistency. Therefore we need to verify the quality of the annotation. Additionally, we want to ensure that relevant algorithms can trace the interrelation between topics and the choice of words in SMS.

In order to verify both requirements, we perform an automatic validation by applying a nuance (Hecht et al., 2009) of the Agglomerative Information Bottleneck (AIB) method (Tishby et al., 1999; Slonim and Tishby, 2000). This derivative of the AIB is a hierarchical clustering algorithm, and as such, it produces a hierarchical topic tree.

The clustering starts with each lower level topic as a singleton. In an iterative process, the two closest topics are merged to form a larger topic, where the two closest topics are defined as the ones that minimize the AIB functional (Eq. 1). The process ends when all topics are merged into a single topic.

$$L[p(\hat{x}|x)] = I(X;\hat{X}) - \beta I(Y;\hat{X}) \qquad (1)$$

X, Y and $\hat{X}$ are the set of topics, set of words and clustered set of topics respectively. $I(A;B)$ is the mutual information between A and B.

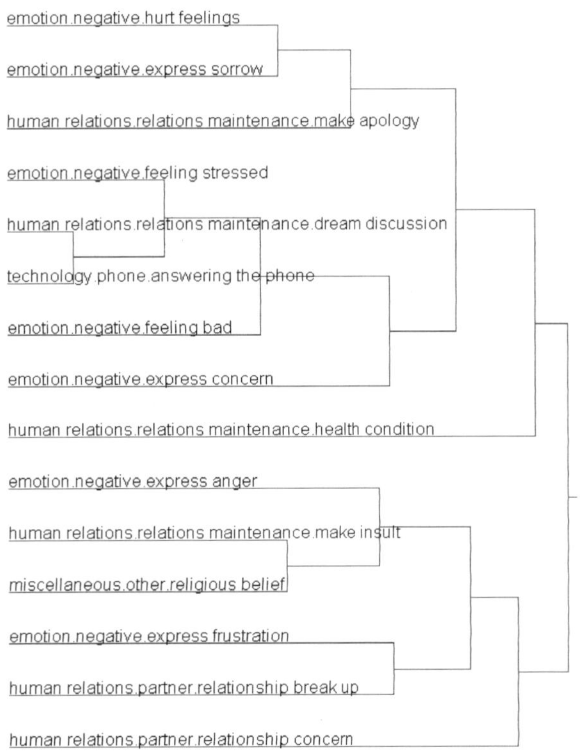

Figure 7: Tree branch of the hierarchical clustering of topics into groups.

Intuitively, the function tries to achieve two goals simultaneously. It minimizes $I(X;\hat{X})$ which can be interpreted as finding the most compact topic representation and at the same time it maximizes $I(Y;\hat{X})$ which can be interpreted as finding the most indicative subset of topics. These two goals contradict one another. Therefore a tradeoff parameter β is added.

Presenting the entire AIB tree is not feasible in this paper. In order to provide some intuition, a sub tree is shown in figure 7. Briefly, each AIB tree branch shows a distribution of topics that is mostly in line with the hand crafted topic tree. Even sentiments are clustered (negative sentiment for all lower level topics in figure 7), a superior achievement to the manual topic tree, where this is done only for "emotion". Moreover, it becomes evident that the interrelation between topics and wording in SMS can likely be captured automatically.

4.2 Method for Relation Discovery

Being confident regarding automatic computation, we can strive for more and aim to discover the interrelation between topics and wording in detail. Any vocabulary used in SMS dialogs can intuitively be viewed as containing information which points to one or a limited group of conversed topics, or as being general vocabulary with respect to topic distinctiveness. Such a view point entails questions. How can we extract a list of distinctive words per topic; words which are dominant in a certain topic but subordinate in others respectively? To what extent are topic distinctive words still ambiguous and are assigned to more than one topic? And ultimately, can we use topic distinctive vocabulary to recognize a list of conversed topics for each SMS dialog based on its choice of words?

Our method evolves from the questions as follows: First, we categorize the SMS vocabulary into topic distinctive vs. general vocabulary by introducing an algorithm which uses topic information as qualitative measurement to extract a list of distinctive words operating as classifiers for topics. In a second step we evaluate for each topic to what extent topic distinctive word list classifiers can recognize topics in SMS dialogs. Finally we compare the classifiers' topic recognition capabilities with unigram language models. We use only the nine first level topic clusters to guarantee that the amount of available dialogs per topic is sufficient.

4.3 Topic Distinctive Vocabulary

To categorize the vocabulary we calculate for each word w_i with at least 4 occurrences in the corpus and topic t_j the ratio between word frequency in the topic and general word frequency in the corpus (known as Term Frequency/Collection Frequency Measure) normalized by the topic size (Eq. 2):

$$Tf \circ Cf(w_i, t_j) = \frac{freq_{t_j}(w_i)}{freq_{corpus}(w_i)} * \frac{1}{size(t_j)} = \frac{count(w_i, t_j)}{\sum_l count(w_i, t_l) * \sum_m count(w_m, t_j)} \quad (2)$$

After scores are calculated for all words, we sort the words for each topic from their highest to lowest score. Then we assign a topic dependent threshold for each topic determined by a Receiver Operating Characteristic (ROC) analysis as described in 4.4. All words above the threshold belong to the distinctive word set (DWS) per topic. In additionally conducted experiments with the corpus this method has proven to outperform other alternatives, such as TF*IDF or Term Discrimination Models (Salton et. al., 1975).

transportation	finance & property	emotion
lane	loan	loss
boarding	payments	xox
tires	printing	beyond
flight	sander	childish
wheel	cheque	love
license	paypal	bitching
roads	discount	mentally
battery	invoice	soo
plane	price	stressed
exit	dollars	nerves

Table 2: Examples of topic distinctive words.

Table 2 illustrates examples of high-scored retrieved distinctive words from several topics. It becomes evident that words with high scores are related to a topic in our intuition or mental concepts. However, frequently used general words, such as pronouns, prepositions, and common nouns, do not receive high scores, because of their vast number of occurrences in other topics, e.g. "never", "flat", "boy", "you", or "from". Topics that are more descriptive or transactional in their orientation, such as "transportation" or "finance", generate better content distinctive word sets than the ones with relational intent, such as "emotion".

4.4 Topic Recognition by Word Sets

In order to determine optimal thresholds (see 4.3) and to analyze the coverage and distinctiveness of the word sets, we divide the corpus into a training batch (90% of all messages) and a test batch (10%). The training batch is used for the calculation of word scores as described in 4.3. By iteratively increasing the score threshold which defines a word set, we calculate per iteration the amount of dialogs from the test batch containing at least one word of the set, for dialogs annotated with the affiliated topic as well as for dialogs tagged differently. Consequently, ROC curves are created for all topics. This process is performed in a cross validation manner (10-fold).

Figure 8 shows the ROC curves for the topics "human relations", "activities & events", "finance & property", and "food & drinks", averaged over the 10-fold iterations.

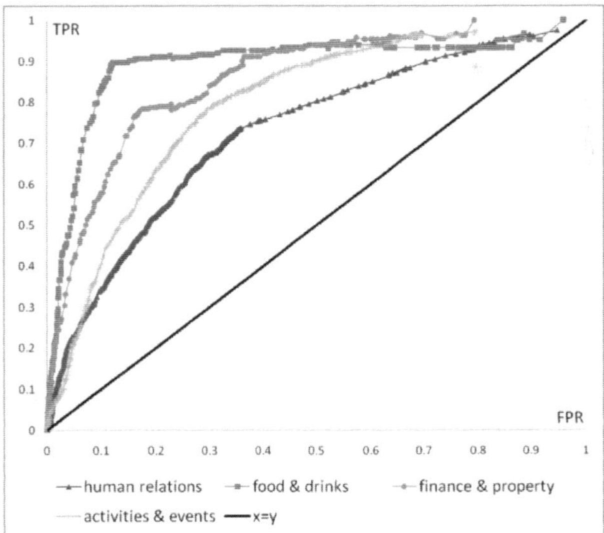

Figure 8: ROC curves for selected topics including best and worst performing topics with x axes for false positive rate (FPR) and y axes for true positive rate (TPR).

These results show that once appropriate thresholds are chosen, relatively small DWS, mostly ranging between 60-120 words per set, have the capability of achieving a true positive rate (TPR, also known as recall) of 80.3% for topic dialogs with an average false positive rate (FPR, also known as fall-out) of 26.8%, even with a relatively naïve classification method. Table 3 provides detailed results of TPR and FPR. Topic DWS for more descriptive or transactional topics (e.g. "transportation", "food & drinks") manage to distinguish better than relational targeted topics, such as "emotion" and "human relations", since words like "love", "babe", or "thank" are highly related to the "emotion" topic, but also appear in many other topics. Hence, these words are increasing the FPR.

Eventually, the word sets chosen by optimal thresholds allow us to quantify topic recognition of dialogs. We automatically assign topics to each dialog in the corpus according to the described algorithm. Then we compare these topics to the manually annotated topics and measure recall and precision per dialog, denoted (Eq. 3):

$$recall = \frac{\#correct\_matched\_topics}{\#annotated\_topics} \qquad prec = \frac{\#correct\_matched\_topics}{\#matched\_topics} \tag{3}$$

The average recall and precision rates over all dialogs are 73.5% and 44.3%, respectively. Taking into account the complexity of the recognition task due to the possibility of multiple topic assignment for each dialog, the results strengthen the hypothesis of the positively measureable interrelation between topics and wording.

4.5 Comparison to Full Vocabulary Models

Finally, we wish to better understand the impact of DWS, in comparison to the general language derived from the topic text, which is motivated by the fact that speech applications rely on SLMs. To this end, we construct a unigram language model binary classifier for each topic as baseline and perform a 10-fold cross validation classification task, to identify whether a given dialog is related to the topic or not, using the following formula (Eq. 4), where D_i is the ith dialog and M_t is the language model of topic t:

$$\begin{aligned} topic^*(D_i) &= \underset{t \in topic, topic}{\arg\max}(D_i \mid M_t) \\ &= \underset{t \in topic, topic}{\arg\max}\left(\prod_{w \in D_i} p(w \mid M_t)\right) \end{aligned} \tag{4}$$

Table 3 summarizes the results of TPR and FPR of the two approaches. As expected, the DWS approach suffers from a higher FPR, due to a lack of weights and relative comparisons to other classes. Since the differences in FPR between the two methods are not immense, we conclude that our chosen word sets are indeed distinctive, and with proper tuning have the potential of achieving better results. On the other hand, the DWS approach manages to outperform language models in terms of TPR. Hence, most of the information needed for the identification of dialog topics is provided by distinctive words to a significant higher extent as by the rest of the vocabulary.

Topic	DWS		Language models	
	TPR	FPR	TPR	FPR
Activities & events	81.9	34.7	64.1	22.8
Appoint. & schedule	69.5	31.0	82.6	21.4
Transportation	78.7	17.3	68.8	9.8
Finance & property	77.9	17.0	76.5	9.6
Food & drinks	88.4	11.7	74.1	10.6
School & work	80.9	22.4	54.3	14.0
Technology	92.4	28.7	75.5	12.6
Emotion	80.7	34.4	71.3	12.7
Human relation	72.2	34.7	69.8	20.8
	80.3	**26.8**	**70.7**	**14.9**

Table 3: True and false positive rates for all topics using DWS classification and language models.

5 Conclusion

The primary motivation of this study has been to estimate and facilitate the potential integration of contextual knowledge, in particular topics, into SMS dictation by voice. We have identified the interrelation between conversed topics and the choice of words in SMS dialogs as a key property, which needs to be quantified. After creating an annotated corpus and developing a classification method based on topic distinctive word lists, we have presented initial, promising results, which encourage further research.

Our study exposes also some challenges, which may not be easy to address. It would be useful to have a larger annotated corpus. Fully automated annotation of topics seems hardly achievable in view of our results. We may therefore rely on semi-supervised or unsupervised learning algorithms. Moreover, the study explores the relation of topics to single words. It needs to be enhanced to phrases, because SMS dictation by voice relies on higher order n-gram SLMs.

In summary, when taking the next step and moving towards speech applications, we expect performance improvement after making topic knowledge useful for SMS dictation.

References

Agar, Jon (2003). Constant touch: A global history of the mobile phone. Cambridge, UK: Icon Books.

Aw, AiTi, Zhang, Min, Xiao, Juan & Su, Jian (2006). A phrase-based statistical model for SMS text normalization. In Proceedings of COLING/ACL, Sidney, AU.

Chafe, Wallace (1976). Givenness, contrastiveness, definiteness, subjects, topics, and point of view. In Li, Charles N. (Ed.), Subject and Topic (pp. 25-55). New York: Academic Press.

Cook, Paul & Stevenson, Suzanne (2009). An unsupervised model for text message normalization. In Proceedings of the NAACL HLT, Boulder, CO.

Fairon, Cédrick & Paumier, Sébastien (2006). A translated corpus of 30,000 French SMS. In Proceedings of LREC, Genova

Goggin, Gerard (2006). Cell phone culture: Mobile technology in everyday life. New York: Routledge.

Hecht, Ron M., et. al. (2009). Information Bottleneck based age verification. In Proceedings of Interspeech, Brighton, UK.

Kobus, Catherine, Yvon, Francois & Damnati, Geraldine (2008). Normalizing SMS: are two metaphors better than one? In Proceedings of COLING, Manchester, UK.

Kothari, Govind, Negi, Sumit & Faruquie, Tanveer A. (2009). SMS based interface for FAQ retrieval. In Proceedings of ACL, Singapore.

Lambert, Lynn & Carberry, Sandra (1992). Using linguistic, world, and contextual knowledge in a plan recognition model of dialogue. In Proceedings of the 14th International Conference on Computational Linguistics.

Lenhart, Amanda, et. al. (2010). Teens and mobile phones. From Pew Research Center http://pewinternet.org/Reports/2010/Teens-and-Mobile-Phones.aspx

Levinson, Stephen C. (1983). Pragmatics. Cambridge: Cambridge University Press.

Li, Charles N. & Thompson, Sandra A. (1976). Subject and topic. A new typology of languages. In Li, Charles N. (Ed.), Subject and Topic (pp. 457-490). New York: Academic Press.

McEnery, Tony, Xiao, Richard & Tono, Yukio (2006). Corpus-based language studies. An advanced resource book. London, New York: Routledge.

Meyer, Charles F. (2002). English corpus linguistics. An introduction. Cambridge: Cambridge University Press.

Molnár, Valería (1993). Zur Pragmatik und Grammatik des Topik-Begriffes. In Reis, Marga (Ed.), Wortstellung und Informationsstruktur (pp. 155-202). Tübingen: Niemeyer.

Pennell, Deana L. & Liu, Yang (2010). Normalization of text messages for text-to-speech. In Proceedings of ICASSP, Dallas, TX.

Salton, Gerard, Wong, Anita & Yang, Chung-Shu (1975). A Vector Space Model for automatic indexing. In Proceedings of Communications of the ACM, 18(11), 613–620.

Slonim, Noam & Tishby, Naftali (2000). Agglomerative Information Bottleneck. In Proceedings of NIPS 12.

Stutterheim, Christiane von (1997). Einige Prinzipien des Textaufbaus. Empirische Untersuchungen zur Produktion mündlicher Texte. Tübingen: Niemeyer.

Thurlow, Crispin (2003). Generation txt? The sociolinguistics of young people's text-messaging. From Discourse Analysis Online http://extra.shu.ac.uk/daol/articles/v1/n1/a3/thurlow2002003-01.html

Thurlow, Crispin & Poff, Michele (2009). The language of text messaging. In Herring, Susan C., Stein, Dieter & Virtanen, Tuija (Eds.), Handbook of the Pragmatics of CMC. Berlin and New York: Mouton de Gruyter.

Tishby, Naftali, Pereira, Fernando C. & Bialek, William (1999). The Information Bottleneck method. In Proceedings of 37th annual Allerton conference on communication, control and computing, Monticello, IL.

Wallis, Sean & Nelson, Gerald (2001). Knowledge discovery in grammatically analysed corpora. Data Mining and Knowledge Discovery, 5(4), 305-335.

Wu, Wei, Ju, Yun-Cheng, Li, Xiao & Wang, Ye-Yi (2010). Paraphrase detection on SMS messages in automobiles. In Proceedings of ICASSP, Dallas, TX.

Multilingual Annotation and Disambiguation of Discourse Connectives for Machine Translation

Thomas Meyer and **Andrei Popescu-Belis**
Idiap Research Institute
Rue Marconi 19, 1920 Martigny, Switzerland
Thomas.Meyer@idiap.ch, Andrei.Popescu-Belis@idiap.ch

Sandrine Zufferey and **Bruno Cartoni**
Department of Linguistics, University of Geneva
Rue de Candolle 2, 1211 Geneva 4, Switzerland
Sandrine.Zufferey@unige.ch, Bruno.Cartoni@unige.ch

Abstract

Many discourse connectives can signal several types of relations between sentences. Their automatic disambiguation, i.e. the labeling of the correct sense of each occurrence, is important for discourse parsing, but could also be helpful to machine translation. We describe new approaches for improving the accuracy of manual annotation of three discourse connectives (two English, one French) by using parallel corpora. An appropriate set of labels for each connective can be found using information from their translations. Our results for automatic disambiguation are state-of-the-art, at up to 85% accuracy using surface features. Using feature analysis, contextual features are shown to be useful across languages and connectives.

1 Introduction

Discourse connectives are generally considered as indicators of discourse structure, relating two sentences of a written or spoken text, and making explicit the rhetorical or coherence relation between them. Leaving aside the cases when connectives are only implicit, the presence of a connective does not unambiguously signal a specific discourse relation. In fact, many connectives can indicate several types of relations between sentences, i.e. they have several possible "senses" in context.

This paper studies the manual and automated disambiguation of three ambiguous connectives in two languages: *alors que* in French, *since* and *while* in English. We will show how the multilingual perspective helps to improve the accuracy of annotation, and how it helps to find appropriate labels for automated processing and MT. Results from automatic annotation experiments, which are close to the state of the art, as well as feature analysis, help to assess the usefulness of the proposed labels.

The paper is organized as follows. Section 2 explains the motivation of our experiments, and offers a wider perspective on our research goals, illustrating them with examples of translation problems which arise from ambiguous discourse connectives. Current resources and methods for discourse annotation are discussed in Section 3. Section 4 analyzes our experiments in manual annotation and in particular the influence of the set of labels on the reliability of annotation. The automatic disambiguation experiments, the features used, the results and the analysis of features are described in Section 5. Section 6 concludes the paper and outlines future work.

2 Explicit Connectives and their Translation

2.1 Three Multi-functional Connectives

Discourse connectives form a functional category of lexical items that are used to mark coherence relations such as *Cause* or *Contrast* between units of discourse. Along with other function words, many connectives appear among the most frequent words, as shown for instance by counts (Cartoni et al., 2011) over the Europarl corpus (Koehn, 2005). The Penn Discourse Treebank (Prasad et al., 2008) (see Section 3.1 below) includes around 100 connective types, but the exact number varies across studies,

Proceedings of the SIGDIAL 2011: the 12th Annual Meeting of the Special Interest Group on Discourse and Dialogue, pages 194–203,
Portland, Oregon, June 17-18, 2011.

depending on the discourse theory used to classify them. Among these types, Pitler et al.(2008) have shown that most of them are unambiguous and easy to identify, but others, especially temporal ones, often signal multiple senses depending on their context.

Following the terminology of Petukhova and Bunt (2009, Section 2), we are interested here in "sequential" multi-functionality, i.e. the fact that the same connective can signal different relations in different contexts. We do not deal with "simultaneous" multi-functionality, i.e. the possibility for a single occurrence to signal several relations, which has been less frequently studied for connectives (see Petukhova and Bunt (2009) for the discourse usage of *and*).

We identified the two English connectives *while* and *since*, along with the French connective *alors que*, as being particularly problematic because they are highly multi-functional, i.e. they can signal multiple senses. For *alors que*, a French database of connectives (LexConn (Roze et al., 2010), see Section 3 below) contains examples of sentences where *alors que* expresses either a *Background* or a *Contrast* relation. For the English connective *since*, Miltsakaki et al. (2005) identified three possible meanings: *Temporal*, *Causal*, and simultaneously *Temporal/Causal*. For *while*, even more senses are observed: *Comparison*, *Contrast*, *Concession*, and *Opposition*. In fact, in the Penn Discourse Treebank, the connective *while* is annotated with more than twenty different senses.

2.2 Wider Research Objectives

Our long-term goal is to identify automatically the senses of connectives for an application to machine translation (MT). Going beyond the labels provided by discourse theories, the goal is thus to find the most appropriate labels in a new multilingual, empirical approach that makes use of parallel corpora to annotate and then learn the various senses of connectives. The disambiguation of such connectives in a source text is crucial for its translation, because each sense may be translated by a different connective and/or syntactical construct in the target language.

More specifically, we hypothesize that correctly labeled connectives are easier to learn and to translate by statistical MT systems than unlabeled ones. To support this hypothesis, we set up an experiment (Meyer, 2011) in which we constrained the translation of the three senses of the discourse connective *while* that were previously annotated as *Temporal*, *Contrast* and *Concession*. The system was forced to use predefined French translations known to be correct, by directly modifying the phrase table of the trained MT system. This modification noticeably helped to improve translation quality and rose the BLEU score by 0.8 for a preliminary test set of 20 sentences.

2.3 Illustration of Mistranslations

Among the connectives that we plan to process in order to improve MT, the three connectives we focus on in this paper are frequent, ambiguous and therefore difficult to translate correctly by MT systems, as illustrated in the following examples.

A first reason why machine translation of connectives can be difficult is that there may be no direct lexical correspondence for the explicit source language connective in the target language, as shown in the reference translation of the first example in Table 1, taken from the Europarl corpus (Koehn, 2005).

EN	*It is also important that we should not leave these indicators floating in the air* ***while*** *congratulating ourselves on the fact that we have produced them.*
FR	*Il est également important de ne pas laisser ces indicateurs flotter,* ***en*** *nous félicit****ant*** *de les avoir instaurés.*
EN	*Finally, and in conclusion, Mr President, with the expiry of the ECSC Treaty, the regulations will have to be reviewed* ***since*** *[causal] I think that the aid system will have to continue beyond 2002 . . .*
FR	**Enfin, et en conclusion, Monsieur le président, à l'expiration du traité ceca, la réglementation devra être revu* ***depuis que*** *[temporal] je pense que le système d'aides devront continuer au-delà de 2002 . . .*
FR	*Oui, bien entendu, sauf que le développement ne se négocie pas,* ***alors que*** *[contrast] le commerce, lui, se négocie.*
EN	**Yes, of course, but development cannot be negotiated,* ***so*** *[causal] that trade can.*
EN	*Between 1998 and 1999, loyalists assaulted and shot 123 people,* ***while*** *[contrast] republicans assaulted and shot 93 people.*
FR	**Entre 1998 et 1999, les loyalistes ont attaqué et abattu 123 personnes, ϕ 93 pour les républicains.*

Table 1: Translation examples from Europarl. Discourse connectives, their translations, and their senses are indicated in bold. The first example is a reference translation from EN into FR, while the others are wrong translations generated by MT (EN/FR and respectively FR/EN), hence marked with an asterisk.

When an ambiguous connective is explicitly translated by another connective, the incorrect rendering of its sense can lead to erroneous translations, as in the second and third examples in Table 1, which are translated by the Moses SMT decoder (Koehn et al., 2007) trained on the Europarl corpus. The reference translation for the second example uses the French connective *car* with a correct causal sense, instead of the wrong *depuis que* generated by SMT, which expresses a temporal relation. In the third example, the French connective *alors que*, in its contrastive usage, is wrongly translated into the English connective *so*, which has a causal meaning (the reference translation uses *whereas* to express contrast). It may even occur that the system fails to translate a connective at all, as in the fourth example where the discourse information provided by *while*, namely a *Contrast* relation, is lost in the French translation, which is hardly coherent any longer.

3 Related Work

3.1 Annotated Resources

One of the very few available discourse annotated corpora is the Penn Discourse Treebank (PDTB) in English (Prasad et al., 2008). For this resource, one hundred types of explicit discourse connectives were manually annotated, as well as implicit relations not signaled by a connective. The sense hierarchy used for annotation consists of three levels, from four top-level senses (*Temporal*, *Contingency*, *Comparison*, and *Expansion*), to 16 subsenses on the second level, and 23 further ones on the third level. The annotators were allowed to assign more than one sense to each occurrence, so 129 simple or complex labels are observed, over more than 18,000 explicit connectives. For French, the ANNODIS project (Péry-Woodley et al., 2009) will provide annotation of discourse on an original corpus. Resources for Czech are also becoming available (Zikánová et al., 2010).

For German, a lexicon of discourse markers named DiMLex exists since the 1990s (Stede and Umbach, 1998). An equivalent, more recent database for French is the LexConn lexicon of connectives (Roze et al., 2010) containing a list of 328 explicit connectives. For each of them, LexConn indicates and exemplifies the possible senses, chosen from a list of 30 labels inspired from Rhetorical Structure Theory (Mann and Thompson, 1988).

3.2 Automatic Disambiguation of Connectives

The release of the PDTB had quite an impact on automatic disambiguation experiments. The state-of-the-art for recognizing all types of explicit connectives in English is therefore already high, at 97% accuracy for disambiguating discourse vs. non-discourse uses (Lin et al., 2010) and 94% for disambiguating the four main senses from the PDTB hierarchy (Pitler and Nenkova, 2009). Lin et al. (2010) recently built the first end-to-end PDTB discourse parser, which is able to parse unrestricted text with an F1 score of 38.18% for senses on the second level of the PDTB hierarchy. Other important contributions to automatic discourse connective classification and feature analysis has been provided by Wellner et al. (2006) and Elwell and Baldrige (2008).

Fewer studies focus on the detailed analysis of specific discourse connectives. In Section 5.3, we will compare our results to Miltsakaki et al. (2005) who report classification results for the connectives *since*, *while* and *when*. In their study, as in the present one, the goal is to disambiguate senses from the second level of the PDTB hierarchy, a level which, as we will show, is appropriate for the translation of these connectives as well.

4 Connective Annotation in Parallel Corpora

The resources mentioned above are either monolingual only (PDTB, LexConn) and/or not yet publicly available (ANNODIS, DiMLex). Moreover, our overall goal is related to multilingualism and translation, as explained in Section 2.2 above. Therefore, we performed manual annotation of connectives in a multilingual, aligned resource: the Europarl corpus (Koehn, 2005). We extracted from Europarl two subcorpora for each translation direction, EN/FR and FR/EN, to take into account the varying distribution of connectives in translated vs. original language, as explained in Cartoni et al. (2011).

As the full PDTB hierarchy seemed too fine-grained given current capabilities for automatic labeling and the needs for translating connectives, we defined a simplified set of labels for the senses of connectives, by considering their usefulness and granularity with respect to translation, focusing on those that may lead to different connectives or syntactical constructs in the target language.

4.1 Method

There are two major ways to annotate explicit discourse connectives. The first approach is to label each occurrence of a connective with a label for its sense, similar to the PDTB or LexConn hierarchies of senses. However, as shown among others by Zikanova et al. (2010), this is a difficult and time-consuming task even when the annotators are trained over a long period of time. This is confirmed by the rather low kappa scores resulting from the manual sense annotations as can be seen for each connective in detail below.

The second approach to annotation, which is the one put forward in this paper, is based on *translation spotting*. In a first step, human annotators work on bilingual sentence pairs, and annotate the translation of each connective in the target language. The translations are either a target language connective (signaling in principle the same sense(s) as the source one), or a reformulation, or a construct with no connective at all. In a second step of the annotation, all translations of a connective are manually clustered by the experimenters to derive sense labels, by grouping together similar translations.

As demonstrated in the following subsections, for the three connectives under study, the second approach to connective annotation not only facilitates the annotation task, but also helps to derive the appropriate level of granularity for the sense labels.

4.2 Annotation of *alors que*

This first manual annotation involved two experienced annotators who annotated *alors que* in 423 original French sentences. The two main senses identified for *alors que* are *Background* (labeled B) *Contrast* (labeled C), as in the LexConn database. Annotators were also allowed to use the J label if they did not know which label to assign, and a D label for discarded sentences – due to a non-connective use of the two words which could not be filtered out automatically (e.g. *Alors, que fera-t-on?*). The annotators found 20 sentences labeled with D, which were removed from the data. 15 sentences were labeled with J by one annotator (but none by both), and it was decided to assign to them the label (either B or C) provided by the other annotator.

The inter-annotator agreement on the B vs. C labels was quite low, showing the difficulty of the task: *kappa* reached 0.43, quite below the 0.7 mark often considered as indicating reliability. The following example from Europarl illustrates the difficulty of choosing between B and C. In particular, the reference translation into English also uses an ambiguous connective, namely *while*.

FR *La monnaie unique va entrer en vigueur au milieu de la tourmente financière,* ***alors que*** *de nombreux compléments, logiques, mais que les États ne semblaient pas avoir prévus, n'ont pas encore été apportés.*

EN *The single currency is going to come into force in the midst of financial turmoil,* ***while*** *a great many additional factors which were only to be expected, but which the states do not seem to have anticipated, have not been taken into consideration.*

Two methods were applied to deal with diverging manual annotations. To prepare the datasets for the automated disambiguation experiments, one solution (named A1, see Table 2) is to use the double-sense label B/C for sentences labeled differently by annotators (B vs. C). This label reflects the difficulty of manual annotation and preserves the ambiguity which might be genuinely present in each occurrence. The relevance of the B/C label is also supported by results from automatic labeling in Section 5.3 below.

For comparison purposes, a second dataset named A2 was derived from translation spotting on the same French sentences aligned to English ones, as explained in Section 4.1. *Alors que* appeared to be mainly translated by the following English equivalents and constructs: *although*, *whereas*, *while*, *whilst*, *when*, *at a time when*. Through this operation, inter-annotator disagreement can sometimes be solved: when the translation is a clearly contrastive English connective (*whereas* or *although*), then the C label was assigned instead of B/C. Conversely, when the English translation was still ambiguous (*while*, *whilst*, or *when*), the experimenters made a decision in favor of either B or C by re-examining source and target sentences.

4.3 Annotation of *since*

For *since*, 30 sentences were annotated by four experimenters in a preliminary round, with a kappa

ID	Connective	Sent.	Labels (nb. of occ.)
A1	alors que	403	B (92), C (191), B/C (120)
A2	alors que	403	B (126), C (277)
B1	since	727	T (375), C (341), T/C (11)
B2	since	727	T (375), C (352)
C1	while	299	T/C (92), CONC (134), C (43) T/CAUSAL (19), T/DUR (7) T/PUNCT (4)
C2	while	299	T (30), C (135), CONC (134)

Table 2: The six datasets resulting from the manual annotation of the three connectives, with total number of sentences, possible labels and their number of occurrences. The explanations of the labels are given in Sections 4.2 through 4.4.

score of 0.77, indicating good agreement. Then, each half of the entire dataset (727 sentences) was annotated by another person with three possible sense labels: T for *Temporal*, C for *Causal* and T/C for a simultaneously *Temporal/Causal* meaning. Two datasets were again derived from this manual annotation. To study the effects of a supplementary label, we kept the label T/C for dataset B1, but condensed it under label C in dataset B2, as shown in Table 2.

4.4 Annotation of *while*

The English connective *while* is highly ambiguous. In the PDTB, occurrences of *while* are annotated with no less than 21 possible senses, ranging from *Conjunction* to *Contrast*, *Concession*, or *Synchrony*.

We performed a pilot annotation of 30 sentences containing *while* with five different experimenters, resulting in a quite low inter-annotator agreement, $\kappa = 0.56$. We therefore decided to perform a translation spotting task only, with two experienced annotators fluent in English and French. The observed translations into French confirm the ambiguity of *while*, as they include several connectives and constructs, quite evenly distributed in terms of frequency: *alors que*, gerundive reformulations, other reformulations, *si*, *tandis que*, *même si*, *bien que*, etc.

The translations were manually clustered to derive senses for *while*, in an empirical manner. For example, *alors que* signals *Temporal/Contrast*, which is also true for *tandis que*. Similarly, *même si* and *bien que* are clustered under the label *Concession*, and so forth. The translation spotting shows that at least *Contrast*, *Concession*, and several temporal senses are necessary to account for a correct translation. These distinctions are comparable to the semantic granularity of the second PDTB hierarchy level.

To generate training sets for automated classification out of a total of 500 sentences, we discarded 201 sentences labeled by annotators with G (gerundive constructions), P (reformulations) or Z (no translation at all) – these cases could be reconsidered in further work, as they represent valid translation problems. For the remaining 299 sentences, we created the following six labels by clustering the spotted translations: T/C (*Temporal/Contrast*), T/PUNCT (*Temporal/Punctual*), T/DUR (*Temporal/Duration*), T/CAUSAL (*Temporal/Causal*), CONC (*Concession*) and C (*Contrast*). These were used to tag the remaining 299 sentences, forming dataset C1. A second dataset (C2) with fewer senses was obtained from C1 by merging T/C to C (*Contrast* only) and all T/x to T (*Temporal* only).

5 Disambiguation Experiments

The features for connective classification, the results obtained and a detailed feature analysis are discussed in this section. We show that an automated disambiguation system can be used to determine the most appropriate set of labels, and thus to corroborate the selection we made using translation spotting.

5.1 Features

For feature extraction, all the datasets described in Section 4 were processed as follows. The English texts were parsed and POS-tagged by Charniak and Johnson's (2005) reranking parser. The French texts were POS-tagged with the MElt tagger (Denis and Sagot, 2009) and parsed with MaltParser (Nivre, 2003). As the English parser provides constituency trees, and the parser for French generates dependency trees, the features are slightly different in the two languages. The other features below were extracted using elementary pre-processing of the sentences.

For English sentences, we used the following features: the sentence-initial character of the connective (yes/no); the POS tag of the first verb in the sentence; the type of first auxiliary verb in the sentence (if any); the word preceding the connective; the word following the connective; the POS tag of the first verb following the connective; the type of the first auxiliary verb after the connective (if any).

For French sentences, the features were the following: the sentence-initial character of the connective (yes/no); the dependency tag of the connective; the first verb in the sentence; its dependency tag; the word preceding the connective; its POS tag; its dependency tag; the word following the connective; its POS tag; its dependency tag; the first verb after the connective; its dependency tag.

The cased connective word forms from the corpus were not lower-cased, thus keeping the implicit indication of the sentence-initial character of the occurrence, i.e. whether it starts a sentence or not. The output of the POS taggers was used for neighboring words, but not for the connectives, which almost always received the same tag. Charniak's parser for English provides POS tags which differentiate the verb tenses, such as VBD (past), VBG (gerund), and so on. These were considered for the verb directly preceding and the one directly following the connective. Tense was believed to be potentially relevant because *since* and *while* can have temporal meanings.

The occurrence of auxiliary verbs (*be*, *have*, *do*, or *need*) may give additional indications about temporal relations in the sentence. We therefore used the types of auxiliary verbs as features, including the elementary conjugations, represented for *to be* as: *be_present*, *be_past*, *be_part*, *be_inf*, *be_gerund* – and similarly for the other auxiliary verbs, as in (Miltsakaki et al., 2005).

As shown by Lin et al. (2010), duVerle and Prendinger (2009) or Wellner et al. (2006), the context of a connective is very important. We therefore extracted the words preceding and following each connective, the verbs and the first and the last word of the sentences. These may include numbers, sometimes indicating a numerical comparison, time expressions, or antonyms, which could indicate contrastive relations, such as *rise* vs. *fall* (e.g. *It is interesting to see the fundamental stock pickers scream "foul" on program trading when the markets* ***decline****, while hailing the great values still abounding as the markets* ***rise****.*).

For French, we likewise extracted the words immediately preceding and following each connective, supplemented by their POS tags. In contrast to constituents, dependency structures contain information about the grammatical function of each word (heads) and link the dependents belonging to the same head. However, as the dependency parser provides no differentiated verb tags, we extracted the verb word forms themselves and added their dependency tags. The same applies to the connective itself, and preceding and following words and their dependency tags.

The dependency tag of the non-connectives varies between *subj* (subject), *det* (determiner), *mod* (modifier) and *obj* (object). The first verb in the sentence often belongs to the *root* dependency while the verb following the connective most often belongs to the *obj* dependency. For *alors que*, the most frequent dependency tags were *mod_mod* and *mod_obj*, indicating the connective's main function as a modifier of its argument.

5.2 Experimental Setting

Our classification experiments made use of the WEKA machine learning toolkit (Hall et al., 2009) to run and compare several classification algorithms: Random Forest (sets of decision trees), Naive Bayes, and Support Vector Machine. The results are reported with 10-fold cross validation on the entire data for each connective, using all features.

Table 3 lists for each method – including the majority classifier as a baseline – the percentage of correctly classified instances (or accuracy, noted *Acc.*), and the *kappa* values. Significance above the baseline is computed using paired t-tests at 95% confidence. When a score is significantly above the baseline, it is shown in *italics* in Table 3. The best scores for each dataset, across classifiers, are indicated in **boldface**. When these scores were not significantly above the baseline, at least they were never significantly below either.

5.3 Results and Discussion

Overall, the SVM classifier performed best, which may be due to the large number of textual features (3 for EN data and 5 for FR data), as SVMs are known to handle them well (Joachims, 1998; du-

ID	Connective	#	Labels	Baseline	R. Forest		N. Bayes		SVM	
				Acc.	*Acc.*	κ	*Acc.*	κ	*Acc.*	κ
A1	*alors que*	403	B, C, B/C	46.9	*53.1*	*0.2*	***55.7***	***0.3***	*54.2*	***0.3***
A2	*alors que*		B, C	68.7	**69.2**	0.1	68.3	***0.2***	64.7	0.1
B1	*since*	727	T, C, T/C	51.6	*79.8*	*0.6*	*82.3*	***0.7***	***85.4***	***0.7***
B2	*since*		T, C	51.6	*80.7*	*0.6*	*84.0*	***0.7***	***85.7***	***0.7***
C1	*while*	299	T/C, T/PUNCT, T/DUR, T/CAUSAL, CONC, C	44.8	43.2	*0.1*	49.9	***0.2***	***52.2***	***0.2***
C2	*while*		T, C, CONC	43.5	*60.5*	***0.3***	*59.9*	***0.3***	***60.9***	***0.3***

Table 3: Disambiguation scores for three connectives (number of occurrences in the training sets), with two sets of labels each, for various classification algorithms. Accuracy (*Acc.*) is in percentage (%), and *kappa* is zero for the baseline method (majority class). The best scores for each data set are in **boldface**, and scores significantly above the baseline (95% t-test) are in *italics*.

Verle and Prendinger, 2009). The maximum accuracy for *alors que* is 55.7%, for *since* it is 85.7%, and for *while* it is 60.9%. While close to other reported values, there is still potential for improvement in the future.

The analysis of results for each data sets leads to observations that are specific to each connective. The high improvement of over the baseline for A1, as opposed to no improvement for A2, confirms the usefulness of the double-sense B/C label for *alors que*, showing that in this case the three-way classification is probably better adapted to the linguistic properties of *alors que* than a two-way classification. Indeed, *alors que*, just as its frequently spotted translation *while*, is linguistically ambiguous in some contexts (see for instance the example in Section 4.2), in which the temporal and the contrastive meaning are likely to co-exist. In the case of A2, where the labels were forced to B or C only, automatic classifiers do not significantly outperform the baseline. While more elaborate features might help, these low scores can be related to the difficulties of human annotators (Section 4.2), and make a strong case against using a two-label schema for *alors que*.

The features used so far lead to high scores for *since* in datasets B1 and B2. The results are comparable to those from Miltsakaki et al. (2005), who used similar features and labels, though with a Maximum Entropy classifier. Moreover, they provide results for individual connectives, and not, as most of the related work for the PDTB, on the whole set of ca. 100 discourse connective types. However, Miltsakaki et al. (2005) used their own datasets for each connective, which are different from the PDTB, because the PDTB was not available at that time. Our SVM classifier outperforms considerably the Maximum Entropy classifier on the three-way classification task (with T, C, T/C), with an accuracy of 85.4% vs. 75.5%, obtained however on different datasets. For the two-way classification (T, C), again on different datasets, our accuracy of 85.7% is slightly lower than the 89.5% given in Miltsakaki et al. (2005).[1]

For *while*, when comparing C1 to C2, it appears that reducing the number of labels from six to three increases accuracy by 8-10%. This is probably due to the small number of training instances for the labels T/PUNCT and T/DUR in C1 for example. However, even for the larger set of labels, the scores are significantly above baseline (52.2% vs. 44.8%), which indicates that such a classifier might still be useful as input to an MT system, possibly improved thanks to a larger training set. The performance obtained by Miltsakaki et al. (2005) on *while* is markedly better than ours, with an accuracy of 71.8% compared to ours of 60.9% with three labels.

5.4 Feature Analysis

The relevance of features can be measured using WEKA by computing the information gain (IG) brought by each feature to the classification task,

[1] In another experiment (Meyer, 2011), we also applied our classifiers to the PDTB data, with less features however. The results were in the same range as those from Miltsakaki et al. (2005), i.e. 75.3% accuracy for *since* and 59.6% for *while*.

R	Feature	IG	
		A1	A2
1	preceding word	1.12	0.64
2	following verb	0.81	0.51
3	first verb	0.74	0.42
4	following word	0.68	0.23
5	preceding word's POS tag	0.15	0.05
5	first verb's dep. tag	0.14	0.06
5	following word's POS tag	0.19	0.03
8	preceding word's dep. tag	0.10	0.03
8	connective's dep. tag	0.09	0.04
10	following word's dep. tag	0.13	0.013
10	following verb's dep. tag	0.04	0.03
12	sentence initial	0.05	0.001

Table 4: Information gain (IG) of features for French connective *alors que*, ordered by decreasing average ranking (R) in experiments A1 and A2. Features 1–4 are considerably more relevant than the following ones.

R	Feature	IG	
		B1	B2
1	preceding word	0.83	0.75
2	following word	0.56	0.52
3	following verb's POS tag	0.24	0.21
4	type of following aux. verb	0.13	0.12
5	type of first aux. verb	0.11	0.11
6	first verb's POS tag	0.02	0.01
7	sentence initial	0.00	0.00

Table 5: Information gain (IG) of features for EN connective *since*, ordered by decreasing average ranking (R) in experiments B1 and B2.

i.e. the reduction in entropy with respect to desired classes (Hall et al., 2009) – the higher the IG, the more relevant the feature. Features can be ranked by decreasing IG, as shown in Tables 4, 5 and 6, in which ranks were averaged over the first and the second data set in each series.

The tables show that across all three connectives and the two languages, the contextual features are always in the first positions, thus confirming the importance of the context of a connective. Following these are verbal features, which are, for these connectives, of importance because the temporal meanings are additionally established by verbal tenses. POS and dependency features seem the least helpful for disambiguation.

R	Feature	IG	
		C1	C2
1	preceding word	1.02	0.65
2	following word	0.83	0.55
3	type of first aux. verb	0.12	0.07
4	following verb's POS tag	0.16	0.04
5	first verb's POS tag	0.07	0.09
5	type of following aux. verb	0.12	0.05
7	sentence initial	0.08	0.07

Table 6: Information gain (IG) of features for EN connective *while*, ordered by decreasing average ranking (R) in experiments C1 and C2. The first two features are considerably more relevant than the remaining ones.

6 Conclusion and Future Work

We have described a translation-oriented approach to the manual and automatic annotation of discourse connectives, with the goal of identifying their senses automatically, prior to machine translation. The manual annotation of the senses of connectives has been enhanced through parallel corpora and translation spotting. This has lead to tag sets that improved both inter-annotator agreement and automatic labeling, which reached state-of-the-art scores. The analysis of relevant features has shown the utility of contextual information.

To improve over these initial results, we will use more semantic information, such as relations found in WordNet between words in the neighborhood of connectives – e.g. word similarity measures and semantic relations such as antonymy. To generate more training instances of the labels found, manual annotation will continue in order to see whether the senses found through translation spotting can improve automatic disambiguation of many more connectives. The annotation of a large parallel corpus will then help to train disambiguation tools along with statistical MT systems that use their output.

Acknowledgments

We are grateful for the funding of this work by the Swiss National Science Foundation (SNSF) under the COMTIS Sinergia Project, n. CRSI22_127510 (see `www.idiap.ch/comtis/`).

References

Bruno Cartoni, Sandrine Zufferey, Thomas Meyer, and Andrei Popescu-Belis. 2011. How comparable are parallel corpora? Measuring the distribution of general vocabulary and connectives. In *Proceedings of 4th Workshop on Building and Using Comparable Corpora*, Portland, OR.

Eugene Charniak and Mark Johnson. 2005. Coarse-to-fine n-best parsing and maxent discriminative reranking. In *Proceedings of ACL 2005 (43rd Annual Meeting of the ACL)*, pages 173–180, Ann Arbor, MI.

Pascal Denis and Benoît Sagot. 2009. Coupling an annotated corpus and a morphosyntactic lexicon for state-of-the-art POS tagging with less human effort. In *Proceedings of PACLIC 2009 (23rd Pacific Asia Conference on Language, Information and Computation)*, pages 110–119, Hong Kong, China.

David duVerle and Helmut Prendinger. 2009. A novel discourse parser based on support vector machine classification. In *Proceedings of ACL-IJCNLP 2009 (47th Annual Meeting of the ACL and 4th International Joint Conference on NLP of the AFNLP)*, pages 665–673, Singapore.

Robert Elwell and Jason Baldridge. 2008. Discourse connective argument identification with connective specific rankers. In *Proceedings of ICSC 2008 (2nd IEEE International Conference on Semantic Computing)*, pages 198–205, Santa Clara, CA.

Mark Hall, Eibe Frank, Geoffrey Holmes, Bernhard Pfahringer, Peter Reutemann, and Ian H. Witten. 2009. The WEKA data mining software: An update. *ACM SIGKDD Explorations Newsletter*, 11:10–18.

Thorsten Joachims. 1998. Text categorization with support vector machines: Learning with many relevant features. In *Proceedings of ECML 1998 (10th European Conference on Machine Learning)*, pages 137–142, Chemnitz, Germany.

Philipp Koehn, Hieu Hoang, Alexandra Birch, Chris Callison-Burch, Marcello Federico, Nicola Bertoldi, Brooke Cowan, Wade Shen, Christine Moran, Richard Zens, Chris Dyer, Ondrej Bojar, Alexandra Constantin, and Evan Herbs. 2007. Moses: Open source toolkit for statistical machine translation. In *Proceedings of ACL 2007 (45th Annual Meeting of the ACL), Demonstration Session*, pages 177–180, Prague, Czech Republic.

Philipp Koehn. 2005. Europarl: A parallel corpus for statistical machine translation. In *Proceedings of MT Summit X*, pages 79–86, Phuket, Thailand.

Ziheng Lin, Hwee Tou Ng, and Min-Yen Kan. 2010. A PDTB-styled end-to-end discourse parser. Technical Report TRB8/10, School of Computing, National University of Singapore, Singapore.

William C. Mann and Sandra A. Thompson. 1988. Rhetorical Structure Theory: towards a functional theory of text organization. *Text*, 8(3):243–281.

Thomas Meyer. 2011. Disambiguating temporal-contrastive discourse connectives for machine translation. In *Proceedings of ACL-HLT 2011 (49th Annual Meeting of the ACL: Human Language Technologies), Student Session*, Portland, OR.

Eleni Miltsakaki, Nikhil Dinesh, Rashmi Prasad, Aravind Joshi, and Bonnie Webber. 2005. Experiments on sense annotations and sense disambiguation of discourse connectives. In *Proceedings of the TLT 2005 (4th Workshop on Treebanks and Linguistic Theories)*, Barcelona, Spain.

Joakim Nivre. 2003. An efficient algorithm for projective dependency parsing. In *Proceedings of IWPT 2008 (8th International Workshop on Parsing Technologies)*, pages 149–160, Tokyo, Japan.

Marie-Paule Péry-Woodley, Nicholas Asher, Patrice Enjalbert, Farah Benamara, Myriam Bras, Cécile Fabre, Stéphane Ferrari, Lydia-Mai Ho-Dac, Anne Le Draoulec, Yann Mathet, Philippe Muller, Laurent Prévot, Josette Rebeyrolle, Ludovic Tanguy, Marianne Vergez-Couret, Laure Vieu, and Antoine Widlöcher. 2009. Annodis: une approche outillée de l'annotation de structures discursives. In *Proceedings of TALN 2009 (16ème Conférence sur le Traitement Automatique des Langues Naturelles)*, Paris, France.

Volha Petukhova and Harry Bunt. 2009. Towards a multidimensional semantics of discourse markers in spoken dialogue. In *Proceedings of IWCS-8 (8th International Conference on Computational Semantics)*, pages 157–168, Tilburg, The Netherlands.

Emily Pitler and Ani Nenkova. 2009. Using syntax to disambiguate explicit discourse connectives in text. In *Proceedings of ACL-IJCNLP 2009 (47th Annual Meeting of the ACL and 4th International Joint Conference on NLP of the AFNLP), Short Papers*, pages 13–16, Singapore.

Emily Pitler, Mridhula Raghupathy, Hena Mehta, Ani Nenkova, Alan Lee, and Aravind Joshi. 2008. Easily identifiable discourse relations. In *Proceedings of Coling 2008 (22nd International Conference on Computational Linguistics), Companion Volume: Posters*, pages 87–90, Manchester, UK.

Rashmi Prasad, Nikhil Dinesh, Alan Lee, Eleni Miltsakaki, Livio Robaldo, Aravind Joshi, and Bonnie Webber. 2008. The Penn Discourse Treebank 2.0. In *Proceedings of LREC 2008 (6th International Conference on Language Resources and Evaluation)*, pages 2961–2968, Marrakech, Morocco.

Charlotte Roze, Laurence Danlos, and Phillippe Muller. 2010. LEXCONN: a French lexicon of discourse connectives. In *Proceedings of MAD 2010 (Multidis-*

ciplinary Approaches to Discourse), pages 114–125, Moissac, France.

Manfred Stede and Carla Umbach. 1998. DiMLex: a lexicon of discourse markers for text generation and understanding. In *Proceedings of ACL 1998 (36th Annual Meeting of the ACL)*, pages 1238–1242, Montreal, Canada.

Ben Wellner, James Pustejovsky, Catherine Havasi, Roser Sauri, and Anna Rumshisky. 2006. Classification of discourse coherence relations: An exploratory study using multiple knowledge sources. In *Proceedings of 7th SIGDIAL Workshop on Discourse and Dialogue*, pages 117–125, Sydney, Australia.

Sárka Zikánová, Lucie Mladová, Jiří Mírovský, and Pavlina Jínová. 2010. Typical cases of annotators' disagreement in discourse annotations in Prague Dependency Treebank. In *Proceedings of LREC 2010 (7th International Conference on Language Resources and Evaluation)*, pages 2002–2006, Valletta, Malta.

Commitments to Preferences in Dialogue

Anais Cadilhac*, Nicholas Asher*, Farah Benamara*, Alex Lascarides**
*IRIT, University of Toulouse, **School of Informatics, University of Edinburgh

Abstract

We propose a method for modelling how dialogue moves influence and are influenced by the agents' preferences. We extract constraints on preferences and dependencies among them, even when they are expressed indirectly, by exploiting discourse structure. Our method relies on a study of 20 dialogues chosen at random from the Verbmobil corpus. We then test the algorithms predictions against the judgements of naive annotators on 3 random unseen dialogues. The average annotator-algorithm agreement and the average inter-annotator agreement show that our method is reliable.

1 Introduction

Dialogues are structured by various moves that the participants make—e.g., answering questions, asking follow-up questions, elaborating prior claims, and so on. Such moves come with commitments to certain attitudes such as intentions and preferences. While mapping utterances to their underlying *intentions* is well studied through the application of plan recognition techniques (e.g., Grosz and Sidner (1990), Allen and Litman (1987)), game-theoretic models of rationality generally suggest that intentions result from a deliberation to find the optimal tradeoff between one's *preferences* and one's *beliefs* about possible outcomes (Rasmusen, 2007). So mapping dialogue moves to *preferences* is an important task: for instance, they are vital in decisions on how to re-plan and repair should the agents' current plan fail, for they inform the agents about the relative importance of their various goals. Classical game theory, however, demands a complete and cardinal representation of preferences for the optimal intention to be defined. This is not realistic for modelling dialogue because agents often lack complete information about preferences prior to talking: they learn about the domain, each other's preferences and even their own preferences through dialogue exchange. For instance, utterance (1) implies that the speaker wants to go to the mall given that he wants to eat, but we do not know his preferences over "go to the mall" if he does not want to eat.

(1) I want to go to the mall to eat something.

Existing formal models of dialogue content either do not formalise a link between utterances and preferences (e.g., Ginzburg (to appear)), or they encode such links in a typed feature structure, where desire is represented as a feature that takes conjunctions of values as arguments (e.g., Poesio and Traum (1998)), making the language too restricted to express *dependencies* among preferences of the kind we just described. Existing implemented dialogue systems likewise typically represent goals as simple combinations of values on certain information 'slots' (e.g., He and Young (2005), Lemon and Pietquin (2007)); thus (1) yields a conjunction of preferences, to go to the mall and to eat something. But such a system could lead to suboptimal dialogue moves—e.g., to help the speaker go to the mall even if he has already received food.

What's required, then, is a method for extracting partial information about preferences and the dependencies among them that are expressed in dialogue, perhaps indirectly, and a method for exploiting that partial information to identify the next optimal action. This paper proposes a method for achieving these tasks by exploiting discourse structure.

We exploited the corpus of Baldridge and Lascarides (2005a), who annotated 100 randomly chosen spontaneous face-to-face dialogues from the Verbmobil corpus (Wahlster, 2000) with their discourse structure according to Segmented Discourse Representation Theory (SDRT, Asher and Lascarides (2003))—these structures represent the types of (relational) speech acts that the agents perform. Here's a typical fragment:

(2) a. *A*: Shall we meet sometime in the next week?
b. *A*: What days are good for you?
c. *B*: Well, I have some free time on almost every day except Fridays.

Proceedings of the SIGDIAL 2011: the 12th Annual Meeting of the Special Interest Group on Discourse and Dialogue, pages 204–215,
Portland, Oregon, June 17-18, 2011.

d. *B*: In fact, I'm busy on Thursday too.
e. *A*: So perhaps Monday?

Across the corpus, more than 30% of the discourse units are either questions or assertions that help to elaborate a plan to achieve the preferences revealed by a prior part of the dialogue—these are marked respectively with the discourse relations *Q-Elab* and *Plan-Elab* in SDRT, and utterances (2b) and (2e) and the segments (2c) and (2d) invoke these relations (see Section 2). Moreover, 10% of the moves revise or correct prior preferences (like (2d)).

We will model the interaction between dialogue content and preferences in two steps. The first maps utterances and their rhetorical connections into a partial description of the agents' preferences. The mapping is *compositional* and *monotonic* over the dialogue's logical form (i.e., the description of preferences for an extended segment is defined in terms of and always subsumes those for its subsegments): it exploits recursion over discourse structure. The descriptions partially describe *ceteris paribus preference nets* or CP-nets with Boolean variables (Boutilier et al., 2004). We chose CP-nets over alternative logics of preferences, because they provide a compact, computationally efficient, qualitative and relational representation of preferences and their dependencies, making them compatible with the kind of partial information about preferences that utterances reveal. Our mapping from the logical form of dialogue to partial descriptions of Boolean CP-nets proceeds in a purely linguistic or domain independent way (e.g., it ignores information such as Monday and Tuesday cannot co-refer) and will therefore apply to dialogue generally and not just Verbmobil.

In a second stage, we "compress" and refine our description making use of constraints proper to CP-nets (e.g., that preference is transitive) and constraints provided by the domain—in this case constraints about times and places, as well as constraints from deep semantics. This second step reduces the complexity of inferring which CP-net(s) satisfy the partial description and allows us to identify the minimal CP-net that satisfies the domain-dependent description of preferences. We can thus exploit dependencies between dialogue moves and mental states in a compact, efficient and intuitive way.

We start by motivating and describing the semantic representation of dialogue from which our CP-net descriptions and then our CP-nets will be constructed.

2 The Logical Form of Dialogue

Our starting point for representing dialogue content is SDRT. Like Hobbs et al. (1993) and Mann and Thompson (1987), it structures discourse into units that are linked together with *rhetorical relations* such as *Explanation*, *Question Answer Pair* (*QAP*), *Q-Elab*, *Plan-Elab*, and so on. Logical forms in SDRT consist of *Segmented Discourse Representation Structures* (SDRSs). As defined in Asher and Lascarides (2003), an SDRS is a set of labels representing discourse units, and a mapping from each label to an SDRS-formula representing its content—these formulas are based on those for representing clauses or elementary discourse units (EDUs) plus rhetorical relation symbols between labels. Lascarides and Asher (2009) argue that to make accurate predictions about acceptance and denial, both of which can be implicated rather than linguistically explicit, the logical form of dialogue should track each agent's commitments to content, including rhetorical connections. They represent a dialogue turn (where turn boundaries occur whenever the speaker changes) as a set of SDRSs—one for each agent representing all his current commitments, from the beginning of the dialogue to the end of that turn. The representation of the dialogue overall—a Dialogue SDRS or DSDRS—is that of each of its turns. Each agent constructs the SDRSs for all other agents as well as his own. For instance, (2) is assigned the DSDRS in Table 1, with the content of the EDUs omitted for reasons of space (see Lascarides and Asher (2009) for details). We adopt a convention of indexing the root label of the nth turn, spoken by agent d, as nd; and $\pi : \phi$ means that ϕ describes π's content (we'll sometimes also write ϕ_π to identify this description).

We now return to our example (2). Intuitively, (2a) commits A to a preference for meeting next week but it does so indirectly: the preference is not asserted, or equivalently entailed at the level of content from the semantics of $Q\text{-}Elab(a,b)$. Accordingly, responding with "I do too" (meaning "I want to meet next week too") is correctly predicted to be highly anomalous. A's SDRS for turn 1 in Table 1 commits him to the questions (2a) and (2b) because *Q-Elab* is veridical: i.e. $Q\text{-}Elab(a,b)$ entails the dynamic conjunction $\phi_a \wedge \phi_b$. Since intuitively (2a) commits A to the implicature that he prefers next week, our algorithm for eliciting preferences from dialogue must ascribe this preference to A on the basis of his move $Q\text{-}Elab(a,b)$. Furthermore, $Q\text{-}Elab(a,b)$ entails that any answer to (2b) must elaborate a plan to achieve the preference revealed by (2a); this makes ϕ_b paraphrasable as "What days next week are good for you?", which does not add new preferences.

B's contribution in the second turn attaches to (2b) with *QAP* and also *Plan-Elab*—he answers with a non-empty extension for *what days*. Lascarides and Asher (2009) argue that this means that B is also committed to the illocutionary contribution of (2b), as shown in Table 1 by the addition of $Q\text{-}Elab(a,b)$ to B's SDRS. This addition commits B also to the preference of meeting next week, with his answer making the preference more precise: (2c) reveals that B prefers any day except Friday; by linking (2d) with *Plan-Correction* he retracts the preference for Thursday. This compels A to revise his inferences about

Turn	A's SDRS	B's SDRS
1	π_{1A} : *Q-Elab*(a,b)	$\emptyset$
2	π_{1A} : *Q-Elab*(a,b)	π_{2B} : *Q-Elab*$(a,b) \wedge$ *QAP*$(b,\pi) \wedge$ *Plan-Elab*(b,π) π : *Plan-Correction*(c,d)
3	π_{3A} : *Q-Elab*$(a,b) \wedge$ *QAP*$(b,\pi) \wedge$ *Plan-Elab*$(b,\pi) \wedge$ *Plan-Elab*(π,e)	π_{2B} : *Q-Elab*$(a,b) \wedge$ *QAP*$(b,\pi) \wedge$ *Plan-Elab*(b,π) π : *Plan-Correction*(c,d)

Table 1: The DSDRS for Dialogue (2).

B's preference for meeting on Thursday. A's *Plan-Elab* move (2e) in the third turn reveals another preference for Monday. This may not match his preferred day when the dialogue started: perhaps that was Friday. He may continue to prefer that day. But engaging in dialogue can compel agents to revise their commitments to preferences as they learn about the domain and each other.

The above discussion of (2) exhibits how different types of rhetorical *relations* between utterances rather than Searle-like speech acts like *question*, construed as a property of an utterance, are useful for encoding how preferences evolve in a dialogue and how they relate to one another. While the Grounding Acts dialogue model (Poesio and Traum, 1998) and the Question Under Discussion (QUD) model (Ginzburg, to appear) both have many attractive features, they do not encode as fine-grained a taxonomy of types of speech acts and their semantic effects as SDRT: in SDRT each rhetorical relation is a different kind of (relational) speech act, so that, for instance, the speech act of questioning is divided into the distinct types *Q-Elab*, *Plan-Correction*, and others. For the QUD model to encode such relations would require implicit questions of all sorts of different types to be included in the taxonomy, in which case the result may be equivalent to the SDRT taxonomy of dialogue moves. We have not explored this eventual equivalence here.

3 CP-nets and CP-net descriptions

A preference is standardly understood as an ordering by an agent over outcomes; at the very least it entails a comparison between one entity and another (outcomes being one sort of entity among others). As indicated in the introduction, we are interested in an ordinal definition of preferences, which consists in imposing an ordering over all (relevant) possible outcomes. Among these outcomes, some are acceptable for the agent, in the sense that the agent is ready to act in such a way as to realize them; and some outcomes are not acceptable. Amongst the acceptable outcomes, the agent will typically prefer some to others. Our method does not try to determine the most preferred outcome of an agent but follows rather the evolution of their commitments to certain preferences as the dialogue proceeds. To give an example, if an agent proposes to meet on a certain day X and at a certain time Y, we infer that among the agent's acceptable outcomes is a meeting on X at Y, even if this is not his most preferred outcome (see earlier discussion of (2e)).

A CP-net (Boutilier et al., 2004) offers a compact representation of preferences. It is a graphical model that exploits conditional preferential independence so as to structure the decision maker's preferences under a *ceteris paribus* assumption.

Although CP-nets generally consider variables with a finite range of values, to define the mapping from dialogue turns to descriptions of CP-nets in a domain independent and compositional way, we use *Boolean* propositional variables: each variable describes an action that an agent can choose to perform, or not. We will then refine the CP-net description by using domain-specific information, transforming CP-nets with binary valued variables to CP-nets with multiple valued variables. This reduces the complexity of the evaluation of the CP-net by a large factor.

More formally, let V be a finite set of propositional variables and L_V the description language built from V via Boolean connectives and the constants $\top$ (*true*) and $\bot$ (*false*). Formulas of L_V are denoted by ϕ, ψ, etc. 2^V is the set of interpretations for V, and as usual for $M \in 2^V$ and $x \in V$, M gives the value *true* to x if $x \in M$ and *false* otherwise. Where $X \subseteq V$, let 2^X be the set of X*-interpretations*. X-interpretations are denoted by listing all variables of X, with a $^{-}$ symbol when the variable is set to false: e.g., where $X = \{a,b,d\}$, the X-interpretation $M = \{a,d\}$ is expressed as $a\bar{b}d$.

A *preference relation* $\succeq$ is a reflexive and transitive binary relation on 2^V with strict preference $\succ$ defined in the usual way (i.e., $M \succeq M'$ but $M' \not\succeq M$). Note that preference orderings are not necessarily complete, since some candidates may not be comparable by a given agent. An agent is said to be indifferent between two options $M, M' \in 2^V$, written $M \sim M'$, if $M \succeq M'$ and $M' \succeq M$.

As we stated earlier, CP-nets exploit conditional preferential independence to compute a preferential ranking over outcomes:

Definition 1 *Let V be a set of propositional variables and $\{X,Y,Z\}$ a partition of V. X is* conditionally preferentially independent *of Y given Z if and only if $\forall z \in 2^Z$, $\forall x_1, x_2 \in 2^X$ and $\forall y_1, y_2 \in 2^Y$ we have: $x_1y_1z \succeq$*

x_2y_1z *iff* $x_1y_2z \succeq x_2y_2z$.

For each variable X, the agent specifies a set of *parent variables* $Pa(X)$ that can affect his preferences over the values of X. Formally, X is conditionally preferentially independent of $V \setminus (\{X\} \cup Pa(X))$. This is then used to create the CP-net.

Definition 2 *Let V be a set of propositional variables. $\mathcal{N} = \langle \mathcal{G}, \mathcal{T} \rangle$ is a* CP-net *on V, where $\mathcal{G}$ is a directed graph over V, and $\mathcal{T}$ is a set of Conditional Preference Tables (CPTs) with indifference. That is, $T = \{\mathrm{CPT}(X_j)$: $X_j \in V\}$, where $\mathrm{CPT}(X_j)$ specifies for each instantiation $p \in 2^{Pa(X_j)}$ either $x_j \succ_p \overline{x_j}$, $\overline{x_j} \succ_p x_j$ or $x_j \sim_p \overline{x_j}$.*

The following simple example illustrates these definitions. Suppose our agent prefers to go from Paris to Hong Kong by day rather than overnight. If he takes an overnight trip, he prefers a non stop flight, but if he goes by day, he prefers a flight with a stop. Figure 1 shows the associated CP-net. The variable T stands for the preference over the period of travel. Its values are T_d for a day trip and T_n for a night one. The variable St stands for the preference over stops. Its values are S for a trip with stops and $\overline{S}$ without.

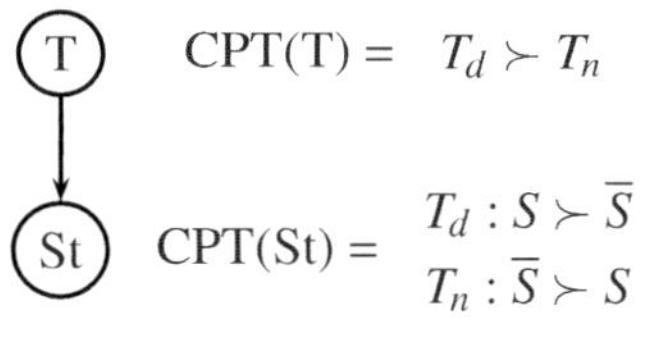

Figure 1: Travel CP-net

With CP-nets defined, we proceed to a description language for them. The description language formula $w \succ y(CPT)$ describes a CP-net where a CPT contains an entry of the form $w \succ_p y$ for some possibly empty list of parent variables p. A CP-net description is a set of such formulas. The CP-net $\mathcal{N} \models x_1, \ldots x_n : w \succ y(CPT)$ iff the CP-net $\mathcal{N}$'s CPT $\mathcal{T}$ contains an entry $w \succ_{\vec{u}} y$—also written $\vec{u} : w \succ y$—where $x_1, \ldots x_n$ figure in $\vec{u}$. Satisfaction of a description formula by a CP-net yields a notion of logical consequence between a CP-net description $\mathcal{D}\mathcal{N}$ and a description formula in the obvious way. Dialogue turns also sometimes inform us that certain variables enter into preference statements. We'll express the fact that the variables $x_1, \ldots, x_n$ are associated with discourse constituent π by the formula $x_1, \ldots, x_n(P(\pi))$, where $P(\pi)$ refers to the partial description of the preferences expressed by the discourse unit π (see Section 4).

The description language allows us to impose constraints on the CP-nets that agents commit to without specifying the CP-net completely, as is required for utterances like (1). In section 6, we describe how to construct a minimal CP-net from a satisfiable CP-net description. One can then use the *forward sweep* procedure for outcome optimisation (Boutilier et al., 2004). This is a procedure of *linear* complexity, which consists in instantiating variables following an order compatible with the graph, choosing for each variable (one of) its preferred values given the value of the parents.

4 From EDUs to Preferences

EDUs are described in SDRT using essentially Boolean formulas over labels (Asher and Lascarides, 2003); thus $\phi(\pi) \wedge \psi(\pi)$ means that ϕ and ψ describe aspects of π's content. $Not(\pi_1, \pi) \wedge \phi(\pi_1)$ means that the logical form of the EDU π is of the form $\neg\pi_1$ and that π_1 is described by ϕ; so π has the content $\neg\phi$. Our task is to map such descriptions of content into descriptions of preferences. Our preference descriptions will use Boolean connectives and operators over preference entries (e.g., of the form $x \succ y$): namely, $\&, \bigtriangledown, \mapsto$, and a modal operator $\Diamond$. The rules below explain the semantics of preference operators (they are in effect defined in terms of the semantics of buletic attitudes and Boolean connectives) and how to recursively calculate preference descriptions from the EDU's logical structure.

Simple EDUs can provide *atomic* preference statements (e.g., *I want X* or *We need X*). This means that with this EDU the speaker commits to a preference for X. X will typically involve a Boolean variable and a preference entry for its CPT. $P(\pi)$ is the label of the preference description associated with discourse unit π. Hence for a simple EDU π, we have $X(P(\pi))$ as its description. Simple EDUs also sometimes express preferences in an indirect way (see (2a)).

More generally, P recursively exploits the logical structure of an EDU's logical form to produce an EDU *preference representation* (EDUPR). For instance, since the logical form of the EDU *I want fish and wine* features conjunction, likewise so does its preference description: $\phi\&\psi(P(\pi))$ means that among the preferences included in π, the agent prefers to have both ϕ and ψ and prefers either one if he can't have both.[1] We also have disjunctions (*let's meet Thursday or Friday*), and negations (*I don't want to meet on Friday*), whose preferences we'll express respectively as $Thurs \bigtriangledown Fri(P(\pi))$ and $\neg\mathrm{Fri}(P(\pi))$.

Some EDUs express commitments to dependencies among preferences. For example, in the sentence *What about Monday, in the afternoon?*, there are two preferences: one for the day Monday, and, given the Monday preference, one for the time afternoon (of Monday), at least on one syntactic disambiguation. We represent this dependency as $\mathrm{Mon} \mapsto \mathrm{Aft}(P(\pi))$. Note that $\mapsto$ is not expressible with just Boolean operators. Finally, EDUs can express commitment to preferences via free choice

[1] The full set of rules also includes a stronger conjunction $\phi\Delta\psi(P(\pi))$ (the agent prefers both ϕ and ψ, but is indifferent if he can't have both).

modalities; *I am free on Thursday*, or $\Diamond\text{Thurs}(P(\pi))$, tells us that Thursday is a possible day to meet. $\Diamond\phi$ says that ϕ is an acceptable outcome (as described earlier, this means the agent is ready to act so as to realize an outcome that entails ϕ). Thus, $\Diamond\phi(\pi)$ entails $\phi(\pi)$, and $\Diamond$-embedded preferences obey reduction axioms permitting $\Diamond$ to be eliminated when combined with other preference operators. But a $\Diamond$ preference statement does affect a preference description when is is conjoined in Boolean fashion with another $\Diamond$ preference statement in an EDU or combined via a discourse relation like *Continuation*. This is because $\Diamond$ is a free choice modality and obeys the equivalence (3) below, which in turn yields a *disjunctive* preference $\phi \bigtriangledown \psi(P(\pi))$ from what appeared to be a conjunction.[2]

(3) $$(\Diamond\phi(P(\pi)) \wedge \Diamond\psi(P(\pi))) \leftrightarrow \Diamond(\phi \bigtriangledown \psi)(P(\pi))$$

The variables introduced by a discourse segment π are integrated into the CP-net description $\mathcal{DN}$ via the operation $Commit(\pi, \mathcal{DN})$. The following seven rules cover the different possible logical structures for the EDU preference representation. In the following, X,Y,Z,W denote propositional variables and ϕ, ψ propositional formulas from EDUPR. $Var(\phi)$ are the variables in ϕ, and $\succ_X$ the preference relation describing $CPT(X)$. $Sat(\phi)$ (or *non-Sat*(ϕ)) is a conjunction of literals from $Var(\phi)$ that satisfy (or do not satisfy) ϕ. $Sat(\phi) - X$ is the formula that results from removing the conjunct with X from $Sat(\phi)$.

1. Where $X(P(\pi))$ (X is a variable of $P(\pi)$, e.g., *I want* X), $Commit(\pi, \mathcal{DN})$ adds the description $\mathcal{DN} \models X \succ \overline{X}(CPT(X))$.[3]
2. Where $\phi \& \psi(P(\pi))$, $Commit(\pi, \mathcal{DN})$ adds descriptions as follows:
   - For each $X \in Var(\phi)$, add $Var(\psi)$ to $Pa(X)$ and modify $CPT(X)$ as follows:
     If $Sat_i(\psi)$, $Sat_j(\phi) \vdash X$ (resp. $\overline{X}$), then $Sat_i(\psi)$, $Sat_j(\phi) - X$: $X \succ \overline{X}$ (resp. $\overline{X} \succ X$), for all satisfiers i and j.
   - Similarly for each $Y \in Var(\psi)$.

   If ϕ and ψ are literals X and Y we get: $\mathcal{DN} \models Y \succ \overline{Y}(CPT(Y))$ and $\mathcal{DN} \models X \succ \overline{X}(CPT(X))$. Graphically, this yields the following preference relation (where one way arrows denote preference, two way arrows denote indifference or equal preference, and no arrow means the options are incomparable):

   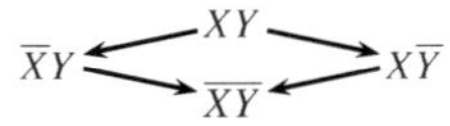

3. Where $\phi \bigtriangledown \psi(P(\pi))$ (the agent prefers to have at least one of ϕ and ψ satisfied). If ϕ and ψ are X and Y, we get:
   - $Var(X) \in Pa(Var(Y))$ and $\mathcal{DN} \models X : Y \sim \overline{Y}(CPT(Y))$, $\mathcal{DN} \models \overline{X} : Y \succ \overline{Y}(CPT(Y))$.
   - $Var(Y) \in Pa(Var(X))$ and $\mathcal{DN} \models Y : X \sim \overline{X}(CPT(X))$, $\mathcal{DN} \models \overline{Y} : X \succ \overline{X}(CPT(X))$.

   This corresponds to the following preference relation:

   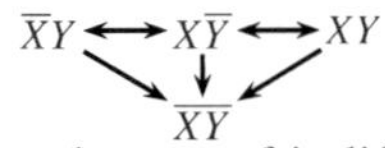

   As before, the use of indifference allows us to find the best outcomes (XY, $X\overline{Y}$ and $\overline{X}Y$) easily.
4. Where $\phi \mapsto \psi(P(\pi))$ (the agent prefers that ϕ is satisfied and if so that ψ is also satisfied. If ϕ is not satisfied, it is not possible to define preferences on ψ). If ϕ and ψ are X and Y, we get:
   - $\mathcal{DN} \models X \succ \overline{X}(CPT(X))$
   - $Var(X) \in Pa(Var(Y))$ and
     $\mathcal{DN} \models X : Y \succ \overline{Y}(CPT(Y))$.

   Note that this description is also produced by $Elab(\pi_i, \pi_j)$ below where $X(P(\pi_i))$ and $Y(P(\pi_j))$ (see rule 8). Thus the implication symbol $\mapsto$ is a "shortcut" in that it represents elaborations whose arguments are in the same EDU.
5. Where $\Diamond\phi(P(\pi))$ (the agent prefers a free choice of ϕ). Given the behaviour of $\Diamond$, this reduces to treating $\phi(P(\pi))$.
6. Where $\neg\phi(P(\pi))$. We can apply rules 1-5 by converting $\neg\phi$ into conjunctive normal form.
7. Where $\phi(P(\pi)) \wedge \psi(P(\pi))$, with ϕ and ψ nonmodal, we simply apply the rule for ϕ and that for ψ.

5 From Discourse Structure to Preferences

We must now define how the agents' preferences, represented as a partial description of a CP-net, are built compositionally from the discourse structure over EDUs. The constraints are different for different discourse relations, reflecting the fact that the semantics of connections between segments influences how their preferences relate to one another.

We will add rules for defining *Commit* over labels π whose content ϕ_π express rhetorical relations $R(\pi_i, \pi_j)$—indeed, we overload the notation and write $Commit(R(\pi_i, \pi_j), \mathcal{DN})$. Since *Commit* applies compositionally, starting with the EDUs and working up

---

[2] We provide here the reduction axioms over preference descriptions

1. $\Diamond(\phi \& \psi)(P(\pi)) \leftrightarrow (\phi \& \psi)(P(\pi))$
2. $\Diamond(\phi \mapsto \psi)(P(\pi)) \leftrightarrow (\phi \mapsto \psi)(P(\pi))$
3. $\Diamond(\phi \bigtriangledown \psi) \leftrightarrow (\phi \bigtriangledown \psi)(P(\pi))$
4. $\Diamond\Diamond\phi(P(\pi)) \leftrightarrow \Diamond\phi(P(\pi))$

[3] Given our description language semantics, this means that any CP-net which satisfies the description $\mathcal{DN}$ contains a preference table $CPT(X)$ with an entry $X \succ \overline{X}$ with at least one instantiation of the variables in $Pa(X)$.

the discourse structure towards the unique root label of the SDRS, we can assume in our definition of $Commit(R(\pi_i,\pi_j),\mathcal{DN})$ that the EDUPRs are already defined. We give rules for all the relations in the Verbmobil corpus, though we will be very brief with those that are less prevalent. A complete example using our rules is in appendix A.

IExplanation, Elab, Plan-Elab, Q-elab

IExplanation(π_i, π_j): i.e., π_j's preferences explain π_i's (e.g., see (1), where $P(\pi_i)$ would be going to the mall and $P(\pi_j)$ is eating something). With *Elab*(π_i, π_j) a preference in π_i is elaborated on or developed in π_j, as in: *I want wine. I want white wine.* That is, a preference for white wine depends on a preference for wine. *Plan-Elab*(π_i,π_j) means that π_j describes a plan for achieving the preferences expressed by π_i, and with *Q-Elab* we have a similar dependence between preferences, but the second constituent is a question (so often in practice this means preference commitments from π_i transfer from one agent to another).

Plan-Elab(π_j,π_i), *Elab*(π_j,π_i) and *IExplanation*(π_i,π_j) all follow the same two-step rule, and so from the point of view of preference updates they are equivalent:

8. i Firstly, preference description $\mathcal{DN}$ is updated according to $P(\pi_j)$ by applying $Commit(\pi_j,\mathcal{DN})$, if π_j expresses a new preference. If not go to step (ii).
   ii. Secondly, description $\mathcal{DN}$ is modified so that each variable in $P(\pi_i)$ depends on each variable in $P(\pi_j)$: i.e., $\forall X \in Var(P(\pi_i))$, $\forall Y \in Var(P(\pi_j)), Y \in Pa(X)$. Then, $\mathcal{DN}$ is enriched according to $P(\pi_i)$, if π_i expresses a preference. If it does not, then end.

We now give some details concerning step (ii) above. To this end, let ϕ denote a formula with SDRS description predicates, ϕ' its corresponding boolean (preference) formula and $\overline{\phi'}$ its negation. Then for $\phi = Y$, we define $\phi' = Y$ and $\overline{\phi'} = \overline{Y}$; for $\phi = Y \mapsto Z$ we define $\phi' = Y \wedge Z$ and $\overline{\phi'} = \overline{Y} \vee \overline{Z}$; and for $\phi = Y \bigtriangledown Z$ and $\phi = Y\&Z$, we have $\phi' = Y \vee Z$ and $\overline{\phi'} = \overline{Y} \wedge \overline{Z}$.

a. $X(P(\pi_i))$ and $\phi(P(\pi_j))$. The agent explains his preferences on X by ϕ. So, if no preferences on X are already defined, ϕ is a reason to prefer X. That is, $\mathcal{DN} \models \phi'$: $X \succ \overline{X}(CPT(X))$. However, it is not possible to define preferences on X if ϕ is false. If, on the other hand, preferences on X are already defined, the agent prefers X if ϕ is satisfied, and does not modify his preferences otherwise—i.e., $\succ_{X,\phi'} = X \succ \overline{X}$, $\succ_{X,\overline{\phi'}} = \succ_X$.[4]

[4]If we have $\succ_X$ such that Z: $\overline{X} \succ X$, $\overline{Z}$: $X \succ \overline{X}$, $\succ_{X,\phi'}$ represents preferences defined by $Z \wedge \phi'$ and $\overline{Z} \wedge \phi'$, whereas $\succ_{X,\overline{\phi'}}$ represents preferences defined by $Z \wedge \overline{\phi'}$ and $\overline{Z} \wedge \overline{\phi'}$.

For $\phi = Y$, if $\succ_X$ is not already defined, we obtain the following preference relation (no information on the preference for X if Y is false makes $X\overline{Y}$ and $\overline{XY}$ incomparable):

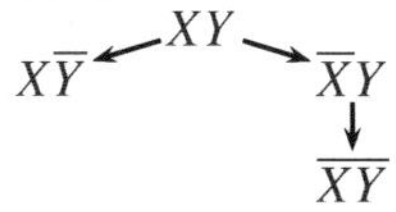

b. $X \bigtriangledown Z(P(\pi_i))$ and $\phi(P(\pi_j))$. The agent explains his preferences $X \bigtriangledown Z$ by ϕ: he wants to satisfy X or Z if ϕ is satisfied.
   First, we set $Var(Z) \in Pa(Var(X))$, $Var(X) \in Pa(Var(Z))$. If $\succ_X$ is not already defined, we have: $\mathcal{DN} \models \phi' \wedge Z$: $X \sim \overline{X}(CPT(X))$, $\mathcal{DN} \models \phi' \wedge \overline{Z}$: $X \succ \overline{X}(CPT(X))$.
   Otherwise, $\succ_{X,\phi',Z} = X \sim \overline{X}$, $\succ_{X,\phi',\overline{Z}} = X \succ \overline{X}$, $\succ_{X,\overline{\phi'},Z} = \succ_{X,\overline{\phi'},\overline{Z}} = \succ_X$.
   $CPT(Z)$ is defined as $CPT(X)$ by inverting X and Z. For $\phi = Y$, if $\succ_X$ and $\succ_Z$ are not already defined, we obtain the following preference relation (again, the lack of preference information on X and Z when Y is false yields incomparability among states where Y is false):

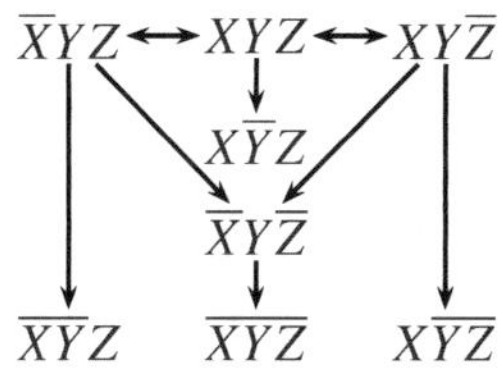

c. $X\&Z(P(\pi_i))$ and $\phi(P(\pi_j))$. The agent explains his preferences on $X\&Z$ by ϕ.
   - If $\succ_X$ is not already defined, we have: $\mathcal{DN} \models \phi' : X \succ \overline{X}(CPT(X))$.
     Otherwise, $\succ_{X,\phi'} = X \succ \overline{X}$, $\succ_{X,\overline{\phi'}} = \succ_X$,
   - $CPT(Z)$ is defined as $CPT(X)$ by replacing X by Z.

d. $X \mapsto Z(P(\pi_i))$ and $\phi(P(\pi_j))$. The agent explains his preferences on $X \mapsto Z$ by ϕ: he wants to satisfy X and after Z if ϕ is satisfied.
   If $\succ_X$ is not already defined, we have $\mathcal{DN} \models \phi'$: $X \succ \overline{X}(CPT(X))$ and we set $Var(X) \in Pa(Var(Z))$.[5]
   If $\succ_Z$ is not yet defined, we have : $\mathcal{DN} \models \phi' \wedge X$: $Z \succ \overline{Z}(CPT(Z))$, $\mathcal{DN} \models \phi' \wedge \overline{X} : Z \sim \overline{Z}(CPT(Z))$.
   Else, $\succ_{Z,(\phi' \wedge X)} = Z \succ \overline{Z}$, $\succ_{Z,(\phi' \wedge \overline{X})} = Z \sim \overline{Z}$, $\succ_{Z,(\overline{\phi'} \wedge X)} = \succ_{Z,(\overline{\phi'} \wedge \overline{X})} = \succ_Z$.

e. $\psi(P(\pi_i))$ and $\phi(P(\pi_j))$. We can apply rules 8 by decomposing ψ.

[5]Otherwise, there is no need to modify $\succ_X$. This is what we call a '*partial elaboration*'. Variables that were evoked since preferences on X were introduced are parents of Z but not of X. For example, if an agent commits to a preference for *Monday* then *Afternoon*, and later in the discourse he commits to *2oclock*, then *Afternoon* is *2oclock*'s parent but not *Monday*'s.

f. $\diamond(\psi)(P(\pi_i))$ and $\diamond(\phi)(P(\pi_j))$. We treat this like a free choice EDU (see rule 5).

g. $\diamond(\psi)(P(\pi_i))$ and $\phi(P(\pi_j))$, where ϕ is non modal. We treat this like $\psi(P(\pi_i))$ and $\phi(P(\pi_j))$ (see rule 8.e)

Let's briefly look at how the rule changes for $Q\text{-}elab_A(\pi_1,\pi_2)$ (where the subscript A identifies the speaker of π_2):

9. $Q\text{-}Elab_A(\pi_1,\pi_2)$ implies that we update A's CP-net description $\mathcal{DN}$ by applying the rule for $Elab(\pi_1,\pi_2)$, where if π_2 expresses no preferences on their own, we simply make the $P(\pi_2)$ description equal to the $P(\pi_1)$ description. Thus A's CP-net description is updated with the preferences expressed by utterance π_1, regardless of who said π_1.

QAP Answers to questions affect preferences in complex ways:

10. The first case concerns yes/no questions and there are two cases, depending on whether B replies *yes* or *no*:

    Yes $QAP_B(\pi_1,\pi_2)$ where π_2 is *yes*. B's preference descriptions are updated by applying $Commit(Elab_B(\pi_1,\pi_2),\mathcal{DN})$ (and so B's preference description include preferences expressed by π_1 and π_2).

    No $QAP_B(\pi_1,\pi_2)$ where π_2 is *no*. If $P(\pi_1)$ and $P(\pi_2)$ are consistent, then B's preference descriptions are updated by applying $Commit_B(Elab_B(\pi_1,\pi_2),\mathcal{DN})$; otherwise, they are updated by applying $Commit(Correction(\pi_1,\pi_2),\mathcal{DN})$ (see rule 13).

11. When π_1 is a *wh*-question and $QAP_B(\pi_1,\pi_2)$, B's preferences over variables in π_1 and π_2 are exactly the same as the ones defined for a yes/no question where the answer is *yes*. Variables in π_2 will refine preferences over variables in π_1. So, B's preference descriptions are updated by applying $Commit_B(Elab_B(\pi_1,\pi_2),\mathcal{DN})$.

In previous rules, it is relatively clear how to update the preference commitments. However, in some cases it's not clear what the answer in a *QAP* targets: in *Could we meet the 25 in the morning? No, I can't.*, we do not know if *No* is about the 25 and the morning, or only about the morning. So, we define the following rule for managing cases where the ***target*** is unknown :

12. If we know the target, we can change the description of the CP-net. Otherwise, we wait to learn more.

Correction and Plan-Correction allow a speaker to rectify a prior commitment to preferences. Self-corrections also occur in the corpus: *I could do it on the 27th. No I can not make it on the 27th, sorry I have a seminar. Correction* and *Plan-Correction* can have several effects on the preferences. For instance, they can correct preference entries. That is, given $Correction(\pi_1,\pi_2)$, some variables in $P(\pi_1)$ are replaced by variables in $P(\pi_2)$ (in the self-correction example, every occurrence of 27 in $P(\pi_1)$ is replaced with $\overline{27}$ and vice versa). We have a set of rules of the form $X \leftarrow \{Y_1,\dots,Y_m\}$, which means that the variable $X \in Var(P(\pi_1))$ is replaced by the set of variables $\{Y_1,\dots,Y_m\} \subseteq Var(P(\pi_2))$. We assume that X can't depend on $\{Y_1,\dots,Y_m\}$ before the *Correction* is performed. Then replacement proceeds as follows:

13. If $Pa(X)=\emptyset$, we add the description $\mathcal{DN} \models Y_k \succ \overline{Y}_k(CPT(Y_k))$ for all $k\in\{1,\dots,m\}$ and remove $X \succ \overline{X}(CPT(X))$ (or $\overline{X} \succ X(CPT(X))$). Otherwise, we replace every description of $CPT(X)$ with an equivalent statement using Y_k (to describe $CPT(Y_k)$), for all $k\in\{1,\dots m\}$.

The specific target of the correction behaves similarly to the target of a *QAP*. In some cases we don't know the target, in which case we apply rule 12.
Plan-Correction can also lead to the modification of an agent's own plan because of other agent's proposals. In this case it corrects the list of parent variables on which a preference depends. We call that list of variables the *operative variables*. Once the operative variables are changed, *Plan-Correction* can elaborate a plan if some new preferences are expressed. For example, all agents have agreed to meet next week, so in their CP-net description, there is the entry $Week1 \succ \overline{Week1}$. Then discussion shows that their availabilities are not compatible and one of them says "okay, that week is not going to work.". That does not mean the agent prefers $\overline{Week1}$ to $Week1$ because both agreed on $Week1$ as preferable. Rather, $Week1$ has been removed as an operative variable in the following discourse segments. This leads us to the following rule:

14. For $Plan\text{-}Correction(\pi_1,\pi_2)$ which corrects the list of parent variables, the operative variable list becomes the intersection of all $Pa(X)$ where $X \in Var(P(\pi_1))$. We can now apply $Commit(Plan\text{-}Elab(\pi_1,\pi_2),\mathcal{DN})$, if $P(\pi_2)$ contains some new preferences ϕ. If the CPT affected by a rule has no entry for the current operative variable list o, then $o:\phi$ has to be added to $\mathcal{DN}$.

Continuation, Contrast and **Q-Cont** pattern with the rule for *Elab*. **Alternation** patterns with rule 8.b.[6] **Explanation, Explanation*, Result, Qclar** (clarification question), **Commentary, Summary** and **Acknowledgment**

[6]The rule for Alternative questions like *Do you want fish or chicken?* is a special case yielding $\phi \bigtriangledown \psi(P(\pi))$, but we don't offer details here.

either do nothing or have the same effect on preference elicitation as *Elab*. Sometimes, adding these preferences via the *Elab* rule may yield an unsatisfiable CP-net description, because an implicit correction is involved. If an evaluation of the CP-net (see next section) is performed after a processing of one of these rules shows that the CP-net description is not satisfiable, then we apply the rule 13, associated with *Correction*.

6 From Descriptions to Models

Each dialogue turn adds constraints monotonically to the descriptions of the CP-nets to which the dialogue participants commit. We have interpreted each new declared variable in our rules as independent, which allows us to give a domain independent description of preference elicitation. However, when it comes to evaluating a CP-net description for satisfiability, we need to take into account various axioms about preference (irreflexivity and transitivity), and axioms for the domain of conversation: in our case, temporal designations (Wednesdays are not Tuesdays and so on). This typically adds dependencies among the variables in the description. In the case of the Verbmobil domain, since the variable *Monday* means essentially "to meet on Monday", *Monday* implies *Meet* , and this must be reflected via a dependency in the CP-net: we must view the variable *Meet* as filling a hidden slot in the variable *Monday* in the preference description, $Meet: Mon \succ \overline{Mon}$. This likewise allows us to fill in the negative clauses of the CP-net description: we can now infer that $\overline{Meet}: \overline{Mon} \succ Mon$. These axioms also predict certain preference descriptions to be unsatisfiable. For instance, if we have $Mon \succ \overline{Mon}$, our axioms imply $Mon \succ Tues$, $Mon \succ Wed$, etc. At this point we can calculate, *ceteris paribus*, inconsistencies on afternoons and mornings of particular days.

Domain knowledge also allows us to collapse Boolean valued variables that all denote, say, days or times of the day into multiple valued variables. So for instance, our domain independent algorithm from dialogue moves to preference descriptions might yield:

(4) $\text{Meet} \wedge \overline{31.01} \wedge \overline{30.01} \wedge 02.02: \text{am} \succ \overline{am}$

Domain knowledge collapses all Boolean variables for distinct days into one variable with values for days to get:

(5) $\text{Meet} \wedge 02.02: \text{am} \succ \text{pm}$

This leads to a sizeable reduction in the set of variables that are used in the CP-net.

We can test any CP-net description for satisfiability by turning the description formulas into CP-net entries. Our description automatically produces a directed graph over the parent variables. We have to check that the $\succ$ statements form an irreflexive and transitive relation and that each variable introduced into the CP-net has a preference entry consistent given these constraints. If the description does not yield a preference entry for a given variable X, we will add the indifference formula $X \sim \overline{X}$ as the entry. If our CP-net description meets these requirements, this procedure yields a minimal CP-net. Testing for satisfiability is useful in eliciting preferences from several discourse moves like *Explanation*, *Qclar* or *Result*, since in the case of unsatisfiability, we will exploit the Correction rule 13 with these moves.

7 Evaluation of the proposed method

We evaluate our method by testing it against the judgments of three annotators on three randomly chosen unseen test dialogues from the Verbmobil corpus. The test corpus contains 75 EDUs and the proportion of discourse relations is the same as in the corpus overall. The three annotators were *naive* in the sense that they were not familiar with preference representations and preference reasoning strategies. For each dialogue segment, we checked if the judges had the same intuitions that we did on: (i) how commitments to preferences are extracted from EDUs, and (ii) how preferences evolve through dialogue exchange.

The judges were given a manual with all the instructions and definitions needed to make the annotations. For example, the manual defined preference to be "a notion of comparison between one thing at least one other". The manual also instructs annotators to label each EDU with the following four bits of information: (1) preferences (if any) expressed in the EDU; (2) dependencies between preferences expressed in the EDU; (3) dependencies between preferences in the current EDU and previous ones; and (4) preference evolution (namely, the appearance of a new factor that affects preferred outcomes, update to preferences over values for an existing factor, and so on). For each of these four components, example dialogues were given for each type of decision they would need to make, and instructions were given on the format in which to code their judgements. Appendix A shows an example of an annotated dialogue.

Table 2 presents results of the evaluation of (i). For each EDU, we asked the annotator to list the preferences expressed in the EDU and we compared the preferences extracted by each judge with those extracted by our algorithm. The triple (a, b, c) respectively indicates the proportion of common preferences (two preference sets Γ_i and Γ_j are common if ($\Gamma_i = \Gamma_j$) or ($\exists x \in \Gamma_i, y \in \Gamma_j, x \rightarrow y$)—for example, the preference $MeetBefore2 \succ MeetAt2$ implies $\overline{MeetAt2} \succ MeetAt2$), the proportion of preferences that one judge extracts and the other judge or our algorithm misses and the proportion of preferences missed by one judge and extracted by the other judge or by our algorithm. The average annotator-algorithm agreement (AAA) is 75.6% and the average inter-annotator agree-

	Our algorithm	J1	J2	J3	% of EDUs that commit to preferences
Our algorithm		(83, 4, 13)	(91, 0, 9)	(91, 0, 9)	76%
J1	(83, 13, 4)		(85, 7, 8)	(91, 4, 5)	80%
J2	(91, 9, 0)	(85, 8, 7)		(92, 4, 4)	86%
J3	(91, 9, 0)	(91, 5, 4)	(92, 4, 4)		84%

Table 2: Evaluating how preferences are extracted from EDUs.

	Our algorithm	J1	J2	J3
Our algorithm		(85, 71)	(96, 100)	(93, 86)
J1	(85, 71)		(89, 71)	(91, 86)
J2	(96, 100)	(89, 71)		(98, 86)
J3	(93, 86)	(91, 86)	(98, 86)	

Table 3: Evaluating how preferences evolve through dialogue.

ment (IAA) is 77.9%; this shows that our method for extracting preferences from EDUs is reliable.

The evaluation (ii) proceeds as follows. For each EDU, we ask the judge if the segment introduces new preferences or if it updates, corrects or deletes preferences commited in previous turns. As in (i), judges have to justify their choices. Table 3 presents the preliminary results where the couple (a,b) indicates respectively the proportion of common elaborations (preference updates or new preferences) and the proportion of common corrections. Since elaboration is also applied in case of other discourse relations (e.g., *Q-Elab*), the measure a evaluates the rules 8, 9, 10 (**yes**) and 11. Similarly, the measure b evaluates the rules 10 (**no**), 13 and 14. We obtain AAA=91% IAA=92.7% for elaboration and AAA=85.7% IAA=81% for correction.

8 Conclusion

We have proposed a compositional method for eliciting preferences from dialogue consisting of a domain-independent algorithm for constructing a partial CP-net description of preferences, followed by a domain-specific method for identifying the minimal CP-net satisfying the partial description and domain constraints. The method supports qualitative and partial information about preferences, with CP-nets benefiting from linear algorithms for computing the optimal outcome from a set of preferences and their dependencies. The need to compute intentions from partially defined preferences is crucial in dialogue, since preferences are acquired and change through dialogue exchange.

Our work partially confirms that CP-nets have a certain naturalness, as the map from dialogue moves to preferences using the CP-net formalism is relatively intuitive. The next step is to implement our method. This depends on extracting discourse structure from text, which, though difficult, is becoming increasingly tractable for simple domains (Baldridge and Lascarides, 2005b). We plan to extract CP-net descriptions from EDUs and to evaluate these descriptions using "multi-valued variables" automatically. We will then evaluate our method on a large number of dialogues.

Our work here is also and more generally a first step towards modelling the complex interaction between what agents say, what their preferences are, and what they take the preferences of other dialogue agents to be. It leads to a conception of dialogue that's more general than one based purely on Gricean cooperative principles (Grice, 1975). On a purely Gricean approach, conversation is cooperative in at least two ways: a basic level concerning the conventions that govern linguistic meaning (basic cooperativity); and a level concerning shared attitudes towards what is said, including shared intentions (content cooperativity). While basic cooperation is needed for communication to work at all, content cooperativity involves strongly cooperative axioms like Cooperativity (interlocutors normally adopt the speaker's intentions) (Allen and Litman, 1987, Grosz and Sidner, 1990, Lochbaum, 1998). Our approach allows for divergent preferences and divergent intentions, i.e. conversations that aren't based on content cooperativity. This will allow us to exploit information about conflicting agents' preferences and game-theoretic techniques that are inherent in the logics of CP-nets for computing optimal moves (Bonzon, 2007). And in contrast to Franke et al. (2009), who analyse conversations where content cooperativity doesn't hold using a game-theoretic framework, our approach allows for partial and qualitative representations of preferences rather than demanding complete and quantitative representations of them.

References

J. Allen and D. Litman. A plan recognition model for subdialogues in conversations. *Cognitive Science*, 11 (2):163–200, 1987.

N. Asher and A. Lascarides. *Logics of Conversation*. Cambridge University Press, 2003.

J. Baldridge and A. Lascarides. Annotating discourse structures for robust semantic interpretation. In *Proceedings of the Sixth International Workshop on Computational Semantics (IWCS)*, Tilburg, The Netherlands, 2005a.

J. Baldridge and A. Lascarides. Probabilistic head-driven parsing for discourse structure. In *Proceedings of the Ninth Conference on Computational Natural Language Learning (CoNLL)*, pages 96–103, 2005b.

E. Bonzon. *Modélisation des Interactions entre Agents Rationnels: les Jeux Booléens*. PhD thesis, Université Paul Sabatier, Toulouse, 2007.

C. Boutilier, R.I. Brafman, C. Domshlak, H.H. Hoos, and David Poole. Cp-nets: A tool for representing and reasoning with conditional *ceteris paribus* preference statements. *Journal of Artificial Intelligence Research*, 21:135–191, 2004.

M. Franke, T. de Jager, and R. van Rooij. Relevance in cooperation and conflict. *Journal of Logic and Language*, 2009.

J. Ginzburg. *The Interactive Stance: Meaning for Conversation*. CSLI Publications, to appear.

H. P. Grice. Logic and conversation. In P. Cole and J. L. Morgan, editors, *Syntax and Semantics Volume 3: Speech Acts*, pages 41–58. Academic Press, 1975.

B. Grosz and C. Sidner. Plans for discourse. In J. Morgan P. R. Cohen and M. Pollack, editors, *Intentions in Communication*, pages 365–388. MIT Press, 1990.

Y. He and S. Young. Spoken language understsanding using the hidden vector state model. *Speech Communication*, 48(3-4):262–275, 2005.

J. R. Hobbs, M. Stickel, D. Appelt, and P. Martin. Interpretation as abduction. *Artificial Intelligence*, 63(1–2): 69–142, 1993.

A. Lascarides and N. Asher. Agreement, disputes and commitment in dialogue. *Journal of Semantics*, 26(2): 109–158, 2009.

O. Lemon and O. Pietquin. Machine learning for spoken dialogue systems. In *Interspeech*, 2007.

K. E. Lochbaum. A collaborative planning model of intentional structure. *Computational Linguistics*, 24(4): 525–572, 1998.

W. C. Mann and S. A. Thompson. Rhetorical structure theory: A framework for the analysis of texts. *International Pragmatics Association Papers in Pragmatics*, 1:79–105, 1987.

M. Poesio and D. Traum. Towards an axiomatisation of dialogue acts. In J. Hulstijn and A. Nijholt, editors, *Proceedings of the Twente Workshop on the Formal Semantics and Pragmatics of Dialogue*. 1998.

E. Rasmusen. *Games and Information: An Introduction to Game Theory*. Blackwell Publishing, 2007.

W. Wahlster, editor. *Verbmobil: Foundations of Speech-to-Speech Translation*. Springer, 2000.

Appendix A : Treatment of an example

We illustrate in this section how our rules work on an example. Since this dialogue was also evaluated by our judges (cf section 7), we give where relevant some details on those annotations. The example is as follows:

(6)
- π_1. *A*: so, I guess we should have another meeting
- π_2. *A*: how long do you think it should be for.
- π_3. *B*: well, I think we have quite a bit to talk about.
- π_4. *B*: maybe, two hours?
- π_5. *B*: how does that sound.
- π_6. *A*: deadly,
- π_7. *A*: but, let us do it anyways.
- π_8. *B*: okay, do you have any time next week?
- π_9. *B*: I have got, afternoons on Tuesday and Thursday.
- π_{10}. *A*: I am out of Tuesday Wednesday Thursday,
- π_{11}. *A*: so, how about Monday or Friday

Table 4 is the DSDRS associated with (6). $Relation(\pi_i, [\pi_j - \pi_k])$ indicates that a rhetorical relation holds between the segment π_i and a segment consisting of $\pi_j, \pi_{j+1}, \ldots, \pi_k$

π_1 provides an atomic preference. We apply the rule 1 and so $Commit_A(\pi_1, \mathcal{DN}_A)$ adds the description $\mathcal{DN}_A \models M \succ \overline{M}(CPT(M))$ where *M* means Meet.

π_2 We have *Q-Elab*(π_1, π_2). *A* continues to commit to *M* in π_2 and no new preferences are introduced by π_2. We apply rule 9, which makes the $P(\pi_2)$ description the same as $P(\pi_1)$'s.

π_3 is linked to π_2 with *QAP*. *B* accepts *A*'s preference and we apply the rule 11 since π_2 is a *wh*-question. Thus $Commit_B(Elab_B(\pi_2, \pi_3), \mathcal{DN}_B)$ adds the description $\mathcal{DN}_B \models M \succ \overline{M}(CPT(M))$. It is interesting to note that some judges consider that agent's utterance in π_3 indicates a preference towards "talking a long time" while other judges consider, as our method predicts, that this segment does not convey any preference.

π_4 is linked to π_3 by *Q-Elab*. *B* commits to a new preference. We apply rule 9, rule 8 and then rule 8.a. The preference on the hour is now dependent on the preference on meeting; i.e., $\mathcal{DN}_B \models M : 2h \succ \overline{2h}(CPT(2h))$, where the variable $2h$ means two hours.

π_5 is related to π_4 with the *Q-Cont* relation. We then follow the same rule as the continued relation, namely *Q-Elab*. We apply rule 9 which does not change the CP-net description of *B* because π_5 does not convey any preference.

π_6 is related to π_5 with *QAP* relation. In this case, it's not clear what is the QAP target and so we apply rule 12: we wait to learn more and we do not change *B*'s CP-net description.

All the Judges indicated that segments π_5 and π_6 are ambiguous and therefore hesitated to say if they commit to preferences. For example in π_6, do we have a preference for meeting more than 2 hours or less than 2 hours? This indecision is compatible with the predictions of rule 12.

π_7 *A* accepts *B*'s preference. We apply rule 9 and then rule 8 to obtain:
$\mathcal{DN}_A \models M \succ \overline{M}(CPT(M))$,
$\mathcal{DN}_A \models M : 2h \succ \overline{2h}(CPT(2h))$.

π_8 is linked to π_7 by *Q-Elab*. *B* introduces a new preference for meeting next week.

We apply rule 9 and then 8 to obtain:
$\mathcal{DN}_B \models M \succ \overline{M}(CPT(M))$,
$\mathcal{DN}_B \models M : 2h \succ \overline{2h}(CPT(2h))$,
$\mathcal{DN}_B \models M \wedge 2h : NW \succ \overline{NW}(CPT(NW))$ where the variable *NW* means next week.

π_9 is linked to π_8 by *Plan-Elab*. π_9 expresses commitments to preference that already involve a CP-net description. *B* introduces three preferences: one for meeting on Tuesday, the other for meeting on Thursday and given the conjunction of preferences $Tues \wedge Thurs$, one for time afternoon (of Tuesday and Thursday). That is, $((\Diamond(Tues) \wedge \Diamond(Thurs)) \mapsto Aft)(P(\pi_9))$. We apply the equivalence (3) and obtain :
$(\Diamond(Tues \bigtriangledown Thurs) \rightarrow Aft)(P(\pi_9))$.
Then, we apply rules 8.g, 8.b and 8.d. The CP-net description of *B* is thus updated as follows:
$\mathcal{DN}_B \models M \wedge 2h \wedge NW \wedge \overline{Tues} : Thurs \succ \overline{Thurs}(CPT(Thurs))$,
$\mathcal{DN}_B \models M \wedge 2h \wedge NW \wedge Tues : Thurs \sim \overline{Thurs}(CPT(Thurs))$,
$\mathcal{DN}_B \models M \wedge 2h \wedge NW \wedge \overline{Thurs} : Tues \succ \overline{Tues}(CPT(Tues))$,
$\mathcal{DN}_B \models M \wedge 2h \wedge NW \wedge Thurs : Tues \sim \overline{Tues}(CPT(Tues))$,
$\mathcal{DN}_B \models M \wedge 2h \wedge NW \wedge (Thurs \vee Tues) : Aft \succ \overline{Aft}(CPT(Aft))$.

Most judges express here a preference ranking over outcomes. For instance, if *B* elaborates by adding the preference "I have got Monday morning too" (as it is in the test corpus), some consider the ranking "(Tuesday or Thursday afternoons) $\succ$ (Monday

Turn	A's SDRS	B's SDRS
1	$\pi_{1A} : Q\text{-}Elab(\pi_1, \pi_2)$	$\emptyset$
2	π_{1A}:is the same as in turn 1	$\pi_{2B} : Q\text{-}Elab(\pi_1, [\pi_2 - \pi_5]) \wedge QAP(\pi_2, [\pi_3 - \pi_5]) \wedge$ $Q\text{-}Elab(\pi_3, \pi)$ $\pi : Q\text{-}Cont(\pi_4, \pi_5)$
3	$\pi_{3A} : Q\text{-}Elab(\pi_1, [\pi_2 - \pi_7]) \wedge QAP(\pi_2, [\pi_3 - \pi_7]) \wedge$ $Q\text{-}Elab(\pi_3, [\pi_4, \pi_7]) \wedge QAP(\pi, \pi')$ $\pi : Q\text{-}Cont(\pi_4, \pi_5), \pi' : Contrast(\pi_6, \pi_7)$	π_{2B}: is the same as in turn 2
4	π_{3A}: is the same as in turn 3	$\pi_{4B} : Q\text{-}Elab(\pi_1, [\pi_2 - \pi_9]) \wedge QAP(\pi_2, [\pi_3 - \pi_9]) \wedge$ $Q\text{-}Elab(\pi_3, [\pi_4 - \pi_9]) \wedge QAP(\pi, [\pi_6 - \pi_9]) \wedge$ $Q\text{-}Elab(\pi', \pi'')$ $\pi : Q\text{-}Cont(\pi_4, \pi_5), \pi' : Contrast(\pi_6, \pi_7)$ $\pi'' : Plan\text{-}Elab(\pi_8, \pi_9)$
5	$\pi_{5A} : Q\text{-}Elab(\pi_1, [\pi_2 - \pi_{11}]) \wedge QAP(\pi_2, [\pi_3 - \pi_{11}]) \wedge$ $Q\text{-}Elab(\pi_3, [\pi_4 - \pi_{11}]) \wedge QAP(\pi, [\pi_6 - \pi_{11}]) \wedge$ $Q\text{-}Elab(\pi', [\pi_8 - \pi_{11}]) \wedge QAP(\pi'', \pi''')$ $\pi : Q\text{-}Cont(\pi_4, \pi_5), \pi' : Contrast(\pi_6, \pi_7)$ $\pi'' : Plan\text{-}Elab(\pi_8, \pi_9), \pi''' : Q\text{-}Elab(\pi_{10}, \pi_{11})$	π_{4B}: is the same as in turn 4

Table 4: The DSDRS for Dialogue (6).

morning) $\succ$ (other days)", while others consider the ranking "(Tuesday or Thursday afternoon) or (Monday morning) $\succ$ (other days)". We did not treat such preference ranking.

π_{10} is related to π_9 by *QAP* where *A* answers no to *B*'s question asked in π_8. We apply rule 10 (**no**). Since $\overline{Tues}\&\overline{Weds}\&\overline{Thurs}(P(\pi_{10}))$ is not consistent with $((\Diamond(Tues) \wedge \Diamond(Thurs)) \mapsto Aft)(P(\pi_9))$, we apply $Commit_A(Correction(\pi_9, \pi_{10}), \mathcal{DN}_A)$, which adds the preference *Weds* to *A*'s description and then the rule 13 where *Tues* and *Thurs* are respectively replaced by $\overline{Tues}$ and $\overline{Thurs}$:
$\mathcal{DN}_A \models M \wedge 2h \wedge NW : \overline{Tues} \succ Tues(CPT(Tues))$,
$\mathcal{DN}_A \models M \wedge 2h \wedge NW : \overline{Thurs} \succ Thurs(CPT(Thurs))$,
$\mathcal{DN}_A \models M \wedge 2h \wedge NW : \overline{Weds} \succ Weds(CPT(Weds))$.

π_{11} Finally, this segment is linked to π_{10} with *Q-Elab* where $Mond \bigtriangledown Fri(P(\pi_{11}))$. We apply rules 9 and 8.b and update *A*'s CP-net description as follows:
$\mathcal{DN}_A \models M \wedge 2h \wedge NW \wedge \overline{Tues} \wedge \overline{Thurs} \wedge \overline{Weds} \wedge \overline{Fri} : Mond \succ \overline{Mond}(CPT(Mond))$,
$\mathcal{DN}_A \models M \wedge 2h \wedge NW \wedge \overline{Tues} \wedge \overline{Thurs} \wedge \overline{Weds} \wedge Fri : Mond \sim \overline{Mond}(CPT(Mond))$,
$\mathcal{DN}_A \models M \wedge 2h \wedge NW \wedge \overline{Tues} \wedge \overline{Thurs} \wedge \overline{Weds} \wedge \overline{Mond} : Fri \succ \overline{Fri}(CPT(Fri))$,
$\mathcal{DN}_A \models M \wedge 2h \wedge NW \wedge \overline{Tues} \wedge \overline{Thurs} \wedge \overline{Weds} \wedge Mond : Fri \sim \overline{Fri}(CPT(Fri))$.

The evaluation of this dialogue also reveals to what extent naive annotators reason with binary (*Monday preferred to not Monday*) or multi-valued variables (*Monday preferred to Tuesday*). Most judges use multi-valued variables to express the preference extracted from an EDU, and the way in which our method exploits domain knowledge to yield the minimal CP-net satisfying the description reflects this. In addition, some judges use a small set of variables (for example the variable *time of meeting* that groups together the notion of week, day, hours, etc.) while others use a distinct variable for each preference. Finally, we also noticed that judges do not describe the same preference dependencies. For example, in:

(7) We could have lunch together and then have the meeting from one to three?

some consider that the preference on having lunch is independent from the preference on the meeting (in this case, they consider that the preference on the period one to three is independent from the preference on meeting) while others consider that the two preferences are dependent.

Using Performance Trajectories to Analyze the Immediate Impact of User State Misclassification in an Adaptive Spoken Dialogue System

Kate Forbes-Riley
Learning Research & Development Ctr (LRDC)
University of Pittsburgh
Pittsburgh, PA 15260
forbesk@cs.pitt.edu

Diane Litman
Dept. Computer Science & LRDC
University of Pittsburgh
Pittsburgh, PA 15260
litman@cs.pitt.edu

Abstract

We present a method of evaluating the *immediate* performance impact of user state misclassifications in spoken dialogue systems. We illustrate the method with a tutoring system that adapts to student uncertainty over and above correctness. First we define a ranking of user states representing local performance. Second, we compare user state trajectories when the first state is accurately classified versus misclassified. Trajectories are quantified using a previously proposed metric representing the likelihood of transitioning from one user state to another. Comparison of the two sets of trajectories shows whether user state misclassifications change the likelihood of subsequent higher or lower ranked states, relative to accurate classification. Our tutoring system results illustrate the case where user state misclassification increases the likelihood of negative performance trajectories as compared to accurate classification.

1 Introduction

Spoken dialogue systems research has shown that natural language processing errors can negatively impact global system performance. For example, automatic speech recognition errors have been shown to negatively correlate with user satisfaction surveys taken after the system interaction is over (e.g., (Walker et al., 2000a; Pon-Barry et al., 2004)).

Automatic user state classification errors have also been shown to negatively impact global performance in spoken dialogue systems (e.g., (Pon-Barry et al., 2006)). For example, in our prior work with an uncertainty-adaptive spoken dialogue computer tutoring system, we found that recognizing and adapting to the user's state of uncertainty, over and above his/her state of correctness, significantly improved global learning over all users (as measured by tests taken before and after the system interaction). However, this was only true when the user uncertainty was manually labeled during the interaction by an unseen human "wizard of oz" (Forbes-Riley and Litman, 2011b); it was not true when the uncertainty was automatically labeled by the system. Further analysis showed that uncertainty classification errors largely accounted for the global performance decrease in our fully automated system. In particular, only a small proportion of users' actual uncertainty was being accurately classified by the system (Forbes-Riley and Litman, 2011a).[1]

The question we address in this study is how to analyze the impact of automatic user state classification errors when analyzing performance at a *local* level. In particular, is there a measurable local performance difference when one compares what happens in a dialogue after a turn is accurately classified versus misclassified? We show here how user state trajectories can be used to answer this question. First, a ranking of user states is defined (Section 3.1). Second, user state trajectories are computed from two sets of system dialogue: one in

[1]In natural language processing (NLP) research, the terms "(in)correct" and "(un)certain" can have multiple interpretations. To avoid confusion, we reserve these terms in this paper *only* to refer to the semantic content and affective/attitudinal expression of user answers (respectively). When referring to the NLP performance of our system, we use the terms "accurately classified" and "misclassified".

Proceedings of the SIGDIAL 2011: the 12th Annual Meeting of the Special Interest Group on Discourse and Dialogue, pages 216–226,
Portland, Oregon, June 17-18, 2011.

which the user state of interest is accurately classified in the first turn in the trajectory, and another in which it is misclassified (Section 3.2). Trajectories are quantified as the likelihood of transitioning from one user state to another (D'Mello et al., 2007). Comparison of the two sets of trajectories indicates how user state misclassifications change the relative likelihood of subsequent states. Transitions to higher ranked states indicate improved local performance while transitions to lower ranked states indicate decreased local performance.

In our research, we are interested in this question because we hypothesize that accurate and inaccurate user state classification in our uncertainty-adaptive system yielded immediate differences in user behavior. We further hypothesize that our uncertainty-adaptive system had a negative immediate impact on the user's state when (un)certainty was misclassified, as compared to when (un)certainty was accurately classified. Our user state trajectory results support these hypotheses. We find that (un)certainty misclassifications increased the likelihood of transitioning to the lowest ranked user state in the next turn. In contrast, accurate (un)certainty classification yielded an increased likelihood of more positive performance trajectories (Section 4).

More generally, this question is relevant to other automatically classified user states and other types of dialogue systems, whenever the goal is to understand the immediate impact of user state classification errors on user behavior during the dialogue (Sections 3.1 and Section 5).

2 The System and Dialogues

We apply this local performance analysis to dialogues between college students and our fully automated spoken dialogue tutoring system, ITSPOKE.[2]

Two sets of dialogues are used here, which come from two versions of ITSPOKE: the uncertainty-adaptive and non-adaptive versions. Both versions automatically classify user (un)certainty and (in)correctness for each turn. However, the non-adaptive version's responses are based only on (in)correctness, while the uncertainty-adaptive version provides an uncertainty adaptation to uncertain+correct answers. All dialogues were collected in our prior experiment comparing global learning across the uncertainty-adaptive and non-adaptive system versions (see Section 1). The uncertainty-adaptive system yielded 120 dialogues (1957 student turns) from 24 subjects. The non-adaptive system yielded 125 dialogues (2065 student turns) from 25 subjects. Our analysis will focus on the dialogues from the uncertainty-adaptive system (Section 4.1); the dialogues from the non-adaptive system will be used for comparison (Section 4.2).

Briefly, ITSPOKE tutors 5 physics problems (one per dialogue), in a Tutor Question - Student Answer - Tutor Response format. The tutor questions serially present topics needed to solve each problem; adjacent questions concern identical or closely related topics. After each tutor question, the student answer is digitized from head-mounted microphone input and sent to the Sphinx2 recognizer, which yields an automatic transcript. The answer's (in)correctness is then automatically classified based on this transcript, using the TuTalk semantic analyzer (Jordan et al., 2007). Simultaneously, the answer's (un)certainty is automatically classified by inputting features of the speech signal, the automatic transcript, and the dialogue context into a logistic regression model.[3] All natural language processing components were trained using prior ITSPOKE corpora.

The dialogue manager determines the appropriate tutor response and sends it to the Cepstral text-to-speech system. The uncertainty-adaptive and non-adaptive system versions give the same response to incorrect answers (regardless of (un)certainty): incorrectness feedback (e.g., "That's not right") followed by additional remedial content to help students understand why their answer was incorrect. Both versions also give the same response to certain+correct answers: correctness feedback only (e.g., "That's right"). The two versions differ in their response to uncertain+correct answers. The non-adaptive version responds with correctness feedback only, while the uncertainty-adaptive version responds with correctness feedback followed by additional remedial content to help students resolve their uncertainty. This uncertainty adaptation is based on

[2]ITSPOKE(**I**ntelligent **T**utoring **SPOKE**n dialogue) is a spoken, modified version of Why2-Atlas (VanLehn et al., 2002).

[3]The uncertainty model includes lexical, pitch, temporal, and energy features as well as tutor question and user gender, and is described further in (Forbes-Riley and Litman, 2011a).

tutor1: Let's begin by looking at the motion of the man and his keys while he's holding them. How does his v compare to that of his keys?

student-automatic1: his also the is the same as that of his keys points force **(certain+incorrect)**

student-manual1: his velocity is the same as that of his keys while he's holding them (uncertain+correct)

tutor2: Actually... Their velocities must be the same, because the man's holding his keys, so they're not moving with respect to each other. [...] What are the forces exerted on the man after he releases his keys?

student-automatic2: gravity **(uncertain+correct)**

student-manual2: gravity?? (uncertain+correct)

non-adaptive-tutor3: Right. So what's the direction of the force of gravity on the man (e.g., vertically up)?

uncertainty-adaptive-tutor3: Right. Gravity is the only force acting on the man. This force is also called the weight of the man. It's always present when an object is in earth's gravitational field. So what's the direction of the force of gravity on the man (e.g., vertically up)?

Figure 1: Annotated Dialogue Example Showing Uncertainty Adaptation and User State Classifications

prior tutoring research, which argues that incorrectness and uncertainty are both signals of a "learning impasse", i.e., an opportunity to better learn the material (VanLehn et al., 2003). Our uncertainty adaptation only provides additional remedial content after the uncertain+correct impasse, because incorrectness impasses (uncertain and certain) already receive remedial content from the non-adaptive system. It is assumed that this content helps resolve both incorrectness and uncertainty (when present).

After the experiment, each student answer (turn) was manually transcribed and labeled for (un)certainty and (in)correctness. One labeler performed the annotation based on schemes developed and evaluated on prior ITSPOKE corpora, where this labeler and another labeler displayed interannotator reliability of 0.85 and 0.62 Kappa on (in)correctness and (un)certainty, respectively (Forbes-Riley and Litman, 2011a).[4] Comparison of the automatic and manual labels yielded 84.7% accuracy for automatic (in)correctness classification and 80.3% accuracy for automatic (un)certainty classification. However, the (un)certainty model had an uncertainty recall of only about 20%, while the (in)correctness model had a correctness recall of about 80% (Forbes-Riley and Litman, 2011a).[5]

Figure 1 illustrates ITSPOKE's natural language processing components and the two system versions. The first answer is classified as certain+incorrect (**student-automatic1**) but manually labeled as uncertain+correct (*student-manual1*); the manual and automatic transcripts are also substantially different. Because this answer was misclassified as incorrect, both versions give the same response (**tutor2**). The second answer is accurately classified as uncertain+correct. The non-adaptive system thus ignores the uncertainty and only provides correctness feedback (**non-adaptive-tutor3**), while the adaptive system responds with correctness feedback and additional remedial content to help resolve the uncertainty (**uncertainty-adaptive-tutor3**).

3 Local Performance Evaluation

Here we discuss how to evaluate the local impact of user state misclassification in dialogue systems.

3.1 Defining a User State Severity Ranking

Building on tutoring research that views both uncertainty and incorrectness as signals of learning impasses (Section 2), we previously defined a severity ranking for the four impasse states corresponding to all combinations of binary (in)correctness

[4]Because these evaluations showed that this trained labeler could reliably annotate (un)certainty and (in)correctness in ITSPOKE dialogues, no further evaluations were performed.

[5]The lower recall for predicting uncertainty is nevertheless higher than always predicting no uncertainty (a majority class baseline has 0% recall), and is on par with prior work in affect-adaptive tutoring systems, e.g. (Walonoski and Heffernan, 2006); in general affective systems research has found it difficult to accurately predict positive occurrences of affect.

Impasse State:	**certain+incorrect**	**uncertain+incorrect**	**uncertain+correct**	**certain+correct**
Severity:	*most*	*less*	*least*	*none*

Figure 2: User Impasse State Severity Ranking

and (un)certainty (Forbes-Riley and Litman, 2011a). This ranking, shown in Figure 2, reflects the assumption that a student must perceive an impasse in order to resolve it. A state of uncertainty reflects this awareness. Therefore, the most severe type of learning impasse occurs when a student is incorrect but not aware of it. Impasse states of decreasing severity occur when the student is incorrect but aware that s/he might be, and correct but believes s/he may not be, respectively. No impasse exists when a student is correct and not uncertain about it.

In our prior work, this ranking of user states was independently validated by showing that average impasse state severity negatively correlates with global learning gain in our system dialogues (Forbes-Riley and Litman, 2011a). In other words, a higher proportion of user states with less severe or no impasses directly relates to higher global learning gain.

More generally, the idea of ranking user states in terms of those that do or do not represent *communication impasses* applies to other dialogue system domains and other user state dimensions as well. For example, in information-seeking domains, frustration and anger are common affective states whose occurrence during the dialogue signals severe communication problems (Batliner et al., 2003), while hang-ups and turns requesting a human operator are other types of user states whose occurrence during the dialogue signals severe communication problems (Walker et al., 2000b).

Moreover, state trajectories can be used to represent abstractions over other types of user (or system) behaviors. In our tutoring system analysis, representing user states in terms of only (un)certainty and (in)correctness is an abstraction that we find useful for analyzing impasse trajectories. However, during run-time, a finite-state dialogue manager consisting of 142 states actually controls the system's operation, and uses many other features besides user uncertainty and incorrectness to determine the system's response (e.g. the physics concepts related to the current system question, the history of prior student answers to similar questions, etc.). Any of these states could be analyzed as well to understand their local performance impact, as could their analogs in other system domains. For example, in a train dialogue system, while the actual state representation used during operation could be quite complex, for a trajectory analysis a simpler representation could be suitable, one which tracks whether the system knows the values of the n attributes needed to query the database. The state ranking in this case would be over equivalence classes of states: states with n attributes known > states with n-1 attributes known > ... > initial state with 0 attributes known.

3.2 Computing User State Trajectories

Local trajectories of user states during a dialogue can be computed as the likelihood of transitioning from the user state in turn *n* to the user state in turn *n+1*. Here we use D'Mello et al.'s metric, *transition likelihood L* (D'Mello et al., 2007).

Transition likelihood L is computed as shown below, where *n* refers to the impasse state in turn *n* and *n+1* refers to the impasse state in turn *n+1*. As shown, L is computed as the conditional probability that the user state in turn *n+1* will occur given that the user state in turn *n* has occurred, adjusted for the base rate of occurrence of the user state in turn *n+1*. The denominator normalizes the result so that L ranges from $-\infty$ to 1. L=1 indicates that *n+1* always follows *n* over and above the probability of n+1 occurring. L=0 indicates that *n+1* follows *n* at the chance level. L<0 indicate that the likelihood of *n+1* following *n* is much lower than the base rate of *n+1* occurring.[6]

$$\mathbf{L(n \rightarrow n+1)} = \frac{P(n+1|n)-P(n+1)}{1-P(n+1)}$$

Transition likelihood L has previously been used to compute the likelihood of transitioning from one affective state to another (e.g., from confusion to

[6]Note that this metric, which assesses the adjusted probability of one user state following another, is equivalent to Kappa in computing agreement among annotators after adjusting for chance (D'Mello et al., 2007).

frustration) in a single set of dialogues between student and computer tutor (D'Mello et al., 2007). Transition likelihood L has also been used to compare how the likelihoods of transitioning from one affective state to another vary across two different sets of dialogues collected with two different versions of an affect-adaptive tutoring system (McQuiggan et al., 2008). Our analysis is based on this analysis, but extends it in three ways: 1) our transitions involve complex user states composed of two dimensions ((un)certainty and (in)correctness), 2) the user states in our transitions are ranked to enable a local performance analysis, 3) our performance analysis is applied to the question of how user state misclassification impacts local performance, by comparing transition likelihoods after accurate and inaccurate user state classifications.

In this prior work and in our work, likelihoods for each transition are computed for each user (over all dialogues of a user). ANOVAs with post-hoc pairwise tests can then determine if there were significant differences between all possible transitions from the current user state in turn *n*.

To investigate how user state misclassifications impact local performance, *two* user trajectories are computed per user for each *n*→*n+1* transition: one when the manual and automatic user state labels for turn *n* agreed, and another when they did not agree. In both cases, using the manual label for turn *n+1* enables the *true* final user state to be compared across the two sets of trajectories. Comparison of the final state in the two sets of trajectories indicates how user state misclassifications change the relative likelihood of the subsequent user states. Transitions to higher ranked states indicate improved local performance while transitions to lower ranked states indicate decreased local performance.

4 Impact of User State Misclassifications in Uncertainty-Adaptive ITSPOKE

We now apply this analysis to the uncertainty-adaptive ITSPOKE dialogues, to investigate how user state misclassification impacts the local performance of the uncertainty adaptation.

Since the complex user state of uncertain+correct triggers the uncertainty adaptation, misclassifying (un)certainty or (in)correctness can potentially impact the local performance of the adaptation. However, as noted in Section 2, we previously found that uncertainty misclassifications in our system were more severe than correctness misclassifications. Thus, to streamline our analysis and avoid data skew issues, we focus on how (un)certainty misclassifications in manually labeled correct answers impact our local performance trajectories. There are 1270 manually labeled correct turns in the dialogues collected with uncertainty-adaptive ITSPOKE. In the dialogues collected with non-adaptive ITSPOKE (which we will use for comparison), there are 1353 manually labeled correct turns.

We hypothesize that when (un)certainty misclassification in correct answers causes the uncertainty adaptation to be erroneously triggered or blocked, we will see a negative performance impact, in terms of an increased likelihood of transitioning to a more severe impasse state when uncertainty is misclassified as compared to when it is accurately classified.

4.1 Uncertainty-Adaptive ITSPOKE Results

Accurate Uncertainty Classification: Figure 3 presents descriptive statistics for the likelihood (L) that a manually labeled uncertain+correct answer *accurately classified as uncertain* in turn *n* will transition to each of the four manually labeled impasse states in turn *n+1*. As noted in Section 3.2, L=0 indicates that the transition likelihood is equal to chance, while $L>0$ and $L<0$ indicate likelihoods greater and less than chance, respectively.

An ANOVA indicated that there were statistically significant differences among the likelihoods in Figure 3 ($F(3,56)=3.87$, $p=.02$). The most likely transitions are shown with stripes. Specifically, post-hoc pairwise tests showed that in turn *n+1*, an uncertain+incorrect answer ($p<.01$) or uncertain+correct answer ($p=.02$) is significantly more likely than a certain+correct answer (but are themselves equally likely). In addition, an uncertain+incorrect answer is significantly more likely than a certain+incorrect answer ($p=.05$), in turn *n+1*. A dialogue example of the most likely transition after accurately classified uncertainty is shown in Figure 5, where it is compared with the misclassified minimal pair in Figure 6 (see Appendix).

These results indicate that accurately classifying (and thus accurately adapting to) uncertain+correct

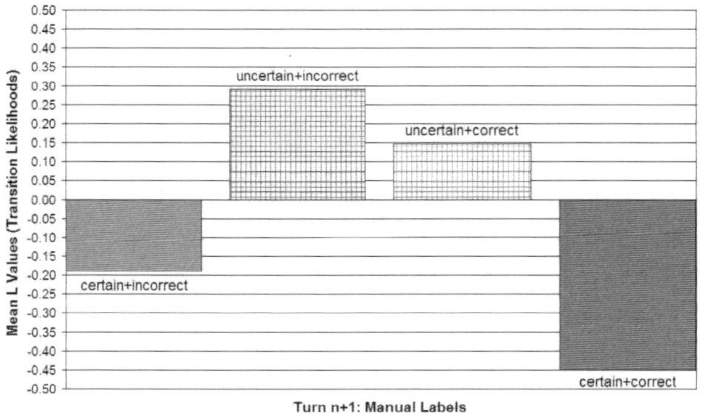

Figure 3: Turn $n \rightarrow$ Turn $n+1$ Transition Likelihoods (L) after a manually labeled uncertain+correct answer in turn n is accurately classified as uncertain and receives the uncertainty adaptation

answers is most likely to yield continued uncertainty (regardless of correctness) in turn $n+1$. Prior research (Craig et al., 2004; Kort et al., 2001) has shown that uncertainty and questioning are positive and crucial aspects of the learning process. The continued uncertainty suggests that the uncertainty adaptation keeps the student engaged in the learning process, and the equal likelihood of correctness or incorrectness accompanying this uncertainty suggests that they have not yet unreservedly adopted either the correct or incorrect line of reasoning about the topic under discussion.

To determine whether any of these transitions are directly tied to global performance, we computed Pearson's correlations over all students between the percentage of each transition and global learning gain.[7] Interestingly, transitioning from an accurately classified correct+uncertain answer to a correct+certain answer is negatively related to global learning gain (R=-.458, p=.025). This indicates that continued uncertainty after the uncertainty adaptation is provided is more beneficial, in the long run, than no uncertainty. No other trajectories are directly related to global learning. Although our prior result, that average impasse severity negatively correlates with global learning gain (Section 3.1), indicates it is better from a global perspective for a student to *be* in a state of no impasse (correct+certain), it does not tell us the best way for the student to attain this state. The results of our transition correlations shed light on this - they tell us that transitioning directly from correct+uncertain is not the best way to attain the no impasse state. We hypothesize that looking at wider transition windows (e.g., trigrams) will shed light on what *is* the best way to attain this state. For example, it may be that the best way to transition to a state of no impasse is to do so after sustained uncertainty (as in Figure 3).

[7]normalized learning gain = (posttest-pretest)/(1-pretest).

Uncertainty Misclassification: Considering now user state misclassifications, our results for accurately classified uncertain+correct answers are in sharp contrast to those for manually labeled uncertain+correct answers *misclassified as certain* in turn n. In particular, an ANOVA indicated that all manually labeled impasse states are equally likely in $n+1$ (F(3,88)=1.22, p=.32) after a misclassified uncertain+correct answer.[8]

These results indicate that misclassifying (and erroneously *not* adapting to) uncertain+correct answers is as likely to have an immediate negative impact on learning as it is to have a neutral or positive impact. In particular, the misclassification is likely to cause some students to transition from the least severe impasse about the concept in turn n to the most severe impasse about the concept in turn $n+1$.[9] When they do not receive the uncertainty adaptation, these students adopt an incorrect line of reasoning in turn $n+1$, without any uncertainty about it at all.

As illustration, compare the example in Figure 5, where uncertainty is accurately classified, with the example in Figure 6, where uncertainty is misclassified (see Appendix). As shown, the uncertainty in *student-manual1* signals that further explanation is needed. When received (Figure 5) the student still makes a math error on the next question, but s/he appears to understand the task. In contrast, when the uncertainty adaptation is erroneously not received (Figure 6), there is no indication that the student's understanding has increased; s/he appears to be simply repeating the number 9.8 (a number which appears frequently in Newtonian physics). User uncertainty misclassification in other domains could have

[8]Since the ANOVA results were non-significant, no figure or correlations are discussed.

[9]As noted in Section 2, adjacent turns within a dialogue will either address the same or closely related topics.

similar effects; in general, if a user is uncertain in turn n about how to perform a task, and the system moves on without supplying information to resolve this uncertainty, there may be an immediate negative impact if that knowledge is required or presupposed again in turn $n+1$.

Accurate Certainty Classification: Turning now to manually labeled certain+correct answers, Figure 4 presents descriptive statistics for the likelihood that when *accurately classified as certain* in turn n, certain+correct answers will transition to each of the four manually labeled impasse states in turn $n+1$. An ANOVA indicated that there were statistically significant differences among these likelihoods (F(3,92)=17.96, p<.01). The most likely transitions are shown with stripes. More specifically, post-hoc pairwise tests showed that in turn $n+1$, a manually labeled certain+correct answer is significantly more likely than any other impasse state (p<.01), and all other impasse states were equally likely. A dialogue example of the most likely transition after accurately classified certainty is shown in Figure 7, where it is compared with the misclassified minimal pair in Figure 8 (see Appendix).

These results indicate that accurately classifying and *not* adapting to certain+correct answers has an immediate positive impact on the learning process, by not introducing learning impasses about concepts already understood. Note however that Pearson's correlations for these transitions showed no significant relation to global performance.

Certainty Misclassification: Again, our results for accurately classified certain+correct answers are in sharp contrast with those found for manually labeled certain+correct answers *misclassified as uncertain* in turn n. An ANOVA indicated that all manually labeled impasse states are equally likely in turn $n+1$ (F(3,72)=0.33, p=.80). These results indicate that misclassifying and erroneously *adapting* to certain+correct answers is as likely to have an immediate negative impact on learning as it is to have a neutral or positive impact. In particular, the misclassification is likely to cause some students to transition from no impasse to the most severe impasse state. When they erroneously receive the uncertainty adaptation, these students go from no impasse at all in turn n to an incorrect line of reasoning in turn $n+1$,

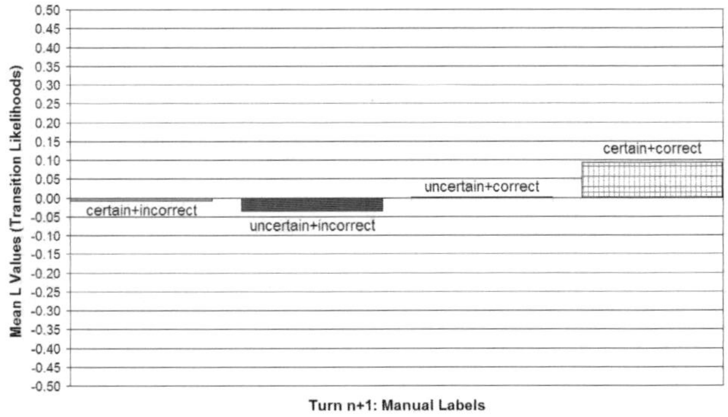

Figure 4: Turn n → Turn $n+1$ Transition Likelihoods (L) after a manually labeled certain+correct answer in turn n is accurately classified as certain and does not receive the uncertainty adaptation

without any uncertainty about it at all.

As illustration, compare the example in Figure 7, where certainty is accurately classified, with the example in in Figure 8, where certainty is misclassified (see Appendix). As shown, the certainty in *student-manual1* signals that no further explanation is needed so the system can move on (Figure 7). When the uncertainty adaptation is erroneously received even though the student is certain (Figure 8), this appears to have caused the student to stop paying close attention and thus provide an obviously incorrect answer to an easy question. User certainty misclassification in other domains could have similar effects; in general, if a user is already certain in turn n about how to perform a task, and the system "wastes" his/her time by resupplying information that is already understood, there may be an immediate negative impact in terms of loss of focus, disengagement, or even decreased understanding, that cause the task in turn $n+1$ to be performed incorrectly.

4.2 Comparing *Non-Adaptive* ITSPOKE

As a sanity check, we performed the same trajectory analysis on the dialogues from the *non-adaptive* version of the system. The purpose here was to confirm the presupposition of the above analysis, that uncertainty-adaptive ITSPOKE was actually producing different local behaviors than non-adaptive ITSPOKE. In other words, since the non-adaptive system ignores uncertainty, there should be no difference in transition likelihoods when uncertainty is accurately classified versus when it is misclassified.

This expectation was borne out. ANOVAs indicated that in the non-adaptive system, a manually labeled uncertain+correct answer is equally likely to transition to any of the four manually labeled impasse states in turn *n+1*, regardless of whether it was accurately classified as uncertain in turn *n* ($F(3,48)=0.25$, $p=.86$) or misclassified as certain in turn *n* ($F(3,92)=0.07$, $p=.98$). Thus as expected, uncertain+correct answers in the non-adaptive system pattern like uncertain+correct answers *misclassified as certain* in the uncertainty-adaptive system. In both cases, we see the same negative immediate performance impact of not giving uncertain+correct answers the uncertainty adaptation.

ANOVAs with post-hoc pairwise tests further indicated that in the non-adaptive system, a manually labeled certain+correct answer is significantly more likely to transition to a certain+correct answer than to any other manually labeled impasse state, regardless of whether it was accurately classified as certain in turn *n* (ANOVA:($F(3,96)=20.81$, $p<.001$), post-hoc tests: $p<.001$) or misclassified as uncertain in turn *n* (ANOVA:($F(3,80)=14.00$, $p<.001$), post-hoc tests: $p<.001$). Thus as expected, certain+correct answers in the non-adaptive system pattern like *accurately classified* certain+correct answers in the uncertainty-adaptive system. In both cases, we see the same positive immediate performance impact of not giving manually labeled certain+correct answers the uncertainty adaptation.

4.3 Comparing Local and Global Performance Results

Finally, in analyses such as this one, comparing local and global performance results can help pinpoint specific areas for future system redesign. In our case, this comparison suggests the most important aspect to focus on with respect to improving our uncertainty model.

In particular, as noted in Section 1, we previously found that the low uncertainty recall of our system (approximately 20%) had a negative global performance impact; mistaking so much true uncertainty for certainty substantially reduced the amount users learned (Forbes-Riley and Litman, 2011a). We also showed in this prior work that mistaking certainty for uncertainty did not negatively impact the amount users learned. These results suggested that the system should be less cautious in applying the uncertainty-adaptive behavior; i.e., applying it whenever there is some possibility that the user is actually uncertain, even if it means applying it to some turns that are actually certain.

On the other hand, our local performance analysis in this paper showed that (un)certainty misclassification increased the likelihood of an immediate negative impact on learning. These results suggest that the system should be more cautious in applying the uncertainty-adaptive behavior; i.e., only applying it when there is a high probability that the user is actually uncertain.

Together these local and global results suggest that we should focus on improving uncertainty recall without decreasing uncertainty precision, in our uncertainty model. With this goal in mind, we are currently exploring the use of features and methods from recent INTERSPEECH emotion and paralinguistic challenges (Schuller et al., 2009; Schuller et al., 2010).

5 Conclusion and Future Directions

This paper presents an approach for analyzing the immediate impact of user state misclassifications in dialogue systems. A ranking of user states is defined, and then user state trajectories are compared when the first state is accurately classified versus misclassified. Trajectories are quantified using a previously proposed metric representing the likelihood of transitioning between states. Comparison of the two sets of trajectories shows whether misclassifications change the likelihood of subsequent higher or lower ranked states, relative to accurate classification. We illustrated the approach with an adaptive tutoring system that automatically detects and adapts to student uncertainty.

As our results indicate, the approach can be used to answer questions which global performance analyses overlook. First, the analysis shows whether user state misclassifications actually matter locally - whether these errors have an immediate effect on user behavior or not. Moreover, the analysis can determine whether this effect is positive or negative or neutral. In our tutoring system data, we found that misclassifying user uncertainty had a negative immediate impact on user behavior, relative to accurate classification.

The analysis can also confirm that a dialogue intervention actually changes user behaviors. In our tutoring system data, we found that the adaptive system yielded significantly different user state trajectories than the non-adaptive system, even though, as noted in Section 1, our prior global performance analysis did not show any overall differences among the global performance metrics that we examined across the adaptive and non-adaptive systems.

In addition, the analysis can confirm that a dialogue intervention shifts user behaviors in the desired direction. In our tutoring system data, we found that the immediate effect of accurately adapting to uncertainty was most likely to be continued uncertainty. Although the adaptation does not yield an immediate transition to the highest ranked user state, the outcome is clearly more positive than that of ignoring uncertainty, which increases the likelihood of transitioning to the lowest ranked user state.

Finally, the local performance results can shed light on the steps needed to improve global performance, by investigating how the two are related. In our tutoring system data, we found that there is not a one-to-one relationship between the most beneficial local and global outcomes. In particular, transitioning directly to the highest ranked (no impasse) state after receiving the uncertainty adaptation was negatively correlated to global learning gain. We hypothesized that looking at wider transition windows (e.g., trigrams) will shed light on what *is* the best local path to the highest ranked state.

We conclude by emphasizing that state trajectories can be used to represent abstractions over various types of user (or system) behaviors, in various domains, whenever their local performance impact is viewed as important to understand.

Acknowledgments

This work is funded by NSF awards #0914615 and #0631930. We thank Reva Freedman and the ITSPOKE group for comments.

References

A. Batliner, K. Fischer, R. Huber, J. Spilker, and E. Noth. 2003. How to find trouble in communication. *Speech Communication*, 40:117–143.

S. Craig, A. Graesser, J. Sullins, and B. Gholson. 2004. Affect and learning: an exploratory look into the role of affect in learning with AutoTutor. *Journal of Educational Media*, 29(3).

S. D'Mello, R. S. Taylor, and A. Graesser. 2007. Monitoring affective trajectories during complex learning. In *Proc. Cognitive Science Society*.

K. Forbes-Riley and D. Litman. 2011a. Benefits and challenges of real-time uncertainty detection and adaptation in a spoken dialogue computer tutor. *Speech Communication*. In Press.

K. Forbes-Riley and D. Litman. 2011b. Designing and evaluating a wizarded uncertainty-adaptive spoken dialogue tutoring system. *Computer Speech and Language*, 25(1):105–126.

P. Jordan, B. Hall, M. Ringenberg, Y. Cui, and C.P. Rose. 2007. Tools for authoring a dialogue agent that participates in learning studies. In *Proc. Artificial Intelligence in Education*.

B. Kort, R. Reilly, and R. Picard. 2001. An affective model of interplay between emotions and learning : Reengineering educational pedagogy-building a learning companion. In *Proc. IEEE Conference on Advanced Learning Technology*.

S. W. McQuiggan, J. L Robison, and J. C. Lester. 2008. Affective transitions in narrative-centered learning environments. In *Proc. Intelligent Tutoring Systems Conference*.

Heather Pon-Barry, Brady Clark, Elizabeth Owen Bratt, Karl Schultz, and Stanley Peters. 2004. Evaluating the effectiveness of SCoT:a spoken conversational tutor. In *Proceedings of ITS Workshop on Dialogue-based Intelligent Tutoring Systems*.

H. Pon-Barry, K. Schultz, E. Bratt, B. Clark, and S. Peters. 2006. Responding to student uncertainty in spoken tutorial dialogue systems. *International Journal of Artificial Intelligence in Education*, 16.

B. Schuller, S. Steidl, and A. Batliner. 2009. The Interspeech 2009 emotion challenge. In *Proc. Interspeech*.

B. Schuller, S. Steidl, A. Batliner, F. Burkhardt, L. Devillers, C. Muller, and S. Narayanan. 2010. The INTERSPEECH 2010 paralinguistic challenge. In *Proc. Interspeech*.

K. VanLehn, P. Jordan, C. Rosé, D. Bhembe, M. Böttner, A. Gaydos, M. Makatchev, U. Pappuswamy, M. Ringenberg, A. Roque, S. Siler, R. Srivastava, and R. Wilson. 2002. The architecture of Why2-Atlas: A coach for qualitative physics essay writing. In *Proc. Intelligent Tutoring Systems Conference*.

K. VanLehn, S. Siler, and C. Murray. 2003. Why do only some events cause learning during human tutoring? *Cognition and Instruction*, 21(3).

Marilyn A. Walker, Candace A. Kamm, and Diane J. Litman. 2000a. Towards developing general models of usability with PARADISE. *Natural Language Engineering*, 6(3).

Marilyn A. Walker, Irene Langkilde, Jerry Wright, Allen Gorin, and Diane Litman. 2000b. Learning to predict problematic situations in a spoken dialogue system: Experiments with How May I Help You? In *Proceedings of the 1st Meeting of the North American Chapter of the Association of Computational Linguistics (NAACL)*.

J. A. Walonoski and N. T. Heffernan. 2006. Detection and analysis of off-task gaming behavior in intelligent tutoring systems. In *Proceedings of the 8th International Conference on Intelligent Tutoring Systems (ITS)*, pages 382–391, Jhongli, Taiwan.

APPENDIX

tutor1: If an object in freefall begins with a velocity of zero, what'll its velocity be a second later? Please specify the units too.

student-automatic1: 9.8 meters per second **(uncertain+correct)**

student-manual1: 9.8 meters per second?? (uncertain+correct)

tutor2: Fine. Because it's in freefall, its acceleration is $9.8 m/s^2$. This tells us that every second, its velocity increases by 9.8 m/s. Therefore, at one second its velocity is 0 m/s, and a second later, its velocity is 9.8m/s. So, what'll its velocity be a second after that?

student-manual2: 18.6 meters per second?? (uncertain+incorrect)

Figure 5: Annotated Dialogue Example of Most Likely Transition after Accurate Uncertainty Classification

tutor1: If an object in freefall begins with a velocity of zero, what'll its velocity be a second later? Please specify the units too.

student-automatic1: 9.8 meters per second **(certain+correct)**

student-manual1: 9.8 meters per second?? (uncertain+correct)

tutor2: Fine. So, what'll its velocity be a second after that?

student-manual2: 9.8 meters per second (certain+incorrect)

Figure 6: Annotated Dialogue Example of Negative Impact of Uncertainty Misclassification

tutor1: There's only one horizontal force exerted on the truck during the collision with the car. What is it?

student-automatic1: impact force **(certain+correct)**

student-manual1: the impact force (certain+correct)

tutor2: Right. Now let's find the forces exerted on the truck in the vertical direction during the collision. First, what vertical force is always exerted on an object near the surface of the earth?

student-manual2: gravity (certain+correct)

Figure 7: Annotated Dialogue Example Showing Most Likely Transition after Accurate Certainty Classification

tutor1: There's only one horizontal force exerted on the truck during the collision with the car. What is it?

student-automatic1: impact force **(uncertain+correct)**

student-manual1: the impact force (certain+correct)

tutor2: Right. The problem statement says the car and the truck are both traveling in a straight horizontal line when they collide. So the impact force of the truck on the truck must be in the horizontal direction. It also says they are driving on a patch of frictionless ice when they collide. So there is no friction to take into account. This means that the impact force is the only horizontal force on the truck. Now let's find the forces exerted on the truck in the vertical direction during the collision. First, what vertical force is always exerted on an object near the surface of the earth?

student-manual2: normal force (certain+incorrect)

Figure 8: Annotated Dialogue Example Showing Negative Impact of Certainty Misclassification

Comparing Triggering Policies for Social Behaviors

Rohit Kumar, Carolyn P. Rosé
Language Technologies Institute, Carnegie Mellon University
Gates Hillman Center, 5000 Forbes Avenue,
Pittsburgh, PA, USA 15213
rohitk , cprose @ cs.cmu.edu

Abstract

Instructional efficacy of automated Conversational Agents designed to help small groups of students achieve higher learning outcomes can be improved by the use of social interaction strategies. These strategies help the tutor agent manage the attention of the students while delivering useful instructional content. Two technical challenges involving the use of social interaction strategies include determining the appropriate policy for triggering these strategies and regulating the amount of social behavior performed by the tutor. In this paper, a comparison of six different triggering policies is presented. We find that a triggering policy learnt from human behavior in combination with a filter that keeps the amount of social behavior comparable to that performed by human tutors offers the most effective solution to the these challenges.

1 Introduction

While Conversational Agents have been shown to be an effective technology for delivering instructional content to students in a variety of learning domains and situations (Grasser et. al., 2005; Kumar et. al., 2007; Arnott et. al., 2008), it has been observed that students are more likely to ignore and abuse the tutor in a collaborative learning setting (with 2 or more students) compared to the case of one-on-one tutoring (Bhatt et. al., 2004; Kumar et. al., 2007). In our prior work (Kumar et. al., 2010a), we have addressed this problem by employing agents that are capable of performing both instructional behavior as well as social behavior. In our initial implementation, the social behavior performed by these agents was composed of eleven social interaction strategies that were triggered by a set of hand crafted rules (Kumar and Rosé, 2010b). Section 2 provides additional details about these strategies.

Comparison between the social behavior triggered by our hand crafted rules and that triggered by a human tutor revealed significant perception benefits (more likeable, higher task satisfaction, etc.) for the human triggering policy. Also, the students in a wizard-of-oz condition who interacted with the tutors whose social behaviors were triggered by humans had better learning outcomes (0.93σ) with respect to a No social behavior baseline. The condition where students interacted with the rule-based automated tutors was also significantly better (0.71σ) than the No social behavior baseline in terms of learning outcomes. While the learning outcomes of the rule-based tutors was not significantly worse than the human tutor, in combination with the perception outcomes, we see the potential for further improvement of conversational agents by employing a better triggering policy.

Building on these prior results, in this paper we explore a way to improve the effectiveness of socially capable tutor agents that uses a triggering policy learnt from a corpus of human behavior. The underlying hypothesis of this approach is that a human-like triggering policy would lead to improvements in the agent's performance and percep-

Proceedings of the SIGDIAL 2011: the 12th Annual Meeting of the Special Interest Group on Discourse and Dialogue, pages 227–238,
Portland, Oregon, June 17-18, 2011.

tion ratings compared to a rule-based triggering policy. As a first step towards verifying this hypothesis, we learnt a collection of triggering policies from a corpus of human behavior. While the focus of this paper is to evaluate the most human-like triggering policy learnt from data in terms of its perception benefits and learning outcomes, Section 4 summarizes our efforts on learning triggering policies.

Before we discuss the details of the evaluation we conducted, Section 3 presents an analysis of mediating factors that provides insights into the reasons behind the effectiveness of social behavior. The design and procedure of the user study we conducted to evaluate the learnt triggering policies is described in Section 5. Finally, Section 6 discusses the results of this evaluation.

2 Social Interaction Strategies

In our prior work (Kumar et. al., 2010; Ai et. al., 2010; Kumar et. al., 2011), we have developed and evaluated automated tutors for two different educational domains equipped with eleven social interaction strategies. These strategies, listed in Table 1, correspond to three positive socio-emotional interaction categories identified by Bales (1950): Showing Solidarity, Showing Tension Release and Agreeing.

Appendix A shows excerpts of an interaction between three students and a tutor during a college freshmen mechanical engineering learning activity. The shaded turns demonstrate realizations of some of the eleven social interaction strategies.

Turns 7-12 shows the tutor initiating and participating in group formation using Strategy 1a (Do Introductions) by greeting the students and asking for their names. In turn 53, the tutor is employing Strategy 3b (Show Comprehension / Approval) in response to a student opinion expressed in turn 52. When one of the students becomes inactive in the interaction, the tutor uses strategy 1e (Encourage) realized as a targeted prompt shown in turn 122 to elicit a response from the inactive student. Turn 148 demonstrates Strategy 1d (Complement / Praise) to appreciate student participation in a conceptual tutoring episode that concluded at turn 147. Finally, turn 152 shows a realization of Strategy 2c (Express Enthusiasm, Elation, Satisfaction) which is tied to either the start or the end of lengthy problem solving steps in the learning activity such as calculating the outcome of certain design choices made by the students during the learning activity.

1. Showing Solidarity *Raises other's status, gives help, reward*
1a. Do Introductions *Introduce and ask names of all participants*
1b. Be Protective & Nurturing *Discourage teasing*
1c. Give Re-assurance *When student is discontent, asking for help*
1d. Complement / Praise *To acknowledge student contributions*
1e. Encourage *When group or members are inactive*
1f. Conclude Socially
2. Showing Tension Release *Jokes, laughs, shows satisfaction*
2a. Expression of feeling better *After periods of tension, work pressure*
2b. Be cheerful
2c. Express Enthusiasm, Elation, Satisfaction *On completing significant steps of the task*
3. Agreeing *Shows passive acceptance, understands, concurs, complies*
3a. Show Attention *To student ideas as encouragement*
3b. Show Comprehension / Approval *To student opinions and orientations*

Table 1. Social Interaction Strategies for three social-emotional interaction categories

3 Effect of Social Behaviors

We have observed the the use of social behavior in collaborative learning settings can help in improving learning outcomes (Kumar et. al., 2010a). This observation is not necessarily consistent with intuition. On the one hand, we could attribute this to the ability to manage the user's (student) attention towards the agent (tutor) by displaying the social behavior. At the same time, we could argue against the use of social behavior by considering it as a potential distraction from the task. In an earlier experiment (Kumar et. al., 2010c), we found that it is important to keep the amount of social behavior at an optimal level in order to observe the learning benefits of the social behavior and to avoid its distraction costs.

1	Tutor	Are you paying attention to this?
2	S006	of course
3	S001	yes
4	Tutor	What would happen if the stress in our Wrench is too high?
5	S006	fail
6	S001	it'd fail
7	S014	it would break.
8	Tutor	That's right. The wrench can break!
9	Tutor	A wrench that can break in normal use is not safe!
10	S006	:(
11	Tutor	In general, to keep a wrench safe, we want to keep the stress in the wrench high or low?
12	S006	lowwww
13	S001	low
14	Tutor	Right, stress should be kept low.
15	Tutor	Which material property determines when the stress is too high?
16	S001	yield strength?

Table 2. Excerpt of a Conceptual Tutoring Episode

In this section, we present a corpus analysis to discover an underlying model of how the social behavior affects learning outcomes. We used a corpus of collaborative learning interactions between teams of three or more students and a tutor. The interactions involve the teams performing a learning activity which lasts approximately 40 minutes. During this time, the tutors provide directions, hints and conceptual tutoring. Each team undergoes up to four conceptual tutoring episodes. An episode is a system-initiated conversation during which the tutor leads the students through a directed line of reasoning to help them reflect upon a concept related to the learning activity. An excerpt of a tutoring episode discussing the relationship between stress and safety is shown in Table 2.

3.1 Coding Tutoring Episodes

Each turn in all the tutoring episodes of the 32 interactions between a team of students and an automated tutor were annotated using a coding scheme described here. The tutor turns were categorized as either Respondable (TR) if the students were expected to the respond to that tutor turn or Not Respondable (TU) otherwise. In Table 2, all the shaded turns are labeled as Respondable.

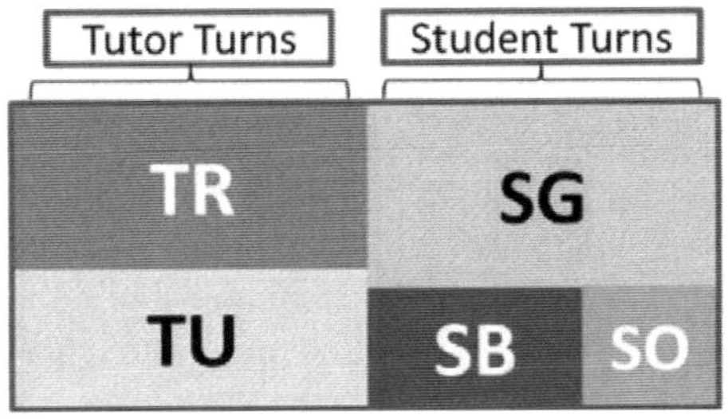

Figure 1. Venn Diagram of Episode Turn Annotations

Student Turns are categorized into one of three categories. Good turns (SG) identifies turns where the students are showing attention to a respondable tutor turn (e.g. Turn 2 & 3 in Table 2) or the students are giving a correct or an incorrect response to a direct question by the tutor (e.g. Turns 5, 6, 7, 12, 13 & 16). Counterproductive (Bad) student turns (SB) include students abusing the tutor or ignoring the tutor (e.g. talking to another student when the students are expected to respond to a tutor turn). Student turns that are not categorized as Good or Bad are labeled as Other (SO). Turn 10 is an example of SO because it is a response to a tutor turn (9) where no student response is expected. Figure 1 shows a Venn diagram of the different annotations. All five categories are mutually exclusive.

3.2 Structural Equation Modeling

In order to discover an underlying model of how the use of social behavior affects student learning, we used a structural equation modeling (SEM) technique (Scheines et. al., 1994).

Data: To measure learning outcomes, our data comprised of scores from pre-test and post-test administered to 88 students who were part of the 32 teams whose data was annotated for this analysis. We normalized the number of Good (SG) and Bad (SB) student turns by the number of Respondable (TR) tutor turns and included normalized SG (*nSG*) and normalized SB (*nSB*) as measures of interaction characteristics of each student in our dataset. Total number of social turns performed by the tutor in each interaction was included as a characteristic of social behavior displayed by the tutor. Finally, the total amount of time (in seconds) that the students spent on the tutoring episodes was included as a characteristic of the interaction quality during the tutoring episodes.

Prior Knowledge: The only prior knowledge input to the model stated that the pre-test occurs before the post-test.

Discovered Models: We used Tetrad IV to discover a structural equation model in the data comprising of 6 fields (*PreTest*, *PostTest*, *nSG*, *nSB*, *SocialTurns*, *EpisodeDuration*) for each of the 88 students. Figure 2 shows the structural equation model discovered by Tetrad using the dataset described above. p-Value of 0.46 for this model confirms the hypothesis used by Tetrad for its statistical analysis i.e. the model was not discovered randomly. Note that unlike other statistical tests, SEM models built using Tetrad are evaluated as significant if the p-Value is greater than 0.05. The numbers on the arrows are correlation coefficients and the numbers on the boxes indicate mean values for each variable.

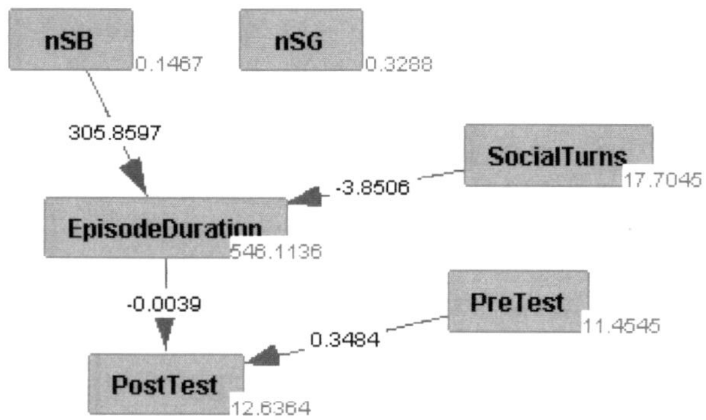

Figure 2. SEM discovered using all 6 variables in our dataset

Besides the obvious causal effect of *PreTest* score on *PostTest* score, we find that as the duration of the tutoring episodes (*EpisodeDuration*) increases, the learning outcomes deteriorate. We notice that an increase in the normalized number of Bad student turns increases *EpisodeDuration* indicating that students who abuse or ignore the tutor are likely to not pay attention to the learning content presented during the tutoring episodes, hence prolonging the tutoring episode as the tutor tries to get the students through the instructional content. Furthermore, we observe that social behavior helps in counteracting the negative learning effect of Bad interaction behaviors of the students. Tutors that perform social behavior are capable of managing the student's attention and get the students through the tutoring episode faster.

3.3 Discussion

The SEM analysis discussed in the previous section helps us better understand the relationship between the use of social behavior and student learning in a collaborative learning setting. Let's consider the duration of the tutoring episodes as an indicator of the students' attention to the tutor (higher duration $\Rightarrow$ lower attention). We see that social behavior helps in managing the students' attention, which may be affected negatively by counterproductive/bad interaction behavior from the students.

Besides suggesting that social behavior could be a useful strategy for directing student attention, it also suggests that social behavior may not serve this function where counterproductive student behavior is not present or where it does not occur enough to negatively impact task behavior. This is because a minimum amount of time needs to be spent on each tutoring episode to deliver the instructional of the concept being discussed. In the absence of counterproductive student behavior, episode duration may be close to that minimum.

Also, in an earlier analysis (Hua et. al., 2010) in a different learning domain where the social behaviors described in Section 2 were employed, we have observed that the number of abusive/negative comment made by the students about the tutor during the interaction were significantly higher in a condition where the tutors performed a high amount of social behavior. This suggests that the relationship between the *SocialTurns* and *EpisodeDuration* variables may not be linear in extreme cases and emphasizes the importance of performing an optimal amount of social behavior.

4 Triggering Social Behavior

Aside from designing, implementing and regulating the amount of social behavior performed by automated tutors, one of the challenges involved in the appropriate use of social interaction strategies is that of triggering these strategies only at the most appropriate moments during the interaction. Our initial implementation of these strategies (Kumar & Rosé, 2010b) achieved this using a set of hand crafted rules that used features such as recent student turns, state of the tutoring plan, etc.

Here we will summarize our efforts on building a better triggering policy using a data-driven approach that models the behavior of human tutors at triggering the social interaction strategies listed in Table 1. Using a corpus of 10 interactions between a group of students and partially automated tutors whose social behaviors were triggered by human tutors, we attempt to learn a triggering policy that predicts when the human tutors will trigger a social strategies. Currently, we focus on only learning a triggering policy that determines if a social behavior should be performed. The choice of which behavior is performed when triggered by the policy is still based on the rules used in our earlier implementation as discussed in Section 5.3.

In order to compare the triggers generated by a policy, we use a binary sequence comparison metric called *kKappa* (Neikrasz & Moore, 2010) developed for evaluating discourse segmentation approaches. The metric allows a soft penalty for misplacing a trigger (or a segment boundary) within a window of *k* turns.

We developed a large margin learning algorithm following McDonald et. al. (2005) that iteratively learns the coefficients of a linear function in the feature space that separates turns where human tutors decided to trigger a social behavior from the rest of the turns. Instead of using an instance-based objective function (like square-loss), our algorithm maximizes the *kKappa* metric over a provided training set. The function learnt this way can be used as a triggering policy by using it at every turn during an interaction to predict if a human tutor would trigger a social behavior. We used a collection of automatically extractable features that represent the lexical and semantic content of recent student and tutor turns, current discourse state and activity levels of the students.

While details of the objective evaluation of the various learnt triggering policies is beyond the scope of this paper, we found that the best performing strategy (k-κ = 0.13) was significantly better than a random baseline (k-κ = 0.01) as well as the rule based triggering policy (k-κ = -0.09) used in our initial implementation. Also, the policy learnt by our algorithm outperformed policies learnt by algorithms such as Linear Regression (k-κ = 0.00) and Logistic Regression (k-κ = 0.05) that use instance-based loss metrics (Hall et. al., 2009).

5 User Study

Here we will present an experiment we conducted to evaluate the effectiveness of various ways to trigger social behavior discussed in Section 4. This experiment is a step towards verifying the hypothesis that a human-like triggering policy could outperform a rule-based triggering policy that was used in our earlier experiments (Kumar et. al., 2010a). We use the same interactive situation for the experiment presented here as in our earlier work. Freshmen mechanical engineering students enrolled at an American university participate in a computer-aided engineering lab that is divided into three parts, i.e., Computer-Aided Design (CAD), Computer-Aided Analysis (CAA) and Computer-Aided Manufacturing (CAM). Students practice the use of various engineering software packages for all three parts as they design, analyze and manufacture an Aluminum wrench. Our experiment is conducted during the second part (CAA) of the lab.

5.1 Procedure & Materials

The Computer-Aided Analysis lab comprises of two activities. The first activity involves analyzing a wrench design given to the students by specifying certain loading conditions and simulating the stresses and deformations in the wrench. Students are led by a teaching assistant during this activity. They spend approximately 25 minutes performing this activity. At the end of the analysis activity, the students see a simulation of the stress distribution in the body of the wrench.

After the analysis activity, a pre-test is administered. Each student spends 10 minutes working on the pre-test individually. The pre-test comprises of 11 questions, 8 of which are multiple-choice questions and the other 3 are short essay type questions.

The second activity of the CAA lab is a collaborative design activity. During this activity, students work in teams of three. Student in the same team are seated in separate parts of the lab and can only communicate using a text-based chatroom application (Mühlpfordt and Wessner, 2005). The chatroom application also provides a shared workspace in the form of a whiteboard.

After the pre-test, students are given written instructions describing the collaborative design activity. The instructions ask the students to design a better wrench in terms of ease of use, cost of materials and safety compared to the wrench they analyzed earlier. The students are expected to come up with three new designs in 40 minutes by varying parameters like dimensions and materials of the wrench. The instructions also include various formulae and data that the students might need to use for their designs. Besides course credit, the instructions mention an additional giftcard for the team that comes up with the best design ($10 for each member of the winning team).

Students are asked to log in to their respective team's chatroom. They spend the next 40 minutes working on the collaborative design activity. Besides the three students, the chatroom for each team includes an automated tutor. The tutor guides the students through the first two designs suggesting potential choices for dimension and materials for each design. As the design activity progresses, the tutor initiates four conceptual tutoring episodes to help the students reflect upon underlying mechanical engineering concepts like stress, force, moment, safety, etc., that are relevant to the design activity.

Our experimental manipulation happens during this 40 minute segment. The tutor in each team's chatroom is configured to perform social behavior using different triggering policies as specified by the condition assigned to the team. The conditions are discussed in the next section. Irrespective of the condition, each team receives the 4 conceptual tutoring episodes. Every student performs all the steps of this procedure like all other students.

At the end of the collaborative design activity, a post-test and a survey are administered. Students are asked to spend 15 minutes to first complete the test and then the survey. The post-test is the same test used for pre-test. The survey comprises of 15 items shown in Appendix B. The students are asked to rate each item on a 7-point Likert scale ranging from Strongly Disagree (1) to Strongly Agree (7). The 15 items on the survey include 11 items eliciting perception of the tutor. 9 of the 11 items state positive aspects of the tutor (e.g. *...tutor was friendly...*). The other 2 items stated negative aspects about the tutor (e.g. *...tutor's responses got in the way...*). Besides the items about the tutor, 2 items elicited the student's rating about the collaborative design activity. The last 2 items were about the student's satisfaction with their performance on the design task.

In total, both the activities that are part of the CAA lab take approximately 1 hour 40 minutes.

5.2 Experimental Design

The teams participating in the experiment described here were divided into six conditions. These conditions determined the triggering policy and the amount of social behavior performed by the automated tutors. Tutors in the **None** condition did not perform any social behavior. Tutors in the **Rules** condition used the same hand crafted rule-based triggering policy employed in our earlier experiment (Kumar et. al., 2010a). Following the results from another experiment (Kumar & Rosé, 2010c), the automated tutors in the Rules condition performed a moderate amount of social behavior (atmost 20% of all tutor turns). On average, the Rules policy triggered 25 social turns per interaction.

The **RandomLow** and **RandomHigh** conditions used a random triggering policy with a social ratio filter to regulate the amount of social behavior. In both the random conditions, the tutor would trigger social behavior using a random number generator to generate the confidence of triggering a social behavior after every turn (by a student or a tutor). In the RandomLow condition, a behavior would be triggered if the confidence was above 0.91. In the RandomHigh condition, a behavior would be triggered if the confidence was above 0.85. On average, the RandomLow condition had 23 behaviors triggered per interaction. About 37 behaviors were triggered in the RandomHigh condition.

The **LearntLow** and **LearntHigh** conditions used the best triggering policy learnt from a corpus of human triggering of social behavior as discussed in Section 4. The same social ratio filter used in the random conditions was used in these two conditions also. As in the case with RandomLow and RandomHigh, different values of a confidence parameter were used for the LearntLow and LearntHigh conditions to control the number of social behaviors triggered. On average, the LearntLow condition had 22 triggers and the LearntHigh condition had 28 triggers.

5.3 Generating Behaviors

The various triggering policies described above for each of our experimental conditions only determine when a tutor agent will perform a social behavior. In order to perform the social behavior in actual use, the agent must not only determine when a behavior should be triggered, but also determine which behavior should be performed when a trigger is received. Our implementation of the tutor agent used in this experiment provides a continuous stream of scores for each of the eleven social interaction strategies that the tutor can perform. The scores are computed using hand-crafted functions that use the same features used in our rule-based triggering policy (Kumar et. al., 2010b). When a social behavior is triggered, a roulette wheel selection is used to determine the strategy to be performed. The circumference of the wheel assigned to each strategy is proportional to the score of each strategy. If the score of all the strategies is zero, a generic social prompt is performed.

6 Results

126 students enrolled in an introductory mechanical engineering course at an American university participated in the experiment described in this paper. The experiment was conducted on two separate days separated by one week. On each day, four sessions of the Computer-Aided Analysis lab were conducted, and students attended only one assigned session. Session assignment was made based on an alphabetic split. The 126 students were divided into 42 teams. 20 teams participated on the first day of the experiment. They were evenly split into four conditions (None, Rules, RandomHigh & LearntHigh). The remaining 22 teams participated on the second day. Out of these, 5 teams each were assigned to the None and RandomLow condition. 6 teams each were assigned to the Rules and LearntLow conditions.

The rest of this section presents detailed results and analysis of this experiment. To summarize, we found that out of the six evaluated policies only the LearntLow policy that uses a triggering model learnt from human triggering data and generates a moderate amount of social behavior is consistently better than the other policies in terms of both performance as well as perception outcomes. Also, the LearntLow policy is found to be most efficient at delivering the instructional content as indicated by the smallest *EpisodeDuration* in Table 5.

6.1 Learning Outcomes

The learning outcomes analysis presented here shows the advantage of using a triggering policy learnt from a corpus of human triggering behavior along with a filtering technique that regulates the amount of social behavior as shown in Table 3.

We first verified that there was no significant difference between the six conditions on the pre-test scores. As in the case of previous experiments using this learning activity, we saw that the learning activity was pedagogically beneficial to the students irrespective of the condition. There was a significant improvement in test scores between pre-test and post-test { $p < 0.0001$, $F(1,250) = 26.01$, effect-size = 0.58σ }.

There was no significant effect of the condition assigned to each team on the total test scores. However, there was a significant effect on the test scores of short-essay type questions using the pre-test score as a covariate and the condition as a factor { $p < 0.05$, $F(5, 119) = 2.88$ }. The adjusted post test scores for the short essay type questions and their standard deviations are shown in Table 3. Post-hoc analysis showed that the LearntLow condition was significantly better than LearntHigh condition { effect-size = 0.65σ }. Also, RandomLow condition was marginally better than LearntHigh condition { $p < 0.07$, effect-size = 0.62σ }.

	Mean	**St.Dev.**
LearntLow	5.12	0.54
RandomLow	5.06	0.67
None	4.75	1.13
RandomHigh	4.59	1.09
Rules	4.38	0.89
LearntHigh	3.98	1.74

Table 3. Mean and Standard Deviation of Adjusted Post Test Scores for Short Essay Type Questions

This result further supports the observation from our earlier experiment (Kumar & Rosé, 2010c) which demonstrated that importance of performing the right amount of social behavior. Both RandomLow and LearntLow conditions employ the non-linear social ratio filter which keeps the amount of allowed social behavior at a level comparable to the amount of social behavior performed by human tutors.

Since the primary objective of the experiment described here was to evaluate a learnt triggering policy with respect to a rule-based triggering policy, we repeated the ANCOVA for the short essay type question using data from only the Rules,

LearntLow and LearntHigh conditions. We found a significant effect of condition on the post-test score using pre-test score as a covariate { $p = 0.01$, $F(2,62) = 4.98$ }. A post-hoc analysis showed that the LearntLow condition was significantly better than the LearntHigh condition as above and the LearntLow condition was marginally better than the Rules condition { $p \approx 0.08$, effect-size = 0.84σ }. We observe that a triggering policy learnt from human triggering behavior can achieve a marginal improvement on learning outcomes compared to our existing rule-based triggering policy. This is consistent with our hypothesis.

6.2 Perception Ratings

We averaged the student's rating for the 11 items about the tutor into a single tutor rating measure used here. Rating on the two negative statements about the tutor were inverted (7→1, 6→2, and so on) for this calculation.

	Mean	St.Dev.
Rules	4.74	1.45
LearntLow	4.56	1.58
None	4.42	1.49
RandomHigh	3.74	1.63
LearntHigh	3.55	1.26
RandomLow	3.18	0.91

Table 4. Mean and Standard Deviation of Tutor Ratings

We found a significant effect of condition on the tutor ratings { $p < 0.01$, $F(5,120) = 3.83$ }. Table 4 shows the mean and standard deviations of tutor ratings for each condition. Post-hoc analysis showed that only the Rules condition was significantly better than the RandomLow condition. Also, we found that Rules was marginally better than LearntHigh condition { $p < 0.08$ } and both LearntLow and None conditions was marginally better than RandomLow condition { $p < 0.08$ }.

While we did not see a significant improvement in perception due the use of a learnt triggering policy when compared to a rule-based triggering policy, we find an advantage over using a random triggering policy (RandomLow) which was as good as a learnt policy on the learning outcomes. The results from the tutor's perception ratings further support the importance of timing and regulating the amount of social behavior.

We did not find any significant effect of condition on the ratings about the design activity or student's task satisfaction.

6.3 Analysis of Tutoring Episodes

In order to understand the results from the experiment presented in this paper, we applied the structural equation model discussed earlier (Figure 2) to the data collected from our current experiment. Figure 3 shows the model for our current experiment (p=0.4492). Only four variables were used because the annotations of good and bad student behavior are not available at this time.

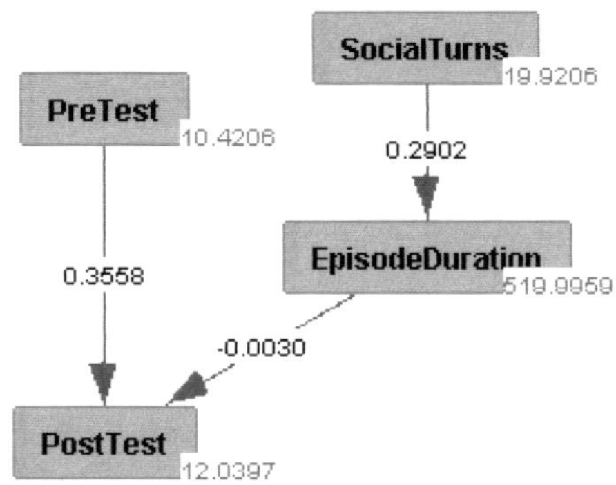

Figure 3. SEM applied to data from this experiment

	Mean	St.Dev.
RandomHigh	540.80	49.50
LearntHigh	534.80	61.00
None	523.88	41.54
Rules	519.80	102.70
RandomLow	519.20	74.40
LearntLow	484.00	69.80

Table 5. Mean and Standard Deviation of Duration of Tutoring Episodes

We see that most of the model parameters (p-Value, means & correlations) are similar to parameters for the model shown in Figure 2. However, the correlation between *SocialTurns* and *EpisodeDuration* is much smaller. Also, note that the mean of *EpisodeDuration* is smaller compared to that in Figure 2 which indicates that lesser counterproductive behavior was displayed by the students in this experiment. The conceptual tutoring episodes are operating closer to the minimum episode duration which leaves a smaller room for improvement by the use of social interaction strategies. As discussed in Section 3.3, this explains the smaller correlation between *SocialTurns* and *EpisodeDuration* in Figure 3.

Table 5 shows the mean and standard deviations of the duration of tutoring episodes for each condition. Even though the differences are not significant, the LearntLow policy has the lowest duration indicating higher student attention than the other conditions.

7 Discussion

Prior work in the field of human-human interaction and human-machine interaction in the form of dialog systems has emphasized the importance of timing the display of behavior to achieve natural and/or productive interactions. In general, timing of interactive behaviors (verbal as well as non-verbal) has been studied in the context of joint activities being performed by the participants. Behaviors are timed to achieve and maintain coordination between the participants (Clark, 2005). Specifically, among other topics, timing of low-level (signal) interaction like turn-taking has been the subject of several investigations (Raux & Eskenazi, 2008; Takeuchi et. al., 2004).

On the other hand, the use of social behavior by conversational agents to support students has been proposed (Veletsianos et. al., 2009; Gulz et. al., 2010). Work in the area of affective computing and its application to tutorial dialog has focused on identification of student's emotional states and using those to improve choice of behavior performed by tutors (D'Mello et. al., 2005). Our prior work (Kumar et. al., 2010; Kumar et. al., 2007) has shown that social behavior motivated from empirical research in small group communication (Bales, 1950) can help in effectively supporting students in collaborative learning settings. Use of social interaction in other applications of conversational agents besides education has been investigated (Bickmore et. al., 2009; Dybala et. al., 2009; Dohsaka et. al., 2009).

The experiments presented here bridges these two tracks of research specifically proposing a solution to the challenge of timing social behavior in the context of a supporting collaborative learning. Compared to the work on timing signal-level joint activities like turn-taking, this work focuses on the timing of joint activities at the conversation level. The success of our algorithm at learning a model of timing conversational behaviors in the context of an interactive task could potentially offer a general approach for realizing such behaviors in other conversational agents.

8 Conclusion

In this paper, we presented an experiment that compared the effectiveness of several social behavior triggering policies. Specifically, we compared a triggering policy learnt from a corpus of human triggering behavior to a rule-based policy which has previously been shown to be successful at triggering effective social behavior in a collaborative learning activity.

The presented experiment provides further evidence in support of the intuition that timing of social behavior and regulating the amount of social behavior are critical to improving performance and perception outcomes. A triggering policy based on human-like timing in combination with a filter that attempts to keep amount of social behavior at the same level as human tutors was shown to be marginally better than the rule-based policy on learning outcomes. Also, on perception measures, we found that the human-like policy is marginally better than a random triggering policy which uses the same filter to control the amount of social behavior. Only the learned model provides a win both on learning and on perception measures.

In order to better understand the effect of use of social behavior by automated tutors on student's learning outcomes, we presented a structured model which suggests that social behavior helps in achieving higher learning outcomes by allowing the tutor to better manage the student's attention. Following this model, we saw that a human-like triggering policy is able to achieve higher student attention as indicated by the smaller duration of tutoring episodes.

We found a significant negative correlation { coefficient = -0.20, $p < 0.05$ } between the tutor's perception rating and number of social behaviors triggered when none of the social interaction strategies were applicable. As next steps, our best triggering policy could be potentially further refined by achieving a closer integration of the triggering model with the social behavior generation mechanism to prevent triggering when none of the eleven strategies could be generated.

References

Hua Ai, Rohit Kumar, Dong Nguyen, Amrut Nagasunder and Carolyn P. Rosé, 2010, Exploring the Effectiveness of Social Capabilities and Goal Alignment in Computer Supported Collaborative Learning, Intelligent Tutoring Systems, Pittsburgh, PA

Elizabeth Arnott, Peter Hastings and David Allbritton, 2008, Research Methods Tutor: Evaluation of a dialogue-based tutoring system in the classroom, Behavior Research Methods, 40 (3), 694-698

Robert F. Bales, 1950, Interaction process analysis: A method for the study of small groups, Addison-Wesley, Cambridge, MA

Khelan Bhatt, Martha Evens, Shlomo Argamon, 2004, Hedged responses and expressions of affect in human/human and human/computer tutorial interactions, CogSci, Chicago, IL

Timothy Bickmore, Daniel Schulman and Langxuan Yin, 2009, Engagement vs. Deceit: Virtual Humans with Human Autobiographies, Proc. of Intelligent Virtual Agents, Amsterdam, Netherlands

Herbert H. Clark, 2005, Coordinating with each other in a material world, Discourse Studies, 7 (4-5), 507-525

Sidney K. D'Mello, Scotty D. Craig, Barry Gholson, Stan Frankin, Rosalind Picard, Arthur C. Graesser, 2005, Integrating Affect Sensors in an Intelligent Tutoring System, Wksp on Affective Interactions: The Computer in the Affective Loop, IUI, San Diego, CA

Pawel Dybala, Michal Ptaszynski, Rafal Rzepka and Kenji Araki, 2009, Humoroids: Conversational Agents that induce positive emotions with humor, AAMAS, Budapest, Hungary

Kohji Dohsaka, Ryoto Asai, Ryichiro Higashinaka, Yasuhiro Minami and Eisaku Maeda, 2009, Effects of Conversational Agents on Human Communication in Though Evoking Multi-Party dialogues, SIGDial 2009, London, UK

Agneta Gulz, Annika Silvervarg and Björn Sjödén, 2010, Design for off-task interaction - Rethinking pedagogy in technology enhanced learning, Intl. Conf. on Advanced Learning Technologies, Tunisia

Arthur C. Graesser, Patrick Chipman, Brian C. Haynes, and Andrew Olney, 2005, AutoTutor: An Intelligent Tutoring System with Mixed-initiative Dialogue, IEEE Transactions in Education, 48, 612-618

Mark Hall, Eibe Frank, Geoffrey Holmes, Bernhard Pfahringer, Peter Reutemann and Ian H. Witten, 2009, The WEKA Data Mining Software: An Update; SIGKDD Explorations, Volume 11, Issue 1

Rohit Kumar, Jack L. Beuth and Carolyn P. Rosé, 2011, Conversational Strategies that Support Idea Generation Productivity in Groups, 9th Intl. Conf. on Computer Supported Collaborative Learning, Hong Kong

Rohit Kumar, Hua Ai, Jack Beuth and Carolyn P. Rosé, 2010a, Socially-capable Conversational Tutors can be Effective in Collaborative-Learning situations, Intelligent Tutoring Systems, Pittsburgh, PA

Rohit Kumar and Carolyn P. Rosé, 2010b, Engaging learning groups using Social Interaction Strategies, NAACL-HLT, Los Angeles, CA

Rohit Kumar and Carolyn P. Rosé, 2010c, Conversational Tutors with Rich Interactive Behaviors that support Collaborative Learning, Workshop on Opportunities for intelligent and adaptive behavior in collaborative learning systems, ITS 2010, Pittsburgh, PA

Rohit Kumar, Gahgene Gweon, Mahesh Joshi, Yue Cui and Carolyn Rosé, Supporting students working together on Math with Social Dialogue, Workshop on Speech and Language Technology in Education, Farmington, PA, 2007

Ryan McDonald, Koby Crammer and Fernando Pereira, 2005a, Online large-margin training of dependency parsers, Proc. of ACL, 91-98, Ann Arbor, MI

Martin Mühlpfordt and Martin Wessner, 2005, Explicit referencing in chat supports collaborative learning, Proc. Computer Support for Collaborative Learning (CSCL)

John Niekrasz and Johanna D. Moore, 2010, Unbiased Discourse Segmentation Evaluation, Proc. of SLT, Berkeley, CA

Antoine Raux and Maxine Eskenazi, 2008, Optimizing Endpointing Thresholds using Dialogue Features in a Spoken Dialogue System, SIGDial 2008, Columbus, OH

Richard Scheines, Peter Spirtes, Clark Glymour, and Christopher Meek, 1994, TETRAD II: Tools for Discovery, Lawrence Erlbaum Associates, Hillsdale, NJ

Masashi Takeuchi, Norihide Kitaoka and Seiichi NakagawaM, 2004, Timing detection for realtime dialog systems using prosodic and linguistic information, Intl Conf. on Speech Prosody 2004, Nara, Japan

Tetrad IV, http://www.phil.cmu.edu/projects/tetrad/tetrad4.html

George Veletsianos, Charles Miller and Aaron Doering, Veletsianos, 2009, EnALI: A Research and Design Framework for Virtual Characters and Pedagogical Agents, Journal of Educational Computing Research, 41(2), 171-194

Appendix A. Excerpts of an interaction between three students and an automated tutor demonstrating some of the social interaction strategies listed in Table 1.

7	Tutor	Hi, I am your tutor for today's lab.
8	Tutor	Lets introduce ourselves briefly. I am Avis.
9	S083	Hey Avis! I'm _name1_
10	S073	Im _name2_
11	S089	i'm _name3_
12	Tutor	Its nice to meet you all. :)
13	Tutor	Let's get started by reviewing the base design in your worksheet.

Strategy 1a: Do Introductions

48	S083	R we using the same material?
49	S073	I assume so
50	S073	just changing the length
51	S089	yeah we have multiple design steps
52	S089	so probably for now
53	Tutor	cool :)
54	S083	O ok

Strategy 3b: Show Comprehension / Approval

119	Tutor	Is this a safe wrench?
120	S073	and then is the same for design 2
121	S073	so yes the wrench is safe
122	Tutor	_name1_ ... any thoughts you'd like to contribute?
123	S083	its a safer wrench if its in steel

Strategy 1e: Encourage (inactive members)

143	S073	high
144	Tutor	Right, higher yield stress is better.
145	S089	so steel or titanium
146	S089	but have fun paying for that...
147	Tutor	All other things being equal, you want to choose a stronger material.
148	Tutor	It's good to have your contributions to the discussion :-)
149	S073	yay

Strategy 1d: Complement / Praise

150	S073	:)
151	Tutor	Let's improve design 1 by using Steel for our 2nd _truncated_
152	Tutor	I am happy to be working with our team
153	S083	thanks :-)
154	Tutor	You can start calculating the fields in the worksheet _truncated_
155	S089	woo...

Strategy 2c: Express Enthusiasm, Elation, Satisfaction

Appendix B. Survey administered to the participants at the end of the Collaborative Design Activity

Using the following scale, Indicate to what extent you agree with each of the following items.

1 Strongly Disagree	2 Mostly Disagree	3 Somewhat Disagree	4 Neutral	5 Somewhat Agree	6 Mostly Agree	7 Strongly Agree

The tutor was part of my team.	1	2	3	4	5	6	7
The tutor provided good ideas for the discussion.	1	2	3	4	5	6	7
The tutor received my contributions positively.	1	2	3	4	5	6	7
The tutor was friendly during the discussion.	1	2	3	4	5	6	7
The tutor responded to my contributions.	1	2	3	4	5	6	7
The tutor helped in lowering the tension in my group.	1	2	3	4	5	6	7
The tutor was paying attention to our conversation.	1	2	3	4	5	6	7
Overall, I liked the tutor very much.	1	2	3	4	5	6	7
I think the tutor was as good as a human tutor.	1	2	3	4	5	6	7
I often ignored what the tutor was saying.	1	2	3	4	5	6	7
The tutor's responses got in the way of our conversation.	1	2	3	4	5	6	7
The design challenge was exciting.	1	2	3	4	5	6	7
I did my best to come up with good designs.	1	2	3	4	5	6	7
I am happy with the discussion I had with my group.	1	2	3	4	5	6	7
Overall, we were successful at meeting our goals during the design challenge.	1	2	3	4	5	6	7

Facilitating Mental Modeling in Collaborative Human-Robot Interaction through Adverbial Cues

Gordon Briggs and **Matthias Scheutz**
Human-Robot Interaction Laboratory
Tufts University, Medford, MA 02155, USA
{gbriggs,mscheutz}@cs.tufts.edu

Abstract

Mental modeling is crucial for natural human-robot interactions (HRI). Yet, effective mechanisms that enable reasoning about and communication of mental states are not available. We propose to utilize adverbial cues, routinely employed by humans, for this goal and present a novel algorithm that integrates adverbial modifiers with belief revision and expression, phrasing utterances based on Gricean conversational maxims. The algorithm is demonstrated in a simple HRI scenario.

1 Introduction

Advances in robotics and autonomous systems are paving the way for the development of robots that can take on increasingly complex tasks without the need of minute human supervision. As a result of this greater autonomy, the interaction styles between humans and robots are slowly shifting from those of humans micromanaging robot behaviors (e.g., via remote controls) to more higher-level interactions (e.g., verbal commands) which are required for many mixed initiative tasks where humans and robots work together in teams (e.g., in search and rescue missions). In order for these joint human-robot interactions to be productive and efficient, robots must have the ability to communicate in *natural* and *human-like* ways (Scheutz et al., 2007). Natural human-like communication in robots, however, requires us to tackle several challenges, including the development of robust natural language (NL) competencies and the ability to understand and utilize a variety of affective, gestural, and other non-linguistic cues that are indicative of the interlocutor's mental states. Hence, natural human-like interaction also requires the construction and maintenance of mental models of other agents, especially in the context of collaborative team tasks where actions among multiple agents must be coordinated, often through natural language dialogues.

Several recent efforts are aimed at endowing robots with natural language processing capabilities to allow for verbal instructions as a first step (e.g., (Brenner, 2007; Dzifcak et al., 2009; Kress-Gazit et al., 2008; Rybski et al., 2007; Kollar et al., 2010)). Independently, user modeling has been extensively explored in order to generate more natural and productive human-machine interactions (Kobsa, 2001), including adapting the natural language output of dialogue systems based on mental models of human users (Wahlster and Kobsa, 1989). However, there is currently no integrated robotic architecture that includes explicit mechanisms for efficiently conveying natural language information about the robot's "mental states" (i.e., beliefs, goals, intentions) to a human teammate. Yet, such mechanisms are not only desirable to make the robot's behavior more intuitive and predictable to humans, but can also be crucial for team success (e.g., quick updates on goal achievement or early corrections of wrong human assumptions).

We propose a novel integrated belief revision and expression algorithm that allows robots to track and update the beliefs of their interlocutors in a way that respects Gricean maxims about language usage. The algorithm explicitly models and updates task-relevant beliefs and intentions of all participating

Proceedings of the SIGDIAL 2011: the 12th Annual Meeting of the Special Interest Group on Discourse and Dialogue, pages 239–247,
Portland, Oregon, June 17-18, 2011.

agents. Whenever a discrepancy is detected between a human belief (as implied in a natural language expression uttered by the human) and the robot's mental model of the human, the robot generates a natural language response that corrects the discrepancy in the most effective way. To achieve effectiveness, the robot uses linguistic rules about the pragmatic implications of adverbial modifiers like "yet", "still", "already", and others that are used by humans to effectively communicate their beliefs and intentions.

The rest of the paper is organized as follows. We start with a motivation of our approach based on Gricean maxims. Then, we introduce formalizations of linguistic devices that humans use to generate effective task-based dialogue interactions and present our algorithm for generating appropriate utterances in response to human queries. Next we use a simple remote human-robot interaction scenario to demonstrate the operation of the algorithm, followed by a discussion and summary of our contributions.

2 Motivation

Joint activity often requires agents to monitor and keep track of each others' mental states to ensure effective team performance. For example, searchers during rescue operations in disaster zones typically coordinate their (distributed and remote) activities through spoken natural language interactions via wireless audio links to keep team members informed of discoveries and plans of other team members. Coordination as part of joint activities requires two important processes in an agent: (1) building and maintaining a *mental model* of the other agents' beliefs and intentions (based on perceived, communicated, and inferred information), which is critical for situational awareness (Lison et al., 2010); and (2) actively supporting the maintenance of others' mental models of oneself (e.g., by proactively communicating new information to the other agents in ways that will allow them to update their mental models).

Cohen et al. (1990), for example, discuss the necessity of various communicative acts that serve to synchronize agent belief-models. These communicative acts include both linguistic and non-linguistic cues, such as utterances of confirmation ("okay.") or signals that indicate intention (putting on a turn-signal). In addition to utilizing explicit cues to synchronize belief-models, humans employ various other mechanisms to convey information about one's own belief-state, in particular, various linguistic devices. A simple, but very powerful linguistic mechanism is the use of *adverbial cues*.

Consider a scenario where one agent wants to know the location of another agent, e.g., whether the agent is at home. A straightforward way to obtain this information is to simply ask "Are you at home?" The other agent can then answer "yes" or "no" accordingly. Now, suppose the first agent knew that the second agent was planning to be at home at some point. In that case, the agent might ask "Are you at home yet?" Note that semantically both questions have the same meaning, but their pragmatic implications are different as the second implies that that agent 1 knows that agent 2 was planning to be at home, while no such implication can be inferred from the first query. Conversely, suppose that agent 2 responded "not yet" in the first example (instead of "no"). While the semantic meaning is the same as "no", "not yet" communicates to agent 1 that agent 2 has the goal to be home. In general, adverbs like "yet" can be used to convey information about one's (or somebody else's) beliefs concerning mutually-recognized goals and intentions. Not surprisingly, humans use them regularly and with ease to aid their interlocutors with maintaining an accurate model of their beliefs and goals.

The challenges that need to be addressed to allow robots to have the above kinds of linguistic exchanges are: (1) how to formalize the functional roles of adverbial modifiers in different sentence types, and how to use the formalized principles to (2) perform belief updates and (3) generate effective natural language responses that are natural, succinct, and complete. To tackle these three challenges, we turn to Gricean principles that have long be used in pragmatics as guiding principles of human communicative exchanges.

3 NL Understanding and Generation

Grice (1975) proposed four general principles to aid in the pragmatic analysis of utterances. Phrased as rules, it is unsurprising that they have been used as an inspiration for NL generation systems before. Dale and Reiter (1995) have enlisted the maxims in their design of an algorithm to generate referring expressions, while others have cited Gricean influence in utterance selection for intelligent tutor systems (Eugenio et al., 2008). The particular maxims we considered are the maxims of *quality* (G1), *quantity* (G2), and *relevance* (G3): (G1) requires one to not say what one believes is false or for which one lacks adequate evidence; (G2) requires one to make contributions as informative as necessary for the current purposes of the exchange, but not more informative; and (G3) tersely states "be relevant."

Our approach to belief-model synchronization and utterance selection is based on the above maxims and attempts to select the most appropriate response to another agent's query based on relevance of semantic content. It uses speech pragmatic meaning postulates for linguistic devices such as adverbial modifiers to search for a succinct and natural linguistic representation that captures the intended updates. Rather than explicitly communicating each and every proposition that needs to be communicated to a human to allow the person to update their mental model of the robot, the algorithm makes heavy use of "implied meanings", i.e., propositions that humans will infer from the way the information is phrased linguistically. This allows for much shorter messages to be communicated than otherwise possible and addresses the second maxim of quantity.

3.1 Formalizing pragmatic implications

We start by introducing four types of sentences as they are found in typical dialogue interactions: *statements* (expressed through declarative sentences), *questions* (expressed through interrogative sentences), *commands* (expressed through imperative sentences) and *acknowledgments* (expressed through words like "okay", "yes", "no", etc.). For simplicity, we restrict the discussion to one predicate $at(\alpha, \lambda)$ which states that agent α is in location λ.

3.1.1 Statements

We will use the form $Stmt(\alpha, \beta, \phi, \mu)$ to express that agent α communicates ϕ to agent β using adverbial modifiers in a set μ. For example, $Stmt(A_2, A_1, \neg at(A_2, home), yet)$ means that agent A_2 tells A_1 that it is not at home yet. Note that we are indifferent about the exact linguistic representation of ϕ here as the goal is to capture the pragmatic implications.

If α informs β that it is at λ without any adverbial modifiers or additional contextual information, then we can assume using (G1) that α is indeed at that location:

$$[[Stmt(\alpha, \beta, at(\alpha, \lambda), \{\})]]_c := at(\alpha, \lambda) \tag{1}$$

Here we use $[[..]]_c$ to denote the "pragmatic meaning" of an expression in context c, which includes task, goal, belief and discourse aspects. Next, we inductively define the pragmatic meanings for several adverbial modifiers "still", "already", "now", and "not yet" (the meanings of compound expressions such as $at(\alpha, \lambda_1) \wedge \neg at(\alpha, \lambda_2)$ are defined recursively in the usual way).

If α states that it is "still" at λ, one can infer that α is at λ and that α will not be at λ at some point in the future:

$$\begin{aligned}&[[Stmt(\alpha, \beta, at(\alpha, \lambda), \{still\})]]_c := \\ &[[Stmt(\alpha, \beta, at(\alpha, \lambda)), \{\}]]_c \wedge Future(\neg at(\alpha, \lambda))\end{aligned} \tag{2}$$

If α states that it is "already" at λ, one can infer that α is at λ and that α had a goal (expressed via the "G" operator) to be at λ at some point in the past:

$$\begin{aligned}&[[Stmt(\alpha, at(\alpha, \lambda), \{already\})]]_c := \\ &[[Stmt(\alpha, \beta, at(\alpha, \lambda), \{\}]]_c \wedge Past(G(\alpha, at(\alpha, \lambda)))\end{aligned} \tag{3}$$

If α states that it is "now" at λ, one can infer that α is at λ and that α had not been at λ at some point in the past:

$$\begin{aligned}&[[Stmt(\alpha, \beta, at(\alpha, \lambda), \{now\})]]_c := \\ &[[Stmt(\alpha, \beta, at(\alpha, \lambda)), \{\}]]_c \wedge Past(\neg at(\alpha, \lambda))\end{aligned} \tag{4}$$

If α states that it is "not...yet" at λ, one can infer that α is not at λ, but has an intention to be at λ.

$$\begin{aligned}&[[Stmt(\alpha, \beta, \neg at(\alpha, \lambda), \{yet\})]]_c := \\ &\neg at(\alpha, \lambda) \wedge G(\alpha, at(\alpha, \lambda))\end{aligned} \tag{5}$$

Even in our limited domain, one must be cognizant of the ambiguities that arise from how adverbial cues are deployed. In addition to the simple presence of an adverbial cue, the location of the adverb in a sentence and prosodic factors may affect the intended meaning of the utterance. For instance, consider the statements: (a) I am now at λ; (b) I am at λ now; (c) I am still at λ; and (d) I am *still* at λ. Statement (a) is a simple situational update utterance as described above, while (b) could be construed as a statement akin to "I am already at λ. Statement (d) could be interpreted as additionally signaling the frustration of the agent, beyond conveying the information from (c).

It should also be noted that our analysis of these adverbial cues is to be understood in the limited context of these simple task-related predicates (e.g. $at(\alpha, \lambda)$). Formal definition of these adverbial cues in general cases is beyond the scope of this paper. For instance, "yet" could be used in a context when the predicate is not intended by the agent to which it applies (e.g. "Has Bill been fired yet?"). In this case, it would probably be incorrect to infer that the agent Bill had a goal to be fired. Instead an inference could be made regarding the probabilistic judgments of the interlocutors regarding the topic agent's future state. However, in the context of this paper, it is assumed that "yet" is used in the context of goals intended by agents.

3.1.2 Questions

Here we will limit the discussion to two question types, the "where" question (regarding locations) and simple "Yes-No" questions.

If α asks β about its location in the general sense ("where are you?"), then one can infer that α has an intention to know (expressed via the "IK" operator, see (Perrault and Allen, 1980)) where β is located:

$$[[Ask_{loc}(\alpha, \beta, \{\})]]_c := IK(\alpha, at(\beta, \lambda)) \tag{6}$$

for some λ.

If α asks β whether it is at λ, then one can infer that α has an intention to know whether β is at λ:

$$[[Ask_{yn}(\alpha, \beta, at(\beta, \lambda), \{\})]]_c := IK(\alpha, at(\beta, \lambda)) \tag{7}$$

If β is asked by α whether it is "still" at λ, β can infer that α believes (expressed via the "B" operator) that β is currently at λ:

$$[[Ask_{yn}(\alpha, \beta, at(\beta, \lambda), \{still\})]]_c := [[Ask_{yn}(\alpha, \beta, at(\beta, \lambda), \{\})]]_c \wedge B(\alpha, at(\beta, \lambda)) \tag{8}$$

If β is asked by α whether it is at λ "yet", β can infer that α believes that β has a goal to be at λ:

$$[[Ask_{yn}(\alpha, \beta, at(\beta, \lambda), \{yet\})]]_c := [[Ask_{yn}(\alpha, \beta, at(\beta, \lambda), \{\})]]_c \wedge B(\alpha, G(\beta, at(\beta, \lambda))) \tag{9}$$

3.1.3 Question-Answer Pairs

Next, we consider how discourse context as provided by question-answer pairs can further specify the pragmatic implications.

If α asks β whether it is at λ with any set of adverbial modifiers μ (i.e., $Prior(Ask_{yn}(\alpha, \beta, at(\beta, \lambda), \mu)) \in c$), and β responds by stating that it is "still" at λ, then one can infer that α has the belief that β was at λ in the recent past:

$$[[Stmt(\beta, \alpha, at(\beta, \lambda), \{still\})]]_c := [[Stmt(\beta, \alpha, at(\beta, \lambda), \{\})]]_c \wedge B(\alpha, RecPast(at(\beta, \lambda))) \tag{10}$$

where $Prior(Ask_{yn}(\alpha, \beta, at(\beta, \lambda), \mu)) \in c$. Also, $RecPast(\phi)$ denotes that ϕ was true in the recent past, as distinct from ϕ holding at some arbitrary point in the past (i.e. $Past(\phi)$). This distinction is necessary as it only makes sense to use the adverbial cue at this point if agent α believed $at(\beta, \lambda)$ at some relative and recent point in the past. Formalizing this would require keeping track of the points in time at which certain propositions are believed. To avoid committing to a particular temporal modeling system, we make the simplifying assumption that the $RecPast$ operator is not applied in rules (10) and (11), which is sufficient for the very simple interactions examined in this paper.

If α asks β whether it is at λ with any set of adverbial modifiers μ, and β responds by stating that it is "now" at λ, then one can infer that α has the belief that β is was not at λ in the recent past:

$$[[Stmt(\beta, \alpha, at(\beta, \lambda), \{now\})]]_c := [[Stmt(\beta, \alpha, at(\beta, \lambda), \{\})]]_c \wedge B(\alpha, RecPast(\neg at(\beta, \lambda))) \tag{11}$$

where $Prior(Ask_{yn}(\alpha, \beta, at(\beta, \lambda), \mu)) \in c$.

3.1.4 Commands

We also briefly describe how command processing (which we have studied elsewhere in much greater detail (Dzifcak et al., 2009)) can be augmented with the inclusion of pragmatic meanings. If α orders β to travel to λ, then one can infer that α has a goal for β to be at λ and that α intends to know whether β has received its new goal:

$$[[Cmd(\alpha, \beta, at(\beta, \lambda), \{\})]]_c := G(\alpha, at(\beta, \lambda)) \wedge IK(\alpha, G(\beta, at(\beta, \lambda))) \tag{12}$$

It would be an oversimplification to assume that the proposition $G(\beta, at(\beta, \lambda))$ is immediately understood by all listening agents. In order to generate the appropriate goal belief in the target agent, additional inference rules need to be considered. The following rule states that β will instantiate the goal $G(\beta, at(\beta, \lambda))$ when it believes α has the same goal and it believes $authority(\alpha, \beta)$, which denotes that α has command authority over β:

$$G(\alpha, at(\beta, \lambda)) \wedge authority(\alpha) \Rightarrow G(\beta, at(\beta, \lambda))$$

Other agents would have to wait for an acknowledgment that this inference has indeed taken place (as β could have not heard the initial command utterance). These acknowledgment utterances are described in the subsequent section.

3.1.5 Acknowledgments

Finally, we consider typical forms of acknowledgment. If α utters an acknowledgment (e.g., "OK.") when the previous utterance was a positive statement of location by β, then one can infer α no longer has the intention to know β's location:

$$[[Ack(\alpha, \beta, \{\})]]_c := \neg IK(\alpha, at(\beta, \lambda)) \quad (13)$$

for some λ where for any M $Prior(Stmt(\beta, \alpha, at(\beta, \lambda), \{M\})) \in c$.

If α utters an acknowledgment (e.g., "OK.") when the previous utterance was a command by β to be at λ, then one can infer that

$$[[Ack(\alpha, \beta, \{\})]]_c := G(\alpha, at(\alpha, \lambda)) \wedge G(\beta, at(\alpha, \lambda)) \wedge \neg IK(\beta, G(\alpha, at(\alpha, \lambda) \quad (14)$$

where $Prior(Cmd(\beta, \alpha, at(\alpha, \lambda), \{M\})) \in c$ for any M.

We should note here that the distinction between explicitly not intending-to-know and the lack of an intention-to-know has been blurred in the above rules for the sake of simplicity. As described in the subsequent section, agent beliefs are removed when contradicted in the current system (i.e. $Remove(\phi, B_\alpha) \Leftrightarrow (\neg\phi) \in B_\alpha$). A more comprehensive belief update system should allow for a mechanism to remove beliefs without the need for explicit contradiction.

3.2 Agent Modeling and Belief Updates

Belief updates occur whenever an agent α receives an utterance Utt from another agent β in context c. First, $[[Utt]]_c$ is computed using the pragmatic principles and definitions developed in Section 3.1. For simplicity, we assume that agents adhere to the Gricean maxim of *quality* and, therefore, do not communicate information they do not believe. Hence, all propositions $\phi \in [[Utt]]_c$ are assumed to be true and to the extent that they are inconsistent with existing beliefs of α as determined by $\alpha's$ inference algorithm $\Rightarrow^b_\alpha$, the conflicting beliefs are removed from the agent's sets of beliefs Bel_{self} (b here denotes some finite bound on the inference algorithm, e.g., resources, computation time, etc.).[1]

To model other agents hearing the utterance, agent α derives the set $B_\alpha B_\gamma = \{\psi | B(\gamma, \psi) \in Bel_{self}\}$ for all other agents $\gamma \neq \alpha$. The agent updates these belief sets by applying the same rules as it does to Bel_{self}.

It should be noted that these belief update rules are indeed simplifications designed to avoid the issue of resolving conflicting information from different sources. These belief update rules would be problematic, for instance, when agents have incorrect beliefs (and proceed to communicate them), as no method for belief disputation exists. For the purpose of illustrating the implementation and utility of adverbial cues, however, they should suffice. We set up our environment and rule sets such that the autonomous agent has perfect information about itself (specifically location), and no utterances exists to communicate propositions that are not about oneself.

3.3 Sentence Generation

Depending on the sentence type α received (and the extent to which meanings can be resolved, an issue we will not address in this paper), different response sentence types are appropriate (e.g., a yes-no ques-

[1]Note that we are not making any assumption about a particular inference algorithm or its (as it will, in general, depend on the expressive power of the employed logic to represent meanings), only that if a contradiction can be reached using the inference algorithm, the existing belief needs to be removed (otherwise existing beliefs are taken to be consistent with the implications of the utterance). In our implemented system, we use a simplified version of the resolution inference principle.

tion requires a statement answering the question). The generation of an appropriate response proceeds in two steps. First, based on the agent's current set of beliefs Bel_{self}, we determine the set of propositions Φ_{comm} that the agent has an interest in conveying. Second, we attempt to find the smallest utterance Utt given a set of pragmatic principles (as specified in Section 3.1) that communicates one or more of these propositions and implies the rest for recipient β.

3.3.1 What to say

In obtaining a set Φ_{comm} of propositions to communicate, α may obey the Gricean maxim of *quality* by adding a proposition ϕ to Φ_{comm} only if $\phi \in Bel_{self}$. The maxims of *relevance* and *quantity* are heeded by restricting believed propositions to be conveyed solely to those that either correct a false belief of β or provide β some piece of information it wants to know. Specifically, we find the set of all propositions used to correct false beliefs Φ_{rev}, defined as:

$$\begin{aligned}\psi \in \Phi_{rev} &\Leftrightarrow \exists \beta, \phi : \\ &B(\beta, \phi) \wedge \phi \in Bel_{self} \wedge (\psi \Rightarrow_{\alpha}^{b} \neg\phi)\end{aligned}$$

The set of all propositions other agents want to know, Φ_{IK}, can be defined as:

$$\begin{aligned}\psi \in \Phi_{IK} &\Leftrightarrow \exists \beta, \phi : \psi \in Bel_{self} \wedge \\ &IK(\beta, \phi \in Bel_{self}) \wedge (\psi \Rightarrow_{\alpha}^{b} \phi \vee \psi \Rightarrow_{\alpha}^{b} \neg\phi)\end{aligned}$$

The final set of propositions to convey is obtained by merging these two sets, $\Phi_{comm} = \Phi_{rev} \cup \Phi_{IK}$. Note that this set is always consistent because propositions are added to Φ_{rev} and Φ_{IK} if and only if they exist in Bel_{self}, which is maintained to be consistent.

3.3.2 How to say it

Once Φ_{comm} has been obtained, α must select potential utterances to produce. It starts by generating an initial set Utt_0 of utterances that in the present context c imply some subset of Φ_{comm}:

$$(u \in Utt_0) \Leftrightarrow \exists \Phi \in \Phi_{comm} \forall \phi \in \Phi : ([[u]]_c \Rightarrow_{\alpha}^{b} \phi)$$

Currently, this is achieved by searching through the set of all utterances defined by rules such as those found in Section 3.1. Note that while this approach is feasible for our quite limited domain, more efficient methods for identifying candidate utterances must be developed as the number of understood utterances grows.

Applying the maxim of *quality*, this set can be pruned of all utterances that are defined by additional propositions that we either have no evidence for ("unsupported") or explicitly believe to be false:

$$False(\phi) \Leftrightarrow \exists \psi : \psi \in Bel_{self} \wedge (\psi \Rightarrow_{\alpha}^{b} \neg\phi)$$

$$NoSupp(\phi) \Leftrightarrow \neg\exists \psi : \psi \in Bel_{self} \wedge (\psi \Rightarrow_{\alpha}^{b} \phi)$$

Using these conditions, we can generate a new subset of utterance candidates Utt_1:

$$\begin{aligned}(u \in Utt_1) \Leftrightarrow \neg\exists \phi : ([[u]]_c \Rightarrow_{\alpha}^{b} \phi) \\ \wedge (False(\phi) \vee NoSupp(\phi)))\end{aligned}$$

Applying the maxim of *quantity*, utterances that revise or add the most beliefs to other agent belief-spaces ought to be favored:

$$\begin{aligned}&RevBel(\beta, \phi) \Leftrightarrow \\ &\quad \exists \psi : B(\beta, \psi) \in B_{self} \wedge (\psi \Rightarrow_{\alpha}^{b} \neg\phi)\end{aligned}$$

$$AddBel(\beta, \phi) \Leftrightarrow B(\beta, \phi) \notin Bel_{self}$$

Using these definitions, we can derive the "correction-score" of an utterance by counting the number of propositions $\phi \in [[u]]_c$ that revise or add a belief for β.

If multiple candidate utterances still exist at this point, we can again apply the maxim of *quantity* to favor utterances that convey the most (true) information. Because all definitions with false propositions have been eliminated, we can simply count the number of true propositions derived from the utterance, thereby favoring semantically richer utterances. At this point, if multiple candidate utterances are still available, the difference is of stylistic nature only and we may choose an arbitrary one. Note that the correct usage of adverbial modifiers emerges naturally from these rules as utterances that include inappropriate adverbs are removed in Utt_1, while utterances that include appropriate adverbial cues are subsequently favored.

4 Case Study

We now demonstrate the operation of the proposed algorithm in a simple joint activity scenario where a robot (R) is located at nav-point 1 and correctly knows its location, having the initial belief-space $B_R = \{at(R, N1)\}$. The remote human operator starts by asking:

`O: R, where are you?`

R updates its beliefs based on this question:

$$\begin{array}{l} u := parse(\text{"O: R, where are you?"}) \\ \rightarrow u := Ask_{loc}(O, R, \{\}) \\ [[u]]_c := \{IK(O, at(R, N1)), IK(O, at(R, N2)), \\ IK(O, at(R, N3))\} \\ P_{contra} := contradictedTerms([[u]]_c, B_{self}) \\ B_R := (B_R - P_{contra}) + [[u]]_c \\ B_R B_O := (B_R B_O - P_{contra}) + [[u]]_c \end{array}$$

which yields a new belief-space:

$$\begin{array}{l} B_R := \{at(R, N1), IK(O, at(R, N1)), \\ IK(O, at(R, N2)), IK(O, at(R, N3)), \\ B(O, IK(O, at(R, N1))), B(O, IK(O, at(R, N2))), \\ B(O, IK(O, at(R, N3)))\} \end{array}$$

Next, R proceeds to respond. For compactness, we refer below to utterance candidates according to the index of the applicable rules from Section 3.1, so that u_{13} denotes $Ack(\alpha, \beta, \{\})$.

$$\begin{array}{l} B_R B_O := \{IK(O, at(R, N1)), IK(O, at(R, N2)) \\ IK(O, at(R, N3))\} \\ \Phi_{rev} := \{\}; \Phi_{IK} := \{at(R, N1)\} \\ \Phi_{comm} := \{at(R, N1)\}; \\ \rightarrow Utt_0 := \{u_1, u_2, u_3, u_4\} \end{array}$$

R now has an initial set of candidate utterances, which it prunes using the rules from Section 3.3.2.

$$\begin{array}{l} [[u_1]]_c := at(R, N1) \\ [[u_2]]_c := at(R, N1) \wedge Future(\neg at(R, N1)) \\ [[u_3]]_c := at(R, N1) \wedge Past(G(R, N1)) \\ [[u_4]]_c := at(R, N1) \wedge Past(\neg at(R, N1)) \\ \rightarrow Utt_1 := \{u_1\} \end{array}$$

Thus, R chooses the utterance of the form, $Stmt(R, O, at(R, N1), \{\})$, and responds:

`R: I am at N1.`

Finally, R processes its own utterance so that it can update its beliefs according to rule (1):

$$\begin{array}{l} B_R := \{at(R, N1), IK(O, at(R, N1)), \\ IK(O, at(R, N2)), IK(O, at(R, N3)), \\ B(O, IK(O, at(R, N1))), B(O, IK(O, at(R, N2))), \\ B(O, IK(O, at(R, N3))), B(O, at(R, N1)\} \end{array}$$

When the operator responds:

`O: Okay.`

R also processes this acknowledgment to update its beliefs according to rule (13):

$$B_R := \{at(R, N1), B(O, at(R, N1)\}$$

R proceeds to respond, but finds that it has nothing to convey.

$$\begin{array}{l} B_R B_O := \{at(R, N1)\} \\ ; \Phi_{rev} := \{\}; \Phi_{IK} := \{\} \\ ; \Phi_{comm} := \{\}; \\ \rightarrow Utt_0 := \{\} \end{array}$$

Thus, R generates no utterance. Now let us suppose that R moves to N2, and enough time elapses such that the operator forfeits his/her conversational turn. R then proceeds to generate an utterance.

$$\begin{array}{l} B_R := \{at(R, N2), Past(at(R, N1))\} \\ B_R B_O := \{at(R, N1)\} \\ \Phi_{rev} := \{at(R, N2)\}; \Phi_{IK} := \{\} \\ \Phi_{comm} := \{at(R, N2)\} \\ \rightarrow Utt_0 := \{u_1, u_2, u_3, u_4\} \\ [[u_1]]_c := at(R, N2) \\ [[u_2]]_c := at(R, N2) \wedge Future(\neg at(R, N2)) \\ [[u_3]]_c := at(R, N2) \wedge G(R, N2) \\ [[u_4]]_c := at(R, N2) \wedge Past(\neg at(R, N2)) \\ \rightarrow Utt_1 := \{u_1, u_4\} \end{array}$$

So, R must now resolve which of these candidate utterances to select by choosing the one that revises the most beliefs of O, or failing that, the one that has the most true propositions.

$$\begin{array}{l} at(R, N2) \Rightarrow \neg at(R, N1) \\ \rightarrow NumRev([[u_1]]_c) := 1; NumRev([[u_4]]_c) := 1; \\ NumTrue([[u_1]]_c) := 1; NumTrue([[u_4]]_c) := 2; \\ \rightarrow Utt_{final} := u_4 \end{array}$$

Thus, R chooses the utterance of the form, $Stmt(R, O, at(R, N2), \{now\})$, and responds:

`R: I am now at N2.`

R again processes its own utterance to update its beliefs according to rule (4). If O then asks:

`O: R, are you still at N2?`

R updates its beliefs according to rule (10):

$$\begin{array}{l} B_R := \{at(R, N2), B(O, at(R, N2)), \\ Past(at(R, N1)), B(O, Past(at(R, N1))), \\ IK(O, at(R, N2)), B(O, IK(O, at(R, N2)))\} \end{array}$$

Next, R generates a response:

$$\begin{array}{l} \Phi_{rev} := \{\}; \Phi_{IK} := \{at(R, N2)\} \\ \Phi_{comm} := \{at(R, N2)\}; \\ \rightarrow Utt_0 := \{u_1, u_2, u_{10}, u_{11}\} \\ [[u_1]]_c := at(R, N2) \\ [[u_2]]_c := at(R, N2) \wedge Future(\neg at(R, N2)) \\ [[u_{10}]]_c := at(R, N2) \wedge B(O, at(R, N2)) \\ [[u_{11}]]_c := at(R, N2) \wedge B(O, \neg at(R, N2)) \\ \rightarrow Utt_1 := \{u_1, u_{10}\} \\ \rightarrow NumRev([[u_1]]_c) := 0; NumRev([[u_{10}]]_c) := 0; \\ NumTrue([[u_1]]_c) := 1; NumTrue([[u_{10}]]_c) := 2; \\ \rightarrow Utt_{final} := u_{10} \end{array}$$

replying with the utterance:

`R: I am still at N2.`

and processes its own utterance to updates its beliefs according to rule (10). O's acknowledgment:

```
O: Okay.
```

causes R to update its beliefs according to rule (13):

$$B_R := \{at(R, N2), B(O, at(R, N2)), Past(at(R, N1)), B(O, Past(at(R, N1)))\}$$

R does not generate a response as there are no beliefs to revise or intentions to know. Now suppose R moves back to N1, without O's knowledge, after which O commands:

```
O: R, go to N1.
```

R, updates its belief according to rule (12):

$$\begin{aligned} B_R := \{&at(R, N1), B(O, at(R, N2)),\\ &Past(at(R, N2)), B(O, Past(at(R, N2))),\\ &G(R, at(R, N1)), G(O, at(R, N1)),\\ &IK(O, G(R, at(R, N1))),\\ &B(O, G(R, at(R, N1))),\\ &B(O, IK(O, G(R, at(R, N1)))),\\ &B(O, G(O, at(R, N1)))\} \end{aligned}$$

and proceeds to generate a response:

$$\begin{aligned} &\Phi_{rev} := \{at(R, N1)\}\\ &\Phi_{IK} := \{G(R, at(R, N1))\}\\ &\Phi_{comm} := \{at(R, N1), G(R, at(R, N1))\}\\ &\rightarrow Utt_0 := \{u_1, u_2, u_3, u_4\}\\ &[[u_1]]_c := at(R, N1)\\ &[[u_2]]_c := at(R, N1) \wedge Future(\neg at(R, N1))\\ &[[u_3]]_c := at(R, N1) \wedge G(R, at(R, N1))\\ &[[u_4]]_c := at(R, N1) \wedge Past(\neg at(R, N1))\\ &\rightarrow Utt_1 := \{u_1, u_3, u_4\}\\ &\rightarrow NumRev([[u_1]]_c) := 1; NumRev([[u_3]]_c) := 2;\\ &NumRev([[u_4]]_c) := 1\\ &\rightarrow Utt_{final} := u_3 \end{aligned}$$

Thus, R responds:

```
R: I am already at N1.
```

5 Discussion and Related Work

While the above case study was kept simple due to space restrictions, it demonstrates the utility of our utterance generation method in adapting NL output at the sentence-level based on a mental-model of an interlocutor. In particular, we adapted utterances by employing adverbial modifiers, which serve to make the speaker's belief-space more transparent and natural, which was the main motivation for the development of the formal framework with rules for adverbial modifiers in the first place. Other examples of adaptations that are intended to make an automated system's reasoning and internal state representations more open and clear to human-users include the sentence-level adaptation of restaurant recommendations (Walker et al., 2007) and the adaptation of query-phrasing in a robotic context (Kruijff and Brenner, 2009). In addition to conveying information about one's own mental state, pragmatic principles and rules, such as those we have presented, may be deployed to reason about the intentions and beliefs of others (Perrault and Allen, 1980).

The current system, while a promising step towards more natural task-based dialogue interactions, has several limitations. Aside from lexical and semantic limitations, the currently implemented adverbial modifiers are restricted to very simple predicates. Clearly, these restrictions will have to be addressed and the formal definitions will have to be widened. Moreover, the system currently does not handle situations where a human's mental state changes without the robot's knowledge, which can cause misunderstandings that need to be detected and corrected effectively. Additionally, agents can be mistaken about their beliefs. Real-world complexities such as these suggest the inclusion of handling uncertainty in a belief modeling system (Lison et al., 2010), potentially by assigning beliefs confidence values. This is clearly an important topic for future work.

User-model based adaptation of NL output at the sentence level that includes multi-modal components (Walker et al., 2004) has also not been addressed. Further study is required to determine whether our Gricean-inspired utterance selection method can also be applied to non-linguistic communication modalities. Finally, the current system can only handle simple perceptual updates and has limitations when handling multi-robot dialogues (neither of which are discussed here for space reasons). The challenges of perceptual updates that will have to be addressed are investigated in the context of a plan-based situated dialogue system for robots in (Brenner, 2007) and extensions to multi-robot scenarios are explored in (Brenner and Kruijff-Korbayova, 2008).

6 Conclusion

Competency in mental modeling is a crucial component in the development of natural, human-like interaction capabilities for robots in mixed initiative settings. We showed that the ability to understand and employ adverbial modifiers can help both in constructing mental models of human operators and conveying one's own mental state to others.

To this end, we made three contributions. First, we introduced a framework for formalizing different sentence types and the pragmatic meanings of adverbial modifiers. Second, we showed how one can perform belief updates based on implied meanings of adverbial modifiers. And third, we introduced a novel algorithm for generating effective responses that obey three Gricean maxims and aid the listener in appropriate belief updates. The core properties of the algorithm are that it corrects false or missing beliefs in other agents, that it provides an agent with information that is wanted, that it never generates an utterance that implies false propositions, and that it first favors utterances that convey more (true) propositions after favoring utterances that revise or add more beliefs to the listener's belief-space. Finally, we demonstrated our algorithm responding to basic operator queries in a simple case study, correctly using adverbial cues to sound more natural and convey more information regarding its beliefs.

There are extensive avenues to pursue future work. For instance, we plan to extend the algorithm to include multi-modal perceptual integration as well as multi-agent multi-dialogue capabilities. A variety of empirical evaluations would be desirable to evaluate the efficacy and naturalness of the proposed adverbial cues in simulated and real HRI tasks. Additionally, empirical evaluations could also be performed to observe additional cues to incorporate into the system.

7 Acknowledgments

This work was supported by an ONR MURI grant #N00014-07-1-1049 to the second author. We wish to extend our thanks to Paul Schermerhorn and the anonymous reviewers for providing valuable feedback.

References

A. Kobsa. 2001. Generic User Modeling Systems. *User Modeling and User-Adapted Interaction* 11: 49–63.

B. Di Eugenio, et al. 2008. Be Brief, And They Shall Learn: Generating Concise Language Feedback for a Computer Tutor. *International Journal of Artificial Intelligence in Education* 18(4).

C. R. Perrault and J. F. Allen. 1980. A Plan-Based Analysis of Indirect Speech Acts. *American Journal of Computational Linguistics*, 6(3-4):167–182.

G. M. Kruijff and M. Brenner. 2009. Phrasing Questions. *AAAI 2009 Spring Symposium.*

H. Kress-Gazit and G. E. Fainekos and G. J. Pappas 2008 Translating Structured English to Robot Controllers *Advanced Robotics* 22, 12, 1343–1359

H. P. Grice. 1975. Logic and conversation. *Syntax and Semantics*, 3(1):43–58.

J. Dzifcak, M. Scheutz, C. Baral, and P. Schermerhorn. 2009. What to do and how to do it: Translating Natural Language Directives into Temporal and Dynamic Logic Representation for Goal Management and Action Execution. *ICRA*.

M. A. Walker, et al. 2004. Generation and evaluation of user tailored responses in multimodal dialogue. *Cognitive Science* 28: 811–840.

M. Walker, et al. 2007. Individual and Domain Adaptation in Sentence Planning for Dialogue. *Journal of Artificial Intelligence Research*. 30: 413–456.

M. Scheutz, et al. 2007. First Steps toward Natural Human-Like HRI. *Autonomous Robots* 22(4):411–423.

M. Brenner. 2007. Situation-Aware Interpretation, Planning and Execution of User Commands by Autonomous Robots. *RO-MAN 2007*.

M. Brenner and I. Kruijff-Korbayova. 2008. Continual planning and acting in dynamic multiagent environments. *12th SEMDIAL Workshop*.

P. R. Cohen, et al. 1990. Task-Oriented Dialogue as a Consequence of Joint Activity. *Pacific Rim International Conference on Artificial Intelligence*.

P. Lison, C. Ehrler, and G. M. Kruijff. 2010. Belief Modelling for Situation Awareness in Human-Robot Interaction. *19th IEEE International Symposium*.

R. Dale and E. Reiter. 1995. Computational Interpretations of the Gricean Maxims in the Generation of Referring Expressions. *Cognitive Science*, 18(1):233–263.

P. Rybski, K. Yoon, J. Stolarz, and M. Veloso. 2007 Interactive robot task training through dialog and demonstration *HRI*, 49–56

T. Kollar and S. Tellex and D. Roy and N. Roy 2010 Toward Understanding Natural Language Directions *HRI*, 259-266

W. Wahlster and A. Kobsa. 1989. User Models in Dialog Systems. *User Models in Dialog Systems*, 4–34. Springer-Verlag, Berlin.

Embedded Wizardry

Rebecca J. Passonneau[1], **Susan L. Epstein**[2,3], **Tiziana Ligorio**[3] and **Joshua Gordon**[1]
[1]Columbia University
New York, NY, USA
(becky|joshua)@cs.columbia.edu
[2,3]Hunter College
[3]The Graduate Center of the City University of New York
New York, NY, USA (susan.epstein@hunter|tligorio@gc).cuny.edu

Abstract

This paper presents a progressively challenging series of experiments that investigate clarification subdialogues to resolve the words in noisy transcriptions of user utterances. We focus on user utterances where the user's specific intent requires little additional inference, given sufficient understanding of the form. We learned decision-making strategies for a dialogue manager from run-time features of our spoken dialogue system and from observation of human wizards we had embedded within it. Results show that noisy ASR can be resolved based on predictions from context about what a user might say, and that dialogue management strategies for clarifications of linguistic form benefit from access to features from spoken language understanding.

1 Introduction

Utterances have literal meaning derived from their linguistic form, and pragmatic intent, the actions speakers aim to achieve through words (Austin, 1962). Because the channel is usually not noisy enough to impede communication, misunderstandings that arise between adult human interlocutors are more often due to confusions about intent, rather than about words. Between humans and machines, however, verbal interaction has a much higher rate of linguistic misunderstandings because the channel is noisy, and machines are not as adept at using spoken language. It is difficult to arrive at accurate rates for misunderstandings of form versus intent in human conversation, because the two types cannot always be distinguished (Schlangen and Fern'andez, 2005). However, one estimate of the rate of misunderstandings of literal meaning between humans, based on text transcripts of the British National Corpus, is in the low range of 4% (Purver et al., 2001), compared with a 30% estimate for human-computer dialogue (Rieser and Lemon, 2011). The thesis of our work is that misunderstandings of linguistic form in human-machine dialogue are more effectively resolved through greater reliance on context, and through closer integration of spoken language understanding (SLU) with dialogue management (DM). We investigate these claims by focusing on noisy speech recognition for utterances where the user's specific intent requires little additional inference, given sufficient understanding of the form.

This paper presents three experiments that progressively address SLU methods to compensate for poor automated speech recognition (ASR), and complementary DM strategies. In two of the experiments, human *wizards* are embedded in the spoken dialogue system while run-time SLU features are collected. Many wizard-of-Oz investigations have addressed the noisy channel issue for SDS (Zollo, 1999; Skantze, 2003; Williams and Young, 2004; Skantze, 2005; Rieser and Lemon, 2006; Schlangen and Fern'andez, 2005; Rieser and Lemon, 2011). Like them, we study how human wizards solve the joint problem of interpreting users' words and inferring users' intents. Our work differs in its exploration of the role context can play in the literal interpretation of noisy language. We rely on knowledge in the backend database to propose candidate linguistic forms for noisy ASR.

Our principal results are that both wizards and our

Proceedings of the SIGDIAL 2011: the 12th Annual Meeting of the Special Interest Group on Discourse and Dialogue, pages 248–258,
Portland, Oregon, June 17-18, 2011.

SDS can achieve high accuracy interpretations, indicating that predictions about what the user might be saying can play a significant role in resolving noise. We show it is possible to achieve low rates of unresolved misunderstanding, even at word error rates (WER) as poor as 50%-70%. We achieve this through machine learned models of DM actions that combine standard DM features with a rich number and variety of SLU features. The learned models predict DM actions to determine whether a reliable candidate interpretation exists for a noisy utterance, and if not, what action to take. The results support an approach to DM design that integrates the two problems of understanding form and intent.

The next sections present related work, our library domain and our baseline SDS architecture. Subsequent sections discuss the SLU settings across the three experiments, and present the experimental designs and results, discussion and conclusion.

2 Related Work

Previous WOz studies of wizards' ability to process noisy transcriptions of speaker utterances include the use of real (Skantze, 2003; Zollo, 1999) or simulated ASR (Kruijff-Korbayová et al., 2005; Williams and Young, 2004). WOz studies that directed their attention to the wizard include efforts to predict: the wizard's response when the user is not understood (Bohus 2004); the wizard's use of multimodal clarification strategies (Rieser and Lemon, 2006; Rieser and Lemon, 2011); and the wizard's use of application-specific clarification strategies (Skantze, 2003; Skantze, 2005). WOz studies that address real or simulated ASR reveal that wizards can find ways to not respond to utterances they fail to understand (Zollo, 1999; Skantze, 2003; Kruijff-Korbayová et al., 2005; Williams and Young, 2004). For example, they can prompt the user for an alternative attribute of the same object. Our work differs in that we address clarifications about the words used, and rely on a rich set of SLU features. Further, we compare behavior across wizards. Our SDS benefits from models of the most skilled wizards.

To limit communication errors incurred by faulty ASR, an SDS can rely on strategies to detect and respond to incorrect recognition output (Bohus, 2004). The SDS can repeatedly request user confirmation to avoid misunderstanding, or ask for confirmation using language that elicits responses from the user that the system can handle (Raux and Eskenazi, 2004). When the user adds unanticipated information in response to a system prompt, two-pass recognition can rely on a concept-specific language model to improve the recognition of the domain concepts within the utterance containing unknown words, and thereby achieve better recognition (Stoyanchev and Stent, 2009). An SDS could take this approach one step further and use context-specific language for incremental understanding of noisy input throughout the dialogue (Aist et al., 2007).

Current work on error recovery and grounding for SDS assumes that the primary responsibility of a dialogue management strategy is to understand the user's intent. Errors of understanding are addressed by ignoring the utterances where understanding failures occur, asking users to repeat, or pursuing clarifications about intent. These strategies typically rely on knowledge sources that follow the SLU stage. The RavenClaw dialogue manager, which represents domain-dependent (task-based) DM strategy as a tree of goals, triggers error handling by means of a single confidence score associated with the concepts hypothesized to represent the user's intent (Bohus and Rudnicky, 2002; Bohus and Rudnicky, 2009). Features for reinforcement learning of MDP-based DM strategies include a few lexical features and a measure of noise analogous to WER (Rieser and Lemon, 2011). The WOz studies reported here yield learned models of specific actions in response to noisy input, such as whether to treat a candidate interpretation as correct, or to pursue one of many possible clarification strategies, including clarifications of form or intent. These models rely on relatively large numbers of features from all phases of spoken language understanding, as well as on typical dialogue management features.

3 CheckItOut

3.1 Domain

Our domain of investigation simulates book orders from the Andrew Heiskell Braille and Talking Book Library, part of the New York Public Library and the Library of Congress. Patrons order books by telephone during conversation with a librarian, and receive them by mail. Patrons typically have identifying information for the books they seek, which they get from monthly newsletters. In a corpus of eighty two calls recorded at the library, we found that most book requests by title were very faithful to the actual title. Challenges to SLU in this domain include the size of the database, the size of the vocabulary, and the average sentence length.

While large databases have been used for investigations of phonological query expansion (Georgila et al., 2003), much of the research on DM strategy relies on relatively small databases. A recent study of reinforcement learning of DM strategy modeled as a Markov Decision Process reported in (Rieser and Lemon, 2011) relies on a database of 438 items. In (Gordon and Passonneau, 2011) we compared the SLU challenges faced by CheckItOut and the Let's Go bus schedule information system, both of which rely on the same architecture (Raux et al., 2005). The Let's Go corpus contained 70 bus routes names and 1300 place names, and a mean utterance length of 4.4 words. The work reported here uses the full 2007 version of Heiskell's database of 71,166 books and 28,031 authors, and a sanitized version of its 2007 patron database of 5,028 active patrons. Authors and titles contribute 45,636 distinct words, with a 10.43% overlap between the two. Average book title length is 5.4 words; 26% of titles are 1-2 words, 44% are 3-5 words, 20% are 6 to 10. Consequently, our domain has relatively long utterances. The syntax of book titles is much richer than typical SDS slot fillers, such as place or person names.

To achieve high-confidence SLU, we integrate voice search into the SLU components of our two SDS experiments (Wang et al., 2008).[1] Our custom voice search query relies on Ratcliff/Obershershelp (R/O) pattern matching (Ratcliff and Metzener, 1988), the ratio of the number of matching characters to the total length of both strings. This simple metric captures gross similarities without overfitting to a specific application domain. The criteria for selecting R/O derive from our first offline experiment, described in Section 4.2.

For an experiment focused only on a single turn

[1]In concurrent work on a new SDS architecture, we use ensembles of SLU strategies (Gordon and Passonneau, 2011; Gordon et al., 2011).

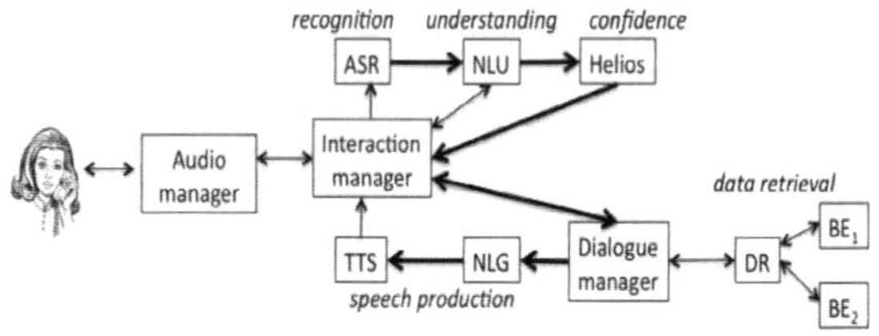

(a) Baseline CheckItOut

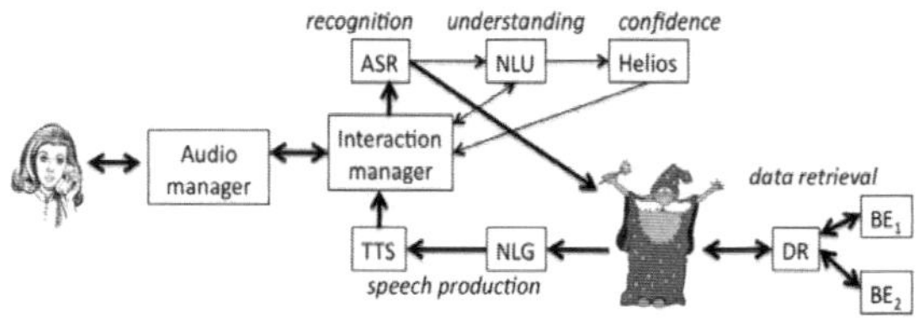

(b) Embedded Wizard

Figure 1: CheckItOut information pipeline

exchange beginning with a user book request, we queried the backend directly with the ASR string. For a subsequent experiment on full dialogues, we queried the backend with a modified ASR string, because the SDS architecture we used permits backend queries to occur only during the dialogue management phase, after natural language understanding. The next section describes this architecture.

3.2 Architecture

CheckItOut, our baseline SDS, employs the Olympus/RavenClaw architecture developed at Carnegie Mellon University (CMU) (Raux et al., 2005; Bohus and Rudnicky, 2009). SDS modules communicate via message passing, controlled by a central hub. However, the information flow is largely a pipeline, as depicted in Figure 1(a). The PocketSphinx recognizer (Huggins-Daines et al., 2006) receives acoustic data segmented by the audio manager, and passes a single recognition hypothesis to the Phoenix parser (Ward and Issar, 1994). Phoenix sends one or more equivalently ranked semantic parses to the Helios confidence annotator (Bohus and Rudnicky, 2002), which selects a parse and assigns a confidence score. The Apollo interaction manager (Raux and Eskenazi, 2007) monitors the three SLU modules–the recognizer, the semantic parser, and the confidence annotator–to determine whether the user or SDS has the current turn. To a limited degree, Apollo can override the early segmentation decisions based solely on pause length.

Confidence-annotated concepts from the semantic parse are passed to the RavenClaw DM, which decides when to prompt the user, present information to her, or query the backend database.

A wizard server communicates with other modules via the hub, as shown in Figure 1(b). For each wizard experiment, we constructed a graphical user interface (GUI). Wizard GUIs display information for the wizard in a manageable form, and allow the wizard to query the backend or select communicative actions that result in utterances directed to the user. Figure 1(b) shows an arrow from the speech recognizer directly to the wizard: the recognition string has been vetted by Apollo before it is displayed to the wizard.

4 Experiments and Results

The experiments reported here are an off-line pilot study to identify book titles under worst case recognition (Title Pilot), an embedded WOz study of a single turn exchange involving book requests by title (Turn Exchange), and an embedded WOz study of dialogues where users followed scenarios that included four books at a time (Full WOz). To evaluate the impact of learned models of wizard actions from the Full WOz wizard data, we evaluated CheckItOut before and after the dialogue manager was enhanced with wizard models for specific actions.

4.1 Experimental Settings

All three experiments use the full database for search. To control for WER, the knowledge sources for speech recognition and semantic parsing vary across experiments. For each experiment, Table 1 indicates the acoustic model (AM) used, the number of hours of domain-specific spontaneous speech used for AM adaptation, the number of titles used to construct the language model (LM), the type of LM, the type of grammar rules in the Phoenix book title subgrammar, and average WER as measured by Levenstein word edit distance (Levenshtein, 1996).

For the first two experiments, we used CMU's Open Source WSJ1 dictation AMs for wideband (16kHz) microphone (dictation) speech. For Full WOz we adapted narrowband (8kHz) WSJ1 dictation speech with about eight hours of data collected from Turn Exchange and two hours of scripted spontaneous speech typical of CheckItOut dialogues.

Logios is a CMU toolkit for generating a pseudo-corpus from a Phoenix grammar. It produces a set of strings generated by Phoenix production rules, which in turn are used to build an LM (Carnegie Mellon University Speech Group, 2008). Before we explain the three rightmost columns in Table 1, we first briefly describe Phoenix, the Phoenix book title subgrammar, and how we combine title strings with a Logios pseudo-corpus.

Phoenix is a context-free grammar (CFG) parser that produces one or more semantic frames per parse. A semantic frame has slots, where each slot is a concept with its own CFG productions (subgrammar). To accommodate noisy ASR, the parser can skip words between frames or slots. Phoenix is well-suited for restricted domains, where a frame represents a particular type of subdialogue (e.g., ordering a plane ticket), and slots represent constrained concepts (e.g., departure city, destination city). Phoenix is not well-suited for book titles, which have a rich vocabulary and syntax, and no obvious component slots. The CFG rules for the Turn Exchange book title subgrammar consisted of a verbatim rule for each book title. Rules that consisted of a bag-of-words (BOW; i.e., unordered) for each title proved to be too unconstrained.[2] In Turn Exchange, interpretation of ASR consisted primarily of voice search; the highly constrained CFG rules (exact words in exact order) had little impact on performance. For baseline CheckItOut dialogues, and for Full WOz, we required more constrained grammar rules that would preserve Phoenix's robustness to noise.

To avoid the brittleness of exact string CFG rules, and the massive over-generation of BOW CFG rules, we wrote a transducer that mapped dependency parses of book titles to CFG rules. When ASR words are skipped, book title parses can consist of multiple slots. We used MICA, a broad-coverage dependency grammar (Bangalore et al., 2009) to parse the entire book title database. When a set of titles is selected for an experiment, the corresponding MICA parses are transduced to the relevant CFG productions, and inserted into a Phoenix grammar. Productions for the *author* subgrammar

[2]BOW Phoenix rules for book titles are used in a more recent Olympus/RavenClaw system inspired in part by CheckItOut (Lee et al., 2010), with a database of 15,088 eBooks.

Exp.	AM	Adapted	# Titles for LM	LM	Grammar rules	WER
Title Pilot	WSJ1 16kHz	NA	500	unigram	NA	0.76
Turn Exchange	WSJ1 16kHz	NA	7,500	trigram	title strings	0.71
Full WOz	WSJ1 8kHz	10 hr.	3,000	Logios + book data	Mica-based	0.50 (est)

Table 1: SLU settings across experiments

consist largely of a first name slot followed by a last name slot. The remaining portions of the Phoenix CheckItOut grammar consist of subgrammars for *book request* prefixes and affixes (e.g., "I would like the book called"), for *confirmations* and *rejections*, *phone numbers*, *book catalogue numbers*, and miscellaneous additional concepts. The set of subgrammars excluding the book title and author subgrammars (*book requests, confirmations*, and so on; the grammar *shell*) are the same for all experiments. The MICA-based book title grammar also provides several features (e.g., number of slots in a parse) for machine learning.

The Title Pilot LM consisted of unigram frequencies of the 1400 word types from a random sample (without replacement) of 500 titles. For Turn Exchange, a trigram LM was constructed from 7,500 titles randomly selected from the 19,708 titles that remained after we eliminated one-word titles and titles with below average circulation. For Full WOz, 3,000 books were randomly selected from the full book database (with no more than three titles by the same author, and no one-word titles). Logios was used on the grammar shell to generate an initial pseudo-corpus, which was combined with the book title and author strings to generate a full pseudo-corpus for the trigram LM (denoted as "Logios + book data" in Table 1).

4.2 Title Pilot

The Title Pilot (Passonneau et al., 2009) was an offline investigation of how reliance on prior knowledge in the database might facilitate interpretation of noisy ASR. It demonstrates that given the context of things a user might say, ASR that is otherwise unintelligible becomes intelligible.

Three males each read 50 randomly selected titles from the LM subset of 500 (see Table 1). Their average WER was 0.75, 0.83 and 0.69, respectively. Three undergraduates (A, B, C) were each given one of the sets of 50 recognition strings from a different speaker. Each also received a plain text file listing all the titles in the database, and word frequency statistics for the book titles. Their task was to try to find the correct title, and to provide a brief description of their overall strategy.

A was accurate on 66.7% of the titles he matched, B and C on 71.7%. We identified similar strategies for A and B, including number of exact word matches, types of exact word matches (e.g., content words were favored over stop words), rarity of exact word matches, and phonetic similarity. Analysis of C's responses showed dependency on number and types of exact word matches, and on miscellaneous strategies that could not be grouped. Through inspection, we determined that similarity in length and number of words were important factors. From this experiment, we concluded that humans are adept at interpreting noisy ASR when provided with context; that voice search (queries to the backend with ASR) would prove useful, given an appropriate similarity metric; and that there would likely always be uncertain cases that might lead to false hits. As we discuss below, two of seven Turn Exchange wizards were fairly adept, and five of six Full WOz wizards were very adept, at avoiding false hits from voice search.

4.3 Turn Exchange

The offline Title Pilot suggested that voice search could lead to far fewer non-understandings, given some predictions as to the actual words a noisy ASR string might represent. The next experiment addressed, in real time, the question of what level of accuracy might be achieved through an online implementation of voice search for book requests by title (Passonneau et al., 2010; Ligorio et al., 2010b). We embedded wizards into the CheckItOut SDS to present them with live ASR, and to collect runtime recognition features. On the GUI, variations in the display fonts for ASR and voice search returns cued the wizard to gross differences in word-level recognition confidence, and similarities between an ASR string and each candidate returned by the search. Learned models of wizard actions indicated that recognition features such as acoustic model fit and speech rate, along with various measures of similarity between the ASR output string and candidate titles, number of books ordered thus far (RecentSuccess), and number of relatively close candidate matches, were useful in modeling the most accurate wizards. These results show that DM strategy for determing what actions to take, given an interpretation of a user request, can depend on subtle recognition metrics.

In Turn Exchange, users requested books by title from embedded wizards. Speech input and output was by microphone and headset, with wizards and users seated in separate rooms, each using a different GUI. Seven undergraduates (one female and six males, including two non-native speakers of English) participated as paid subjects. Each of the 21 possible pairs of students met for five trials. A trial had two sessions. In the first, one student served as wizard and the other as user for a session in which the user requested 20 books by title. In the second session, the students reversed roles. We collected 4,192 turn exchanges.

The GUI displayed the ASR corresponding to the user utterance, with confident words in bolder font. The wizard could query the backend with some or all of the ASR. Voice search results displayed a single candidate above a high R/O threshold with all matching words in boldface, or three candidates of moderate similarity with matching words in medium bold, or five to ten candidates of lower similarity in grayscale. There were four available wizard actions: to offer a candidate title to the user in a confident manner (through Text-to-Speech), to offer a title tentatively, to select two or more candidates and ask a free-form question about them (here the user would hear the wizard's speech), or to give up. The user indicated whether an offered candidate was correct, or indicated the quality and appropriateness of a wizard's question. A prize would go to the wizard who offered the most correct titles.

The top ranked search return was correct 65.24% of the time. The two wizards who most often offered the top ranked return (81% and 86% of the time) both achieved 69.5% accuracy. The two best wizards (W4 and W5) could detect search returns that did not contain the correct title, thus avoiding false hits. On average, they offered the top return only 73% of the time and both achieved the highest accuracy (83.4%).

Several classification methods were used to predict the four wizard actions: firm offer, tentative offer, question, and give up. Features (N=60) included many ASR metrics, such as word-level confidence, AM fit, and three measures of speech rate; various measures of the average similarity or overlap between the ASR string and the candidate titles from the R/O query; the dialogue history; the number of candidates titles returned; and so on. The learned classifiers, including C4.5 decision trees (Quinlan, 1993), all had similar performance. Learned trees for W4 and W5 both had F measures of 0.85. Decision trees give a transparent view of the relative importance of features; those nearer the root have greater discriminatory power. Common features at the tops of trees for all wizards were the type and size of the query return, how often the wizard had chosen the correct title in the last three title cycles, the average of the maximum number of contiguous exact word matches between the ASR string and the candidate titles, and the Helios confidence score.

We trained an additional decision tree to learn how W4 (the best wizard) chose between offering a title versus asking a question (F=0.91 for making an offer; F=0.68 for asking a question). The tree is distinctive in that it splits at the root on a measure of speech rate. If the ASR is short (as measured both by the number of recognition frames and the words), W4 asks a question if the query return is not a single title, and either RecentSuccess=1 or ContiguousWord-Match=0, and the acoustic model score is low. Note that shorter titles are more confusable. If the ASR is long, W4 asks a question when ContiguousWordMatch=1, RecentSuccess=2, and either CandidateDisplay = NoisyList, or Helios Confidence is low, and there is a choice of titles.

4.4 Full WOz

The third experiment was a full WOz study demonstrating that embedded wizards could achieve high task success by relying on a large number of actions that included clarifications of utterance form or intent. Here we briefly report results on task success and time on task in a comparision of baseline CheckItOut with an enhanced version, CheckItOut+, that incorporates learned models of wizard actions. The evaluation demonstrates improved performance with more books ordered, more correct books ordered, and less elapsed time per book, or per correct book.

For Full WOz (Ligorio et al., 2010a), CheckItOut relied on VOIP (Voice over Internet Protocol) telephony. Users interacted with the embedded wizards by telephone, and wizards took over after CheckItOut answered the phone. After familiarization with the task and GUI, nine wizards auditioned and six were selected. There were ten users. Both groups were evenly balanced for gender. Users were directed to a website that presented scenarios for each call. The scenario page gave the user a patron identity and phone number, and author, title and catalogue number information for four books they were to order. Each user was to make at least fifteen calls to each wizard; we recorded 913 usable calls.

A single trainer prepared the original nine wizard volunteers one at a time. First, each trainee practiced on data from the experiments described above. Next, the trainer explained the wizard GUI and demonstrated it, serving as wizard on a sample call. Finally, the trainee served as wizard on five test calls with guidance from the trainer. The trainer chose the six most skilled and motivated trainees as wizards.

The GUI had two screens, one for user login and one for book requests. Users identified themselves by scenario phone number. The book request screen had a scrollable frame displaying the ASR for each user utterance. Separate frames on the GUI displayed the query return, dialogue history, basic actions (e.g., querying the backend with a custom R/O query, or prompting the user for a book), and auxiliary actions (e.g., removing a book from the order in progress). Finally, wizards could select among four types of dialogue acts: signals of non-understanding, or clarifications about the ASR, the book request or the query return. A dialogue act selected by the wizard was passed to a template-based natural language generator, and then to a Text-to-Speech component. Due to their complexity, calls could be time consuming. A clock on the GUI indicated call duration; wizards were instructed to finish the current book request and then terminate the call after six minutes.

A wizard's *precision* is the proportion of books she offer that correctly match the user's request; five of the six wizards had precision over 90%. A wizard's *recall* is the number of books in the scenario that she correctly identified. The two best wizards, WA and WB, had the highest recall, 63% and 67% respectively.

The number of book requests per dialogue was tallied automatically. Some dialogues were terminated before all scenario books could be requested. Also, a wizard who experienced problems with a book request could abandon the current request and prompt the user for a new book. The user could resume the abandoned book request later in the dialogue. In such cases, the abandoned and resumed requests for the same book would count as two distinct book requests. Given these facts, the ratio of number of correct books to number of book requests yields only an approximate estimate of how many scenario books were correctly identified. WA correctly identified 2.69 books per call from 3.64 requests per call, yielding a total success rate of 73.9% per book request, and 67.25% per 4-book scenario. WB correctly identified 2.54 books per call from 4.44 requests per call, yielding success rates of 57.21% per request and 63.50% per 4-book scenario. WA and WB had quite distinct strategies. WA persisted with each book request and exploited a wide range of the available GUI actions, with the greatest number of actions per book request among all wizards (N=8.24). WB abandoned book requests early and moved on to the next book request, exploited relatively fewer GUI actions, and had the fewest actions per book request (N=5.10).

From 163 features that characterize the ASR, search, current user utterance, current turn exchange, current book request, and the entire dialogue, we learned models for three types of wizard actions: select a non-understanding prompt, perform a search, or select a prompt to disambiguate among search returns. We used three machine learning methods for classification: decision trees, logistic regression and support vector machines. Table 2 gives the accuracies and overall F measures for decision trees that model WA and WB. (All learning methods have similar performance.)

Of note here is the range of features that predict when the best wizards selected a non-understanding, shown in Table 3. In addition, the two models depend partly on different features. Trees for the other actions in Table 2 have similarly diverse features.

Wizard	Action	Acc	F
A	Non-Understanding	0.71	0.71
B	Non-Understanding	0.73	0.73
A	Disambiguate	0.80	0.81
B	Disambiguate	0.86	0.87
A	Search	0.94	0.95
B	Search	0.93	0.94

Table 2: Performance of learned trees

To evaluate the benefit of learned models of wizard actions for SDS, we conducted two data collections where subjects placed calls following the same types of scenarios used in Full WOz. For our baseline evaluation of CheckItOut, 10 subjects were recruited from Columbia University and Hunter College. Each was to place a minimum of 50 calls over a period of three days; 562 calls were collected. For each call, subjects visited a web page that presented a new scenario. Each scenario included mock patron data for the caller to use (e.g., name, address and phone number), a list of four books, and instructions to request one book by catalogue number, one by title, one by author, and one by any of those methods. At three points during their calls, subjects completed a user satisfaction survey containing eleven questions adapted from (Hone and Graham, 2006).

CheckItOut+ is an enhanced version of our SDS in which the DM was modified to include learned models for three decisions. The first determines whether the system should signal non-understanding in response to the caller's last utterance, and executes before voice search would take place. The second determines whether to perform voice search with the ASR (i.e., before the parse, in contrast to CheckItOut). The third executes after voice search, and determines whether to offer the candidate with the highest R/O score to the user. The evaluation setup for CheckItOut+ also included 10 callers who were to place 50 calls each; 505 calls were collected.

Here we report results that compare the number of books ordered per call, the number of correct books per call, the elapsed time per book ordered, and elapsed time per correct book. T-tests show all differences to be highly significant. (A full discussion of the evaluation results will appear in future publications.) Callers to CheckItOut+ nearly always ordered four books (3.998), compared with 3.217 for the baseline ($p < 0.0001$). There was an increase of correct books in the order from 2.40 in the baseline to 2.70 in CheckItOut+ ($p < 0.0001$). The total elapsed time per call increased by only 13 seconds from 210.93 to 223.96 ($p < 0.0175$). Given that CheckItOut+ callers ordered more books and more correct books, CheckItOut+ performed much faster. The elapsed time per ordered book decreased from 65.57 to 56.01 seconds, and decreased from 87.89 to 82.95 seconds per correct books.

Feature	WA	WB
# books ordered so far	Y	Y
% unparsed ASR words	Y	N
Avg. word confidence	Y	N
# explicit confirms in call	Y	Y
# MICA slots per concept	Y	N
# searches in call	Y	N
Most recent wizard action	N	Y
Most frequent concept in call	N	Y
Speech rate	N	Y
# user utts. this request	N	Y
# author searches in call	Y	Y
Normalized LM score this utt	Y	Y

Table 3: Features that predict wizards' non-understanding

5 Discussion

Spoken language understanding has been relatively under-investigated in SDS design. Our experiments suggest that tighter integration of all phases of SLU with dialogue management can lead to more robust system behavior. We illustrate here with an example of WA's strategic questioning in which a non-understanding is avoided, and WA builds on partial understanding to identify the user's objective.

In response to ASR `MARY .JO. EARTH`, where the `'.'`s bracket an unconfident word, WA's search returned three authors with first name `Mary`, and last names that had moderate character overlap with `.JO. EARTH`. WA first asked whether the book was by `Mary O'Hara`. When the user responded negatively, WA confirmed the first name, prompted for the last name, and got `SURE` as the ASR. WA finally confirmed that the book was by *Mary Stewart*. Although it took four turns, WA was able to identify the correct book.

In general, the Full WOz corpus contains a very high proportion of wizard questions. In the total corpus of 20,415 caller utterances, there were 11,562 wizard questions. The types of questions

S1: What's the next book?
U1: .BARBARA. THREE THREE
S2: Is the author barbara freethy?
U2: YES
S3: Would you like 'some kind of wonderful' by BARBARA FREETHY?
U3: YES

(a) Example 1

S1: Sorry, I misunderstood. Can you repeat the author?
U1: DIDN'T I AM THE .GOLDEN. ARM
S2: Is the title 'THE man with THE golden ARM '?
U2: NO
S3: Sorry, I misunderstood. Can you repeat the title please?
U3: .A. .AMBLING. .THE. .GAME. .EDELMAN. STORY
S4: Is the title 'up and running the jami goldman STORY '?
U4: YES

(b) Example 2

Figure 2: Sample Clarification Subdialogues

wizard's ask not only often lead to successful concept identification, they also avoid prompting the user to repeat what they said. Previous work has presented results showing that the hyperarticulation associated with user repetitions often leads users to slow their speech, speak more loudly, and pronounce words more carefully, which hurts recognition performance (Hirschberg et al., 2004).

Figure 2 illustrates two clarification subdialogues from CheckItOut+. The first illustrates how prior knowledge about what a user might say provides sufficient constraints to interpret ASR that would otherwise be unintelligible. The first word in the ASR for the caller's first utterance is bracketed by '.', which again represents low word confidence. The high confidence words `THREE THREE` are phonologically and orthographically similar to the actual author name, *Freethy*. Note that from the caller's point of view, the same question shown in S3 could be motivated by confusion over the words alone, as in this case, or confusion over the words and multiple candidate referents (e.g., *Barbara Freethy* versus *Freeling*).

The second clarification subdialogue illustrates how confusions about the linguistic input can be resolved through strategies that combine questions about words and intents. The prompt at system turn 3 indicates that the system believes that the caller provided a title in user turn 1, which is incorrect. The caller responds with the title, however, which provides an alternative means to guess the intended book, Jami Goldman's memoir *Up and Running*.

6 Conclusion

The studies reported here are premised on two hypotheses about the role spoken language understanding plays in SDS design. First, prior knowledge derived from the context in which a dialogue takes place can yield predictions about the words a user might produce, and that these predictions can play a key role in interpreting noisy ASR. Here we have used context derived from knowledge in the application database. Similar results could follow from predictions from other sources, such as an explicit model of the *alignment of linguistic representations* proposed in the work of Pickering and Garrod (e.g., (Pickering and Garrod, 2006). Second, closer integration of spoken language understanding and dialogue management affords a wider range of clarification subdialogues.

Our results from the experiments reported here support both hypotheses. Our first experiment demonstrated that words obscured by very noisy ASR ($50\% \leq WER \leq 75\%$) can be inferred by reliance on what might have been said, predictions that came from the database of entities in the domain. We assume that an SDS that interacts well when ASR quality is poor will perform all the better when ASR quality is good. Our second experiment demonstrated that two of five human wizards were able to achieve high accuracy in on-line resolution of noisy ASR, when presented with no more than ten candidate matches. Run-time recognition features not available to the wizards were nonetheless useful in modeling the ability of the two best wizards to avoid false hits. Our third experiment demonstrated that wizards could achieve high task success on full dialogues where callers requested four books, and an enhancement of our baseline SDS with learned models of three wizard actions led to improved task success with less time per subtask. The variety of features that contribute to learned models of wizard actions demonstrates the advantages of embedded wizardry, as well as the benefit of DM clarification strategies that include features from all phases of SLU.

Acknowledgments

The Loqui project is funded by the National Science Foundation under awards IIS-0745369, IIS-0744904 and IIS-084966. We thank those at Carnegie Mellon University who helped us construct CheckItOut through tutorials and work sessions held at Columbia University and Carnegie Mellon University, and who responded to numerous emails about the Olympus/RavenClaw architecture and component modules: Alex Rudnicky, Brian Langner, David Huggins-Daines, and Antoine Raux. We also thank the many undergraduates from Columbia College, Barnard College, and Hunter College who assisted with tasks that supported the implementation of CheckItOut, including the telephony.

References

Gregory Aist, James Allen, Ellen Campana, Carlos Gomez Gallo, Scott Stoness, Mary Swift, and Michael K. Tanenhaus. 2007. Incremental dialogue system faster than and preferred to its nonincremental counterpart. In *COGSCI 2007*, pages 779–74.

John L. Austin. 1962. *How to Do Things with Words*. Oxford University Press, New York.

Srinivas Bangalore, Pierre B. Boullier, Alexis Nasr, Owen Rambow, and Benoîit Sagot. 2009. Mica: a probabilistic dependency parser based on tree insertion grammars. In *NAACL/HLT*, pages 185–188.

Dan Bohus and Alex Rudnicky. 2002. Integrating multiple knowledge sources for utterance-level confidence anno-tation in the CMU Communicator spoken dialogue system. Technical Report CS-02-190, Carnegie Mellon University, Department of Computer Science.

Dan Bohus and Alex Rudnicky. 2009. The RavenClaw dialog management framework. *Computer Speech and Language*, 23:332–361.

Dan Bohus. 2004. *Error awareness and recovery in conversational spoken language interfaces*. Ph.D. thesis, Carnegie Mellon University, Computer Science.

Carnegie Mellon University Speech Group. 2008. The Logios tool. `https://cmusphinx.svn.sourceforge.net/svnroot/cmusphinx/trunk/logios`.

Kallirroi Georgila, Kyrakos Sgarbas, Anastasios Tsopanoglou, Nikos Fakotakis, and George Kokkinakis. 2003. A speech-based human-computer interaction system for automating directory assistance services. *International Journal of Speech Technology, Special Issue on Speech and Human-Computer Interaction*, 6:145–59.

Joshua Gordon and Rebecca J. Passonneau. 2011. An evaluation framework for natural language understanding in spoken dialogue systems. In *7th LREC*.

Joshua Gordon, Rebecca J. Passonneau, and Susan L. Epstein. 2011. Helping agents help their users despite imperfect speech recognition. In *Proceedings of the AAAI Spring Symposium 2011 (SS11): Help Me Help You: Bridging the Gaps in Human-Agent Collaboration*.

Julia Hirschberg, Diane Litman, and Marc Swerts. 2004. Prosodic and other cues to speech recognition failures. *Speech Communication*, 43(1-2):155–75.

Kate S. Hone and Robert Graham. 2006. Towards a tool for the subjective assessment of speech system interfaces (sassi). *Natural Language Engineering, Special ISsue on Best Practice in Spoken Dialogue Systems*, 6(3-4):287–303.

David Huggins-Daines, Mohit Kumar, Arthur Chan, Allen W. Black, Mosur Ravishankar, and Alex I. Rudnicky. 2006. PocketSphinx: A free, real-time continuous speech recognition system for hand-led devices. In *Proceedings of ICASSP*, volume I, pages 185–188.

Ivana Kruijff-Korbayová, Nate Blaylock, Ciprian Gerstenberger, Verena Rieser, Tilman Becker, Michael Kaisser, Peter Poller, and Jan Schehl. 2005. An experiment setup for collecting data for adaptive output planning in a multimodal dialogue system. In *10th ENLG*, pages 191–196.

Cheongjae Lee, Alexander Rudnicky, and Gary Geunbae Lee. 2010. Let's buy books: finding ebooks using voice search. In *IEEE-SLT 2010*, pages 442–447.

Vladimir I. Levenshtein. 1996. Binary codes capable of correcting deletions, insertions and reversals. *Soviet Physics Doklady*, 10(8):707–710.

Tiziana Ligorio, Susan L. Epstein, and Rebecca J. Passonneau. 2010a. Wizards' dialogue strategies to handle noisy speech recognition. In *IEEE-SLT 2010*.

Tiziana Ligorio, Susan L. Epstein, Rebecca J. Passonneau, and Joshua Gordon. 2010b. What you did and didn't mean: Noise, context and human skill. In *COGSCI 10*.

Rebecca J. Passonneau, Susan L. Epstein, and Joshua Gordon. 2009. Help me understand you: Addressing the speech recognition bottleneck. In *Proceedings of the AAAI Spring Symposium 2009 (SS09): Agents that Learn from Human Teachers*, pages 23–25.

Rebecca J. Passonneau, Susan L. Epstein, Tiziana Ligorio, Joshua Gordon, and Pravin Bhutada. 2010. Learning about voice search for spoken dialogue systems. In *NAACL-HLT 2010*, pages 840–848.

Martin J. Pickering and Simon Garrod. 2006. Alignment as the basis for successful communication. *Research on Language and Communication*, 4(2):203–228.

Matthew Purver, Jonathan Ginzburg, and Patrick Healey. 2001. On the means for clarification in dialogue. In *Proceedings of the 2nd SIGdial Workshop on Discourse and Dialogue*, pages 116–125.

J. Ross Quinlan. 1993. *C4.5: Programs for Machine Learning*. Morgan Kaufmann, San Mateo, CA.

John W. Ratcliff and David Metzener. 1988. Pattern matching: the gestalt approach.

Antoine Raux and Maxine Eskenazi. 2004. Non-native users in the Let's Go! spoken dialogue systems. In *HLT/NAACL*, pages 217–224.

Antoine Raux and Maxine A. Eskenazi. 2007. A multi-layer architecture for semi-synchronous event-driven dialogue management. In *ASRU 2007*, pages 514–519.

Antoine Raux, Brian Langner, Allan W. Black, and Maxine Eskenazi. 2005. Let's Go Public! taking a spoken dialogue system to the real world. In *Interspeech - Eurospeech 2005*, pages 885–888.

Verena Rieser and Oliver Lemon. 2006. Using machine learning to explore human multimodal clarification strategies. In *COLING/ACL*, pages 659–666.

Verena Rieser and Oliver Lemon. 2011. Learning and evaluation of dialogue strategies for new applications: Empirical methods for optimization from small data sets. *Computational Linguistics*, 37:153–96.

David Schlangen and Raquel Fern'andez. 2005. Speaking through a noisy channel – experiments on inducing clarification behaviour in human-human diaogue. In *8th Annual Converence of the International Speech Communication Association (INTERSPEECH 2007)*, pages 1266–1269.

Gabriel Skantze. 2003. Exploring human error handling strategies: Implications for spoken dialogue systems. In *Proceedings of ISCA Tutorial and Research Workshop on Error Handling in Spoken Dialogue Systems*, pages 71–76.

Gabriel Skantze. 2005. Exploring human recovery strategies: Implications for spoken dialogue systems. *Speech Communication*, 45:325–41.

Svetlana Stoyanchev and Amanda Stent. 2009. Predicting concept types in user corrections in dialog. In *EACL Workshop SRSL*, pages 42–49.

Ye-Yi Wang, Yu Dong, Yun-Cheng Ju, and Alex Acero. 2008. An introduction to voice search. *IEEE Signal Processing Magazine: Special ISsue on Spoken Language Technology*, 25(3):28–38.

Wayne Ward and Sunil Issar. 1994. Recent improvements in the CMU spoken language understanding system. In *Proceedings of the ARPA Human Language Technology Workshop*, pages 213–216.

Jason D. Williams and Steve Young. 2004. Characterizing task-oriented dialog using a simulated ASR channel. In *ICSLP/Interspeech*, pages 185–188.

Teresa Zollo. 1999. A study of human dialogue strategies in the presence of speech recognition errors. In *Proceedings of the AAAI Fall Symposium on Psychological Models of Communication in Collaborative Systems*, pages 132–139.

Toward Construction of Spoken Dialogue System that Evokes Users' Spontaneous Backchannels

Teruhisa Misu, Etsuo Mizukami, Yoshinori Shiga, Shinichi Kawamoto,* Hisashi Kawai and Satoshi Nakamura

National Institute of Information and Communications Technology (NICT), Kyoto, Japan.

teruhisa.misu@nict.go.jp

Abstract

This paper addresses a first step toward a spoken dialogue system that evokes user's spontaneous backchannels. We construct an HMM-based dialogue-style text-to-speech (TTS) system that generates human-like cues that evoke users' backchannels. A spoken dialogue system for information navigation was implemented and the TTS was evaluated in terms of evoked user backchannels. We conducted user experiments and demonstrated that the user backchannels evoked by our TTS are more informative for the system in detecting users' feelings than those by conventional reading-style TTS.

1 Introduction

One of the most enduring problems in spoken dialogue systems research is realizing a natural dialogue in a human-human form. One direction researchers have been utilizing spontaneous nonverbal and paralinguistic information. For example,

This paper focuses on backchannels, one of the most common forms of para-linguistic information in human-human dialogue. In particular, we focus on users' verbal feedback, such as *"uh-huh"* (called *Aizuchi* in Japanese), and non-verbal feedback in the form of nods. Such backchannels are very common phenomena, and considered to be used to facilitate smooth human-human communications. In this regard, Maynard (Maynard, 1986) indicated that such backchannels are listener's signals to let the speaker continue speaking (continuer), to indicate that the listener understands and consents. It was also hypothesized that humans detect feelings expressed via backchannels, and the correlation between backchannel patterns and user interests was examined (Kawahara et al., 2008). These studies indicate that detection of spontaneous user backchannels can benefit spoken dialogue systems by providing informative cues that reflect the user's situation. For instance, if a spoken dialogue system can detect user's backchannels, it can facilitate smooth turn-taking. The system can also detect user's feelings and judge if it should continue the current topic or change it.

Despite these previous studies and decades of analysis on backchannels, few practical dialogue systems have made use of them. This is probably due to the fact that users do not react as spontaneously to dialogue systems as they do to other humans. We presume one of the reasons for this is the unnatural intonation of synthesized speech. That is, conventional speech synthesizers do not provide users with signs to elicit backchannels; an appropriate set of lexical, acoustic and prosodic cues (or backchannel-inviting cues (A. Gravano and J. Hirschberg, 2009)), which tends to precede the listener's backchannels in human-human communication. Though recorded human speech can provide such cues, it is costly to re-record system's speech every time system scripts are updated. In this work, we therefore tackle the challenge of constructing dialogue-style text-to-speech (TTS) system that inspires users to make spontaneous backchannels under the hypothesis of:

People will give more spontaneous backchannels to a spoken dialogue system that makes more spontaneous backchannel-inviting cues than a spoken dialogue system that makes less spontaneous ones.

which is derived from the Media Equation (Reeves and Nass, 1996).

2 Related Works

A number of studies have aimed at improving the naturalness of TTS. Though most of these have focused on means of realizing a clear and easy-to-listen-to reading-style speech, some attempts have been made at spontaneous conversational speech. Andersson (Andersson et al., 2010) and Marge (Marge et al., 2010) focused on lexi-

* currently with Japan Advanced Institute of Science and Technology (JAIST)

Proceedings of the SIGDIAL 2011: the 12th Annual Meeting of the Special Interest Group on Discourse and Dialogue, pages 259–265, Portland, Oregon, June 17-18, 2011.

cal phenomena such as lexical filler and acknowledgments in spontaneous speech, and showed that inserting them improves the naturalness of human-computer dialogues. In this work, we tackle constructing a natural dialogue-style TTS system focusing on prosodic phenomena such as intonation and phoneme duration.

In the field of conversation analysis, many studies analyzed backchannels in human-human dialogue focusing on lexical and non-verbal cues (Koiso et al., 1998; Ward and Tsukahara, 2000; A. Gravano and J. Hirschberg, 2009). For instance these cues were examined in preceding utterances, such as in part-of-speech tags, length of pause, power contour pattern, and F_0 contour pattern around the end of the Inter-Pausal Units (IPUs). (A. Gravano and J. Hirschberg, 2009) showed that when several of the above cues occur simultaneously, the likelihood of occurrence of a backchannel will increase.

Several studies also utilized the above findings for spoken dialogue systems. Okato (Okato et al., 1996) and Fujie (Fujie et al., 2005) trained models to predict backchannels, and implemented spoken dialogue systems that make backchannels. Our goal differs in that it is to inspire users to give backchannels.

3 Construction of Spoken Dialogue TTS

3.1 Spoken Dialogue Data collection for TTS

In order to make spontaneous dialogue-style TTS that can evoke backchannels, we construct a spontaneous dialogue-style speech corpus that contains backchannel-inviting cues, and then train an HMM acoustic model for synthesis.

We collected our training data by dubbing a script of our Kyoto Sightseeing Guidance Spoken Dialogue Corpus (Misu et al., 2009), a set of itinerary-planning dialogues in Japanese. In the dialogue task, the expert guide has made recommendations on sightseeing spots and restaurants until has decided on a plan for the day. With the guide's recommendations, many users give spontaneous backchannels. We made a set of dialogue scripts from the corpus, and asked voice actors to act them out.

When preparing the dialogue script for dubbing, we first removed fillers and backchannels from the transcripts of the dialogue corpus. We then annotated the guide's end of the IPUs, where the the user made backchannels, with #. A sample dialogue script is shown in Figure 6. We asked two professional voice actresses to duplicate the spoken dialogue of the script, with playing the role of the tour guide, and the other as the tourist, sitting face-to-face. During the recording, we asked the tour guide role to read the scenario with intonation so that the tourist role would spontaneously make backchannels at the points marked with #. The tourist was allowed to make backchannels at will at any pause segments the guide made. We recorded 12 dialogue sessions in total. The speech data was manually labeled, and 239.3 minutes of tour guide utterances, which are used to train our HMM for the TTS system, were collected. The training data is complemented by the ATR 503 phonetically balanced sentence set (Abe et al., 1990), so as to cover deficiencies in the phoneme sequence. The sentence set is collected from news articles, and data consists of 43.1 minutes of reading-style speech.

3.2 Analysis of Collected Speech Data

Before training the HMM, we analyzed the collected spoken dialogue data to confirm if the recorded dialogue speech data contained backchannel-inviting prosodic cues. We compared prosodic features of the dialogue speech data with those of the reading-style speech data (phonetically balanced sentences that we collected). Following the findings of a previous study (Koiso et al., 1998), we investigated the duration, F_0 contour pattern and power contour pattern of the final phoneme of the IPUs[1].

In conversation analysis of Japanese, the F_0 contour pattern label of the final phoneme is often used. While the contour pattern is usually manually labeled, we roughly determined the patterns based on the following procedure. We first normalized the log F_0 scale using all utterances so that it has zero mean and one standard deviation (z-score: $z = (x-\mu)/\sigma$). We then divided each final phoneme of the IPU into former and latter parts, and calculated the F_0 slope of each segment by linear regression. By combination of following three patterns, we defined nine F_0 contour patterns for the final phonemes of the IPUs. The pattern of the segment was judged as *rise* if the slope was larger than a threshold θ. If the slope was less than the threshold $-\theta$, the pattern was judged as *fall*. Otherwise, it was judged as *flat*. Here, θ was empirically set to 5.0. The power contour patterns of the IPUs were estimated by a similar procedure.

We analyzed 3,311 IPUs that were not followed

[1]For this study, we define an IPU as a maximal sequence of words surrounded by silence longer than 200 ms. This unit usually coincides with one Japanese phrasal unit.

Table 1: Prosodic analysis of final phonemes of IPUs (dialogue script vs. newsarticle script)

	dialogue	newsarticle
dur. phoneme [msec]	177.1 (± 83.6)	119.4 (± 31.3)

average (± standard deviation)

	F_0		power	
pattern	dialogue	news	dialogue	news
rise-rise	3.7 %	10.4 %	0.0 %	0.0 %
rise-flat	2.6 %	2.1 %	0.0 %	0.0 %
rise-fall	18.8 %	3.2 %	0.0 %	0.0 %
flat-rise	4.8 %	11.5 %	0.0 %	0.0 %
flat-flat	3.5 %	1.8 %	0.0 %	9.2 %
flat-fall	12.6 %	2.7 %	13.6 %	0.1 %
fall-rise	29.2 %	47.0 %	0.0 %	0.0 %
fall-flat	7.7 %	9.0 %	86.0 %	90.7 %
fall-fall	17.1 %	12.3 %	0.0 %	0.0 %

by a turn-switch in the dialogue-style speech data and 645 non-sentence-end IPUs in the reading-style speech data. The prosodic features of final phonemes of these IPUs are listed in Table 1.

According to a study (Koiso et al., 1998), in which prosodic features of IPUs followed by a turn-hold with backchannel, without backchannel and turn-switch were compared, a long duration in the final phoneme is a speaker's typical sign to keep floor. The same study also reported that the *flat-fall* and *rise-fall* pattern of F_0 and power are more likely to be followed by a backchannel than a turn-hold without a backchannel and turn-switch. In our collected speech corpus, there were actually significant ($p < 0.01$) differences in the duration of the final phoneme between that in the dialogue-style speech and in reading-style speech. There was also significant ($p < 0.01$) difference in the occurrence probability of the above two prosodic patterns between dialogue-style speech and reading-style speech data. These figures indicate that as a whole the collected dialogue-style data contains more backchannel-inviting cues than collected reading-style speech data.

We trained HMM for our TTS system Ximera using the HMM-based Speech Synthesis System (HTS) (Zen et al., 2007). We adopted mel log spectrum approximation (MLSA) filter-based vocoding (SPTK, 2011), a quint-phone-based phoneme set and five state HMM-based acoustic modeling. All training data including reading-style speech data were used for model training.

4 User Experiment

4.1 Dialogue System used for Experiment

To evaluate our TTS system based on users' reactions, a sightseeing guidance spoken dialogue system that assist users in making decision was implemented. The system can explain six sightseeing spots in Kyoto. The system provides responses to user requests for explanation about a certain spot. Each descriptive text on a sightseeing spot consists of 500 (±1%) characters, 30 phrases. The text is synthesized using section 3 TTS[2]. We set the speech rate of our TTS as nine phoneme per second.

Figure 1: Screen shot of the dialogue system

A display is used to present photos of the target sightseeing spot and an animated 3D desktop avatar named Hanna. Figure 1 shows the GUI the user sees. The avatar can express its status through several motions. For example, when the user begins speaking, it can express the state of listening using the listener's motion, as shown in the figure. A sample dialogue with the system is shown in Table 7. A video (with English subtitles) of an sample dialogue with a user can be seen at http://mastarpj.nict.go.jp/~xtmisu/video/TTS.wmv.

To compare the effectiveness of our TTS in evoking users' spontaneous backchannels, we constructed a comparison system that adopts a conventional reading-style TTS system. An HMM model was trained using 10-hour reading-style speech by another professional female narrator. Other settings, such as the descriptive text and avatar agent, were the same as those of the base system.

4.2 Comparison of Prosodic Features of the Synthesized Speech

Prior to the experiments, we investigated the prosodic features of the final phoneme of IPUs in the synthesized explanations on six spots to confirm if they contain backchannel-inviting cues. The results are given in Table 2.

Tendencies in the duration of the final phoneme and prosody pattern distribution of the synthesized

[2]The descriptive texts are not included in the training data.

Table 2: Prosodic analysis of final phonemes of IPUs (dialogue-style TTS vs. reading-style TTS)

	dialogue synth.	reading synth.
dur. phoneme [msec]	172.9 ($\pm$ 29.6)	126.1 ($\pm$ 19.1)

average ($\pm$ standard deviation)

	F_0		power	
pattern	dialogue	reading	dialogue	reading
rise-rise	5.4 %	0.0 %	0.0 %	0.0 %
rise-flat	2.0 %	0.0 %	1.7 %	0.0 %
rise-fall	23.5 %	0.0 %	46.3 %	5.3 %
flat-rise	5.0 %	0.0 %	0.0 %	0.0 %
flat-flat	1.7 %	0.0 %	4.0 %	9.2 %
flat-fall	15.8 %	0.0 %	22.8 %	18.1 %
fall-rise	15.8 %	0.0 %	0.7 %	0.0 %
fall-flat	3.4 %	0.0 %	7.0 %	0.0 %
fall-fall	27.5 %	100.0 %	17.4 %	76.5 %

speech by the dialogue-style TTS system were similar to that of recorded dialogue speech, suggests that the constructed dialogue-style TTS system can duplicate the backchannel-inviting cues of the recorded original speech. The synthesized dialogue-style speech also contained much more *rise-fall* and *flat-fall* patterns in F_0 and power than that generated by the reading-style TTS system. The average duration of the final phoneme was also longer. Considering the fact that the speech data was generated from the same script, this indicates that the synthesized speech by the dialogue-style TTS system contains more backchannel-inviting features than that by the reading-style TTS system.

4.3 Experimental Setup

We evaluated the TTS systems using 30 subjects who had not previously used spoken dialogue systems. Subjects were asked to use the dialogue system in two settings; dialogue-style TTS system and reading-style TTS system. The experiment was conducted in a small (about 2 m^2) soundproof room with no one else present.

We instructed the subjects to speak with the avatar agent Hanna (not with the system). We also told them that the avatar agent was listening to their speech at all times using the microphone, and was observing their reactions using the camera above the display[3]. Subjects were given the task of acquiring information about three candidate sightseeing spots in Kyoto shown on the display and then selecting one that they liked. An example dialogue with the system is shown in Table 7. A video (with English subtitles) showing a real user dialogue can be seen at http://mastarpj.nict.go.jp/~xtmisu/video/exp.avi.

[3]The system did not actually sense the subjects' reactions.

Table 3: Questionnaire items

1. Overall, which speech was better?
2. Which speech had easier-to-understand explanations?
3. For which speech did you feel compelled to give backchannels?
4. Which speech was more appropriate for this system?
5. Which speech had more human-like explanation?

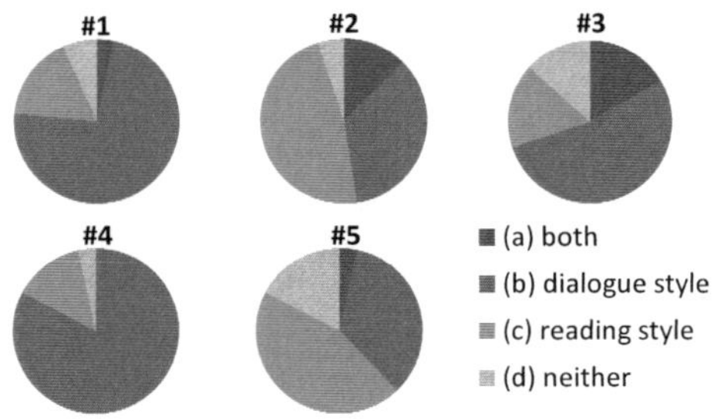

Figure 2: Questionnaire results

After the subject selected from candidate spots, we changed the TTS system settings and instructed the user to have another dialogue session selecting one of another three spots. Considering the effects of the order, the subjects were divided into four groups; the first group (Group 1) used the system in the order of "Spot list A with dialogue-style speech → Spot list B with reading-style speech," the second group (Group 2) worked in reverse order. Groups 3 and 4 used a system alternating the order of the spot sets.

5 Experimental Results

5.1 Questionnaire Results

After the experiments, subjects were asked to fill in a questionnaire about the system. Table 3 shows the questionnaire items. The subjects selected (a) both are good, (b) dialogue-style speech was better, (c) reading-style speech was better, or (d) neither were good. Figure 2 shows the results.

The dialogue-style speech generally earned higher ratings, but reading-style was slightly higher in items #2 and #5. This tendency is likely attributable to the fact that the dialogue-style speech had worse clarity and naturalness than reading-style. The mean opinion score (MOS), which is often used to measure clarity and naturalness of TTS, of the dialogue-style TTS was in fact 2.79, worse than 3.74 for the reading-style.

5.2 Analysis of Frequency of Backchannels

We analyzed the number of backchannels that users made during the dialogue session. We manually annotated subjects' verbal feedbacks, such as *"uh-huh"* and nodding of the head using the recorded video. Out of 30 subjects, 26 gave some form of

Table 4: Percentages and average number of users who made backchannels

	TTS	% users made BCs	# average BCs taken
Group 1: (Dialogue → Reading)	Dialogue-style	100.0% (50.0%, 100.0%)	30.4 (1.8, 28.6)
(Spot list A → Spot list B)	Reading-style	100.0% (50.0%, 87.5%)	26.1 (3.1, 23.0)
Group 2: (Reading → Dialogue)	Dialogue-style	75.0% (25.0%, 62.5%)	12.7 (0.5, 12.2)
(Spot list A → Spot list B)	Reading-style	75.0% (25.0%, 62.5%)	12.9 (1.3, 11.6)
Group 3: (Dialogue → Reading)	Dialogue-style	100.0% (28.6%, 100.0%)	14.0 (0.4, 13.6)
(Spot list B → Spot list A)	Reading-style	100.0% (0%, 100.0%)	19.3 (0, 19.3)
Group 4: (Reading → Dialogue)	Dialogue-style	87.5% (42.9%, 87.5%)	28.2 (4.7, 23,5)
(Spot list B → Spot list A)	Reading-style	100.0% (71.4%, 87.5%)	24.8 (6.5, 18.3)
All:	Dialogue-style	86.7% (36.7%, 86.7%)	21.1 (1.7, 19.4)
	Reading-style	90.0% (40.0%, 83.3%)	20.6 (2.4, 18.2)

Total backchannel (verbal feedback [Aizuchi], nodding)

backchannel to the system. Table 4 shows the percentages and average number of times subjects gave backchannels. Many users made more backchannels using the dialogue-style TTS system. Despite the significant difference in questionnaire item #3, there were no significant differences in the average number of users' backchannels.

5.3 Informativeness of Backchannels

We then evaluated the TTS in terms of the informativeness of evoked backchannels. The spontaneous prosodic pattern of the backchannels is expected to suggest positive/negative feelings on regarding the recommended candidate. One promising use of backchannels in our application is for detecting users' feelings about the currently focused on spot, and choosing to continue the explanation on the current topic if the user seems interested, or otherwise change the topic. We therefore label backchannels made during the systems explanation of the spot that the user finally selected as "positive" and those made during the explanations of the other two spots as "negative" and consider distinguishing between them. In human-human dialogues, it was confirmed that when a user responds promptly, the majority of responses are positive, and more backchannels also suggest positive responses (Kawahara et al., 2008).

We investigated the informativeness of the backchannels based on their classification rate, or whether the system can distinguish positive and negative backchannels, using 10-fold cross-validation. That is, the backchannels evoked by the dialogue-style TTS system were divided into 10 groups and nine were used for training and the other for classification tests. We trained decision trees using J4.8 algorithm using timing, frequency, total frequency throughout the session and type of backchannel (verbal feedback or nod) as the feature set. The classification error cost of the positive sample was set to (# negative samples / # positive samples) considering the difference in the number of positive and negative samples. Ten trials were conducted by changing the test set and the average classification rate was calculated. The classification rate of backchannels evoked by the system with dialogue-style TTS was 71.4%, The confusion matrix of the classification is shown below. We obtained precisions of 62.8% in the classification of the positive backchannels, and 73.2% in that of the negative backchannels. The rates are significantly higher than chance rates of 33.5% and 66.5%. This result indicates the backchannels evoked by the dialogue-style TTS were informative for the system.

Table 5: Confusion matrix of classification

→ classified as ↓ label	positive	negative
positive	76	141
negative	45	386

The classification rate of the reading-style TTS system was calculated in the same way. The average classification rate of backchannels evoked by reading-style TTS was a significantly lower 47.4%, meaning they were not informative at all.

These results suggest that our dialogue-style TTS system can evoke more spontaneous and informative backchannels that reflects users' intentions than the conventional reading-style one. This classification rate is not completely satisfactory, but we expect that users' feeling can be detected after observing several backchannels. We also believe that we can estimate users' interest more precisely by combining verbal information of dialogue acts (Misu et al., 2010).

6 Conclusions

This paper presented our first steps toward a spoken dialogue system that evokes users' spontaneous listener's reactions. We constructed a dialogue-style TTS and confirmed that by generating human-like backchannel-inviting cues, the system can evoke user's spontaneous backchannels, which are informative for the system.

References

A. Gravano and J. Hirschberg. 2009. Backchannel-inviting cues in task-oriented dialogue. In *Proc. Interspeech*, pages 1019–1022.

M. Abe, Y. Sagisaka, T. Umeda, and H. Kuwabara. 1990. *Speech Database User's Manual*. ATR Technical Report TR-I-0166.

S. Andersson, K. Georgila, D. Traum, and R. Clark M. Aylett. 2010. Prediction and Realisation of Conversational Characteristics by Utilising Spontaneous Speech for Unit Selection. In *Proc. Speech Prosody*.

S. Fujie, K. Fukushima, and T. Kobayashi. 2005. Backchannel feedback generation using linguistic and nonlinguistic information and its application to spoken dialogue system. In *Proc. Interspeech*, pages 889–892.

T. Kawahara, M. Toyokura, T. Misu, and C. Hori. 2008. Detection of Feeling Through Back-Channels in Spoken Dialogue. In *Proc. Interspeech*, pages 1696–1696.

H. Koiso, Y. Horiuchi, S. Tutiya, A. Ichikawa, and Y. Den. 1998. An Analysis of Turn-Taking and Backchannels based on Prosodic and Syntactic Features in Japanese Map Task Dialogue. *Language and Speech*, 41(3-4):295–322.

M. Marge, J. Miranda, A. Black, and A. I. Rudnicky. 2010. Towards Improving the Naturalness of Social Conversations with Dialogue Systems. In *Proc. SIGDIAL*, pages 91–94.

S. Maynard. 1986. On back-channel behavior in japanese and english casual conversation. *Linguistics*, 24(6):1079–1108.

T. Misu, K. Ohtake, C. Hori, H. Kashioka, and S. Nakamura. 2009. Annotating Communicative Function and Semantic Content in Dialogue Act for Construction of Consulting Dialogue Systems. In *Proc. Interspeech*.

Teruhisa Misu, Komei Sugiura, Kiyonori Ohtake, Chiori Hori, Hideki Kashioka, Hisashi Kawai, and Satoshi Nakamura. 2010. Dialogue Strategy Optimization to Assist User's Decision for Spoken Consulting Dialogue Systems. In *Proc. IEEE-SLT*, pages 342–347.

Y. Okato, K. Kato, M. Yamamoto, and S. Itahashi. 1996. Insertion of interjectory response based on prosodic information. In *Proc. of IEEE Workshop Interactive Voice Technology for Telecommunication Applications*, pages 85–88.

B. Reeves and C. Nass. 1996. *The Media Equation: How People Treat Computers, Television, and New Media Like Real People and Places*. Cambridge University Press.

SPTK, 2011. *Speech Signal Processing Toolkit (SPTK)*. http://sp-tk.sourceforge.net/.

N. Ward and W. Tsukahara. 2000. Prosodic features which cue backchannel responses in English and Japanese. *Journal of Pragmatics*, 32(8):1177–1207.

H. Zen, T. Nose, J. Yamagishi, S. Sako, T. Masuko, A.W. Black, and K. Tokuda. 2007. The HMM-based speech synthesis system version 2.0. In *Proc. ISCA SSW6*.

A Appendix

Table 6: Example dialogue scenario used for recording (translation of Japanese)

Guide	And Kyomizu-dera.
Guide	Yeah, it is very famous for.
Guide	There is this like wooden balcony#, and you can't see the whole city#, but you can see a good part of the city from there. And it is a beautiful view.
User	It is nice. You have been there?
Guide	Yes, many a times.
Guide	Unfortunately, in winter it is not very green#, and there are not any flowers.
User	So if there is snow will they close the stairs or will they - we are just going to be careful walking the steps?
Guide	You have to be careful going up.
Guide	Basically, it's a slope it's a slope#, so if it's very icy - if there is, you know, like black ice#, you might want to rethink hiking up that slope. But usually it is okay# in the winter. I mean, Kyomizu-dera and this whole area, like every tourist eventually makes their way here#, whether they are Japanese or foreign.
Guide	So, I am sure the paths should be clear.
Guide	Yeah, that is a good spot too.

Table 7: Example dialogue with the system (translation of Japanese)

System	Hello, my name is Hanna, a tour guide for sightseeing in Kyoto. Nice to meet you. Please say "Okay" when you have decided which spot you would like to know about first.
User	Okay.
System	Which spot would you like to know about?
User	Tell me about Shinnyo-do temple.
System	Sure, I'll explain Shinnyo-do temple.
System	Shinnyo-do is a Buddhist Tendai Temple in Sakyo-ku, Kyoto City and the formal name is Shinsho Gokuraku-ji. You may take the bus directly from Kyoto Station for about thirty minutes, and the fee is two hundred twenty yen. The admission fee for the temple is five hundred yen. The temple was established in nine hundred eighty-four A.D., when Amida Nyorai-zo; a principle image from Mt. Hiei was placed in the Imperial villa of this area.
System	Shall I continue?
User	Sure.
System	The temple is famous, especially for its coloring of autumn leaves; Red Maple stand on both sides of the stone-paved approach, and it appears as though the temple is placed inside a maple forest. ...
...	
System	That's all about this spot.
System	Which spot would you like to know about next?
User	Daitoku-ji please.
...	

Learning to Balance Grounding Rationales for Dialogue Systems

Joshua Gordon
Department of Computer Science
Rebecca J. Passonneau
Center for Computational Learning Systems
Columbia University
New York, NY, USA
(joshua|becky)@cs.columbia.edu

Susan L. Epstein
Department of Computer Science
Hunter College and
The Graduate Center of the City University of New York
New York, NY, USA
susan.epstein@hunter.cuny.edu

Abstract

This paper reports on an experiment that investigates clarification subdialogues in intentionally noisy speech recognition. The architecture learns weights for mixtures of grounding strategies from examples provided by a human wizard embedded in the system. Results indicate that the architecture learns to eliminate misunderstandings reliably despite high word error rate.

1 Introduction

We seek to develop spoken dialogue systems (*SDSs*) that communicate effectively despite uncertain input. Our thesis is that a task-oriented SDS can perform well despite a high degree of recognizer noise by relying on context. The SDS described here uses *FORRSooth*, a semi-synchronous architecture under development for task-oriented human-computer dialogue. Our immediate goals are to reduce non-understandings of user utterances (where the SDS produces no interpretation) and to eliminate *misunderstandings* (where the SDS misinterprets user utterances). The experiment recounted here investigates subdialogues consisting of an initial user response to a system prompt, and any subsequent turns that might be needed to result in full understanding of the original response. Our principal finding is that a FORRSooth-based SDS learns to build on partial understandings and to eliminate misunderstandings despite noisy ASR.

A FORRSooth-based SDS is intended to interact effectively "without the luxury of perfect components" (Paek and Horvitz, 2000), such as high-performance ASR. FORRSooth relies on portfolios of strategies for utterance interpretation and grounding, and learns to balance them from its experience. Its confidence in its interpretations is dynamically calibrated against its past experience. At each user utterance, FORRSooth selects grounding actions modulated to build upon partial interpretations in subsequent exchanges with the user.

The experiment presented here bootstraps the SDS with human expertise. In a Wizard of Oz (*WOz*) study, a person (the *wizard*) replaces selected SDS components. Knowledge is then extracted from the wizard's behavior to improve the SDS. FORRSooth uses the Relative Support Weight Learning (*RSWL*) algorithm (Epstein and Petrovic, 2006) to learn weights that balance its individual strategies. Training examples for grounding strategies are based upon examples produced by an *ablated* wizard who was restricted to the same information and actions as the system (Levin and Passonneau, 2006).

Our domain is the Andrew Heiskell Braille and Talking Book Library. Heiskell's patrons order their books by telephone, during conversation with a librarian. The next section of this paper presents related work. Subsequent sections describe the weight learning, the SDS architecture, and an experiment that challenges the robustness of utterance interpretation and grounding with intentionally noisy ASR. We

Proceedings of the SIGDIAL 2011: the 12th Annual Meeting of the Special Interest Group on Discourse and Dialogue, pages 266–271,
Portland, Oregon, June 17-18, 2011.

conclude with a discussion of the results.

2 Related Work

Despite increasingly accurate ASR methods, dialogue systems often contend with noisy ASR, which can arise from performance phenomena such as filled pauses (*er, um*), false starts (*fir- last name*), or noisy transmission conditions. SDSs typically experience a higher WER when deployed. For example, the WER reported for Carnegie Mellon University's Let's Go Public! went from 17% under controlled conditions to 68% in the field (Raux et al., 2005).

To limit communication errors, an SDS can rely on strategies to detect and recover from incorrect recognition output (Bohus, 2007). One such strategy, to ask the user to repeat a poorly understood utterance, can result in hyperarticulation and decreased recognition (Litman, Hirschberg and Swerts, 2006). Prior work has shown that users prefer explicit confirmation over dialogue efficiency (fewer turns) (Litman and Pan, 1999). We hypothesize that this results from an inherent tradeoff between efficiency and user confidence. We assume that evidence of partial understanding increases user confidence more than evidence of non-understanding does. FORRSooth learns to ask more questions that build on partial information, and to make fewer explicit confirmations and requests to the user to repeat herself.

While many techniques exist in the literature for semantic interpretation in task-oriented, information-seeking dialogue systems, there is no single preferred approach. SDSs rarely combine a portfolio of *NLU* (natural language understanding) resources. FORRSooth relies on "multiple processes for interpreting utterances (e.g., structured parsing versus statistical techniques)" as in (Lemon, 2003). These range from voice search (querying a database directly with ASR results) to semantic parsing.

Dialogue systems should ground their understanding of the user's objectives. To limit communication errors, an SDS can rely on strategies to detect and recover from incorrect recognition output (Bohus, 2007). In others' work, the grounding status of an utterance is typically binary (i.e., understood or not) (Allen, Ferguson and Stent, 2001; Bohus and Rudnicky, 2005; Paek and Horvitz, 2000) or ternary (i.e., understood, misunderstood, not understood) (Bohus and Rudnicky, 2009). FORRSooth's grounding decisions rely on a mixture of strategies, are based on degrees of evidence (Bohus and Rudnicky, 2009; Roque and Traum, 2009), and disambiguate among candidate interpretations. Work in (DeVault and Stone, 2009) on disambiguation in task-oriented dialogue differs from ours in that it addresses genuine ambiguities rather than noise resulting from inaccurate ASR.

3 FORR and RSWL

FORRSooth is based on *FORR* (FOr the Right Reasons), an architecture for learning and problem solving (Epstein, 1994). FORR uses sequences of decisions from multiple rationales to solve problems. Implementations have proved robust in game learning, simulated pathfinding, and constraint solving. FORR relies on an adaptive, hierarchical mixture of resource-bounded procedures called *Advisors*. Each Advisor embodies a decision rationale. Advisors' opinions (*comments*) are combined to arrive at a decision. Each comment pairs an action with a strength that indicates some degree of support for or opposition to that action. An Advisor can make multiple comments at once, and can base its comments upon descriptives. A *descriptive* is a shared data structure, computed on demand, and refreshed only when required. For each decision, FORR consults three tiers of Advisors, one tier at a time, until some tier reaches a decision.

FORR learns weights for its tier-3 Advisors with RSWL. *Relative support* is a measure of the normalized difference between the comment strength (confidence) with which an Advisor supports an action compared to other available choices. RSWL learns Advisors' weights from their comments on training examples. The degree of reinforcement (positive or negative) to an Advisor's weight is proportional to its strength and relative support for a decision.

4 FORRSooth

FORRSooth is a parallelized version of FORR. It models task-oriented dialogue with six FORR-based services that operate concurrently: INTE-

RACTION, INTERPRETATION, SATISFACTION, GROUNDING, GENERATION, and DISCOURSE. These services interpret user utterances with respect to system expectations, manage the conversational floor, and consider competing interpretations, partial understandings, and alternative courses of action. All services have access to the same data, represented by descriptives. In this section, we present background on SATISFACTION and INTERPRETATION, and provide additional detail on GROUNDING.

The role of SATISFACTION is to represent dialogue goals, and to progress towards those goals through spoken interaction. Dialogue goals are represented as *agreements*. An agreement is a subdialogue about a *target concept* (such as a specific book) whose value must be grounded through collaborative dialogue between the system and the user (Clark and Schaefer, 1989). Agreements are organized into an agreement graph that represents dependencies among them. Task-based agreements are domain specific, while grounding agreements are domain independent (cf. (Bohus, 2007)). An interpretation *hypothesis* represents the system's belief that the value of a specific target (e.g., a full name or a first name) occurred in the user's speech.

The role of INTERPRETATION is to formulate hypotheses representing the meaning of what the user has said. INTERPRETATION relies on tier-3 Advisors (essentially, mixtures of heuristics). Each Advisor constructs comments on speech recognition hypotheses. A *comment* is a semantic concept (*hypothesis*) with an associated strength. More than one Advisor can vote for the same hypothesis. Confidence in any one hypothesis is a function of votes, learned weights for Advisors, and comment strengths.

In previous work, we showed that INTERPRETATION Advisors can produce relatively reliable hypotheses given noisy ASR, with graceful degradation as recognition performance decreases (Gordon, Passonneau and Epstein, 2011). For example, at WER between 0.2 and 0.4, the concept accuracy of the top hypothesis was 80%. That work left open how to decide whether to use the top INTERPRETATION hypothesis. Here FORRSooth learns how to assess its INTERPRETATION confidence, and what grounding actions to take given different levels of confidence.

Over the life of a FORRSooth SDS, INTERPRETATION produces hypotheses for the values of target concepts. FORRSooth records the mean and variance of the comment strengths for each INTERPRETATION hypothesis, and uses them to calculate INTERPRETATION's *merit*. Merit represents FORRSooth's INTERPRETATION confidence as a dynamic, normalized estimate of the percentile in which the value falls. Merit computations improve initially with use of the SDS, and can then shift with the user population and the data. FORRSooth's approach differs from supervised confidence annotation methods that learn a fixed confidence threshold from a corpus of human-machine dialogues (Bohus, 2007).

The role of GROUNDING is to monitor the system's confidence in its interpretation of each user utterance, to provide evidence to the user of its interpretation, and to elicit corroboration, further information, or tacit agreement. To ground a target concept, FORRSooth considers one or more hypotheses for the value the user intended, and chooses a grounding action commensurate with its understanding and confidence.

GROUNDING updates the agreement graph by adding *grounding agreements* to elicit confirmations or rejections of target concepts, or to disambiguate among target concepts. A grounding agreement's *indicator target* represents the expectation of a user response. Once a sufficiently confident INTERPRETATION hypothesis is bound to an indicator target, the grounding agreement executes side effects that strengthen or weaken the hypothesis being grounded. *Recursive grounding* (where the system grounds the user's response to the system's previous grounding action) can result if the system's expectation has not been met by the next system turn.

GROUNDING makes two kinds of decisions, each with its own set of tier-3 Advisors. The first, *commit bindings*, indicates that the system is confident in the value of a target concept. In this experiment, decisions to commit to a value are irrevocable. The other kind of decision selects the next grounding utterance for any target concepts that have not yet been bound. The decision to ground a target concept is made by tier-3 Advisors that consider the distribution of hypothesis merit, as well as the success or failure of the grounding actions taken thus far.

5 FX2

FX2 is a FORRSooth SDS constructed for the current experiment. The ten FX2 INTERPRETATION Advisors are described in (Gordon, Passonneau and Epstein, 2011). Here we describe its GROUNDING actions and Advisors.

FX2 can choose among six grounding actions. Given high confidence in a single interpretation, it commits to the binding of a target value without confirmation. At slightly lower confidence levels, it chooses to implicitly confirm a target binding, with or without a hedge (e.g., the tag question "*right?*"). At even lower confidence, the grounding action is to explicitly confirm. Given competing interpretations with similarly high confidence, the grounding action is to disambiguate between the candidates. Finally, FX2 can request the user to repeat herself.

We give two examples of the twenty-three FX2 grounding Advisors. Given two interpretation hypotheses with similar confidence scores, a disambiguation Advisor votes to prompt the user to disambiguate between them. The strength for this grounding action is proportional to the ratio of the two hypotheses' scores. To avoid repeated execution of the same grounding action, one grounding Advisor votes against actions to repeat a prompt for the same target, especially if ASR confidence is low. In FX2, RSWL facilitates the use of multiple Advisors for INTERPRETATION and GROUNDING by learning weights for them that reflect their relative reliability. We describe next how we collect training examples through an ablated wizard experiment.

6 Experimental Design

This experiment tests FX2's ability to learn INTERPRETATION and GROUNDING weights. In each dialogue, FX2 introduces itself, prompts the subject for her name or a book title, and then continues the dialogue until FX2 commits to a binding for the concept, or gives up.

Four undergraduate native English speakers (two female, two male) participated. Speech input and output was through a microphone headset. The PocketSphinx speech recognizer produced ASR output (Huggins-Daines et al., 2006) with Wall-Street Journal dictation acoustic models adapted with ten hours of spontaneous speech. We built distinct trigram statistical language models for each type of agreement using names and titles from the Heiskell database.

We collected three data sets, referenced here as *baseline*, *wizard*, and *learning*. Each had two agreement graphs: *UserName* seeks a grounded value for the patron's full name, and *BookTitle* seeks a grounded value for a book title. 120 dialogues were collected for each dataset.

FX2 includes an optional *wizard component*. When active, the wizard component displays a GUI showing the current interpretation hypotheses for target concepts, along with their respective merit. A screen shot for the wizard GUI appears in Figure 1.

A *wizard dialogue* activates the wizard component and uses INTERPRETATION as usual, but embeds a person (the *wizard*) in GROUNDING. The wizard's purpose in this experiment is to provide training data for GROUNDING. After each user turn, the wizard makes two decisions based on data from the GUI: whether to consider any target as grounded, and which in a set of possible grounding actions to use next. The GUI displays what FX2 would choose for each decision; the wizard can either accept or override it.

Ordinarily, a FORR-based system begins with uniform Advisor weights and learns more appropriate values during its experience. Because correct interpretation and grounding are difficult tasks, however, we chose here to *prime* these weights and hypothesis merits using training examples collected during development. Development data for INTERPRETATION included 200 patron names, 400 book titles, and 50 indicator

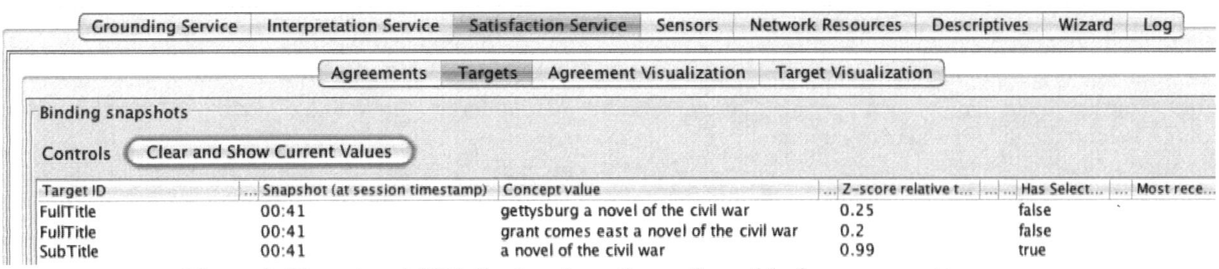

Figure 1. The wizard GUI displays hypotheses for a title from a user utterance.

Condition	Precision	Recall	F	Length
Baseline	0.65	0.78	0.72	4.36
Wizard	0.89	0.76	0.83	4.05
Learned	1.00	0.71	0.86	3.86

Table 1. Performance across three data sets.

Condition	Conf	Disambig	Repeat	Other
Baseline	0.23	0.19	0.50	0.08
Wizard	0.09	0.50	0.35	0.06
Learned	0.15	0.52	0.32	0.01

Table 2. Distribution of grounding actions.

concepts. ASR output for each item, along with its correct value, became a training example. Development data for GROUNDING came from 20 preliminary wizard dialogues. The development data also served to prime hypothesis merit.

Each subject had 30 dialogues with the system for the baseline dataset. For the wizard data set, FX2 used the same primed weights and merits as the baseline. The wizard's grounding actions and the target graphs on which they were based were saved as training examples. Weights for GROUNDING Advisors were learned from the development data training examples and the training examples saved from the wizard data set together before collecting the learned data set.

7 Results and Discussion

We assess system performance as follows. A *true positive (tp)* here is a dialogue that made no grounding errors and successfully grounded the root task agreement; a *false positive (fp)* made at least one grounding error (where the system entirely misunderstood the user). A *false negative (fn)* occurs when the system gives up on the task. Precision is *tp/(tp+fp)*, recall is *tp/(tp+fn)*, and F is their mean. We measure WER using Levenshtein edit distance (Levenshtein, 1966). Because the audio data is not yet transcribed, we estimated average WER from the speaker's first known utterance (*n*=360). Overall estimated WER was 66% (54% male, 78% female).

An ideal system engages in dialogues that have high precision, high recall, and economical *dialogue length* (as measured by number of system turns). Table 1 reports that data. There is a significant increase in precision across the three data sets, a small corresponding decrease in recall, and an overall gain in F measure. The precision demonstrated by the system during dialogues in the learned data set is as good or better than that reported for our best embedded human wizards in full dialogue experiments (Ligorio, Epstein and Passonneau, 2010).

Table 2 shows the distribution of the system's grounding actions for the three data sets. The grounding actions in the learned data set are similar to the wizard's; clearly, RSWL learned well. Figure 2 illustrates an effective learned grounding behavior in which GROUNDING votes to abandon the current grounding strategy on turn 5 in favor of an approach designed to elicit an utterance from the user more likely to be processed correctly by the speech recognizer.

Our experiment suggests that misunderstandings due to ASR errors can be significantly reduced by a close integration between spoken language understanding resources and grounding behavior, together with the use of fine-grained confidence measures. Despite intentionally noisy ASR with an estimated average WER of 66%, FX2 did not experience a single misunderstanding during 120 clarification dialogues after it had trained with RSWL on examples provided by an embedded wizard. After training, the system's actions closely resembled the wizard's, indicating that the system's grounding strategies were sufficiently expressive to approximate the wizard's actions. FX2 accommodates a variety of independent spoken language understanding resources. It relies on RSWL and on merit, a self-normalizing estimate of the confidence percentile in which an interpretation hypothesis falls.

Turn	Utterance	ASR
1	What title would you like?	
2	Family and Friends	family .friends.
3	I have two guesses. The first is *Family and Friends*. The second is *Family Happiness*. Is it either of these?	
4	The first one	.nest. .first.
5	Let's try something else. Is the full title *Family and Friends*?	
6	Yes	yes

Figure 2. Example of learned GROUNDING behavior. The rightmost column is the top ASR hypothesis. Periods delimit unconfident words in the ASR.

References

James Allen, George Ferguson and Amanda Stent. 2001. An architecture for more realistic conversational systems. *Proc. 6th Int'l Conference on Intelligent User Interfaces*. ACM**:** 1-8.

Dan Bohus. 2007. Error awareness and recovery in conversational spoken language interfaces. Ph.D. thesis, Carnegie Mellon University, Pittsburgh,PA.

Dan Bohus and Alexander I. Rudnicky. 2005. Error handling in the RavenClaw dialog management framework. *Proc. Human Language Technology and Empirical Methods in Natural Language Processing*, ACL**:** 225-232.

Dan Bohus and Alexander I. Rudnicky. 2009. The RavenClaw dialog management framework: Architecture and systems. *Comput. Speech Lang.* 23(3): 332-361.

Herbert H. Clark and Edward F. Schaefer. 1989. Contributing to discourse. *Cognitive Science* 13(2): 259 - 294.

David Devault and Matthew Stone. 2009. Learning to interpret utterances using dialogue history. *Proc. 12th Conference of the European Chapter of the Association for Computational Linguistics*. ACL**:** 184-192.

Susan L. Epstein. 1994. For the Right Reasons: The FORR Architecture for Learning in a Skill Domain. *Cognitive Science* 18(3): 479-511.

Susan L. Epstein and Smiljana Petrovic. 2006. Relative Support Weight Learning for Constraint Solving. *AAAI Workshop on Learning for Search*: 115-122.

Joshua B. Gordon, Rebecca J. Passonneau and Susan L. Epstein. 2011. Helping Agents Help Their Users Despite Imperfect Speech Recognition. *AAAI Symposium Help Me Help You: Bridging the Gaps in Human-Agent Collaboration.*

David Huggins-Daines, Mohit Kumar, Arthur Chan, Alan W. Black, Mosur Ravishankar and Alex I. Rudnicky. 2006. Pocketsphinx: A Free, Real-Time Continuous Speech Recognition System for Hand-Held Devices. In *Proc. IEEE ICASSP, 2006.* 185-188.

Oliver Lemon. 2003. Managing dialogue interaction: A multi-layered approach. In *Proc. 4th SIGDial Workshop on Discourse and Dialogue*.

Vladimir Levenshtein. 1966. Binary codes capable of correcting deletions, insertions, and reversals. *Soviet Physics Doklady*. 10**:** 707-710.

Esther Levin and Rebecca Passonneau. 2006. A WOz Variant with Contrastive Conditions. *In Proc. of Interspeech 2006 Satelite Workshop: Dialogue on Dialogues.*

Tiziana Ligorio, Susan L. Epstein and Rebecca J. Passonneau. 2010. Wizards' dialogue strategies to handle noisy speech recognition. *IEEE workshop on Spoken Language Technology (IEEE-SLT 2010)*. Berkeley, CA.

Diane Litman, Julia Hirschberg and Marc Swerts. 2006. Characterizing and predicting corrections in spoken dialogue systems. *Comput. Linguist.* 32(3): 417-438.

Diane J. Litman and Shimei Pan. 1999. Empirically evaluating an adaptable spoken dialogue system. *Proc. 7th Int'l Conference on User Modeling*. Springer-Verlag New York, Inc.**:** 55-64.

Tim Paek and Eric Horvitz. 2000. Conversation as action under uncertainty. *Proc. 16th Conference on Uncertainty in Artificial Intelligence*, Morgan Kaufmann Publishers Inc.**:** 455-464.

Rebecca J. Passonneau, Susan L. Epstein, Tiziana Ligorio, Joshua B. Gordon and Pravin Bhutada. 2010. Learning about voice search for spoken dialogue systems. *Human Language Technologies: NAACL 2010*. ACL**:** 840-848.

Antoine Raux, Brian Langner, Allan W. Black and Maxine Eskenazi. 2005. Let's Go Public! Taking a spoken dialog system to the real world. *Interspeech 2005 (Eurospeech)*. Lisbon, Portugal.

Antonio Roque and David Traum. 2009. Improving a virtual human using a model of degrees of grounding. *Proc. IJCAI-2009*. Morgan Kaufmann Publishers Inc.**:** 1537-1542.

An Annotation Scheme for Cross-Cultural Argumentation and Persuasion Dialogues

Kallirroi Georgila[†], **Ron Artstein**[†], **Angela Nazarian**[†]
Michael Rushforth[†,*] **David Traum**[†], **Katia Sycara**[‡]
[†]Institute for Creative Technologies, University of Southern California
[‡]Robotics Institute, Carnegie Mellon University
kgeorgila@ict.usc.edu

Abstract

We present a novel annotation scheme for cross-cultural argumentation and persuasion dialogues. This scheme is an adaptation of existing coding schemes on negotiation, following a review of literature on cross-cultural differences in negotiation styles. The scheme has been refined through application to coding both two-party and multi-party negotiation dialogues in three different domains, and is general enough to be applicable to different domains with few if any extensions. Dialogues annotated with the scheme have been used to successfully learn culture-specific dialogue policies for argumentation and persuasion.

1 Introduction

In both cooperative and non-cooperative negotiation the nature of the arguments used can be crucial for the outcome of the negotiation. Argumentation and persuasion are basic elements of negotiation. Moreover, different cultures favor different types of arguments (Koch, 1983; Han and Shavitt, 1994; Zaharna, 1995; Brett and Gelfand, 2006). For example, it is claimed that Western individualistic cultures favor arguments based on logic over arguments that appeal to emotions. On the other hand, people from Eastern collectivistic cultures are more likely to use arguments in which the beneficiary is not themselves. Furthermore, Arab cultures tend to favor more indirect ways of argumentation and expression (Koch, 1983; Zaharna, 1995).

In order to analyze negotiation in detail, including aspects such as persuasion, negotiation, and cross-cultural differences, we have developed a novel annotation scheme. General purpose annotation schemes such as DAMSL (Core and Allen, 1997) and DIT++ (Bunt, 2006) represent moves in the dialogue but do not capture enough details of the interaction to distinguish between different styles of persuasion and argumentation, especially cross-cultural differences.

Our goal for developing this coding scheme is two-fold. First, we aim to fill the gap in the literature of cross-cultural argumentation and persuasion. To our knowledge this is the first annotation scheme designed specifically for coding cross-cultural argumentation and persuasion strategies. Previous work on cross-cultural negotiation, e.g. Brett and Gelfand (2006), has not focused on argumentation or persuasion in particular. Also, previous work on argumentation, e.g. Prakken (2008), has not attempted to capture cross-cultural differences in argumentation and persuasion strategies. Second, we use this coding scheme to annotate negotiation dialogues to automatically learn argumentation and persuasion dialogue policies for different cultures (Georgila and Traum, 2011).

2 Related Work

2.1 Non-Culture Related Argumentation and Persuasion

The topic of negotiation has widely been studied across various fields including social and behavioral science (Kern et al., 2005), and computer science (Sidner, 1994; Rosé and Torrey, 2004). Our specific focus is on the role of argumentation and per-

* Now at the University of Texas at San Antonio.

Proceedings of the SIGDIAL 2011: the 12th Annual Meeting of the Special Interest Group on Discourse and Dialogue, pages 272–278,
Portland, Oregon, June 17-18, 2011.

suasion. Sycara (1990) studied the role of argumentation in negotiation with regard to the role of arguments in changing the decision process of the interlocutor. Most attempts have focused on studying the structure of argumentation and persuasion, often using formal logic (Cohen, 1987; Prakken, 2008). Dung (1995) showed that argumentation can be viewed as a special form of logic programming with negation as failure. An *argumentation scheme* is defined as a structure or template for forming an argument. Schemes are necessary for identifying arguments, finding missing premises, analyzing arguments, and evaluating arguments (Pollock, 1995; Katzav and Reed, 2004; Walton et al., 2008).

Recently, there has been some work on using machine learning techniques for automatically interpreting (George et al., 2007) and generating arguments (Zukerman, 2001). Note also the work of Piwek (2008) who performed a study on how arguments can be presented as fictive dialogues. Finally, there are a few persuasive dialogue systems, e.g. *Daphne* (Grasso et al., 2000) and *BIAS (Bayesian Interactive Argumentation System)* (Zukerman, 2001).

2.2 Cross-Cultural Argumentation and Persuasion

There is a vast amount of research on cultural effects on negotiation. Brett and Gelfand (2006) identify three aspects in cross-cultural negotiation: individualism vs. collectivism, egalitarianism vs. hierarchy, and low context vs. high context communication. Typically Western individuals are individualistic, egalitarian, and use low context communication while Eastern individuals are collectivistic, hierarchical, and use high context communication.[1]

Although there has been a considerable amount of work on building agents that can negotiate (Traum et al., 2003; Rosé and Torrey, 2004), little has been done towards building agents that can take into account culture aspects of negotiation (Cassell, 2009; Paruchuri et al., 2009; Traum, 2009).

Our literature review on cross-cultural argumentation and persuasion showed that there are comparatively few papers related to cross-cultural argumentation and persuasion in dialogue. Most work on cross-cultural studies is based on survey experiments rather than dialogue analysis. Below we summarize the works that we were influenced by the most.

Peng and Nisbett (1999) studied the way Chinese vs. European-American people reason about contradiction. By contradiction, here, we mean opposing pieces of information. Chinese individuals adopt a dialectical or compromise approach by retaining basic elements of the opposing perspectives. European-American people select one of the perspectives as correct and dismiss the opposing ones.

Koch (1983) linguistically analyzed several persuasive texts in contemporary Arabic in which there was both repetition of form and repetition of content. She found that Arabs use repetition as a means for persuasion. This strategy is called "presentation as proof" or "argumentation by presentation". Thus in Arabic argumentation it is the presentation of an idea that is persuasive, not the logical structure of proof which Westerners see behind the words. Zaharna (1995) examined how the Arab and American cultures have two distinct perspectives for viewing the role of language, for structuring persuasive messages, and for communicating effectively with their audiences. For Arabs emphasis is on form over function, affect over accuracy, and image over meaning, which is in line with the work of Koch (1983).

Finally, Cialdini's work (1998) identified six principles of persuasion: reciprocation (tendency to return favors), scarcity (associated with high value), authority (tendency to follow authority figures), social proof (one is looking to the behavior of other individuals to determine her own actions), liking (one tends to do things for people that she likes), and commitment and consistency (one has difficulty to reverse her commitments).

3 Our Annotation Scheme

We have developed a novel scheme for coding cross-cultural argumentation and persuasion strategies. This scheme is based on the literature review presented in section 2.2, as well as our own analysis of three very different kinds of negotiation (section 4). To develop this annotation scheme, we started by adapting existing coding schemes on negotiation developed by Pruitt and Lewis (1975), Carnevale et al. (1981), and Sidner (1994). We were also influenced by the work of Prakken on argumentation and dialogue (2008), and the work of Cialdini (1998) on persuasion (see section 2.2). Our annotation scheme

[1] In high-context cultures the listener must understand the contextual cues in order to grasp the full meaning of the message. In low-context cultures communication tends to be specific, explicit, and analytical.

was further refined by iteratively applying it to three different negotiation domains.

In our coding scheme, we use three dimensions for annotating an utterance: *speech act*, *topic*, and *response or reference to a previous utterance*. We have divided our codes for speech acts in categories. Below we can see each category and the codes that are included in it with explanatory examples, mostly drawn from the florist-grocer dialogues described in section 4.1.

3.1 Topic Tracking

start_topic *Let's talk about the design.*
end_topic *We are done with the design.*
redirect_topic *We need to get back to the task.*

3.2 Information Exchange

This category includes providing and requesting information, broken down into three kinds of information that are about the negotiation (priority, value, preference) as well as a fourth category (fact) which can be further subdivided, depending on the issue being negotiated (e.g. for the toy domain in section 4.3, there are specializations for origin, function, and utility of the toy).

request_info.priority *Which issue is the most important to you?*

request_info.value *How much money will I get if I give you this?*

request_info.preference *What do you think about the blue color?*

request_info.fact *What will happen to the flowers if the temperature gets higher?*

provide_info.priority *I care most about temperature.*

provide_info.value *You get $50 more if you agree to lower the temperature by one degree.*

provide_info.preference *I like design A.*

provide_info.fact (just a simple fact, neither preference nor priority nor value) *So one of them will be yours and one mine.*

3.3 Information Comparison

note_similarities *We both need the temperature to be relatively low.*

note_differences *It seems that you want design A and I prefer design C.*

project_otherspositition *So you want an equal distribution of rent.*

3.4 Clarifications/Confirmations

request_clarification *I am not getting any more money with more customers coming in?*

provide_clarification *Not necessarily.*

request_confirmation *Did you say 68 degrees?*

self_clarification (when the speaker tries to expand on her ideas) *Because when I thought temperature, I was thinking temperature for the products, not temperature for the atmosphere.*

3.5 Offer

We use the following format for an offer: offer.⟨type⟩.⟨beneficiary⟩.⟨directness⟩. For a "request_offer", generally only the *directness* field is used.

Type can take the following values: "standard", "tradeoff", "compromise", "concession", and "retraction". The difference between "compromise" and "concession" is subtle. "Concession" means that "I don't really want to do this but I'll do it because there is no other way". "Compromise" is like splitting the difference and it does not imply that the speaker does not like the option.

Beneficiary can be "me", "you", "both", "else", or "null". By *beneficiary* we mean who the offer or argument would be good for (see also section 3.7). So for example, if one's argument is "it will be too cold for the customers" then "beneficiary=else".

Directness can be "direct" or "indirect". An offer or argument is "indirect" when it needs to be inferred. For example, when the grocer says "well let's say there are lots of other local florists competing for your prices", she means that this is why advertising is important, but this needs some kind of inference, so the argument is indirect.

Below we can see examples of various types of offers (the *beneficiary* and *directness* dimensions are omitted for brevity).

offer.standard *How about 62 degrees?*

offer.tradeoff (between different issues) *I'll agree on 64 degrees if you agree on design A.*

offer.compromise *Well should we just say 50/50?*

offer.concession *There is no other way so I agree on 64 degrees.*

offer.retraction *I changed my mind, I don't want design A.*

request_offer *What temperature do you suggest?*

3.6 General Reaction

accept *Okay, 62 degrees is fine.* or *Yes, I said 62 degrees.*

reject *62 degrees is too low for me.* or *No, I didn't say that.*

acknowledge *I see.*

Note that "accept" is used for accepting offers and confirmation requests but also for agreement, for example, when one interlocutor agrees with the argument of the other interlocutor. "Reject" is used for rejecting offers and confirmation requests but also for disagreement.

3.7 Argumentation

An argument follows the following format: $\langle$role$\rangle$.$\langle$type$\rangle$.$\langle$beneficiary$\rangle$.$\langle$directness$\rangle$. The *role* can be "provide_argument", "attack_argument", "rebut_argument", "undercut_argument", and "accept_defeat". *Beneficiary* and *directness* are defined as in section 3.5. Below we can see examples of different argument roles.

provide_argument *The temperature must be low for my flowers to stay fresh.*

attack_argument (without necessarily providing a counter-argument) *What you say does not make sense.*

rebut_argument (provide a counter-argument) *Yes, but my customers wouldn't want to shop in such a low temperature.*

undercut_argument (invalidate an argument) *You don't need a low temperature in the shop. Your flowers can be refrigerated to stay fresh.*

accept_defeat *You are right, I could use a refrigerator.*

We have identified the following argument types: ideology (what is "right"), logic, fairness, precedent, God's will, promise for the future, honor, duty, identity, authority, refer to relationship, appeal to feelings, social responsibility, assurance (abstract promises), stories/metaphors, ordinance, design (aesthetics and functionality), effect/consequence, cost/means. These types are mostly inspired by our literature review (see section 2.2), as well as our observations in the domains that we used for developing the annotation scheme.

An example logical argument is "my flowers need low temperatures to stay fresh". An example argument that appeals to fairness is "I helped you last time so it's fair to help me now". Arguments that appeal to logic are more likely to appear in individualistic cultures. Arguments that appeal to duty, honor, social responsibility, ideology, and fairness are more common in collectivistic cultures. Stories/metaphors are very common in Arab cultures (Koch, 1983; Zaharna, 1995).

3.8 Other Speech Acts

repetition *I prefer design A. I said design A.*

heavy_commitment *$50 is all I can give, not a cent more.*

weak_commitment *Let's assume that we agree on this and continue.*

meta_task_discussion (try to figure out the task) *You are the grocer and I am the florist.*

self_contradiction *Speaker A: I like design C. Speaker A (later): Design C is terrible.*

show_concern *I understand that this solution would not be good for you.*

putdown *You are stubborn.*

show_frustration *I'm really sick and tired of this.*

threat *If you don't accept my offer I won't do business with you again.*

miscellaneous *Yes, flowers are beautiful.*

4 Applications of the Annotation Scheme on Various Corpora

In order to prove its generality we applied this coding scheme to three different negotiation domains.

4.1 Florist-Grocer Domain

The first domain was dialogues between American undergraduates playing the role of a florist and a grocer who share a retail space. The dialogues were collected by Laurie R. Weingart, Jeanne M. Brett, and Mary C. Kern at Northwestern University. The florist and the grocer negotiate on four issues: the design of the space, the temperature, the rent, and their advertising policy. Using the above coding scheme we annotated 21 dialogues. Example annotations of speech acts are given in Figure 1, as well as the examples in section 3, above.

The final scheme was the result of several cycles of dialogue annotations and revisions of the coding manual. We used the florist-grocer annotations to measure inter-annotator reliability between four annotators. In three cycles of annotation, we measured agreement on speech acts only and complex speech acts were unified, for example, all the "provide_argument" are treated as a single category. Krippendorff's α (Krippendorff, 1980) rose from 0.375 to 0.463 to 0.565.[2]

After analyzing these results we noticed that the main problems in terms of inter-annotator reliability were the confusion between "accept" and "acknowledge" (e.g. the utterance "yeah" could be either, depending on the context), and the confusion between "provide_argument.logic", "provide_argument.effect", and "provide_info". So we revised the manual as follows: in order for something to be annotated as "accept" vs. "acknowledge" we need to look forward in the dialogue; if an argument's type is both "logic" and "effect" then "effect" supersedes; "provide_info" is just provision of a piece of information with no argumentative role.

4.2 SASO Domain

In this second domain (Traum et al., 2008), we annotated role-play dialogues in English between a US Army captain and a Spanish doctor in Iraq. We have annotated five dialogues so far. An example is given in Figure 2.

4.3 Toy-Naming Domain

Finally, in the third domain groups of four people negotiate in English, Spanish, and Arabic about how to name a toy. The dialogues were part of the UTEP-ICT Cross-Cultural dialogue corpus (Herrera et al., 2010). We have annotated five dialogues in English and three in Arabic so far, and are currently working on Spanish. An example is given in Figure 3. The "redirect_topic" act was added based on this domain (to cover cases where one person consciously redirects the group's attention to the task when they drift off-topic for an extended period of time). Also, we added three domain-specific specializations of "provide_info.fact" and "request_info.fact": "provide_info.fact.function" (discussion about what one can do with the toy or things that it does or has, e.g. a secret compartment); "provide_info.fact.origin" (where the toy was manufactured or bought); "request_info.fact.utility" (a person prompts the others for ideas or examples of how the toy could be used and marketed).

[2]Krippendorff's α is 0.460 in the first cycle if we exclude one of the annotators who annotated only 72% of the items.

5 Discussion

We believe that this annotation scheme can be used for analyzing and modeling the fine differences of argumentation and negotiation styles, cross-task, and cross-culture, as well as providing a basis for artificial agents to engage in differentiated negotiation behavior.

Our first use of the annotated florist-grocer dialogues was for learning dialogue policies using simulated users and Reinforcement Learning (RL) (Georgila and Traum, 2011). To facilitate RL we had to make a few simplifications, for example, focus only on the temperature issue. In particular, we built policies for individualistic vs. altruistic florists (and grocers). Our results in simulation were consistent with our reward functions, i.e. the florist individualist agreed on low temperatures while interacting with the grocer altruist, the florist altruist agreed on high temperatures vs. the grocer individualist, etc. Details are given in (Georgila and Traum, 2011).

6 Conclusion

We presented a novel annotation scheme for cross-cultural argumentation and persuasion dialogues. This scheme is based on a review of literature on cross-cultural argumentation and persuasion, and adaptation of existing coding schemes on negotiation. Our annotation scheme is also based on our observations from its application to coding both two-party and multi-party negotiation dialogues in three different domains, and is general enough to be applicable to different domains with minor or no modifications at all. Furthermore, dialogues annotated with the scheme have been used to successfully learn culture-specific dialogue policies for argumentation and persuasion.

Acknowledgments

This research was funded by a MURI award through ARO grant number W911NF-08-1-0301. We are grateful to Laurie R. Weingart, Jeanne M. Brett, and Mary C. Kern who provided us with the florist-grocer dialogues, and to David A. Herrera, David G. Novick, and Dusan Jan who developed the UTEP-ICT corpus, as well as Hussein Sadek for transcriptions and translations of the Arabic dialogues.

References

J.M. Brett and M.J. Gelfand. 2006. A cultural analysis of the underlying assumptions of negotiation theory. In *Frontiers of Negotiation Research, L. Thompson (Ed)*, pages 173–201. Psychology Press.

H. Bunt. 2006. Dimensions in dialogue act annotation. In *Proc. of LREC*.

P.J. Carnevale, D.G. Pruitt, and S.D. Seilheimer. 1981. Looking and competing: Accountability and visual access in integrative bargaining. *Journal of Personality and Social Psychology*, 40(1):111–120.

J. Cassell. 2009. Culture as social culture: Being enculturated in human-computer interaction. In *Proc. of HCI International*.

R.B. Cialdini. 1998. *Influence: The psychology of persuasion, Revised*. Collins.

R. Cohen. 1987. Analyzing the structure of argumentative discourse. *Computational Linguistics*, 13(1-2):11–24.

M.G. Core and J.F. Allen. 1997. Coding dialogs with the DAMSL annotation scheme. In *Proc. of the AAAI Fall Symposium on Communicative Actions in Humans and Machines*.

P.M. Dung. 1995. On the acceptability of arguments and its fundamental role in nonmonotonic reasoning, logic programming and n-person games. *Artificial Intelligence*, 77(2):321–357.

S. George, I. Zukerman, and M. Niemann. 2007. Inferences, suppositions and explanatory extensions in argument interpretation. *User Modeling and User-Adapted Interaction*, 17(5):439–474.

K. Georgila and D. Traum. 2011. Learning culture-specific dialogue models from non culture-specific data. In *Proc. of HCI International*.

F. Grasso, A. Cawsey, and R. Jones. 2000. Dialectical argumentation to solve conflicts in advice giving: A case study in the promotion of healthy nutrition. *International Journal of Human-Computer Studies*, 53:1077–1115.

S. Han and S. Shavitt. 1994. Persuasion and culture: Advertising appeals in individualistic and collectivistic societies. *Journal of Experimental Social Psychology*, 30:326–350.

D. Herrera, D. Novick, D. Jan, and D. Traum. 2010. The UTEP-ICT cross-cultural multiparty multimodal dialog corpus. In *Proc. of the LREC Multimodal Corpora Workshop: Advances in Capturing, Coding and Analyzing Multimodality (MMC)*.

J. Katzav and C. Reed. 2004. On argumentation schemes and the natural classification of arguments. *Argumentation*, 18(2):239–259.

M.C. Kern, J.M. Brett, and L.R. Weingart. 2005. Getting the floor: Motive-consistent strategy and individual outcomes in multi-party negotiations. *Group Decision and Negotiation*, 14:21–41.

B. Johnstone Koch. 1983. Presentation as proof: The language of Arabic rhetoric. *Anthropological Linguistics*, 25(1):47–60.

K. Krippendorff. 1980. *Content analysis: An introduction to its methodology, chapter 12*. Sage, Beverly Hills, CA.

P. Paruchuri, N. Chakraborty, R. Zivan, K. Sycara, M. Dudik, and G. Gordon. 2009. POMDP based negotiation modeling. In *Proc. of the IJCAI Workshop on Modeling Intercultural Collaboration and Negotiation (MICON)*.

K. Peng and R.E. Nisbett. 1999. Culture, dialectics, and reasoning about contradiction. *American Psychologist*, 54(9):741–754.

P. Piwek. 2008. Presenting arguments as fictive dialogue. In *Proc. of the ECAI Workshop on Computational Models of Natural Argument (CMNA)*.

J.L. Pollock. 1995. *Cognitive Carpentry: A blueprint for how to build a person*. Bradford Books, MIT Press.

H. Prakken. 2008. A formal model of adjudication dialogues. *Artificial Intelligence and Law*, 16:305–328.

D.G. Pruitt and S.A. Lewis. 1975. Development of integrative solutions in bilateral negotiation. *Journal of Personality and Social Psychology*, 31(4):621–633.

C. Rosé and C. Torrey. 2004. DReSDeN: Towards a trainable tutorial dialogue manager to support negotiation dialogues for learning and reflection. In *Proc. of ITS*.

C.L. Sidner. 1994. An artificial discourse language for collaborative negotiation. In *Proc. of the National Conference on Artificial Intelligence*.

K. Sycara. 1990. Persuasive argumentation in negotiation. *Theory and Decision*, 28(3):203–242.

D. Traum, J. Rickel, S. Marsella, and J. Gratch. 2003. Negotiation over tasks in hybrid human-agent teams for simulation-based training. In *Proc. of AAMAS*.

D. Traum, S. Marsella, J. Gratch, J. Lee, and A. Hartholt. 2008. Multi-party, multi-issue, multi-strategy negotiation for multi-modal virtual agents. In *Proc. of IVA*.

D. Traum. 2009. Models of culture for virtual human conversation. In *Proc. of HCI International*.

D. Walton, C. Reed, and F. Macagno. 2008. *Argumentation Schemes*. Cambridge University Press.

R.S. Zaharna. 1995. Understanding cultural preferences of Arab communication partners. *Public Relations Review*, 21(3):241–255.

I. Zukerman. 2001. An integrated approach for generating arguments and understanding rejoinders. In *Proc. of the International Conference on User Modeling*.

Appendix

Florist: How does that work for you? **(request_info.preference)**

Grocer: Well, personally for the grocery I think it is better to have a higher temperature. **(provide_argument.logic.me.indirect)**

Grocer: Just because I want the customers to feel comfortable. **(elaborate)**

Florist: Okay. **(acknowledge)**

Grocer: And also if it is warm, people are more apt to buy cold drinks to keep themselves comfortable and cool. **(elaborate)**

Florist: That's true. **(accept)**

Florist: But what about your products staying fresh? Don't they have to stay fresh or otherwise? **(rebut_argument.logic.you.direct)**

Figure 1: Example annotated dialogue with speech acts in the florist-grocer domain.

Captain: I think if you just made the compromise, we could provide so much for you if you just agreed to let us move the clinic. **(offer.standard.you.direct)**

Doctor: Look I need to get back to my patients. They're dying now. They're dying. **(show_frustration)**

Captain: They wouldn't be dying if you let us move the clinic to the US Army base with the additional medical support. **(provide_argument.logic.else.direct)**

Doctor: Well they wouldn't be dying if I was there. **(rebut_argument.logic.else.direct)**

Doctor: Why don't you provide us with additional medical support and get out of our lives? **(request_offer.direct)**

Figure 2: Example annotated dialogue with speech acts in the SASO domain.

Speaker 3: Blue pal. **(offer.standard.null.direct)**

Speaker 4: Blue pal. **(acknowledge)**

Speaker 2: Blue pal. **(acknowledge)**

Speaker 4: That sounds pretty good. I actually like the idea. **(accept)**

Speaker 1: What if it's a different color? **(provide_argument.logic.null.direct)**

Speaker 2: Yeah, what if it's like pink and purple... **(elaborate)**

Speaker 4: Uh I like blue pal. I think that one's pretty cool... **(provide_info.preference)**

Speaker 2: Something pal like your pal. **(offer.standard.null.direct)**

Speaker 4: Blue pal the singing singing pal the singing pal the singing and dancing buddy. The beast you don't want to get angry. **(offer.standard.null.direct)**

Speaker 2: That's too long. **(reject)**

Speaker 2: It has to be short. **(provide_argument.logic.null.direct)**

Speaker 1: Furball. **(offer.standard.null.direct)**

Speaker 4: A short name... Actually a good really long name might work because everything out there is short... **(rebut_argument.logic.null.direct)**

Figure 3: Example annotated dialogue with speech acts in the toy-naming domain.

An Approach to the Automated Evaluation of Pipeline Architectures in Natural Language Dialogue Systems

Eliza Margaretha* and **David DeVault**
USC Institute for Creative Technologies, 12015 Waterfront Dr., Playa Vista, CA 90094
elizam@coli.uni-saarland.de
devault@ict.usc.edu

Abstract

We present an approach to performing automated evaluations of pipeline architectures in natural language dialogue systems. Our approach addresses some of the difficulties that arise in such automated evaluations, including the lack of consensus among human annotators about the correct outputs within the processing pipeline, the availability of multiple acceptable system responses to some user utterances, and the complex relationship between system responses and internal processing results. Our approach includes the development of a corpus of richly annotated target dialogues, simulations of the pipeline processing that could occur in these dialogues, and an analysis of how system responses vary based on internal processing results within the pipeline. We illustrate our approach in two implemented virtual human dialogue systems.

1 Introduction

Natural language dialogue systems are typically implemented as complex modular systems, with a range of internal modules performing tasks such as automatic speech recognition (ASR), natural language understanding (NLU), dialogue management (DM), natural language generation (NLG), and speech synthesis (TTS). A common design is for systems to adopt a pipeline architecture. In a pipeline, each user utterance is processed in a series of successive processing steps, with the output of each module serving as the input of the next module, until the system's response is determined.

*Now at Saarland University, Germany.

While there are many approaches to dialogue system evaluation (see e.g. (Walker et al., 1997; Eckert et al., 1997; Walker, 2005)), in many ways, the primary data for assessing the performance of a dialogue system comes from the collection of live interactive dialogues between an implemented system and members of its intended user population. Yet, live dialogue-based evaluation suffers from a number of limitations and drawbacks. Each dialogue set can be expensive and time-consuming to collect, and may only reflect a specific version of a system under active development. Additional effort is also generally necessary to identify specific system responses as problematic or unacceptable. Further annotation and analysis is then necessary to diagnose and pinpoint the cause of the problematic responses, so that the relevant pipeline module(s) may be improved.

In this paper, we present and discuss an approach to performing automated evaluations of pipeline architectures. Our approach involves the development of a corpus of annotated *target dialogues,* starting from Wizard-of-Oz data. Our automated evaluation assesses the support for these target dialogues in a pipeline system architecture. It is not designed as a substitute for live system evaluations, but rather as a complement to them which may help to alleviate some of these challenges to understanding system performance and streamlining development. In particular, unlike the PARADISE framework (Walker et al., 1997), which aims to evaluate dialogue agent *strategies* — by relating overall user satisfaction to various other metrics (task success, efficiency measures, and qualitative measures) — our approach takes the agent's dialogue strategy for granted (in

Proceedings of the SIGDIAL 2011: the 12th Annual Meeting of the Special Interest Group on Discourse and Dialogue, pages 279–285,
Portland, Oregon, June 17-18, 2011. ©2011 Association for Computational Linguistics

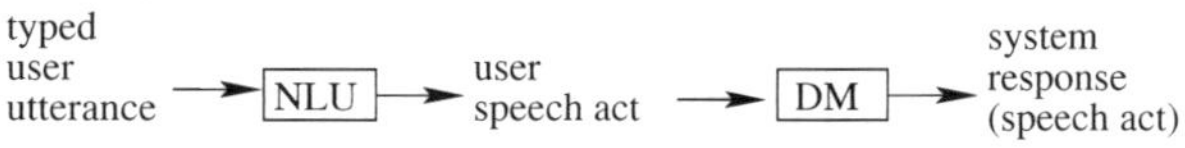

Figure 1: Simplified pipeline architecture.

the form of a set of target dialogues that exemplify the desired strategy), and instead zooms in and aims to directly evaluate the dialogue system's *module pipeline*. Specifically, our approach quantifies the ability of the pipeline to replicate the processing steps needed to reproduce a set of target responses. In our analysis, we place a special emphasis on the possible lack of consensus among human annotators about what the processing results should be. We do not aim to further analyze the system's live dialogue behavior in terms of user satisfaction, task success, or other global measures.

2 Research Setting

The work presented in this paper has been designed to support the dialogue behavior of two virtual human systems, the SimCoach and Tactical Questioning (TACQ) systems. SimCoach (Rizzo et al., 2011) is an on-going project aiming at empowering military personnel and their significant others with online healthcare assistance for Post-Traumatic Stress Disorder (PTSD), depression, and family-related problems. The SimCoach character encourages users to talk about any concerns or problems they may have. TACQ (Gandhe et al., 2008) is designed to support simulation and training for tactical questioning skills, and provides virtual humans who have information but will not answer certain questions unless the user cooperates by agreeing to their requests, offering promises in their favor, and so on. In this work, we have developed target dialogues for the Amani character, who has been an eyewitness of a recent shooting incident.

For simplicity, in the experiments reported in this paper, we have used simplified versions of these two dialogue systems. The simplification removes ASR from TACQ,[1] and removes NLG and TTS from both systems. This yields a simple two-module pipeline architecture that we depict in Figure 1. Note that the input to NLU is a typed English utterance, and the output of the NLU module (also the input to the DM module) is a speech act representation. The output of the DM, which we treat here as the system's response to the user, is also a speech act representation. Both of these systems use statistical classification models for NLU (Leuski and Traum, 2010; Sagae et al., 2009), and finite state machine models for DM (Gandhe et al., 2008; Rizzo et al., 2011).

3 Target Dialogues

Target dialogues are annotated versions of dialogues a system designer would like the system to support.

3.1 Developing Target Dialogues

Wizard-of-Oz (WoZ) and role play dialogues provide valuable data to designers of dialogue systems, especially in the form of natural dialogue data and insights into human-level performance and strategies for the specific dialogue task. However, in practice, system builders may not be able to implement all of the strategies and competences of the wizards or role players, and simplifications may be needed.

SimCoach target dialogues were developed from a collection of 10 WoZ dialogues in which clinicians (wizards) and veterans (users) interacted with each other. We also built Amani target dialogues for TACQ starting from 19 WoZ dialogues. Each user utterance and wizard's response was annotated with a target NLU speech act and one or more target DM speech acts (i.e., the system response).[2] The 10 SimCoach target dialogues contain 376 user utterances and 547 target system response speech acts. The 19 Amani target dialogues contain 317 user utterances and 354 target system response speech acts. For excerpts of the SimCoach and Amani target dialogues, see Tables A.1 and A.2 in the Appendix.

To create our target dialogues, we adjusted the WoZ dialogues to reflect a number of system design limitations as well as wizard deviations from the desired dialogue policy. These changes included removing unsupported wizard utterances and subdialogues, inserting or reordering system responses due to wizard mistakes, and introducing clarification subdialogues for unsupported user utterances.

[1] SimCoach always uses an instant messaging style typed input interface.

[2] For both SimCoach and TACQ, the DM may generate one or multiple speech acts in response to a user utterance.

3.2 Formalizing Target Dialogues

Let $P = \langle p_1, ..., p_k \rangle$ be the pipeline in a system containing k modules. We use S_t to denote the *pipeline state*, which includes the internal states of any modules that maintain an internal state, at time t.

For a user input x_t that occurs at time t, when the pipeline state is S_t, we write $A(P, S_t, x_t) = \langle y_1, ..., y_k \rangle$ to represent the actual sequence of outputs from the pipeline modules, where y_i is the output of module p_i for $i = 1...k$.

For a variety of reasons, these actual module outputs may differ from the target module outputs for this input and pipeline state. Let $T(P, S_t, x_t) = \langle z_1, ..., z_k \rangle$ be the *target pipeline response* to input x_t, i.e. the sequence of target outputs from each of the pipeline modules.

A target dialogue $\mathcal{D} = \langle (x_1, T_1), ..., (x_N, T_N) \rangle$, then, is a sequence of user inputs and corresponding target pipeline responses. Specifically, for time $t = 1...N$, $T_t = T(P, S_t^*, x_t) = \langle z_1, ..., z_k \rangle$ is the target pipeline response to input x_t, where S_t^* is the *target pipeline state* at each time t.

An important detail is that the *target pipeline state* S_t^* is the state that the pipeline *would* be in if all previous user inputs had triggered exactly the target pipeline responses. Formally, let S_1^* be the initial state of the dialogue system pipeline. Then, let $S_{t+1}^* = \text{update}(S_t^*, x_t, T_t)$, where we use an update function to capture the effect on the internal state of the pipeline of the target response T_t to x_t. Note that the target pipeline state may differ from the actual pipeline state, if an actual pipeline response differs from the target pipeline response. For example, if a previous user utterance was misunderstood by an NLU module, then at run-time, the actual information state inside the DM module would reflect this earlier misunderstanding, while the target pipeline state would include a corrected version of the information state. Using corrected information states, and corrected pipeline states more generally, enables the utterances within a target dialogue to be considered independently in a pipeline evaluation.[3]

We can say that a pipeline P is *compatible* with a target dialogue $\mathcal{D} = \langle (x_1, T_1), ..., (x_N, T_N) \rangle$ iff $A(P, S_t^*, x_t)[k] = T_t[k]$ for all $t = 1...N$. In other words, for every user utterance, the actual system response, as emitted by the last (k^{th}) module in the pipeline, matches the target system response.[4] Both the SimCoach and TACQ pipelines are *compatible* in this sense with their target dialogues (Section 3.1).

User Utterance	NLU Speech Act	DM Response
Having difficulty sleeping... bad dreams.. Wake up a few times every night	answer.observable. sleeping-problems	question. depression-pre-check-list.1
	answer.observable. wakeup-generic	question. depression-pre-check-list.1
	answer.observable. wakeup-nightmare	question. ptsd-pre-checklist.1

Table 1: Sample of Different NLU Speech Acts

3.2.1 Addressing the Lack of Consensus

A considerable challenge in the improvement of pipeline performance is the *lack of consensus* about the desired internal processing steps: different system designers or human annotators often disagree about what the intermediate results should be. For example, in a system such as TACQ or SimCoach, there may be substantial disagreement among human annotators about the correct NLU output for each utterance; see e.g. (Artstein et al., 2009). Table 1 exemplifies 3 different possible NLU speech act annotations for a user utterance to SimCoach. Note that for the first two, the DM outputs the same system response (which incidentally is the target response). However, the third speech act yields a different response. In our automated evaluations, rather than trying to resolve all disagreements, our approach is to characterize the frequency with which these kinds of phenomena occur in the pipeline.

To support this analysis, for a target dialogue $\mathcal{D} = \langle (x_1, T_1), ..., (x_N, T_N) \rangle$, we assume then that each input x_t is associated not only with the target pipeline response T_t, but also with a collection of annotations $A_t = \langle a_1, ..., a_k \rangle$. These annotations may be derived from a number of independent sources

[3]It also highlights how our pipeline evaluation results do not translate directly into performance metrics for live dialogues, as deviations and errors in system responses in live dialogues may affect the subsequent interaction in ways that are difficult to predict and deviate substantially from the target dialogues.

[4]A technical detail: for both SimCoach and TACQ, the DM sometimes emits multiple speech acts; to accommodate these cases, for now we treat the target DM output as a set of speech acts $\mathcal{A}$, and count each actual output DM speech act as an independent match if it matches *any* speech act in $\mathcal{A}$ (ignoring order). A more complex matching scheme could be employed.

$\mathcal{S} = \{s_1, ..., s_l\}$, and we write $a_i(s) = w_i$ to denote the correct output w_i for module p_i according to annotation source $s \in \mathcal{S}$. These independent "annotation sources" might be human annotators, or competing module algorithms, for example.

We can then capture the hypothetical effect of using annotation source s in place of some module p_i within the pipeline. To do so, we consider the effect of replacing the output of module p_i with $a_i(s)$, and using this as the input to subsequent modules in the pipeline. Let $P_{i+1}^k = \langle p_{i+1}, ..., p_k \rangle$ be the remainder of the pipeline, starting at module p_{i+1}. For input x_t, we can notate the *hypothetical pipeline response*, if module i were replaced by annotation source s, by $H(P_{i+1}^k, S_t^*, a_i(s)) = \langle y_{i+1}, ..., y_k \rangle$. We will write $h_t^{s\backslash i}$ for the hypothetical system response to the user input at time t, if source s were substituted for the output of module i: $h_t^{s\backslash i} = H(P_{i+1}^k, S_t^*, a_i(s))[k] = y_k$. For a target dialogue of length N, we can summarize the frequency with which the hypothetical pipeline response would match the target system response by a performance measure:

$$\mathcal{P}_{\text{strict}} = \frac{1}{N} \sum_{t=1}^{N} \text{match}(h_t^{s\backslash i}, T_t[k])$$

where $\text{match}(x, y) = 1$ if $x = y$ and 0 otherwise.[5]

A second form of lack of consensus issue is the existence of *multiple acceptable system responses* within a system. Returning to the example in Table 1, system designers might decide that either of the two system responses here would be acceptable. In some cases, actual NLU outputs which differ from the target NLU output will simply result in the system giving alternative acceptable system responses, as in this example. In other cases, they may lead to unacceptable system responses.

We measure the frequency with which these phenomena occur as follows. For a target dialogue $\mathcal{D} = \langle (x_1, T_1), ..., (x_N, T_N) \rangle$, let each input x_t be associated with a set $R_t = \{r_1, ..., r_m\}$ of system responses which differ from the target system response $T_t[k]$, but are also acceptable in design terms. Given these alternative responses, we can then define a more permissive performance measure:

$$\mathcal{P}_{\text{multiple}} = \frac{1}{N} \sum_{t=1}^{N} \text{match}(h_t^{s\backslash i}, T_t[k], R_t)$$

[5]This strict agreement measure can be easily generalized to measure the proportion of matches in a set of target dialogues.

NLU speech act source	Percent of NLU speech acts identical to... (N=317)		Percent of system response speech acts identical to... (N=354)	
	the target NLU speech act (target)	the target or other acceptable NLU speech act ($\text{human}_{\text{all}}$)	a target system response speech act	a target or acceptable system response speech act
target	100%	100%	99.4%	100%
human_1	79.3%	95.4%	84.2%	88.4%
human_2	76.7%	99.7%	86.7%	93.8%
human_3	59.3%	90.2%	69.6%	78.8%
NPCEditor	42.3%	50.5%	55.3%	57.4%

Table 2: TACQ Amani Evaluation Results

where

$$\text{match}(h_t^{s\backslash i}, T_t[k], R_t) = \begin{cases} 1 & \text{if } h_t^{s\backslash i} = T_t[k] \\ 1 & \text{if } h_t^{s\backslash i} \in R_t \\ 0 & \text{otherwise} \end{cases} .$$

4 Results

4.1 Annotations and Results for TACQ

We collected a range of annotations for the 19 TACQ Amani target dialogues, including 6 sources of NLU speech acts for the 317 user utterances: target (the target NLU speech act for each utterance); 3 independent human annotations of the best NLU speech act for each utterance; $\text{human}_{\text{all}}$ (a set containing *all* of the alternative acceptable NLU speech acts for each utterance, according to the same single researcher who prepared target); and NPCEditor, the NLU speech act output from NPCEditor (Leuski and Traum, 2010), the NLU module for TACQ.

We analyzed the effect of differing NLU speech act sources on the responses given by the system. We present the results in Table 2. (For a detailed processing example, see Table A.2 in the Appendix.) The first (leftmost) column of numbers shows the percentage of NLU speech acts from each source that are identical to the target NLU speech act. These results highlight how human annotators do not always agree with each other, or with the target. The agreement among the human annotators themselves, measured by Krippendorf's alpha (Krippendorff, 2007) is 0.599 (see also (Artstein et al., 2009)). In the second column of numbers, we tabulate the frequency with which the NLU speech acts are present in $\text{human}_{\text{all}}$. While these numbers are higher, they do not reach 100% for the human annotators, suggesting that a single annotator is unlikely to be able to circumscribe all the NLU speech acts that other annotators might find acceptable.

Despite the frequent disagreements among human annotators, this evaluation shows that the impact on the target system responses is less than might be expected. In the third column of numbers, we calculate $\mathcal{P}_{\text{strict}}$ which measures the effect of using each of NLU sources, in place of the NLU module's actual output, on the pipeline's ability to produce the target response. As the table implies, the pipeline often produces the target system response (third column) even when the NLU source disagrees with the target (first column). Indeed, for all the NLU sources except for target, the pipeline is significantly more likely to produce the target system response than the NLU source is to produce the target NLU speech act (Wilcoxon test, $p < 0.001$ for each source).

We also calculate $\mathcal{P}_{\text{multiple}}$ (last column) which measures the effect of using each NLU source on the pipeline's ability to produce either the target or any other acceptable system response. As the table shows, the actual system responses are often acceptable when they differ from the target responses. Although this effect seems weaker for NPCEditor, Wilcoxon tests reveal that for every source other than target, the differences between $\mathcal{P}_{\text{strict}}$ and $\mathcal{P}_{\text{multiple}}$ are significant at $p < 0.005$. This evaluation confirms that the pipeline is significantly more likely to deliver an acceptable system response than a target response, and helps quantify to what extent NLU outputs that differ from the target remain problematic for the pipeline performance.

4.2 Annotations and Results for SimCoach

We gathered a set of annotations for the 10 SimCoach target dialogues, including 3 sources of NLU speech acts for the 376 user utterances: target, human_1, and mxNLU (the NLU speech act output from mxNLU (Sagae et al., 2009), the NLU module for SimCoach). We present the evaluation results in Table 3. As the table shows, our independent human annotator often disagreed with the target NLU speech act. Despite the 72.1% agreement rate, the system's response to the human NLU speech act agreed with the target response 93.3% of the time.

In comparison, mxNLU shows somewhat higher

NLU speech act source	NLU speech acts identical to target (N = 376)	System response speech acts identical to target (N = 547)
target	100%	100%
human_1	72.1%	93.3%
mxNLU	75.3%	91.1%

Table 3: SimCoach Evaluation Results

agreement (75.3%) with the target NLU annotation. While this might at first suggest "super-human" NLU performance, in reality it is because the target NLU annotation was constructed in very close consultation with the training data for mxNLU.[6] Despite showing higher agreement with target NLU speech acts, the system responses were not more likely to match the target system responses with mxNLU. The explanation is that disagreements for mxNLU were more serious, reflecting more misunderstandings and failures to understand than occur with a human annotator, and more deviations from the target responses. This highlights the value of looking beyond the performance of individual modules.

5 Conclusions and Future Work

We have presented an approach to performing automated evaluations of pipeline architectures, and demonstrated its application in two implemented virtual human dialogue systems. The pipeline evaluation provided several insights into the current pipeline performance, including what performance would be attainable if human-level NLU were possible. In future work, we would like to expand beyond our simplified two-module pipeline, and investigate the connection between our automated pipeline evaluations and performance in live dialogues.

Acknowledgments

We thank our reviewers, Sudeep Gandhe, Fabrizio Morbini, and David Traum. The project effort described here has been sponsored by the U.S. Army Research, Development, and Engineering Command (RDECOM). Statements and opinions expressed do not necessarily reflect the position or the policy of the United States Government, and no official endorsement should be inferred.

[6]The exact target dialogue utterances were not in the mxNLU training data, but similar utterances were inspected in constructing the target dialogues.

References

R. Artstein, S. Gandhe, M. Rushforth, and D. Traum. 2009. Viability of a simple dialogue act scheme for a tactical questioning dialogue system. In SemDial Workshop, pages 43–50.

W. Eckert, E. Levin, and R. Pieraccini. 1997. User modeling for spoken dialogue system evaluation. In *Proc. IEEE ASR Workshop*, pages 80–87.

S. Gandhe, D. DeVault, A. Roque, B. Martinovski, R. Artstein, A. Leuski, and et al. 2008. From domain specification to virtual humans: An integrated approach to authoring tactical questioning characters. Proceedings of Interspeech-08.

K Krippendorff. 2007. Computing krippendorff's alpha-reliability, June.

A. Leuski and D. Traum. 2010. NPCEditor: A tool for building question-answering characters. In LREC.

A. Rizzo, B. Lange, J.G. Buckwalter, E. Forbell, J. Kim, K. Sagae, J. Williams, B.O. Rothbaum, J. Difede, G. Reger, T. Parsons, and P. Kenny. 2011. An intelligent virtual human system for providing healthcare information and support. In et al. Westwood, J.D., editor, *Technology and Informatics*. IOS Press.

K. Sagae, G. Christian, D. DeVault, and D. R. Traum. 2009. Towards natural language understanding of partial speech recognition results in dialogue systems. In Short Paper Proceedings of NAACL HLT.

M. A. Walker, D. J. Litman, C. A. Kamm, A. A. Kamm, and A. Abella. 1997. Paradise: A framework for evaluating spoken dialogue agents. pages 271–280.

M. A. Walker. 2005. Can we talk? methods for evaluation and training of spoken dialogue systems. *Language Resources and Evaluation*, 39(1):pp. 65–75.

Appendix

t	User Utterance (x_t)	Target NLU Speech Act (t_1)	Target System Response (t_2)	Textual Version of Target System Response
9	my husband seems distant, and we have been arguing a lot more lately	answer.observable. family-problem	question.bio-info. has-kids	Does he have children?
10	yes, 2	answer.yes	question.family-pre-checklist.6	In his family, do people collaborate together to find the best way to solve problems?

Table A.1: Excerpt from a SimCoach Target Dialogue.

t	User Utterance (x_t)	Source of NLU Speech Act	NLU Speech Act (gloss)	System Response Speech Acts (gloss)
1	hi amani.	NPCEditor	*hello*	*hello*
		target NLU	*hello*	*hello*
2	i wanted to talk to you about the recent shooting that occurred	NPC Editor	*Tell me more about the_ incident*	*location of the_incident is the_shop*
		target NLU	*Is amani willing to talk?*	*amani is willing to talk*
3	do you know who was responsible?	NPC Editor	*What is perpetrator of the_ incident ?*	*perpetrator of the_incident is Saif*
		target NLU	*What is name of strange_man ?*	*player should offer 'give-safety'*

Table A.2: Excerpt from a TACQ target dialogue, including pipeline module processing.

Perception of Personality and Naturalness through Dialogues by Native Speakers of American English and Arabic

Maxim Makatchev
Robotics Institute
Carnegie Mellon University
Pittsburgh, PA, USA
mmakatch@cs.cmu.edu

Reid Simmons
Robotics Institute
Carnegie Mellon University
Pittsburgh, PA, USA
reids@cs.cmu.edu

Abstract

Linguistic markers of personality traits have been studied extensively, but few cross-cultural studies exist. In this paper, we evaluate how native speakers of American English and Arabic perceive personality traits and naturalness of English utterances that vary along the dimensions of verbosity, hedging, lexical and syntactic alignment, and formality. The utterances are the turns within dialogue fragments that are presented as text transcripts to the workers of Amazon's Mechanical Turk. The results of the study suggest that all four dimensions can be used as linguistic markers of all personality traits by both language communities. A further comparative analysis shows cross-cultural differences for some combinations of measures of personality traits and naturalness, the dimensions of linguistic variability and dialogue acts.

1 Introduction

English has been used as a lingua franca across the world, but the usage differs. The variabilities in English introduced by dialects, cultures, and non-native speakers result in different syntax and words expressing similar meanings and in different meanings attributed to similar expressions. These differences are a source of *pragmatic failures* (Thomas, 1983): situations when listeners perceive meanings and affective attitudes unintended by speakers. For example, Thomas (1984) reports that usage of Illocutionary Force Indicating Devices (IFIDs, such as "I warn you", (Searle, 1969)) in English by native speakers of Russian causes the speakers to sometimes appear "inappropriately domineering in interactions with English-speaking equals." Dialogue systems, just like humans, may misattribute attitudes and misinterpret intent of user's utterances. Conversely, they may also cause misattributions and misinterpretations on the user's part. Hence, taking into account the user's dialect, culture, or native language may help reduce pragmatic failures.

This kind of adaptation requires a mapping from utterances, or more generally, their linguistic features, to meanings and affective attributions for each of the target language communities. In this paper we present an exploratory study that evaluates such a mapping from the linguistic features of verbosity, hedging, alignment, and formality (as defined in Section 3.1) to the perceived personality traits and naturalness across the populations of native speakers of American English and Arabic.

Estimating the relationship between linguistic features and their perception across language communities faces a number of methodological difficulties. First, language communities shall be outlined, in a way that will afford generalizing within their populations. Defining language communities is a hard problem, even if it is based on the "mother tongue" (McPherson et al., 2000). Next, linguistic features that are potentially important for the adaptation must be selected. These are, for example, the linguistic devices that contribute to realization of *rich points* (Agar, 1994), i.e. the behaviors that signal differences between language communities. To be useful for dialogue system research, the selected linguistic features should be feasible to implement in natural language generation and interpretation mod-

Proceedings of the SIGDIAL 2011: the 12th Annual Meeting of the Special Interest Group on Discourse and Dialogue, pages 286–293, Portland, Oregon, June 17-18, 2011.

ules. Then, a corpus of stimuli that span the variability of the linguistic features must be created. The stimuli should reflect the context where the dialogue system is intended to be used. For example, in case of an information-giving dialogue system, the stimuli should include some question-answer adjacency pairs (Schegloff and Sacks, 1973). Finally, scales should be chosen to allow for scoring of the stimuli with respect to the metrics of interest. These scales should be robust to be applied within each of the language communities.

In the remainder of this paper, we describe each of these steps in the context of an exploratory study that evaluates perception of English utterances by native speakers of American English and Arabic. Our application is an information-giving dialogue system that is used by the robot receptionists (roboceptionists) in Qatar and the United States (Makatchev et al., 2009; Makatchev et al., 2010). In the next section, we continue with an overview of the related work. Section 3 introduces the experiment, including the selection of stimuli, measures, design, and describes the recruitment of participants via Amazon's Mechanical Turk (MTurk). We discuss results in Section 4 and provide a conclusion in Section 5.

2 Related work

2.1 Cross-cultural variability in English

Language is tightly connected with culture (Agar, 1994). As a result, even native speakers of a language use it differently across dialects (e.g. African American Vernacular English and Standard American English), genders (see, for example, (Lakoff, 1973)) and social statuses (e.g. (Huspek, 1989)), among other dimensions.

Speakers of English as a second language display variabilities in language use that are consistent with their native languages and backgrounds. For example, Nelson et al. (1996) reports that Syrian speakers of Arabic tend to use different compliment response strategies as compared with Americans. Aguilar (1998) reviews types of pragmatic failures that are influenced by native language and culture. In particular, he cites Davies (1987) on a pragmatic failure due to *non-equivalence of formulas*: native speakers of Moroccan Arabic use a spoken formulaic expression to wish a sick person quick recovery, whereas in English the formula "get well soon" is not generally used in speech. Feghali (1997) reviews features of Arabic communicative style, including indirectness (concealment of wants, needs or goals (Gudykunst and Ting-Toomey, 1988)), elaborateness (rich and expressive language use, e.g. involving rhetorical patterns of exaggeration and assertion (Patai, 1983)) and affectiveness (i.e. "intuitive-affective style of emotional appeal" (Glenn et al., 1977), related to the patterns of organization and presentation of arguments).

In this paper, we are concerned with English usage by native speakers of American English and native speakers of Arabic. We have used the features of the Arabic communicative style outlined above as a guide in selecting the dimensions of linguistic variability that are presented in Section 3.1.

2.2 Measuring pragmatic variation

Perception of pragmatic variation of spoken language and text has been shown to vary across cultures along the dimensions of personality (e.g. (Scherer, 1972)), emotion (e.g. (Burkhardt et al., 2006)), deception (e.g. (Bond et al., 1990)), among others. Within a culture, personality traits such as extraversion, have been shown to have consistent markers in language (see overview in (Mairesse et al., 2007)). For example, Furnham (1990) notes that in conversation, extraverts are less formal and use more verbs, adverbs and pronouns. However, the authors are not aware of any quantitative studies that compare linguistic markers of personality across cultures. The present study aims to help fill this gap.

A mapping between linguistic dimensions and personality has been evaluated by grading essays and conversation extracts (Mairesse et al., 2007), and by grading utterances generated automatically with a random setting of linguistic parameters (Mairesse and Walker, 2008). In the exploratory study presented in this paper, we ask our participants to grade dialogue fragments that were manually created to vary along each of the four linguistic dimensions (see Section 3.1).

3 Experiment

In the review of related work, we presented some evidence supporting the claim that linguistic markers of personality may differ across cultures. In this section, we describe a study that evaluates perception of personality traits and naturalness of utterances by native speakers of American English and Arabic.

3.1 Stimuli

The selection of stimuli attempts to satisfy three objectives. First, our application: our dialogue system is intended to be used on a robot receptionist. Hence, the stimuli are snippets of dialogue that include four dialogue acts that are typical in this kind of embodied information-giving dialogue (Makatchev et al., 2009): a greeting, a question-answer pair, a disagreement (with the user's guess of an answer), and an apology (for the robot not knowing the answer to the question).

Second, we would like to vary our stimuli along the linguistic dimensions that are potentially strong indicators of personality traits. Extraverts, for example, are reported to be more verbose (use more words per utterances and more dialogue turns to achieve the same communicative goal), less formal (Furnham, 1990) (in choice of address terms, for example), and less likely to hedge (use expressions such as "perhaps" and "maybe") (Nass et al., 1995). Lexical and syntactic alignment, namely, the tendency of a speaker to use the same lexical and syntactic choices as their interlocutor, is considered, at least in part, to reflect the speaker's co-operation and willingness to adopt the interlocutor's perspective (Haywood et al., 2003). There is some evidence that the degree of alignment is associated with personality traits of the speakers (Gill et al., 2004).

Third, we would like to select linguistic dimensions that potentially expose cross-cultural differences in perception of personality and naturalness. In particular, we are interested in the linguistic devices that help realize *rich points* (the behaviors that signal differences) between the native speakers of American English and Arabic. We choose to realize indirectness and elaborateness, characteristic of Arabic spoken language (Feghali, 1997), by varying the dimensions of verbosity and hedging. High *power distance*, or influence of relative social status on the language (Feghali, 1997), can be realized by the degrees of formality and alignment.

In summary, the stimuli are dialogue fragments where utterances of one of the interlocutors vary across (1) dialogue acts: a greeting, question-answer pair, disagreement, apology, and (2) four linguistic dimensions: verbosity, hedging, alignment, and formality. Each of the linguistic dimensions is parameterized by 3 values of valence: negative, neutral and positive. Within each of the four dialogue acts, stimuli corresponding to the neutral valences are represented by the same dialogue across all four linguistic dimensions. The four linguistic dimensions are realized as follows:

- Verbosity is realized as number of words within each turn of the dialogue. In the case of the greeting, positive verbosity is realized by increased number of dialogue turns.[1]
- Positive valence of hedging implies more tentative words ("maybe," "perhaps," etc.) or expressions of uncertainty ("I think," "if I am not mistaken"). Conversely, negative valence of hedging is realized via words "sure," "definitely," etc.
- Positive valence of alignment corresponds to preference towards the lexical and syntactic choices of the interlocutor. Conversely, negative alignment implies less overlap in lexical and syntactic choices between the interlocutors.
- Our model of formality deploys the following linguistic devices: in-group identity markers that target positive face (Brown and Levinson, 1987) such as address forms, jargon and slang, and deference markers that target negative face, such as "kindly", terms of address, hedges. These devices are used in Arabic politeness phenomena (Farahat, 2009), and there is an evidence of their pragmatic transfer from Arabic to English (e.g. (Bardovi-Harlig et al., 2007) and (Ghawi, 1993)). The set of stimuli that vary along the formality are presented in Table 2.

Each dialogue fragment is presented as a text on

[1]The multi-stage greeting dialogue was developed via ethnographic studies conducted at Alelo by Dr. Suzanne Wertheim. Used with permission from Alelo, Inc.

an individual web page. On each page, the participant is asked to imagine that he or she is one of the interlocutors and the other interlocutor is described as "a female receptionist in her early 20s and of the same ethnic background" as that of the participant. The description of the occupation, age, gender and ethnicity of the interlocutor whose utterances the participant is asked to evaluate should provide minimal context and help avoid variability due to the implicit assumptions that subjects may make.

3.2 Measures

In order to avoid a possible interference of scales, we ran two versions of the study in parallel. In one version, participants were asked to evaluate the receptionist's utterances with respect to measures of the Big Five personality traits (John and Srivastava, 1999), namely the traits of extraversion, agreeableness, conscientiousness, emotional stability, and openness, using the ten-item personality questionnaire (TIPI, see (Gosling et al., 2003)). In the other version, participants were asked to evaluate the receptionist's utterances with respect to their naturalness on a 7-point Likert scale by answering the question "Do you agree that the receptionist's utterances were natural?" The variants of such a naturalness scale were used by Burkhardt et al. (2006) and Mairesse and Walker (2008).

3.3 Experimental design

The experiment used a crossed design with the following factors: dimensions of linguistic variability (verbosity, hedging, alignment, or formality), valence (negative, neutral, or positive), dialogue acts (greeting, question-answer, disagreement, or apology), native language (American English or Arabic) and gender (male or female).

In an attempt to balance the workload of the participants, depending on whether the participant was assigned to the study that used personality or naturalness scales, the experimental sessions consisted of one or two linguistic variability conditions—12 or 24 dialogues respectively. Hence valence and dialogue act were within-subject factors, while linguistic variability dimension were treated as an across-subject factor, as well as native language and gender. Within each session the items were presented in a random order to minimize possible carryover effects.

Language	Country	N
Arabic	Algeria	1
	Bahrain	1
	Egypt	56
	Jordan	32
	Morocco	45
	Palestinian Territory	1
	Qatar	1
	Saudi Arabia	5
	United Arab Emirates	13
	Total	155
American English	United States	166

Table 1: Distribution of study participants by country.

3.4 Participants

We used Amazon's Mechanical Turk (MTurk) to recruit native speakers of American English from the United States and native speakers of Arabic from any of the set of predominantly Arabic-speaking countries (according to the IP address).

Upon completion of each task, participants receive monetary reward as a credit to their MTurk account. Special measures were taken to prevent multiple participation of one person in the same study condition: the study website access would be refused for such a user based on the IP address, and MTurk logs were checked for repeated MTurk user names to detect logging into the same MTurk account from different IP addresses. Hidden questions were planted within the study to verify the fluency in the participant's reported native language.

The distribution of the participants across countries is shown in Table 1. We observed a regional gender bias similar to the one reported by Ross et al. (2010): there were 100 male and 55 female participants in the Arabic condition, and 63 male and 103 female participants in the American English condition.

4 Results

We analyzed the data by fitting linear mixed-effects (LME) models (Pinheiro and Bates, 2000) and performing model selection using ANOVA. The comparison of models fitted to explain the personality and naturalness scores (controlling for language and gender), shows significant main effects of valence and dialogue acts for all pairs of personality traits (and naturalness) and linguistic features. The results also show that for every personality trait (and naturalness) there is a linguistic feature that results in a significant three-way interaction between its valence, the native language, and the dialogue act. These results suggest that (a) for both language communities, every linguistic dimension is associated with every personality trait and naturalness, for at least some of the dialogue acts, (b) there are differences in the perception of every personality trait and naturalness between the two language communities.

To further explore the latter finding, we conducted a post-hoc analysis consisting of paired t-tests that were performed pairwise between the three values of valence for each combination of language, linguistic feature, and personality trait (and naturalness). Note, that comparing raw scores between the language conditions would be prone to find spurious differences due to potential culture-specific tendencies in scoring on the Likert scale: (a) perception of magnitudes and (b) appropriateness of the intensity of agreeing or disagreeing. Instead, we compare the language conditions with respect to (a) the relative order of the three valences and (b) the binarized scores, namely whether the score is above 4 or below 4 (with scores that are not significantly different from 4 excluded from comparison), where 4 is the neutral point of the 7-point Likert scale.

The selected results of the post-hoc analysis are shown in Figure 1. The most prominent cross-cultural differences were found in the scoring of naturalness across the valences of the formality dimension. Speakers of American English, unlike the speakers of Arabic, find formal utterances unnatural in greetings, question-answer and disagreement dialogue acts. Formal utterances tend to also be perceived as indicators of openness (omitted from the plot) and conscientiousness by Arabic speakers, and not by American English speakers, in disagreements and apologies respectively. Finally, hedging in apologies is perceived as an indicator of agreeableness by American English speakers, but not by speakers of Arabic.

Interestingly, no qualitative differences across language conditions were found in the perception of extraversion and stability. It is possible that this cross-cultural consistency confirms the view of the extraversion, in particular, as one of most consistently identified dimensions (see, for example, (Gill and Oberlander, 2002)). It could also be possible that our stimuli were unable to pinpoint the extraversion-related rich points due to a choice of the linguistic dimensions or particular wording chosen. A larger variety of stimuli per condition, and an ethnography to identify potentially culture-specific linguistic devices of extraversion, could shed the light on this issue.

5 Conclusion

We presented an exploratory study to evaluate a set of linguistic markers of Big Five personality traits and naturalness across two language communities: native speakers of American English living in the US, and native speakers of Arabic living in one of the predominantly Arabic-speaking countries of North Africa and Middle East. The results suggest that the four dimensions of linguistic variability are recognized as markers of all five personality traits by both language communities. A comparison across language communities uncovered some qualitative differences in the perception of openness, conscientiousness, agreeableness, and naturalness.

The results of the study can be used to adapt natural language generation and interpretation to native speakers of American English or Arabic. This exploratory study also supports the feasibility of the crowdsourcing approach to validate the linguistic devices that realize rich points—behaviors that signal differences across languages and cultures.

Future work shall evaluate effects of regional dialects and address the issue of particular wording choices by using multiple stimuli per condition.

Acknowledgments

This publication was made possible by the support of an NPRP grant from the Qatar National Research Fund. The statements made herein are solely the responsibility of the authors.

The authors are grateful to Ameer Ayman Abdulsalam, Michael Agar, Hatem Alismail, Justine Cassell, Majd Sakr, Nik Melchior, and Candace Sidner for their comments on the study.

References

Michael Agar. 1994. *Language shock: Understanding the culture of conversation.* William Morrow, New York.

Maria Jose Coperias Aguilar. 1998. Intercultural (mis)communication: The influence of L1 and C1 on L2 and C2. A tentative approach to textbooks. *Cuadernos de Filología Inglesa*, 7(1):99–113.

Kathleen Bardovi-Harlig, Marda Rose, and Edelmira L. Nickels. 2007. The use of conventional expressions of thanking, apologizing, and refusing. In *Proceedings of the 2007 Second Language Research Forum*, pages 113–130.

Charles F. Bond, Adnan Omar, Adnan Mahmoud, and Richard Neal Bonser. 1990. Lie detection across cultures. *Journal of Nonverbal Behavior*, 14:189–204.

P. Brown and S. C. Levinson. 1987. *Politeness: Some universals in language usage.* Cambridge University Press, Cambridge.

F. Burkhardt, N. Audibert, L. Malatesta, O. Trk, Arslan, L., and V Auberge. 2006. Emotional prosody—does culture make a difference? In *Proc. Speech Prosody.*

Eirlys E. Davies. 1987. A contrastive approach to the analysis of politeness formulas. *Applied Linguistics*, 8(1):75–88.

Said Hassan Farahat. 2009. *Politeness phenomena in Palestinian Arabic and Australian English: A cross-cultural study of selected contemporary plays (PhD thesis).* Australian Catholic University, Australia.

Ellen Feghali. 1997. Arab cultural communication patterns. *International Journal of Intercultural Relations*, 21(3):345–378.

A. Furnham. 1990. Language and personality. In H. Giles and W. Robinson, editors, *Handbook of Language and Social Psychology*, pages 73–95. Wiley.

Mohammed Ghawi. 1993. Pragmatic transfer in Arabic learners of English. *El Two Talk*, 1(1):39–52.

A. Gill and J. Oberlander. 2002. aking care of the linguistic features of extraversion. In *Proceedings of the 24th Annual Conference of the Cognitive Science Society*, pages 363–368.

A. Gill, A. Harrison, and J. Oberlander. 2004. Interpersonality: Individual differences and interpersonal priming. In *Proceedings of the 26th Annual Conference of the Cognitive Science Society*, pages 464–469.

E. S. Glenn, D. Witmeyer, and K. A. Stevenson. 1977. Cultural styles of persuasion. *International Journal of Intercultural Relations*, 1(3):52–66.

Samuel D. Gosling, Peter J. Rentfrow, and Jr. William B. Swann. 2003. A very brief measure of the Big-Five personality domains. *Journal of Research in Personality*, 37:504–528.

W. B. Gudykunst and S. Ting-Toomey. 1988. *Culture and interpersonal communication.* Sage, Newbury Park, CA.

S. Haywood, M. Pickering, and H. Branigan. 2003. Co-operation and co-ordination in the production of noun phrases. In *Proceedings of the 25th Annual Conference of the Cognitive Science Society*, pages 533–538.

Michael Huspek. 1989. Linguistic variability and power: An analysis of you know/I think variation in working-class speech. *Journal of Pragmatics*, 13(5):661 – 683.

Oliver P. John and Sanjay Srivastava. 1999. The Big Five trait taxonomy: History, measurement, and theoretical perspectives. In Lawrence A. Pervin and Oliver P. John, editors, *Handbook of Personality: Theory and Research*, pages 102–138.

Robin Lakoff. 1973. Language and woman's place. *Language in Society*, 2(1):45–80.

Francois Mairesse and Marilyn Walker. 2008. Trainable generation of big-five personality styles through data-driven parameter estimation. In *Proc. of 46th Annual Meeting of the Association for Computational Linguistics (ACL).*

F. Mairesse, M. A. Walker, M. R. Mehl, and R. K. Moore. 2007. Using linguistic cues for the automatic recognition of personality in conversation and text. *Journal of Artificial Intelligence Research*, 30:457–500.

Maxim Makatchev, Min Kyung Lee, and Reid Simmons. 2009. Relating initial turns of human-robot dialogues to discourse. In *Proc. of the Int. Conf. on Human-Robot Interaction (HRI)*, pages 321–322. ACM.

Maxim Makatchev, Imran Aslam Fanaswala, Ameer Ayman Abdulsalam, Brett Browning, Wael Mahmoud Gazzawi, Majd Sakr, and Reid Simmons. 2010. Dialogue patterns of an arabic robot receptionist. In *Proc. of the Int. Conf. on Human-Robot Interaction (HRI)*, pages 167–168. ACM.

M. McPherson, L. Smith-Lovin, and J. M. Cook. 2000. What is a language community? *American Journal of Political Science*, 44(1):142–155.

Clifford Nass, Y. Moon, B. Fogg, and B. Reeves. 1995. Can computer personalities be human personalities? *Journal of Human-Computer Studies*, 43:223–239.

Gaylel Nelson, Mahmoud Al-Batal, and Erin Echols. 1996. Arabic and english compliment responses: Potential for pragmatic failure. *Applied Linguistics*, 17(4):411–432.

R. Patai. 1983. *The Arab mind.* Charles Scribner's Sons, New York.

J. C. Pinheiro and D. M. Bates. 2000. *Mixed-Effects Models in S and S-PLUS.* Springer.

Joel Ross, Lilly Irani, M. Six Silberman, Andrew Zaldivar, and Bill Tomlinson. 2010. Who are the crowdworkers?: shifting demographics in mechanical turk.

In *Proceedings of the 28th of the international conference extended abstracts on Human factors in computing systems*, CHI EA '10, pages 2863–2872, New York, NY, USA. ACM.

Emanuel A. Schegloff and Harvey Sacks. 1973. Opening up closings. *Semiotica*, 8(4):289–327.

Klaus R. Scherer. 1972. Judging personality from voice: A cross-cultural approach to an old issue in interpersonal perception. *Journal of Personality*, 40:191–210.

John Searle. 1969. *Speech acts: An essay in the philosophy of language*. Cambridge University Press.

Jenny Thomas. 1983. Cross-cultural pragmatic failure. *Applied Linguistics*, 4(2):91–112.

Jenny Thomas. 1984. Cross-cultural discourse as 'unequal encounter': Towards a pragmatic analysis. *Applied Linguistics*, 5(3):226–235.

Greeting	Question-Answer	Disagreement	Apology
A: Good morning. B: What's up? Need anything?	A: Could you tell me where the library is? B: Just go to the end of the hallway, you can't miss it.	A: Could you tell me where the library is? B: Go to the second floor. A: I thought it was on the first floor. B: No, honey, there is none on the first floor.	A: Could you tell me where the library is? B: Sorry about that, I have no idea.
A: Good morning. B: Good morning. How may I help you?	A: Could you tell me where the library is? B: It's at the end of the hallway on your left.	A: Could you tell me where the library is? B: It's on the second floor. A: I thought it was on the first floor. B: No, there is no library on the first floor.	A: Could you tell me where the library is? B: Sorry, I don't know.
A: Good morning. B: Good morning, sir (madam). Would you allow me to help you with anything?	A: Could you tell me where the library is? B: Kindly follow this hallway and you will encounter the entrance on your left.	A: Could you tell me where the library is? B: Yes, you may find the library on the second floor. A: I thought it was on the first floor. B: I am afraid that is not correct, there is no library on the first floor.	A: Could you tell me where the library is? B: I have to apologize, but I don't know.

Table 2: Stimuli that correspond to negative (top row), neutral (middle row), and positive (bottom row) formality.

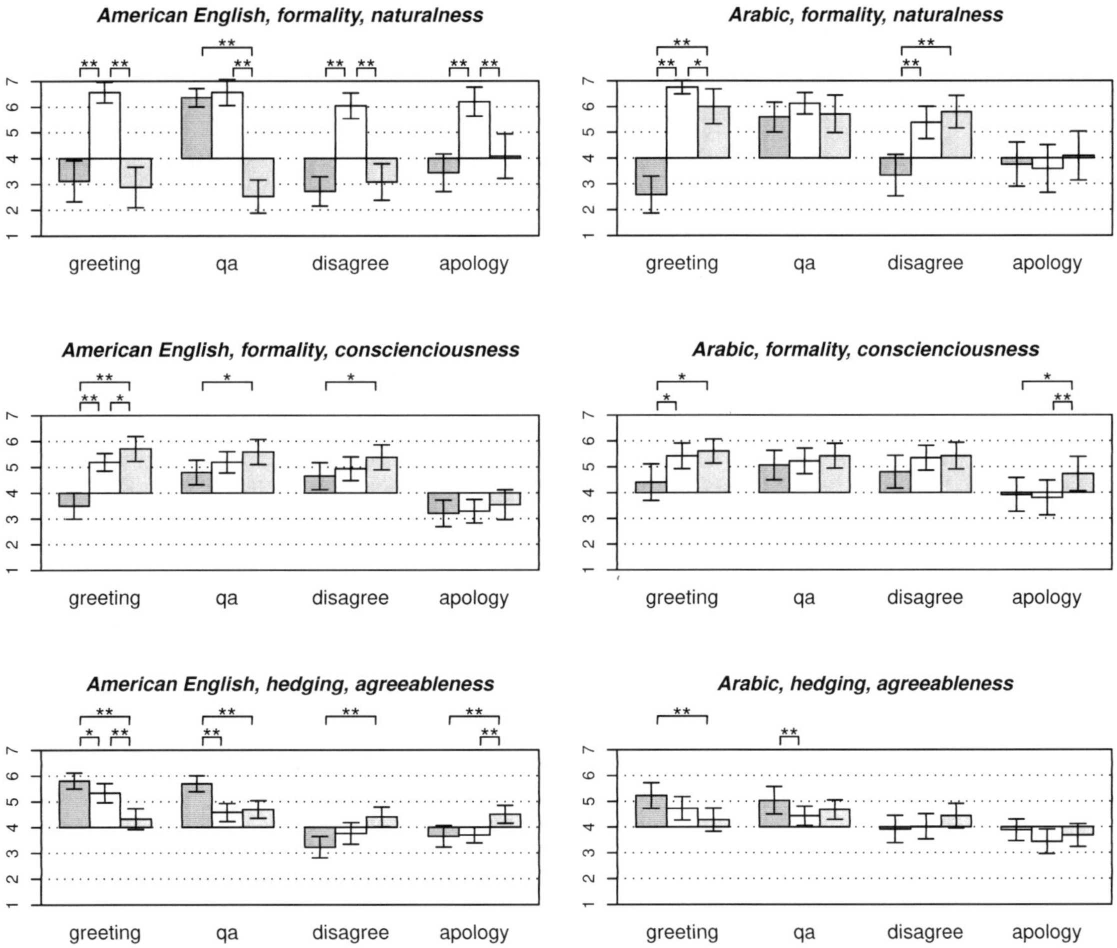

Figure 1: A subset of data comparing scores on the Big Five personality traits and naturalness as given by native speakers of American English (left half of the page) and Arabic (right half of the page). Blue, white, and pink bars correspond to negative, neutral, and positive valences of the linguistic features respectively. Dialogue acts listed along the horizontal axis are a greeting, question-answer pair, disagreement, and apology. Error bars the 95% confidence intervals, brackets above the plots correspond to p-values of paired t-tests at significance levels of 0.05 ($*$) and 0.01 ($**$) after Bonferroni correction.

Multi-Policy Dialogue Management

Pierre Lison
Logic and Natural Language Group
Department of Informatics
University of Oslo, Norway

Abstract

We present a new approach to dialogue management based on the use of multiple, interconnected policies. Instead of capturing the complexity of the interaction in a single large policy, the dialogue manager operates with a collection of small local policies combined concurrently and hierarchically. The meta-control of these policies relies on an activation vector updated before and after each turn.

1 Introduction

Many dialogue domains are naturally open-ended. This is especially the case in situated dialogue, where the conversational agent must operate in continuously changing environments where there is often no single, pre-specified goal to achieve. Depending on the situation and the (perceived) user requests, many distinct tasks may be performed. For instance, a service robot for the elderly might be used for cleaning, monitoring health status, and delivering information. Each of these tasks features a specific set of observations, goals, constraints, internal dynamics, and associated actions.

This diversity of tasks and models poses significant challenges for dialogue systems, and particularly for dialogue management. Open-ended interactions are indeed usually much more difficult to model than classical slot-filling applications, where the application domain can provide strong constraints on the possible dialogue transitions. Using machine learning techniques to learn the model parameters can help alleviate this issue, but only if the task can be efficiently factored and if a sufficient amount of data is available. Once a model of the interaction and its associated environment is available, a *control policy* then needs to be learned or designed for the resulting state space. The extraction of good control policies can be computationally challenging, especially for interactions which simultaneously combine *partial observability* (to deal with noisy and incomplete observations) and *large state spaces* (if the optimal behaviour depends on a wide range of user- and context-specific factors) – which is the case for many open-ended domains.

In this paper, we present ongoing work on a new approach to dialogue management which seeks to address these issues by leveraging prior knowledge about the interaction structure to break up the full domain into a set of smaller, more predictable subdomains. Moving away from the idea of capturing the full interaction complexity into a unique, monolithic policy, we extend the execution algorithm of the dialogue manager to directly operate with a *collection* of small, interconnected local policies.

Viewing dialogue management as a decision process over multiple policies has several benefits. First, it is usually easier for the application developer to model several small, local interactions than a single large one. Each local model can also be independently modified, extended or replaced without interfering with the rest of the system, which is crucial for system maintenance. Finally, different theoretical frameworks can be used for different policies, which means that the developer is free to decide which approach is most appropriate to solve a specific problem, without having to commit to a unique theoretical framework for the whole application. For instance, one policy might be expressed as a solution to a Partially Observable Markov Decision Process (POMDP) while another policy is encoded as a

Proceedings of the SIGDIAL 2011: the 12th Annual Meeting of the Special Interest Group on Discourse and Dialogue, pages 294–300,
Portland, Oregon, June 17-18, 2011.

hand-crafted finite-state controller, and the two can be integrated in the same control algorithm.

One of the challenges when operating with multiple policies is the "meta-control" of these policies. At each turn, the system must know which policy is currently in focus and is responsible for deciding the next action to perform. Since dialogue management operates under significant uncertainty, the system can never be sure whether a given policy is terminated or not. We thus need a "soft" *control mechanism* which is able to explicitly account for the uncertainty about the completion status of each policy. This is precisely what we present in this paper.

The rest of the paper is as follows. We first provide general definitions of dialogue policies, and present an algorithm for dialogue management operating on multiple policies. We then present an implementation of the algorithm together with an empirical evaluation of its performance, and conclude the paper by comparing our approach to related work.

2 Background

We start by providing a generic definition of a policy which can hold independently of any particular encoding. Dialogue policies can indeed generally be decomposed in three basic functions, which are called consecutively upon each turn: (1) *observation update*, (2) *action selection* and (3) *action update*.

2.1 Observation update

The role of *observation update* is to modify the policy's current state[1] upon receiving a new observation, which can be linguistic or extra-linguistic.

Observation update is formally defined as a function OBS-UPDATE : $\mathcal{S} \times \mathcal{O} \rightarrow \mathcal{S}$ which takes as input the current state s and a new observation o, and outputs the updated state s'. For instance, a finite-state controller is expressed by a set of nodes $\mathcal{N}$ and edges $\mathcal{E}$, where the state is expressed by the current node, and the update mechanism is defined as:

$$\text{OBS-UPDATE}(s, o) = \begin{cases} s' & \text{if } \exists \text{ an edge } s \xrightarrow{o} s' \\ s & \text{otherwise} \end{cases}$$

In information-state approaches (Larsson and Traum, 2000), the update is encoded in a collection of *update rules* which can be applied to infer the new state. In POMDP-based dialogue managers (Young et al., 2010), the observation update corresponds to the *belief monitoring/filtering* function.

2.2 Action selection

The second mechanism is *action selection*, whose role is to select the optimal (communicative) action to perform based on the new estimated state. The action selection is a function $\pi : \mathcal{S} \rightarrow \mathcal{A}$ which takes the updated state as input, and outputs the optimal action to execute (which might be void).

Different encodings are possible for the action selection mechanism. Finite-state controllers use a straightforward mechanism for π, since each state node in the graph is directly associated with a unique action. Information-state approaches provide a mapping between particular sets of states and actions by way of selection rules. Decision-theoretic approaches such as MDPs and POMDPs rely on an estimated *action-value function* which is to be maximised: $\pi(s) = \arg\max_a Q(s, a)$. The utility function $Q(s, a)$ can be either learned from experience or provided by the system designer.

2.3 Action update

Once the next action is selected and sent for execution, the final step is to re-update the dialogue state given the action. Contrary to the two previous functions which can be found in all approaches, this third mechanism is optional and is only implemented in some approaches to dialogue management.

Action update is formally defined as a function ACT-UPDATE : $\mathcal{S} \times \mathcal{A} \rightarrow \mathcal{S}$. Finite-state and information-state approaches typically have no explicit account of action update. In (PO)MDPs approaches, the action update function is computed with the *transition function* of the model.

3 Approach

3.1 Activation vector

To enable the dialogue manager to operate with multiple policies, we introduce the notion of *activation value*. The activation value of a policy i is the probability $P(\phi_i)$ that this policy is in focus for the interaction, where the random variable ϕ_i denote the activation of policy i. In the rest of this paper, we

[1] We adopt here a broad definition of the term "state" to express any description of the agent's current knowledge. In a POMDP, the state thus corresponds to the *belief state*.

shall use $b_t(\phi_i)$ to denote the activation value of policy ϕ at time t, given all available information. The $b_t(\phi_i)$ value is dependent on both the completion status of the policy itself and the activations of the other policies: $b_t(\phi_i) = P(\phi_i|s_i, b_t(\phi_1), ...b_t(\phi_n))$. We group these values in an *activation vector* $b_\Phi = \langle b(\phi_1)...b(\phi_n)\rangle$ which is updated after each turn.

3.2 Activation functions

To compute the activation values, we define the two following functions associated with each policy:

1. LIKELIHOOD$_i(s, o) : \mathcal{S} \times \mathcal{O} \rightarrow [0, 1]$ computes the *likelihood* of the observation o if the policy i is active and currently in state s. It is therefore an estimate of the probability $P(o|\phi_i, s)$.

2. ACTIVATION$_i(s) : \mathcal{S} \rightarrow [0, 1]$ is used to determine the probability of policy i being active at a given state s. In other words, it provides an estimate for the probability $P(\phi_i|s)$.

These functions are implemented using heuristics which depend on the encoding of the policy. For a finite-state controller, we realise the function LIKELIHOOD(s, o) by checking whether the observation matches one of the outward edges of the current state node – the likelihood returns a high probability if such a match exists, and a low probability otherwise. Similarly, the ACTIVATION function can be defined using the graph structure of the controller:

$$\text{ACTIVATION}(s) = \begin{cases} 1 & \text{if } s \text{ non-final} \\ \delta & \text{if } s \text{ final with outgoing edges} \\ 0 & \text{if } s \text{ final w/o outgoing edges} \end{cases}$$

where δ is a constant between 0 and 1.

3.3 Constraints between policies

In addition to these activation functions, various *constraints* can hold between the activation of related policies. Policies can be related with each other either *hierarchically* or *concurrently*.

In a *hierarchical mode*, a policy A triggers another policy B, which is then executed and returns the control to policy A once it is finished. As in hierarchical planning (Erol, 1996; Pineau, 2004), we implement such hierarchy by distinguishing between *primitive actions* and *abstract actions*. An abstract action is an action which corresponds to the execution of another policy instead of leading directly to a primitive action. With such abstract actions, the system designer can define a hierarchical structure of policies as illustrated in Figure 1. When a policy A executes an abstract action pointing to policy B, the activation value of policy B is increased and the one of policy A proportionally decreased. This remains so until policy B terminates, at which point the activation is then transferred back to policy A.

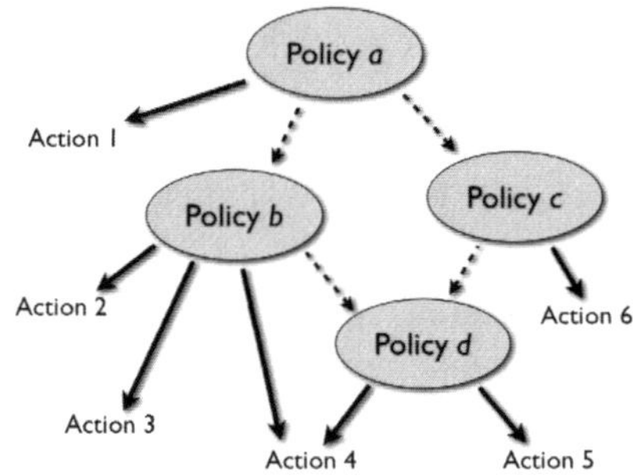

Figure 1: Graphical illustration of a hierarchical policy structure. Dotted lines denote abstract actions.

In a *concurrent mode*, policies stand on an equal footing. When a given policy takes the turn after an observation, the activations of all other concurrent policies are decreased to reflect the fact that this part of the interaction is now in focus. This redistribution of the activation mass allows us to run several policies in parallel while at the same time expressing a "preference" for the policy currently in focus. The "focus of attention" is indeed crucial in verbal interactions, and in linguistic discourse in general (Grosz and Sidner, 1986) – humans do not arbitrarily switch from one topic to another and back, but rather concentrate on the most salient elements.

The set of constraints holding between the activation values of hierarchical and concurrent policies is encoded in a simplified Bayesian network.

3.4 Execution algorithm

Algorithm 1 illustrates how the activation values are exploited to select the optimal action for multiple policies. The algorithm relies on a set of processes $\mathcal{P}$, where a process i is associated with a specific policy, a current state s_i for the policy, and a current activation value $b(\phi_i) \in b_\Phi$. As we have seen, each policy is fully described with five functions: LIKELIHOOD(s, o), OBS-UPDATE(s, o), $\pi(s)$, ACT-UPDATE(s, a), and ACTIVATION(s). A network of conditional constraints $\mathcal{C}$ on the activation vector is also given as input to the algorithm.

Algorithm 1 operates as follows. Upon receiving a new observation, the procedure loops over all processes in $\mathcal{P}$ and updates the activation values $b'(\phi_i)$ for each given the likelihood of the observation (with η as a normalisation factor). Once this update is completed, the process p with the highest activation is selected, and the function GET-OPTIMAL-ACTION(p, o) is triggered.

Algorithm 1 : MAIN-EXECUTION $(\mathcal{P}, o)$

Require: $\mathcal{P}$: the current set of processes
Require: $\mathcal{C}$: network of constraints on b_Φ
Require: o: a new observation

for all $i \in \mathcal{P}$ **do**
  $P(o|\phi_i, s_i) \leftarrow$ LIKELIHOOD$_i(s_i, o)$
  $b'(\phi_i) \leftarrow \eta \cdot P(o|\phi_i, s_i) \cdot b(\phi_i)$
end for
Select process $p \leftarrow \arg\max_i b'(\phi_i)$
$a^* \leftarrow$ GET-OPTIMAL-ACTION(p, o)
for all $i \in \mathcal{P}$ **do**
  $P(\phi_i|s_i) \leftarrow$ ACTIVATION$_i(s_i)$
  Prune i from $\mathcal{P}$ if inactive
  Compute $b(\phi_i)$ given $P(\phi_i|s_i)$ and $\mathcal{C}$
end for
return $a*$

Within GET-OPTIMAL-ACTION, the state of the process is updated given the observation, the next action a^* is selected using $\pi(s)$ and the state is updated again given this selection. If the action is abstract, the above-mentioned procedure is repeated until a primitive action is reached. The resulting hierarchical structure is recorded in children(p) which details, for each process $p \in \mathcal{P}$, the list of its children processes. To ensure consistency among the activation values in this hierarchy, a constraint is added to $\mathcal{C}$ for each process visited during execution.

Once the action a^* is found, the activation values $b(\phi_i)$ are recomputed according to the local activation function combined with the constraints $\mathcal{C}$. Processes which have become inactive (i.e. which have transferred control to one parent process) are also pruned from $\mathcal{P}$. Finally, the action a^* is returned.

Algorithm 2 : GET-OPTIMAL-ACTION (p, o)

Require: p: process with current state s_p
Require: o: a new observation
Require: children(p): list of current processes directly or indirectly forked from p

$s_p \leftarrow$ OBS-UPDATE$_p(s_p, o)$
$a^* \leftarrow \pi_p(s_p)$
$s_p \leftarrow$ ACT-UPDATE$_p(s_p, a^*)$
if a^* is an abstract action **then**
  Fork new process q with policy from a^*
  Add q to set of current processes $\mathcal{P}$
  $a^* \leftarrow$ GET-OPTIMAL-ACTION(q, o)
  children$(p) \leftarrow \langle q \rangle +$ children(q)
else
  children$(p) \leftarrow \langle\rangle$
end if
Add to $\mathcal{C}$ the constraint $b(\phi_p) = (1 - \sum_{i \in \text{children}(p)} b(\phi_i)) \cdot P(\phi_p|s_p)$
return $a*$

4 Evaluation

The described algorithm has been implemented and tested with different types of policies. We present here a preliminary experiment performed with a small dialogue domain. The domain consists of a (simulated) visual learning task between a human and a robot in a shared scene including a small number of objects, described by various properties such as color or shape. The human asks questions related to these object properties, and subsequently confirms or corrects the robot's answers – as the case may be. We account for the uncertainty both in the linguistic inputs and in the visual perception.

We model this domain with two connected policies, one top policy handling the general interaction (including engagement and closing acts), and one bottom policy dedicated to answering each user question. The top policy is encoded as a finite-state controller and the bottom policy as a POMDP solved using the SARSOP algorithm, available in the APPL toolkit[2] (Kurniawati et al., 2008). A sample run is provided in Appendix **A**.

The experiment was designed to empirically compare the performance of the presented algorithm

[2] http://bigbird.comp.nus.edu.sg/pmwiki/farm/appl/

with a simpler hierarchical control algorithm which does not use any activation vector, but where the top policy is blocked until the sub-policy releases its turn. The policies themselves remain identical in both scenarios. We implemented a handcrafted user simulator for the domain, and tested the policies with various levels of artificial noise.

The average return for the two scenarios are provided in Figure 2. The results show that activation values are beneficial for multi-policy dialogue management, especially in the presence of noise.. This is due to the soft control behaviour provided by the activation vector, which is more robust than hierarchical control. Activation values provide a more fine-grained mechanism for expressing the completion status of a policy, and therefore avoid fully "blocking" the control at a given level.

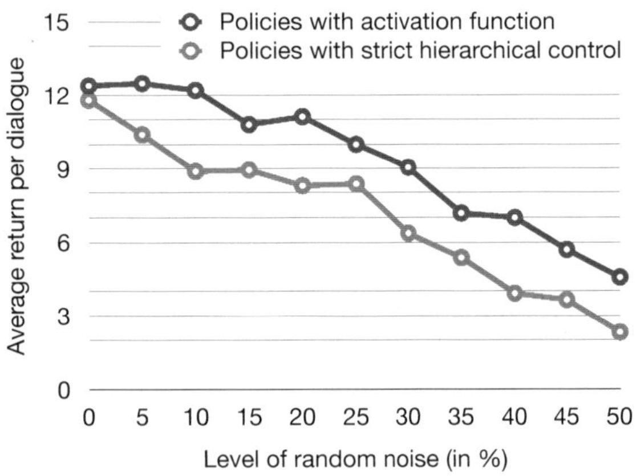

Figure 2: Average return (as generated by the handcrafted user simulator) for the two connected policies, using either the present algorithm or strict hierarchical control. 400 runs are used for each level of noise.

5 Related work

The exploitation of prior structural knowledge in control has a long history in the planning community (Erol, 1996; Hauskrecht et al., 1998), and has also been put forward in some approaches to dialogue modelling and dialogue management – see e.g. (Grosz and Sidner, 1990; Allen et al., 2000; Steedman and Petrick, 2007; Bohus and Rudnicky, 2009). These approaches typically rely on a task decomposition in goals and sub-goals, and assume that the completion of each of these goals can be fully observed. The novel aspect of our approach is precisely that we seek to relax this assumption of perfect knowledge of task completion. Instead, we treat the activation/termination status of a given policy as a *hidden variable* which is only indirectly observed and whose value at each turn is determined via probabilistic reasoning operations.

The idea of combining different dialogue management frameworks in a single execution process has also been explored in previous work such as (Williams, 2008), but only as a filtering mechanism – one policy constraining the results of another. Related to the idea of concurrent policies, (Turunen et al., 2005) describes a software framework for distributed dialogue management, mostly focussing on architectural aspects. In the same vein, (Lemon et al., 2002; Nakano et al., 2008) describe techniques for dialogue management respectively based on multi-threading and multi-expert models. (Cuayáhuitl et al., 2010) describe an reinforcement learning approach for the optimisation of hierarchical MDP policies, but is not extended to other types of policies. Closest to our approach is the PolCA+ algorithm for hierarchical POMDPs presented in (Pineau, 2004), but unlike our approach, her method does not support temporally extended actions, as the top-down trace is repeated after each time step.

6 Conclusion

We introduced a new approach to dialogue management based on multiple, interconnected policies controlled by activation values. The values are updated at the beginning and the end of each turn to reflect the part of the interaction currently in focus.

It is worth noting that the only modification required in the policy specifications to let them run in a multi-policy setting is the introduction of the two functions LIKELIHOOD(s, o) and ACTIVATION(s). The rest remains untouched and can be defined independently. The presented algorithm is therefore well suited for the integration of dialogue policies encoded in different theoretical frameworks.

Future work will focus on various extensions of the approach and the use of more extensive evaluation metrics. We are also investigating how to apply reinforcement learning techniques to learn the model parameters in such multi-policy paradigms.

Acknowledgements

This work was supported by the EU FP7 IP project "*'ALIZ-E: Adaptive Strategies for Sustainable Long-Term Social Interaction*" (FP7-ICT-248116) and by a PhD research grant from the University of Oslo. The author would like to thank Stephan Oepen, Erik Velldal and Alex Rudnicky for their comments and suggestions on earlier drafts of this paper.

References

J. Allen, D. Byron, M. Dzikovska, G. Ferguson, L: Galescu, and A. Stent. 2000. An architecture for a generic dialogue shell. *Natural Language Engineering*, 6:213–228, September.

D. Bohus and A. I. Rudnicky. 2009. The RavenClaw dialog management framework: Architecture and systems. *Computer Speech & Language*, 23:332–361, July.

H. Cuayáhuitl, S. Renals, O. Lemon, and H. Shimodaira. 2010. Evaluation of a hierarchical reinforcement learning spoken dialogue system. *Computer Speech & Language*, 24:395–429, April.

K. Erol. 1996. *Hierarchical task network planning: formalization, analysis, and implementation.* Ph.D. thesis, College Park, MD, USA.

B. J. Grosz and C. L. Sidner. 1986. Attention, intentions, and the structure of discourse. *Computational Linguistics*, 12:175–204, July.

B. J. Grosz and C. L. Sidner. 1990. Plans for discourse. In P. R. Cohen, J. Morgan, and M. E. Pollack, editors, *Intentions in Communication*, pages 417–444. MIT Press, Cambridge, MA.

M. Hauskrecht, N. Meuleau, L. P. Kaelbling, T. Dean, and C. Boutilier. 1998. Hierarchical solution of markov decision processes using macro-actions. In *Proceedings of Uncertainty in Artificial Intelligence (UAI)*, pages 220–229.

H. Kurniawati, D. Hsu, and W.S. Lee. 2008. SARSOP: Efficient point-based POMDP planning by approximating optimally reachable belief spaces. In *Proc. Robotics: Science and Systems.*

S. Larsson and D. R. Traum. 2000. Information state and dialogue management in the trindi dialogue move engine toolkit. *Natural Language Engineering*, 6:323–340, September.

O. Lemon, A. Gruenstein, A. Battle, and S. Peters. 2002. Multi-tasking and collaborative activities in dialogue systems. In *Proceedings of the 3rd SIGDIAL workshop on Discourse and Dialogue*, pages 113–124, Stroudsburg, PA, USA.

M. Nakano, K. Funakoshi, Y. Hasegawa, and H. Tsujino. 2008. A framework for building conversational agents based on a multi-expert model. In *Proceedings of the 9th SIGDIAL Workshop on Discourse and Dialogue*, pages 88–91, Stroudsburg, PA, USA.

J. Pineau. 2004. *Tractable Planning Under Uncertainty: Exploiting Structure.* Ph.D. thesis, Robotics Institute, Carnegie Mellon University, Pittsburgh, PA.

M. Steedman and R. P. A. Petrick. 2007. Planning dialog actions. In *Proceedings of the 8th SIGDIAL Workshop on Discourse and Dialogue (SIGdial 2007)*, pages 265–272, Antwerp, Belgium, September.

M. Turunen, J. Hakulinen, K.-J. Räihä, E.-P. Salonen, A. Kainulainen, and P. Prusi. 2005. An architecture and applications for speech-based accessibility systems. *IBM Syst. J.*, 44:485–504, August.

J. D. Williams. 2008. The best of both worlds: Unifying conventional dialog systems and POMDPs. In *International Conference on Speech and Language Processing (ICSLP 2008)*, Brisbane, Australia.

S. Young, M. Gašić, S. Keizer, F. Mairesse, J. Schatzmann, B. Thomson, and K. Yu. 2010. The hidden information state model: A practical framework for pomdp-based spoken dialogue management. *Computer Speech & Language*, 24:150–174, April.

A Example of execution with two policies

We provide here an example of execution of Algorithm 1 with the two policies described in the evaluation section. Figure 3 illustrates the policy hierarchy, which consists of two policies connected with an abstract action. The finite-state graph of the top policy is shown in Figure 4.

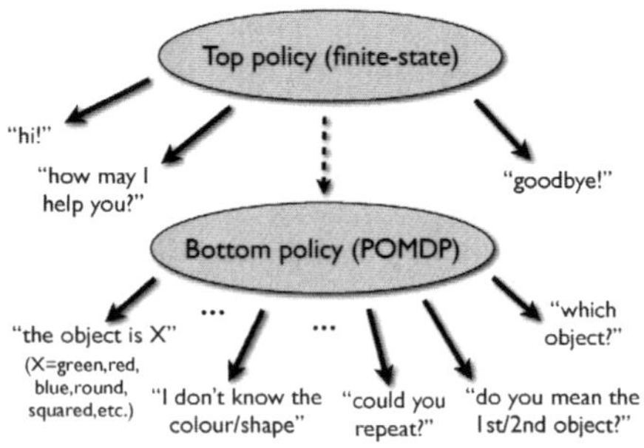

Figure 3: Hierarchical structure of the two policies.

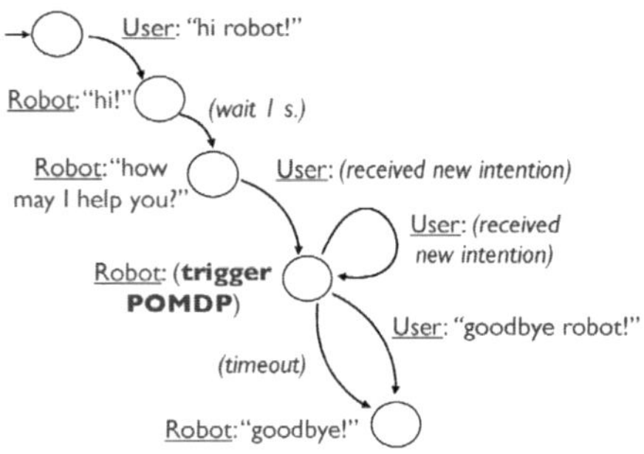

Figure 4: Finite-state controller for the top policy.

A.1 Example of interaction

Transcript A.1 provides a full example of interaction as generated by the user simulator. Human utterances can contain variable noise levels, which makes it necessary to use clarification requests when the user intention is unclear (lines 5 and 10).

Contextual knowledge can also influence how the dialogue unfolds – here, the robot knows that the first object is blue but is uncertain about the second object. Such contextual knowledge is expressed in terms of hidden variables in the POMDP model.

The execution of Algorithm 1 for the above example proceeds as follows. From line 1 to line 4, the set $\mathcal{P}$ contains one single process, based on the top policy. This process is fully activated. At line 5, the new user intention is mapped to the abstract action, and thus to the creation of a second process based the POMDP policy. This second process becomes highly activated due its function ACTIVATION(s). Given the constraint holding between the activation values of two processs, the high activation of the bottom process leads to a proportional reduction of the activation value of the top process.

The utterance at line 8 is interpreted as a signal that the user intention has been met, and the activation value of the bottom process is subsequently decreased. The top process is then partially reactivated, and interprets the utterance at line 9 as a new user intention, leading to the creation of a new POMDP process. This process handles the interaction until the line 14, where the control is transferred back to the finite-state controller.

The better performance of Algorithm 1 compared to strict hierarchical control is due to the lines 8 – 9. In the presence of noise, the transition to the second question might not be detected (if the confidence scores of the utterance is below a fixed threshold). In such case, the dialogue manager might stay "stuck" in the first POMDP process instead of interpreting the utterance as a new question.

Transcript A.1 Example of interaction

1: HUMAN: Hi robot!
2: ROBOT: Hi! [*wait 1 s.*]
3: ROBOT: How may I help you?
4: HUMAN: Could you tell me the colour of the first object? [*trigger POMDP*]
5: ROBOT: Sorry, could you repeat?
6: HUMAN: What colour is the first object?
7: ROBOT: It is blue
8: HUMAN: That's right
9: HUMAN: Now, could you tell me the colour of the second object? [*trigger POMDP*]
10: ROBOT: Do you mean the second object?
11: HUMAN: Yes
12: ROBOT: I don't know
13: HUMAN: It is green
14: ROBOT: Thanks
15: HUMAN: Ok I'm done. Goodbye!
16: ROBOT: Goodbye! [*close interaction*]

A Robotic World Model Framework Designed to Facilitate Human-robot Communication

Meghann Lomas, E. Vincent Cross II, Jonathan Darvill, R. Christopher Garrett, Michael Kopack, and Kenneth Whitebread
Lockheed Martin Advanced Technology Laboratories
3 Executive Campus, Suite 600, Cherry Hill, NJ 08002
1 856.792.9681
{mlomas, ecross, jdarvill, rgarrett, mkopack, kwhitebr}@atl.lmco.com

Abstract

We describe a novel world model framework designed to support situated human-robot communication through improved mutual knowledge about the physical world. This work focuses on enabling a robot to store and use semantic information from a human located in the same environment as the robot and respond using human-understandable terminology. This facilitates information sharing between a robot and a human and subsequently promotes team-based operations. Herein, we present motivation for our world model, an overview of the world model, a discussion of proof-of-concept simulations, and future work.

1 Introduction

As robots become more ubiquitous, their interactions with humans must become more natural and intuitive for humans. One of the main challenges to natural human-robot interaction is the "language barrier" between humans and robots. While a considerable amount of work has gone into making robot dialogue more human-like (Fong et al., 2005), the content of the conversation is frequently highly scripted.

An essential precondition to intuitive human-robot dialogue is the establishment of a common ground of understanding between humans and robots (Kiesler, 2005). Operators expect information to be presented in a way such that they can connect it with their own world information. This implies a need for robots to be capable of expressing information in human-understandable terms. By shifting some responsibility for establishing common ground to robots, interactions between humans and robots become considerably more natural for humans by reducing the need for humans to "translate" the robot's information.

Ultimately, the robot's world model is a key contributor to the "language barrier." Because humans and robots view and think about the world differently (having different "sensors" and "processing algorithms"), they subsequently have different world representations (Figure 1). Humans tend to think of the world as objects in space, while robotic representations vary based on sensors, but are typically coordinate-based representations of

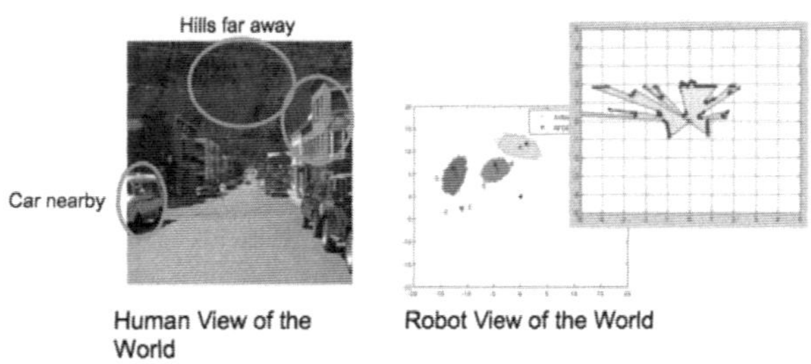

Figure 1. Humans and robots think and subsequently communicate about the world using different terminology.

Proceedings of the SIGDIAL 2011: the 12th Annual Meeting of the Special Interest Group on Discourse and Dialogue, pages 301–306,
Portland, Oregon, June 17-18, 2011.

free and occupied space. This presents a considerable challenge when humans want to communicate naturally with robots. For robots to become active partners for humans, they must be better able to share the information they have gathered about the world. To that end, we have begun to address the "language barrier" by focusing on how information is stored by the robot.

We have developed a novel world model representation that will enable a robot to merge information communicated by its human teammates with its own situational awareness data and use the resulting "operating picture" to drive planning and decision-making for navigation in unfamiliar environments. The ultimate aim of this research is to enable robots to communicate with humans *and* maintain an "actionable awareness" of the environment. This provides a number of benefits:

- *Increased robot situational awareness.* The robots will be able to learn about, store, and recall environmental information obtained from humans (or other robots). This can include information the robot would be incapable of getting on its own, either because it has not visited that region of the environment or because it is not capable of sensing that information.
- *Increased human situational awareness.* Humans will be able to receive information from robots in human-understandable terms.
- *Reduced workload and training for human-robot interaction.* Because robots will be able to communicate in human-understandable terms, people will be able to interact with robots in ways that are more natural to humans. As a result, people will need fewer specialized interfaces to interact with robots and subsequently less training.
- *Improved collaboration.* Because people and robots will be able to share information, the team will be able to operate more efficiently. Each team member will be able to contribute to team knowledge, which will allow for better planning.

2 World Model Overview

Our world model framework was designed using several key principles: that information must be stored in both human-understandable terms and in a format usable by the robot; that information must be capable of being added, deleted, or modified during operations; and that the world model framework should be capable of integrating with a wide variety of external systems including preexisting perception and planning systems.

To meet these principles, we have developed a layered framework that has internal functions for managing the world model and can integrate with external systems that use the world model, such as systems that populate it (perception systems) or use it to govern robotic actions (planning systems) (Figure 2).

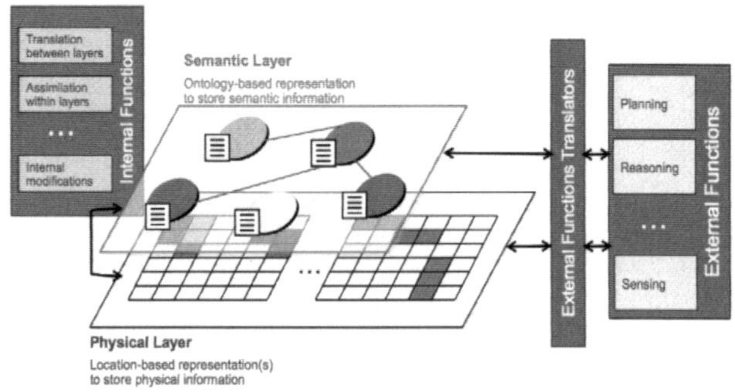

Figure 2. We have developed a two-layer world model that integrates with external functions via translation functions to support the use of a variety of robotic capabilities.

Layered world models have shown promise for both robot navigation (Kuipers and Byun, 1991; Mataric, 1990) and for communication with humans (Kennedy et al., 2007; Zender et al., 2008). Additionally, work in symbol grounding has supported robotic actions based on natural language interactions (Jacobsson et al., 2008, Hsiao et al., 2008). We leverage this research and extend it with the aim of supporting human-robot information sharing, robot navigation, and use by external systems.

The bottom layer stores a spatiotemporal description of the environment expressed in metrical terms. While there are several different possibilities for how this location-based information could be stored, we use a grid-based representation because it is commonly used by existing planners (e.g., a cost map-based planner) and it allows for flexibility of information storage. While our framework supports the inclusion of an arbitrary number of grids, our experimental prototype uses three: an occupancy grid that stores free and occupied space, an "object" grid, and a "terrain" grid. The object grid stores the types of objects in each cell in ascending order of vertical position (e.g., "table, plate, apple"). The terrain grid stores terrain type in each cell and may also have multiple entries per cell (e.g., "sand, boulders" or "grass").

The top layer stores a relational description of the situation in semantic terms compatible with typical human descriptions of the physical environment. We use node-attribute structures in which objects (e.g., chairs, keys, trees, people, buildings) are represented as nodes that have a list of corresponding attributes (e.g., type, color, GPS coordinates, last time sensed, source of information, etc.). The nodes are connected by their relationships, which are human-understandable concepts (e.g., "near" or "above"). The graph form of the semantic layer supports the many, varied types of relationships between objects. There are many ways to express the physical relationships between objects, and humans often use ambiguous terms (Crangle et al., 1987). By establishing the semantic layer as a connected graph, we aim to support these ambiguous terms and ultimately provide a way for the robot to process their meaning.

In the top layer of the world model, we use an ontological representation to model the world, and include both an "upper ontology" that provides a template for what information can be included in the world as well as an instantiated world built from experience. In addition to providing a framework that stores the list of all objects that could be present in the world, their associated attributes, and the possible relationship between the objects, this upper layer includes other information such as the robot's goals and current high level plans and additional information the robot has about itself or the world (e.g., domain theory or object affordances). An additional benefit of an ontology-based representation is that it supports the inclusion of objects despite uncertainty. If a perception algorithm cannot confidently identify an object but can classify it, this class of object can be stored in the semantic layer of the world model and refined as more information is made available.

To support a consistent, complete view of the world, translation functions translate the information between the layers and assimilation functions merge information within layers. These translation functions support symbol grounding and enable the robot to use both semantically-described information along with sensed data. The translation functions are a set of functions, each of which translates an attribute, for example, a color translation function that translates between RGB values and a semantic label. More interesting are the location-based translation functions, for example "near A" translates to "within 2 meters of A's position." This introduces uncertainty into the position of the object and so we use a probabilistic approach for placing any unsensed (but described) object in the bottom layer. The location of the object is updated once the object is sensed by the robot.

The assimilation algorithms, which are also still in development, are built upon data fusion ideas because they merge data from multiple sources. Because a considerable amount of existing work has been done on integrating (assimilating) information at the sensor level, to date we have focused on assimilation in the semantic layer of our world model. We have developed heuristic-based algorithms that compare information stored in the world model with actively sensed information (essentially creating a temporary world model of the area currently being sensed by the robot). During operation, the robot's sensor detects an object and outputs a vector of possible object classifications. Each object classification has an associated confidence along with attributes of the object including size, color, etc. The assimilation component pulls all objects within a prescribed radius of the newly sensed object's location from the world model to compare them with the newly sensed object. The assimilation algorithm starts with the object closest in position to the newly sensed object and stops comparing objects if an object is determined to be "same as" the newly sensed object or if all objects with the prescribed radius are compared and none match.

To compare our newly sensed object with one of the objects already in the world model, the assimilation algorithm compares the object vectors, which contain the list and confidence in each object type and object attributes such as color, size, and location. Some attributes (like source of information) are ignored in this calculation. To compare two objects, we compute the distance between the object vectors. This distance is computed through a pairwise comparison of attributes in the vector lists. These distances are then weighted according to "importance" in assimilation process, for example objects with similar type should be more likely to be merged than objects that only have similar color. We then sum the weighted distances; if sum is less than a prescribed threshold, we assume the objects are the same and then merge them. If not the same, the algorithm checks this object against the other objects within the radius and if none are found, adds the object as a new object. To merge objects, the algorithm merges the attribute vectors of the temporary object and the original object. Some parts of the vectors are averaged (e.g., color), some amalgamated (e.g., data source), and some pick one of the values (e.g., pick most recent time). Additionally, because it is stored in the world model, we can incorporate logic about the world to facilitate assimilation (e.g., "this object is immovable so it must not have changed position"). While this algorithm has served as an initial assimilation algorithm, we will continue researching and designing assimilation algorithms to better support the uncertainty present in the sensing outputs (e.g., false positives).

One of the key requirements of our world model is that it be able to integrate with external robotic systems. To accomplish this, the world model layers integrate with external functions that serve as translators to existing (or future) functions. These external translation functions pull relevant information from the world model and present it in a form usable by a planner. For example, we have created a planning translator that takes the grids from the physical layer and produces a cost map for a ground robot (with set parameters), which can then be used by any cost map-based planner.

3 Proof-of-Concept Simulations

To evaluate the feasibility of our world model framework, we performed several proof-of-concept simulations designed to both demonstrate and test the capabilities of our world model and subsequently to help the design process. We created different environments using Player/Stage and ran the robot through two scenarios. In both scenarios, humans needed robotic assistance to escape from a burning building and communicated with the robot using natural language. In the first scenario, a mobile robot was asked by a group of trapped people to unlock a door and alert them when the door was open. In the second scenario, two mobile robots were tasked with searching for trapped people and coordinating with first responders. Because the focus of the simulations was on evaluating the world model itself, we made the assumption that the robot had both camera and LIDAR sensors and had processing algorithms capable of outputting an object classification and a confusion matrix. We assumed the robot had both a speech processing and synthesis mechanism with which it could communicate verbally with people in the environment. We assumed the robot had a common A* planner that used a cost map representation for planning.

The first scenario highlighted the ability for the robot to understand and use human-communicated information by adding a human-described object to its world model and planning based on this assimilated information. At the beginning of the scenario, a human described the location of a key ("near the desk in the room with one table and one desk") and told the robot to open the locked east door. The human did not tell the robot to use the key to unlock the door, instead the robot used object affordances stored in its world model to establish a high-level plan of getting the key, then unlocking the door. When the human told the robot about the location of the key, the robot stored this location in the top layer and translated the object's position down to the bottom layer using a probabilistic translation algorithm that placed the key in the bottom layer at the most likely position within a certain region (whose size and position corresponded to "nearness"). The robot used a simple cost map-based planner to plan its movements and so the system created a cost map from all the relevant bottom layer information in a format used by a classic A* planner. As a result, this scenario showed that our world model enabled the robot to use information gathered by a human teammate and expressed in semantic terminology without a specially designed planner.

The second scenario illustrated the merits of our world model for *responding* to humans. In this scenario, once the robot had searched the environment, it was asked a series of questions by a first responder including: "How many people did you find?" and "How do I get to the fire extinguisher?" The latter question was particularly interesting because it forced the robot to describe a path in semantic terminology (as opposed to a list of waypoints). The robot used information from its top layer to describe the path from the first responder's current position to the fire extinguisher. This scenario highlighted the ability for the robot to produce human-understandable and useful information despite having gathered the information using its low-level sensors and planner.

In both of the scenarios, the robot was given both instructions and information verbally from one or more of the people in the robot's environment. The robot stored this described information in the world model and merged it with the information the robot had gathered with its own sensors to form a cohesive view of the world. The robot then used both the described and sensed information to formulate a plan to accomplish its goals. At the end of the mission, the robot was asked questions about the environment and was able to answer using *human understandable* terminology.

In these simulations we were able to show the robot formulating a plan based on information it had not sensed by itself. Because the robot had only a simple cost map-based planner, it was essential that the semantic information be translated to the grid representations in the bottom layer. This allowed the planning translator to produce a cost map in the form expected by the planner.

We used these simulations to inform key design decisions including the need to have multiple grids in the bottom layer of the world model and to incorporate object affordances in the semantic layer. Another key insight was that uncertainty must be included in the semantic layer and that it is an important element in semantic layer assimilation.

4 Conclusions and Future Work

We have designed and developed a world model framework that supports situated information sharing between robots and humans. By integrating semantic and sensor-based terminology, we have enabled a robot to integrate information described in natural human terms with its own sensed information. In addition, we have shown how a robot with a standard A* planning algorithm can thereby plan and respond appropriately using information obtained in semantic terms.

Because this world model framework was designed to support a variety of robotic operations and capabilities, there are many areas of potential future work. These include facilitating robotic dialogue systems, developing reasoning systems that can use the semantic level information to predict certain aspects of the world model (such as how an event will affect the physical layout of the world or where an object will be in a certain amount of time), and enabling semantic-level planners that can perform high-level planning.

To further improve the functionality supported by this world model framework, there are a number of areas of future work within the framework itself. We are exploring the design changes needed to support modeling of dynamic objects and the types of assimilation algorithms that exist or need to be developed to truly integrate tracks generated by external perception systems into our world model. We are also looking into how to better reason about spatial relationships, particularly those that are only true when described from a specific vantage point. Additionally, we would like to improve the translation algorithms by exploring additional scenarios and determining what mechanisms are needed. In the area of multi-robot coordination, we want to explore physical layer assimilation, which includes the ability to align reference frame for heterogeneous robots. Finally, we would also like to apply our world model on multiple real robots with speech systems and evaluate the world model in a series of real-world operations.

References

Terrence W. Fong, Illah Nourbakhsh, Robert Ambrose, Reid Simmons, Alan Schultz, and Jean Scholtz. The peer-to-peer human-robot interaction project. AIAA Space, 2005.

S. Kiesler. Fostering common ground in human-robot interaction. Robot and Human Interactive Communication Proceedings. ROMAN 2005. The 14th IEEE International Workshop. Nashville, TE. Aug 2005.

Benjamin Kuipers and Yung-Tai Byun. A robot exploration and mapping strategy based on a semantic hierarchy of spatial representation. Journal of Robotics and Autonomous Systems, 8:47–63, 1991.

Maja Mataric. A distributed model for mobile robot environment-learning and navigation. Technical Report, MIT Artificial Intelligence Laboratory, 1990.

William G. Kennedy, Magdalena D. Bugajska, Matthew Marge, William Adams, Benjamin R. Fransen, Dennis Perzanowski, Alan C. Schultz, and J. Gregory Trafton. Spatial representation and reasoning for human-robot collaboration. In Proceedings of the

Twenty-Second Conference on Artificial Intelligence, 2007.

C. Crangle, P. Suppes, and S. Michalowski. Types of verbal interaction with instructable robots. In Proceedings of the Workshop on Space Telerobotics, Vol 2, 1987.

H. Zender, O. Martinez Mozos, P. Jenselt, G.-J. M. Kruijff, and W. Burgard. Conceptual Spatial Representations for Indoor Mobile Robots. Robotics and Autonomous Systems, Special Issue "From Sensors to Human Spatial Concepts." Vol. 56, Issue 6. pp. 493-502. Elsevier. June 2008.

H. Jacobsson, N. Hawes, G-J. Kruijff, J. Wyatt, Cross-modal Content Binding in Information-Processing Architectures. Proceedings of the 3rd ACM/IEEE International Conference on Human-Robot Interaction (HRI). March 2008. Amsterdam, The Netherlands.

Kai-yuh Hsiao, Soroush Vosoughi, Stefanie Tellex, Rony Kubat, Deb Roy. (2008). Object Schemas for Responsive Robotic Language Use. Proceedings of the 3rd ACM/IEEE International Conference on Human-Robot Interaction, pages 233-240.

Improving Pronominal and Deictic Co-Reference Resolution with Multi-Modal Features

Lin Chen, Anruo Wang, Barbara Di Eugenio
Department of Computer Science
University of Illinois at Chicago
851 S Morgan ST, Chicago, IL 60607, USA
{lchen43,awang28,bdieugen}@uic.edu

Abstract

Within our ongoing effort to develop a computational model to understand multi-modal human dialogue in the field of elderly care, this paper focuses on pronominal and deictic co-reference resolution. After describing our data collection effort, we discuss our annotation scheme. We developed a co-reference model that employs both a simple notion of markable type, and multiple statistical models. Our results show that knowing the type of the markable, and the presence of simultaneous pointing gestures improve co-reference resolution for personal and deictic pronouns.

1 Introduction

Our ongoing research project, called RoboHelper, focuses on developing an interface for older people to effectively communicate with a robotic assistant that can help them perform *Activities of Daily Living (ADLs)* (Krapp, 2002), so that they can safely remain living in their home (Di Eugenio et al., 2010). We are devising a multi-modal interface since people communicate with one another using a variety of verbal and non-verbal signals, including haptics, i.e., force exchange (as when one person hands a bowl to another person, and lets go only when s/he senses that the other is holding it). We have collected a mid size multi-modal human-human dialogue corpus, that we are currently processing and analyzing. Meanwhile, we have started developing one core component of our multi-modal interface, a co-reference resolution system. In this paper, we will present the component of the system that resolves pronouns, both personal (*I, you, it, they*), and deictic (*this, that, these, those, here, there*). Hence, this paper presents our first steps toward a full co-reference resolution module, and ultimately, the multi-modal interface.

Co-reference resolution is likely the discourse and dialogue processing task that has received the most attention. However, as Eisenstein and Davis (2006) notes, research on co-reference resolution has mostly been applied to written text; this task is more difficult in dialogue. First, utterances may be informal, ungrammatical or disfluent; second, people spontaneously use hand gestures, body gestures and gaze. Pointing gestures are the easiest gestures to identify, and vision researchers in our project are working on recognizing pointing and other hand gestures (Di Eugenio et al., 2010). In this paper, we replicate the results from (Eisenstein and Davis, 2006), that pointing gestures help improve co-reference, in a very different domain. Other work has shown that gestures can help detect sentence boundaries (Chen and Harper, 2010) or user intentions (Qu and Chai, 2008).

The rest of the paper is organized as follows. In Section 2 we describe the data collection and the ongoing annotation. In Section 3 we discuss our co-reference resolution system, and we present experiments and results in Section 4.

2 The ELDERLY-AT-HOME corpus

Due to the absence of multi-modal collaborative human-human dialogue corpora that include haptic data beyond what can be acquired via point-and-touch interfaces, and in the population of interest,

Proceedings of the SIGDIAL 2011: the 12th Annual Meeting of the Special Interest Group on Discourse and Dialogue, pages 307–311,
Portland, Oregon, June 17-18, 2011.

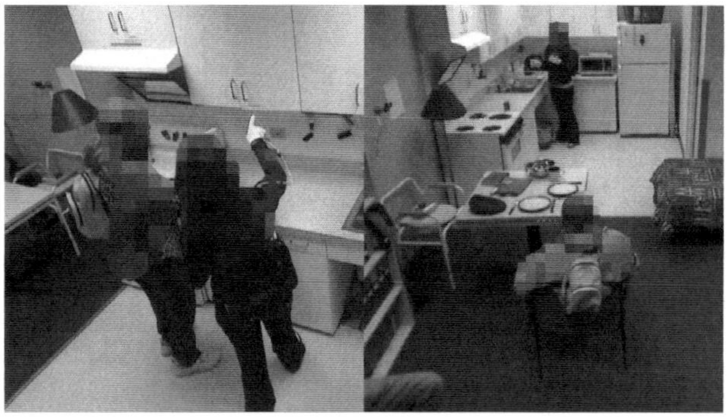

Figure 1: Experiment Excerpts

we undertook a new data collection effort. Our experiments were conducted in a fully functional studio apartment at Rush University in Chicago – Figure 1 shows two screen-shots from our recorded experiments. We equipped the room with 7 web cameras to ensure multiple points of view. Each of the two participants in the experiments wears a microphone, and a data glove on their dominant hand to collect haptics data. The ADLs we focused on include ambulating, getting up from a bed or a chair, finding pots, opening cans and containers, putting pots on a stove, setting the table etc. Two students in gerontological nursing play the role of the helper (HEL), both in pilot studies and with real subjects. In 5 pilot dialogues, two faculty members played the role of the elderly person (ELD). In the 15 real experiments, ELD resides in an assisted living facility and was transported to the apartment mentioned above. All elderly subjects are highly functioning at a cognitive level and do not have any major physical impairment.

The size of our collected video data is shown in Table 1. The number of subjects refers to the number of different ELD's and does not include the helpers; we do include our 5 pilot dialogues though, since those pilot interactions do not measurably differ from those with the real subjects. Usually one experiment lasts about 50' (recording starts after informed consent and after the microphones and data gloves have been put on). Further, we eliminated irrelevant content such as interruptions, e.g. by the person who accompanied the elderly subjects, and further explanations of the tasks. This resulted in about 15 minutes of what we call *effective* data for each subject; the effective data comprises 4782 turns (see Table 1).

Subjects	Raw(Mins)	Effective(Mins)	Turns
20	482	301	4782

Table 1: ELDERLY-AT-HOME Corpus Size

The effective portion of the data was transcribed by the first two authors using the Anvil video annotation tool (Kipp, 2001). A subset of the transcribed data was annotated for co-reference, yielding 114 sub-dialogues corresponding to the tasks subjects perform, such as finding bowls, filling a pot with water, etc. (see Table 2).

An annotation excerpt is shown in Figure 2. Markable tokens are classified into *PLC(Place)*, *PERS(Person)*, *OBJ(Object)* types, and numbered by type, e.g., PLC#5. Accordingly, we mark pronouns with types as well, *RPLC, RPERS, ROBJ*, e.g. RPLC#5. If a subject produced a pointing gesture, we generate a markable token to mark what is being pointed to at the end of the utterance (see Utt. 4 and 5 in Figure 2). Within the same task, if two markables have the same type and the same markable index, they are taken to co-refer (hence, longer chains of reference across tasks are cut into shorter spans).

Haptics annotation is at the beginning. We have identified *grab*, *hold*, *give* and *receive* as high-level haptics phonemes that may be useful from the language point of view. We have recently started annotating our corpus with those labels.

Subjects	Tasks	Utterances	Gestures	Pronouns
12	114	1920	896	1635

Table 2: Annotated Corpus Size

In order to test the reliability of our annotation, we double coded about 18% of the data, namely 21 sub-dialogues comprising 213 pronouns, on which we computed the Kappa coefficient (Carletta, 1996). Similar to (Rodrıguez et al., 2010), we measured the reliability of **markable** annotations, and of **link to the antecedent** annotations. As concerns the **markable** level, we obtained κ=0.945, which is high but no surprisingly for such a simple task. At the **link to the antecedent** level, we compared the links from pronouns to antecedents in a specified context of 4 utterances, obtaining a reasonable κ=0.723.

3: PERS#1(HEL/NNP) : RPERS#1(I/PRP) do/VBP n't/RB see/VB any/DT OBJ#3(pasta/NN) ./.
4: PERS#2(ELD/NNP) : Try/VB over/IN RPLC#5(there/RB) ./. {PLC#5(cabinet/NN)}
5: PERS#1(HEL/NNP) : This/DT RPLC#5(**one/NN**) ?/. {PLC#5(cabinet/NN)}
6: PERS#2(ELD/NNP) : Oh/UH ,/, yes/RB ./.

Figure 2: Annotation Excerpt

3 Our approach

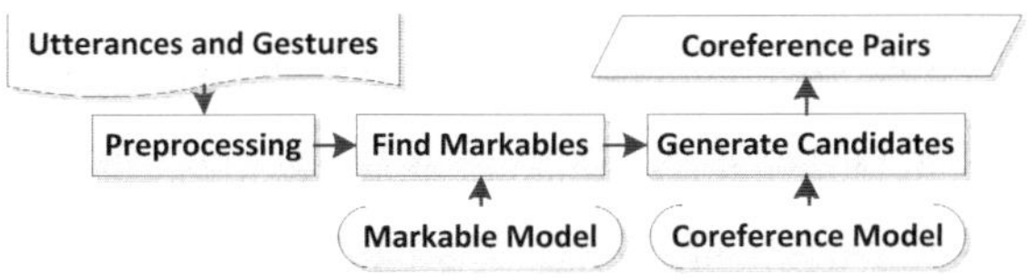

Figure 3: Co-reference System Architecture

The architecture of our co-reference resolution system is shown in Figure 3.

We first pre-process a dialogue by splitting turns into sentences, tokenizing sentences into tokens, POS tagging tokens. The *Markable* model is used to classify whether a token can be referred to and what type of markable it is. The *Markable* model's feature set includes the POS tag of the token, the word, the surrounding tokens' POS tags in a window size of 3. The model outputs markable classes: Place/Object/Person, or None, which means the token is not markable. A pointed-to entity serves as a markable by default.

To perform resolution, each pronoun to be resolved (*I, you, it, they; this, that, these, those, here, there*) is paired with markables in the context of the previous 2 utterances, the current utterance and the utterance that follows, by using {pronoun, markable type} compatibility rules. For example, let's consider the excerpt in Figure 2. To resolve *one* in utterance 5, the system will generate 3 candidate token pairs: <one(5,2), pasta(3,6)>, <one(5,2), cabinet(4,-1)>, <one(5,2), cabinet(5,-1)> (including the pointed-to markable is a way of roughly approximating information that will be returned by the vision component). The elements in those pairs are tokens with their coordinates in the format (*SentenceIndex, TokenIndex*); markables pointed to are given negative token indices.

The *Co-reference* model will filter out the pairs <pronoun, markable> that it judges to be incorrect. For the *Co-reference* model, we adopted a subset of features which are commonly used in co-reference resolution in written text. These features apply to each <pronoun, markable> pair and include: *Lexical* features, i.e. words and POS tags for both anaphora and antecedent; *Syntactic* features, i.e. syntactic constraints such as number and person agreement; *Distance* features, i.e. sentence distance, token distance and markable distance. Additionally, the Co-reference model uses pointing gesture information. If the antecedent in the <pronoun, markable> was pointed to, the pair is tagged as *Is-Pointed*. In our data, people often use pronouns and hand gestures instead of nouns when introducing new entities. It is not possible to map these pronouns to a textual antecedent since none exists. This confirms the findings from (Kehler, 2000): in a multi-modal corpus, he found that no pronoun is used *without* a gesture when it refers to a referent which is not in focus.

4 Experiments and Discussion

The classification models described above were implemented using the Weka package (Hall et al., 2009). Specifically, for each model, we experimented with J48 (a decision tree implementation) and LibSVM (a Support Vector Machine implementation). All the results reported below are calculated using 10 fold cross-validation.

We evaluated the performances of individual models separately (Tables 3 and 4), and of the system as a whole (Table 5).

Algorithm	Precision	Recall	F-Measure
J48	0.984	0.984	0.984
LibSVM	0.979	0.936	0.954
Baseline	0.971	0.971	0.971

Table 3: Markable Model Performance

The results in Table 3 are not surprising, since detecting the type of markables is a simple task. Indeed the results of the baseline model are extremely

Method	J48			LibSVM		
	Precision	Recall	F-Measure	Precision	Recall	F-Measure
Text + Gesture	0.700	0.684	0.686	0.672	0.669	0.670
Text Only	0.655	0.656	0.656	0.624	0.624	0.624

Table 4: Co-reference Model Performance

Words	Method	Features	Precision	Recall	F-Measure
All Pronouns	J48	Text Only	0.544	0.332	0.412
		Text + Gesture	0.482	0.783	0.596
	LibSVM	Text Only	0.56	0.27	0.364
		Text + Gesture	0.522	0.6	0.559
	Baseline	Text Only	0.367	0.254	0.300
		Text + Gesture	0.376	0.392	0.384
3rd Person + Deictic	J48	Text Only	0.264	0.028	0.05
		Text + Gesture	0.438	0.902	0.589
	LibSVM	Text Only	0.6	0.009	0.017
		Text + Gesture	0.525	0.695	0.598
	Baseline	Text Only	0.172	0.114	0.137
		Text + Gesture	0.301	0.431	0.354

Table 5: Co-reference System Performance (Markable + Co-reference Models)

high as well. We compute the baseline by assigning to the potential markable (i.e., each word) its most frequent class in the training set (recall that the four classes include *None* as well).

For the *Co-reference* model, we conducted 2 sets of experiments to ascertain the effect of including *Gesture* in the model. As shown in Table 4, both J48 and LibSVM obtain better results when we include gestures in the model. χ^2 shows that differences in precision and recall [1] are significant at the $p \leq 0.01$ level, though the absolute improvement is not high.

As concerns the evaluation of the whole system, we ran a 4-way experiment, where we examine the performance of the system on all pronouns, and on those pronouns left after eliminating first and second person pronouns, without and with *G*esture information. We also ran two sets of baseline experiments. In the baseline experiments, we link each pronoun we want to resolve, to the most recent utterance-markable token and to a pointed-to markable token (if applicable). Markables are filtered by the same compatibility rules mentioned above.

Regarding the metrics we used for evaluation, we used the same method as Strube and Müller (2003), which is also similar to MUC standard (Hirschman, 1997). As the golden set, we used the human annotated links from the pronouns to markables in the same context of four utterances used by the system. Then, we compared the co-reference links found by the system against the golden set, and we finally calculated precision, recall and F-Measure.

Table 5 shows that the F-measure is higher when including gestures, no matter the type of pronouns. When we include gestures, there is no difference between "All Pronouns" and "$3rd$ Person + Deictic". In the "$3rd$ Person + Deictic" experiments, we observed huge drops in recall, from 0.902 to 0.028 for J48, and from 0.695 to 0.009 for LibSVM algorithm. This confirms the point we made earlier, that 3rd person pronouns/deictic words (Kehler, 2000) often do not have textual antecedents, since when accompanied by simultaneous pointing they introduce new entities in a dialogue.

Comparison to previous work is feasible only at a high level, because of the usage of different corpora and/or measurement metrics. This said, our model with gestures outperforms Strube and Müller (2003), who did not use gesture information to resolve pronouns in spoken dialogue. Strube and Müller (2003) used the 20 Switchboard dialogues as their experiment dataset, and used the MUC metrics. Our re-

[1] χ^2 does not apply to the F-Measure.

sults are similar to Eisenstein and Davis (2006), but there are two main differences. First, the corpus they used is smaller than what we used in this paper. Their corpus was collected by themselves and consisted of 16 videos, each video was 2-3 minutes in length. Second, they used a difference measurement metrics called CEAF (Luo, 2005).

5 Conclusions

In this paper, we presented the new ELDERLY-AT-HOME multi-modal corpus we collected. A co-reference resolution system for personal and deictic pronouns has been developed on the basis of the annotated corpus. Our results confirm that gestures improve co-reference resolution; a simple notion of type also helps. The *Markable* and *Co-reference* modules we presented are a first start in developing a full multi-modal co-reference resolution module. Apart from completing the annotation of our corpus, we will develop an annotation scheme for haptics, and investigate how haptics information affects co-reference and other dialogue phenomena. Ultimately, both pointing gestures and haptic information will automatically be recognized by the collaborators in the project we are members of.

Acknowledgments

This work is supported by award IIS 0905593 from the National Science Foundation. Thanks to the other members of the RoboHelper project, for their many contributions, especially to the data collection effort.

References

Jean Carletta. 1996. Assessing agreement on classification tasks: The kappa statistic. *Computational Linguistics*, 22:249–254.

Lei Chen and Mary P. Harper. 2010. Utilizing gestures to improve sentence boundary detection. *Multimedia Tools and Applications*, pages 1–33.

Barbara Di Eugenio, Miloš Žefran, Jezekiel Ben-Arie, Mark Foreman, Lin Chen, Simone Franzini, Shankaranand Jagadeesan, Maria Javaid, and Kai Ma. 2010. Towards Effective Communication with Robotic Assistants for the Elderly: Integrating Speech, Vision and Haptics. In *Dialog with Robots, AAAI 2010 Fall Symposium*, Arlington, VA, USA, November.

Jacob Eisenstein and Randall Davis. 2006. Gesture Improves Coreference Resolution. In *Proceedings of the Human Language Technology Conference of the NAACL, Companion Volume: Short Papers*, pages 37–40.

Mark Hall, Eibe Frank, Geoffrey Holmes, Bernhard Pfahringer, Peter Reutemann, and Ian H. Witten. 2009. The WEKA data mining software: An update. *SIGKDD Explorations*, 11(1).

Lynette Hirschman. 1997. Muc-7 coreference task definition.

Andrew Kehler. 2000. Cognitive Status and Form of Reference in Multimodal Human-Computer Interaction. In *AAAI 00, The 15th Annual Conference of the American Association for Artificial Intelligence*, pages 685–689.

Michael Kipp. 2001. Anvil-a generic annotation tool for multimodal dialogue. In *Proceedings of the 7th European Conference on Speech Communication and Technology*, pages 1367–1370.

Kristine M. Krapp. 2002. *The Gale Encyclopedia of Nursing & Allied Health*. Gale Group, Inc. Chapter Activities of Daily Living Evaluation.

Xiaoqiang Luo. 2005. On coreference resolution performance metrics. In *Proceedings of the conference on Human Language Technology and Empirical Methods in Natural Language Processing*, HLT '05, pages 25–32, Stroudsburg, PA, USA. Association for Computational Linguistics.

Shaolin Qu and Joyce Y. Chai. 2008. Beyond attention: the role of deictic gesture in intention recognition in multimodal conversational interfaces. In *Proceedings of the 13th international conference on Intelligent user interfaces*, pages 237–246.

Kepa Joseba Rodrıguez, Francesca Delogu, Yannick Versley, Egon Stemle, and Massimo Poesio. 2010. Anaphoric annotation of wikipedia and blogs in the live memories corpus. In *Proceedings of the 7th International Conference on Language Ressources and Evaluation (LREC 2010)*, pages 157–163.

Michael Strube and Christoph Müller. 2003. A machine learning approach to pronoun resolution in spoken dialogue. In *Proceedings of the 41st Annual Meeting on Association for Computational Linguistics-Volume 1*.

Examining the Impacts of Dialogue Content and System Automation on Affect Models in a Spoken Tutorial Dialogue System

Joanna Drummond
Department of Computer Science
University of Pittsburgh
Pittsburgh, PA 15260
jmd73@cs.pitt.edu

Diane Litman
Department of Computer Science
Learning Research & Development Ctr.
University of Pittsburgh
Pittsburgh, PA 15260
litman@cs.pitt.edu

Abstract

Many dialogue system developers use data gathered from previous versions of the dialogue system to build models which enable the system to detect and respond to users' affect. Previous work in the dialogue systems community for domain adaptation has shown that large differences between versions of dialogue systems affect performance of ported models. Thus, we wish to investigate how more minor differences, like small dialogue content changes and switching from a wizarded system to a fully automated system, influence the performance of our affect detection models. We perform a post-hoc experiment where we use various data sets to train multiple models, and compare against a test set from the most recent version of our dialogue system. Analyzing these results strongly suggests that these differences do impact these models' performance.

1 Introduction

Many dialogue system developers use data gathered from previous versions of a system to train models for analyzing users' interactions with later versions of the system in new ways, e.g. detecting users' affect enables the system to respond more appropriately. However, this training data does not always accurately reflect the current version of the system. In particular, differences in the levels of automation and the presentation of dialogue content commonly vary between versions. For example, Raux et al (2006) changed dialogue strategies for their Let's Go bus information system after real-world testing.

Previous work in dialogue systems with regards to analyzing the impact of using differing training data has primarily been in the domain adaptation field, and has focused on two areas. First, previous work empirically analyzed the *need* for domain adaptation, i.e. methods for porting existing classifiers to unrelated domains. For example, Webb and Liu (2008) developed a cue-phrase-based dialogue act classifier using the Switchboard corpus, and tested on call center data. While this performed reasonably, training on the call center corpus and testing on Switchboard performed poorly.

The second research direction involves proposing *methods* for domain adaptation. Margolis et al. (2010) observed similar poor performance when porting their dialogue act classifier between three corpora: Switchboard, the Meeting Recorder Dialog Act corpus, and a machine-translated version of the Spanish Callhome corpus. They report promising results through varying their feature set. Blitzer et al. (2007) also observed poor performance and the *need* for adaptation when porting product review sentiment classifiers. They used four review corpora from Amazon (books, DVDs, electronics, and small appliances), which yielded 12 cross-domain training/testing pairs. Their algorithmic adaptation methods showed promising results.

Our work is in the first direction, as we also empirically analyze the impact of differences in training and testing corpora to demonstrate the *need* for adaptation methods. However, our work differs from domain adaptation, as the corpora in this experiment all come from one intelligent spoken physics tutor. Instead, we analyze differences resulting from vary-

Proceedings of the SIGDIAL 2011: the 12th Annual Meeting of the Special Interest Group on Discourse and Dialogue, pages 312–318,
Portland, Oregon, June 17-18, 2011.

ing levels of **automation** and small changes in dialogue **content** between versions of our system.

With respect to analyzing **automation**, we empirically compare the impact of differences in training on data from wizarded (WOZ) versus fully automated systems. Though many systems use data from a WOZ version of the system to train models which are then used in fully automated versions of the system, the effectiveness of this method of dialogue system development has not been tested. We hypothesize that models built with automated data will outperform models built with wizarded data.

Additionally, minor dialogue **content** changes typically exist between versions of systems. While large changes, like changing domains, have been shown to affect model performance, no work has investigated the impact of these more minute changes. We hypothesize that these differences in dialogue **content** presentation will also affect the models.

Finally, the amount of training data is a well known factor which affects performance of models built using supervised machine learning. We hypothesize that combining some, but not all, types of training corpora will improve the performance of the trained models, e.g. adding automated data to WOZ data will improve performance, as this provides fully automated examples. We hypothesize only providing more WOZ data will not be as useful.

2 Data

The data used for this work comes from two prior experiments using ITSPOKE, a spoken tutorial dialogue system, which tutors physics novices. Table 1 describes all data used, displaying the number of users per data set, the number of dialogues between the system and each user, the total number of user turns per corpus, and the percentage of turns labeled uncertain. See Appendix A for more information.

The first experiment, in 2007, compared two dialogue-based strategies for remediating user uncertainty over and above correctness (Forbes-Riley and Litman, 2011b). The goal of this work was to not only test the hypothesis that this uncertainty remediation would improve users' learning, but to investigate what types of dialogue remediation would improve users' learning the most. Since this experiment, WOZ-07, was designed to be a gold-standard case of uncertainty remediation, all natural language understanding and uncertainty annotation was performed by a human wizard, in real time (WOZ). All annotations were made at the turn-level.

For WOZ-07, users' dialogue interactions with the system would change based on which remediation strategy they were assigned to. There were two different dialogue-based remediation strategies. In addition to varying the strategies, the two control conditions in this experiment also varied when the remediation strategy was applied.

The *simple* remediation dialogue strategy provided additional information about the physics concept the user was struggling with, or asked them further questions about the concept. Both control conditions used the *simple* remediation strategy; one only applied the strategy when the user was incorrect, the other applied it if the user was incorrect and randomly when the user was correct. The *simple* remediation experimental condition applied the remediation when the user was incorrect, or correct but uncertain about their answer. The fourth condition in WOZ-07 used the second dialogue strategy, *complex* remediation. This strategy changed the way the remediation was presented, depending on a combination of the user's correctness and certainty in their answer. Only users in the *simple* remediation experimental condition learned more than users in other conditions. Figure 1 shows an example of *simple* remediation; the tutor acknowledges that the user is incorrect, saying "Well...", and then explains the concept the previous question tested. Appendix B compares *simple* and *complex* remediation strategies.

Another experiment was performed in 2008, where users interacted with either a fully automated (ASR) version of ITSPOKE or a wizarded version. The goal of this experiment was to see if the learning gains found in the 2007 experiment would hold in the ASR version of the system. To mimic the WOZ-07 experiment, the wizarded version (WOZ-08) only used the *simple* remediation experimental condition found in WOZ-07, while the ASR version contained the *simple* remediation experimental condition and both *simple* remediation control conditions. The *complex* remediation strategy was not included due to its poor performance in WOZ-07. Thus, WOZ-08 and ASR-08 used identical dialogue strategies, with minor differences in where the reme-

TUTOR$_{p5}$: *(Response to an incorrect answer)* Well... We just discussed that by Newton's Third law, when two objects collide, the forces they exert on each other are equal in magnitude and opposite in direction. This is true regardless of the objects' differing masses. So the first question's answer is that the impact forces on the truck and the car will have the same magnitude but opposite direction. Now, the second question asks about the vehicles' change in motion. We can use Newton's Second law to answer this. What does this law say?

TUTOR$_{p6}$: *(Response to a correct, certain answer)* Fine. So the first question's answer is that the impact forces on the bus and the motorbike will have the same magnitude, but opposite direction. Now, the second question asks about the vehicles' change in motion. We can use Newton's second law to answer this. What does this law say?

Figure 1: Corpus Excerpt: Remediation in Dialogue 5, and No Remediation in Isomorphic Dialogue 6

diation would be applied. For the ASR conditions, all models were trained on WOZ-07 data; users were randomly assigned to the WOZ-08 or ASR-08 condition as they participated.

In addition to eliminating the *complex* remediation condition, a sixth dialogue, completely isomorphic to the fifth dialogue, was added to all conditions. See Appendix B dialogue examples, highlighting their content differences. Figure 1 displays two ASR-08 tutor turns with the same user. These turns are from the fifth problem, and the isomorphic sixth problem. Note that two things change between these two answers. First, the system responds to the user's incorrectness in the first example. Had the user been correct and uncertain, this is also the dialogue s/he would have seen. Second, notice that problem five discusses a car, while problem six discusses a motorcycle. To create a completely isomorphic problem, the scenario for the dialogue was changed from a car to a motorcycle.

For both the 2007 and 2008 corpora, all gold-standard uncertainty annotations were performed by a trained human annotator. Development and previous testing of the annotation scheme between this annotator and another trained annotator resulted in *kappa* = 0.62. All wizarded conditions were annotated in real-time; all ASR conditions were annotated in a post-hoc manner.

Data Set	#Usr	#Dia	#Turn	%Unc
WOZ-07	81	5	6561	22.73
WOZ-08	19	6	1812	21.85
ASR-08	72	6	7216	20.55
ASR-08-Train	19	6	1911	21.51
ASR-08-Test	53	6	5305	20.21

Table 1: Description of data sets

In sum, the main differences between the two systems' data are differences in **automation** (i.e. WOZ and ASR) and **content** (i.e. presentation of content, reflected by differing dialogue strategies, and number of physics dialogues).

3 Post-Hoc Experiment

In this post-hoc analysis, we will analyze the impact of **content** differences by comparing the performance of models built with WOZ-07 and WOZ-08, and **automation** differences by comparing models built with WOZ-08 and ASR-08 data. Instead of the original study design, where WOZ-08 and ASR-08 subjects were run in parallel, we could have gathered the WOZ data first, and used the WOZ data and the first few ASR users for system evaluation and development purposes. Thus, for the post-hoc analysis, we mimic this by using WOZ-08 as a training set, and splitting ASR-08 into two data sets–ASR-08-Train (the first few users), and ASR-08-Test. (Please see the last two rows of Table 1.) We held out the first 19 users for ASR-08-Train, since this approximates the amount of data used to train the model built with WOZ-08. For our post-hoc study, the remaining 53 ASR users were used as a test set for all training sets, to mimic an authentic development lifestyle for a dialogue system. Additionally, this guaranteed that no users appear in both the training and testing set given any training set.

As all uncertainty remediation happens at the turn-level, we classified uncertainty at the turn-level, and compared these automated results with the gold-standard annotations. We used all the features that were designed for the original model. Since previous experiments with our data showed little variance between different machine learning algorithms, we chose a J48 decision tree, implemented by WEKA,[1]

[1]http://www.cs.waikato.ac.nz/ml/weka/

for all experiments due to its easy readability. Since our class distribution is skewed (see Table 1), we also used a cost matrix which heavily penalizes classifying an uncertain instance as certain.

We use simple lexical, prosodic and system-specific features described in (Forbes-Riley and Litman, 2011a) to build our models. These features were kept constant through all experiments, so the results could be directly comparable. For all lexical features for all data sets, ASR text was used.[2] For all WOZ conditions, we gathered ASR text post-hoc.

We trained models on individual training sets, to inspect the impact of **content** and **automation** differences. We then trained new models on combinations of these original training sets, to investigate possible interactions. To allow for direct comparison, we used ASR-08-Test to evaluate all models.

Since detecting uncertainty is related to detecting affective user states, we use the evaluation measures Unweighted Average (UA) Recall and UA Precision, presented in (Schuller et al., 2009).We also use UA F-measure. Note that because only one hold-out evaluation set was used, rather than using multiple sets for cross-fold validation, we do not test for statistical significance between models' results.

4 Results

The first three rows of Table 2 present the results of training a model on each possible training set individually. Note that the number of instances per training set varies. WOZ-07 simply has more users in the training set than WOZ-08 or ASR-08-Train. While WOZ-08 and ASR-08-Train have the same number of users, the number of turns slightly varies, since dialogues vary depending on users' answers.

When comparing WOZ-08 to WOZ-07, first notice that WOZ-08 outperforms WOZ-07 with a much smaller amount of data. Both are wizarded versions, but **content** differences exist between these experiments; WOZ-08 only used the *simple* remediation strategy, and added a dialogue.

When comparing ASR-08-Train to the other two individual training sets, note that it best approximates the test set. This training condition outperforms all others, while using less data than WOZ-07. While WOZ-08 and ASR-08 have the same **content**, the system changes from wizarded to automated language recognition. This allows us to directly compare how differences due to **automation** (e.g. errors in detecting correct answers) can affect performance of the models. Note that even though we used ASR transcriptions of WOZ-08 turns, the effects of ASR errors on later utterances are only propagated in ASR-08-Train. As ASR-08-Train noticeably outperforms WOZ-08, with approximately the same amount of training data, we conclude that using automated data for training better prepares the model for the data it will be classifying.

As we also wish to investigate how incorporating more diverse training data would alter the performance of the model, we combined ASR-08-Train and WOZ-08 with the WOZ-07 training set, shown in Table 2. We combined these sets practically, as we wish to test how our model could have performed if we had used our first few 2008 users to train the model in the actual 2008 experiment.

First, note that all combination training sets outperform individual training sets. As ASR-08-Train outperformed WOZ-08 for individual training sets, it is not surprising that WOZ-07+ASR-08-Train outperforms WOZ-07+WOZ-08.

However, we could have used WOZ-07 for feature development only, and trained on WOZ-08 + ASR-08-Train. Since the training and testing sets contain identical **content**, it is unsurprising that the precision for this classifier is high. This classifier does not perform as well with respect to recall, perhaps since its training data is not as varied. Also note, while this model trained on few data points, we used additional data for feature development purposes.

Combining all three possible training sets does not outperform WOZ-07+ASR-08-Train; it performs equivalently, and uses much more data. We hypothesize that, since WOZ-07 constitutes the majority of the training set, the benefit of including WOZ-08 may be mitigated. Downsampling WOZ-07 could test this hypothesis. Alternatively, the benefit of combining WOZ-07+ASR-08-Train could be that we provide many varied examples in this combined training set. Since WOZ-07 already accounts for differences in both **content** and **automation**, WOZ-08 doesn't introduce novel examples for the classifier, and adding it may not be beneficial.

[2]We used ASR instead of manual transcriptions, to better approximate automated data.

Training Set	n	UA Rec.	UA Prec.	UA F1
WOZ-07	6561	54.6%	53.0%	53.79%
WOZ-08	1812	58.0%	55.4%	56.67%
ASR-08-Train	1911	60.5%	57.2%	58.80%
WOZ-07 + WOZ-08	8373	66.1%	61.0%	63.45%
WOZ-07 + ASR-08-Train	8472	**68.3%**	63.5%	65.81%
WOZ-08 + ASR-08-Train	3723	64.0%	**73.4%**	**68.38%**
WOZ-07 + WOZ-08 + ASR-08-Train	10284	**68.3%**	63.6%	65.86%

Table 2: Results; Testing on ASR-08-Test ($n = 5305$). Bold denotes best performance per metric.

In sum, different training set combinations provide different benefits. With respect to UA F1 and UA Precision, WOZ-08 + ASR-08-Train outperforms all other training sets. Using only 3723 turns to train the model, this configuration uses the least amount of training data. However, this requires previously collected data, such as WOZ-07, for feature development purposes. Alternatively, WOZ-07 + ASR-08-Train performs better than WOZ-08 + ASR-08-Train with respect to UA Recall, and does not require a separate feature development set. Thus, the 'best' training set would depend on both the experimental design, and the preferred metric.

5 Discussion and Future Work

In this paper, we provided evidence that the degree of **automation** of a system used to collect training data can impact the performance of a model when used in a fully automated system. Since one common technique of building fully automated dialogue systems uses a semi-automated wizarded version, this result suggests incorporating a small amount of automated data could greatly improve performance of the models. Our results also suggest that the type of data is more important than the quantity when building these models, since well-performing models were built with small amounts of data. We also investigated the impact of building models trained with different dialogue **content**, another common method of developing dialogue systems. As the WOZ-08 model outperforms the WOZ-07 model, it appears that this has a noticeable impact.

However, the WOZ-08 and WOZ-07 experiments may not have had identical user population, due to the timing differences between studies. We wish to perform further post hoc-experiments to analyze the impact of population differences in our data. To do so, we will eliminate all dialogue strategy differences between WOZ-07 and WOZ-08. To further support our results regarding **content** differences, we wish to split WOZ-08 into two training sets, one including the sixth problem, and one excluding it. After controlling for differences in quantity of data, we will analyze the resulting models. To further strength our results regarding **automation** differences, we will eliminate all differences in when the remediation dialogue strategy was applied between the WOZ-08 and ASR-08-Test corpus, and try to replicate the results found in this paper.

As our results suggest the *need* for applying domain adaptation methods to improve models' performance when there are differences in **automation** and **content**, future work could investigate applying already existing *methods* for domain adaptation, and developing new ones for this problem. In particular, the results we presented suggest a method for building a dialogue system that could mitigate the effects of changes in automation and content. A small wizarded condition, with changes in dialogue content, could be used for feature development. This data, or data from another small wizarded condition, could then be used to train a preliminary model. This preliminary model could be tested with a small number of users using an automated version. Then, the data from the preliminary conditions could be used to build the final model, which would be used for the current, fully automated version of the system.

Acknowledgments

We thank Michal Valko, Michael Lipschultz, Wenting Xiong, and the ITSPOKE group for helpful comments and suggestions, and an REU supplement to NSF Grant #0631930 for funding this work.

References

J. Blitzer, M. Dredze, and F. Pereira. 2007. Biographies, bollywood, boom-boxes and blenders: Domain adaptation for sentiment classification. In *Annual Meeting-Association For Computational Linguistics*, volume 45, page 440.

K. Forbes-Riley and D. Litman. 2011a. Benefits and challenges of real-time uncertainty detection and adaptation in a spoken dialogue computer tutor. *Speech Communication*.

K. Forbes-Riley and D. Litman. 2011b. Designing and evaluating a wizarded uncertainty-adaptive spoken dialogue tutoring system. *Computer Speech & Language*, 25(1):105–126.

A. Margolis, K. Livescu, and M. Ostendorf. 2010. Domain adaptation with unlabeled data for dialog act tagging. In *Proceedings of the 2010 Workshop on Domain Adaptation for Natural Language Processing*, pages 45–52. Association for Computational Linguistics.

A. Raux, D. Bohus, B. Langner, A.W. Black, and M. Eskenazi. 2006. Doing research on a deployed spoken dialogue system: One year of Lets Go! experience. In *Proc. Interspeech*, pages 65–68. Citeseer.

B. Schuller, S. Steidl, and A. Batliner. 2009. The interspeech 2009 emotion challenge. In *Tenth Annual Conference of the International Speech Communication Association*.

N. Webb and T. Liu. 2008. Investigating the portability of corpus-derived cue phrases for dialogue act classification. In *Proceedings of the 22nd International Conference on Computational Linguistics-Volume 1*, pages 977–984. Association for Computational Linguistics.

Data Set	Dialogue #5		Dialogue #6	
	Avg. #Turn	Avg. %Unc	Avg. #Turn	Avg. %Unc
WOZ-07	15.21	26.87	N/A	N/A
WOZ-08	14.37	28.21	13.42	9.02
ASR-08	16.26	19.90	16.28	9.73
ASR-08 -Train	16.05	19.67	16.00	11.84
ASR-08 Test	16.38	19.98	16.38	8.99

Table 3: Dialogue-level description of corpora

Appendix A Differences between corpora

We note that one possible difficulty in using dialogues with differing **content** could be differing levels of users' uncertainty between those dialogues. Thus, Table 3 depicts the average percent of uncertain turns over all users, per dialogue. Only Dialogues #5 and #6 are presented; average number of turns and average percent uncertainty do change between all problems. While the average number of turns are similar, the percentage of uncertain turns drops greatly between the two isomorphic problems.

Appendix B Dialogue Examples

We also present dialogue examples from our corpora to illustrate various **content** differences between versions of ITSPOKE. The changes between Dialogues #5 and #6 are as follows: every instance of "car" in Dialogue #5 with "motorbike," and every instance of "truck" is replaced with "PAT bus." Since users discuss Problem #6 with ITSPOKE immediately after discussing Problem #5, the drop in percentage of user uncertainty between Dialogue #5 and Dialogue #6 show in Table 3 might be explained by this. However, all of the domain-specific words and all of the knowledge concepts will remain the same between these two problems.

Figures 1 (in the main paper) and 2 give examples of the two types of remediation found in the 2007 corpus. ITSPOKE can change its dialogue based on not only how it presents the content, but also what feedback it gives. *Complex* remediation changes both of these attributes. Table 4 displays possible feedbacks given to the user, depending on their levels of correctness and certainty. In Figure 2, the segment of the tutor's turn is labeled after that segment is completed (e.g. the Feedback is "That's not correct... resolve it."). The type of remediation can also change. While Figure 1 depicts the normal remediation path as if the user had answered incorrectly or correct but uncertain, *complex* remediation, shown in Figure 2, first gives the user a short version of the answer that they should have given, before moving down the normal remediation path.

Tutor: What's the overall net force on the truck equal to?
User: Zero?? *[Incorrect & Uncertain]*
Tutor: That's not correct, but don't worry. You seem to be aware of your mistake. Let's resolve it. *[FEEDBACK]* The net force on the truck is equal to the impact force on it. Let's walk through this answer step by step. *[NEW SHORT ANSWER]* We can derive the net force on the truck by summing the individual forces on it, just like we did for the car. First, what horizontal force is exerted on the truck during the collision? *[EXISTING SUBDIALOGUE]*

Figure 2: Example of *Complex* uncertainty remediation.

User Answer	Examples of Feedback Phrases	
	Simple	*Complex*
Correct & Certain	That's right.	That's right.
Correct & Uncertain	That's right.	That's right, but you don't sound very certain, so let's recap.
Incorrect & Uncertain	Well...	Good try, but that's not right. It sounds like you knew there might be an error in your answer. Let's fix it.
Incorrect & Certain	Well...	I'm sorry, but there's a mistake in your answer that we need to work out.

Table 4: Example Feedback Phrases used in *Simple* and *Complex* Remediation

Error Return Plots

Ron Artstein
Institute for Creative Technologies, University of Southern California
12015 Waterfront Drive, Playa Vista, CA 90094-2536, USA
`<lastname>@ict.usc.edu`

Abstract

Error-return plots show the rate of error (misunderstanding) against the rate of non-return (non-understanding) for Natural Language Processing systems. They are a useful visual tool for judging system performance when other measures such as recall/precision and detection-error tradeoff are less informative, specifically when a system is judged on the correctness of its responses, but may elect to not return a response.

1 Introduction

Many Natural Language Processing systems make a distinction between *misunderstanding*, where the system interprets an input incorrectly, and *non-understanding*, where the system is aware that it is not able to interpret an input (Bohus and Rudnicky, 2005). This distinction is common in dialogue systems, where it pertains to Natural Language Understanding components which pass their output to a dialogue manager: a dialogue manager will act on the contents of misunderstood input, but if it knows that the input is not understood then it can engage in a variety of recovery techniques, such as asking for clarification, moving on, or changing the topic. For this reason non-understanding is usually preferred to misunderstanding. While common to dialogue systems, the concept of non-understanding is useful for other tasks as well, whenever a system can benefit from the knowledge that its best interpretation is likely to be incorrect (see below for an example in question answering).

Detecting non-understanding is a tradeoff: a system that is prone to non-understanding will inevitably miss some inputs that it would have understood correctly under a forced interpretation. This is similar but not identical to the familiar tradeoffs between recall and precision (van Rijsbergen, 1979) and between detection and error (Martin et al., 1997). Recall and precision are measures taken from information retrieval, where there are typically multiple documents relevant to a query, and ideal performance is defined as retrieving all and only the relevant documents: recall measures the "all" part while precision measures the "only" part, and tuning a system to increase one measure typically implies decreasing its counterpart. Detection and error apply to forced choice tasks: each input must be classified as either positive or negative, and decreasing false positives typically implies increasing false negatives and vice versa. The tradeoff between misunderstanding and non-understanding is similar to recall-precision in that a response need not be given to each input, and is similar to detection-error in that when a response is given, we only care about its correctness and not about its exhaustiveness.

There is presently no accepted measure for the tradeoff between misunderstanding and non-understanding. A recent example illustrating the confusion, and need for a standard measure, comes from the QALD-1 Open Challenge (Question Answering over Linked Data).[1] The task is defined as giving a complete and correct answer to a natural language question, but systems are allowed to not return an answer. The evaluation metric uses recall and precision, but they are defined in a non-standard way. Precision is defined as the number

[1] http://www.sc.cit-ec.uni-bielefeld.de/sites/www.sc.cit-ec.uni-bielefeld.de/files/sharedtask.pdf (dated 2011-03-28)

Proceedings of the SIGDIAL 2011: the 12th Annual Meeting of the Special Interest Group on Discourse and Dialogue, pages 319–324, Portland, Oregon, June 17-18, 2011.

of correctly answered questions divided by the total number of answered questions; given that each question receives at most one answer, this is equivalent to the standard definition of correct answers divided by the total number of answers provided by the system – it penalizes misunderstanding and gives credit to non-understanding. Recall is also defined in a non-standard way.

$$\frac{\text{number of correctly answered questions}}{\text{number of questions}}$$

This would normally be considered the definition of accuracy, and it penalizes misunderstanding and non-understanding equally; the standard definition of recall is the number of correct answers divided by the number of available correct answers, and it does not normally penalize incorrect answers. The reason for the confusion between recall and accuracy is that in a task where each question has a unique correct answer, failure to provide a correct answer to a question implies that an available answer has not been retrieved. What the QALD-1 evaluation does, in effect, is penalize non-understanding through accuracy, and penalize misunderstanding more, through both accuracy and precision.

To properly evaluate the tradeoff between misunderstanding and non-understanding we need to look at each type of error separately. If each input receives a response, then accuracy is the complement of error; if some responses are not returned, then accuracy is the complement of the sum of errors (misunderstandings) and non-returns (non-understandings). The relative severity of misunderstanding and non-understanding will vary based on the application: a question-answering system that is required to provide accurate information might have a low tolerance for misunderstanding, while a story-driven dialogue system might have a low tolerance for asking clarification questions as a result of non-understanding. The relation between misunderstanding and non-understanding is not fixed – a system with lower error rates under a forced interpretation may turn out to have higher error rates than a competitor after allowing for non-understanding. It is therefore useful to look at the entire range of return rates when evaluating systems. The remainder of this paper introduces the error-return plot as a graphical representation for comparing error rates across different return rates, and presents examples for its use from recent experiments.

2 Characteristics of the tradeoff

A Natural Language Processing component that is capable of indicating non-understanding consists of two distinct processes: figuring out the best (or most likely) response to an input, and deciding whether the best response is likely to be appropriate. These two processes may be implemented as distinct software components, as in the system used for the experiments in section 4, NPCEditor (Leuski and Traum, 2010) – a classification-based system for Natural Language Understanding that chooses the best interpretation from a fixed set. NPCEditor first calculates the appropriateness of each available interpretation, and then compares the score of the best interpretation to a predetermined threshold; if the best interpretation falls below the threshold, NPCEditor indicates non-understanding. Other implementations are, of course, possible – for example, Patel et al. (2006) describe an architecture where the system first decides if it can understand the input, and then tries to determine the interpretation only if the answer is positive. The two processes may also be linked more intimately together, but in order to determine the tradeoff between misunderstanding and non-understanding, there must be some way to isolate the decision of whether or not the input has been understood. By varying the sensitivity of this decision, we can compare the rates of misunderstanding across different rates of non-understanding.

Decomposing Natural Language Understanding into two distinct processes helps illustrate the inapplicability of the popular measures of ROC curves (relative operating characteristic, Swets, 1973) and DET curves (detection error tradeoff, Martin et al., 1997). These measures only look at the decision of whether an interpretation is good enough, while abstracting away the decision about the actual interpretation. ROC and DET curves were developed for detection and verification tasks, where performance is determined by the rate of errors – misses and false alarms – irrespective of the composition of the input. They plot the false alarm rate against the hit rate (ROC) or miss rate (DET) – that is, the returned errors as a proportion of all errors against the returned (ROC) or missed (DET) correct responses as a proportion of all correct responses. Consequently, ROC and DET curves say nothing about the actual error rate. A system with an error rate of 10%, where errors are uniformly spread among correct responses when ranked by the system's confidence, will have identical ROC and DET curves to a system with an error rate of 40%, 50% or 90% with the errors spread uniformly.

For investigating the tradeoff between misunderstanding and non-understanding, we want to look not only at the system's decision about whether or not to return an interpretation, but also at the correctness of the chosen interpretation. We therefore need a plot that reflects the actual error rate as a function of the return rate.

3 Definition

An error-return plot is a graphical representation of the tradeoff between errors (misunderstandings) and failures to return a response (non-understandings). It applies to systems that react to each input in one of three possible ways – a correct response, an incorrect response, or a failure to respond to the input. The error rate and non-return rate are defined as follows.

$$\text{Error rate} = \frac{\text{incorrect responses}}{\text{number of inputs}}$$

$$\text{Non-return rate} = \frac{\text{failures to respond}}{\text{number of inputs}}$$

In order to plot the entire range of the tradeoff, the system is set to make a forced-choice response to each input. The responses are then ranked according to the system's confidence (or whatever other measure is used to decide when to issue a non-return), and at each possible cutoff, the non-return rate is plotted on the horizontal axis against the error rate on the vertical axis. As the number of non-returns grows, the number of errors can only go down, so the plot is monotonically decreasing; at the extreme right, where no responses are returned, error rates are necessarily zero, while at the extreme left, the error rate is equivalent to accuracy under a forced choice. Lower curves indicate better performance.

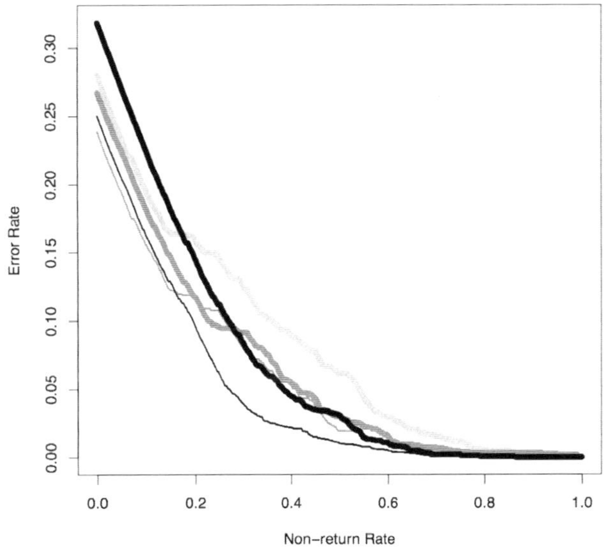

Figure 1: Comparing tokenizers, SGT Star data (Wang et al., 2011, black = baseline)

4 Examples

An example error-return plot is shown in Figure 1. The plot is taken from Wang et al. (2011), an experiment which tested the effect of using phonetic information in a Natural Language Understanding component in order to recover from speech recognition errors. The base system is NPCEditor (Leuski and Traum, 2010), trained for SGT Star, a virtual character who provides information about the U.S. Army to potential recruits (Artstein et al., 2009). For each input utterance, NPCEditor selects one output out of a fixed set, based on a learned mapping between input and output training examples; it also has the capability of not returning a response if the classifier's confidence in the appropriateness of the best choice falls below a certain threshold. The specific experiment in Figure 1 tested alternative methods to tokenize the input: the base tokenizer is represented by the thick black curve, and uses words as tokens; alternative tokenizers are shown in thinner lines or in shades of gray, and they use tokens with various mixtures of phonetic and word information (phone unigrams, bigrams etc.). The test data consisted of utterances for which the correct interpretation is known, but which NPCEditor would occasionally fail to classify due to speech recognition errors.

Figure 1 shows several properties at a glance. The base tokenizer has a fairly high error rate (over 30%)

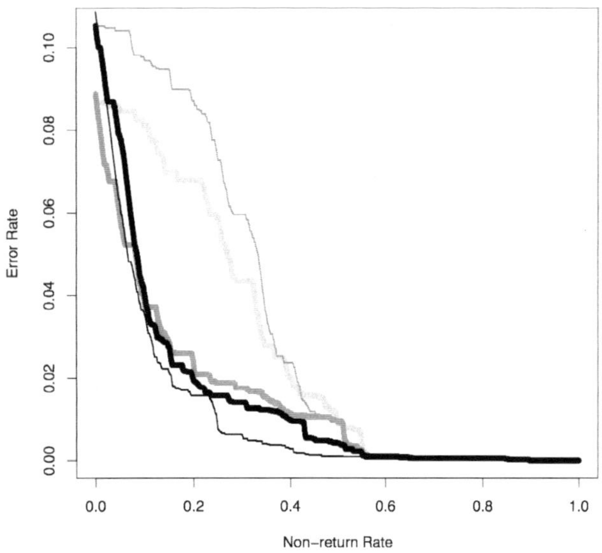

Figure 2: Comparing tokenizers, Twins data (Wang et al., 2011, black = baseline)

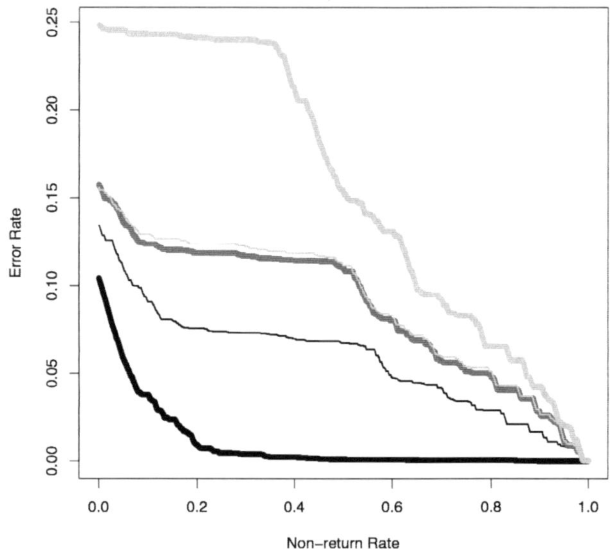

Figure 3: Augmented classifiers (black = baseline)

under forced choice, but the error rate decreases rapidly when non-understanding is allowed (on the left-hand side of the plot the slope is close to -1, which is the steepest possible decline). When tolerance for non-understanding is low, all the alternative tokenizers produce lower error rates than the baseline; however, increasing the non-understanding does not affect all tokenizers equally, and the error rate of the baseline tokenizer improves more rapidly than others, so that at 30% non-return rate it is better than most of the alternative tokenizers. Finally, one alternative tokenizer – the thin black line – shows best or almost-best performance at all return rates, supporting the hypothesis of the original experiment, that adding phonetic information to a Natural Language Understanding component can help in recovery from speech recognition errors.

Figure 2 is from the same experiment but using a different data set – the one developed for the the twins Ada and Grace, two virtual guides at the Museum of Science in Boston who answer questions about their neighboring exhibits and about science in general (Swartout et al., 2010). The overall error rate is much lower than in Figure 1. Otherwise, the pattern is similar, though we see that the thin gray tokenizer has shifted from a close second-best to being the worst performer. Once again, the thin black tokenizer beats all the others across most return rates.

Figure 3 shows a different experiment, also using NPCEditor. This experiment tested the effect of taking an existing virtual character – the twins Ada and Grace – and expanding the character's understanding by adding training input-output pairs extracted automatically from text (the method for extracting training data is described in Chen et al., 2011; the present experiment is currently under review for publication). The baseline classifier is the thick black line, trained on the Twins' original question-answer links; the alternative classifiers add automatically extracted questions-answer training links from successive orthogonal domains. All classifiers were evaluated using the same test set of questions from the original domain, in order to test how the addition of orthogonal training data affects performance on inputs from the original domain. The plot shows that the effect is quite noticeable: the original classifier has a 10% absolute error rate, which drops to virtually zero at a non-return rate of 20% and above; the augmented classifiers display a higher initial error rate, and moreover this higher error rate is not easily mitigated by accepting higher non-return rates. The augmented classifiers have the advantage of being able to understand inputs from the added domains, but the cost is some confusion on the original domain, both in terms of understanding the input, and in the ability to identify non-understanding.

5 Discussion

The error-return plot is a graphical representation for looking at the tradeoff between misunderstanding and non-understanding. Evaluating systems capable of indicating non-understanding is somewhat tricky, and error-return plots can show information that is useful when comparing such systems. If the curve of one system completely dominates the other, then we can say with confidence that the first system has better performance. If the curves intersect, then we need to compare the parts of the curve where we expect actual system performance to fall, and this will vary by application. The systems described above all use the same strategy for dealing with non-understanding: they issue an "off-topic" response which asks for clarification, stalls, or changes the conversation topic. The systems are intended for fairly short question-answer dialogues, for which an off-topic response rate of about 1 in 5 is usually acceptable, so the critical region is around 20% non-understanding. In applications where it is possible to judge the relative severity of misunderstanding and non-understanding, a weighted average could identify the optimal setting for the non-understanding threshold. Such an average should give non-understanding a lower weight than misunderstanding, since treating them as equal would obviate the need for identifying non-understanding.

A counterpart to the error rate would be the "missed chance rate" – the proportion of responses that would have been correct under forced choice but were not returned. Curves for missed chances start at zero (when all responses are returned) and increase with the non-return rate to a maximum of one minus the absolute error rate. The relation between the missed chance curve and the error return plot is straightforward: wherever the error return curve goes down, the missed chance curve stays level, and wherever the error return plot stays level, the missed chance curve goes up. The curves intersect at the point where the number of misunderstandings is identical to the number of non-understandings that would have been correct under forced choice; it is not clear, however, whether this point has any practical significance.

Error-return plots suffer from the usual problem of evaluating single components in a dialogue system: since subsequent input is to a certain extent contingent on system actions, it is conceivable that a system prone to misunderstanding would trigger different user utterances than a system prone to non-understanding. Determining the full consequences of non-understanding would require running a full dialogue system with real users under varying settings; error-return plots show the performance of Natural Language Understanding under the assumption of fixed input.

Overall, error return plots provide useful information about the tradeoff between misunderstanding and non-understanding in cases where recall/precision, ROC and DET curves are less informative. They have been used in several recent experiments, and hopefully may gain acceptance as a standard tool for system evaluation.

Acknowledgments

The project or effort described here has been sponsored by the U.S. Army Research, Development, and Engineering Command (RDECOM). Statements and opinions expressed do not necessarily reflect the position or the policy of the United States Government, and no official endorsement should be inferred.

References

Ron Artstein, Sudeep Gandhe, Jillian Gerten, Anton Leuski, and David Traum. 2009. Semi-formal evaluation of conversational characters. In Orna Grumberg, Michael Kaminski, Shmuel Katz, and Shuly Wintner, editors, *Languages: From Formal to Natural. Essays Dedicated to Nissim Francez on the Occasion of His 65th Birthday*, volume 5533 of *LNCS*, pages 22–35. Springer, May.

Dan Bohus and Alexander I. Rudnicky. 2005. Sorry, I didn't catch that! – An investigation of non-understanding errors and recovery strategies. In *Proceedings of the 6th SIGdial Workshop on Discourse and Dialogue*, pages 128–143, Lisbon, Portugal, September.

Grace Chen, Emma Tosch, Ron Artstein, Anton Leuski, and David Traum. 2011. Evaluating conversational characters created through question generation. In *Proceedings of the Twenty-Fourth International Florida Artificial Intelligence Research Society Conference*, pages 343–344, Palm Beach, Florida, May.

Anton Leuski and David Traum. 2010. Practical language processing for virtual humans. In *Proceedings of the Twenty-Second Innovative Applications of Artificial Intelligence Conference (IAAI-10)*, pages 1740–1747, Atlanta, Georgia, July.

Alvin Martin, George Doddington, Terri Kamm, Mark Ordowski, and Mark Przybocki. 1997. The DET curve in assessment of detection task performance. In *Eurospeech 1997*, pages 1895–1898, Rhodes, Greece, September.

Ronakkumar Patel, Anton Leuski, and David Traum. 2006. Dealing with out of domain questions in virtual characters. In Jonathan Gratch, Michael Young, Ruth Aylett, Daniel Ballin, and Patrick Olivier, editors, *Intelligent Virtual Agents: 6th International Conference, IVA 2006, Marina Del Rey, CA, USA, August 21–23, 2006 Proceedings*, volume 4133 of *Lecture Notes in Artificial Intelligence*, pages 121–131, Heidelberg, August. Springer.

William Swartout, David Traum, Ron Artstein, Dan Noren, et al. 2010. Ada and Grace: Toward realistic and engaging virtual museum guides. In Jan Allbeck, Norman Badler, Timothy Bickmore, and Alla Pelachaud, Catherine Safonova, editors, *Intelligent Virtual Agents*, volume 6356 of *LNAI*, pages 286–300. Springer, September.

John A. Swets. 1973. The relative operating characteristic in psychology. *Science*, 182(4116):990–1000.

C. J. van Rijsbergen. 1979. *Information Retrieval*. Butterworths, London, 2nd edition.

William Yang Wang, Ron Artstein, Anton Leuski, and David Traum. 2011. Improving spoken dialogue understanding using phonetic mixture models. In *Proceedings of the Twenty-Fourth International Florida Artificial Intelligence Research Society Conference*, pages 329–334, Palm Beach, Florida, May.

PARADISE-style Evaluation of a Human-Human Library Corpus

Rebecca J. Passonneau
Center for Computational Learning Systems
Columbia University
becky@cs.columbia.edu

Irene Alvarado
School of Engineering and Applied Science
Columbia University
ia2178@columbia.edu

Phil Crone
Simon Jerome
Columbia College
Columbia University
ptc2107@columbia.edu
sgj2111@columbia.edu

Abstract

We apply a PARADISE-style evaluation to a human-human dialogue corpus that was collected to support the design of a spoken dialogue system for library transactions. The book request dialogue task we investigate is informational in nature: a book request is considered successful if the librarian is able to identify a specific book for the patron. PARADISE assumes that user satisfaction can be modeled as a regression over task success and dialogue costs. The PARADISE model we derive includes features that characterize two types of qualitative features. The first has to do with the specificity of the communicative goals, given a request for an item. The second has to do with the number and location of overlapping turns, which can sometimes signal rapport between the speakers.

1 Introduction

The PARADISE method for evaluating task-based spoken dialogue systems (SDSs) assumes that user satisfaction can be modeled as a multivariate linear regression on measures of task success and dialogue costs (Walker, et al. 1998). Dialogue costs address efficiency, such as length of time on task, and effort, such as number of times the SDS fails to understand an utterance and re-prompts the user. It has been used to compare subjects performing the same or similar tasks across distinct SDSs (Sanders, et al. 2002). To our knowledge, it has not been applied to human-human dialogue.

For human-human task-based dialogues, we hypothesized that user satisfaction would not be predicted well by measures of success and dialogue costs alone. We expected that qualitative characteristics of human-human dialogue, such as the manner in which a dialogue goal is pursued, could counterbalance high dialogue costs. To test this hypothesis, we performed a PARADISE-like evaluation of a corpus of human-human library transaction dialogues that was originally collected to support the design of our SDS (Passonneau, et al. 2010). The communicative task we examine is to identify a specific set of books of interest from the library's holdings. This can be straightforward if the patron requests a book by catalogue number. It can be complex if the patron does not have complete bibliographic information, or if the request is non-specific. A book request is successful when the librarian identifies a specific book that addresses the patron's request.

Task success was predictive on a training set, but not on a held-out test set. Dialogue costs were less reliably predictive. Two additional factors we found to be moderate predictors pertained to the number of book requests that were non-specific in nature, and the amount and location of overlapping turns. We refer to these as qualitative features. A non-specific book request can lead to a collaborative identification of a specific book, and the costs incurred can be worth the effort. We speculate that overlapping turns during non-task-oriented subdialogue reflects positive rapport between the speakers, while the role of overlapping turns during task-oriented subdialogue is contingent on other characteristics of the task, such as whether the goal is specific or non-specific.

The three following sections discuss related work, our corpus, and our annotation procedures and reliability. We then present how we measure

Proceedings of the SIGDIAL 2011: the 12th Annual Meeting of the Special Interest Group on Discourse and Dialogue, pages 325–331,
Portland, Oregon, June 17-18, 2011.

user satisfaction, informational task success on book requests, and various dialogue costs. This is followed by results of the application of PARADISE to the human-human corpus.

2 Related Work

It is commonly assumed that human-computer interaction should closely resemble human-human interaction. For example, the originators of social presence theory propose that media that more closely resemble face-to-face communication provide a higher degree of social presence, or awareness of the communicative partner (Short, et al. 1976), which in turn leads to communicative success. A similar idea is seen in the origins of media richness theory (Daft and Lengel 1984), which defines media with more "richness" as having more communication cues, and thus enhancing task success. A key component of this assumption is that, if computers are created with human-like qualities then people will view computers similarly to humans. We hypothesize that human-machine dialogue need not resemble human-human dialogue in all respects, thus we earlier proposed a method to investigate human-machine dialogue despite the large disparity in the spoken language processing abilities of humans versus machines (Levin and Passonneau 2006), and applied it work described in this proceedings (Gordon, et al. 2011). Here, we apply PARADISE to human-human dialogue to facilitate comparison.

Turn-taking in conversation has received a significant amount of attention. Early work examined the types of turn-taking attempts and the reasons why such attempts either succeed or fail (Beattie 1982). Recent research has focused on the acoustic, lexical, and discourse-relevant cues that indicate a transition between speakers (Beňuš 2009, Gravano and Hirschberg 2009). More recently, turn-taking has been examined in the context of multi-tasking dialogues (Yang, et al. 2011). The Loqui human-human dialogues often involve multiple tasks. We do not annotate who has the floor, but we do transcribe overlapping speech, where there may be competition for the turn (see below).

3 Loqui Human-Human Corpus

Our baseline SDS, CheckItOut, is modeled on library transactions for the Andrew Heiskell Braille and Talking Book Library of New York City, and is part of the Library of Congress. Patrons request books from librarians by telephone, and receive book orders (primarily in recorded format) by mail. Early in the project, we recorded 175 patron-librarian calls at the Heiskell Library, 82 of which we identified to be primarily about book information and book orders. These were transcribed with an XML transcription tool, and utterances were aligned with the speech signal. The total number of words is approximately 24,670, or about 300 words per dialogue. Our transcription conventions are documented on our website.[1]

To facilitate analysis of the interactive structure of many types of interaction, such as spontaneous spoken dialogue, email, and task-oriented dialogue, we previously developed Dialogue Function Unit (DFU) annotation (Hu, et al. 2009). The primary motivation was to capture information about *adjacency pairs*, sequences of communicative acts in which an initial utterance calls forth a responding one (Sacks, et al. 1974). DFUs encode links between the elements of an adjacency pair, and a restricted set of dialogue acts designed to generalize across genres of interaction. Trained annotators applied DFU annotations to all 82 dialogues.

To measure task success and dialogue costs, we developed an additional annotation process that builds on DFU annotation, as described next.

4 TSC Annotation

In our human-human corpus, each patron has a different set of goals. For most of the dialogues, at least some of the patron's goals are to request books from the librarian. Other goals include requesting an update to the patron's profile information, requesting new equipment for listening to recorded books, and so on. The three-step method developed for annotating task success, dialogue costs and qualitative features (TSC Annotation) consists of an annotation step to determine what tasks are being executed, and two tabulation steps. The 82 dialogues that had already been annotated for DFUs were then annotated for task success and dialogue costs.[2] Three annotators were trained in the annotation over the course of several one-hour sessions, each of which was devoted to a different

[1]See resources link at http://www1.ccls.columbia.edu/~Loqui/.
[2] The guidelines are at http://www1.ccls.columbia.edu/~Loqui/resources.html.

16.1.0	L	*wh- wha- do you have the author?*
		[Request-Info: author of book]
17.1.0	P	*Cesar Millan*
		[Inform: author is Cesar Millan]
18.1.0	L	*M I L A N?*
		[Request-Info: is librarian's spelling correct]
19.1.0	P	yes
20.1.0	L	<non-speaking-librarian-activity>
21.1.1	P	can you hold on just {one second}
		[Request-Action: can librarian hold]
21.1.2	L	{sure sure}
		[Confirm]
22.1.0	P	I'm back
23.1.1	L	I'm sorry I'm not seeing anything {by him}
		[Inform: Nothing by this author]
23.1.2	P	{really}
		[Request-Info: yes/no]
24.1.0	L	no
		[Disconfirm]
		BOOK REQUEST 1.1

Figure 1. Book request DTU

sample dialogue. Pairs of annotators worked on each dialogue, with one annotator reviewing the other's work. Disagreements were adjudicated, and interannotator agreement was measured on three dialogues.

4.1 Annotation

The annotation procedure starts by dividing a transcription of a dialogue into a covering sequence of communicative tasks (Dialogue Task Units, or DTUs). Each DTU encompasses a complete idea with a single goal. It ends when both speakers have collaboratively closed the topic, per the notion of *collaborative contributions to discourse* found in (Clark and Schaefer 1989). Each DTU is labeled with its type. The two types of DTUs of most relevance here are book requests (BRs; where a patron requests a book), and librarian proposals (LPs; where the librarian proposes a book for the patron). Each BR or LP is numbered. Other DTU types include Inform (e.g., patron requests the librarian to provide a synopsis of a book), and Request-Action (e.g., patron requests the librarian update the patron's profile). After the DTUs have been annotated, success and task measures are tabulated for the book requests (BR and LP): the start and end lines, the specificity of the request (a request for any book by a given author is non-specific), and whether the task was successful.

Figure 1 shows part of a *book request* DTU. The DTU in Figure 1 is unsuccessful; the librarian is unable to identify the book the patron seeks. Several DTUs might pertain to the same goal, pursued in different ways. For example, the DTU illustrated here is the second of three in which the patron tries to request a book called *The Dog Whisperer*. The dialogue contains 7 DTUs devoted to this request, which is ultimately successful.

Figure 1 also illustrates how we transcribe overlapping utterances. Each line in Figure 1 corresponds to an utterance, or in the case of overlapping speech, to a time segment consisting of an utterance with some overlap. Patron utterance 21.1.1 is transcribed as ending with overlapping speech (in curly braces) where the librarian is also speaking within the same time segment (21.1.2). This is followed by the patron's utterance 22.1.0. The next time segment (23) also has an overlap, followed by the librarian's turn 24.1.0. As a result, we can investigate the proportion of utterances in a dialogue or subdialogue with overlapping speech, and the types of segments where overlaps occur.

4.3 Interannotator Agreement

To assess interannotator agreement among the three annotators, we randomly selected dialogues from a set that had already been annotated until we identified three that had been annotated by distinct pairs of annotators. Each was then annotated by a different third annotator who had not been a member of the original pair. Interannotator agreement on DTU boundaries and labels was measured using Krippendorff's alpha (Krippendorff 1980). Alpha ranges from 0 for no agreement above chance prediction, given the rate at which each annotation value is used, to 1 or -1, for perfect agreement or disagreement.

The three dialogues had alpha values of 0.87, 0.77 and 0.66, thus all well above agreement that could have resulted from chance. The dialogue with the highest agreement had 1 book request consisting of 2 DTUs. The first DTU had a non-specific request for two books by a given author, that was later reformulated in the second DTU as a specific request--by author and titles--for the two books. The dialogue with the next highest agreement had 12 specific book requests by catalogue number, and one DTU per book request. The dialogue with the lowest agreement had 5 book requests, with one DTU per book request. Two were by catalogue number, one was by author, and one was by author and title.

5. Perceived User Satisfaction

An indirect measure of User Satisfaction for each dialogue was provided by two annotators who listened to the audio while reviewing the transcripts. The annotators completed a user satisfaction survey that was nearly identical to one used in an evaluation of CheckItOut, the SDS modeled on the library transactions; references to *the system* were replaced with *the librarian*. It contained ten questions covering the librarian's clarity, friendliness, helpfulness, and ability to communicate. The annotators rated the perceived response of the caller with regard to the survey questions. On a 1 to 5 scale where 5 was the greatest satisfaction, the range was [3.8, 4.7], thus overall, patrons were perceived to be quite satisfied.

6. Task Success

The dialogue task investigated here is informational in nature, rather than a borrowing task. That is, a book request is considered successful if the librarian is able to identify the specific book the caller is requesting, or if the librarian and patron are able to specify a book in the library's holdings that the caller wants to borrow. The actual availability of the book is not relevant. Some patrons request a specific book, and provide alternative means to identify the book, such as catalogue number versus title. Some seek unspecified books by a particular author, or books in a given genre.

We calculate task success as the ratio of successfully identified books to requested books. The total number of books requested ranged from 1 to 24. Patron-initiated book requests as well as librarian-initiated proposals are included in the tabulation. In addition, we tabulate the number of specific book requests that change in the type of information provided (RC, title, author, genre, etc.) as well as the number of book requests that change in their specificity (non-specific to specific). Finally, we tabulate how many of these changes lead to successful identifications of books.

In general, task success was extremely high. More than 90% of book requests were successful; for 78% of the dialogues, all book requests were successful. This high success rate is to be expected, given that most callers are requesting specificc books they learn about from a library newsletter, or making non-specific requests that the librarian can satisfy.

7. Dialogue Costs and Qualitative Features

Along with two measures of task success (number of successfully identified books: Successful.ID; percent of requested books that are successfully identified: Percent.Successful), we have 48 measures of dialogue costs and qualitative features. The full list appears in column 1 of the table in Appendix A. Dialogue costs consist of measures such as the total number of turns, the total number of turns in book requests, the total number of utterances, counts of interruptions and misunderstandings by either party, and so on. Qualitative features include extensive clarifications, the types of book request, and overlapping utterances.

An extensive clarification serves to clarify some misunderstanding by the caller, and generally these segments take at least ten turns.

We classify each book request into one of seven types. These are non-specific by author, non-specific by genre, specific author, specific title, specific author and title, specific set, and specific catalogue number. As shown in the Appendix, we also tabulate the total number of specific book requests per dialogue (S.Total) and the total number of non-specific requests (NS.Total).

We tabulate overlapping utterances in a variety of ways. The average number of overlapping utterances per dialogue is 13.9. A breakdown of overlapping utterances into those that occur in book requests versus other types of DTU gives a mean of 4.36 for book requests compared with 8.74 otherwise. We speculate that the difference results from the potential for overlapping utterances to impede understanding when the utterance goals are to request and share information about books. In these contexts, overlap may reflect competition for the floor. In contrast, overlapping utterances at points in the dialogue that pertain to the social dimension may be more indicative of rapport between the patron and the librarian, as a reflection of sharing the floor. We do not attempt to distinguish overlaps with positive versus negative effects. We do, however, tabulate overlapping speech in different types of DTUs, such as book request DTUs versus other DTUs.

To illustrate the role of the qualitative features, we discus one of the dialogues in our corpus that exemplifies a property of these human-human dialogues that we believe could inform SDS design: high user satisfaction can occur despite low success rate on the communicative tasks. Dialogue 4 had the lowest task success of all dialogues (62.5%), yet perceived user satisfaction was quite high (4.7). This dialogue had a large number of book requests and librarian proposals, with a mix of requests for specific books by catalogue number, title, or author and title, along with non-specific requests for works by given authors. It also had a fairly high proportion of overlapping speech. As we discuss next, both dimensions are represented in the quantitative PARADISE models for predicting user satisfaction.

8. PARADISE Results

PARADISE predicts user satisfaction as a linear combination of task success and cost variables. Here we apply PARADISE to the Loqui library corpus, and add qualitative features to task success and dialogue costs. Six of the dialogues had no book requests, thus did not exemplify the task, namely to identify books for the patron in the library's holdings. These six were eliminated.

We split the data into independent training and test sets. From the 76 dialogues with book requests, we randomly selected 50 for deriving a regression model. These dialogues had a total of 211 book requests (mean=4.22). We reserved 26 dialogues for an independent test of how well the features from the user satisfaction model on the training set predicted user satisfaction on the test set. The test set had 73 book requests (mean=2.81).

To explore the data, we first did Analysis of Variance (ANOVA) tests on the 50 individual features as predictors of perceived user satisfaction on the training set. Certain features that are typically predictive for SDSs were also predictive here. Those that were most predictive on their own included the proportion of book requests successfully identified (Pct.Successful), and several cost measures such as total length in utterances, and the total number of interruptions and misunderstandings. However, other features that were predictive here that are not typical of human-machine dialogue were the number of utterances with overlapping speech (Simultaneous.Utterances), and the number of book requests that evolved from non-specific to specific (Change.NS.to.S).

Given the relatively small size of our corpus, and the large number of variables, we pruned the 30 features from the trained model before using them to build a regression on the test set. All analyses were done in the R Statistical Package (http://www.r-project.org/). We used the R function `step` to apply the Akaike Information Criterion to guide the search through the model space. The resulting model relies on 30 of the 50 variables, and has a multiple R-squared of 0.9063 (p= 0.0001342). Appendix A indicates the 30 features selected, and their p-values. For the pruned model, we selected half of the 30 features that contributed most to the best model found through the step function on the training set. The pruned model had a multiple R-squared of 0.5334 (p=0.0075). When we used the same features on the test set, the R-squared was 0.7866 (p=0.0416). However, the significance of individual features differed in training versus test. Appendix A lists the 15 features and their p-values on the training and test sets.

On the training data, the most significant features were Pct.Successful, the total number of dialogue segments pertaining to book requests (including librarian proposals; BR.request.segs), and the total number of book requests (Total.BR). The number of non specific book requests that evolved into specific requests (Change.NS.to.S) and the number of utterances per turn (Utterances.Turns) were marginally significant.

On the test data, the most significant variables were the ratio of overlapping utterances in segments that were not about book requests to book request segments (noBRLP.Overlap.per.TotalRequestSegments), the total number of non-specific book requests (NS.Total), and the number of overlapping utterances (Overlap.Utterances).

9. Conclusion

The human-human corpus examined here is an appropriate corpus to compare with human-machine dialogue, in that our SDS was modeled on the book requests in the human-human corpus. The R^2 values indicate that the regression models based on the 15 features fit the data well, yet the coefficients and probabilities are very different. In part, this is due to the large number of variables we investigated, relative to the small size of the corpus. Nevertheless, the results presented here point to a number of dimensions of human-human dialogue that contribute to user satisfaction beyond those that are typically considered when evaluating human-machine dialogue.

References

Beattie, G. W. 1982. Turn-taking and interruption in political interviews: Margaret Thatcher and Jim Callaghan compared and contrasted. Semiotica, 39 (1-2): 93-114.

Beňuš, Š. 2009. Are we 'in sync': Turn-taking in collaborative dialogues. In 10th Interspeech, pp. 2167-2170.

Clark, H. H. and E. F. Schaefer 1989. Contributing to discourse. Cognitive Science, 13 259-294.

Daft, R. L. and R. H. Lengel 1984. Information richness: A new approach to manager behavior and organization design. Research in Organizational Behavior, 6 191-233.

Gordon, J., et al. 2011. Learning to balance grounding rationales for dialogue systems. In 12th Annual SIGdial Meeting on Discourse and Dialogue (SIGdial 12).

Gravano, A. and J. Hirschberg. 2009. Turn-yielding cues in task-oriented dialogue. In 10th Annual Meeting of SIGDIAL, pp. 253-261.

Hu, J., et al. 2009. Contrasting the interaction structure of an email and a telephone corpus: A machine learning approach to annotation of dialogue function units. In 10th SIGDIAL on Dialogue and Discourse, pp. 357-366.

Krippendorff, K. 1980. Content Analysis: An Introduction to Its Methodology. Beverly Hills, CA: Sage Publications.

Levin, E. and R. J. Passonneau. 2006. A WOz Variant with Contrastive Conditions. In Interspeech Satelite Workshop, Dialogue on Dialogues: Multidisciplinary Evaluation of Speech-based Interactive Systems.

Passonneau, R. J., et al. 2010. Learning About Voice Search for Spoken Dialogue Systems. In 11th Annual Conference of the North American Chapter of the Association for Computational Linguistics (NAACL HLT 2010), pp. 840-848.

Sacks, H., et al. 1974. A simplest systematics for the organization of turn-taking for conversation. Language, 50 (4): 696-735.

Sanders, G. A., et al. 2002. Effects of word error rate in the DARPA Communicator data during 2000 and 2001. International Journal of speech Technology, 7 293-309.

Short, J., et al. 1976. The social psychology of telecommunications. Chichester: John Wiley.

Walker, M. A., et al. 1998. Evaluating Spoken Dialogue Agents with PARADISE: Two Case Studies. Computer Speech and Language, 12 317-348.

Yang, F., et al. 2011. An Investigation of interruptions and resumptions in multi-tasking dialogues. Computational Linguistics, 37 (1): 75-104.

Appendix A: Features

	Variable	Training Coeff.	Training p-value	Pruned Coeff	Pruned p-value	Test Coeff.	Test p-value
1	Successful.ID						
2	Pct.Successful	**0.504001**	**0.005118**	**0.356516**	**0.01219**	-0.04154	0.86744
3	Change.NS.to.S	**1.440471**	**0.023525**	**0.287376**	**0.05761**	0.10284	0.22876
4	Successful.NS.to.S	**-1.450301**	**0.048656**				
5	Change.S.to.S						
6	Successful.S.to.S						
7	BR.request.segs	-0.201228	0.119857	**-0.147057**	**0.00837**	0.02566	0.79277
8	LP.request.segs	**0.146464**	**0.073138**				
9	Total.Request.Segments						
10	Total.BR	**0.448858**	**0.001813**	**0.147945**	**0.01220**	-0.09960	0.35796
11	Segments.per.BR	**0.296577**	**0.047333**	0.123411	0.17907	-0.08707	0.59903
12	NS.Author	-0.216559	0.090830				
13	NS.Genre	-0.138867	0.249339				
14	S.Title						
15	S.AuthorTitle						
16	S.Set	**-0.953284**	**6.61e-05**				
17	S.RC	-0.158897	0.104752				
18	S.Author						
19	S.Total						
20	NS.Total			0.013265	0.75986	-0.27280	**0.00716**
21	Turns.in.BR						
22	Utterances	**-0.005613**	**0.013967**				
23	Interruptions	**0.187876**	**0.002704**	-0.050500	0.29683	-0.29078	**0.05378**
24	Misunderstandings						
25	Simultaneous.Utterances	**-0.151491**	**0.001967**	-0.008705	0.21024	0.02329	**0.04179**
26	Extensive.Clarifications	**-0.181057**	**1.76e-05**	-0.022723	0.25767	-0.08685	0.11608
27	S.U.Conventional	**0.142152**	**0.006168**				
28	S.U.Inform	**0.141891**	**0.001619**				
29	S.U.Sidebar	**0.107238**	**0.047303**				
30	S.U.BR.RC	**0.142538**	**0.006467**				
31	S.U.BR.Title	**0.245880**	**0.000415**				
32	S.U.BR.Title.and.Author	**0.136412**	**0.002581**				
33	S.U.BR.Genre						
34	S.U.LP	**0.176515**	**0.015598**				
35	S.U.R.A.	**0.171413**	**0.001459**				
36	S.U.IR.IRA	**0.166315**	**0.001994**				
37	Utterances.Turns	**-0.392267**	**0.020190**	-0.256307	0.08077	0.01731	0.95674
38	Total.Turns.BR						
39	Turns.in.BR.BR	-0.015623	0.093573				
40	BR.Utterances	**-8.875951**	**0.000603**	-1.104338	0.55174	2.59438	0.33439
41	NS.Total.per.BR	0.183761	0.177739	-0.102524	0.33547	0.31111	0.10004
42	S.U.BRLP						
43	S.U.BRLP.per.BR						
44	S.U.BRLP.per.TotalRequestSegs						
45	S.U.nonBRLP						
46	S.U.nonBRLP.per.BR						
47	S.U.nonBRLP.per.TotalRequestSegs	0.024492	0.117363	0.007839	0.33727	-0.06000	**0.00848**
48	S.nonRC						
49	S.nonRC.per.BR	-0.370227	0.064299	-0.062149	0.46085	-0.08072	0.47704
50	S.nonRC.per.TotalRequestSegs						

An Incremental Architecture for the Semantic Annotation of Dialogue Corpora with High-Level Structures. A case of study for the MEDIA corpus.*

Lina Maria Rojas-Barahona and **Matthieu Quignard**
LORIA/INRIA, France
{lina.rojas,matthieu.Quignard}@loria.fr

Abstract

The semantic annotation of dialogue corpora permits building efficient language understanding applications for supporting enjoyable and effective human-machine interactions. Nevertheless, the annotation process could be costly, time-consuming and complicated, particularly the more expressive is the semantic formalism. In this work, we propose a bootstrapping architecture for the semantic annotation of dialogue corpora with rich structures, based on Dependency Syntax and Frame Semantics.

1 Introduction

We propose a cooperative architecture that incrementally generates and improves the annotation of the French MEDIA dialogue corpus with high-level semantics (HLS), as a result of the cooperation of several linguistic modules. MEDIA is a French corpus that has collected about 70 hours of spontaneous speech from the task of hotel room reservation. It contains transcribed utterances[1] that have been manually segmented[2] and annotated with a **flat semantics** i.e.,concept-value pairs (Bonneau-Maynard et al., 2005).

The **HLS semantics**, namely the MultiModal Interface Language formalism (MMIL) (Denis et al., 2010), augments the expressivity of the flat semantics by representing communicative actions, predicates, arguments and fine-grained features. Communicative actions are **components** built up from two types of entity (i.e. *events* and *participants*), which are linked together by *relations* and described by sets of **features** (attribute-value pairs). It is possible to identify in entities a set of **main features**, which can be domain-specific. For the semantic annotation, components are mapped to segments in utterances. Figure 1 shows the canonical representation of an utterance in the corpus in compliance with the specifications for the annotation[3].

2 The Architecture

The architecture (Figure 2) for the automatic annotation has been formulated as a post-interpretation process that takes place after the syntactic analysis and semantic role labeling (SRL). Two linguistic resources interact within the architecture, the corpus and the Frames[4]. Four linguistic modules are involved in the annotation: the Part-Of-Speech (POS) tagger, the parsing, the semantic-role labeling (SRL) and the HLS Builder. The common knowledge base comprises two knowledge-bases (one for the domain and the other for the HLS formalism) together with a relational database management system (RDBMS). The knowledge bases assure the coherence of the an-

*This work is supported by the *Agence Nationale de la Recherche (ANR)* in France and is part of the French Project PORT-MEDIA.

[1]Utterances with ellipsis, disfluencies, false starts, reformulations, repetitions and ungrammaticalities and special characters such as the symbol '*' that indicates uncertainty due to noise in the communication channel.

[2]The term *Segment* means sequence of words in utterances.

[3]http://www.port-media.org/doku.php?id=mmil_for_annotating_media

[4]Frames is the process in which the frames and frame elements (FE) are defined.

Proceedings of the SIGDIAL 2011: the 12th Annual Meeting of the Special Interest Group on Discourse and Dialogue, pages 332–334,
Portland, Oregon, June 17-18, 2011. ©2011 Association for Computational Linguistics

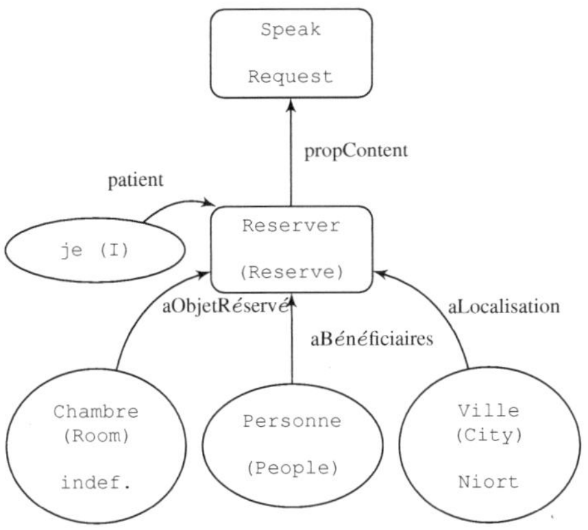

Entities	Segment	Features=Value
Communicative Act:Request	je voudrais ... à Niort	
Main Event:Reserve	faire une réservation	
Participant 1:Pronoun	je	
Participant 2:Chambre	d' une chambre	
	une	refType=indefinite
	chambre	objType=Chambre

Figure 1: HLS representation for the French utterance "je voudrais faire une réservation d' une chambre pour une personne à Niort" (*So I would like to make a reservation for a room for one person in Niort*). It shows a *request to reserve*: the communicative action is *Request* the main event is *Reserve*. Note that the beneficiary and the patient are two different roles, the beneficiary is the person, not necessarily the same speaker, who will use the object reserved (e.g. rooms). The patient is the speaker. The segmentation of the HLS Component is presented in the Table, the component is mapped to the whole utterance. The fine-grained segmentation of features is shown for the Participant 2.

notation while the database assures persistence and data integrity. The database stores the corpus, the frames, the results at each level of analysis, as well as the progress in the annotation. The persistence permits progressively optimizing the algorithms until the desired annotation is obtained and integrated into the corpus files. The corpus manager is in charge of the resources management. Last but not least, two annotation tools were built: one for the SRL gold standard (web-based) and the other for the HLS gold standard (standalone).

Syntactic Analysis. We decided to employ statistical approaches that could learn the irregularities of spoken language: the French Tree-Tagger[5] and the dependency-based MALT-PARSER (Nivre et al., 2007). The parser has been trained with 1449 utterances annotated according to the annotation guidelines described in (Cerisara and Gardent, 2009).

[5]http://www.ims.uni-stuttgart.de/~schmid/

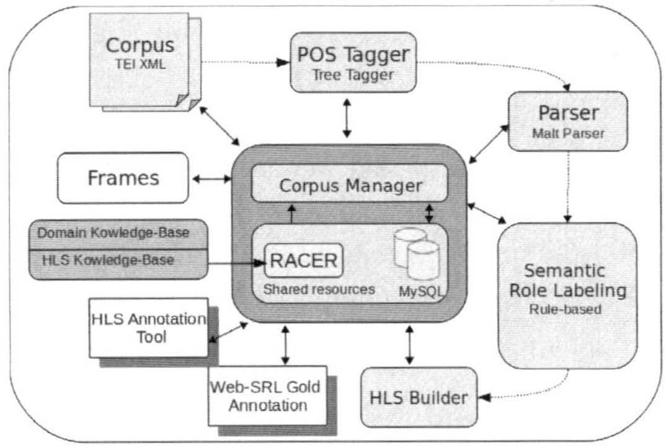

Figure 2: General Architecture for the HLS Annotation.

Definition of Frames. Frame Semantics, (Baker et al., 1998) arranges common background knowledge for situations by grouping verbal, nominal causative and non-causative predicates. Nevertheless, paraphrases are more used in spoken language than explicitly uttered nouns, adjectives or verbs for referring to a situation (e.g.'ask', 'request' or 'demand'). Here we introduce the term: **Frame Evoking Phrase** (FEP) for evoking frames and we include syntactic templates that mirror these phrases in frames and frame elements (FE). Table 1 summarizes the differences between PORT-MEDIA frames and FrameNet (Baker et al., 1998).

	FrameNet	PORT-MEDIA
Frames	Lexical Units	Lexical Units, POS tags and templates MEDIA Flat Semantics
Frame Elements	Lexical Units, Phrase Type and Grammatical Function Semantic Type	Lexical Units, POS tags, templates and dependency relation Semantic Type and MEDIA flat semantics

Table 1: Static Characteristics of Frames in FrameNet and in PORT-MEDIA.

Semantic Role Labeling. We built a rule-based semantic role labeling for detecting frames and FE (roles) by using dependency tree-template pattern matchers that exploit the information already compressed in frames. The SRL detects the boundaries of FEP and FE by measuring the syntactic and semantic similarity between the utterance and the frame.

HLS Builder. The HLS Builder is the last phase in the annotation process: it is rule-based and it takes utterances in the corpus with their flat semantics, dependency trees and predicates-arguments and builds the HLS representation (See Figure 1), according to the specifications for the annotation and the knowledge bases. The *dialogue act* and *main event* in HLS components can be detected from the predicates. Similarly, *secondary events* and *participants* with their *features* can be detected from the roles and the flat semantics.

3 Evaluation and Discussion

For evaluating the system we separately computed the accuracy of its linguistic components. **The parser** achieved a label attachment score (LAS) (Nivre et al., 2007) of 86.16%, with a training set of 1097 utterances and a test-set of 100 utterances. **The SRL** was evaluated with metrics adapted from the CONLL 2005 evaluation (Carreras and Màrquez, 2005) f*or supporting FEP and allowing overlapped FEP for different frames*. The LAS was computed by comparing the semantic dependencies of *system's and gold's propositions*[6] and their segments. The gold standard comprises 115 utterances annotated with the major frames in the domain: Request, Reserve and Attributes. The F1-measure computed for propositions with exactly the same segments was 56.66%. When verifying whether the segments contain the same syntactic governor, the SRL achieves a better score: 71.30%. Finally, varying the number of excluded words in both segments[7] yielded a constant increase of the F1-measure until a maximum of 84.27%. **The HLS annotation** was evaluated by measuring the similarity between *gold's and system's components* with a gold standard of 330 complex utterances related to the reservation task. When rigorously measuring the *equality of components*[8], we obtained a F1-measure of 57.79%. Measuring equality of components without being so rigorous with features' segmentation, yielded a slightly higher score 63.31%. Finally, when measuring equality of components by taking into account only the **main features** of entities, we obtained a higher score: 70.65%.

We proposed an architecture for corpus management that allows incremental updates over persistent information until a more accurate semantic annotation is obtained. The preliminary results show a general agreement when defining *the main features and the main entities in HLS components* and a disagreement when segmenting fine-grained features. We observed that the system tends to create new entities when it detects repetitions or references in long utterances. Defining a more precise segmentation policy in the manual annotation guidelines, augmenting the training data for parsing, as well as integrating reference resolution and disambiguation techniques, will enhance the annotation process. An appealing research direction would be to integrate and evaluate machine learning components in the architecture.

[6]A proposition is a structure containing the predicate, their arguments and the semantic relation between them.

[7]From 1 to n words not common in both segments.

[8]Two HLS components are equal if their entities and relations are equal. Two entities are equal if they have the same segment and features (feature name and feature value) and if these features are mapped to the same segments in the utterance. Two relations are equal if they have the same source and target entities as well as the same name

References

Hélène Bonneau-Maynard and Matthieu Quignard and Alexandre Denis. 2005. MEDIA: A semantically annotated corpus of task oriented dialogs in French. *Language Resources and Evaluation.*

Alexandre Denis and Lina M. Rojas-Barahona and Matthieu Quignard. 2010. Extending MMIL Semantic Representation: Experiments in Dialogue Systems and Semantic Annotation of Corpora. *In: Proceedings of the Fifth ISO-ACL/SIGSEM Workshop on Interoperable Semantic Annotation (ISA-5), Hong Kong.*

Collin Baker and Charles Fillmore and John Lowe. 1998. The Berkeley FrameNet Project. *Proceedings of the 17th International Conference on Computational linguistics*, 86–90. Association for Computational Linguistics.

Joakim Nivre and Johan Hall and Sandra Kübler and Ryan McDonald and Jens Nilsson and Sebastian Riedel and Deniz Yuret. 2007. The CoNLL 2007 Shared Task on Dependency Parsing. *Proceedings of the CoNLL Shared Task Session of EMNLP-CoNLL 2007.* Prague, Czech Republic:915–932. Association for Computational Linguistics.

Christophe Cerisara and Claire Gardent. 2009. Analyse syntaxique du français parlé. *Journée thématique ATALA Quels analyseurs syntaxiques pour le français.*

Xavier Carreras and Lluís Màrquez. 2005. Introduction to the CoNLL-2005 shared task: Semantic role labeling. CONLL '05: Proceedings of the Ninth Conference on Computational Natural Language Learning. 152–164. Association for Computational Linguistics.

The CODA System for Monologue-to-Dialogue Generation

Svetlana Stoyanchev
Centre for Research in Computing
The Open University
Walton Hall, Milton Keynes, UK
s.stoyanchev@open.ac.uk

Paul Piwek
Centre for Research in Computing
The Open University
Walton Hall, Milton Keynes, UK
p.piwek@open.ac.uk

Abstract

This paper describes an implemented monolingual Text-to-Text generation system. The system takes monologue and transforms it to two-participant dialogue. The system uses mappings between discourse relations in text and dialogue acts in dialogue. These mappings are extracted from a parallel monologue and dialogue corpus.

1 Introduction

This paper describes the CODA system,[1] a Text-to-Text generation system that converts text parsed with discourse relations (Mann and Thompson, 1988) into information-delivering dialogue between two characters. By information-delivering dialogue, we mean dialogue (akin to that used by Plato) that is used primarily to convey information and possibly also to make an argument; this in contrast with dramatic dialogue which focuses on character development and narrative.

Several empirical studies show that delivering information as dialogue, rather than monologue, can be particularly effective for education (Craig et al., 2000; Lee et al., 1998) and persuasion (Suzuki and Yamada, 2004). Information-delivering dialogue also lends itself well for presentation through computer-animated agents (Prendinger and Ishizuka, 2004).

[1]CODA stands for COherent Dialogue Automatically generated from text (see http://computing.open.ac.uk/coda/). The CODA project is funded by the UK's Engineering and Physical Sciences Research Council under Grant EP/G020981/1.

With most information locked up in text (books, newspapers, leaflets, etc.), automatic generation of dialogue from text in monologue makes it possible to convert information into dialogue on demand.

In contrast to previous Text-to-Dialogue systems (Piwek et al., 2007), the CODA system is data-driven and modular. The system is composed of three modules: *Dialogue Modeller, Verbalizer,* and *Dialogue Merger*.

The *Dialogue modeller* determines appropriate dialogue act sequences that can be used for converting a segment of input text containing a single discourse relation into dialogue. The module is data-oriented in that the mappings it uses between discourse structure and dialogue act sequences have been derived from the CODA parallel monologue/dialogue corpus (Stoyanchev and Piwek, 2010).

The *Verbalizer* converts text segments together with a specification of the target dialogue act types into dialogue utterances.

The Dialogue modeller and verbaliser components overgenerate possible outputs for each discourse relation in monologue. The *Dialogue Merger* component selects one of the proposed outputs for each text segment of the input and merges them into a single coherent dialogue.

2 System Design

In this section we describe the three components of the system: dialogue modeller, verbalizer, and dialogue merger.

Before we look at each of the modules, we, however, first need to specify more precisely what the

Proceedings of the SIGDIAL 2011: the 12th Annual Meeting of the Special Interest Group on Discourse and Dialogue, pages 335–337,
Portland, Oregon, June 17-18, 2011.

Input	MANNER-MEANS [In September, Ashland settled the long-simmering dispute] [by agreeing to pay Iran $325 million.]
Dialogue Modeller	1. (ComplexQ; Explain) 2. (Explain; ComplexQ; Explain) 3. (Explain; YesNoQ; Explain)
Verbalizer DA Seq1	A: How did Ashland settle the long-simmering dispute in September? B: By agreeing to pay Iran $325 million.
Verbalizer DA Seq2	A: In September, Ashland settled the long-simmering dispute. B: How? A: By agreeing to pay Iran $325 million.
Verbalizer DA Seq3	A: In September, Ashland settled the long-simmering dispute. B: By agreeing to pay Iran $325 million? A: Correct.
Dialogue Merger	Select one of the DA sequences based on overall dialogue

Table 1: Example of the output from each component

input for our system is. The system expects text that has already been annotated with a discourse structure. There have been recent encouraging advances in the automatic parsing of discourse structure, e.g., see duVerle and Prendinger (2009), but the state-of-the-art is not yet at a point where it provides sufficiently reliable inputs for our purposes. To demonstrate the functionality of our system without relying on still imperfect discourse parsing, we use the RST-parsed Wall Street Journal corpus as input (Carlson et al., 2001).

Throughout the remainder of this section, we use the outputs for each of the modules in Table 1 as a running example.

2.1 Dialogue Modeller

The *Dialogue Modeller* component takes as input a snippet of monologue text annotated with discourse structure. For each input Discourse Relation structure (DR), the dialogue modeller outputs a set of dialogue act (DA) sequences appropriate for expressing the same information, but now in dialogue form.

The *Dialogue modeller* uses a configuration XML file to look up possible DA sequences for the input

DA sequence
YesNoQ; Explain
YesNoQ; Yes; Explain
Explain; ComplexQ; Explain
ComplexQ; Explain
Explain; YesNoQ; Resp-Answer-Yes
Explain; Contradict
Factoid-Info-Req;Factoid-Resp;Explain
Exlain; Resp-Agree;Explain

Table 2: Dialogue act sequences

discourse structure. In the current system configuration we extract these mappings from the CODA parallel corpus of professionally authored dialogues and parallel monologues. We use the eight most frequent DA sequences (see Table2) that occur on the dialogue side of discourse relations in the parallel dataset. Each discourse relation is mapped to one or more DA sequences with a score indicating frequency of this mapping in the CODA corpus.

The dialogue modeller can be customised with mappings from other sources such as a different corpus, manually authored mappings or a mapping arrived at through experimental methods.

The current version of the dialogue modeller supports input with only one level of discourse structure annotation. As a result, all input structures contain parts made of two segments and one discourse relation between these segments. In the future work, we plan to implement a dialogue modeller that accepts more complex (nested) discourse structures.

2.2 Verbalizer

The verbalizer is rule-based and has three types of rules: discourse relation (DR)-specific, generic, and canned. All of the rules take as input a monologue segment and a target dialogue act. DR-specific rules also use the discourse relation and segment nuclearity of the input segment.[2] The verbalization rules are ordered according to their priority with DR-specific rules having a higher priority.

Generic and DR-specific rules use the CMU question generation tool (Heilman and Smith, 2010) in combination with syntactic and lexical manipulation rules. Canned text rules are used to generate *AnswerYes, Agree* and *Clarify* dialogue acts by proba-

[2]Nucleus is the more salient segment in a relation.

bilistic selection from a set of utterances extracted from the CODA corpus. For example, the *Agree* dialogue act is verbalized as one of the statements: *I agree with you; I agree; I couldn't agree more; I completely agree; Absolutely; Very true; Right; True*. Probabilistic selection from a list allows us to generate non-repetitive dialogues. The system is extendible, such that new rules can be easily added to the implementation.

2.3 Dialogue Merger

The Dialogue Merger component takes as input verbalized dialogue act sequences. The tasks of the Dialogue Merger include: 1) selecting the best verbalized sequence and 2) assigning speaker roles (TEACHER or STUDENT) to dialogue turns.

We aim to create diverse dialogues, in particular, by avoiding repetitive use of the same dialogue act sequences. This is achieved as follows. Selection of DA sequence is incremental, considering one relation at a time. For each relation, the dialogue merger selects a dialogue act sequence that has been successfully verbalized by the *verbalizer* and which, so far, has been used the smallest number of times (out of all the sequences that have been used up to this point).

Although in the original authored dialogues, both TEACHER and STUDENT ask questions and give explanations, in our preliminary experiments observers made negative comments about mixing initiative between the STUDENT and the TEACHER in the generated dialogues. In the current version, the speaker roles are assigned based on the dialogue act. All questions and clarification requests are assigned to the STUDENT and other dialogue acts are assigned to the TEACHER.

As an additional post-processing step, to maintain perspective in the dialogue, we change pronouns in the dialogue turns. The turns assigned to the TEACHER character remain unchanged. The turns assigned to the STUDENT character change the perspective: non-possessive pronouns are inverted, e.g. *you* $\rightarrow$ *I*, *we* $\rightarrow$ *us*, *my* $\rightarrow$ *your*.

3 Conclusions and Further Work

In this paper, we described a Text-to-Dialogue generation system that converts text annotated with discourse relations into dialogue. The system is modular, data-driven, and takes advantage of state-of-the-art question generation tools. Our evaluation of the dialogue modeller and verbalizer components described in (Piwek and Stoyanchev, 2011) shows that both accuracy and fluency of generated dialogues are not worse than that of human-written dialogues.

We plan to release the CODA Text-to-Dialogue system as open source code later this year. The system can be used as a starting point for researchers interested in evaluating NLP tools for question generation, dialogue modelling and paraphrasing in a dialogue generation task.

References

L. Carlson, D. Marcu, and M. E. Okurowski. 2001. Building a discourse-tagged corpus in the framework of rhetorical structure theory. In *Proceedings of the Second SIGdial Workshop on Discourse and Dialogue*, SIGDIA.

S. Craig, B. Gholson, M. Ventura, A. Graesser, and the Tutoring Research Group. 2000. Overhearing dialogues and monologues in virtual tutoring sessions. *International Journal of Artificial Intelligence in Education*, 11:242–253.

D. duVerle and H. Prendinger. 2009. A novel discourse parser based on support vector machines. In *Procs of ACL-IJCNLP)*, pages 665–673, Singapore, August.

M. Heilman and N. A. Smith. 2010. Good question! statistical ranking for question generation. In *Proc. of NAACL/HLT*, Los Angeles.

J. Lee, F. Dinneen, and J. McKendree. 1998. Supporting student discussions: it isn't just talk. *Education and Information Technologies*, 3:217–229.

W. C. Mann and S. A. Thompson. 1988. Rhetorical structure theory: Toward a functional theory of text organization. *Text*, 8(3):243–281.

P. Piwek and S. Stoyanchev. 2011. Data-oriented Monologue-to-Dialogue Generation. In *Procs of ACL*.

P. Piwek, H. Hernault, H. Prendinger, and M. Ishizuka. 2007. T2D: Generating Dialogues between Virtual Agents Automatically from Text. In *Procs of IVA07*, LNAI 4722, pages 161–174. Springer Verlag.

H. Prendinger and M. Ishizuka, editors. 2004. *Life-Like Characters: Tools, Affective Functions, and Applications*. Cognitive Technologies Series. Springer, Berlin.

S. Stoyanchev and P. Piwek. 2010. Constructing the CODA corpus. In *Procs of LREC*, Malta.

S. V. Suzuki and S. Yamada. 2004. Persuasion through overheard communication by life-like agents. In *Procs of the 2004 IEEE/WIC/ACM International Conference on Intelligent Agent Technology*, Beijing.

BEETLE II: an adaptable tutorial dialogue system

Myroslava O. Dzikovska and **Amy Isard** and **Peter Bell** and **Johanna D. Moore**
School of Informatics, University of Edinburgh, Edinburgh, United Kingdom
{m.dzikovska,j.moore,amy.isard,peter.bell}@ed.ac.uk

Natalie Steinhauser and **Gwendolyn Campbell**
Naval Air Warfare Center Training Systems Division, Orlando, FL, USA
{gwendolyn.campbell,natalie.steihauser}@navy.mil

Abstract

We present BEETLE II, a tutorial dialogue system which accepts unrestricted language input and supports experimentation with different dialogue strategies. Our first system evaluation compared two dialogue policies. The resulting corpus was used to study the impact of different tutoring and error recovery strategies on user satisfaction and student interaction style. It can also be used in the future to study a wide range of research issues in dialogue systems.

1 Introduction

There has recently been much interest in developing tutorial dialogue systems that understand student explanations (Graesser et al., 1999; Aleven et al., 2001; Nielsen et al., 2008; VanLehn et al., 2007), because it has been shown that high percentages of self-explanation and student contentful talk are correlated with better learning in human-human tutoring (Chi et al., 1994; Litman et al., 2009). However, most existing systems use pre-authored tutor responses for addressing student errors. The advantage of this approach is that tutors can devise remediation dialogues that are highly tailored to specific misconceptions, providing step-by-step scaffolding and potentially suggesting additional exercises. The disadvantage is a lack of adaptivity and generality: students often get the same remediation for the same error regardless of their past performance or dialogue context. It also becomes more difficult to experiment with different dialogue policies (including error recovery and tutorial policies determining the most appropriate feedback), due to the complexities in applying tutoring strategies consistently in a large number of hand-authored remediations.

The BEETLE II system architecture is designed to overcome these limitations (Callaway et al., 2007). It uses a deep parser and generator, together with a domain reasoner and a diagnoser, to produce detailed analyses of student utterances and to generate feedback automatically. This allows the system to consistently apply the same tutorial policy across a range of questions. The system's modular setup and extensibility also make it a suitable testbed for both computational linguistics algorithms and more general questions about theories of learning.

The system is based on an introductory electricity and electronics course developed by experienced instructional designers, originally created for use in a human-human tutoring study. The exercises were then transferred into a computer system with only minor adjustments (e.g., breaking down compound questions into individual questions). This resulted in a realistic tutoring setup, which presents interesting challenges to language processing components, involving a wide variety of language phenomena.

We demonstrate a version of the system that underwent a user evaluation in 2009, which found significant learning gains for students interacting with the system. The experimental data collection compared two different dialogue policies implemented in the system, and resulted in a corpus supporting research into a variety of questions about human-computer dialogue interaction (Dzikovska et al., 2010a).

Proceedings of the SIGDIAL 2011: the 12th Annual Meeting of the Special Interest Group on Discourse and Dialogue, pages 338–340,
Portland, Oregon, June 17-18, 2011. ©2011 Association for Computational Linguistics

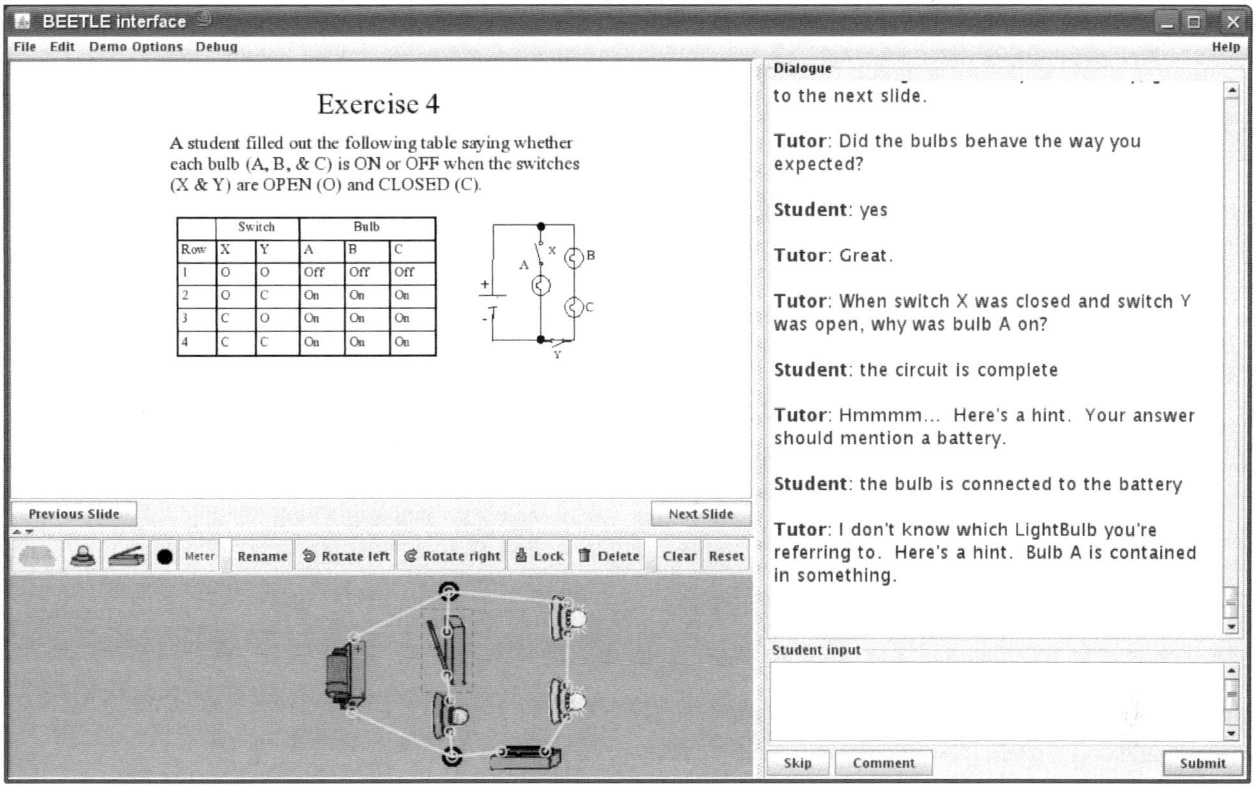

Figure 1: Screenshot of the BEETLE II system

2 Example Interaction

The BEETLE II system delivers basic electricity and electronics tutoring to students with no prior knowledge of the subject. A screenshot is shown in Figure 1. The student interface includes an area to display reading material, a circuit simulator, and a dialogue history window. Currently all interactions with the system are typed. Students read pre-authored curriculum slides and carry out exercises which involve experimenting with the circuit simulator and explaining the observed behaviour. The system also asks some high-level questions, such as "What is voltage?".

An example dialogue with the system, taken from the evaluation corpus, is shown in Figure 2. It shows three key system properties: after the student's first turn, which was correct but incomplete, the system rephrases the correct part of the student answer and prompts for the missing information. In the second turn, the system cannot interpret the student utterance, so it responds with a targeted help message and a hint about the object that needs to be mentioned. Finally, in the last turn the system combines the information from the tutor's hint and the student's answers and restates the complete answer since the current answer was completed over multiple turns.

3 Data Analysis and Future Work

The data collected with the BEETLE II system has been used to investigate several research questions regarding discourse and dialogue: the effectiveness of different error recovery strategies (Dzikovska et al., 2010b); the underlying dimensions of user satisfaction and their relationship with learning gain (Dzikovska et al., 2011); the relationship between (student) alignment in dialogue and learning gain (Steinhauser et al., 2011); and the differences between students' social and metacognitive statements depending on the interaction style (Dzikovska et al., 2010a). We are currently annotating the data with additional interaction parameters, including correctness of student answers and appropriateness of system hints. This will allow us to apply PARADISE

Tutor:	Why was bulb A on when switch Y was open and switch Z was closed?
Student:	because it had a closed path
Tutor:	Right. There is a closed path. Keep going.
Student:	there was a closed path not effected by the switch
Tutor:	I'm sorry, I'm having a problem understanding. I don't understand the word 'effect' here. Here's a hint. Your answer should mention a battery.
Student:	it has a closed path with the battery
Tutor:	You're on the right track. Here's the answer. Bulb A is still contained in a closed path with the battery.

Figure 2: Example interaction with the system from our corpus

methodology to get additional insight into which parameters of tutorial dialogue affect learning gain and user satisfaction.

We are also adding a speech interface to the system, which will open new and interesting research questions. Students often fail to use domain terminology correctly, and in the tutoring domain it is important to teach students to use proper terminology, so incorrect usage must be detected and corrected. This means that grammar-based language models are not appropriate for the language modelling, and opens new questions about robust ASR and language interpretation in such domains.

Acknowledgements

This work has been supported in part by US Office of Naval Research grants N000141010085 and N0001410WX20278. We thank Katherine Harrison, Leanne Taylor, Charles Scott, Simon Caine, Charles Callaway and Elaine Farrow for their contributions to this effort.

References

V. Aleven, O. Popescu, and K. R. Koedinger. 2001. Towards tutorial dialog to support self-explanation: Adding natural language understanding to a cognitive tutor. In *Proceedings of the 10th International Conference on Artificial Intelligence in Education (AIED '01)"*.

Charles B. Callaway, Myroslava Dzikovska, Elaine Farrow, Manuel Marques-Pita, Colin Matheson, and Johanna D. Moore. 2007. The Beetle and BeeDiff tutoring systems. In *Proceedings of SLaTE'07 (Speech and Language Technology in Education)*.

Michelene T. H. Chi, Nicholas de Leeuw, Mei-Hung Chiu, and Christian LaVancher. 1994. Eliciting self-explanations improves understanding. *Cognitive Science*, 18(3):439–477.

Myroslava Dzikovska, Natalie B. Steinhauser, Johanna D. Moore, Gwendolyn E. Campbell, Katherine M. Harrison, and Leanne S. Taylor. 2010a. Content, social, and metacognitive statements: An empirical study comparing human-human and human-computer tutorial dialogue. In *Proceedings of ECTEL-2010*, pages 93–108.

Myroslava O. Dzikovska, Johanna D. Moore, Natalie Steinhauser, and Gwendolyn Campbell. 2010b. The impact of interpretation problems on tutorial dialogue. In *Proceedings of the 48th Annual Meeting of the Association for Computational Linguistics(ACL-2010)*.

Myroslava O. Dzikovska, Johanna D. Moore, Natalie Steinhauser, and Gwendolyn Campbell. 2011. Exploring user satisfaction in a tutorial dialogue system. In *Proceedings of the 12th annual SIGdial Meeting on Discourse and Dialogue*.

A. C. Graesser, K. Wiemer-Hastings, P. Wiemer-Hastings, and R. Kreuz. 1999. Autotutor: A simulation of a human tutor. *Cognitive Systems Research*, 1:35–51.

Diane Litman, Johanna Moore, Myroslava Dzikovska, and Elaine Farrow. 2009. Using natural language processing to analyze tutorial dialogue corpora across domains and modalities. In *Proc. of 14th International Conference on Artificial Intelligence in Education*.

Rodney D. Nielsen, Wayne Ward, and James H. Martin. 2008. Learning to assess low-level conceptual understanding. In *Proceedings 21st International FLAIRS Conference*, Coconut Grove, Florida, May.

Natalie B. Steinhauser, Gwendolyn E. Campbell, Leanne S. Taylor, Simon Caine, Charlie Scott, Myroslava O. Dzikovska, and Johanna D. Moore. 2011. Talk like an electrician: Student dialogue mimicking behavior in an intelligent tutoring system. In *Proceedings of the 15th International Conference on Artificial Intelligence in Education (AIED-2011)*.

Kurt VanLehn, Pamela Jordan, and Diane Litman. 2007. Developing pedagogically effective tutorial dialogue tactics: Experiments and a testbed. In *Proceedings of SLaTE Workshop on Speech and Language Technology in Education*, Farmington, PA, October.

Engagement-based Multi-party Dialog with a Humanoid Robot

David Klotz and **Johannes Wienke** and **Julia Peltason** and **Britta Wrede** and **Sebastian Wrede**
Applied Informatics Group
Bielefeld University
{dklotz, jwienke, jpeltaso, bwrede, swrede}@techfak.uni-bielefeld.de

Vasil Khalidov and **Jean-Marc Odobez**
IDIAP Research Institute
{vasil.khalidov, odobez}@idiap.ch

Abstract

When a robot is situated in an environment containing multiple possible interaction partners, it has to make decisions about when to engage specific users and how to detect and react appropriately to actions of the users that might signal the intention to interact.

In this demonstration we present the integration of an engagement model in an existing dialog system based on interaction patterns. As a sample scenario, this enables the humanoid robot Nao to play a quiz game with multiple participants.

1 Introduction

Giving robotic systems the ability to join in conversation with one or multiple users poses many new challenges for the development of appropriate dialog systems and models. When a dialog system is situated in the real, physical world and used in more open settings, more effort needs to be spent on establishing and maintaining clear communication channels between the system and its users. E.g. the system first needs to detect that there are potential users with whom interacting would be possible, it needs to decide if a detected person wants to interact with the system at all and it needs to make decisions when and how it should try to start an interaction with that person.

Bohus and Horvitz (2009) have developed a model for representing the current relation of a user with such a system (their *engagement state*) and determining if they want to be involved in an interaction with the system (using explicit *engagement actions* and the more abstract *engagement intention*). Each user can be *engaged* in specific *interactions* (denoting different "basic unit[s] of sustained, interactive problem-solving") and there can be multiple such interactions, each with potentially different users.

This demonstration shows how an engagement model inspired by these ideas was integrated into an existing dialog system and how it helps in realizing interactive scenarios with a robot that incorporate cues for the dialog from the system's environment. Section 3 gives more details about this model and how it is used by the dialog.

2 Scenario

As a scenario for this demonstration we chose a simple quiz game involving the robot Nao as a host playing with one or multiple human users. At first, the robot waits until one of the human interaction partners approaches. When the person opens the interaction (i.e. by greeting the robot), the system responds with an appropriate greeting. While the person continues to show the intention to interact with the robot (determined by the process described in section 3.1), the robot will ask questions randomly chosen from a predefined set and will try to judge if the person answered them correctly.

When another person enters the robot's field of view, the system also tries to determine if they have the intention to interact with it. If that is the case, the system suspends the current interaction with the first person and actively tries to engage the second person, encouraging him or her to join the ongoing quiz game. The prospective new player can then choose

Proceedings of the SIGDIAL 2011: the 12th Annual Meeting of the Special Interest Group on Discourse and Dialogue, pages 341–343,
Portland, Oregon, June 17-18, 2011.

Figure 1: Two persons interacting with the developed system.

to join or decline the request.

As long as one of the engaged participants shows the intention to interact, the robot continues to ask questions which all participants can try to answer. The quiz game is stopped either by an explicit request of one the users or after all participants have left the scene.

This scenario serves as a good testbed for the integration of different cues for the engagement model and how that model affects the actions taken by the dialog system. The right-hand side of figure 1 shows two people interacting with the robot during the quiz game.

3 System Overview

Figure 2 shows an overview of the different components involved in the demonstrated system. This includes components for the perception (e.g. accessing images from the robot's camera and audio from its microphones), for generating actions (e.g. using the robot's text-to-speech system), the dialog system itself and a memory system for connecting these diverse components.

The dialog system used for this demonstration is called PaMini, which is short for "Pattern-based Mixed-Initiative human-robot Interaction" and is described in more detail by Peltason and Wrede (2010). This dialog system was modified in Klotz (2010) with a model of engagement based on the ideas presented by Bohus and Horvitz (2009). In our adaptation of this model, there are extension points for integrating different sources of information about the user's engagement intentions and actions, described in the following section.

3.1 Determining the User's Actions & Intention

For determining the user's actions (e.g. if the user explicitly wants to start an interaction with the system), this demonstration uses a set of possible utterances which are simply matched against the results of a speech recognition module.

To get an estimation of the user's intention to interact, the image from the robot's camera is first used to detect the faces of users and to estimate their current visual focus of attention. A module based on a framework by Ba and Odobez (2009) is used to determine probabilities that the user is looking at each of a pre-defined list of possible focus targets, including the robot itself and other users visible in the scene. The upper left of figure 1 shows a visualization of this module's output. *Nao* denotes the robot as the focus target with the highest probability, while the designation *UN* is short for the "unfocused" target.

This list of probabilities is then stored in a mem-

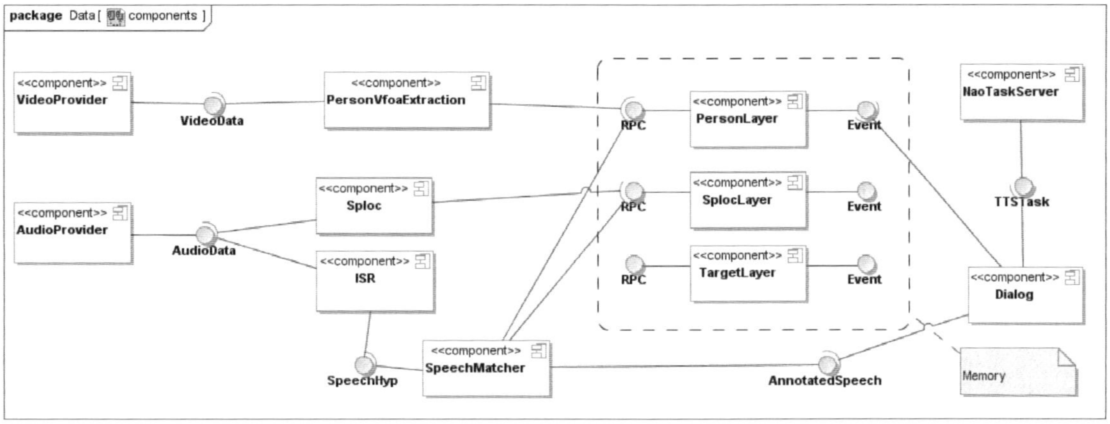

Figure 2: Components of the developed system.

ory system developed by Wienke and Wrede (2011). The memory system provides temporal query capabilities which are finally used to guess a user's current intention of interacting with the robot based on the history of the probabilities that the robot was the user's current visual focus of attention target. This result is also stored in the memory system together will all other information known about a user.

3.2 Engagement Cues for the Dialog

The dialog system receives the information about the user's state and intention from the memory system and uses it in several rules for controlling its own engagement actions. The intention is e.g. used to determine if there is a new user that should be persuaded to join the quiz game described in section 2 and if any of the users still shows interest so that a new question should be asked. The general state of the detected users is also used e.g. to observe when the users leave the robot's field of view for a longer period of time which causes the dialog system to close its current interaction.

4 Conclusion

We have shown how an existing dialog system that was enhanced using an explicit model of engagement can be used to realize interactive scenarios with a robot that is situated in the physical world. An estimation of the user's current visual focus of attention is used to gauge their intention to engage the robot in conversation.

A video recording of two people interacting with the developed system is available online at `http://youtu.be/pWZLVF2Xa8g`

Acknowledgments

This work was done in the HUMAVIPS project, funded by the European Commission Seventh Framework Programme, Theme Cognitive Systems and Robotics, Grant agreement no. 247525.

References

S. Ba and J.-M. Odobez. 2009. Recognizing Visual Focus of Attention from Head Pose in Natural Meetings. *IEEE Trans. on System, Man and Cybernetics: part B, Cybernetics*, 39:16–34.

Dan Bohus and Eric Horvitz. 2009. Models for multiparty engagement in open-world dialog. In *Proceedings of the SIGDIAL 2009 Conference*, pages 225–234, London, UK. Association for Computational Linguistics.

David Klotz. 2010. Modeling engagement in a multiparty human-robot dialog. Master's thesis, Bielefeld University.

Julia Peltason and Britta Wrede. 2010. Modeling human-robot interaction based on generic interaction patterns. In *AAAI Fall Symposium: Dialog with Robots*, Arlington, VA, USA.

Johannes Wienke and Sebastian Wrede. 2011. A spatiotemporal working memory for multi-level data fusion. In *Proc. of IEEE/RSJ International Conference on Intelligent Robots and Systems*. submitted.

POMY: A Conversational Virtual Environment for Language Learning in POSTECH

Hyungjong Noh Kyusong Lee Sungjin Lee Gary Geunbae Lee

Department of Computer Science and Engineering
Pohang University of Science & Technology, Pohang, South Korea
{nohhj, kyusonglee, junion, gblee}@postech.ac.kr

Abstract

This demonstration will illustrate an interactive immersive computer game, POMY, designed to help Korean speakers learn English. This system allows learners to exercise their visual and aural senses, receiving a full immersion experience to increase their memory and concentration abilities to a greatest extent. In POMY, learners can have free conversations with game characters and receive corrective feedback to their errors. Game characters show various emotional expressions based on learners' input to keep learners motivated. Through this system, learners can repeatedly practice conversations in everyday life setting in a foreign language with no embarrassment.

1 Introduction

The needs for computer-based methods for learning language skills and components are increasing. One of the ultimate goals of computer-assisted language learning is to provide learners with an immersive environment that facilitates acquiring communicative competence. According to Second Language Acquisition (SLA) theories, there are some essential factors for improving learners' conversational skills: 1) comprehensible inputs and outputs, 2) corrective feedback, and 3) motivation and attitude. SLA theories imply that providing learners with the opportunity to have free conversations with someone who can correct their errors is very important for successful acquisition of foreign languages. Moreover, motivation is another crucial factor; therefore a good CALL system should have elements which can interest learners [1].

Considering these requirements, we have developed a conversational English education framework, POMY (POstech iMmersive English studY). The program allows users to exercise their visual and aural senses to receive a full immersion experience to develop into independent English as a Foreign Language (EFL) learners and increase their memory and concentration abilities to a greatest extent [2].

Figure 1: Example screenshots of POMY: path-finding, post office, and market

Proceedings of the SIGDIAL 2011: the 12th Annual Meeting of the Special Interest Group on Discourse and Dialogue, pages 344–346,
Portland, Oregon, June 17-18, 2011.

Figure 2: Various character animations

2 Demonstrated System

In order to provide learners with immersive world, we have developed a virtual reality environment using the Unity 3D game engine[1]. For the domains that learners are exposed to, we select such domains as path-finding, market, post office, library, and movie theater (Figure 1) to ensure having learners practice conversations in everyday life setting. To keep learners motivated and interested during learning sessions, learners are encouraged to accomplish several missions. For example, the first mission in the post office is to send a camera to one's uncle in England. The package must be insured and delivered by the next week. In order to send the package, a learner must talk to Non-Player Characters (NPCs) to fill in the zip-code properly.

All NPCs can perceive the utterances of learners, especially Korean learners of English. Korean learners' production of the sound is different from those of native speakers, resulting in numerous pronunciation errors. Therefore, we have collected a Korean-English corpus to train acoustic models. In addition, since language learners commit numerous grammatical errors, we should consider this to understand their utterances. Thus, we statistically infer the actual learners' intention by taking not only the utterance itself but also the dialog context into consideration, as human tutors do [1].

While free conversation is invaluable to the acquisition process, it is not sufficient for learners to fully develop their L2 proficiency. Corrective feedback to learners' grammatical errors is necessary for improving accuracy in their interlanguage. For this purpose, we designed a special character, Ghost Tutor, which plays the role of English tutor and helps learners to use more appropriate words and expressions during the game. When a learner produces ungrammatical utterances, the Ghost Tutor provides both implicit and explicit negative and positive feedback in a form of elicitation or recast, which was manifested as effective ways in the second language acquisition processes [3]. To provide corrective feedback on grammatical errors, we use a method which consists of two sub-models: the grammaticality checking model and the error type classification model [4]. Firstly, we automatically generate grammatical errors that learners usually commit [5-6], and construct error patterns based on the articulated errors. Then the grammaticality checking model classifies the recognized user speech based on the similarity between the error patterns and the recognition result using confidence scores. After that, the error type classification model chooses the error type based on the most similar error pattern and the error frequency extracted from a learner corpus.

Finally, the human perception of NPC's emotional expressions plays a crucial role in human computer interaction. Thus, all NPCs are provided with a number of communicative animations such as talking, laughing, waving, crying, thinking, and getting angry (Figure 2).The total number of animations is over thirty from which the system can select one based on the response of a learner. The system generates positive expressions such as clapping and laughing when the learner answers correctly, and negative expressions such as crying and getting angry for incorrect answers.

[1] http://unity3d.com/

Acknowledgments

This work was supported by the Industrial Strategic technology development program, 10035252, development of dialog-based spontaneous speech interface technology on mobile platform, funded by the Ministry of Knowledge Economy (MKE, Korea), and by Basic Science Research Program through the National Research Foundation of Korea (NRF) funded by the Ministry of Education, Science and Technology (2010-0019523).

References

Lee, S., Noh, H., Lee, J., Lee, K., Lee, G. G., Sagong, S., Kim, M. 2011. On the Effectiveness of Robot-Assisted Language Learning, ReCALL Journal, Vol.23(1).

Lee, S., Noh, H., Lee, J., Lee, K., Lee, G. G. 2010. POSTECH Approaches for Dialog-based English Conversation Tutoring. Proceedings of the APSIPA annual summit and conference, Singapore.

Long, M. H., Inagaki, S., Ortega, L. 1998. The Role of Input and Interaction in Second Language Acquisition. The Modern Language Journal, 82, 357-371.

Lee, S., Noh, H., Lee, K., Lee, G. G. 2011. Grammatical error detection for corrective feedback provision in oral conversations. Proceedings of the 25th AAAI conference on artificial intelligence (AAAI-11), San Francisco.

Lee, S., Lee J., Noh, H., Lee, K., Lee, G. G, 2011. Grammatical Error Simulation for Computer-Assisted Language Learning, Knowledge-Based Systems (to be published).

Lee, S. and Lee, G. G. 2009. Realistic grammar error simulation using markov logic. Proceedings of the ACL, Singapore.

Rapid Development of Advanced Question-Answering Characters by Non-experts

Sudeep Gandhe and **Alysa Taylor** and **Jillian Gerten** and **David Traum**
USC Institute for Creative Technologies
12015 Waterfront Drive, Playa Vista, CA 90094, USA
<lastname>@ict.usc.edu

Abstract

We demonstrate a dialogue system and the accompanying authoring tools that are designed to allow authors with little or no experience in building dialogue systems to rapidly build advanced question-answering characters. To date seven such virtual characters have been built by non-experts using this architecture and tools. Here we demonstrate one such character, PFC Sean Avery, which was developed by a non-expert in 3 months.

1 Introduction

Our goal is to allow *non-experts* to build advanced question-answering Virtual Human characters. By *non-experts*, we mean that scenario authors need not have any background in computational linguistics or any experience in building dialogue systems; although they can be an expert in the specific domain of interaction. The advanced question-answering characters we want to build should have the ability to decide whether to answer a specific question truthfully or to lie about it or to simply refuse to answer depending on the dialogue context and scenario design. Interviewers can practice their questioning skills by interacting with virtual characters that can engage in simple bargaining behavior. In order to reveal certain information marked as *sensitive*, interviewers may have to employ several different tactics like building rapport, offering to provide what the virtual character wants or threatening the character with consequences for not cooperating. The Amani character (Artstein et al., 2009) is an example advanced question-answering character.

Several different architectures have been used for building Virtual Human dialogue systems (Traum, 2008). Leuski et al. (2006; 2010) describe one such architecture that can be used to build simple question-answering characters. In this architecture, scenario designers author a list of questions, a list of answers and all possible links between these. Although this approach allows *non-experts* to develop virtual characters, it falls short of maintaining coherence over sequence of utterances greater in length than two. Traum et al. (2008) describe an architecture that models such dependencies by using an information-state based dialogue model (Traum and Larsson, 2003), but this architecture is not currently accessible to *non-experts* for authoring, due to expertise needed in designing task model plans and thematic-role based framebanks.

We choose an intermediate approach, using a simple information-state dialogue manager, making authoring accessible to *non-experts* through use of the accompanying integrated authoring tool, *DomainEditor* (Gandhe et al., 2009).

2 PFC Sean Avery

Private First Class (PFC) Sean Avery is a virtual character who has witnessed a fellow soldier and his accomplice smuggling something suspicious on a U.S. Army base. Avery can be questioned about what he saw, who the soldier and the accomplice were. But the soldier involved in the smuggling is from Avery's platoon and Avery wants to cover up the incident. He may choose to lie and will need more persuasion in the form of threats & offers (see figure 1).

Proceedings of the SIGDIAL 2011: the 12th Annual Meeting of the Special Interest Group on Discourse and Dialogue, pages 347–349, Portland, Oregon, June 17-18, 2011. ©2011 Association for Computational Linguistics

Player	ynq	Are you Sean Avery?
Avery	yes	Yes
Avery	assert	My name is PFC Sean Avery.
Player	whq	Tell me what you saw.
Avery	assert	The soldier got out of the car and took a package from the back seat.
Player	whq	Do you know who the soldier was?
Avery	assert-lie	I have no clue what the soldier's name is.
Player	threat	If you don't tell me your privileges will be revoked.
Avery	response-threat	I don't want to be on restriction
Player	whq	Who was the soldier?
Avery	assert	The soldier's name is Ryan Benton.
Player	whq	Tell me more about the soldier.
Avery	assert	The PFC is in my platoon and one of my closest friends.
Player	whq	What was inside the package?
Avery	assert	He was carrying a puppy.
Player	whq	What was inside the package?
Avery	self-repeat	As I said earlier,
Avery	assert	The suspicious package contained a puppy.
Player	whq	Whose idea was it to smuggle the puppy on the base.
Avery	elicit-offer	Will you give the soldier a less severe punishment if I talk?
Player	accept	yes
Avery	response-offer	That's comforting, I wouldn't want him to get thrown off base or anything.
Avery	assert	I think the soldier told his girlfriend it wouldn't be a big deal to sneak a puppy on base.

Figure 1: A sample dialogue with **PFC Sean Avery** character. *Player* refers to the human trainee.

3 Authoring Process

The authoring process for such characters has two phases. The first phase is a top-down process which begins with defining the character's domain knowledge using the authoring tool, *DomainEditor* (See Figure 2). The basic unit of domain knowledge is an <*object*, *attribute*, *value*> triple. DomainEditor automatically generates all relevant Dialogue Acts (DAs) following a dialogue act schema. The default schema was authored by experts specifically for tactical questioning, but can be easily tailored to add different types of DAs for other scenarios. Each DA has a detailed XML representation and a pseudo-natural language gloss generated using templates. E.g. a template like "*Attribute* of *Object* is *Value*" for an *assert* dialogue act type. The growth in number of DAs represents the growth in character's domain knowledge (See figure 3). Our experience with several non-expert authors is that the domain reaches a stable level relatively early. Most of the domain authoring occurs during this phase. Scenario designers author one or two utterances for each of the character's DAs and substantially more examples for player's DAs in order to ensure robust NLU performance. These utterances are used as training data for NLU and NLG.

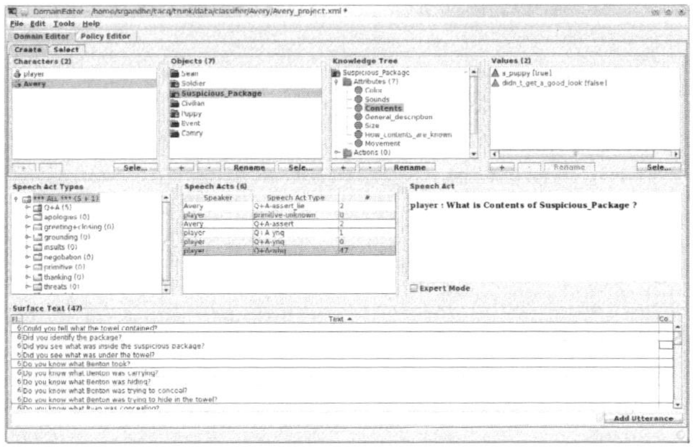

Figure 2: DomainEditor: An Integrated Authoring tool for designing the conversational domain, and specifying the utterances that map to various dialogue acts.

The second phase is a bottom-up phase which involves collecting a dialogue corpus by having volunteers interview the virtual character that has been built. The utterances from this corpus can then be annotated with the most appropriate DA. This second phase is responsible for a rapid growth in player utterances. It can also lead to minor domain expansion and small increase in character utterances, as needed to cover gaps found in the domain knowledge.

4 System Architecture

Figure 4 depicts the architecture for our dialogue system. CMU pocketsphinx[1] is used for speech

[1]http://cmusphinx.sourceforge.net/

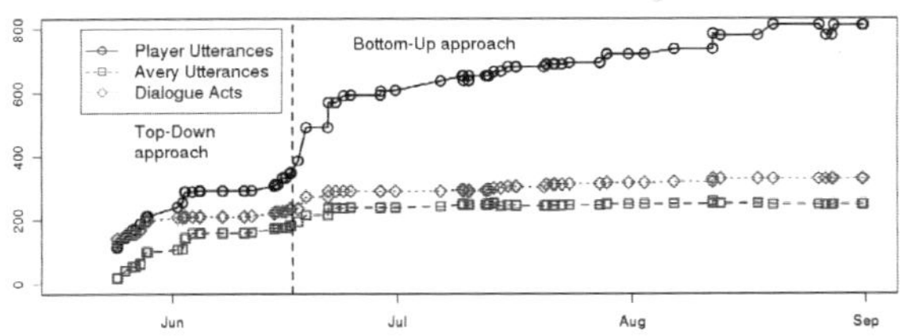

Figure 3: Amount of resources collected across time for the character, PFC Sean Avery

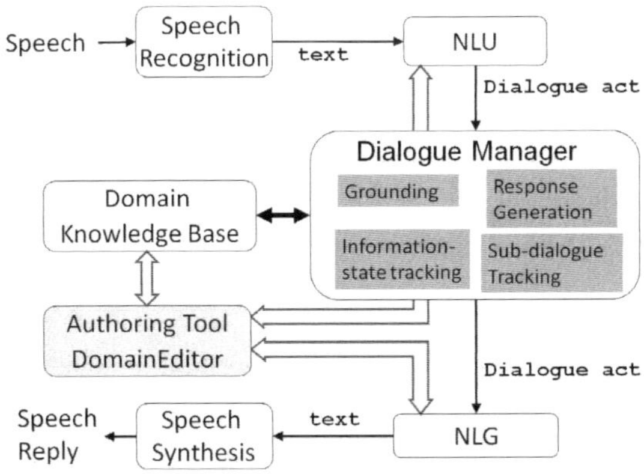

Figure 4: Architecture for the Advanced Question-Answering Conversational Dialogue System

recognition and CereVoice (Aylett et al., 2006) for speech synthesis. The information-state based dialogue manager (DM) communicates with NLU and NLG using dialogue acts (DAs). NLU maps recognized speech to one of the DAs from the set that is automatically generated by the *DomainEditor*. If the confidence for the best candidate DA is below a certain threshold, NLU generates a special non-understanding DA – *unknown*. The information-state is in part based on conversational game theory (Lewin, 2000). The main responsibilities of the DM are to update the information state of the dialogue based on the incoming DA and to select the response DAs. The information state update rules describe grammars for conversational game structure and are written as state charts using SCXML[2]. These state charts model various subdialogues like question-answering, offer, threat, greetings, closings, etc. The DM also implements advanced features like topic-tracking and grounding (Roque and Traum, 2009). The virtual human character delivers synthesized speech and corresponding non-verbal behavior, based on additional components of the ICT Virtual Human Toolkit[3].

Acknowledgments

This work was sponsored by the U.S. Army Research, Development, and Engineering Command (RDECOM). The content does not necessarily reflect the position or the policy of the U.S. Government, and no official endorsement should be inferred. We would like to thank other members of the TACQ team who helped design the architecture.

References

Ron Artstein, Sudeep Gandhe, Michael Rushforth, and David Traum. 2009. Viability of a simple dialogue act scheme for a tactical questioning dialogue system. In *proc. of 13th SemDial workshop : DiaHolmia*.

M. P. Aylett, C. J. Pidcock, and M. E. Fraser. 2006. The cerevoice blizzard entry 2006: A prototype database unit selection engine. In *Blizzard Challenge Workshop*, Pittsburgh.

Sudeep Gandhe, Nicolle Whitman, David Traum, and Ron Artstein. 2009. An integrated authoring tool for tactical questioning dialogue systems. In *6th Workshop on Knowledge and Reasoning in Practical Dialogue Systems*, Pasadena, California, July.

Anton Leuski and David R. Traum. 2010. NPCEditor: A tool for building question-answering characters. In *proc. of LREC' 10*.

Anton Leuski, Ronakkumar Patel, David Traum, and Brandon Kennedy. 2006. Building effective question answering characters. In *Proceedings of the 7th SIGdial Workshop on Discourse and Dialogue*, Australia.

I. Lewin. 2000. A formal model of conversational game theory. In *4th SemDial workshop: Gotalog 2000*.

Antonio Roque and David Traum. 2009. Improving a virtual human using a model of degrees of grounding. In *Proceedings of IJCAI-09*.

David Traum and Staffan Larsson. 2003. The information state approach to dialogue management. In Jan van Kuppevelt and Ronnie Smith, editors, *Current and New Directions in Discourse and Dialogue*. Kluwer.

David Traum, William Swartout, Jonathan Gratch, and Stacy Marsella. 2008. *A Virtual Human Dialogue Model for Non-Team Interaction*, volume 39 of *Text, Speech and Language Technology*. Springer.

David Traum. 2008. Talking to virtual humans: Dialogue models and methodologies for embodied conversational agents. In Ipke Wachsmuth and Günther Knoblich, editors, *Modeling Communication with Robots and Virtual Humans*, pages 296–309. Springer.

[2]State Chart XML – http://www.w3.org/TR/scxml/
Apache commons SCXML – http://commons.apache.org/scxml

[3]http://vhtoolkit.ict.usc.edu/

A Just-in-Time Document Retrieval System for Dialogues or Monologues

Andrei Popescu-Belis, Majid Yazdani, Alexandre Nanchen, and Philip N. Garner
Idiap Research Institute
Rue Marconi 19, Case Postale 592
1920 Martigny, Switzerland
{apbelis,myazdani,ananchen,pgarner}@idiap.ch

Abstract

The Automatic Content Linking Device is a just-in-time document retrieval system that monitors an ongoing dialogue or monologue and enriches it with potentially related documents from local repositories or from the Web. The documents are found using queries that are built from the dialogue words, obtained through automatic speech recognition. Results are displayed in real time to the dialogue participants, or to people watching a recorded dialogue or a talk. The system can be demonstrated in both settings.

1 Introduction

The Automatic Content Linking Device (ACLD) is a system that analyzes speech input from one or more speakers using automatic speech recognition (ASR), in order to retrieve related content, in real time, from a variety of repositories. This paper describes the main components of the system and summarizes evaluation results. The remainder of this section introduces scenarios of use and previous systems with similar goals.

The first scenario of use involves people taking part in meetings, who often mention documents containing facts that are relevant to the current discussion, but cannot search for them without interrupting the discussion flow. Our goal is to perform such searches automatically. In a second scenario, search is performed for live or recorded lectures, for instance in a computer-assisted learning environment. The ACLD enriches the lectures with related course material, receiving real-time feedback from the user.

The ACLD improves over past systems by using speech, by giving access to multimedia documents, and by using semantic search. Its first precursors were the Fixit query-free search system (Hart and Graham, 1997), the Remembrance Agent for just-in-time retrieval (Rhodes and Maes, 2000), and the Implicit Queries system (Dumais et al., 2004). A version of the Remembrance Agent called Jimminy was conceived as a wearable assistant for taking notes, but ASR was only simulated (Rhodes, 1997). Watson monitored the user's operations in a text editor, and selected terms for web search (Budzik and Hammond, 2000). Another authoring assistant was developed in the A-Propos project (Puerta Melguizo and al., 2008). Recently, several speech-based search engines have been proposed, as well as systems for searching spoken documents. For human dialogues in meetings, the FAME interactive space (Metze and al., 2006) provided multi-modal access to recordings of lectures via a table top interface, but required specific voice commands from one user only, and did not spontaneously follow a conversation as the ACLD does.

2 Description of the ACLD

The architecture of the ACLD comprises modules for: (1) document preparation and indexing; (2) input sensing and query construction; (3) search and integration of results; (4) user interaction.

2.1 Document Preparation and Indexing

The preparation of the local database of documents available for search requires text extraction from various file formats (like MS Office or PDF), and

Proceedings of the SIGDIAL 2011: the 12th Annual Meeting of the Special Interest Group on Discourse and Dialogue, pages 350–352,
Portland, Oregon, June 17-18, 2011. ©2011 Association for Computational Linguistics

document indexing, here using Apache Lucene. Past meetings, when available, are automatically transcribed, then chunked into smaller units, and indexed along with the other documents. For searching the Web, the system does not build indexes but uses the Google Search API.

2.2 Sensing the User's Information Needs

The ACLD uses the AMI real-time ASR system for English (Garner and al., 2009), which has an acceptable accuracy for use with conversational speech in the ACLD. When processing past recordings, the ASR system can run slower than real-time to maximize its accuracy. If one or more pre-specified keywords (based on domain knowledge) are detected in the ASR output, then their importance is increased for searching. Otherwise, all the words from the ASR (except stopwords) are used for constructing the query.

2.3 Querying the Document Database

The Query Aggregator component uses the ASR words in order to retrieve the most relevant documents from a given database. The latest version of the ACLD makes use of semantic search (see below), but earlier versions used keyword-based search from Apache Lucene for local documents. Queries are formulated and launched at regular time intervals, typically every 15-30 seconds, or on demand. The search results are integrated with previous ones, using a persistence model that smoothes variations in time by keeping track of the salience of each result. Salience is initialized from the ranking of search results, then decreases in time, or increases if the document appears again among results. A history of all results is also accessible.

2.4 Semantic Search over Wikipedia

The goal of semantic search is to improve the relevance of results with respect to the spoken words, and to make search more robust to noise from ASR. The method used here is adapted from a graph-based measure of semantic relatedness between text fragments (Yazdani and Popescu-Belis, 2010). Relatedness is computed using random walk in a large network of documents, here about 1.2 milion Wikipedia articles from the WEX data set (Metaweb Technologies, 2010). These are linked by directional hyperlinks, and also by lexical similarity links that we construct upon initialization. The random walk model allows the computation of the visiting probability (VP) from one document to another, and then of the VP between sets of documents. This functions as a measure of semantic relatedness, and has been applied to several NLP problems by projecting the text fragments to be compared onto the documents in the network (Yazdani and Popescu-Belis, 2010).

For the ACLD, the use of semantic relatedness for document retrieval amounts to searching, in a very large collection, the documents that are the most closely related to the words obtained from the ASR in a given time frame. Here, we set the document collection to Wikipedia (WEX). As the search is hard to perform in real time, we made a series of justified approximations to make it tractable.

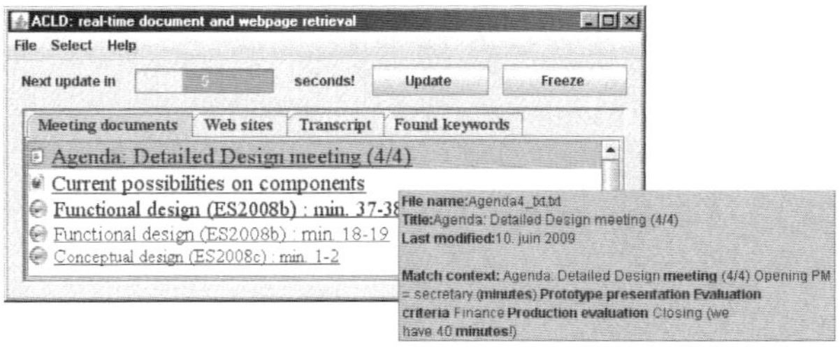

Figure 1: Unobtrusive UI of the ACLD displaying document results. The pop-up window shows more details for the first results.

2.5 The User Interface

The goal of the UI is to make ACLD information available in a configurable way, allowing users to see more or less information according to their own needs. The UI displays up to four widgets, which can be arranged at will, and contain: (1) ASR words with highlighted keywords; (2) tag-cloud of keywords, coding for recency and frequency; (3) links to the current results from the local repository; (4) links to the current Web search results.

Two main arrangements are intended: an informative full-screen UI (not shown here from lack of space) and an unobtrusive UI, with superposed tabs, shown in Figure 1 with the document result widget. When hovering over a document name, a pop-up window displays metadata and document excerpts that match words from the query, as an explanation for why the document was retrieved.

3 Evaluation of the ACLD

Four types of evidence for the relevance and utility of the ACLD are summarized here. Firstly, the ACLD was demonstrated to about 50 potential users (industrial partners, focus groups, etc.), who found the concept useful, and offered positive verbal evaluation, along with suggestions for smaller and larger improvements.

Secondly, a pilot experiment was conducted with a group using an earlier version of the UI. Two pilot runs have shown that the ACLD was consulted about five times per meeting, but many more runs are (still) needed for statistical significance of observations.

Thirdly, the UI was tested in a usability evaluation experiment with nine non-technical subjects, who rated it as 'acceptable' (68%) on the System Usability Scale, following a series of tasks they had to perform using it. Additional suggestions for changes were received.

Finally, we compared offline the results of semantic search with the keyword-based ones. We asked eight subjects to read a series of nine meeting fragments, and to decide which of the two results was the most useful one (they could also answer 'none'). Of a total of 36 snippets, each seen by two subjects, there was agreement on 23 (64%) snippets and disagreement on 13 (36%). In fact, if 'none' is excluded, there were only 7 true disagreements. Over the 23 snippets on which the subjects agreed, the result of semantic search was judged more relevant than that of keyword search for 19 (53% of the total), and the reverse for 4 only (11%). Alternatively, if one counts the votes cast by subjects in favor of each system, regardless of agreement, then semantic search received 72% of the votes and keyword-based only 28%. Hence, semantic search already outperforms keyword based one.

4 Conclusion

The ACLD is, to the best of our knowledge, the first just-in-time retrieval system to use spontaneous speech and to support access to multimedia documents and to websites, using a robust semantic search method. Future work should aim at improving the relevance of semantic search, at modeling context to improve the timing of results, and at inferring relevance feedback from users. The ACLD should also be applied to specific use cases, and an experiment with group discussions in a learning environment is under way.

Acknowledgments

We are grateful to the EU AMI and AMIDA Integrated Projects and to the Swiss IM2 NCCR (Interactive Multimodal Information Management) for supporting the development of the ACLD.

References

Jay Budzik and Kristian J. Hammond. 2000. User interactions with everyday applications as context for just-in-time information access. In *IUI 2000 (5th International Conference on Intelligent User Interfaces)*, New Orleans, LA.

Susan Dumais, Edward Cutrell, Raman Sarin, and Eric Horvitz. 2004. Implicit Queries (IQ) for contextualized search. In *SIGIR 2004 (27th Annual ACM SIGIR Conference) Demonstrations*, page 534, Sheffield.

Philip N. Garner and al. 2009. Real-time ASR from meetings. In *Interspeech 2009 (10th Annual Conference of the International Speech Communication Association)*, pages 2119–2122, Brighton.

Peter E. Hart and Jamey Graham. 1997. Query-free information retrieval. *IEEE Expert: Intelligent Systems and Their Applications*, 12(5):32–37.

Metaweb Technologies. 2010. Freebase Wikipedia Extraction (WEX). http://download.freebase.com/wex/.

Florian Metze and al. 2006. The 'Fame' interactive space. In *Machine Learning for Multimodal Interaction II*, LNCS 3869, pages 126–137. Springer, Berlin.

Maria Carmen Puerta Melguizo and al. 2008. A personalized recommender system for writing in the Internet age. In *LREC 2008 Workshop on NLP Resources, Algorithms, and Tools for Authoring Aids*, pages 21–26, Marrakech.

Bradley J. Rhodes and Pattie Maes. 2000. Just-in-time information retrieval agents. *IBM Systems Journal*, 39(3-4):685–704.

Bradley J. Rhodes. 1997. The Wearable Remembrance Agent: A system for augmented memory. *Personal Technologies: Special Issue on Wearable Computing*, 1:218–224.

Majid Yazdani and Andrei Popescu-Belis. 2010. A random walk framework to compute textual semantic similarity: a unified model for three benchmark tasks. In *ICSC 2010 (4th IEEE International Conference on Semantic Computing)*, pages 424–429, Pittsburgh, PA.

Author Index

Alvarado, Irene, 325
Arizmendi, Iker, 110
Artstein, Ron, 272, 319
Asher, Nicholas, 204

Baumann, Timo, 120
Bell, Peter, 338
Ben-Aharon, Roni, 185
Benamara, Farah, 204
Benotti, Luciana, 68
Bergmann, Kirsten, 88
Black, Alan W, 2
Bohus, Dan, 98
Boyer, Kristy, 49
Briggs, Gordon, 239
Burger, Susanne, 2

Cadilhac, Anaïs, 204
Campbell, Gwendolyn, 162, 338
Cartoni, Bruno, 194
Chaudhuri, Sourish, 30
Chen, Lin, 307
Chernobrov, Daniel, 185
Conkie, Alistair, 2
Crone, Phil, 325
Cross, Ernest, 301
Cuayáhuitl, Heriberto, 78

Darvill, Jonathan, 301
Denis, Alexandre, 68
Dethlefs, Nina, 78
DeVault, David, 39, 279
Di Eugenio, Barbara, 307
Drummond, Joanna, 312
Dzikovska, Myroslava, 338
Dzikovska, Myroslava O., 162

Epstein, Susan L., 248, 266
Eskenazi, Maxine, 2

Forbes-Riley, Kate, 216
Funakoshi, Kotaro, 18

Gandhe, Sudeep, 347
Garner, Philip N., 350
Garrett, Robert, 301
Georgila, Kallirroi, 272
Gerten, Jillian, 347
González-Brenes, José, 8
Gordon, Joshua, 248, 266

Ha, Eun Young, 49
Hastie, Helen, 2, 142
Hecht, Ron, 185
Heeman, Peter, 110
Hirschberg, Julia, 152
Horvitz, Eric, 98

Isard, Amy, 338

Janarthanam, Srinivasan, 142
Jerome, Simon, 325

Kawahara, Tatsuya, 59
Kawai, Hisashi, 259
Kawamoto, Shinichi, 259
Keizer, Simon, 2
Khalidov, Vasil, 341
Klotz, David, 341
Komatani, Kazunori, 18
Kopack, Michael, 301
Kopp, Stefan, 88
Kumar, Rohit, 227

Lascarides, Alex, 1, 204
Lee, Gary Geunbae, 344
Lee, Kyusong, 344
Lee, Sungjin, 344
Lemon, Oliver, 2, 142
Lester, James, 49

Leuski, Anton, 39
Ligorio, Tiziana, 248
Lison, Pierre, 294
Litman, Diane, 216, 312
Liu, Xingkun, 142
Lomas, Meghann, 301

Makatchev, Maxim, 286
Margaretha, Eliza, 279
Matsuyama, Kyoko, 18
Merigaud, Nicolas, 2
Meyer, Thomas, 194
Minker, Wolfgang, 173
Misu, Teruhisa, 259
Mizukami, Etsuo, 259
Moore, Johanna, 338
Moore, Johanna D., 162
Mori, Shinsuke, 59
Mostow, Jack, 8

Nakamura, Satoshi, 259
Nakano, Mikio, 18
Nanchen, Alexandre, 350
Nazarian, Angela, 272
Noh, Hyungjong, 344

Odobez, Jean-Marc, 341
Okuno, Hiroshi G., 18

Parent, Gabriel, 2
Passonneau, Rebecca J., 248, 266, 325
Peltason, Julia, 341
Phillips, Robert, 49
Piwek, Paul, 335
Popescu-Belis, Andrei, 194, 350

Quignard, Matthieu, 332

Raj, Bhiksha, 30
Rieser, Hannes, 88
Rojas-Barahona, Lina Maria, 332
Rosé, Carolyn, 227
Rushforth, Michael, 272

Sagae, Kenji, 39
Sato, Shun, 18
Schatz, Benjamin, 173
Scheutz, Matthias, 239
Schlangen, David, 120
Schmitt, Alexander, 173
Schubiner, Gabriel, 2
Selfridge, Ethan, 110
Shiga, Yoshinori, 259
Simmons, Reid, 286
Steinhauser, Natalie, 162, 338
Stoyanchev, Svetlana, 335
Sycara, Katia, 272

Tanenhaus, Michael K., 67
Taylor, Alysa, 347
Thomson, Blaise, 2
Traum, David, 272, 347

Viethen, Jette, 78

Wang, Anruo, 307
Wang, William Yang, 152
Whitebread, Kenneth, 301
Wienke, Johannes, 341
Williams, Jason, 110, 130
Williams, Jason D., 2
Winter, Ute, 185
Wrede, Britta, 341
Wrede, Sebastian, 341

Yazdani, Majid, 350
Yoshino, Koichiro, 59
Young, Steve, 2
Yu, Kai, 2

Zufferey, Sandrine, 194

Association for Computational Linguistics
209 N. Eighth Street
Stroudsburg, Pennsylvania 18360

CURRAN ASSOCIATES INC
proceedings.com